914.2

London

timeout.com/london

Penguin Books

'DUNCAN OF
JORDANSTONE COLLEGE
LIBRARY

PENGUIN BOOKS

Published by the Penguin Group
Penguin Books Ltd, 80 Strand, London WC2R ORL, England
Penguin Books USA Inc., 375 Hudson Street, New York, New York 10014, USA
Penguin Books Australia Ltd, 250 Camberwell Road, Camberwell, Victoria, Australia
Penguin Books Canada Ltd, 10 Alcorn Avenue, Toronto, Ontario, Canada M4V 3B2
Penguin Books (NZ) Ltd, cnr Rosedale and Airborne Roads, Albany, Auckland, New Zealand

Penguin Books Ltd, Registered Offices: Harmondsworth, Middlesex, England

First published 1989
First Penguin edition 1990
Second edition 1992
Third edition 1994
Fourth edition 1995
Fifth edition 1997
Sixth edition 1998
Seventh edition 1999
Eighth edition 2000
Ninth edition 2001
Tenth edition 2002
10 9 8 7 6 5 4 3 2 1

Colour reprographics by Icon, Crown House, 56-58 Southwark Street, London SE1
and Precise Litho, 34-35 Great Sutton Street, London EC1
Printed and bound by Cayfosa-Quebecor, Ctra. de Caldes, Km 3 08 130 Sta, Perpètua de Mogoda, Barcelona, Spain

Edited and designed by
Time Out Guides Limited
Universal House
251 Tottenham Court Road
London W1T 7AB
Tel + 44 (0) 20 7813 3000
Fax + 44 (0) 20 7813 6001
Email guides@timeout.com
www.timeout.com

Editorial
Editor Rhonda Carrier
Deputy Editor Sam Le Quesne
Listings Editors Eli Dryden, Cathy Limb
Proofreader Tasmin Shelton
Indexer Jackie Brind

Editorial Director Peter Fiennes
Series Editor Ruth Jarvis
Deputy Series Editor Jonathan Cox
Guides Co-ordinator Jenny Noden

Design
Group Art Director John Oakey
Art Director Mandy Martin
Art Editor Scott Moore
Designers Benjamin de Lotz, Lucy Grant
Picture Editor Kerri Littlefield
Deputy Picture Editor Kit Burnet
Picture Librarian Sarah Roberts
Scanning & Imaging Dan Conway
Ad make-up Glen Impey

Advertising
Group Commercial Director Lesley Gill
Sales Director/Sponsorship Mark Phillips
Sales Manager Alison Gray
Sales Executives James Coulbault, Terina Rickit,
Jason Trotman
Copy Controller Oliver Guy
Advertising Assistant Sabrina Ancilleri

Administration
Publisher Tony Elliott
Managing Director Mike Hardwick
Group Financial Director Kevin Ellis
Marketing Director Christine Cort
Marketing Manager Mandy Martinez
US Publicity & Marketing Associate Rosella Albanese
Group General Manager Nichola Coulthard
Production Manager Mark Lamond
Production Controller Samantha Furniss
Accountant Sarah Bostock

Features in this guide were researched and written by:
Introduction Rhonda Carrier. **History** Liz Wyse. **London Today** Will Fulford-Jones (*Who he? Ken Livingstone* Bradfield Read).
Architecture Rhonda Carrier. **The Melting Pot** Rebecca Taylor. **Fictional London** Nicholas Royle (*Word up* Cathy Limb; *Who he? Derek Raymond* Conrad Williams) **Accommodation** Rebecca Taylor, Rhonda Carrier. **Sightseeing Introduction** Bradfield Read; **South Bank & Bankside** Rhonda Carrier. **The City** Conrad Williams. **Holborn & Clerkenwell** Bradfield Read.
Bloomsbury & Fitzrovia Jaclyn Kelly. **Marylebone** Lou Read. **Mayfair & St James's** Conrad Williams. **Soho & Leicester Square** Jaclyn Kelly. **Covent Garden & St Giles's** Bradfield Read (*On location: Hitchcock's Frenzy* Conrad Williams). **Westminster** Tosca Ford (*The Black Museum* Conrad Williams). **Knightsbridge & South Kensington** Gala Blau (*On location: Polanski's Repulsion* Conrad Williams). **Chelsea** Gala Blau. **North London** Rebecca Taylor (*Noble rot* Lou Read). **East London** Lance Benest (*The melting pot: Vietnamese London* Rebecca Taylor). **South London** Richard Lines (*Who he? Raymond Chandler* Conrad Williams; *Whatever happened to? Bedlam* Kitty Devine; *The melting pot: Caribbean London* Rebecca Taylor); **West London** Sapphire Hammond (*The melting pot: Punjabi London* Rebecca Taylor). **Restaurants** Sam Le Quesne (*Look who's cooking* Conrad Williams; *Who he? Sivadas Shreedharan* Rebecca Taylor). **Pubs & Bars** Sam Le Quesne. **Shops & Services** Sapphire Hammond (*Who she? Sparkle Moore* and *Who he? Vittorio Radice* Rebecca Taylor). **By Season** Bradfield Read. **Children** Nana Ocran. **Clubs** Francesca Gavin. **Comedy** Sharon Lougher. **Dance** Donald Hutera. **Film** Conrad Williams. **Galleries** Marc Werner. **Gay & Lesbian** Tom Coates. **Music** *Classical* Tim Rowbottom (*Who he? George Frideric Handel* Conrad Williams), *Rock, Roots & Jazz* Alistair Newton. **Sport & Fitness** Richard Lines (*In the swim* Jaclyn Kelly; *Relax!* Sapphire Hammond). **Theatre** Liz Wyse (*Who they? The Generating Company* Lou Read). **Trips Out of Town** Colette Arnesby (*A sea change* Mary Alexander). **Directory** Sharon Lougher.

The Editor would like to thank:
Sophie Blacksell, Gareth Bunn, Sophie Bureau, Ayesha Braganza, David Carrier, Ric Coady, Alex Dahm, Christi Daugherty, Kevin Ebbutt, Mary and Tim Freeman, Gerontion, Sarah Guy, Malcolm Hay, Gemma Hirst, Ram Kumar, Pippa Le Quesne, Rock Le Roc, Jane London, Vernon Lord, Lesley McCave, Cathy Phillips, Ros Sales, Dave Swindells, Adi Welch, Reddy Williams, France Zarza, and all the contributors from previous editions, whose work formed the basis for parts of this book.

Maps by JS Graphics, 17 Beadles Lane, Old Oxted, Surrey RH8 9JG.

Photography by Amanda Edwards except: p7, p17, 132 Hulton Archive; p10, p11, p87 AKG; p14 Jewish Museum; p18, p19 Corbis; p100 Courtesy of the Trustees of Sir John Soane's Museum/Martin Charles; p119 Neil Massey; p37, p137 Jon Perugia; p155 Museum of London; p117, p169, p121, p263 Corbis Images; p202 Rob Greig; p209 Tony Gibson; p215 Tricia de Courcy Ling; p216 Alys Tomlinson; p217 Dominic Dibbs; p259 Matt Carr; p240 James Winspear; p25, p33, p267 Press Association; p280 PYMCA/David Swindells; p350 The National Trust Photographic Library/Eric Crichton; p353 Tricia Moxey; p347 (left) Paul Avis; p299 Andrew Burman. **The following images were provided by the featured establishments/artists:** p38, p42, p61, p68/Nigel Young, p115, p118, p126, p139, p142, p235, p273, p276, p287, p291, p297, p312, p319/ John Mannion, p328, p332, p333, p335, p337, p342, p343, p344, p345, p349.

Contents

Introduction

London defies definitition, as anyone who has ever tried to fathom out where it begins and ends, and where its heart lies, will vouchsafe. Geographically speaking, it's to the statue of Charles I in Trafalgar Square that British mileposts measure distances to the centre of London, but it's in the square mile of the City that Londinium, as the Romans had it, had its seed. In 1999, meanwhile, when a site was being chosen for a giant observation wheel to mark the millennium, planners drew a circle around London and pronounced the current dead centre to be Jubilee Gardens on the South Bank. The London Eye now marks the spot.

As for its perimeters, well, Apsley House at Hyde Park Corner used to be known as 'No.1 London', since it was the first building visitors to the city came to on their way from the village of Kensington, while these days central London covers about 12 square miles (30 square kilometres) and Greater London's tentacles reach out as far as the M25 at various points. Yet ask any local to pinpoint either of these areas without the assistance of a map and chances are they won't have a clue where to start.

Historically, too, London is an elusive concept, with invasions and internal strife repeatedly reducing the fledgling city to a ghost town over the course of its first millennium, making it impossible to posit any real 'beginning'. In fact, in many ways the urban landscape we know today only began to come into being after 1666, when the Great Fire proved to the authorities the wisdom of building in brick and stone and had rich folk hurrying to set up home in the West End.

All of which is to say that London is a slippery entity, an evolving mass with constantly shifting boundaries. With its wildly cosmopolitan population and its perpetual influx of new restaurants, bars, clubs, shops and other attractions, it's a place that you can never quite grasp or pin down. It's this that makes it one of the world's most exhilarating cities – however well you may think you know it, however long you spend here, London will constantly surprise you.

Our job is to reacquaint you with the London you think you know and to open up the one you don't yet know – to help you find your own London, in fact. Because as with most things in life, London is above all a state of mind.

ABOUT THE TIME OUT CITY GUIDES

The *Time Out London Guide* is one of an expanding series of *Time Out* City Guides, now numbering 35, produced by the people behind London and New York's successful listings magazines. Our guides are all written and updated by resident experts who have striven to provide you with all the most up-to-date information you'll need to explore the city or read up on its background, whether you're a local or a first-time visitor.

THE LOWDOWN ON THE LISTINGS

Above all, we've tried to make this book as useful as possible. Addresses, telephone numbers, websites, transport information, opening times, admission prices and credit card details have all been included in the listings. And, as far as possible, we've given details of facilities, services and events, all checked and correct as we went to press. However, owners and managers can change their arrangements at any time. Before you go out of your way, we'd advise you to telephone and check opening times, ticket prices and other particulars.

While every effort has been made to ensure the accuracy of the information contained in this guide, the publishers cannot accept responsibility for any errors it may contain.

PRICES AND PAYMENT

We have noted where venues such as shops, hotels and restaurants accept the following credit cards: American Express (**AmEx**), Diners Club (**DC**), MasterCard (**MC**), Visa (**V**) and JCB. Many businesses will also accept other cards, including Switch or Delta. Most shops, restaurants and attractions will accept sterling travellers' cheques issued by a major financial institution such as American Express.

THE LIE OF THE LAND

Thanks to the chaotic street plan – or, rather, the lack of one – London is one of the most complicated of all major world cities to find

> There is an online version of this guide, as well as weekly events listings for more than 30 international cities, at www.timeout.com.

your way around. To make it a little easier, we've included an area designation for every venue in this guide (such as Soho, Covent Garden, Westminster, et cetera), along with map references that point to our street maps at the back of the book (starting on page 394). However, for the sake of comprehensiveness, we recommend that you follow the example of the locals and invest in a standard *A-Z* map of the city the minute you arrive.

TELEPHONE NUMBERS
The area code for London is 020. All telephone numbers given in this guide take this code unless otherwise stated: add 020 to the numbers listed throughout the book if calling from outside London; otherwise, simply dial the number as written. Numbers priced at non-

standard rates – for example, mobile phone numbers (starting 07), free numbers (which take an 0800 or 0808 code) and premium rate numbers (beginning 09) – have been designated as such in the listings. For more details of phone codes and charges, *see p374*. The international dialling code for the UK is 44.

ESSENTIAL INFORMATION
For all the practical information you might need for visiting London, including visa and customs information, advice on disabled facilities and access, emergency telephone numbers and local transport, turn to the **Directory** chapter at the back of the guide. It starts on page 356.

MAPS
The map section at the back of this book includes a trips out of town map, orientation and overview maps of the area and city, and street maps of most of central London, with a comprehensive street index. The maps start on page 389.

LET US KNOW WHAT YOU THINK
We hope you enjoy the *Time Out London Guide*, and we'd like to know what you think of it. We welcome tips for places that you consider we should include in future editions and take note of your criticism of our choices. There's a reader's reply card at the back of this book for your feedback, or you can email us at londonguide@timeout.com.

Teamsys.

A WORLD OF SERVICES

 Teamsys is always with you, ready to assure you all the tranquillity and serenity that you desire for your journeys, 365 days a year.

Roadside assistance always and everywhere, infomobility so not to have surprises, insurance... and lots more.

To get to know us better contact us at the toll-free number **00-800-55555555**.

...and to discover Connect's exclusive and innovative integrated infotelematic services onboard system visit us at:

www.targaconnect.com

In Context

Boudicca and her troops set London alight.

History

From the chief city of Roman Britannia Superior to the 'capital of cool', London has long been leader of the pack.

London's origins as a settlement date back to the invasion of the Roman emperor Claudius' legions in AD 43, when the Thames was forded at its shallowest point and, later, a timber bridge was built here (near the site of today's London Bridge). It was over the following decade that the north side of this strategically vital crossing became settled. During the first two centuries AD, the Romans built roads, towns and forts in the area, and trade flourished. The first mention of London (Londinium) was in AD 60, when Roman historian Tacitus described it as 'filled with traders… a celebrated centre of commerce'.

Progress came to a halt in AD 61 when Boudicca, the fearsome widow of an East Anglian chieftain, rebelled against the Imperial forces who had seized her land, flogged her and raped her daughters. She led the Iceni in a savage revolt, destroying the Roman colony at Colchester, and then marching on London. The inhabitants were massacred and the settlement was burned to the ground.

After order was restored, the town was rebuilt and, around AD 200, a two-mile (three-kilometre) long, six-metre (18-foot) high defensive wall was constructed around it. Chunks of the wall survive today, and the names of the original gates – Ludgate, Newgate, Bishopsgate and Aldgate – are preserved on the map of the city. The street known as London Wall traces part of its original course.

By the fourth century, racked by barbarian invasions and internal strife, the Empire was in decline. In 410 the last troops were withdrawn and London became a ghost town. The Roman way of life vanished, their only enduring legacies being roads and early Christianity.

SAXON & VIKING LONDON

During the fifth and sixth centuries, history gives way to legend. The Saxons crossed the North Sea and settled in eastern and southern England, apparently avoiding the ruins of London; they built farmsteads and trading posts outside the walls.

In 596 Pope Gregory sent Augustine to convert the English to Christianity. Ethelbert, Saxon King of Kent, proved a willing convert, and Augustine was appointed the first Archbishop of Canterbury. Since then Canterbury has remained the centre of the English Christian Church. London's first Bishop, though, was Mellitus: one of Augustine's missionaries, he converted the East Saxon King Sebert and, in 604, founded a wooden cathedral dedicated to St Paul inside the old city walls. On Sebert's death, his followers reverted to paganism, but later generations of Christians rebuilt what is now St Paul's Cathedral.

London, meanwhile, continued to expand. In 731 the Venerable Bede described 'Lundenwic' as 'the mart of many nations resorting to it by land and sea'. This probably refers to a settlement west of the Roman city in the area of today's Aldwych (Old English for 'old settlement').

In the ninth century the city faced a new danger from across the North Sea: the Vikings. The city was sacked in 841 and, in 851, the Danish raiders returned with 350 ships, leaving London in ruins. It was not until 886 that King Alfred of Wessex – aka Alfred the Great – regained the city, soon re-establishing London as a major trading centre with a merchant navy and new wharfs at Billingsgate and Queenhithe.

> **'Londoners threw their dead animals into the furrow that formed the city's eastern boundary.'**

Throughout the tenth century, the Saxon city prospered. Churches were built, parishes established and markets set up. However, the 11th century brought more Viking harassment, and the English were even forced to accept a Danish king, Cnut (Canute, 1016-40), during whose reign London replaced Winchester as the capital of England.

In 1042 the throne reverted to an Englishman, Edward the Confessor, who devoted himself to building the grandest church in England two miles (three kilometres) west of the City at Thorney ('the isle of brambles'). He replaced the timber church of St Peter's with a huge abbey, 'the West Minster' (Westminster Abbey; consecrated in December 1065), and moved his court to the new Palace of Westminster. A week after the consecration Edward died and was buried in his new church. London now grew around two hubs: Westminster as the centre for the royal court, government and law; and the City of London as the commercial centre.

THE NORMAN CONQUEST

On Edward's death there was a succession dispute. William, Duke of Normandy, claimed that the Confessor (his cousin) had promised him the English crown but the English chose Edward's brother-in-law Harold. Piqued, William gathered an army and invaded, and, on 14 October 1066, defeated Harold at the Battle of Hastings and marched on London. City elders had little option but to offer William the throne, and the conqueror was crowned in Westminster Abbey on Christmas Day, 1066.

Recognising the need to win over the prosperous city merchants by negotiation rather than force, William granted the Bishop and burgesses of London a charter – which is still kept at Guildhall – that acknowledged their rights and independence in return for taxes. But, 'against the fickleness of the vast and fierce population', he also ordered strongholds to be built alongside the city wall, including the White Tower (the tallest building in the Tower of London) and the now-lost Baynard's Castle at Blackfriars. The earliest surviving written account of contemporary London was written 40 years later by a monk, William Fitz Stephen, who vividly conjured up the walled city and, outside, pastures and woods for hunting, youths wrestling and fencing in Moorfields, and skating on frozen ponds.

THE MIDDLE AGES

In the growing city of London, much of the politics of the Middle Ages – the late 12th to the late 15th centuries – revolved around a three-way struggle for power between the king and the aristocracy, the Church, and the Lord Mayor and city guilds.

In the early Middle Ages, the king and his court frequently travelled to other parts of the kingdom and abroad. However, in the 14th and 15th centuries, the Palace of Westminster became the seat of law and government. The noblemen and bishops who attended court built themselves palatial houses along the Strand from the City to Westminster, with gardens stretching to the river.

The Model Parliament, agreeing the principles of government, was held in Westminster Hall in 1295, presided over by Edward I and attended by barons, clergy and representatives of knights and burgesses. The first step towards establishing personal rights and political liberty – not to mention curbing the power of the king – had already been taken in 1215 with the signing of the Magna Carta by King John. In the 14th century, subsequent assemblies gave rise to the House of Lords (which met at the Palace of Westminster) and the House of Commons (which met in the Chapter House at Westminster Abbey).

Relations between the monarch and the City were never easy; indeed, they were often outright hostile. Londoners guarded their privileges with self-righteous intransigence, and resisted all attempts by successive kings to squeeze money out of them to finance wars and building projects. Subsequent kings were forced to turn to Jewish and Lombard money-lenders, but the City merchants were as intolerant of foreigners as of the royals. Rioting, persecution and the occasional lynching and pogrom were all commonplace in medieval London.

CITY STATUS & COMMERCIAL CLOUT

The privileges granted to the City merchants under Norman kings, allowing independence and self-regulation, were extended by the monarchs who followed, in return for financial favours. In 1191, during the reign of Richard I, the City of London was formally recognised as a commune – a self-governing community – and, in 1197, won control of the Thames that included lucrative fishing rights, which it retained until 1857. In 1215 King John confirmed the city's right 'to elect every year a mayor', a position of great authority with power over the Sheriff and the Bishop of London. A month later the Mayor joined the rebel barons in signing the Magna Carta.

Over the next two centuries, the power and influence of the trade and craft guilds – later known as the City Livery Companies – increased as trade with Europe grew, and the wharfs by London Bridge were crowded with imports such as fine cloth, furs, wine, spices and precious metals. Port dues and taxes were paid to Customs officials such as part-time poet Geoffrey Chaucer, whose *Canterbury Tales* became the first published work of English literature.

The city's markets, already established, drew produce from miles around: livestock at Smithfield, fish at Billingsgate and poultry at Leadenhall. The street markets, or 'cheaps', around Westcheap (now Cheapside) and Eastcheap were crammed with a variety of goods. As commerce increased, foreign traders and craftsmen settled around the port; the population within the city wall grew from about 18,000 in 1100 to well over 50,000 in the 1340s.

BLACK DEATH & REVOLTING PEASANTS

However, perhaps unsurprisingly, lack of hygiene became a serious problem in the city. Water was provided in cisterns at Cheapside and elsewhere, but the supply, which came more or less direct from the Thames, was limited and polluted. The street called Houndsditch was so named because Londoners threw their dead animals into the furrow that formed the city's eastern boundary. There was no proper sewerage system; in the streets around Smithfield (the Shambles) butchers dumped the entrails of slaughtered animals.

These conditions provided the breeding ground for the greatest catastrophe of the Middle Ages: the Black Death of 1348 and 1349. The plague came to London from Europe, carried by rats on ships. During this period, about 30 per cent of England's population died of the disease. Although the epidemic abated, it was to recur in London on several occasions during the next three centuries, each time devastating the city's population.

These outbreaks of disease left the labour market short-handed, causing unrest among the overworked peasants. The imposition of a poll tax – a shilling a head – proved the final straw, leading to the Peasants' Revolt. In 1381 thousands marched on London, led by Jack Straw from Essex and Wat Tyler from Kent. In the rioting and looting that followed, the Savoy Palace on the Strand was destroyed, the Archbishop of Canterbury was murdered, and hundreds of prisoners were set free. When the 14-year-old Richard II rode out to Smithfield to face the rioters, Wat Tyler was fatally stabbed by Lord Mayor William Walworth. The other ringleaders were subsequently rounded up and hanged. But no more poll taxes were imposed.

CHURCHES & MONASTERIES

Like every other medieval city, London had many parish and monastic churches, as well as the great Gothic cathedral of St Paul's. Though the majority of Londoners were allowed access to the major churches, the lives of most of them revolved around their own local parish places of worship, where they were baptised, married and buried. Many churches were linked with particular craft and trade guilds.

Monasteries and convents were also established, all owning valuable acres inside and outside the city walls. The crusading Knights Templars and Knights Hospitallers were two of the earliest religious orders to settle, though the increasingly unruly Templars were disbanded in 1312 by the Pope and their land eventually became occupied by the lawyers of Inner and Middle Temple.

The surviving church of St Bartholomew-the-Great (founded 1123) and the names of St Helen's Bishopsgate, Spitalfields and St Martin's-le-Grand are reminders of these early monasteries and convents. The friars, who were active social workers among the poor living outside the city walls, were known by the colour of their habits: the Blackfriars

(Dominicans), the Whitefriars (Carmelites) and the Greyfriars (Franciscans). Their names are still in evidence around Fleet Street and the west of the City.

TUDORS, STUARTS & DIVORCE

Under the Tudor monarchs (who reigned from 1485 until 1603), spurred by the discovery of America and the ocean routes to Africa and the Orient, London became one of Europe's largest cities. Henry VII brought to an end the Wars of the Roses by defeating Richard III at the Battle of Bosworth and marrying Elizabeth of York. Henry VII's other great achievements included the building of a merchant navy, and the Henry VII Chapel in Westminster Abbey, the eventual resting place for him and his queen.

Henry VII was succeeded in 1509 by arch wife-collector (and dispatcher) Henry VIII. Henry's first marriage to Catherine of Aragon failed to produce an heir, so the King, in 1527, determined that the union should be annulled. As the Pope refused to co-operate, Henry defied the Catholic Church, demanding that he himself be recognised as Supreme Head of the Church in England and ordering the execution of anyone who refused to go along with the plan (including his chancellor Sir Thomas More). Thus England began the transition to Protestantism. The subsequent dissolution of the monasteries transformed the face of the medieval city with the confiscation and redevelopment of all property owned by the Catholic Church.

On a more positive note, Henry did manage to develop a professional navy in between beheading his wives, founding the Royal Dockyards at Woolwich in 1512 and at Deptford the following year. He also established palaces at Hampton Court and Whitehall, and built a residence at St James's Palace. Much of the land he annexed for hunting became the Royal Parks, including Hyde, Regent's, Greenwich and Richmond Parks.

There was a brief Catholic revival under Queen Mary (1553-8), and her marriage to Philip II of Spain met with much opposition in London. She had 300 Protestants burned at the stake at Smithfield, earning her the nickname 'Bloody Mary' (*see p11* **Who she?**).

ELIZABETHAN LONDON

Elizabeth I's reign (1558-1603) saw a flowering of English commerce and arts. The founding of the Royal Exchange by Sir Thomas Gresham in 1566 gave London its first trading centre, allowing it to emerge as Europe's leading commercial centre. The merchant venturers and the first joint-stock companies (Russia Company and Levant Company) established new trading enterprises, and Drake, Raleigh and Hawkins sailed to the New World and beyond. In 1580 Elizabeth knighted Sir Francis Drake on his return from a three-year circumnavigation; eight years later, Drake and Howard defeated the Spanish Armada.

As trade grew, so did London. By 1600, it was home to some 200,000 people, many living in dirty, overcrowded conditions, with plague and fire constant hazards. The most complete picture of Tudor London is given in John Stow's *Survey of London* (1598), a fascinating first-hand account by a diligent Londoner whose monument stands in the City church of St Andrew Undershaft.

The glory of the Elizabethan era was the development of English drama, popular with all social classes but treated with disdain by the Corporation of London, which went as far as to ban theatres from the City in 1575. Two theatres, the Rose (1587) and the Globe (1599), were erected on the south bank of the Thames at Bankside, and provided homes for the works of Marlowe and Shakespeare. Deemed 'a naughty place' by royal proclamation, Bankside was the Soho of its time: home not just to the theatre, but also to bear-baiting, cock-fighting, taverns and 'Stewes' (brothels).

The Tudor dynasty ended with Elizabeth's death in 1603. Her successor, the Stuart King James I, narrowly escaped assassination on 5 November 1605, when Guy Fawkes and his gunpowder were discovered underneath the Palace of Westminster. The Gunpowder Plot was a protest at the failure to improve conditions for the persecuted Catholics, but only resulted in several messy executions and an

Early bard: **Christopher Marlowe**.

Who she? Bloody Mary

The reign of 'Bloody Mary', a devout Catholic who sought to return her land to the 'true faith', will be forever tainted by the barbaric treatment she meted out to Protestant 'heretics'. The daughter of Henry VIII and his first wife, Catherine of Aragon, Mary Tudor was born in 1516. After repudiating Henry's divorce of her mother and subsequent marriage to Anne Boleyn, she was stripped of her title of princess, but when Anne fell out of favour and became the first of Henry's wives to go to the execution block, father and daughter were reconciled.

In 1547 Mary's younger brother succeeded his father as King Edward VI. Swayed by religious fervour, and surrounded by over-zealous advisers, he embarked on a series of swingeing Protestant reforms. Mary risked her own life to continue celebrating the Roman Catholic mass in her private chapel. In 1553, after a brief hiatus when Lady Jane Grey usurped the throne, Mary was proclaimed the rightful ruler. On 3 August 1553, at the age of 37, she made a triumphant entry into London. According to a contemporary observer, she rode through London streets 'so full of people shouting "Jesus save her Grace", with weeping tears for joy, that was never seen before'.

The Venetian ambassador described her as short, rather thin, with a red and white complexion and a poor dress sense. In the opinion of an imperial envoy, she was 'inexperienced in worldly matters and a novice all round'. Longing to bring her people back to the Church of Rome, she resolved, against the wishes of her advisors, to marry Philip II of Spain, son of Emperor Charles V. A Protestant insurrection broke out under the leadership of Sir Thomas Wyatt, who, in February 1554, crossed the River Thames at Richmond and marched on London accompanied by 3,000 armed rebels. At the Guildhall, Mary rallied Londoners to the city's defence. Wyatt led his men past Charing Cross, along Fleet Street, and was halted by troops at Ludgate, where he gave himself up. Along with 100 rebels, he was executed for treason, and Mary's Spanish marriage went ahead.

Fearful of Mary's Catholicism, some 700 Protestant refugees fled to Frankfurt, Zurich and Geneva. From the safety of these cities, they waged an unceasing propaganda war on Mary's Catholic reforms. In 1555 the

persecution of Protestants began. A total of 237 men and 52 women were burnt at the stake, about 60 of them in London alone, and the Queen's informers and spies generated an atmosphere of fear and paranoia that did little to serve Mary's pro-Catholic cause. Mary's husband persuaded her to wage an unsuccessful war with France, which further alienated her from her people.

After what turned out to be an unhappy and childless marriage, Mary died on November 17 1588, disliked, feared and slandered. Her Catholic reforms died with her.

intensification of anti-papist feelings in ever-intolerant London. The date is commemorated – and, a little incongruously, celebrated with fireworks galore – as Bonfire Night to this day.

But aside from his unwitting part in the Gunpowder Plot, James I merits remembering for other, more important reasons. For it was he who hired Inigo Jones to design court masques and what ended up as the first examples of classical Renaissance style in London, the Queen's House in Greenwich (1616) and the Banqueting House in Westminster (1619).

CIVIL WAR

Charles I succeeded his father in 1625, but gradually fell out with the City of London (from whose citizens he tried to extort taxes) and an increasingly independent-minded and antagonistic Parliament. The last straw finally came in 1642 when he intruded on the Houses of Parliament in an attempt to arrest five MPs. The country soon slid into a civil war (1642-9) between the supporters of Parliament (led by Puritan Oliver Cromwell) and those of the King.

> **'Many poor Londoners drank excessive amounts in an attempt to escape the horrors of daily life.'**

Both sides knew that control of the country's major city and port was vital for victory. London's sympathies were firmly with the Parliamentarians and, in 1642, 24,000 citizens assembled at Turnham Green, west of the city, to face Charles's army. Fatally, the King lost his nerve and withdrew, and was never to seriously threaten the capital again; eventually, the Royalists were defeated. Charles was tried for treason and, though he denied the legitimacy of the court, he was declared guilty. On 30 January 1649, he was beheaded outside the Banqueting House in Whitehall, declaring himself to be a 'martyr of the people'.

For the next 11 years the country was ruled as a Commonwealth by Cromwell. However, the closing of the theatres and the banning of the supposedly Catholic superstition of Christmas, along with other Puritan strictures on the wickedness of any sort of fun, meant that the restoration of the exiled Charles II in 1660 was greeted with relief and rejoicing by the populace.

PLAGUE, FIRE & REVOLUTION

However, two major catastrophes marred the first decade of Charles's reign in the capital. In 1665 the most serious outbreak of bubonic plague since the Black Death killed so many of the capital's population. By the time the winter cold had put paid to the epidemic, nearly 100,000 Londoners had died.

On 2 September 1666, just as the city was breathing a sigh of relief, a second disaster struck. The fire that spread from a carelessly tended oven in Farriner's Baking Shop on Pudding Lane was to rage for three days and consume four-fifths of the city, including 87 churches, 44 livery company halls and more than 13,000 houses.

Despite the obvious tragic element, the Great Fire at least allowed planners the chance to rebuild London as a spacious, rationally planned modern city. Many blueprints were drawn up and considered, but, in the end, Londoners were so impatient to get on with business as soon as possible that the city was reconstructed largely on its medieval street plan, albeit this time in brick and stone rather than wood. The towering figure of the period turned out to be the extraordinarily prolific Sir Christopher Wren (*see p86* **Who he?**), who oversaw the work on 51 of the 54 churches that were rebuilt. Among them was his masterpiece, the new St Paul's, completed in 1711 and, effectively, the world's first Protestant cathedral.

After the Great Fire, many well-to-do former City residents moved to new residential developments that were springing up in the West End. In the City, the Royal Exchange was rebuilt, but merchants increasingly used the new coffee houses in which to exchange news. With the expansion of the joint-stock companies and the chance to invest capital, the City was emerging as a centre not of manufacturing, but of finance.

Anti-Catholic feeling still ran high, however. The accession of Catholic James II in 1685 aroused fears of a return to Catholicism, and resulted in a Dutch Protestant, William of Orange, being invited to take the throne with his wife, Mary Stuart (James's daughter); James later fled to France in 1688 in what became known – by its beneficiaries – as the 'Glorious Revolution'. One of the most significant developments during William III's reign was the founding of the Bank of England in 1694, initially to finance the King's wars with France.

GEORGIAN LONDON

After the death of Queen Anne, and in accordance with the Act of Settlement (1701), the throne passed to George, great-grandson of James I, who had been born and brought up in Hanover, Germany. Thus, a German-speaking king – who never learned English – became the first of four long-reigning Georges in the Hanoverian line.

Jewish London

The first Jewish settlers came to England with the Normans, with the earliest documentary evidence of a Jewish quarter in London dating back to 1128. Little more than half a century later, in 1189, this fledgling Jewish community fell victim to the first of London's anti-semitic riots, which may have been initiated by people who owed money to the Jews (who weren't permitted to engage in ordinary commerce but were allowed to lend money, since usury was forbidden by the Christian Church). Their 'houses were besieged by roaring people' and burnt to the ground, and many people who tried to flee were clubbed or beaten to death.

This was just the start of it. In 1272 hundreds of Jews were hung on suspicion of adulterating the coinage, and further mob slaughters occurred in 1215 and 1290. Finally, following the carnage of 1290, Jews were expelled from the city. Over the next four centuries, some Jews returned, quietly and unobtrusively, but it was not until the mid 17th century, following a 'Humble Petition of the Hebrews at present residing in this City of London', that Oliver Cromwell officially sanctioned their presence. They were granted their wish that 'we may therewith meete at our said private devotions in our particular houses without feere of Molestation either to our persons, famillys or estates'.

The first official settlers were mainly Sephardic Jews from Spain and Portugal, but the 17th and 18th centuries saw the arrival of Ashkenazi Jews from central and eastern Europe; the first Ashkenazi synagogue was established in Aldgate in 1722. These new settlers, often fleeing persecution, were less affluent and less well educated than their predecessors. Their poverty, and the self-containment of their communities, made them frequent targets of public opprobrium and hatred. Whitechapel was long established as the first port of call for migrants, with Huguenots, Jews and Irish migrants all settling there. The number of Jewish arrivals swelled after the assassination of Tsar Alexander II in 1881 led to anti-semitic pogroms in Russia and Poland. Many new arrivals found work in the clothing and tailoring trades, which were centred on Petticoat Lane, as well as other branches of commerce and finance.

By the beginning of the 20th century, many newly affluent Jews had moved out of the East End and put down roots elsewhere, especially in areas in the north and west of London, such as St John's Wood, Golders Green, Islington and Stoke Newington. Today London's orthodox Jewish communities are concentrated in the Stamford Hill area. Famous old East End landmarks, such as Bloom's restaurant, the Kosher Luncheon club and the Garden Street Synagogue, have all disappeared, though you can still see a piece of old Jewish London at 19 Princelet Street, Spitalfields, which began life as a home for Huguenots fleeing persecution in France but later, in 1869, had a synagogue built in its grounds by Jewish emigrants (*see p153*).

During his reign (1714-27), and for several years afterwards, the Whig party – led by Sir Robert Walpole – had the monopoly of power in Parliament. Their opponents, the Tories, supported the Stuarts and had opposed the exclusion of the Catholic James II. On the King's behalf Walpole chaired a group of ministers (the forerunner of today's Cabinet), becoming, in effect, Britain's first prime minister. Walpole was presented with 10 Downing Street as a residence; it remains the official home of all serving prime ministers.

During the 18th century, London grew with astonishing speed, in terms of both population and built-up area. New squares and streets of terraced houses spread all over Soho, Bloomsbury, Mayfair and Marylebone as wealthy landowners and speculative developers who didn't mind taking a risk given the size of the potential rewards cashed in on the demand for leasehold properties.

South London, too, became more accessible with the opening of the first new bridges for several centuries, Westminster Bridge (1750)

In Context

and Blackfriars Bridge (1763). Until then, London Bridge had been the only bridge over the Thames. The old city gates, most of the Roman Wall and the remaining houses on Old London Bridge were demolished, allowing easier access to the City for traffic and people.

POVERTY & CRIME

In the older districts, however, people were still living in terrible squalor and poverty, far worse than that of Victorian times. Some of the most notorious slums were around Fleet Street and St Giles's (north of Covent Garden), only a short distance from streets of fashionable residences maintained by large numbers of servants. To make matters worse, gin ('mother's ruin') was readily available at very low prices, and many poor Londoners drank excessive amounts in an attempt to escape the horrors of daily life. The well-off seemed complacent, amusing themselves at the popular Ranelagh and Vauxhall Pleasure Gardens or with organised trips to Bedlam (see p169 **Whatever happened to?**) to mock the mental patients. On a similar level, public executions at Tyburn – near today's Marble Arch – were among the most popular events in the social calendar.

The outrageous imbalance in the distribution of wealth encouraged crime: robberies in the West End took place in daylight. Reformers were few, though there were exceptions. Henry Fielding, author of the picaresque novel *Tom Jones*, was also an enlightened magistrate at Bow Street Court. In 1751 he established, with his blind brother John, a volunteer force of 'thief-takers' to back up the often ineffective efforts of the parish constables and watchmen who were the only law-keepers in the city. This group of early cops, known as the Bow Street Runners, were the forerunners of today's Metropolitan Police (established in 1829).

Disaffection was also evident in the activities of the London mob during this period. Riots were a regular reaction to middlemen charging extortionate prices, or merchants adulterating their food. In June 1780 London was hit by the anti-Catholic Gordon Riots, named after ringleader George Gordon; the worst in the city's violent history, they left 300 people dead.

Some attempts were made to alleviate the grosser ills of poverty with the setting up of five major new hospitals by private philanthropists. St Thomas's and St Bartholomew's were already long established as monastic institutions for the care of the sick, but Westminster (1720), Guy's (1725), St George's (1734), London (1740) and the Middlesex (1745) went on to become world-famous teaching hospitals. Thomas Coram's Foundling Hospital for abandoned children was another remarkable achievement of the time.

However, it wasn't just the indigenous population of London that was on the rise in the 18th century. Country people (who had lost their own land because of enclosures and were faced with starvation wages or unemployment) drifted into the towns in large numbers. The East End increasingly became the focus for poor immigrant labourers, especially with the building of the docks towards the end of the 18th century. By 1801, London's population had grown to almost a million, the largest of any city in Europe. And by 1837, when Queen Victoria came to the throne, five more bridges and the capital's first railway line (from London Bridge to Greenwich) gave off further hints that a major expansion might be around the corner.

THE VICTORIAN ERA

As well as being the administrative and financial capital of the British Empire, spanning a fifth of the globe, London was also its chief port and the world's largest manufacturing centre, with breweries, distilleries, tanneries, shipyards, engineering works and many other grimy industries lining the south bank of the Thames. On the one hand, London boasted splendid buildings, fine shops, theatres and museums; on the other, it was a city of poverty, disease and prostitution. The residential areas were becoming polarised into districts with fine terraces maintained by squads of servants, and overcrowded, insanitary, disease-ridden slums.

> **'After the trauma of World War I, a "live for today" attitude prevailed in the "Roaring '20s".'**

The growth of the metropolis in the century before Victoria came to the throne had been spectacular enough, but during her reign, which lasted until 1901, thousands more acres were covered with housing, roads and railway lines. Today, if you pick any street within five miles (eight kilometres) of central London, chances are that its houses will be mostly Victorian. By the end of the 19th century, the city's population had swelled to in excess of six million.

Despite the social problems – memorably depicted in the writings of Charles Dickens – major steps had been taken to improve conditions for the great majority of Londoners by the turn of the century. The Metropolitan Board of Works installed an efficient sewerage system, street lighting and better roads, while the worst slums were replaced by low-cost building schemes funded by philanthropists such as the American George Peabody and by the London County Council (created in 1888).

The Victorian expansion of London would not have been possible without an efficient public transport network with which to speed workers into and out of the city from the new suburbs. The horse-drawn bus appeared on London's streets for the first time in 1829, but it was the opening of the first passenger railway seven years later, running from Greenwich to London Bridge, that hailed the London of the future. In 1863 the first underground line – which ran between Paddington and Farringdon Road – proved an instant success, attracting more than 30,000 travellers on the first day. Soon thereafter, the world's first electric track in a deep tunnel (the 'Tube') opened in 1890 between the City and Stockwell, later becoming part of the present-day Northern line.

THE GREAT EXHIBITION

The Great Exhibition of 1851 captured the zeitgeist: confidence and pride, discovery and invention. Prince Albert, the Queen's Consort, was involved in the organisation of this triumphant event, for which the Crystal Palace, a giant building of iron and glass – designed not by a professional architect but by the Duke of Devonshire's talented gardener, Joseph Paxton – was erected in Hyde Park. During the five months it was open, the Exhibition drew some six million visitors from Great Britain and abroad, and the profits inspired the Prince Consort to establish a permanent centre for the study of the applied arts and sciences: the result is the South Kensington museums and Imperial College. After the Exhibition the Palace was moved to Sydenham and used as an exhibition centre until it was destroyed by fire in 1936.

When the Victorians were not colonising the world by force, they had the foresight to combine their conquests with scientific developments. The Royal Geographical Society sent navigators to chart unknown waters, botanists to bring back new species, and geologists to study the earth. Many of the specimens that were brought back ended up at the Royal Botanic Gardens at Kew.

THE 20TH CENTURY

During the brief reign of Edward VII (1901-10), London regained some of the gaiety and glamour it lacked in the dour last years of Victoria's reign. A touch of Parisian chic came to London with the opening of the Ritz Hotel in Piccadilly; the Café Royal hit the heights of its popularity as a meeting place for artists and writers; and 'luxury catering for the little man' was provided at the Lyons Tea Shops and new Lyons Corner Houses (the Coventry Street branch, which opened in 1907, could accommodate an incredible 4,500

people). Meanwhile, the first American-style department store, Selfridges, opened to an eager public on Oxford Street in 1909.

Road transport, too, was revolutionised. Motor cars put-putted around the city's streets, before the first motor bus was introduced in 1904. Double-decked electric trams had started running in 1901 (though not through the West End or the City), and continued doing so for 51 years. In fact, by 1911 the use of horse-drawn buses had been abandoned.

WORLD WAR I (1914-18)

London suffered its first air raids in World War I. The first bomb over the city was dropped from a Zeppelin near Guildhall in September 1915, and was followed by many nightly raids; bombing raids from planes began in July 1917. Cleopatra's Needle, on Victoria Embankment, was a minor casualty, receiving damage to the plinth and one of its sphinxes that can still be seen. In all, around 650 people lost their lives as a result of Zeppelin raids.

BETWEEN THE WARS

Political change happened quickly after World War I. Lloyd George's government averted revolution in 1918-19 by promising (but not delivering) 'homes for heroes' for the embittered returning soldiers. But the Liberal Party's days in power were numbered, and by 1924 a Labour Party, led by Ramsay MacDonald, had enough MPs to form its first government.

After the trauma of World War I, a 'live for today' attitude prevailed in the 'Roaring '20s' among the young upper classes, who flitted from parties in Mayfair to dances at the Ritz. But this meant little to the mass of Londoners, who were suffering greatly in the post-war slump. In 1921 Poplar Council in east London refused to levy the rates on its impoverished population. The entire council was sent to prison but was later released, having achieved an equalisation of the rates over all London boroughs that relieved the burden on the poorest ones.

Still, things didn't improve immediately. Civil disturbances brought on by an increased cost of living and rising unemployment resulted in the nationwide General Strike of 1926, when the working classes downed tools in support of the striking miners. Prime Minister Baldwin encouraged volunteers to take over the public services and the streets teemed with army-escorted food convoys, aristocrats running soup kitchens and students driving buses. After nine days of chaos, the strike was called off by the Trades Union Congress (TUC).

The economic situation only worsened in the early 1930s following the New York Stock Exchange crash of 1929; by 1931, more than

WORLD WAR II (1939-45)

Neville Chamberlain's policy of appeasement towards Hitler's increasingly aggressive Germany during the 1930s finally collapsed when the Germans invaded Poland, and on 3 September 1939, Britain declared war. The government implemented precautionary measures against the threat of air raids – including the digging of trench shelters in London parks, and the evacuation of 600,000 children and pregnant mothers – but the expected bombing raids did not happen during the autumn and winter of 1939-40, a period that became known as the 'Phoney War'. In July 1940, though, Germany began preparations for an invasion of Britain with three months of aerial attack that came to be known as the Battle of Britain.

'London Transport and the NHS were particularly active in encouraging West Indians to emigrate to Britain.'

For Londoners the Phoney War came to an abrupt end on 7 September 1940 when hundreds of German bombers dumped their loads of high explosives on east London and the docks. Entire streets were destroyed; the dead and injured numbered more than 2,000. The Blitz had begun. The raids on London continued for 57 consecutive nights, then intermittently for a further six months. Londoners reacted with tremendous bravery and stoicism, a period still nostalgically referred to as 'Britain's finest hour'. After a final massive raid on 10 May 1941 the Germans focused their attention elsewhere, but by the end of the war about a third of the City and the East End was in ruins.

From 1942 the tide of the war began to turn, but Londoners still had a new terror to face: the V1, or 'doodlebug'. In 1944 dozens of these explosives-packed pilotless planes descended on the city, causing widespread destruction. Later in the year, the more powerful V2 rocket was launched, and over the winter, 500 of them dropped on London, mostly in the East End. The last fell on 27 March 1945 in Orpington, Kent, around six weeks before Victory in Europe (VE Day) was declared on 8 May 1945. Thousands of people took to the streets of London to celebrate.

POST-WAR LONDON

World War II left Britain almost as shattered as Germany. Soon after VE Day a general election was held and Churchill was heavily defeated by the Labour Party under Clement Attlee. The

Lyons Tea Shops: 'little luxuries'. *See p16.*

three million people in Britain were jobless. During these years, the London County Council began to have a greater impact on the city's life, undertaking programmes of slum clearance and new housing, creating more parks and taking under its wing education, transport, hospitals, libraries and the fire service.

London's population increased dramatically between the wars too, peaking at nearly 8.7 million in 1939. To accommodate the influx, the suburbs expanded at a tremendous rate, particularly to the north-west with the extension of the Metropolitan line to an area that became known as Metroland. Identical gabled, double-fronted houses sprang up in their hundreds of thousands, from Golders Green to Surbiton.

All these new Londoners were entertained by the new media of film, radio and TV. London's first radio broadcast was beamed from the roof of Marconi House in the Strand in 1922, and families were soon gathering around their enormous Bakelite wireless sets to hear the latest sounds from the British Broadcasting Company (the BBC; from 1927 called the British Broadcasting Corporation). Television broadcasts started on 26 August 1936, when the first BBC telecast went out live from Alexandra Palace studios.

Londoners shelter from the **Blitz**. *See p17.*

in 1953 had been the biggest television broadcast in history, and there was the feeling of a new age dawning.

However, many Londoners were moving out of the city. The population dropped by half a million in the late 1950s, causing a labour shortage that prompted huge recruitment drives in Britain's former colonies. London Transport and the National Health Service were particularly active in encouraging West Indians to emigrate to Britain. Unfortunately, as the Notting Hill race riots of 1958 illustrated, the welcome these new emigrants received was rarely friendly. Yet there were areas of tolerance, among them Soho, which, during the 1950s, became famed for its seedy, bohemian pubs, clubs and jazz joints, such as the still-jumping Ronnie Scott's.

By the mid '60s London had started to swing. The innovative fashions of Mary Quant and others broke Paris's stranglehold on couture: boutiques blossomed along King's Road, while Biba set the pace in Kensington. Carnaby Street became a byword for hipness as the city basked in its newfound reputation as the music and fashion capital of the world.

new government established the National Health Service in 1948, and began a massive nationalisation programme that included public transport, electricity, gas, postal and telephone services. But for all the planned changes, life for most people was drab, regimented and austere.

In London, the most immediate problem was a critical shortage of housing. Prefabricated bungalows provided a temporary solution (though many were still occupied 40 years later), but the huge new high-rise housing estates that the planners began to erect were often badly built and proved to be very unpopular with residents.

However, there were bright spots during this otherwise rather dour time. London hosted the Olympics in 1948; three years later came the Festival of Britain (100 years after the Great Exhibition), a celebration of British technology and design. The exhibitions that took over derelict land on the south bank of the Thames for the Festival provided the incentive to build the South Bank Centre.

THE 1950S AND 1960S

As the 1950s progressed, life and prosperity gradually returned to London, leading Prime Minister Harold Macmillan in 1957 to proclaim that 'most of our people have never had it so good'. The coronation of Queen Elizabeth II

'So effective was the GLC, in fact, that Thatcher abolished it in 1986.'

The year of student unrest in Europe, 1968, saw the first issue of *Time Out* (a fold-up sheet for 5p) appear on the streets in August. The decade ended with the Beatles naming their final album *Abbey Road* after their recording studios in London, NW8, and the Rolling Stones playing a free gig in Hyde Park (July 1969) that drew around half a million people.

THATCHERISM

The bubble, though, had to burst, and burst it did. Many Londoners remember the 1970s as a decade of economic strife: inflation, the oil crisis and international debt caused chaos, and the IRA began its bombing campaign on mainland Britain. The explosion of punk in the second half of the decade, sartorially inspired by the idiosyncratic genius of Vivienne Westwood, provided some nihilistic colour.

History will regard the 1980s as the Thatcher era. When the Conservatives won the general election in 1979, Britain's first woman prime minister – the propagandist for 'market forces' and Little Englander morality – set out to expunge socialism and the influence of the 1960s and 1970s. A monetarist policy and cuts in public services savagely widened the divide between rich and poor. While the professionals and 'yuppies' (Young Urban Professionals) profited from tax cuts and easy credit, unemployment soared. In London, riots erupted in Brixton (1981) and Tottenham (1985); mass unemployment and heavy-handed policing methods were seen as contributing factors.

The Greater London Council (GLC), led by Ken Livingstone (*see p25* **Who he?**), mounted spirited opposition to the Thatcher government with a series of populist measures, the most famous of which was a revolutionary fare-cutting policy on public transport. So effective was the GLC, in fact, that Thatcher decided to abolish it in 1986.

The spectacular rise in house prices at the end of the 1980s (peaking in August 1988) was followed by an equally alarming slump and the onset of a severe recession that only started to lift in the mid 1990s. The Docklands development – one of the Thatcher enterprise schemes, set up in 1981 in order to create a new business centre in the Docklands to the east of

The great smog

On 6 December 1952 London was swathed in a lethal combination of fog and smoke that, over the next four days, left an astonishing 4,000 people dead, mainly from respiratory and cardiac conditions, and even asphyxiated cattle at Smithfield Market. The British capital was no stranger to smog, the main culprit for which was the burning of coal: in 1661 John Evelyn had written of the 'hellish and dismall cloud of sea-coale' that lay over the city. But the authorities ignored him and the pollution continued.

In 1813 a persistent fog that cloaked London for a week was so dense it took the mail coach from London seven hours to reach Uxbridge. By the 19th century factories were belching gases and huge numbers of particles into the atmosphere, compounding the poisonous cocktail. Acrid-smelling, yellow-tinted fogs – known as 'pea-soupers' – became a common phenomenon, with serious fogs occurring in 1873, 1880, 1882, 1891 and 1892, each of them accompanied by a marked increase in death rate. The worst afflicted areas were invariably the East End, with its high density of factories and houses; the fact that it is low-lying also made it difficult for the fog to disperse.

In December 1952 the weather was colder than average. A large high-pressure centre hung over London, forming an 'inversion' – a shallow layer of cool air that trapped the pollution near the ground. On the night of 5-6 December the fog thickened, forming a dense yellow cloud, and visibility dropped to less than half a metre. Cyclists found themselves covered in soot, while pedestrians blundered through the murky darkness. In the Isle of Dogs the fog was so thick that people could not even see their own feet. Choked by acrid fumes, people resorted to face masks and even gas masks. A performance at Sadler's Wells Theatre was halted because of choking

fog in the auditorium, while films had to be cancelled because people couldn't see the screens. Road, rail and air transport was brought to a complete standstill.

But the infamous great smog was the last of its kind – the Clean Air Acts of 1956 and 1968 banned emissions of black smoke, decreeing that residents and factories converted to smokeless fuels, and after several centuries and thousands of human deaths, pea-soupers finally became a thing of the past.

the City – has faltered many times, although it can now be counted as a qualified success in terms of attracting business and a rapidly increasing number of residents to the Isle of Dogs and surrounding areas.

RECENT PAST & NEAR FUTURE

The replacement of the by-now hated Thatcher by John Major as leader of the Conservative Party in October 1990 signalled an upsurge of hope in London. A riot in Trafalgar Square had helped to see off both Maggie and her inequitable Poll Tax.

Yet the early years of the decade were scarred by continuing recession and an all-too-visible problem of homelessness on the streets of the capital. Shortly after the Conservatives were elected for another term in office in 1992, the IRA detonated a massive bomb in the City, killing three people. This was followed by a second bomb a year later, which shattered buildings around Bishopsgate, and by another Docklands bomb in February 1996, which broke a fragile 18-month ceasefire. The Good Friday agreement raised hopes for permanent peace in the province, and although disagreements about the decommissioning of weapons have given rise to sporadic violence in Northern Ireland, these questions now appear to have been resolved, and the terrorist threat to the capital has been massively reduced – at least from those quarters.

In May 1997 the British people ousted the tired Tories, and Tony Blair's notably unsocialist Labour Party swept to victory on a wave of enthusiasm. But a sequence of woes did much to obliterate that enthusiasm. Although the millennium celebrations went off with a bang, London's hugely hyped assortment of celebratory projects had a mixed reception. Tate Modern and the Millennium wheel were considered an unqualified success, but the Millennium Dome, the unlikely recipient of nearly £1 billion of public money, was badly mismanaged from the outset. Despite attracting around six million visitors over the year in which it was open, it never shook off its negative image, and was not much mourned when it closed at the end of the year.

In 2000 there was a nationwide petrol crisis, during which protesters against fuel taxes effectively blockaded the country's petrol supply, leaving London without vehicle fuel for 48 hours. A series of serious rail accidents, most notably at Ladbroke Grove and Hatfield, brought the train network to a near standstill in the winter of 2000/2001, as railway companies embarked on a panic-stricken, and long-overdue, overhaul of Britain's railway lines. Finally, in the spring of 2001, the English

countryside was hit by an epidemic of foot and mouth disease. London was not directly affected, but grim scenes of pyres of burning carcasses and the virtual closure of parts of the countryside had an immediate impact on tourist figures, in London as elsewhere.

In May 2000 Ken Livingstone, ex-Labour MP and former leader of the ill-fated GLC (*see p19*), became London's first directly elected mayor, heading up the Greater London Assembly (GLA), which, it is hoped, will provide London with a democratic voice on local issues. The GLA immediately became embroiled in an issue that deeply concerns most Londoners, the parlous state of the Underground system, with Livingstone contending that the government's proposed public-private partnership scheme (PPP) will jeopardise public safety (*see p70* **Rumblings**).

Despite all this controversy, when Blair finally called a general election in June 2001 the public reacted with indifference and inertia. Lacking any credible opposition, Blair and the Labour party were re-elected, though with a reduced majority, and they continue to dominate London's politics.

In 1996, before Blair's triumphant victory, *Newsweek* magazine proclaimed London was the 'capital of cool', a city effervescing with creativity and unrivalled for its clubs, fashion industry, art world, architecture and general lifestyle. But the last five years have brought their share of troubles, from strikes by disgruntled tube workers to violent riots by anti-capitalist protesters. The government's vision for London is expansive: the eastern river corridor is being redeveloped, and leading architects such as Richard Rogers and Norman Foster are continuing their transformation of the city. Culturally, the city is very much alive – as a glance at Tate Modern, the newly refurbished Wallace Collection, Somerset House or the British Museum will prove. But the people who live in this overwhelming city – beset by chaos on the tube, rising crime, congested traffic and the sheer size of the place – often find that their own lives fall far short of the government's visions and promises.

As we go to press, in the wake of the terrorist outrages that took place in New York and Washington in September 2001, Londoners are once again on their guard, more alert than ever to threats to their security. Visitor numbers are down, and the impact is being felt in theatreland, hotels, restaurants and all of London's many tourist attractions. It remains to be seen whether the city will be able to rise above these challenges, as it has done with other challenges in its history.

Key events

AD 43	The Romans invade; a bridge is built on the Thames; Londinium is founded.	**1802**	The Stock Exchange is founded.
61	Boudicca burns Londinium; the city is rebuilt and made the provincial capital.	**1803**	The first public railway opens, horse-drawn from Croydon to Wandsworth.
200	A city wall is built; Londinium becomes capital of Britannia Superior.	**1812**	Prime Minister Spencer Perceval is assassinated at Parliament.
410	Roman troops evacuate Britain.	**1824**	The National Gallery is founded.
c600	Saxon London is built to the west.	**1827**	Regent's Park Zoo opens.
604	St Paul's is built by King Ethelbert; Mellitus becomes Bishop of London.	**1829**	London's first horse-drawn bus runs from Paddington to the City; the Metropolitan Police Act is set up.
841	The Norse raid for the first time.		
c871	The Danes occupy London.		
886	King Alfred of Wessex retakes London.	**1833**	The London Fire Brigade is established.
1013	The Danes take London back.	**1835**	Madame Tussaud's opens.
1042	Edward the Confessor builds a palace and 'West Minster' upstream.	**1836**	The first passenger railway opens, from Greenwich to London Bridge; the University of London is founded.
1066	William I is crowned in Westminster Abbey; London is granted a charter.		
1067	Work begins on the Tower of London.	**1837**	Parliament is rebuilt after a fire.
1191	Henry Fitzalwin is the first mayor.	**1843**	Trafalgar Square is laid out.
1213	St Thomas's Hospital is founded.	**1848-9**	A cholera epidemic sweeps London.
1215	The Mayor of London signs the Magna Carta, strengthening the City's power.	**1851**	The Great Exhibition takes place.
1240	First Parliament sits at Westminster.	**1853**	Harrods opens its doors.
1290	Jews are expelled from London.	**1858**	The Great Stink: pollution in the Thames reaches hideous levels.
1327	The first Common Council of the City of London.	**1863**	The Metropolitan line, the world's first underground railway, opens.
1348-9	The Black Death devastates London.	**1864**	The Peabody buildings, cheap housing for the poor, are built in Spitalfields.
1381	Wat Tyler leads the Peasants' Revolt.		
1397	Richard Whittington is Lord Mayor.	**1866**	London's last major cholera outbreak; the Sanitation Act is passed.
1476	The first ever printing press is set up by William Caxton at Westminster.	**1868**	The last public execution is held at Newgate Prison.
1513	The Royal Dockyard at Woolwich and Deptford is founded by Henry VIII.	**1884**	Greenwich Mean Time is established.
1534	Henry VIII cuts off the Catholic Church.	**1888**	Jack the Ripper prowls the East End.
1566	Gresham opens the Royal Exchange.	**1889**	A London County Council is created.
1599	The Globe Theatre is built on Bankside.	**1890**	The Housing Act enables the LCC to clear the slums; the first electric underground railway opens.
1605	Guy Fawkes fails to blow up James I.		
1642	The start of the Civil War; Royalists are defeated at Turnham Green.	**1915-8**	Zeppelins bomb London.
1649	Charles I is executed; Commonwealth is established under Cromwell.	**1940-4**	The Blitz devastates much of London.
1664-5	The Great Plague.	**1948**	The Olympic Games are held.
1666	The Great Fire.	**1951**	The Festival of Britain takes place.
1675	Building starts on the new St Paul's.	**1953**	Queen Elizabeth II is crowned.
1692	Lloyd's first insurance market opens.	**1966**	England win World Cup at Wembley.
1694	The Bank of England is established.	**1982**	The last of London's docks close.
1717	Hanover Square and Cavendish Square are laid out, signalling the start of the development of the West End.	**1986**	The GLC is abolished.
		1990	Poll Tax protesters riot.
		1991	Riots in Brixton.
1750	Westminster Bridge is built.	**1992**	Canary Wharf opens; an IRA bomb ravages the Baltic Exchange in the City.
1766	The city wall is demolished.		
1780	The anti-Catholic, anti-Irish Gordon Riots take place.	**1997**	Princess Diana dies.
		2000	Ken Livingstone is elected mayor; new attractions include Tate Modern and the London Eye.
		2001	The Labour government is re-elected.

London Today

History in the making.

Night time is the right time, but daylight isn't too shabby, either. It's probably best seen from somewhere around the Tower of London; certainly, the north bank of the Thames, around the City of London, is the optimum viewing point for this south-side cityscape. So, view...

To your left? The handsome yet daunting Tower Bridge, low-lit for optimum dramatic effect. A powerful, unselfconsciously garish construct, dripping with history, gall and an indisputable arrogance. On your right? The squat Greater London Authority building, its gonadal silhouette seemingly loved and hated in equal measure .

OK, so it's basically just a couple of buildings. But to look at them together is to come face to face with the dilemmas faced by London as the 21st century snaps into gear. On the one hand, its past, constantly making itself known to visitors and locals alike, refusing to be defeated by the march of time. On the other, the city's solutions to the albatrosses of its history, and of the problems it's made for itself down the years.

It's this to and fro that defines London, among visitors who come to soak up a backlog of riches at the Tower of London, Shakespeare's Globe and Buckingham Palace, but also among locals, who, while often dismissive of the city's past lives, are also typically British in their reactionary attitudes to progress. And nowhere

is progress needed more than in the perennial problem of London's traffic. That much everyone agrees; how to fix it, though, is something on which few concur.

WALKING BACK TO HAPPINESS

Let's start, though, with public transport. The government have realised it's basically rubbish and have decided to try and fix it, to liberate it from the horrors of its past.

Sorry, its past? Ah, yes: a shabby, unreliable tube service relied upon by locals only because the perpetually clogged-up traffic precludes travelling above ground. And the future, proclaims the government? A shiny happy tube service, with drivers who'll ensure every train arrives on time at its new station, and passengers who have nary a complaint about this stunning service, and are quite delighted that the government decided to fix it.

Ho-hum. We've been down this railroad before. And driving the bandwagon were the previous government. In the early 1990s, the Conservatives decided to privatise British Rail, the national overground rail network that for years had been in a parlous state, under the umbrella control of a new authority named Railtrack. Sure enough, the rail network got worse. Much, much worse. But, worst of all, safety became compromised, so in late 2001, the government shut down Railtrack.

It all sounds OK so far. Until you learn that while the government have been pronouncing rail privatisation a mess, they've been planning to introduce private funding on the tube under a scheme known as PPP (*see p70* **Rumblings**). Absolutely no one outside of the Cabinet has expressed confidence that it will help in any way whatsoever; many maintain, with good reason, that it's basically privatisation by another name, Railtrack redux. So, why are they going ahead with it? Well, in the absence of any evidence that it will actually improve the tube, the only answer is that they're doing it as a way of getting back at a man by the name of Ken Livingstone.

TURN AGAIN, KEN LIVINGSTONE

Ah, yes. Ken Livingstone. The past? Red Ken: radically left-wing and the only well-known independent politician in the country. And the future, said the voters in 2000? The first ever Mayor of London.

To scythe a long story down to its bare bones (for the uncut version, *see p25*, **Who he?**), the Labour Party still have the hump with Ken, because he had the temerity to quit the party and beat Labour's official candidate in the inaugural London mayoral election two years ago. It's likely that, were Ken not in power, the Labour government would have quietly dropped its plans for tube privatisation aeons ago. But to back down now would be viewed as a victory for Ken, and Labour couldn't countenance that.

The tube battle all but lost, Livingstone is now free to turn his attention, and that of the GLA, to his Big Idea. Essentially, the plan is that cars entering central London – an area bounded by King's Cross, Tower Bridge, Vauxhall and Park Lane – will have to pay a £5 congestion charge (road toll meets stealth tax, in essence, but 'congestion charge' sounds nicer than either of them). This fee, says Ken, will deter people from driving into busy areas, easing the traffic burden while raising money with which to improve public transport.

Like all Big Ideas, it's eye-catching, daring and revolutionary. But will it work? Though it'll raise money for public transport, it seems less likely to solve London's traffic chaos. Ken's own authority, Transport for London, predicts that traffic will drop by a mere 15 per cent in the affected area; even this sounds a little optimistic. And traffic outside the zone – in many places, as bad as that within it – is unlikely to decrease. After all, people will only ditch their cars and take public transport if public transport's worth taking, and London's isn't… especially not, says Ken without a hint of irony, if the government brings in PPP. In terms of solving London's

traffic nightmare, the congestion charge may end up as folly. Certainly, if the government had brought it in, there'd have been an outcry. But because everyone loves the media-friendly, media-savvy Ken, no one complains, and the scheme looks scheduled to start in January 2003.

CRIME AND THE CITY SOLUTION

It's far from the only problem facing Ken, though; and going on column inches alone, crime and poverty are up there at the top of the table. Few issues are as headline-grabbing as the gun violence (often drug-related) waged by gangs in pockets of east and south London. Indeed, one stretch of street in Hackney, the Lower Clapton Road, has seen so many shootings on and around it that it's become known countrywide as Murder Mile. With locals too scared to go to police for fear of reprisals, and gangs keeping their own turf wars to themselves, those investigating the crimes have been left with an impossible job, and the violence shows no signs of abating.

> ### 'People will only ditch their cars if public transport's worth taking.'

Amid these disruptions, London continues to try to position itself as a tourist-friendly town. It's done well in recent years, too, with the ill-fated Dome, the infamously unstable Millennium Bridge and the almighty governmental screw-up over the World Athletics Championships (no longer coming to London in 2005, as originally planned) the only real blots on an otherwise successful landscape of new projects. September 11 didn't even put the mockers on governmental approval for the building of a new terminal for Heathrow airport, which they rubber-stamped in November 2001 after a four-year enquiry, despite huge objections from local residents.

Yet the short-term future for London looks troubled. As a planet-wide recession begins to kick in and fewer tourists choose to fly – particularly Americans, on whom London depends for an incalculable amount of tourism income each year – the city's businesses, particularly the service industries, look set for a miserable year. Ironic, really, that while it starts to deal with many of its self-made problems of bygone years, the most hellacious prospect facing London – global economic slowdown – is one it could do little about, and that seems sure to hamper its attempts at progress in the months to come. The past looks set to hold firm and steady for a while yet. No change there, then.

Amsterdam | Barcelona | Berlin | Boston | Brussels | Budapest

Buenos Aires | Chicago | Copenhagen | Dublin | Edinburgh | Florence

Havana | Hong Kong | Istanbul | Las Vegas | Lisbon | London

Los Angeles | Madrid | Miami | Moscow | Naples | New Orleans

New York | Paris | Prague | Rome | San Francisco | South of France

Sydney | Tokyo | Venice | Vienna | Washington, DC

The **Time Out City Guides** spectrum

Who he? Ken Livingstone

Ken Livingstone's victory in the mayoral election of May 2000 was just one chapter in the career of the colourful political figure once described by the *Sun* newspaper as 'the most odious man in Britain'. A Londoner through and through (he was born in Streatham, south London, in 1945), Livingstone had his eye on a career in politics from an early age, though for eight years he worked as an animal technician in a cancer research lab. It was in 1971, two years after joining the Labour Party and while he was training as a teacher, that he was elected to Lambeth borough council. In 1973 he became a member of the infamous Greater London Council (GLC), the body responsible for coordinating London's local councils and its governing boards.

In 1981, two years after Margaret Thatcher was elected prime minster, the 36-year-old Livingstone became the most powerful figure in local government when he was made leader of the GLC. Among the positive measures he brought in were the Fares Fair initiative to cut the cost of travelling by tube, and – in the teeth of Conservative cuts – financial support for public health and housing and for the arts. Yet he revealed himself early on as a provocateur and a showman: he boycotted Charles' and Di's wedding, and, in an antagonistic gesture at the government almost directly across the Thames, hoisted a red flag alongside a banner showing unemployment figures over the GLC's HQ at County Hall.

Thatcher was livid: though the GLC didn't really have a great deal of sway, Red Ken, as he came to be known, was popular among Londoners, in many ways because of the mischievous relish with which he assumed the role of populist underdog. By 1986 the 'Iron Lady' had had enough and axed the GLC, returning London's government to local councils and unelected regional authorities. Livingstone retreated, spending his time writing books such as *If Voting Changed Anything They'd Abolish It* (1987) and

breeding newts in his backyard – a passion since childhood. The following year he was elected Labour MP for Brent East, but unable to shake off the 'Loony Left' tag it had acquired in the '80s, the party found itself on a losing streak at the next two general elections.

It was John Smith (Labour leader 1992-4) who vowed to introduce a system of regional government that included an elected mayor for Greater London. Smith's successor, Tony Blair, inherited this pledge, but found himself running scared of Red Ken, an obvious candidate but unforgiven as one of the hardliners who made the party unelectable for so long. Labour tried to limit the powers of the mayoral role; more disastrously, it also ruled out Livingstone as its candidate by imposing its own choice.

Though he'd sworn he wouldn't, Ken left the party he loved and ran as an independent candidate. On 4 May he was elected mayor by a wide margin – an extraordinary victory for the man who had said that global capitalism has killed more people than Hitler and that World Trade Organisation members should be pelted with fruit. In this respect, Ken seems very much a part of the *No Logo* generation. Yet he's also shown himself an unlikely apologist for big business in his defence of tall corporate buildings (*see 26*).

Irascible, unpredictable and, according to some, egotistical, Livingstone isn't everyone's cup of tea, yet with the limited powers afforded him and his media-friendliness he's made Londoners really think about the future of their city – what it should look like and what its role in the modern world might be – and given the government a run for its money. And that, in the end, may be his greatest legacy, for in voting for his unrepentant socialist (whether for ideological reasons or because they thought he looked like a nice guy), the public sent out a powerful message about the current state of the Labour Party.

The **GLA building**: Fostering a new image for Ken and co. *See p27*

Architecture

From medieval infernos to fiery debates, London's architecture has always been contentious.

Way back in 2000, London was heady with the excitement of a rash of millennial development, some of it more successful than others – the Tate Modern (*see p79*) was a triumph, reigniting public interest in both museum-going and architecture, while the Millennium Bridge linking the Tate to St Paul's across the river was closed almost immediately after its inauguration due to an 'unexpected wobble' (it was due to reopen as we went to press; *see p75*).

TALL STORIES

In 2001 this mood changed, with this sense of a new dawn giving way to a ferocious debate about the future of the London skyline – a debate that largely took place between Mayor Ken Livingstone and Sir Neil Cossons, chairman of English Heritage. Livingstone, who as leader of the now-defunct GLC (*see p25* **Who he?**) waged a successful war against Richard Rogers' scheme to build a stretch of offices across Coin Street on the South Bank, ousting it with a scheme to build low-rise community housing, is an unlikely champion of modern skyscrapers, and a strangely vehement one: first he described Cossons' antipathy towards them as more dangerous to the future of London as a world city than the Luftwaffe, then he went totally overboard and described English Heritage as 'the Taliban of British architecture'.

In retaliation, Cossons commissioned an opinion poll showing that most Londoners are against the construction of tall buildings that affect the city's historic skyline, which has St Paul's Cathedral as its focal point. In June he spoke out against Renzo Piano's proposed London Bridge Tower, describing it as 'a stake through London's Heart'. The tower, which at 1,014 feet (309 metres) would be Europe's tallest, will be the subject of a public enquiry at some as yet unspecified date in 2002.

Also the subject of a public enquiry as we went to press is the Heron Bishopsgate Tower designed by Kohn Pedersen Fox. The 37-storey tower, which Cossons believes would destroy the 'Canaletto view' of the Thames in front of Somerset House, is seen as a bit of a test case for the future of tower block proposals in London, especially those that would block views of St Paul's and ruin the famous view from Waterloo Bridge – immortalised by the Kinks in *Waterloo Sunset*. This too is supported by Livingstone, as well as by the Corporation of London, who want towers in the City to staunch the flow of companies to Canary Wharf, the site of two new tower blocks, including Norman Foster's Hong Kong & Shanghai Bank building.

> **'In 2001 the sense of a new dawn gave way to a ferocious debate about the future of London's skyline.'**

Livingstone's volte-face with regard to skyscrapers seemed to have been echoed by a similar switch with regard to his future home, the new GLA building on the South Bank (*see p81*): after seeing Norman Foster's plans in 2000, he pronounced the building 'a glass testicle', while in the middle of 2001 he hailed it as 'one of the most spectacular examples of architecture to be seen in the capital for years'. Likened to a huge headlamp by detractors, the building is already mired in controversy (in mid 2001 a report commissioned by the government office for London questioned its much-vaunted green credentials) and will certainly not be universally popular, but only time will tell whether it functions as the democratic powerhouse that it is intended to be.

As far as Livingstone is concerned, it's beginning to look as though, for all his talk of the importance of tall buildings for London's future as a financial centre, he's determined to make his mark on the capital in the same way that Mitterrand did with his *grands projets* in Paris. However, his new allegiance with modern architects will be sorely tested in 2002 by the vociferous opposition that is growing towards plans to demolish part of Spitalfields Market to make room for a new Norman Foster designed office complex (*see p153*).

In the meantime, English Heritage has relented somewhat in its opposition to tall buildings, conceding that it would not be reasonable to stand in the way of all skyscrapers that are planned for London. It is, however, insisting that it should have a say in both the location and the design of the new buildings, which seems fair enough.

Meanwhile, events in Manhattan in September 2001 have made us all a little less comfortable with the idea of tall buildings, particularly those connected with financial institutions, as skyscrapers tend to be. Whatever the future holds, London will be getting at least one lanky new landmark in the coming year in the form of the 'erotic gherkin', Norman Foster's building for Swiss Reinsurance, which is going up on the site of the Baltic Exchange, itself the victim of a terrorist attack. As such, it's a powerful symbol of the city as a living, changing entity, whether we want it that way or not.

CH-CH-CH-CH-CHANGES...

Unlike many other major cities, London has never really been planned. Instead, it's a hotch-potch, the product of a gradual accumulation of towns and villages and subject to adaptation, renewal and disfigurement by the changing needs of its population. Among the many events that have left their imprint on its architecture, the Great Fire of 1666 provides a useful historical marker, signalling the end of medieval London and the start of the city that we know today. Commemorated by Christopher Wren's **Monument** (*see p92*), the fire destroyed five-sixths of the city, including 13,200 houses and 89 churches. London at that time was a densely populated city built of wood, with uncollected rubbish and primitive fire control. It was only after the three-day inferno that the authorities began to insist on basic building regulations; from then on, brick and stone were the materials of choice, and key streets were widened to act as fire breaks. Most of what can now be seen is a testament to the talents of Wren (*see p86* **Who he?**) and his successors.

In spite of grand proposals from architects hoping to remodel the city from scratch, London reshaped around the old street lines. And the buildings that had survived the fire stood as monuments to earlier ages, including **St Ethelburga-the-Virgin** (68-70 Bishopsgate, EC2), noteworthy as the city's smallest chapel. Sadly, where the fire failed, the IRA succeeded, destroying two-thirds of this 13th-century building in a 1993 bomb attack. The Norman **Tower of London** (*see p92*), begun soon after William's 1066 conquest and extended over the course of the next 300 years, remains the country's most perfect example of a medieval fortress thanks to the Navy, which cheated the advancing flames by clearing the surrounding houses before the fire could get to them six centuries later.

Then there's **Westminster Abbey** (*see p133*), begun in 1245 when the borough lay far outside London's walls and completed in 1745 when Nicholas Hawksmoor added the west towers. Though the abbey is the most French of England's Gothic churches, deriving its geometry, flying buttresses and rose windows from across the Channel, the chapel, added by Henry VII and completed in 1512, is pure Tudor. 'Stone seems, by the winning labour of the chisel, to have been robbed of its weight and

density, suspended aloft, as if by magic,' gushed US author Washington Irving centuries later.

The Renaissance came late to Britain, making its London debut with Inigo Jones's 1622 **Banqueting House** (*see p133*). The addition of a sumptuously decorated ceiling by Rubens in 1635, celebrating the benefits of wise rule, made the building a must for the public, who could watch from the balconies as Charles I dined. As it turned out, the king's wisdom was a trifle lacking: 14 years later, he provided the public with an even greater spectacle as he was led from the building and beheaded.

Tourists have Jones to thank for **Covent Garden** (*see p123*) and the **Queen's House** at Greenwich (*see p166*), but these are not his only legacies. By the 1600s, Italian architecture, rooted in the forms and geometries of the Roman era, was all the rage. As a dedicated follower of fashion, Inigo Jones became proficient in the art

Is it terminal?

If first impressions count, it's almost criminal that most transport terminals are uninspiring entry and exit points for their various cities — places for watching the clock and wishing one were elsewhere. But visitors to London lucky enough to come in via one of its great Victorian rail stations or one of its new hi-tech termini such as the Waterloo International terminal or Stansted airport will find themselves face to face with some of the capital's most splendid architecture.

That St Pancras Station as we know and love it almost never came to be is a chastening thought. In 1867, midway through construction of its marvellous glass and iron train shed by William Barlow, a competition was held to find an architect for the Midland Grand Hotel that was to form the station's façade. One of the Midland Railway's directors attempted to persuade Sir George Gilbert Scott to enter but was rebuffed more than once before he agreed. In 1868-72 the vast edifice of external pinnacles, towers and gables and glorious interior (including a long curved dining hall) was constructed, and Scott recognised that 'it is possibly too good for its purpose' (it spookily resembled the government office he never got to build; *see p31*). Today you can take a guided tour of the interior, St Pancras Chambers (*see p104*).

Nicholas Grimshaw's hi-tech Waterloo International Terminal, which opened in 1994, was conceived with the intention

of reviving the tradition of great railway engineers such as William Barlow and Isambard Kingdom Brunel, both of whom created large-span, iron-roofed stations. Largely successful (despite emergency restoration work in 2000, when panes began to fall out of the glorious, sinuous but alas all-too gravity-prone glass and steel roof), the Eurostar is one of the finest pieces of public transport architecture in recent years.

In 2000 Grimshaw was also responsible for transforming the listed but run-down Paddington Station into an airy, civilised place where you don't actually mind waiting for your train. Isambard Kingdom Brunel's wonderful vaulted roof was cleaned, while at the front of the station a mezzanine level for cafés and bars was created, sheltered by a new glass roof supported by stainless-steel rods that, without even trying to compete with Brunel's vaults, are a thing of beauty.

But perhaps most modern and most successful of all is Stansted, which functions as London's third airport. Built by Norman Foster Associates between 1985 and 1991, the low, single-storey building with its vast, open-plan interior, stunning floating roof and views out over the runway and the surrounding countryside from the glazed perimeter walls – was designed to capture the elegant simplicity of early airport terminals and, unlike, say, Gatwick, could not be more user-friendly.

of *piazze*, porticos and pillasters, changing British architecture forever. His work not only influenced the careers of succeeding generations of architects, it also introduced the unhealthy habit of venerating the past. Even today, London has a knack for glueing fake classical extras over the doors of cheap kit buildings in the hope it will lend them a little dignity.

UNHOLY DESIGNS

Nothing cheers a builder like a natural disaster, so one can only guess at the relish with which Christopher Wren and co began rebuilding in the aftermath of the Great Fire. Taking their cue from Jones, they brandished classicism like a new broom: the pointed arches of English Gothic were rounded off, Corinthian columns made an appearance and church spires became as multi-layered and complex as a baroque wedding cake.

Wren blazed the trail with daring plans for **St Paul's Cathedral** (*see p86*), but the scheme, which incorporated a Catholic dome rather than a Protestant steeple, was too Roman for the reformist tastes of the establishment and the design was rejected. The undaunted architect quickly produced a redesign and gained planning permission by incorporating the much-loved spire, then set about a series of mischievous U-turns once work had commenced, giving us the building – domed and heavily suggestive of an ancient temple – that has survived to this day.

So prolific was the building of churches that Londoners managed to turn a blind eye to the odd synagogue. Allowed back into England by Oliver Cromwell in 1657, the city's Sephardic community from Spain and Portugal (*see p14*) went on to commission a Quaker to build them a home in a square in a quiet enclave. **Bevis Marks Synagogue** (2 Heneage Lane, EC3), the UK's oldest synagogue, was completed in 1701

St Pancras: Scott lays it on the line.

and gives little of its semitic purpose away from the outside… and very little internally. The rabbi even jokes that the once-trendy baroque cupboard (or ark) at one end of the building is more the 18th-century equivalent of Ikea than Jewish iconography.

Wren's architectural baton was picked up by Nicholas Hawksmoor and James Gibbs, who received a huge career opportunity when anxieties that London's population was becoming ever more ungodly led to a 1711 initiative to construct 50 churches. Gibbs busied himself in and around Trafalgar Square, building the steepled Roman temple that constitutes **St Martin-in-the-Fields** (*see p130*), the baroque **St Mary-le-Strand** (Strand, WC2) and the tower of **St Clement Danes** (*see p96*).

While Gibbs' work was well received, the more prolific and experimental Hawksmoor encountered a rougher ride. His imposing **St Anne's** (Commercial Road, E14) and **St George's** in Bloomsbury (*see p105*) both broke the bank, though **Christ Church Spitalfields** (*see p153*) remains one of London's best-loved buildings.

NEW DIRECTIONS

One of a large family of Scottish architects, Robert Adam found himself at the forefront of a movement that came to see Italian baroque as a corruption of the real thing. Architectural exuberance was eventually dropped in favour of a simpler interpretation of the ancient forms.

The best surviving work of Adam and his brothers James, John and William can be found in London's great suburban houses **Osterley Park** (*see p186*), **Syon House** (*see p184*) and the library of **Kenwood House** (*see p149*), but the project for which they are most famous no longer stands – the cripplingly expensive Adelphi housing estate (after the Greek for 'brothers') embarked upon off the Strand in 1768. Built over vaults used to store goods offloaded from river barges, most of the complex was pulled down in the 1930s and replaced by an office block of the same name, but part of the original development survives in what is now the **Royal Society for the Arts** (8 John Adam Street, WC2).

Just as the first residents were moving into the Adelphi, a young unknown called John Soane was embarking on a tour of his own. In

Love 'em or hate 'em?

Canary Wharf Tower, E14
Postmodern megalump or hi-tech landmark?
Centrepoint, W1
Pop or pap architecture? *See p128.*
Barbican Centre, EC2
Artistic/residential blueprint or soulless '80s development? *See p95.*
Brunswick Centre, WC1
Hideous goldfish bowl or successful social experiment?
GLA building, SE1
Giant testicle or showpiece of democratic architecture? *See p27.*
Marco Polo House, SW8
Liquorice Allsort or popular postmodern office building?
Portcullis House, SW1
Award-winning model of sustainable architecture or government folly? *See p268.*
National Theatre, SE1
Concrete monstrosity or modernist masterpiece? *See p74.*
Trellick Tower, W10
Seminal modern tower block or giant carbuncle? *See p182.*
Vauxhall Cross, SE1
Imposing secret services HQ or vile Lego-like monolith? *See p134.*

Portcullis House snuggles up to Big Ben.

Rome, the 25-year-old Soane met the wealthy Bishop of Derry, who persuaded him to abandon his travels and accompany him to Ireland to build a house. Though the project came to nothing (Soane dealt with the setback by working hard and marrying into money), he went on to build the **Bank of England** and the recently remodelled **Dulwich Picture Gallery** (*see p171*). Sadly, the Bank was demolished between the wars, leaving nothing but the perimeter walls and depriving London of what is said to have been Soane's masterpiece, though a hint of what the bankers might have enjoyed can be gleaned from a visit to Soane's house, now **Sir John Soane's Museum** (*see p31*). Soane fans should also visit the family tomb in **St Pancras Gardens** (*see p105*).

A near-contemporary of Soane, John Nash was a less talented architect, but his contributions to the fabric of London have proved greater than any other individual. Among his buildings are **Buckingham Palace** (*see p131*), the **Haymarket Theatre** (Haymarket, W1) and **Regent Street** (W1), which began as a proposal to link the West End to the planned **Regent's Park** (*see p109*) further north, as well as a device to separate the toffs and the riff-raff.

NEW ROMANTICS

By the 1830s, the classical form had been established for 200 years, and a handful of upstarts began pressing for change. In 1834 the **Houses of Parliament** burned down, leading to the construction of Charles Barry's Gothic masterpiece (*see p133*). This was the beginning of the Gothic revival, a move by the new romantics to replace what they considered to be foreign and pagan with a style that was not only native but Christian. The architectural profession was divided, but the argument was never resolved, merely made irrelevant by the advent of modernism a century later.

Barry would have preferred a classical design, but the brief was unambiguous and Gothic was to prevail. In need of assistance, he sought out August Pugin, whose Victorian fantasy, while a fine example of the perpendicular form, shows how the Middle Ages had become distorted in the minds of 19th-century architects: new buildings were constructed as a riot of turrets, towers and winding staircases that would today be condemned as the Disney-fication of history.

Even in renovating ancient buildings, architects often decided that they weren't Gothic enough; this was the case with the 15th-century **Guildhall** (*see p91*), which gained its corner turrets and central spire in 1862. Bombed by the Luftwaffe, the Guildhall was rebuilt largely as the Victorians had left it, apart from

RIBA: instituting a new style. *See p32.*

the interior statues of Gog and Magog, the protagonists in a legendary battle between ancient Britain and Troy. In the post-war reconstruction of this stately building, these two ugly bastards got even uglier. There's also a good statue of Churchill, looking stereotypically grumpy.

The argument between the classicists and goths erupted in 1857, when the government commissioned Sir George Gilbert Scott, a leading light of the Gothic movement, to design a new HQ for the **Foreign Office**. Scott's design incensed anti-goth Lord Palmerston, the then prime minister, whose diktats prevailed, but Scott exacted his revenge by building an office in which everyone hated working, and by going on to construct Gothic edifices all over the capital, among them the **Albert Memorial** (*see p138*) and **St Pancras Station** (*see p105*). The latter was lambasted by some critics of the time for its 'incongruous medievalism' but today is widely admired as one of the capital's loveliest buildings (*see p28* **Is it terminal?**).

The Gothic style continued to dominate until the 20th century, leaving London littered with other charming, imposing but anachronistic buildings such as the **Royal Courts of Justice** (*see p96*), the **Natural History Museum** (*see p138*), **Liberty** (*see p236*) and **Tower Bridge** (*see p92*).

RENEWAL AND REBIRTH

World War I and the onset of modernism led to tentative renewal in London architecture; the **Royal Institute of British Architects** (aka RIBA; *see p300*) and the BBC's **Broadcasting House** on Portland Place are good examples of the pared-down style of the '20s and '30s. But perhaps the finest example of between-the-wars modernism is the Penguin Pool at **London Zoo** (*see p109*). Built by Russian emigré Bethold Lubetkin and the Tecton group, the pool's spiral ramps were a showcase for the possibilities of concrete, which was also being put to good use on the Underground, where it enabled the quick and cheap building of large, cavernous spaces with the sleek lines and curves associated with speed. The Piccadilly Line was a particular beneficiary: its 1930s expansion yielded the likes of Charles Holden's **Arnos Grove Station**, the first of many circular station buildings and the model for the new and acclaimed **Canada Water Station**.

> ### 'Post-war architecture has left many Londoners wary of new buildings.'

World War II left large areas of London ruined, providing another opportunity for builders to cash in. Lamentably, the city was little improved by the rebuild; in fact, in many cases it was left worse off. The destruction left the capital with a dire housing shortage, giving architects a chance to demonstrate the speed and efficiency with which they could house large numbers of families in tower blocks. Most were not a success and deserve to be pulled down. Some of them have gone already.

But post-war architecture has left many Londoners wary of new buildings, and this experience has both tempered the arrogance of the architectural profession and created a planning process that places so many hurdles in the way of developers that it's a wonder anything gets built at all. There are diamonds among the coal, however, including the **Royal Festival Hall** on the South Bank: the sole survivor of the 1951 Festival of Britain, it was built to celebrate the war's end and the centenary of the Great Exhibition, and, though it can be crowded and awkward, it's a much-loved

piece of London's fabric. As with the rest of the South Bank arts complex, it's undergoing a long-overdue renovation (*see p74*).

Elsewhere, Richard Rogers' 1980s **Lloyd's Building** (Lime Street, EC3) achieves the seemingly impossible by combining office space with oil-refinery aesthetics and still managing to make it look good. Mocked upon completion in 1986, the building still manages to outclass more recent projects, a fact not lost on Channel 4 when it commissioned Rogers to design its new HQ in Horseferry Road, SW1, in the early 1990s.

It is largely the doing of Rogers and his rival (and close friend) Norman Foster that London is becoming a showcase for brave and innovative buildings. Future Systems' **NatWest Media Centre** at Lord's Cricket Ground (*see p326*), built from aluminium in a boatyard and perched high above the pitch like a giant bar of soap, is arguably London's most daring construction to date, especially given its traditional setting. Meanwhile, Will Alsop's multicoloured **Peckham Library** (171 Peckham Hill Street, SE15) redefined community architecture so comprehensively that it fully deserved the £20,000 Stirling Prize awarded in late 2000.

But it's not just new buildings that define the landscape of London: the city's architecture is also affected by the presence of a 'green belt', a slice of protected countryside that prevents the city from bursting its banks and obliges architects to work with old buildings rather than pull them down. Done well, the new is grafted on to the old in a way that is often invisible from street level; visitors will be surprised by the way contemporary interiors have been inserted into elderly buildings.

Some of the best examples of this can be found in public museums and art galleries, many of which underwent millennium make-overs and expansion programmes. The **National Portrait Gallery** (*see p130*), the **Royal Opera House** (*see p125*), **Tate Britain** (*see p134*) and **Tate Modern** (*see p75*) are good examples of architects redefining old buildings to a greater or lesser degree, while the **British Museum** (*see p101*), the **National Maritime Museum** (*see p166*) and the **Wallace Collection** (*see p108*) have all, with the help of large grants from the National Lottery and glass roofs, considerably added to their facilities by invading what were once external courtyards.

This, after all, is what London does best: it integrates, absorbs, juxtaposes, allowing the new and the old, the traditional and the innovative, to co-exist in such a way that each throws a new, fascinating light on the other.

Trafalgar Square, earmarked as a showcase for London's cultural diversity. *See p36.*

The Melting Pot

London's ethnic diversity is a cause for celebration.

It's a Thursday night at Holborn's Kuch Kuch club. Indian sitars twang against a background of bhangra beats and thumping house music, and clubbers kitted out in white flares, spangly boob tubes and flame-coloured sari-tops wiggle their heads and sway their arms to the swirling sounds as if they were extras on a Bollywood movie set. Meanwhile, down in Brixton, the Soul of Black Folk café is heaving. On the tiny stage a young black man has just finished an alto sax set and a woman from Compton, LA, is reading out a long poem about her local police. Back up in the West End, at the Fitz & Firkin pub on Great Portland Street, Irish-Iranian comic Patrick Monahan is reducing the crowd to tear-dabbing hysterics.

Wherever you choose to look, whether it's in the arts, in food, in the political sphere or in the everyday experiences of people all over the city – the massive impact of London's different races and cultures is unmistakable. From the energy of the music scene to arguments over community policing, cultural diversity is at the core of London life.

NEW BEGINNINGS

The influx of different cultures and races into the city is no modern phenomenon; it was invading Roman who established the place, after all, and since then its development has been fuelled by the talents and contributions of a huge range of peoples.

Small communities of Jews, Flemish and Dutch immigrants were well established in London by the end of the 14th century. They were followed by Protestant refugees from France and the Netherlands in the 17th century and by black Africans who were brought to Britain by force in the 17th and 18th centuries to be kept as slaves or servants. It's estimated that by the end of the 18th century there were about 20,000 black people in London.

▶ For more on some of London's ethnic communities, see p14 **Jewish London**, p148 **Turkish London**, p158 **Vietnamese London**, p174 **Caribbean London** and p180 **Punjabi London**.

Thousands of people arrived during the 19th century from Ireland, eastern and southern Europe and Asia, escaping from persecution, poverty or famine. Working on the docks, building canals, roads and railways, or toiling in sweatshops or factories, these Irish, Jewish, Indian and Chinese workers contributed greatly to London's prosperity and industrial expansion.

Following World War II, Britain looked to its colonies to help rebuild its shattered workforce. Arriving by boat at Tilbury, Caribbean immigrants dispersed to areas such as Brixton and Notting Hill, from which strong Afro-Caribbean communities flourished. The end of the 1970s, however, brought in strict controls on immigration. Most immigrants in London today come from other parts of Europe, or are work-permit holders from the USA, India, Australia, Japan and South Africa. Others are admitted as refugees from a huge range of countries, including Lebanon, Vietnam, Nigeria, Iraq and the former Yugoslavia. There are an estimated 330,000 refugees and asylum-seekers living in London, with most recent arrivals coming from eastern Europe, North Africa and Kurdistan.

STORM CLOUDS

Today as many as 300 different languages are spoken in the capital, and within ten years 40 per cent of Londoners will be from ethnic minorities. Such a mix of cultures and races is not without its problems. Brixton was the scene of infamous riots in 1981, 1985 and 1995, and in 1993 the brutal murder of the black teenager Stephen Lawrence created an outcry about the nature of racism in the capital. The public inquiry that followed, the Macpherson Report, highlighted the need for London to rethink its approach to racism, particularly with regard to institutions such as the Metropolitan Police. Ken Fero's recent controversial film, *Injustice*, much of which was shot in Brixton, confirms that this issue still needs to be urgently addressed.

London was also the focus of a spate of racially motivated attacks in summer 1999, when nail bombs targeted the heart of Brixton and Brick Lane, the core of the East End's Asian community. Meanwhile, statistics show that ethnic communities still experience higher rates of ill health, poor housing and unemployment than their white counterparts, though this varies from community to community.

Yet the cultural richness that such communities bring to the capital is something that cannot be understated. Following the 2001 attacks on New York and Washington, London mayor Ken Livingstone (*see p25* **Who he?**) said, 'London's international status means that we are home to the most diverse population in Europe. Our ability to live and work together means refusing to allow racists to exploit the current climate. London will celebrate its diversity while I am mayor.'

And celebrate it does. From South Africa to Poland, Canada to Japan, the world has made its way to London, making it possible to converse, buy food or order a minicab in a rich range of tongues. And there is a burgeoning array of festivals and celebrations that highlight the experiences of these communities: the Jewish Arts and Culture Festival, the Turkish Film Festival and the Keralan Food Festival are just some of the events that might be taking place in any one month across the capital.

A FRESH EYE

Of the 25 million tourists who will descend on London this year, however, it's unlikely that any but the most adventurous will visit Southall, Wembley, Brick Lane, or any of the other areas that illustrate the city's diversity.

'When London is marketed abroad, what is marketed is Big Ben, perhaps the Royal Opera House, St Paul's Cathedral, the Tower of London and the Houses of Parliament. This does not necessarily reflect the magnitude and diversity of London,' says Claudia Webbe, Ken Livingstone's adviser on culture (a portfolio that includes tourism).

'There are distinct and unique communities that make up London and that make London unique. What people on the outside have perhaps seen is a Britain that exists with an average, white Englishman, and certainly that is not London. A third of Londoners are from ethnic groups, and the city is diverse in language and in religious make-up.'

The time has come for change, says Webbe, not just because tourism earns us billions of pounds a year, but because at the moment a third of Londoners are being treated as though they don't exist.

> **'Within ten years 40 per cent of Londoners will be from ethnic minorities.'**

There are various ways in which this change is being implemented. Tourist companies are fast catching on to the fact that this is an area ripe for developing. Ethnic Tours, set up last year by Heather Pickering, aims to highlight areas of London not usually included in most tourists' itineraries. Her day trips take visitors to places such as Brixton Market, Southall, Chinatown, and the Islamic Culture Centre and London Central Mosque in Regent's Park, providing a glimpse of London they might otherwise never see.

The London Tourist Board (LTB) is also anxious to ensure that the message sent out to visitors accurately reflects the ethnic background of the city. In fact, so successful has the LTB's promotion of the Notting Hill Carnival been to overseas visitors that the Mayor has requested that its profile be played down due to fears of overcrowding. More recently, the LTB has been offering information on everything from ethnic restaurants to Bollywood film locations.

The current interest in Bollywood is a prime example of London's reincarnation as a multicultural mecca. London's love affair with the genre was highlighted last summer, when a star-studded crowd filed in to the Millennium Dome to celebrate the first International Indian Film Awards, or 'Bollywood Oscars'. 'Wake up and smell the curry,' said Leslee Udwin, director of cult Asian comedy *East is East*.

Meanwhile, cinemas such as the Himalaya Palace in Southall (*see p294*) are showing a healthy quota of Bollywood films, and the Kuch Kuch Bollywood club night in the West End has been a massive hit with Asian and non-Asian clubbers alike. Even Andrew Lloyd Webber is getting in on the act with his musical, *Bombay Dreams*, scheduled to hit the West End in spring 2002. London is also a prime location for Bollywood film locations, attracting hundreds of Indian tourists every year. In recognition of this fact, the British Tourist Board has devoted a section on its website to Bollywood film locations in Britain, with Big Ben, Trafalgar Square and Harrods making regular star turns. But the real sign that things have changed is a recent addition to Madame Tussaud's – a wax figure of Bollywood legend Amitabh Bachchan.

THE VOICES OF LONDON

While the Asian and black communities in London have become relatively well established, however, there's a whole new wave of immigrants whose voices are all too often overlooked. On a balmy summer evening at Covent Garden's Poetry Café (*see p40*), a group of refugee writers, poets and journalists are meeting to read and discuss their work. Their assured delivery and relaxed demeanour make it difficult to believe that many of them have fled from some of the world's most brutal regimes, often having undergone torture and imprisonment in their home countries. The group, Exiled Writers Ink, was set up by Jennifer Langer, the daughter of Jewish survivors of the Holocaust, in an attempt to provide a voice for professional writers, academics and journalists, many of whom have not been able to pick up their careers in the United Kingdom.

The list of countries from which the group's members have come reads like a roll call of political hotspots, including Iran, Somalia and Chile. One writer, Tomor Bahja, fled Albania after receiving death threats following the publication of his novel criticising his native government. He arrived in London having been crammed into a melon lorry for a 48-hour journey across Europe to Britain and spent his first few weeks here sleeping on the streets. The process of seeking asylum is often extremely dehumanising and Exiled Writers Ink offers one of the few outlets for Bahja and writers like him to express their thoughts and feelings about their new lives here.

> ### 'The Mayor hopes to turn the waters of Trafalgar Square's fountains green and saffron to celebrate St Patrick's Day and Diwali.'

Ironically, the ultimate outcome of promoting multiculturalism is that boundaries that defined groups are eventually broken down. Talvin Singh, a critically acclaimed London-based DJ and tabla virtuoso, helped kickstart the huge interest in Asian music a few years ago with his popular Hoxton club night Anokha. He went on to win the Mercury Music Prize and heralded a wave of London-based Asian musicians, such as Badmarsh & Shri and Nitin Sawhney.

'With me being from Asian origin, I am a minority, and this [the music] is celebrating the struggle of our forefathers,' says Singh. 'Yet I am not a minority any more, I am a majority. This [the Mercury Prize] is celebrating that.'

Such artists have emerged from the ethnic underground to make music that bends – and transcends – traditional pop categories. Now, with the novelty of the 'Asian underground' fading, Asian musicians are demanding recognition as mainstream British artists with global appeal.

FOOD FOR THOUGHT

One obvious example of how ethnic influences have made an impact on the capital is in what Londoners are eating these days. Whereas ten years ago London's restaurants were the laughing stock of Europe, they're now lauded as being some of the best in Europe. Much of that improvement has to do with the infusion of variety from its ethnic eateries.

'London's restaurants reflect the history of London's people,' says Jenny Linford, author of *The Food Lover's London*, which looks at the capital's ethnic cuisines. 'Shops and restaurants

'Maybe it's because I'm a Londoner'

We asked a selection of city-dwellers what London represents to them and how they feel they fit into it.

Robert Eckford, 40, owner of the Juice Bar, Brixton, from Jamaica

'London is the only place where I can express myself as a black person. If I go to Bath, Sheffield, or to any other city in Britain, or even to Paris or Berlin, I don't feel safe. The police don't understand our culture in other towns and I don't feel I have the same clout there. London has so many minorities that it gives me a real sense of security. I absolutely love London for that. People who have come here from the Caribbean say, "If I leave London, I leave England".'

Thai Nu Trahn, 32, works in IT, from Vietnam

'London is a very good city, especially for foreigners [...] because it's a city of many cultures and therefore it makes them feel less intimidated. I feel that this city has a lot of opportunities for everyone. They don't feel like strangers in town. I don't feel like an outsider here.'

Janet Banana, 63, asylum seeker, former teacher and First Lady of independent Zimbabwe

'I live with the fear of being liable to be detained and I ask myself "why?", and "what for?". However, I have learnt to find ways of keeping sane by accessing learning centres, attending workshops, worshipping freely. I find that there is so much diversity here, in culture, class, ethnicity and sexual orientation. I love the freedom of expression and association.'

Shaun Levin, 38, writer, from South Africa

'London doesn't accept you and it doesn't reject you. I can live without being accountable to anyone, that is I don't have to report back to anyone with ID cards. As a foreigner, you can create whatever life you want to here and no one has a tag on you.'

Sofia Buchuck, 29, student, from Peru

'I believe I am a true Londoner in a certain sense, because London is a multicultural city, you can't avoid the changes that happen to you after living with so many

that started out as specialised ethnic food stores have now become a mainstream part of London life. For example, Italian stores that catered specifically to the Italian community 50 years ago have metamorphosed into the trendy delis we see everywhere in London, run by hip young Brits today. A trend I have noticed, however, is that earlier immigrants, who used to set up restaurants as a way of making money easily and quickly, no longer need to look towards catering as a way of breaking into life here. The Chinese community is now an assimilated, educated community, with many professional Chinese such as doctors and lawyers. Running a takeaway isn't as attractive an option – and isn't the only option that's open to them.'

THIS IS THE MODERN WORLD

Just as ethnic influences are being absorbed by London to become part of the mainstream, a transformation has occurred among the bastions of white London. Organisations that haven't traditionally been part of the multicultural environment are taking stock and reinventing themselves to better reflect the diversity around them. Venues such as the

Theatre Royal in Stratford East are focusing on multicultural work in an attempt to embrace the experiences of their audiences; the Barbican's Iranian film season was booked out weeks ahead; and the Serpentine Gallery's exhibition by female Iranian photographer and video installation artist Shirin Neshet was packed out. At the reopening of Tate Britain in 2001 the statue of Britannia at the entrance was draped with a colourful hanging made of African textiles by black artist Yinka Shonibare, and even that staple of the chattering classes, the London Philharmonic Orchestra, now puts on an annual event bringing together culturally diverse musical influences.

Perhaps the most prominent example of how London's diversity can be recognised is Trafalgar Square, the only venue the Mayor has the power to programme. The square is being developed as part of a World Squares For All project (*see p129*), and Livingstone has placed great emphasis on its symbolic potential. It has already hosted a spectacular South Africa Freedom Day concert; upcoming festivals will feature Cuban dance bands and bhangra

people of so many countries. Because I'm from an Andean culture, I believe in mysticism... London has its own mysticism, especially in the nights of winter and even in the summer nights.'

Bill Broun, 35, journalist, from the USA

'I feel an outsider here when a rude bus driver slams the doors shut on my face and lurches off while I'm late for work. But the things I like about London are the great, secret and not-so-secret nests of deeply eccentric beings cached all over this city; it's an absolute treasure trove of delicate human weirdness; Russian minicab drivers who drive like Formula 1 drop-outs; the zoological gardens; the memento mori of Westminster Abbey; Norman Foster; those surreal goat carcasses and piles of dead eels at several East End markets.'

Abol Froushan, 44, works in computer technology/multimedia poet, from Iran

Excerpt from a poem: 'In London I feel closer to cosmos as it manifests/in its chaos, its tempo beat of tubes and trains and bustle of cars and/bus lanes, as we sit round a Soho/brasserie five friends of five continents, the most unlikely/bunch round a table anywhere in the cosmic stew.'

John Nassari, 31, producer of www.photoinsight.org.uk, 3rd generation Greek Cypriot

'My website is totally interested in cultural difference and identity. For me it is about celebrating and raising awareness of cultural difference... That's why I like London so much, because communities and identities are so fragmented and diverse, and that can only be good with so many people on the move around Europe and the globe. As borders blur, and single currencies develop, a multicultural nation is a natural and normal nation.'

groups; and Livingstone hopes to turn the waters of the square's fountains green and saffron to celebrate St Patrick's Day and Diwali respectively. There are ongoing negotiations with the Chinese and African communities to decide ways to showcase their cultures there, and even the buskers who will be allowed to perform in the square will be chosen to represent the city's cultural diversity.

But any changes are no more than token gestures unless they're followed up with proper investment, and, historically, organisations that cater to the cultures of ethnic minority communities have been woefully underfunded. Promisingly, however, the Greater London Authority (GLA) has already successfully lobbied the Arts Council of England to invest more than £13 million in black and Asian projects in London, and the GLA and London Tourist Board also heavily support Black History Month. In 2001 the GLA announced large grants to Talawa, a leading black theatre company, as well as funding for the planned new Stephen Lawrence Centre in Deptford. Meanwhile, smaller organisations such as Exiled

Writers Ink are beginning to benefit from grants from bodies such as the London Boroughs Grants Committee and London Arts, although as Jennifer Langer points out, the larger an organisation is, the easier it is to get money.

Claudia Webbe says that the GLA is constantly pushing for greater investment into multicultural initiatives. 'London will not survive if one third of London's community are ignored, and are not given opportunities,' she says. In the light of this, the words of Exiled Writers Ink member Tomor Bahja, in his poem 'Thank You London', are particularly humbling:

London gave me freedom,
the right to be alive,
to be a human being
bound up with being
(and not being) human.
In the century of the atom
that's the hardest hardship,
the finest offering.

Ethnic Tours can be contacted on 8314 1031, Exiled Writers Ink on 8458 1910.

Home, sweet home:
a resident of the
Death Line. *See p39*.

Fictional London

London through a lens.

As with any city, much of our experience of London is mediated through writers, filmmakers and other creative types, each of whom interprets the metropolis in his or her unique fashion, from Dickens with his ragged urchins and workhouses via the genteel modernism of Virginia Woolf to the psycho-geographical speculations of Iain Sinclair. We take a selective look at how modern-day artists have reimagined the urban landcape.

AN UNCERTAIN TERRAIN

In *Junk Mail* (1995), **Will Self** recalls answering the door to a schizophrenic who asked Self to drive him to Leytonstone. Halfway there, Self challenged the man to pinpoint his destination in the *A–Z*. Replied the man: 'You and I know that the *A–Z* is a plan of what's going to be built.' In this man's version of London, the Geographers' A–Z Map Co Ltd has dreamed up the entire city.

Undergoing brainwashing in **Sidney J Furie**'s 1965 film *The Ipcress File*, Harry Palmer (Michael Caine) learns from his captors that he is being held in a Stalinist country ('What's the matter with these zombies? Can't they speak?' 'You don't speak English in Albania.'). Imagine his surprise when, upon his escape, the first thing he sees is a Routemaster bus. Finding a phone box, he establishes his location as Austin's Wharf Lane. No such street exists, but in **Len Deighton**'s original novel, the unnamed agent – he was only named in the films – discovers he's been held in Wood Green.

When shooting Cold War thrillers in the '60s, it was mandatory to include a shot of traffic flowing over Westminster Bridge. Nowadays, the preferred shot is of the MI6 building by Vauxhall Bridge (*see p30* **Love 'em or hate 'em**), though traffic hardly *flows* over any of the bridges any more. Also made in the '60s, swinging London pictures would be incomplete without a montage of strip clubs and neon signs; Soho having since been sanitised, they now look somewhat dated. Recent cinema's most enchanting representation of the district must be **Michael Winterbottom**'s *Wonderland* (1999), filmed *vérité*-style with hand-held 16mm cameras in venues such as Duke's Café on Old Compton Street.

Soho is the setting for much of *Robinson* (1994), the first novel by writer and filmmaker **Chris Petit**. Petit takes the 'shivering, naked heart of the city' and makes it his setting for a study of disintegrating personalities. The narrator is a film editor whose career has run aground when he meets Robinson, a shady but charismatic Soho character. The narrator's interest in Robinson grows into obsession as the pair frequent Soho pubs and the narrator avoids going home to his wife. 'My horizons shrank until it became hard to leave the area. It felt as though I would be breaking a spell.' Soho becomes a special, idealised place, like Alain-Fournier's lost domain; indeed, it has its own 'border post', the archway at the western end of Manette Street where the narrator and Robinson first meet, at which 'all obligation could be left behind'. Petit's latest novel, *The Hard Shoulder* (2001), is set among the Irish community in Kilburn.

WAY OUT WEST

In his first feature film, *Radio On* (1979) – an English road movie that found in the Westway a stretch of macadam worthy of the genre – Petit created a fusion of electronic/new wave music and dreamlike monochrome cinematography to enhance the ambiguous qualities of its locations. The David Beames character parks his old Rover opposite the Plaza cinema in Camden (demolished in 2000). Later, he stops at Gillette Corner off the Great West Road, then heads west out of town on the M4 past the Agfa building at Brentford, listening to David Bowie's *Always Crashing in the Same Car*. One of the film's most haunting shots is of the car leaving the Westway to join the M41. The camera is way up above, on top of one of the tower blocks near Latimer Road, granting us an aerial view of Shepherd's Bush that encompasses the old Franco-British Exhibition Halls and White City's Central line tube depot.

The White City Estate is fictionalised in *The Scholar* (1997), the first novel by **Courttia Newland**, who was himself born and raised in the Bush. It's the powerful story of teenage cousins raised on the Greenside Estate; one gets into petty crime and soft drugs, while the other studies. Both are seeking an escape route. 'Greenside – a term the police use for all of west London – is every estate I've ever been to, both in London and all over the country,' Newland explained in an interview.

It's further west, in Hammersmith, that the hapless Jack Vail, hero of **Trevor Hoyle**'s extraordinary novel *Vail* (1984), enjoys the

▶ For more **London fiction**, see *p378-9*.

hospitality of TV vamp Virgie Hance. 'Lord Napier Place, Upper Mall,' she tells him. 'Nine o'clock. Bring an erection.' Vail also wanders through Harrods after a bomb attack: 'The goods on display, despite being bomb-blasted and blackened by the smoke, were still of the usual first-rate quality, and amazingly varied. Black Mamba snakeskin belts. Piano-shaped fudge in 3-kilo boxes. Platinum "His 'n' Hers" roller skates… Pearl-inlaid toilet roll holders.'

Down the road from Harrods, on Old Brompton Road, you'll find Hotel 167 (*see p59*), the setting for **Jane Solomon**'s debut novel *Hotel 167*, published by Picador in 1993 when the author was just 20. It tells the story of Maud, who sees a psychiatrist for psychotic depression. The hotel of the title – 'Faintly Tunisian in style… Painted a medium mint green, with a black sign' – is both an aid to auto-erotic/suicidal fantasies and a prop that anchors her chaotic intellect in reality.

UNDERGROUND, OVERGROUND

The fictional possibilities of the Underground have long fascinated London wordsmiths, including **Barbara Vine**; in *King Solomon's Carpet* (1991) the main character lives in a house overlooking the Jubilee line, and rooms are let out to characters variously linked with the tube (one train-surfs, another busks).

If there's one London film location to which we would like to consign all those responsible for 'chick fic' and 'lad lit' – as well as the makers of *Sliding Doors* (1997), for that matter – it's Russell Square tube station. In **Gary Sherman**'s *Death Line* (1972), plague-ridden ghouls survive in the tunnels by feasting on human flesh. When one of the creatures loses his wife, he emerges into Russell Square station in search of fresh meat.

The main characters in **Tobias Hill**'s first novel, *Underground* (1999), are alive and do not eat people, but still choose to spend their lives below street level. A fictional character who does not make this choice, but who is trapped in the tube nevertheless, appears in 'South Kentish Town', an short story by **John Betjeman** that was reprinted in Candida Lycett-Green's anthology of his prose, *Coming Home*. Disembarking his train at the station, now disused, Betjeman's character finds it impossible to leave the station.

Geoff Ryman's *253*, set on the Bakerloo line between Embankment and Elephant & Castle, was published online in 1996 (www.ryman-novel.com), later appearing in a 'print remix'. The title refers to the number of passengers there would be on a Bakerloo line train if every seat were taken, plus the driver. Ryman uses 253 words to describe each character and tell us what they are thinking. Readers who enjoy *253* may also appreciate **Giles Gordon**'s experimental short story 'Fourteen Stations on the Northern Line', published in *The New SF* (1969, edited by Langdon Jones).

The Northern line calls at King's Cross, until recently home to the UK's most photographed gasholders. The huge listed Victorian structures, which have just been dismantled for building work connected with the Channel tunnel link (though three of them will ultimately be reassembled), are used to good effect in director **Mike Leigh**'s *High*

Hopes (1988): leading couple Cyril and Shirley live in the scruffy splendour of the Battle Bridge Road/Stanley Buildings community. And up the Jubilee line, the interiors in **Clive Barker**'s *Hellraiser* (1987) were shot in an empty house on a leafy Dollis Hill avenue. Despite the obvious London location, when Andy Robinson and family move in they're aided by removal men whose transatlantic overdubs are not even in synch. Come the climactic conflagration, we seem to be standing not on Dollis Hill, but on some desolate docklands plain ten miles away.

Word up

London's spoken word scene is more exciting than ever, with many of the capital's hippest venues, including the Bug Bar and Momo, now hosting regular evenings of literary readings by novelists, short-story writers and poets. Well established on the circuit, **Vox 'n' Roll** at Filthy McNasty's (68 Amwell Street, Finsbury, EC1; 7837 6067) holds regular events during which authors as diverse as Howard 'Mr Nice' Marks, ex-grebo rocker Mark Manning (aka Zodiac Mindwarp), Giles Smith, Roddy Doyle and Will Self read extracts from their work in tandem with chosen music, to emphasise the link between music and literature. A recent offshoot of the event, **seriously...Vox 'n' Roll** at North African bar and restaurant Momo (25 Heddon Street, W1; 7434 4040) consists of live readings interspersed with music that has inspired each author. Held one Thursday a month, it has welcomed, to date, Alexei Sayle, Nick Hornby, Hanif Kureishi and Helen Fielding. Entry is free but attendees should phone ahead to book, as spaces are limited to 40.

Covent Garden's Poetry Café (22 Betterton Street, WC2; 7420 9880) is a café/bar presenting a range of events, including **Poetry Unplugged** (open-mic performances), book readings, alternative cabaret, improvised music and dance, and **Cats Night Out** (held on the last Wednesday of each month), a successful season of women's contemporary poetry.

Down in Brixton, **Singers & Poets** at the Bug Bar (The Crypt, St Matthew's Church, Brixton Hill, SW2; 7738 3184), now in its fourth year, is a monthly hosted session with new and up-and-coming live bands and singers, and an open-mic spot for budding poets. **Poetry Kitchen**, held at the same venue bi-monthly, is a new night of live

readings from south London poetry collective Renaissance One. Guests can chill out on comfy sofas and play board games.

Also in south London, **Apples & Snakes**, based at Battersea Arts Centre (Lavender Hill, Battersea, SW1; 7223 222), is a progressive organisation promoting cross-cultural and accessible poetry to a wide-ranging audience. Recent acts include US performance poet Will Power with his fusion of hip hop culture and contemporary theatre, and Helen East's stories of urban London lore, interwoven with riddles, music and song.

Voicebox (Level 5, Royal Festival Hall, South Bank, SE1; 7960 4242), a small live venue attached to the Poetry Library, is one of several used by the RFH for its literature and talks programme. The Purcell Room and Queen Elizabeth Hall also host frequent poetry events, talks and readings from novelists such as Alan Bennett, Oliver Sacks, Jenny Diski and Esther Freud.

Further north, in Chalk Farm, **Express Excess** (The Enterprise, 2 Haverstock Hill, NW3; 7485 2659) is a weekly mix of poetry and storytelling, and has occasional open-mic performances too. Readings from leading authors and spoken word events featuring the likes of Salford poet John Cooper-Clarke also take place in this pleasant candle-lit venue.

London offers a number of literary festivals too, of which the biggest is September's **The Word** (7837 2555/www.theword.org.uk), while many central London bookstores, **Borders** and **Waterstone's** among them (for both, *see p232*), host regular readings by writers who have a book to plug. For up-to-the-minute information, as well as the latest book reviews, see *Time Out* magazine's weekly Books section.

Iconic **gasholders** at King's Cross. *See p40.*

Docklands locations had been put to better use in **John Mackenzie**'s *The Long Good Friday* (1979), in which Bob Hoskins played a gangster with a vision for developing the area. Hoskins also played a villain in **Neil Jordan**'s *Mona Lisa* (1986), in which he's hired as Cathy Tyson's chauffeur. Jordan might have overdone King's Cross – the area hasn't seen quite that many tarts for years – but the film takes its locations seriously, from Tyson's assignations in the Park Lane Hotel to her flat in Trinity Court, an art deco block on Gray's Inn Road.

THE STREETS OF LONDON

In **Nicolas Roeg** and **Donald Cammell**'s *Performance* (1970), on-the-run hood Chas (James Fox) seeks refuge chez rock star Turner (Mick Jagger), at the north-west corner of Powis Square, W11. Numbered 81 in the film, the house is, in fact, No.25. As Chas walks up the west side of the square, he passes Nos.23-4 before arriving at No.81… and this is *before* trying Turner's hallucinogenic mushrooms. Disappointingly, the interiors were filmed in Belgravia, but the exteriors linger in the mind.

If you walk south down the west side of Powis Square – the direction taken by the white Rolls in the final shot of the film – and go right at the bottom, in a few blocks you hit Portobello Road. Turn right and across the street is the

newly reopened Electric Cinema (*see p293* **Electric dreams**), where **Stuart Cooper**'s *The Disappearance*, based on **Derek Marlowe**'s novel *Echoes of Celandine* (some nice, melancholy South Kensington locations), played in 1977. We're now just yards away from the Travel Bookshop in Blenheim Crescent, as featured in **Roger Michell**'s *Notting Hill* (1999).

The title of **Maxim Jakubowski**'s '71-73 Charing Cross Road', part of his own *London Noir* anthology (1994), is double-edged with irony: the address is that of his own Murder One bookshop (*see p233*). It's the saddest piece in the book, and one can only hope that it draws lightly from experience. Stories by **Derek Raymond** (*see p42* **Who he?**) and **Mark Timlin** are shot through with the spirit of London. When **Christopher Fowler**'s Dutch filmmakers are casting a film in an old warehouse in 'Perfect Casting', actor Peter Tipping arrives in the Edgware Road 'skirting filthy puddles to locate a small turning between the kebab shops and falafel bars'.

> **'Neil Jordan might have overdone King's Cross – the area hasn't seen quite that many tarts for years.'**

Graham Greene was also familiar with the Edgware Road. He wrote the same haunted cinema story twice. In 'A Little Place Off the Edgware Road', Craven 'knew all the side streets round the Edgware Road only too well'. And well he might. The narrator of a shorter piece, 'All But Empty', passed 'out of the Edgware Road and found it [the same cinema] in a side street'.

DIGGING DEEPER

If the last decades of the old millennium belong to any London writers above others, it's those who dig beneath the surface of our metropolitan existence and fiddle around in the interstices of history, those who conjure strange new tales out of the zone between myth and reality; the Mythical Realists, if you like. **Peter Ackroyd**, with his compelling popular blend of London past and present, is one; **JG Ballard**, with his unique, increasingly popular and now even respectable blend of science fiction, surrealism and fetishistic obsession, is another. *Crash* (1971), *Concrete Island* (1974) and *High-Rise* (1975) are classic London novels, although technically *Crash* is more a London Airport (as was) work. The concrete island where Robert Maitland is marooned after his Jaguar leaves the road is the one we see in the aerial shot of *Radio On* (*see p39*).

Who he? Derek Raymond

That Derek Raymond isn't more recognised is a crime: his 'Factory' series, which took urban noir into its blackest territories, kicks most modern detective fiction into touch. Next to his anonymous Detective Sergeant, even the best of today's pet 'tecs', including Rankin's Rebus, look as pale as watered-down milk.

Raymond was born Robin Cook in 1931 but changed his name so he wouldn't be mistaken for the American author who wrote medical thrillers such as *Coma*. An old Etonian, Raymond portrayed – at least in early work such as *The Crust on its Uppers* – an England that was on its knees and filled with a marvellous but almost impenetrable jargon. The themes of English decay followed him into his Factory novels – short, sharp explorations of the criminal badlands in and around London. Shot

through with bilious humour, these books – *The Devil's Home on Leave, He Died With His Eyes Open, I Was Dora Suarez, Dead Man Upright* and *How the Dead Live* – introduced us to a crime fighter the likes of whom we had never seen before and who was a million miles away from the comforting detectives offered by Christie, Dexter and James.

The sarcastic, foul-mouthed Detective Sergeant – unpromotable, unpredictable and unpalatable, especially to his superiors – was dedicated to the unsavoury task of hunting down the most depraved killers, out of the Poland Street offices that was A14, 'Unexplained Deaths' (a fictional adjunct to the public face of police work at New Scotland Yard). The DS pulls no punches when it comes to belittling his colleagues at the Yard, especially the oleaginous Inspector Bowman. Yet Raymond rescues his creation from being totally repellent by giving him a heart when it comes to the poor souls of the victims. In perhaps his best, and bleakest, novel, *I Was Dora Suarez*, the DS shows so much compassion for the murdered Dora that he visualises himself living out the last, desperate days of her life.

A stalwart of dingy backstreet watering holes such as the Troy Club on Hanway Street, Raymond – nicknamed 'Cookie' – could often be seen propping up the bar in his trademark beret. At the point of his untimely death in 1994, the BBC were planning to film the 'Factory 'series, but the project was shelved – perhaps for the best, because the books are uniquely disturbing and would have had to be heavily sanitised for the small screen. Nevertheless, this masterful quintet is an important stopping place for anybody interested in British crime fiction and was an unmistakeable influence on today's urban crime writers, including Mark Timlin, Jake Arnott and Adam Baron.

For a more in-depth look at the man and his work, get hold of his excellent autobiography, *The Hidden Files*.

The most uncompromising writer around, Welsh-born, Dublin-educated, East End-naturalised **Iain Sinclair** used to work as a book dealer and parks gardener, self-publishing his own darkly intuitive poetry. Sinclair, who calls his work 'future memories', has become *the* London authority (at least before Ackroyd's *London: The Biography*), a *Newsnight* conscript and a merciless iconoclast. Speculations about the mythology of London run as deep in his fiction as the city's lost rivers.

The films Sinclair has made with Chris Petit – *The Cardinal and the Corpse* (1993), *The Falconer* (1998), *Asylum* (2000) – explore the rich territory where fiction and documentary overlap. In *Asylum*, they visit **Michael**

Moorcock, who is said to embody 1,000 years of London's literary history. His *Mother London* (1988; reprinted in 2000) is probably the best London novel of all time.

If you have time to watch only one London film, *London* (1994), directed by **Patrick Keiller**, is both the oddest and most engaging film ever made about the capital. There's no real plot as such, and no characters apart from the voices of the narrator (Paul Scofield) and his friend, Robinson. A slyly humorous blend of satire, anecdote and myth-making, *London* is a unique triumph.

Nicholas Royle is the editor of 'The Time Out Book of London Short Stories Vol 2' (Penguin).

Accommodation

Accommodation   **45**

Features

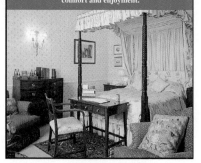

Accommodation

Whether laid-back luxe or budget chic is your bag, London
is getting better at coming up with the goods.

Though London achieved its 1995 target of
10,000 new rooms by the turn of the millennium,
the end of 2001 saw much uncertainty in the
hotel world in the aftermath of the terrorist
attacks on America, and many hotels began to
struggle to fill rooms as travellers chose to stay
at home and airlines slashed their services. It's
impossible to predict what this will mean for
the hotel industry in 2002 or in the longer run,
though one consequence may be a welcome drop
in London's notoriously steep prices, with hotels
obliged to offer discounts and special deals to
win customers. In any case, visitors should
always ask for a special rate when booking,
especially in the traditional 'off-season' months
of January and February. But in spite of this
downturn, bear in mind that it's always wise to
book a hotel in advance of your trip.

In terms of openings, the plush but hip
Trafalgar (*see p53*), the new Hilton hotel in the
heart of town, was the most high-profile and
glamorous launch of the year. Designer hotels
continued to dominate the accommodation
scene, though the austerity and all-out
minimalism of many '90s newcomers has been
tempered by a new emphasis on comfort.

London's greatest concentration of seriously
plush hotels is in Mayfair, but some people
are finally recognising the East End's potential
– the Hilton is getting in on the buzz with a
Petticoat Lane address scheduled for 2003 –
while the City and Canary Wharf are taking
their lead from the **Great Eastern Hotel** (*see
p46*) and the **Four Seasons Canary Wharf**
(*see p60*) respectively.

Further down the ladder, Bloomsbury brims
with mid-priced hotels. For cheaper beds, try
Ebury Street near Victoria (SW1), Gower Street
in Bloomsbury (WC1), and Earl's Court (SW5).
Other areas worth exploring for small, budget
hotels include Bayswater and Paddington (W2)
and South Kensington (SW7). For gay and
lesbian accommodation, *see p308*.

INFORMATION AND BOOKING

If you haven't booked ahead, staff at a London
Tourist Board centre (*see p375*) will look for a
place within your area and price range for a £5
fee (if you book a few weeks in advance, a
deposit may be required). The LTB also
publishes *Where to Stay & What to Do* (£4.99),
available at its centres or in good bookshops.

Most hotels now have their own websites,
through which bookings can be made. You can
also see what's available and make reservations
at LTB's website.
**London Tourist Board Hotel
Booking Line**
*7604 2890/8759 3909/7802 5480/
www.londontown.com.* **Open** 9am-6pm Mon-Fri;
9am-1pm Sat.

PRICES AND CLASSIFICATION

Though British hotels are classified according
to a star system agreed by the English Tourism
Council, the AA and the RAC, we don't list star
ratings, which tend to reflect facilities rather
than overall quality; instead, we've classified
hotels, within their area headings, according to
the price of the cheapest double room per night.

Note that all the room rates listed here are
inclusive of 17.5 per cent VAT (sales tax).
Despite the fact that VAT is included in the
quoted price of almost everything in the UK,
most of the hotels listed below under the Deluxe and
Expensive brackets sneakily quote room
prices exclusive of the tax, presumably to
soften the shock of the bill. Don't be taken in,
and always ask whether the price you're being
quoted includes tax or not. After adding the
VAT, we've rounded the rates up or down to
the nearest pound; to check the rates without
VAT, simply divide the quoted price by 1.175.

All hotels in the **Deluxe** and **Expensive**
categories come with an en suite bath and/or
shower and toilet. All **Deluxe** hotels (over
£250) offer air-conditioning, bar(s), concierge,
laundry, limousine service and restaurant(s),
and can arrange babysitting; in-room services
for all include dataport, minibar, phone,
turndown and 24-hour room services. Other
services are listed by each hotel's review.

Expensive hotels (£151-£250) offer
concierge, laundry and a limousine service,
and can arrange babysitting; in-room services
include a dataport and a phone. As before, any
extras are listed below each review.

All **Moderate** hotels (£101-£150) provide a
laundry, a limo service (unless otherwise stated)
and an in-room phone over and above the
services detailed beneath each review, while
those in the **Moderate to cheap** bracket
(£75-£100) offer an in-room telephone in
addition to the services listed.

Cheap means less than £75. Staying at most cheaper hotels involves sharing bathrooms.

'Including breakfast' often means that of the continental variety (sometimes little more than tea and toast); 'English breakfasts' are of the glorious, fried-everything variety.

VISITORS WITH DISABILITIES

While we've tried to indicate which hotels offer rooms adapted for the needs of disabled guests, check specifics with the hotel directly before booking. A useful organisation is **Holiday Care** (01293 774535/www.holidaycare.org.uk), which has information on accessible hotels in the UK for the disabled and elderly.

COMPLAINTS

To lodge a complaint about any hotel, inform the management in person, and then, if necessary, in writing. The LTB will, depending on the circumstances, look into complaints, regardless of whether you booked through it. *Time Out* always appreciates any feedback on any of the hotels listed here.

EMERGENCY ACCOMMODATION

Shelter is a national charity that provides advice on housing and homelessness. If you get stranded in London without anywhere to stay, call its 24-hour helpline on 0808 800 4444.

The South Bank & Bankside

Cheap

London County Hall Travel Inn Capital

County Hall, Belvedere Road, SE1 7PB (7902 1600/ fax 7902 1619/www.travelinn.co.uk). Waterloo tube/rail. **Rooms** 313 (all en suite). **Rates** £74.95. **Credit** AmEx, DC, MC, V. **Map** p401 M9.
While no one in their right mind would come to a Travel Inn in search of character or luxury, this hotel in the former County Hall is great value given its location right in the shadow of the London Eye and within spitting distance of the manifold attractions of the South Bank. There's a flat room rate of £74.95 per night; rooms are homogeneous but clean and comfy. There are other Travel Inns at Euston, Kensington, Putney Bridge and Tower Bridge. **Hotel services** *Bar. Disabled: adapted rooms. No-smoking rooms. Payphone. Restaurant.* **Room services** *Dataport. Telephone. TV.*

Mad Hatter Hotel

3-7 Stamford Street, SE1 9NY (7401 9222/fax 7401 7111/www.fullers.co.uk). Southwark tube/Waterloo tube/rail. **Rooms** 30. **Rates** £79-£95. **Credit** AmEx, DC, MC, V. **Map** p404 N8.
The Fuller's pub chain's foray into the hotel world has been a success so far, largely thanks to its value for money and good level of service. Called, rather anachronistically, 'English Inns', the growing number of hotels (a new one, the Chamberlain, opened in the City in November 2001) are all attached to cosy and traditional bars and restaurants serving Fuller's famous beer. The Mad Hatter has large, pleasant rooms, three of which are adapted for the disabled. Other guestrooms with interlinking doors are ideal for families.
Hotel services *Bar. Disabled: adapted rooms. No-smoking floor. Payphone. Restaurant.* **Room services** *Telephone. TV.*

The City

For the **Chamberlain**, *see p46* Mad Hatter Hotel; for **Threadneedles**, *see p63* Colonnade Town House.

Deluxe

Great Eastern Hotel

Liverpool Street, EC2M 7QN (7618 5000/ fax 7618 5001/www.great-eastern-hotel.co.uk). Liverpool Street tube/rail. **Rooms** 267. **Rates** £264 single; £305-£381 double; £452-£605 suite. **Credit** AmEx, DC, MC, V. **Map** p405 Q6.
With its breathtaking Guggenheim-style rotunda, a six-storey atrium that overlooks a Zen rock garden lounge, and rooms boasting Eames chairs, Jacobsen desk lamps and chocolate shagpile rugs, this formerly decaying Victorian edifice is a style mag editor's wet dream. The hotel also sports a large collection of modern art from local East End artists, as well as Patrick Caulfield prints. When you've finished gawping at the interior, head for a drink at the George Bar, a glorious wood-panelled affair, or chow down at the Aurora restaurant, which boasts a stunning stained-glass dome. Rooms here aren't huge, but it's the style that counts.
Hotel services *Beauty salon. Business services. Disabled: adapted rooms. Gym. No-smoking floor.* **Room services** *TV: cable/satellite.*

Holborn & Clerkenwell

Deluxe

One Aldwych

1 Aldwych, WC2B 4RH (7300 1000/fax 7300 1001/www.onealdwych.com). Covent Garden or Temple tube/Charing Cross tube/rail. **Rooms** 105. **Rates** £340 single; £364-£435 double; £556-£1,345 suite. **Credit** AmEx, DC, JCB, MC, V. **Map** p401 M7.
Housed in a listed Edwardian bank, One Aldwych is luxurious rather than ostentatious and interesting rather than gimmicky. The double-height lobby and its bar are reminiscent of a fantastic metropolitan railway station, with limestone flooring, dramatic modern sculpture and outlandish furniture. While some of the bedrooms are tiny, all are sleek, chic and chintz-free, and come decorated with gravity-defying flower arrangements and original modern

A bedroom at the **Sanderson**: far too stylish to waste on sleep.

art. Every detail has been considered, down to fibre optic reading lights, mini-televisions on bendable stems in the bathroom and taps designed by Philippe Starck. The hotel's bar, along with its restaurants Axis and Indigo, are all very highly rated on the London scene.

Hotel services *Beauty salon. Business services. Disabled: adapted rooms. Gym. No-smoking floors. Parking. Swimming pool (indoor).* **Room services** *TV: cable/pay movies/satellite/VCR.*

Expensive

Rookery

12 Peter's Lane, Cowcross Street, EC1M 6DS (7336 0931/fax 7336 0932/www.rookeryhotel.com). Farringdon tube/rail. **Rooms** 33. **Rates** £223-£241 single; £264 double; £323-£583 suite. **Credit** AmEx, DC, JCB, MC, V. **Map** p402 O5.

Inspired by fashionably raffish roots – the area was reputedly home to Charles Dickens' Fagin – the Rookery is refreshingly eccentric. Tucked away in a street off fashionable Smithfields, it occupies six restored Georgian townhouses and boasts bedrooms imaginatively named after 18th- and 19th-century locals, including prostitutes and thieves. Vast oak beds with ornately carved Gothic headboards, Victorian commodes and inlaid tables fill the bedrooms, while the magnificent bathrooms are outfitted with Victorian fittings, deep tubs and polished copper pipework. Meals are served in the oak-panelled library. Despite the olde English feel, there's a defiantly modern ambience – the service is impeccable and all mod cons are available.

Hotel services *Business services. Disabled: adapted rooms. Garden. No-smoking floors.* **Room services** *Room service (7am-10pm). TV: satellite/VCR.*

Bloomsbury & Fitzrovia

Deluxe

Sanderson

50 Berners Street, W1T 3NG (7300 1400/ fax 7300 1401/www.schragerhotels.com). Oxford Circus or Tottenham Court Road tube. **Rooms** 150. **Rates** £229-£317 single; £258-£347 double; £441-£881 suite. **Credit** AmEx, DC, MC, V. **Map** p398 J5.

The bland '50s office block exterior gives nothing away (though the male model doormen provide a hint of what's to come). Inside, however, the Sanderson is a fantasy world, where guests are greeted by a giant red lips sofa, a naked woman sashaying along a plasma screen on the front desk, billowing translucent curtains and cutting-edge furniture alongside gold-leaf trimmings and a giant-size Louis XV armoire. A central courtyard garden with fountains, mosaics and magnolias completes the scene. The latest Schrager-Starck creation (or 'urban spa') comes with all their trademark touches, and then some. Daring and drop-dead gorgeous, the rooms share the dream-like quality: bathrooms are encased in a glowing floor-to-ceiling glass box wrapped in layers of diaphanous curtains, and paintings hang over silver-leafed sleigh beds. For a piece of the action, head for the lushly theatrical residents-only Purple Bar, or people-watch at the Long Bar. Expect to pay dear for drinks either way.

The best Hotels

For aspiring literati
Hazlitt's (see p53).

For rural wannabes
Dorset Square Hotel (see p51).

For would-be Hollywood starlets
Dorchester (see p51).

For midnight feasters
Lanesborough (see p59); No.5 Maddox Street (see p53).

For modern art lovers
Great Eastern Hotel (see p46);
Westbourne Hotel (see p62).

Hotel services *Beauty salon. Business services. Disabled: adapted rooms. Garden. Gym. No-smoking floors. Parking.* Room services *TV: cable/ satellite/DVD.*

Expensive

Academy Hotel
21 Gower Street, WC1E 6HG (7631 4115/fax 7636 3442/www.etontownhouse.com). Goodge Street or Tottenham Court Road tube. Rooms 49. Rates £153 single; £179-£217 double; £241-£265 suite. Credit AmEx, DC, MC, V. Map p399 K5.

Housed in three Georgian terraces dating from 1776, the Academy evokes English country-house living, but despite its chintzy tendencies, the interior retains a cool, urbane and restrained ambience. Plain, light walls flatter bright contemporary fabrics and tasteful modern prints, but period features, including glass panelling and colonnades, are still intact. The rooms, filled with *Country Life*-style overstuffed armchairs and half-canopied beds, are restful and serene. If you're looking to unwind, check your room comes with a bath, as some rooms have showers only. The small library-lounge opens on to lush patio gardens, and in the evening, live jazz often plays in the Alchemy, the sleek basement dining club.
Hotel services *Business services. Garden. No-smoking rooms.* Room services *Turndown. TV.*

Blooms Townhouse Hotel
7 Montague Street, WC1B 5BP (7323 1717/fax 7636 6498/www.bloomshotel.com). Holborn or Russell Square tube. Rooms 27. Rates £130 single; £175-£205 double. Credit AmEx, DC, MC, V. Map p399 L5.

Blooms combines state-of-the-art mod cons and quality service in an 18th-century townhouse setting. Besides the books, board games and copies of *The Times* spread liberally over the place, there's a malt 'library' and a secluded walled garden overlooking the British Museum. Spice up your visit by staying in one of the themed bedrooms: choose from the plush Theatre Royal room, the cricket-themed Lord's room, and the Dickens' suite. Bedrooms are medium to small-ish, but all are elegantly designed with muted tones and well-equipped bathrooms.
Hotel services *Garden.* Room services *TV: satellite.*

Charlotte Street Hotel
15 Charlotte Street, W1P 1HB (7806 2000/fax 7806 2002/www.charlottestreethotel.com). Goodge Street or Tottenham Court Road tube. Rooms 52. Rates £206 single; £229-£329 double; £347-£529 suite. Credit AmEx, MC, V. Map p399 J5.

With its buzzy bar that opens on to the street, basement screening room and prime West End location this is a popular hangout for the local media brigade. Surprisingly subtle and understated in comparison with its hipper competitors, the hotel, designed by the rated Kit Kemp, combines elegant period decor with contemporary comfort. The spacious lobby is dotted with deep brown leather armchairs, bare floorboards, and open fireplaces, while the rooms are decorated in soft pinks and purples, with the odd splash of colour or bold print thrown in. Bathrooms are equally easy on the eye, with oak-panelled baths and pretty granite wall mosaics. For something special, choose a loft suite with soaring windows and ceilings, or the open-plan penthouse suite, which has private elevators and spectacular views.
Hotel services *Business services. Cinema. Disabled: adapted rooms. Gym. Library. No-smoking rooms. Parking.* Room services *TV: DVD/satellite/VCR.*

Montague on the Gardens
15 Montague Street, WC1B 5BJ (7637 1001/fax 7637 2516/www.redcarnationhotels.com). Holborn or Russell Square tube. Rooms 104. Rates £194 single; £223-£259 double; £394-£494 suite. Credit AmEx, DC, MC, V. Map p399 L5.

The Montague comes at you like a Victorian Christmas on acid: a tent-like affair of flowery fabric greets you in the lobby, while the lounge is a gorgeous melange of crimson walls, velvet drapes, extravagant chandeliers and richly patterned sofas. A conservatory, lush garden, period bar and gym/sauna complete the relaxing air. The smallish rooms border on the kitsch but are extremely comfortable, with all the usual mod cons, as well as tea- and coffee-making facilities. Room service is very reasonable and staff are helpful.
Hotel services *Business services. Disabled: adapted room. Garden. Gym. No-smoking rooms. Parking.* Room services *TV: pay movies/satellite.*

myhotel bloomsbury
11-13 Bayley Street, WC1B 3HD (7667 6000/ fax 7667 6001/www.myhotels.co.uk). Goodge Street or Tottenham Court Road tube. Rooms 78. Rates £200 single; £247-£294 double; £417 suite; £529-£1,175 penthouse. Credit AmEx, DC, MC, V. Map p399 K5.

Designed using feng shui principles, myhotel pulls all the right strings in attempting to achieve a soothing eastern aesthetic, but cosy it isn't. The minimalist lobby is decorated with artfully arranged flowers and candles, while oriental-style corridors lead to Conran-designed rooms that have a rather sparse, sinewy feel to them (some of the back ones are surprisingly poky). Jinja beauty therapies are offered in the downstairs treatment rooms, and there's a modern fitness studio and a library with Internet access. A branch of Yo! Sushi on the ground floor completes the trip east.

Hotel services *Beauty salon. Business services. Gym. No-smoking floors.* **Room services** *TV: pay movies/satellite/VCR.*

Moderate to cheap

Harlingford Hotel

61-3 Cartwright Gardens, WC1H 9EL (7387 1551/fax 7387 4616/www.harlingfordhotel.com). Russell Square tube/Euston tube/rail. **Rooms** 43. **Rates** £70 single; £88 double; £98 triple; £105 quad. **Credit** AmEx, DC, JCB, MC, V. **Map** p399 L3.

On a lovely Georgian crescent packed with townhouse hotels, the Harlingford stands out because of its varnished-wood bathrooms. Run by the same family for three generations, it's relaxed and friendly. Rooms, though recently refurbished, are a bit lacklustre, and there's no lift. But you do get access to the private tennis courts in the pretty garden square. **Room services** *TV.*

Jenkins Hotel

45 Cartwright Gardens, WC1H 9EH (7387 2067/ fax 7383 3139/www.jenkinshotel.demon.co.uk). Russell Square tube/Euston tube/rail. **Rooms** 14 . **Rates** £72 single; £85 double; £105 triple. **Credit** MC, V. **Map** p399 L3.

Like some of its neighbours on this quiet crescent, the Jenkins, which featured in the TV series *Poirot*, allows its guests access to a private garden square and tennis courts. Rooms are modest but comfortable. The hand-embroidered silk flowers framed with poems that you see throughout the hotel, found by the owner in a box belonging to his grandfather, are a nice personal touch.

Hotel services *No-smoking throughout.* **Room services** *minibar. TV.*

Morgan Hotel

24 Bloomsbury Street, WC1B 3QJ (7636 3735/fax 7636 3045). Tottenham Court Road tube. **Rooms** 21. **Rates** £58-£68 single; £85 double; £115 suite; £130 triple. **Credit** JCB, MC, V. **Map** p399 K5.

Homely and clean if slightly worn in terms of its furnishings, the family-run Morgan is very popular for its big, bargain-priced apartment-style suites in an annexe several doors down the street. A functional but cheerful option in a great location (back rooms look out over the British Museum).

Hotel services *Air-conditioning. Payphone.* **Room services** *TV.*

Cheap

Arosfa

83 Gower Street, WC1E 6HJ (tel/fax 7636 2115). Euston Square or Goodge Street tube. **Rooms** 16. **Rates** £37 single; £50-£66 double; £68-£79 triple; £92 quad. **Credit** JCB, MC, V. **Map** p399 K4.

This spartan but clean and homely bed and breakfast (the name means 'place to stay' in Welsh) is in an elegant Georgian house that was once home to artist John Everett Millais. There's a pretty back garden and a large lounge with a coffee machine and paperbacks. But take note, there's a 2% surcharge for credit card bookings.

Hotel services *Garden. Lounge. No-smoking floors. Payphone. TV room.* **Room services** *TV.*

Ashlee House

261-5 Gray's Inn Road, WC1X 8QT (7833 9400/fax 7833 9677/www.ashleehouse.co.uk). King's Cross tube/rail. **Rooms** 26 (175 beds). **Rates** (per person) £17-£19 4-6-bed room; £15-£17 8-10-bed room; £13-£15 16-bed room; £22-£24 twin; £34-£36 single. **Credit** MC, V. **Map** p399 M3.

A friendly, modern and clean hostel located just a couple of minutes' walk from King's Cross, Ashlee House offers single and twin rooms and large and small dorms. There's a 24-hour reception and security system, no curfew and free luggage storage.

Hotel services *Cooking facilities. Internet access. Laundry. No-smoking rooms. Payphone. TV room.*

The Generator: power 'packing. See p51.

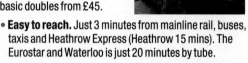

Generator

*37 Tavistock Place, WC1H 9SD (7388 7666/fax
7388 7644/www.the-generator.co.uk). Russell
Square tube.* **Rooms** 217 (833 beds; none en suite).
Rates (per person, incl breakfast) *Nov-Feb* £40
single; £23.50 twin; £20 multi; £15 dormitory.
Mar-Oct £42 single; £26.50 twin; £22.50 multi;
£15 dormitory. **Credit** MC, V. **Map** p399 K4.
Not for the fainthearted, this huge, hyper-modern
hostel with its industrial interior design of stainless
steel and exposed ventilation offers basic accommodation (rooms have just bunks and washbasins)
but provides a great atmosphere in which to meet
other young visitors and backpacker-tailored facilities. There's an Internet room, a 24-hour games area
with pool tables, satellite TV, table football, video
games and refreshments, and a lively bar, and the
location is great for West End nightlife. Wide screen
TV and evening meals are available.
Hotel services *Air-conditioning. Bar. No-smoking
rooms. Payphone. Restaurant. TV room.*

St Margaret Hotel

*26 Bedford Place, WC1B 5JL (7636 4277/fax 7323
3066). Holborn or Russell Square tube.* **Rooms** 64.
Rates £48.50-£50.50 single; £60.50-£95 double;
£87.50-£105.50 triple. **Credit** MC, V. **Map** p399 L5.
On a relatively quiet, tree-lined Georgian street
well situated for the British Museum and other
Bloomsbury pleasures, this value-for-money hotel is
run by friendly Italians. Rooms are plain but well
sized, with high ceilings; those at the back overlook
the Duke of Bedford's private garden (guests have
access to the hotel's own small garden).
Hotel services *Concierge. Disabled: adapted
rooms. Garden. No-smoking rooms. Payphone.
TV room.* **Room services** *Telephone. TV:
satellite.*

Marylebone

Expensive

Dorset Square Hotel

*39 Dorset Square, NW1 6QN (7723 7874/
fax 7724 3328/www.firmdale.com). Baker Street
tube/Marylebone tube/rail.* **Rooms** 38. **Rates** £135
single; £164-£247 double; £282 suite. **Credit** AmEx,
MC, V. **Map** p384 F4.
This elegantly restored Regency townhouse overlooks the original Marylebone site of Lord's cricket
ground, and is more like a traditional English country villa than a city hotel. Masses of flowerpots guide
punters to the wacky Potting Shed basement bar
and restaurant, with its mountains of terracotta pots
and seed boxes, dried flowers and fake fence panelling. The hotel itself, another Kit Kemp creation,
is staggeringly beautiful. The graceful bedrooms are
treasure troves of original oils and antiques, covetable paintings and acres of sumptuous fabrics.
Hotel services *Business services. Garden. No-
smoking rooms.* **Room services** *Turndown. TV:
satellite/VCR.*

Mayfair & St James's

Deluxe

Browns

*Albermarle Street, W1S 4BP (7493 6020/
fax 7393 9381/www.brownshotel.com). Green Park
tube.* **Rooms** 118. **Rates** £317 single; £358-£446
double; £552-£958 suite. **Credit** AmEx, DC, MC, V.
Map p400 7J.
Mr Brown, Lord Byron's entrepreneurial valet,
opened this dignified property in 1837 to cater
for the gentry. These days, you're more likely to
stumble over Americans or Japanese lapping up the
quintessentially English atmosphere. The rooms
combine conservative elegance – wood panelling
and antique furnishings – with all the usual modern
comforts, and there's an aura of a refined gentlemen's club about the place. If cigars and smoking
gowns aren't to your taste, there's also a state-of-the-
art health club. Brown's famous afternoon tea is
served in the drawing room.
Hotel services *Disabled: adapted rooms. Gym.
No-smoking rooms. Parking.* **Room services**
TV: cable/pay movies/satellite.

Dorchester

*Park Lane, W1A 2HJ (7629 8888/fax 7409 0114/
www.dorchesterhotel.com). Green Park or Hyde Park
Corner tube.* **Rooms** 248. **Rates** £334-£358 single;
£376-£441 double; £558-£2,467 suite. **Credit** AmEx,
DC, JCB, MC, V. **Map** p400 G7.

Accommodation

Chest lovely: **No.5 Maddox Street**, *p53.*

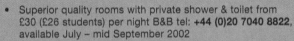

If your idea of luxury is Cinderella ballrooms, Corinthian columns and – er – gold-leaf toilet seats, head for the Dorchester. The place oozes old school (and slightly faded) glamour; you half expect Vivien Leigh or Douglas Fairbanks to waltz through the opulent marbled lobby. The hotel has certainly had more than its fair share of big-name visitors: Liberace's piano is in the bar, Prince Philip had his stag night here, and Liz Taylor and Richard Burton famously honeymooned in the Oliver Messel suite (which hides its minibar behind a row of fake bookshelves). The rooms are decorated in classic 1930s style with etched glass and chrome fittings, while the more expensive suites have private terraces overlooking Hyde Park.

Hotel services *Beauty salon. Business services. Disabled: adapted rooms. Garden. Gym. No-smoking floors. Parking.* **Room services** *TV: cable/pay movies/satellite/VCR.*

Metropolitan

Old Park Lane, W1Y 4LB (7447 1000/fax 7447 1147/www.metropolitan.co.uk). Green Park or Hyde Park Corner tube. **Rooms** 155. **Rates** £282 single; £282-£393 double; £522-£1,880 suite. **Credit** AmEx, DC, MC, V. **Map** p400 G8.

With its zeitgeist minimalist design and achingly trendy clientele (often indistinguishable from the DKNY-clad staff), the Metropolitan has become something of a London institution since opening in 1997. Rooms are simple with little ornamentation, though soft purples, olives and warm natural woods offset the stark aesthetic. All rooms boast the usual high-tech gadgetry, plus huge expanses of windows that overlook Hyde Park. Organic meals are available on room service, and holistic beauty therapies are on offer in the hotel's treatment rooms. The Met's fashionable eaterie Nobu has attracted as much notoriety for its celebrity goings-on (such as Boris Becker's broom cupboard canoodlings) as for its top-quality Japanese nosh.

Hotel services *Beauty salon. Business services. Gym. No-smoking rooms. Parking.* **Room services** *TV: cable/pay movies/satellite/VCR.*

No.5 Maddox Street

5 Maddox Street, W1R 9LE (7647 0200/fax 7647 0300/www.living-rooms.co.uk). Oxford Circus tube. **Rooms** 12. **Rates** £265 double; £294-£370 suite; £470 2-bedroom loft; £646 3-bedroom suite. **Credit** AmEx, DC, MC, V. **Map** p398 J6.

If it wasn't for the posh West End address, you might think you were entering a dodgy establishment – No.5 Maddox Street's innocuous black front door is squeezed between two shops, and to get in you have to register your details over the entrance intercom. Inside, it's as if time stood still sometime around 1985, when chrome was cool, blond wood floors were exotic and black was, well, the original new black. The rooms combine bachelor pad credentials – shagpile rugs, chocolate leather pouffes, fireplaces and wide screen TVs – with oriental touches such as bamboo flooring, sliding doors,

lacquered chests and linen kimonos. Each of the suites has a kitchen stocked with groceries and folding Muji ten-speed bikes can be hired.

Hotel services *Business services. Cooking facilities.* **Room services** *Room service (7am-4.30pm). TV: satellite/VCR.*

Ritz

150 Piccadilly, W1J 9BR (7493 8181/fax 7493 2687/www.theritzhotel.co.uk). Green Park tube. **Rooms** 133. **Rates** £358 single; £417-£499 double; £582-£1,586 suite. **Credit** AmEx, MC, V. **Map** p400 J8.

Not to be outdone by young pretenders to the hotel throne, the centenarian Ritz is getting groovy. Although it's still the venue of choice for Charles and Camilla, a recent birthday bash by Elton John brought in the likes of Damien Hirst and Joe Strummer – staff even waived the 'tie and no trainers' dress code. But while it might have shifted upwards in the hipness stakes, much about the Piccadilly pleasure palace remains resolutely old school (as in Louis XVI). The restaurant (where the Queen Mum keeps a corner table) drips with elaborate gold-leaf mouldings, chandeliers and rococo mirrors, while afternoon tea in the Palm Court remains a refined affair. The rooms, furnished in peach and cream, are similarly lavish, with 24-carat gold-leaf trim, silk bedspreads, antique furniture and marble bathrooms. There's a staff-to-guest ratio of two to one to cater for your every whim.

Hotel services *Beauty salon. Business services. Disabled: adapted rooms. Garden. Gym. No-smoking floors. Parking.* **Room services** *TV: cable/satellite/VCR.*

The Trafalgar

2 Spring Gardens, SW1A 2TS (7870 2900/fax 7870 2911/www.thetrafalgar.hilton.com). Charing Cross tube/rail. **Rates** £317-£435 double; £505-£552 suite. **Credit** AmEx, DC, MC, V. **Map** p401 K7.

Hilton's positioning of the Trafalgar as its first 'lifestyle hotel' is a little misleading: it's far classier than such PR would suggest. While design-aware, it's sleek rather than desperately chic, and its minimalism comes over more as plain good taste. In any case, no design guru in the world could come up with anything to compete with the views – the best from the ground-floor bourbon bar and rooms 203, 503, 603 and 703 – over London's restless main square, into which the wedge-shaped neo-classical building (formerly the offices of the Cunard cruise line) nuzzles like the prow of a ship. Rooms vary in shape and size; some are split level, and all are simply furnished in muted taupe tones and decorated with works by local artists. The luxury is in the quality of the fittings rather than fancy accoutrements. Quibbles? The price of the 'lifestyle' rooms, which don't have views, and the occasional blip in service. Special mention? The carbon-neutral energy policy.

Hotel services *Business services. Disabled: adapted rooms. Garden (rooftop). No-smoking rooms. Parking.* **Room services** *CD player. Dataport. TV: cable/DVD/games/pay movies/web TV.*

Soho & Leicester Square

Expensive

Hazlitt's

6 Frith Street, W1D 3JA (7434 1771/fax 7439 1524/ www.hazlittshotel.com). Tottenham Court Road tube. **Rooms** 23. **Rates** £182 single; £230 double; £260 triple; £352 suite. **Credit** AmEx, DC, MC, V. **Map** p399 K6.

This charming 18th-century hotel is steeped in history and culture: the writer William Hazlitt lived and died here, and the hotel is a favourite stopover for visiting authors and media types. More characterful than luxurious, the small-ish rooms boast clawfoot baths, oil paintings and antique hardwood furnishings. Modern gadgetry is largely absent, though there are modem points in the rooms.
Hotel services *Business services. No-smoking rooms.* **Room services** *TV: satellite/VCR.*

Covent Garden & St Giles's

Deluxe

Covent Garden Hotel

10 Monmouth Street, WC2H 9HB (7806 1000/fax 7806 1100/www.firmdale.com). Covent Garden or Leicester Square tube. **Rooms** 58. **Rates** £223 single; £258-£329 double; £382-£699 suite. **Credit** AmEx, MC, V. **Map** p399 L6.

From the outside it looks like a small brasserie; inside, the curtains and bare boards of the lobby give the place a theatrical air – a theme that continues with the upholstered mannequins in the rooms, a screening room in the basement and a clientele of models, ad execs and film industry types. Designer duo Tim and Kit Kemp (also responsible for the well-received interiors of Charlotte Street Hotel, Dorset Square Hotel and the Pelham) have given the place a dose of their signature style: think Regency fop meets Hollywood starlet. The rooms are decked out with dramatic textiles, four-poster beds, chandeliers, and mahogany and marble bathrooms (with Molton Brown supplies). The richly decorated and cosy main drawing room (guests only) is almost more suited to a private home than a hotel.
Hotel services *Beauty salon. Business services. Gym.* **Room services** *TV: pay movies/satellite/VCR.*

St Martin's Lane

45 St Martin's Lane, WC2N 4HX 0800 634 5500/7300 5500/fax 7300 5501/ www.ianschragerhotels.com). Covent Garden or Leicester Square tube. **Rooms** 204. **Rates** £247 single; £270-£329 double; £493-£558 suite; £1,410-£1,645 penthouse. **Credit** AmEx, DC, MC, V. **Map** p401 L7.

Entered through tall revolving doors of luminescent yellow glass, the lobby of St Martin's Lane encapsulates the Schrager-Starck vision; part soaring theatre, part bustling meeting point, it's seen everyone from Kate Moss to Robert de Niro navigating their way around its oversized columns, tiny garden gnomes, gold molar-teeth stools and giant chess pieces. The public areas are beautiful, as are the staff, and the cocktails – pretty much everything apart from the occasional ordinary-looking but loaded guest. Rooms are light, bright and space shuttle white, with floor-to-ceiling windows that command sweeping views of London's theatre district. The minimalist aesthetic is set off by bold, Starck-designed furniture and bathrooms, state-of-the-art technology, and an interactive light installation for that Studio 54 disco effect.
Hotel services *Business services. Disabled: adapted rooms. Garden. Gym. No-smoking floors. Parking.* **Room services** *TV: satellite/VCR.*

Savoy

Strand, WC2R OEU (7836 4343/fax 7240 6040/www.savoy-group.co.uk). Covent Garden or Embankment tube/Charing Cross tube/rail. **Rooms** 233. **Rates** £341-£376 single; £405-£441 double; £582-£1,469 suite. **Credit** AmEx, DC, MC, V. **Map** p401 L7.

Black cabs and limos glide past the entrance hall, which is decked with marble reliefs. Behind lie a trio of celebrated restaurants where guests get through more than 9,500 sides of smoked salmon and 52,000 oysters a year. More understated than the Ritz, the Savoy has its own palatial grandeur: many of its restored art deco bedrooms have incredible river

Hip **Trafalgar**: not for squares. *See p52.*

Stair case or head case? The curious, cultish **Hotel 167**. *See p59.*

views. The spacious rooms have the restrained elegance of a gentlemen's club, though the mirrored bathroom ceilings and enormous showerheads add a touch of decadence. Rooms are comfortable (though if you want a double bed make sure you're not given a twin room), but the air-conditioning can be a little noisy. The lovely rooftop health club offers steam rooms, saunas and a small pool. A galaxy of stars has stayed here, including Monet, who painted the Thames from his fifth-floor room, and Bob Dylan. **Hotel services** *Beauty salon. Business services. Gym. No-smoking rooms. Parking. Swimming pool (indoor).* **Room services** *TV: cable/pay movies/satellite/VCR.*

West Street

13-15 West Street, WC2H 9NE (7010 8700/ fax 7010 8601). Leicester Square tube. **Rooms** 3. **Rates** £294-£529 double. **Credit** AmEx, DC, MC, V. **Map** p399 6K.
Not strictly a hotel in the traditional sense of the word, this six-floor building has a strikingly contemporary interior with two restaurants, a cocktail bar, a private dining room and three luxurious apartment suites on the top two floors. The White Room comes complete with white marble flooring and an opulent marble bathroom and the Stone Room with a spectacular roof terrace, while the Loft is kitted out like a chi-chi Italian furniture showroom. Guests reach the main desk via a bridge flanked by deep drops and a hanging sculpture suspended over the basement. As befits a hotel in the heart of theatreland, the effect is breathtakingly dramatic.
Hotel services *Bar. Disabled: adapted rooms. No-smoking rooms. Parking. Restaurants.*
Room services *Minibar. Room service (24hrs). TV: cable/pay movies/satellite/DVD.*

Knightsbridge & South Kensington

Deluxe

Blakes

33 Roland Gardens, SW7 3PF (7370 6701/fax 7373 0442/www.blakeshotels.com). Gloucester Road or South Kensington tube. **Rooms** 49. **Rates** £200 single; £299-£393 double; £640-£1,051 suite. **Credit** AmEx, DC, MC, V. **Map** p397 D11.
While designer Anoushka Hempel's star may have fallen at The Hempel (*see p61*), Blakes, the sumptuous hotel she opened in South Kensington in the 1970s, remains resolutely in fashion. The original boutique hotel, Blakes offers a discreet and luxurious hideaway for the beautiful and glamorous. Each room is a unique, self-contained fantasy in extravagant colour schemes evoking an oriental exoticism. The rooms spill over with antique treasures, silk embroidered cushions and lacquered chests. Marble bathrooms sport the requisite fluffy towels and expensive toiletries.
Hotel services *Business services. Cooking facilities. Garden. No-smoking rooms. Parking.* **Room services** *TV: satellite/VCR.*

Expensive

The Gore

189 Queen's Gate, SW7 5EX (7584 6601/fax 7589 8127/www.gorehotel.com). Gloucester Road tube. **Rooms** 53. **Rates** £164-£182 single; £206-£311 double; £335 suite. **Credit** AmEx, DC, MC, V. **Map** p397 D9.

This 19th-century townhouse spills over with English Victoriana in the form of hunting prints, oil paintings, potted ferns, velvet drapes and Gothic cornices, while well-worn tomes of Victorian classics are left invitingly open on the tables. The warm and welcoming rooms are decorated in rich wood panelling, oriental rugs, leather armchairs and ornate mirrors; some contain four-posters the size of boats, antique-style wooden thrones that open up to reveal (thankfully modern) loos, and stunning, tiled bath alcoves. The Tudor room comes with its own floor-to-ceiling minstrel's gallery, while the Venus room has a florid mural over the bath and a gilt-edged bed that was owned by Judy Garland.

Hotel services *Bar. Business services. No-smoking floor. Restaurants.* **Room services** *minibar. Room service (7am-11pm).* TV: *satellite/VCR.*

Kensington House Hotel

15-16 Prince of Wales Terrace, W8 5BQ (7937 2345/fax 7368 6700/www.kenhouse.com). High Street Kensington tube. **Rooms** 41. **Rates** £135 single; £155-£175 double; £195 suite. **Credit** AmEx, DC, MC, V.

A newcomer to the London hotel scene (it opened in 2000), Kensington House markets itself very consciously as a modern hotel; there's not a scrap of chintz to be seen, though the exterior itself has been restored to its 19th-century elegance and the spacious rooms have the benefit of high ceilings and large arch windows. Decor-wise, it's all cool cream walls and dazzlingly white bedlinen with flashes of colour, such as red leather sofas in the executive rooms, one of which has a beautiful balcony. The Tiger Bar can lack atmosphere on a slow evening but provides an attractive breakfast venue. Its slightly more expensive sister hotel, **London Bridge Hotel** (8-18 London Bridge Street, SE1 9SG, 7855 2200), is a good choice on the South Bank.

Hotel services *Bar. Business services. No-smoking rooms. Restaurant.* **Room services** TV: *pay movies/satellite.*

Pelham

15 Cromwell Place, SW7 2LA (7589 8288/fax 7584 8444/www.firmdale.com). South Kensington tube. **Rooms** 51. **Rates** £176 single; £211-£294 double; £529-£811 suite. **Credit** AmEx, MC, V. **Map** p397 D10.

The Pelham has long been the hotel of choice for the fashion pack – as much, one suspects, for its over-sized wardrobes and proximity to Harvey Nicks as for its handy location during London Fashion Week. Boasting some 18th-century pine panelling, original oils and generous helpings of designer fabrics and flowers, the Pelham is a classic example of Kit Kemp's 'classic yet contemporary' trademark. Soft pastel shades, florals and tartans dominate the rooms, while the bathrooms have tubs large enough to get lost in.

Hotel services *Air-conditioning. Bar. Business services. Restaurant.* **Room services** *minibar. Room service (24hrs). Turndown.* TV: *cable/pay movies/satellite/VCR.*

Moderate

Aster House

3 Sumner Place, SW7 3EE (7581 5888/ fax 7584 4925/www.asterhouse.com). South Kensington tube. **Rooms** 14. **Rates** £75-£99 single; £135-£180 double. **Credit** JCB, MC, V. **Map** p397 11D.

Aster House is located on a quiet, upmarket street that doesn't allow hotel signs. Its florally decorated guestrooms are rather uninspired, but all of them have been fully refurbished within the last couple of years, and the bathrooms have marble floors and power showers. The public areas, including the L'Orangerie breakfast conservatory, are plusher, and there's a lovely garden at the back.

Hotel services *Air-conditioning. Business services. Garden. Iron. No smoking throughout.* **Room services** TV: *satellite.*

Cranley Gardens Hotel

8 Cranley Gardens, SW7 3DB (7373 3232/fax 7373 7944/www.cranleygardenshotel.com). Gloucester Road tube. **Rooms** 85. **Rates** £85 single; £115 double; £135 triple. **Credit** AmEx, DC, JCB, MC, V. **Map** p397 D11.

A hop and a skip away from the shopping delights of the King's Road, Kensington High Street, Harrods and Harvey Nicks, this pleasant if unatmospheric mid-range hotel occupies four listed Victorian townhouses. The rooms, some of which have balconies over a pretty garden square, are a little chintzy but generously proportioned. There's no limo service, but staff are eager to please.

Hotel services *Babysitting. Bar. Business services. Restaurant (7.30am-10am Mon-Sat; 8am-10am Sun).* **Room services** *Room service (8am-midnight).* TV: *satellite.*

Five Sumner Place

5 Sumner Place, SW7 3EE (7584 7586/fax 7823 9962/www.sumnerplace.com). South Kensington tube. **Rooms** 15. **Rates** £99 single; £150 double. **Credit** AmEx, MC, V. **Map** p397 D11.

This delightful and friendly little hotel, which has won a raft of awards, aims to whisk you out of the 21st century and take you back in time to a more genteel era. Handy for shopping, it's set in a listed terrace of white townhouses built around 1848. Rooms, while not overly large, are furnished in a restrained period style, and there's lift access to all floors. The airy Victorian-style conservatory is a lovely place for a long breakfast over free newspapers and magazines.

Hotel services *Garden. No-smoking floors.* **Room services** *Dataport. minibar. Room service (8am-8pm).* TV.

Gainsborough Hotel

7-11 Queensberry Place, SW7 2DL (7957 0000/fax 7957 0001/www.eeh.co.uk). South Kensington tube. **Rooms** 49. **Rates** £79-£102 single; £141 double; £235 suite. **Credit** AmEx, DC, JCB, MC, V. **Map** p397 D10.

Part of the Elegant English Hotels mini-chain, the Gainsborough lives up to the communal epithet, with its country-house feel and understated period decor in the public rooms (the bedrooms are a little more exuberant). In this case, elegance doesn't preclude a relaxed atmosphere, or value for money. In the spacious lounge and reception there is a portrait of the Duchess of Richmond by Gainsborough, after whom the hotel is named, while the Picasso Bar has yellow silk walls and tasselled drapes – not at all Picassoesque, but rather glam all the same. There's also a complimentary three-day pass to some of the museums and galleries nearby.
Hotel services *Air-conditioning. Babysitting. Bar. Business services. Concierge. No-smoking rooms.* **Room services** *Room service (24hrs). TV: satellite.*

Gallery Hotel

8-10 Queensberry Place, SW7 2DL (7915 0000/fax 7915 4400/www.eeh.co.uk). South Kensington tube. **Rooms** 36. **Rates** £137-£147 double; £237 suite. **Credit** AmEx, DC, JCB, MC, V. **Map** p397 D10.
Set in an imposing but fabulously comfortable Victorian residence across the road from its sister the Gainsborough (*see p57*), the Gallery is quietly refined, with its mahogany-panelled reception, bar and lounge and original, framed artworks in both the common parts and the guestrooms. The lounge resembles a gentlemen's club, with its plush leather and velvet armchairs and sofas, heavy drapes and oriental carpets, while the rooms are subtly luxurious, with pinstriped or floral bedlinen and muted colours. Suites have private roof terraces, Jacuzzis, minibars and VCRs. Three-night stays get you free passes to several London museums and galleries.
Hotel services *Air-conditioning. Babysitting. Bar. Business services. Concierge.* **Room services** *Dataport. Room service (24hrs). TV: satellite/VCR.*

Moderate to cheap

Hotel 167

167 Old Brompton Road, SW5 0AN (7373 0672/fax 7373 3360/www.hotel167.com). Gloucester Road tube. **Rooms** 19. **Rates** £72-£86 single; £90-£99 double; extra bed £16. **Credit** AmEx, DC, JCB, MC, V. **Map** p397 D11.
This idiosyncratic and somewhat cultish hotel (it inspired both an unreleased Manic Street Preachers track and a now out-of-print novel, *Hotel 167*, by Jane Solomon; *see p39*) offers a cheery, relaxed retreat. In terms of decor, it's a hybrid of Victorian and modern (marble, wrought-iron, antique knick-knacks and potted palms rub shoulders with Scandinavian-style furnishings and modern paintings).
Room services *TV: satellite.*

Swiss House Hotel

171 Old Brompton Road, SW5 0AN (7373 2769/fax 7373 4983/www.swiss-hh.demon.co.uk). Gloucester Road tube. **Rooms** 15. **Rates** £48-£68 single; £85-£99 double; £114 triple; £128 quad. **Credit** AmEx, DC, JCB, MC, V. **Map** p397 D11.

A little piece of the countryside in the heart of South Ken, this lovingly run B&B (the name is down to the fact that it used to be a residence for Swissair crews), with its trailing ivy without and dried flowers and pine furniture within, is a calm haven. Rooms are less heavy on the rustic theme, with smart navy bedlinen, wooden floors and fireplaces. Fans are provided, and the back rooms have garden views. Price hikes are scheduled for spring 2002.
Hotel services *Babysitting. Concierge. Laundry. Limousine service. No-smoking rooms.* **Room services** *Dataport. Room service on request. TV: cable.*

Cheap

Abbey House

11 Vicarage Gate, W8 4AG (7727 2594/fax 7727 1873/www.abbeyhousekensington.com). High Street Kensington or Notting Hill Gate tube. **Rooms** 16. **Rates** £45 single; £74 double; £90 triple; £100 quad. **No credit cards. Map** p394 B8.
An excellent B&B for the price, the family-run Abbey House is set in an elegant Victorian house that has retained many of its original fittings. The well-maintained rooms, which are refurbished annually, are overly floral but spacious and comfortable, with orthopaedic beds.
Hotel services *Babysitting. Payphone.* **Room services** *TV.*

Vicarage Hotel

10 Vicarage Gate, W8 4AG (7229 4030/fax 7792 5899/www.londonvicaragehotel.com). High Street Kensington or Notting Hill Gate tube. **Rooms** 18. **Rates** £46 single; £76-£100 double; £93 triple; £100 quad. **No credit cards. Map** p394 B8.
Family-run and with a loyal base of fans, the Vicarage must be doing something right, though visitors with heavy luggage should be warned that the stairs are a bit daunting. This five-storey Victorian house, which has retained many original features, is in a calm and leafy garden square. Rooms are pleasantly furnished with period furniture and subtle floral decor, and there's a cosy TV lounge.
Hotel services *Payphone. TV room.* **Room services** *TV (some rooms).*

Belgravia & Pimlico

Deluxe

Lanesborough

Hyde Park Corner, SW1X 7TA (7259 5599/fax 7259 5606/www.lanesborough.com). Hyde Park Corner tube. **Rooms** 95. **Rates** £311-£376 single; £435-£529 double; £670-£5,288 suite. **Credit** AmEx, DC, MC, V. **Map** p400 G8.
Unashamed hedonism is the key to the Lanesborough's reputation as the most opulent of London's hotels (*see p62* **Rock hotels**). The rooms all combine elegant Regency-period furnishings with space-age

technology, and the range of facilities is awesome: in-room computers and software, Internet access, private phone lines, digital movies, music libraries and mobile phones. Other touches, such as the personalised stationery, use of hotel cars, and personal 24-hour butler service, elevate the hotel into a league of its own. The glass-roofed conservatory is a fantasy of chinoiserie, trickling fountains and exotic vegetation, and the Library bar, a gentleman's bolt-hole complete with wall to wall books, a cocktail piano and a deserved reputation for serving some of the best Martinis in London.

Hotel services *Business services. Disabled: adapted rooms. Gym. No-smoking rooms. Parking.* **Room services** *TV: cable/DVD/satellite/web TV.*

Moderate

Topham's Belgravia

28 Ebury Street, SW1W 0LU (7730 8147/fax 7823 5966/www.tophams.co.uk). Victoria tube/rail. **Rooms** 39. **Rates** £115 single; £130-£150 double; £170 triple; £260 family room. **Credit** AmEx, DC, JCB, MC, V. **Map** p400 H10.

This lovely townhouse hotel in the heart of Belgravia has been owned by the Topham family for more than 60 years (its founder, Diana Topham, took over her brother's somewhat wild drinking club and gradually extended into the neighbouring four houses) and has built up a solid base of satisfied customers, many of whom originally came here for their honeymoon (it was, until recently, called the Ebury Court Hotel). It's a suitably romantic and characterful setting, with its cosy restaurant and bar, rabbit-warren passages and creaking floors, yet the cool white and cream bedrooms are blessedly chintz-free.

Hotel services *Babysitting. Bar. Disabled: adapted rooms. Restaurant.* **Room services** *Dataport. Room service (24hrs). Turndown. TV: satellite.*

Cheap

Woodville House & Morgan House

107 Ebury Street, SW1W 9QU (7730 1048/fax 7730 2574/www.woodvillehouse.co.uk) & 120 Ebury Street, SW1W 9QQ (7730 2384/fax 7730 8442/ www.morganhouse.co.uk). Victoria tube/rail. **Rooms** *Woodville* 12 (none en suite); *Morgan* 11 (3 en suite). **Rates** (incl English breakfast) £42 single; £62-£80 double; £80 triple; £90-£115 quad. **Credit** MC, V. **Map** p400 H10.

Run by the friendly Rachel Joplin and Ian Berry, these Georgian B&Bs complement one another – the Woodville is traditional, with somewhat florid decor, while the Morgan has a more modern feel. The comfortable rooms have orthopaedic mattresses. The Woodville also boasts a pretty patio.

Hotel services *Air-conditioning (selected rooms, Woodville). Babysitting. Garden. No-smoking rooms. Payphone (Woodville).* **Room services** *Kitchenette (Woodville). TV.*

North London

Moderate to cheap

30 King Henry's Road

30 King Henry's Road, Primrose Hill, NW3 3RP (7483 2871/fax 7209 9739/www.30kinghenrys road.co.uk). Chalk Farm tube/Primrose Hill rail. **Rooms** 3. **Rates** £80 single; £100 double. **No credit cards.**

Refreshingly distant from the budget hotel hubs of Bloomsbury, Bayswater and South Kensington, this tiny, old-fashioned B&B set in a mid-Victorian house is run by the affable Carole and Andrew Ingram with the help of their greyhounds Grace and Joe. The lovely rooms, which don't have phones, have queen-sized beds with crisp white bedlinen; bathrobes are provided. Breakfast (using organic ingredients where possible) is taken around the kitchen table looking out into the beautiful garden.

Hotel services *Air-conditioning. No-smoking throughout.* **Room services** *TV.*

Cheap

Hampstead Village Guesthouse

2 Kemplay Road, Hampstead, NW3 1SY (7435 8679/fax 7794 0254/www.hampstead guesthouse.com). Hampstead tube/Hampstead Heath rail. **Rooms** 6. **Rates** £48-£66 single; £72-£84 double; £90-£150 studio. **Credit** AmEx, DC, JCB, MC, V.

This lovingly restored Victorian house, home to Dutchwoman Annemarie van der Meer, her husband Jim and Marley the dog, offers modern amenities in a setting of antique and handmade furniture, books, Delft earthenware and general bohemian clutter. Each of the six rooms has its own individual flavour and boasts a comfy bed with good reading lamps. A separate outhouse with a tiny corner kitchenette sleeps up to five people, while the back garden is a fine setting for full English breakfasts in summer. Credit card payments are subject to a 5% surcharge.

Hotel services *Babysitting. Cooking facilities. Garden. Laundry. No-smoking throughout. Parking.* **Room services** *Telephone. TV.*

East London

Deluxe

Four Seasons Canary Wharf

46 Westferry Circus, Canary Wharf, E14 8RS (7510 1999/fax 7510 1998/www.fourseasons.com). Canary Wharf tube/Westferry DLR. **Rooms** 142. **Rates** £306-£364 single; £329-£388 double; £588-£1,763 suite. **Credit** AmEx, DC, MC, V. **Map** p394 C6.

Apparently designed (by United Designers) with an ice cube in mind, this slick Docklands hotel has a pleasingly symmetrical aesthetic, from the clean lines of the lobby pillars to the boxy window seats in the bedrooms. Views from the riverside rooms are stunning, taking in one of the broadest sweeps of the Thames, and the swimming pool at the neighbouring Holmes Place health club (to which guests have free access) exploits one of London's most picturesque settings with floor-to-ceiling windows. An understated mineral colour scheme, a menu of decent Italian food and lobby-side cocktails complete the restful tableau of East 14's only hotel of substance.

Hotel services *Business services. Disabled: adapted rooms. Gym. No-smoking rooms. Parking. Swimming pool (indoor).* **Room services** *TV: cable/pay movies/satellite/web TV/VCR.*

South London

Moderate to cheap

Riverside Hotel

23 Petersham Road, Richmond-upon-Thames, Surrey TW10 6UH (8940 1339/fax 8948 0967/ www.riversidehotelrichmond.co.uk). Richmond tube/rail. **Rooms** 22. **Rates** £65 single; £85-£90 double; £125 suite (call for details of special rates). **Credit** AmEx, DC, MC, V.

A fine choice for those wishing to steer clear of the West End yet only 15 minutes from Waterloo by train, the Riverside offers spacious if plain rooms, some of which have splendid Thames views (as do the lounge and breakfast room). It's superbly situated for Hampton Court, Kew Gardens and more. **Hotel services** *Laundry. No-smoking rooms. Parking (free).* **Room services** *Dataport. Room service (10am-11.30pm). TV: satellite.*

West London

Deluxe

Halcyon Hotel

81 Holland Park, Kensington, W11 3RZ (7727 7288/ fax 7729 8516/www.thehalcyon.com). Holland Park tube. **Rooms** 42. **Rates** £206-£259 single; £323 double; £370-£776 suite. **Credit** AmEx, DC, MC, V.

Situated in two peach stucco townhouses in the midst of genteel and leafy Holland Park, the Halcyon is perfectly placed to offer a tranquil, if lavish, getaway for the rock musicians and film stars who head its star-studded guest list. The feel is romantic; some of the spacious and airy rooms have French windows and ivy-covered balconies, others have four-poster beds and gorgeously clashing upholstery. The exotic Halcyon Suite has a private conservatory that overlooks gardens and lawn tennis courts. The relaxed air is complemented by Jacuzzis and corner baths in some of the bathrooms. A secluded al fresco lunch (cooked by Nigel Davis, former head chef at the celeb-adored Ivy) on the pretty back patio offers all the privacy you could need.

Hotel services *Garden. Parking.* **Room services** *TV: cable/pay movies/satellite/VCR.*

The decadent **Lanesborough**. *See p59.*

Hempel

31-55 Craven Hill Gardens, Bayswater, W2 3EA (7298 9000/fax 7402 4666/www.the-hempel.co.uk). Lancaster Gate or Queensway tube/Paddington tube/rail. **Rooms** 41, 5 apartments. **Rates** £300 single; £347 double; £517-£1,527 suite. **Credit** AmEx, DC, MC, V. **Map** p394 C6.

A room full of white orchids greets you at Anoushka Hempel's homage to minimalism. Although Anoushka and the hotel have parted ways, her vision of a pared-down, Eastern aesthetic lives on in the cool spare design and monochromatic interiors. There's a mausoleum-like feel to the rooms, with their heavy doors, white-on-white wall panelling and stone floors and bathrooms, but there's no denying the effect is impressive. The restaurant, I-Thai, is equally stunning in a stark, vault-like sort of way, and the food is good. The surprisingly relaxed and friendly staff provide a welcome antidote to the 'don't-touch-or-you'll-mess-it-up' aura.

Hotel services *Disabled: adapted rooms. Garden. Parking.* **Room services** *TV: cable/pay movies/ satellite/VCR.*

Expensive

Pembridge Court Hotel

34 Pembridge Gardens, Notting Hill, W2 4DX (7229 9977/fax 7727 4982/www.pemct.co.uk). Notting Hill Gate tube. **Rooms** 20. **Rates** £125-£165 single; £160-£195 double. **Credit** AmEx, DC, MC, V. **Map** p394 A7.

Pembridge Court is home to Churchill, possibly the largest cat ever to walk the planet, and his furry mate Spencer, so cat lovers will feel immediately at home (manager Valerie hands out boxes of chocolate cats to children who are staying, too). Rooms are large and airy, decorated in chintzy florals that are a little mumsy in style but soothing nonetheless. The ambience is comfortable, with power showers, VCRs and CD players in all the rooms. The hotel walls are covered in a fascinating collection of 19th-century accessories including delicate evening gloves, fans and jewellery that wouldn't look out of place in the V&A. There's a large restaurant and bar, and the back door opens directly on to Portobello Road.

Hotel services *Air-conditioning. Bar. Business services.* **Room services** *Room service (24hrs). TV: satellite/VCR.*

Portobello Hotel
22 Stanley Gardens, Notting Hill, W11 2NG (7727 2777/fax 7792 9641/www.portobello-hotel.co.uk). Notting Hill Gate tube. **Rooms** 24. **Rates** £150 single; £195-£375 double. **Credit** AmEx, DC, MC, V. **Map** p394 A6.

For a spot of exotica, the Portobello can't be beat; the rock star clientele, certainly, can't get enough of the place (*see below* **Rock hotels**). Rooms are gorgeously and imaginatively decorated with billowing white drapes, vivid throws and cushions, oriental mirrors, palm trees and intricately decorated Indian screens. A visit to the eccentric and beautiful restaurant Julie's round the corner is the perfect way to complement your bohemian fantasies.

Hotel services *Air-conditioning. Bar. Business services. Restaurant.* **Room services** *minibar. Room service (24hrs). TV: cable/VCR.*

Westbourne Hotel
163-5 Westbourne Grove, Notting Hill, W11 2RS (7243 6008/fax 7229 7201/www.westbourne hotel.com). Notting Hill Gate tube. **Rooms** 20. **Rates** £206-£300 double. **Credit** AmEx, MC, V. **Map** p394 A6.

With its low-slung reception area kitted out like an upmarket airport lounge and the young and friendly staff gliding around in what appear to be factory overalls, you know you're in deeply trendy territory. Walls have a smattering of Britart pieces, and the rooms feature some original large-scale art pieces by the likes of Sarah Lucas and Bridget Riley. They form a striking contrast with their surroundings – rooms have a minimum of fuss and furniture (the bright white-tiled bathrooms with their tiny sinks are more reminiscent of a hospital than a hotel).

Rock hotels

If you happen to fancy yourself as a bit of a Lenny Kravitz or a Rolling Stone, a pretty B&B in a quiet Kensington street is not going to be your ideal London stopover. So for all you aspiring rock gods, we've compiled a rundown of London hotels that have been graced by the stars. Just don't get carried away and try to eject your TV set from the window.

Columbia Hotel
95-9 Lancaster Gate, W2 (7402 0021). Double £83.
Who: The Teardrop Explodes started the trend back in 1983. Since then the Columbia has been the temporary abode of Simple Minds, Marc Almond, the Eurythmics and, er, Slade frontman Noddy Holder.
High points: Great price, a central location, and a bar that stays open until until the wee small hours (well, 3am).
Low point: Bland interiors.
Did you know? During World War I one of the two houses that makes up the Columbia was an American Red Cross hospital.

Conrad International London
Chelsea Harbour, SW10 (7823 3000). Suites only: £185-£247.
Who: David Bowie, Prince, Neil Diamond.

High points: Indoor pool; marina views; free limo service to Harrods.
Low point: Naff decor.
Did you know? After their sixth stay, Take That were told not to come back, not for their rock star behaviour but because of the number of last-minute bookings made by young fans, many not legally old enough to stay in a hotel by themselves.

Hyatt Carlton Tower
Cadogan Place, SW1 (7235 1234). Double £295.
Who: Madge (*In Bed with Madonna* features several scenes shot in her room).
High point: Glass-roofed pool.
Low point: Large and a bit impersonal.
Did you know? The presidential suite on the 18th floor has bulletproof windows.

Lanesborough
See p59.
Who: Madonna, Michael Jackson, Geri Halliwell, Mariah Carey, Celine Dion.
High points: London's most expensive hotel suite, the Royal Suite (£5,288 a night), which has three double bedrooms, a drawing room, a dining room and kitchen, a gym, 24-hour butler service, and a chauffeured Bentley; the famous Martinis in the Library Bar.

Hotel services *Air-conditioning. Bar. Business services. Garden. No-smoking rooms.* **Room services** *Room service (24hrs). TV: satellite/DVD.*

Moderate

Colonnade Town House
2 Warrington Crescent, Little Venice, W9 1ER (7286 1052/fax 7286 1057/www.etontownhouse.com). Warwick Avenue tube. **Rooms** 43. **Rates** £90 single; £120-£235 double; £258-£276 suite. **Credit** AmEx, DC, JCB, MC, V.

Originally two Victorian mansions, the delightfully situated Colonnade was massively refurb ished a couple of years back, and it looks stunning. The individually designed rooms, which take advantage of the building's existing architectural features, are warm and inviting, with antiques, rich fabrics, luxurious Egyptian cotton bedlinen and Penhaligon's toiletries. Some of the deluxe ones have four-poster beds or balconies. The suites, which include the JFK Suite complete with the four-poster made for his visit in 1962, the Freud Suite commemorating Sigmund's stay in 1938, are stunning. The breakfast room is chic and modern. Call for details of the Colonnades'

new boutique sister hotel, **Threadneedles**, in the City; it was about to open as we went to press. **Hotel services** *Air-conditioning. Babysitting. Business services. Concierge. Garden. No-smoking rooms. Parking.* **Room services** *Dataport. minibar. Room service (24hrs). Turndown. TV: satellite.*

London Elizabeth Hotel
Lancaster Terrace, Bayswater, W2 3PF (7402 6641/ fax 7224 8900/www.londonelizabethhotel.co.uk). Lancaster Gate tube. **Rooms** 49. **Rates** £100 single; £115 double; £180-£250 suite. **Credit** AmEx, DC, JCB, MC, V. **Map** p395 D6.

This glitzy hotel on the northern edge of Hyde Park is set in a Victorian building whose unique shape explains the very varied character of its guestrooms. The cheaper rooms are somewhat functional, but some of the suites, especially the split-level semi-circular Conservatory Suite (£180) with its panoramic stained-glass windows and private veranda, are alluring. This year a 'secret room' not shown on any of the hotel plans and unseen since the 1800s was uncovered during redecoration and has become the hotel's sixth suite, the split-level Lancaster Suite, with an original fireplace and small patio (£140).

Low point: A bit stuffy.
Did you know? Some of the sex scenes for Kubrick's *Eyes Wide Shut* were filmed in the Royal Suite's junior bedroom (*see p290* **On location: Kubrick's London**).

Portobello Hotel
See p62.
Who: the Sex Pistols, Oasis, Blur (Damon Albarn tended bar here), U2, Mick Jagger, George Michael, Tina Turner (who loved it so much, she bought the house next door).
High points: Room 16 (*pictured*) a favourite with Catherine Deneuve, which has the round bed built for Alice Cooper and the 'Jules Verne fantasy bath', a Victorian bathing machine; the 24-hour bar.
Low point: Poky rooms.
Did you know? The Portobello established itself in 1969 by providing cheap rooms (£3 a night) for struggling rock musicians.

St James's Club
7-8 Park Place, SW1 (7629 7688).
Double £241 (with temporary membership).
Who: David Bowie, Tina Turner, Robert Palmer.
High points: Penthouse suite with two bathrooms, a Jacuzzi, a dining room, two terraces and a private elevator; new restaurant with dishes by Gary Rhodes.

Sweet 16: the **Portobello Hotel**.

Low point: The chintz.
Did you know? The St James's Club's honorary committee includes such thespian big-wigs as Sir John Mills, Michael Caine, Liza Minnelli and Dudley Moore.

The Garden Terrace is a fine spot for afternoon tea or an aperitif, and there's a fragrant herb garden that supplies the kitchen. No limo service.
Hotel services *Air-conditioning (deluxe rooms & suites only). Babysitting. Bar. Business services. Concierge. Garden. Parking. Restaurant.* **Room services** *Dataport. Room service (24hrs). TV.*

Mornington Lancaster Hotel

12 Lancaster Gate, Bayswater, W2 3LG (7262 7361/ fax 7706 1028/www.mornington.se). Lancaster Gate tube. **Rooms** 66. **Rates** £120 single; £135-£145 double; £160 suite. **Credit** AmEx, DC, JCB, MC, V. **Map** p395 D7.

Swedish-owned and -run, the Mornington is ideal for visitors who like a little luxury but worry about the effects of tourism on the environment – it has a committee charged with making the hotel function in as ecologically friendly a fashion as possible. Situated in a quiet residential street, it's a schizophrenic mix of regal Victorian exterior and library-like lobby, and clean, modern, IKEA-influenced bedrooms. Swedish guests are welcomed with Swedish newspapers in the bar and marinated herring for breakfast, but English versions of both are available. There's no limo service.
Hotel services *Bar. Business services. Concierge. No-smoking rooms.* **Room services** *Dataport. Room service (7-10am, 4-11pm). TV: cable/pay movies.*

Moderate to cheap

Amsterdam Hotel

7 Trebovir Road, Earl's Court, SW5 9LS (7370 2814/fax 7244 7608/www.amsterdam-hotel.com). Earl's Court tube. **Rooms** 27. **Rates** £76-£84 single; £86-£98 double; £100-£160 suite. **Credit** AmEx, DC, JCB, MC, V. **Map** p396 B11.

Bright and cheerful in terms of both welcome and decor, this hotel has a modern, slightly glitzy feel, with its plant-filled lobby, pastel hues, floral fabrics and wicker and bamboo furniture. A recent refurbishment means there's a fresh feel to it. Rooms and suites are pleasant; the latter have kitchenettes.
Hotel services *Business services. Concierge. Garden. Laundry. No-smoking rooms.* **Room services** *Room service 7.30am-9.30pm. TV.*

Kensington Gardens Hotel

9 Kensington Gardens Square, Bayswater, W2 4BH (7221 7790/fax 7792 8612/www.kensingtongardens hotel.co.uk). Bayswater or Queensway tube. **Rooms** 16. **Rates** £55-£65 single; £85 double; £105 triple. **Credit** AmEx, DC, MC, V. **Map** p394 B6.

Freshly refurbished, this good-value hotel situated in a restored Victorian townhouse has an elegant black and white tiled entrance. The rooms are rather uninspired decor-wise, but the hotel is spotless throughout, and it's handy both for Hyde Park and increasingly hip Westbourne Grove. The main door is manned round the clock, and there's CCTV for added security.
Room services *minibar. TV: satellite.*

Mayflower Hotel

26-8 Trebovir Road, Earl's Court, SW5 9NJ (7370 0991/fax 7370 0994/www.mayflower hotel.activehotels.com). Earl's Court tube. **Rooms** 48. **Rates** £59 single; £79 double; £109 triple. **Credit** AmEx, JCB, MC, V. **Map** p396 B11.

This friendly independent hotel has been conceived with an eye for design: its grey lobby has black leather couches, and some rooms are studiously modern in feel (though others have more run-of-the-mill budget hotel decor). Ask about the adjoining Court Apartments, where you can sometimes get a special deal on a contemporary four-room suite.
Hotel services *Business services. Concierge. Parking (£17 per night). Payphone.* **Room services** *TV.*

Rushmore Hotel

11 Trebovir Road, Earl's Court, SW5 9LS (7370 3839/fax 7370 0274/www.rushmorehotel. co.uk). Earl's Court tube. **Rooms** 22. **Rates** £59-£69 single; £79-£85 double; £89-£95 triple; £99-£110 family. **Credit** AmEx, DC, JCB, MC, V. **Map** p396 B11.

One of the most stylish of the budget options, this small, family-run hotel has a charming breakfast conservatory with black granite counters, wrought-iron chairs and glass tables. The Rushmore's rooms, although less eye-catching, are nonetheless individually designed and very comfortable; those at the back overlook a courtyard.
Hotel services *Business services. No-smoking rooms. Parking. Payphone.* **Room services** *TV: cable.*

Vancouver Studios

30 Prince's Square, Bayswater, W2 4NJ (7243 1270/fax 7221 8678/www.vienna-group.co.uk). Bayswater or Queensway tube. **Rooms** 45. **Rates** £75 single; £95-£110 double; £130 triple; (10% discount if you stay for over a week). **Credit** AmEx, DC, MC, V. **Map** p394 B6.

This 'concept apartment-hotel' owned by the Vienna Group combines the convenience of a hotel (it has a 24-hour reception, daily maid service and pleasant public areas, including a lovely ivy-covered walled garden) with the privacy of a flat. The well-appointed apartments are pleasantly decorated and boast power showers and mini-kitchens.
Hotel services *Business services. Concierge. Cooking facilities. Garden. Laundry.* **Room services** *Dataport. Kitchenette. TV.*

Cheap

Garden Court Hotel

30-31 Kensington Gardens Square, Bayswater, W2 4BG (7229 2553/fax 7727 2749/www.garden courthotel.co.uk). Bayswater or Queensway tube. **Rooms** 32 (16 en suite). **Rates** (incl English breakfast) £39-£58 single; £58-£88 double; £72-£99 triple; £82-£120 quad. **Credit** MC, V. **Map** p394 B6.

Situated in two listed 1854 townhouses overlooking a pretty Victorian square, the deservedly popular Garden Court has been run by the same family for almost half a century. The individually designed rooms are clean and comfortable, and the large lounge, with its modern leather armchairs, wooden floor and beefeater statue, is welcoming. Guests have access to the square, but the hotel also has an attractive paved garden of its own.

Hotel services *Garden.* **Room services** *Telephone. TV: satellite.*

Youth hostels

Hostel beds are either in twin rooms or dorms. If you're not a member of the International Youth Hostel Federation (IYHF), you have to pay an extra £2 a night to stay at hostels (after six nights you automatically become a member). Alternatively, join the IYHF for £13 (£6.50 for under-18s) at any hostel, or through www.yha.org.uk, which also allows you to book rooms. Always phone first to check the availability of beds. The following hostels take MasterCard, Visa and travellers' cheques.

City of London *36-38 Carter Lane, EC4V 5AB (7236 4965/fax 7236 7681). St Paul's tube/ Blackfriars tube/rail.* **Beds** 195. **Reception open** 7am-11pm daily; 24hr access. **Rates** (incl breakfast) £21.50-£27.80; £19.90-£23.70 under-18s. **Map** p404 O6.

Earl's Court *38 Bolton Gardens, Earl's Court, SW5 0AQ (7373 7083/fax 7835 2034). Earl's Court tube.* **Beds** 154. **Reception open** 7.30am-10pm daily; 24hr access. **Rates** (incl breakfast) £21.80; £18.50 under-18s; (bed only) £18.50; £16.50 under-18s. **Map** p396 B11.

Hampstead Heath *4 Wellgarth Road, Golders Green, NW11 7HR (8458 9054/fax 8209 0546). Golders Green tube.* **Beds** 199. **Reception open** 6.45am-11pm daily; 24hr access. **Rates** (incl breakfast) £20.40; £18 under-18s.

Holland House *Holland House, Holland Walk, W8 7QU (7937 0748/fax 7376 0667). High Street Kensington tube.* **Beds** 201. **Reception open** 7am-11pm daily; 24hr access. **Rates** (incl breakfast) £20.50; £18.50 under-18s. **Map** p394 A8.

Oxford Street *14 Noel Street, W1F 8GJ (7734 1618/fax 7734 1657). Oxford Circus tube.* **Beds** 75. **Reception open** 7am-11pm daily; 24hr access. **Rates** £21.50-£23.50; £17.50 under-18s. **Map** p398 J6.

Rotherhithe *Island Yard, Salter Road, Rotherhithe, SE16 5PR (7232 2114/fax 7237 2919). Rotherhithe or Canada Water tube.* **Beds** 320. **Reception open** 7am-11pm; 24hr access. **Rates** (incl breakfast) £23.50; £19.90 under-18s.

St Pancras *79-81 Euston Road, NW1 2QS (7388 9998/fax 7388 6766). King's Cross tube/rail.* **Beds** 152. **Open** *Reception* 7am-11pm daily; 24hr access. **Rates** £23.50; £19.90 under-18s. **Map** p399 L3.

YMCAs

You may need to book months ahead to stay at a YMCA: many specialise in long-term accommodation. A few of the larger hostels are listed below (all are unisex), but you can get a full list from the National Council for YMCAs

(8520 5599/www.ymca.org.uk). Prices are around £25-£30 per night for a single room and £40-£45 for a double.

Barbican YMCA *2 Fann Street, EC2Y 8BR (7628 0697/fax 7638 2420). Barbican tube.* **Beds** 240. **Map** p402 P5.

London City YMCA *8 Errol Street, EC1Y 8SE (7628 8832/fax 7628 4080). Barbican tube/Old Street tube/rail.* **Beds** 111. **Map** p402 F4.

Wimbledon YMCA *200 The Broadway, Wimbledon, SW19 1RY (8542 9055/fax 8540 2526). South Wimbledon tube/Wimbledon tube/ rail/.* **Beds** 110.

Staying with the locals

Staying in a Londoner's home is often more fun than being in an impersonal hotel. The following organisations can arrange accommodation; rates include breakfast.

At Home in London *70 Black Lion Lane, Hammersmith, W6 9BE (8748 1943/fax 8748 2701/www.athomeinlondon.co.uk).* **Open** *Phone enquiries* 9.30am-5.30pm Mon-Fri. **Rates** (per room incl breakfast) £29-£65 single; £52-£90 double. **Credit** AmEx, JCB, MC, V.

Bulldog Club *14 Dewhurst Road, Kensington, W14 0ET (7371 3202/fax 7371 2015/www.bulldog club.com).* **Rates** from £105. *Membership* £25/3yrs. **Credit** AmEx, MC, V.

Host & Guest Service *103 Dawes Road, Fulham, SW6 7DU (7385 9922/fax 7386 7575/ www.host-guest.co.uk). Fulham Broadway tube.* **Open** 9am-5.30pm Mon-Fri. **Rates** from £16.50/ person. *Students* from £95/wk. **Credit** MC, V. **Minimum stay** 2 nights.

London Bed & Breakfast Agency *71 Fellows Road, Swiss Cottage, NW3 3JY (7586 2768/fax 7586 6567/www.londonbb.com).* **Open** *Phone enquiries* 9am-6pm Mon-Fri; 10am-2pm Sat. **Rates** £20-£60. **Credit** MC, V. **Minimum stay** 2 nights.

London Homestead Services *Coombe Wood Road, Kingston-upon-Thames, Surrey KT2 7JY (8949 4455/8541 0044/fax 8549 5492).* **Open** *Phone enquiries* 9am-7pm daily. **Rates** from £18 single; from £36 double. **Credit** MC, V. **Minimum stay** 3 nights.

Self-catering apartments

It can be expensive to rent in London, but if you're in a group, you may save money by renting a flat from one of the following places: all specialise in holiday lettings. *See also p308* **Accommodation outlet**.

Apartment Service *1st floor, 5-6 Francis Grove, Wimbledon, SW19 4DT (8944 1444/fax 8944 6744). Wimbledon tube/rail.* **Open** 9am-6.30pm Mon-Fri. **Rates** from £90 double studio. **Credit** AmEx, DC, MC, V.

Astons Apartments *31 Rosary Gardens, South Kensington, SW7 4NH (7590 6000/fax 7590 6060/www.astons-apartments.com). Gloucester*

Road tube. **Open** 8am-9pm daily. **Rates** £76.40 single studio; £105.75 double studio. **Credit** AmEx, MC, V. **Map** p396 C11.

Holiday Serviced Apartments *273 Old Brompton Road, Earl's Court, SW5 9JA (7373 4477/fax 7373 4282/www.holidayapartments.co.uk). Earl's Court tube.* **Open** 9.30am-6pm Mon-Fri. **Rates** from £80 single/double studio. **Credit** AmEx, MC, V. **Map** p396 C11.

Independent Traveller *Thorverton, Exeter, Devon EX5 5NT (01392 860807/fax 01392 860552/www.gowithit.co.uk).* **Rates** *apartments* £250-£2,000/wk. **Credit** MC, V. **Minimum stay** 3 nights.

Palace Court Holiday Apartments *1 Palace Court, Bayswater Road, Bayswater, W2 4LP (7727 3467/fax 7221 7824/www.palacecourt.co.uk). Notting Hill Gate or Queensway tube.* **Open** 8.30am-11pm daily. **Rates** £65 single studio; £79 double studio; £86 triple studio. **Credit** MC, V.

Perfect Places *53 Margravine Gardens, Hammersmith, W6 8RN (8748 6095/fax 8741 4213/www.perfectplaceslondon.co.uk).* **Open** *Phone enquiries* 9am-7pm daily. **Rates** from £550/wk. **Credit** AmEx, MC, V.

University residences

During university vacations much of London's student accommodation is open to visitors, providing a basic but cheap place to stay.

Arcade Halls *The Arcade, 385-401 Holloway Road, Holloway, N7 ORN (7607 5415/fax 7609 0052/www.unl.ac.uk/accommodation). Holloway Road tube.* **Rooms** *Self-contained flats for 4-6 people.* **Rates** £18/night; £83/wk. **Available** 1 July-2 Sept 2001.

Goldsmid House *36 North Row, Mayfair, W1K 6DN (bookings 01273 207481/fax 7491 0586). Bond Street or Marble Arch tube.* **Rooms** *Single* 10. *Twin* 120. **Rates** £23 single; £32 twin. **Available** 8 June-22 Sept 2002. **Map** p398 G6.

High Holborn Residence *178 High Holborn, Holborn, WC1V 7AA (7379 5589/fax 7379 5640/www.lse.ac.uk/vacations). Holborn tube.* **Rooms** *Single* 400. *Twin* 48. **Rates** £35 single; £57 twin; £67 triple. **Available** July-end Sept 2002 *(no definite 2002 dates released yet).* **Map** p399 M5.

International Students House *229 Great Portland Street, Marylebone, W1W 5PN (7631 8300/8310/fax 7631 8315/www.ish.org.uk). Great Portland Street tube.* **Rooms** *Single* 170. *Twin* 76. **Rates** £31 single; £25 twin; £12-£18 dormitory. **Available** all year. **Map** p398 H5.

King's College Conference & Vacation Bureau *Strand Bridge House, 138-142 Strand, Covent Garden, WC2R 1HH (7848 1700/fax 7848 1717/www.kcl.ac.uk/services/conbro/vehelo.html). Temple tube.* **Rooms** *approx 2,000 beds in 6 halls.* **Rates** £18-£33 single; £33-£52 twin. **Available** 26 Mar-18 Apr, 12 June-12 Sept 2002. **Map** p404 N8.

Passfield Hall *1-7 Endsleigh Place, Bloomsbury, WC1H 0PW (7387 3584/fax 7387 0419/www.lse.ac.uk/vacations). Euston tube/rail.* **Rooms** *Single* 100. *Twin* 36. *Triple* 8. **Rates** £25

single; £46 twin; £60 triple. **Available** 17 Mar-21 Apr, 30 June-27 Sept 2001. **Map** p399 K4.

Walter Sickert Hall *29 Graham Street, Islington, N1 8LA (7477 8822/fax 7477 8825/www.city.ac.uk/ems). Angel tube.* **Rooms** 226. *Twin* 6. **Rates** £30-£40 single; £55-£60 twin. **Available** 24 June-15 Sept 2002 (selected rooms available year round). **Map** p402 P3.

Camping & caravanning

None of these campsites is especially central, and transport into town isn't what it might be, but all are conveniently cheap.

Crystal Palace Caravan Club Site

Crystal Palace Parade, SE19 1UF (8778 7155). Crystal Palace rail/3 bus. **Open** *Office Mar-Oct* 8.30am-8pm daily. *Nov-Feb* 9am-8pm daily. **Rates** £13.80-£16 caravan pitch. **Credit** MC, V.

Lee Valley Campsite

Sewardstone Road, Chingford, E4 7RA (8529 5689/fax 8559 4070/scs@leevalleypark.org.uk). Walthamstow Central tube/rail then 215 bus. **Open** *Apr-Oct* 8am-10pm daily. *Nov-Mar* closed. **Rates** £5.60; £2.50 under-16s. **Credit** MC, V.

Lee Valley Leisure Centre Camping & Caravan Park

Meridian Way, Edmonton, N9 0AS (8803 6900/fax 8884 4975/leisurecentre@leevalleypark.org.uk). Edmonton Green rail/W8 bus. **Open** 8am-10pm daily. **Rates** £5.65; £2.35 5-16s. **Credit** MC, V.

Longer stays

If you're staying for months rather than weeks, it may be cheaper to rent a place. Even so, accommodation is still very expensive – plus you'll normally have to pay a month's rent in advance and a further month's rent as a deposit – and competition is fierce. The best source for places to rent is *Loot*, published daily. Capital Radio publishes a flatshare list, available from the foyer (30 Leicester Square, WC2) on Friday at around 5pm. Also try the small ads in *Time Out* magazine (available from newsstands and newsagents from Tuesday in central London and Wednesday further out), and *Midweek* (free outside tube stations on Thursdays).

You're unlikely to get a studio (no separate bedroom or, often, kitchen) or a one-bedroom flat for less than £500 per month. If you're intent on staying in a hip area, expect to fork out around double that, perhaps more. If, however, you can stomach a room in a shared flat/house, you can find accommodation for less than £300 a month in the further reaches of the East End and south London, rising to around £600 a month in the swankier likes of Fulham or Hampstead.

Sightseeing

Introduction

A rise in the number of free attractions means
there are more reasons to visit London than ever before.

In December 2001, when national museums
(with a few exceptions) became free of charge
to all visitors, London became an even better
place to visit. Find your way around with
our pick of the best sights (*see p69*) and our
chapter by chapter area guide, which has
detailed reviews of the area's sights.

London Pass

The **London Pass**, which offers free entry
to more than 60 attractions and free travel on
public transport, is available for one, two, three
and six days, priced at £24/£16 child, £44/£27
child, £55/£34 child and £89/£45 child,
respectively. Before you rush in, consider that
many of London's major attractions, including
the British Museum and Tate Modern, are free
anyway, and some of those that charge
admission offer free entry in the late afternoon,
though the pass does provide value-added
services in certain venues, such as free access
to paying exhibitions or a free printed guide.
Other 'extras' include £5 worth of free phone
calls, commission-free currency exchange, free
Internet access at specified venues and five
days' free Orange mobile phone rental.

For more info, and to buy online, go to
www.londonpass.com, or call 0870 242 9988
for credit card bookings (8.30am-8pm Mon-Fri;
10am-4pm Sat). Passes are also available from
Exchange International (there are 20 offices in
London, including at the major train stations).

Trips & tours

Balloon tours

Adventure Balloons *Winchfield Park, London
Road, Hartley Wintney, Hampshire RG27 8HY
(01252 844222/www.adventureballoons.co.uk).*
Flights *Apr-Oct* morning & evenings daily, weather
permitting. **Fares** *Home Counties flights* £130 per
person. *London* £150 per person. No child reductions.
Credit MC, V.

Bicycle tours

See p361.

Bus tours

Big Bus Company *48 Buckingham Palace
Road, SW1 (0800 169 1365/7233 9533/
www.bigbus.co.uk).* **Open-top bus tours** three
different routes, 2hrs; both with live commentary.
Departures every 15min from Green Park,
Victoria & Marble Arch. *Summer* 8.30am-7pm
daily. *Winter* 8.30am-4.30pm daily. **Pick-up**
Green Park (near the Ritz); Marble Arch (Speaker's
Corner); Victoria (outside Thistle Victoria Hotel,
48 Buckingham Palace Road, SW1). **Fares** £15;
£6 5-15s; free under-5s. Tickets are valid for 24hrs
and are interchangeable between routes.
Credit AmEx, DC, MC, V.
Original London Sightseeing Tour *8877
1722/www.theoriginaltour.com.* **Departures**
Summer 9am-7pm daily. *Winter* 9.30am-5pm
daily. **Pick-up** Victoria Street; Marble Arch
(Speakers' Corner); Baker Street tube (forecourt);
Coventry Street; Embankment station; Trafalgar
Square (northside). **Fares** £15; £7.50 concessions.
Credit MC, V.

Take time out to see what London has to offer.

The best Sights

New to view

Handel House Museum (*p113*); Wellington Arch (*p115*); Stratford Circus (*p287*); Museum in Docklands (*p161*); Firepower (*p165*); Thames Barrier Park (*p163*).

For high times

British Airways London Eye (*p73*); The Monument (*p94*); St Paul's Cathedral (*p89*); Primrose Hill (*p145*).

For going underground

London Dungeon (*p80*); the crypt at Sir John Soane's Museum (*p99*); Cabinet War Rooms (*p133*); the tube (*p70*).

For modern art

Tate Modern (*p79*); ICA Gallery (*p132*); Serpentine Gallery (*p137*); Saatchi Gallery (*p146*); Camden Arts Centre (*p147*); Whitechapel Art Gallery (*p156*).

For modern architecture

National Theatre (*p333*); Waterloo Station (*p75*); British Museum Great Court (*p103*); 2 Willow Road (*p148*); Trellick Tower (*p179*).

For animal encounters

London Zoo (*p110*); St James's Park (*p130*); Natural History Museum (*p140*); Coram's Fields (*p272*).

For crime & punishment

Clink Prison Museum (*p77*); Inns of Court (*p96*); Old Bailey (*p89*); Royal Courts of Justice (*p97*); Madame Tussaud's Chamber of Horrors (*p110*).

For famous tombs

St Pancras Gardens (*p106*); Westminster Abbey (*p134*); Highgate Cemetery (*p150*).

For something a little macabre

Old Operating Theatre, Museum & Herb Garrett (*p81*); Jeremy Bentham's 'auto-icon' (*p101*); Petrie Museum of Egyptian Archaeology (*p105*).

For escape

Hampstead Heath (*p149*); Highgate Wood (*p150*); Royal Botanic Gardens at Kew (*p174*); WWT Wetland Centre (*p175*); Osterley House (*p186*).

Helicopter tours

Cabair Helicopters *Elstree Aerodrome, Borehamwood, Hertfordshire WD6 3AW (8953 4411/www.cabair.com). Edgware tube or Elstree rail.* **Flights** from 9.45am Sun. **Fares** £125. No child reductions. **Credit** AmEx, DC, MC, V. **Map** p389.

Personal tours

Tour Guides *7495 5504/www.tourguides.co.uk.* Tailor-made tours with Blue Badge guides for individuals or groups, on foot, by car, coach or boat.

River tours

See p359.

Specialist tours

Architectural Dialogue *39-51 Highgate Road, NW5 (7267 7697/www.architecturaldialogue.co.uk).* **Departures** 10.15am Sat; 10.45am Sun. **Meeting point** in front of Royal Academy of Arts, Piccadilly, W1 (Piccadilly Circus tube). **Duration** 3hrs (& occasional one-day tours). **Tickets** £18.50; £13 students; advance booking advisable. **Credit** MC, V.

Beatles Walks *7624 3978/www.walks.com* Beatles Magical Mystery Tour **Departures** 2pm Wed; 11am Thur; 10.45am Sun. **Pick-up** Dominion Theatre, Tottenham Court Road, W1 (Tottenham Court Road tube). **Duration** 2hrs. Beatles In My Life Tour **Departures** 11.20am Tue, Sat. **Meeting point** Marylebone tube. **Duration** *Both* 2hrs 30min. **Tickets** *Both* £5; £4 concessions.

Gentle Journeys Garden Day Tours *01935 815924/from USA 1-800 873 7145/ www.gentlejourneys.co.uk.* **Departures** *May-Sept* 9am Tue-Thur, Sun (return approx 6.30pm). **Meeting point** Victoria Coach Station. **Tickets** £58 per day (lunch not included).

Jack the Ripper Mystery Walk *8558 9446/ mobile 07957 388280/www.mysterywalks.com.* **Departures** 8pm Wed, Sun; 7pm Fri. **Duration** 2hrs. **Meeting point** Aldgate tube. **Tickets** £5; £4 concessions.

Taxi tours

Black Taxi Tours of London *7289 4371/ www.blacktaxitours.co.uk.* **Cost** £70. A tailored two-hour tour for up to five people.

Walking tours

Arguably the best company running walks around London is **Original London Walks** (7624 3978/ www.walks.com), which encompasses sorties on everything from Sherlock Holmes to riverside pubs. Other walks companies include **Citisights** (8806 4325), **Historical Tours** (8668 4019), **Cityguide Walks** (01895 675389) and **Stepping Out** (8881 2933). If you'd prefer to do it yourself and at your own pace, the excellent **Green Chain** walks connect a number of green spaces in south-east London (8921 5028/www.greenchain.com).

For more self-guided walks, see *Time Out London Walks* volumes 1 and 2 (£9.99 and £11.99).

Rumblings

Love it or hate it – and most people who have to use it every day have few kind words to say about it – the tube is an indispensable facet of London life. While neither as cheap nor as characterful as the red double-decker buses that have become a kind of visual shorthand for the city, it's the quickest way, given our traffic-clogged streets, of getting around.

But it's not been a good year for this most essential of transport systems. The future of the tube has been a matter of heated debate for many years, but in the sweltering days of summer 2001, things came to a head. First, at the beginning of July, about 4,000 passengers were trapped for 90 minutes in the morning rush hour, at temperatures close to 100°F, when four packed trains got stuck behind one another on the Victoria line. In what the London Ambulance Service called 'a major incident', more than 620 had to be treated at the scene and ten were taken to hospital. A subsequent investigation revealed that, in the absence of sufficient ventilation, tube passengers often have to endure temperatures higher than those permitted when transporting animals.

The incident revealed how urgently London Underground (LU) needs to be modernised, an issue that has been on the political agenda for some time but that was still, as we went to press, unresolved. The government's £13-billion solution, the public-private partnership (PPP) plan, was already unpopular when, at the beginning of August 2001, LU's annual report and accounts revealed that the network had failed to reach its seven key performance targets, including safety (not that that stopped MD Derek Smith raking in a £17,000 bonus, taking his salary up to almost £230,000). Critics, who are legion, said that these failures prove that the government and the tube management, which would still run the network under PPP, can't be relied upon to improve it. Many also object to the fact that between £2 billion and £5 billion from the public coffers would be required.

Among the critics, the most vocal are mayor Ken Livingstone (*see p25* **Who he?**) and his transport commissioner Bob Kiley, an American who saved the ailing New York subway. Kiley was taken on by the Labour government as chairman of London Transport in the hope that he would do the same for the British capital, but he was sacked in mid July 2001 when Downing Street found out he was about to attack the PPP scheme. Despite this, and despite the fact that in August Livingstone and Kiley dropped their proposed legal action against the PPP, they continue to be outspoken critics of it. Towards the end of the year, the collapse of Railtrack, the company assigned with running the national rail network, added fuel to their fire.

Meanwhile, tube users had to deal with the usual strikes and, in July, the news that a further £100 million of taxpayers' money is going to be needed to replace a signalling system on the Jubilee line extension, which had only opened in 1999, and which, at £3.4 billion, had come in £1 billion over budget. Add to this fears, after the US terrorist attacks, of gas attacks on the tube, and it becomes clear that it's not been a happy few months for travellers. Is there light at the end of the tunnel? Only, it seems, if the Labour government can swallow its pride and pull out of the PPP scheme. If it doesn't, commuters are likely to demonstrate their displeasure at the next general election.

Yet it's not all doom and gloom where the Underground is concerned. The Jubilee line, for all its problems, needed new stations, and these have provided the capital with some of its best modern architecture. Norman Foster's Canary Wharf station was shortlisted for the 2000 Stirling Prize, while Westminster tube station won a RIBA Award for Architecture last year, together with Portcullis House under which it was built (*see p268* **Grand openings**). Others deserving of more than a passing glance include Borough and Canada Water, the latter a reinterpretation of Charles Holden's modernist Arnos Grove.

The South Bank
& Bankside

London's riverside renaissance means there
are more cultural delights on offer than ever before.

Maps p403, p406 & p407

London's riverside has always been integral
to both work and play, but for much of the 20th
century it's been somewhat neglected, at least in
comparison with other world cities and with its
own rich history. Over the past few years, all
this has been changing, and nowhere, with the
possible exception of Docklands (*see p158*), is
more indicative of this boom than the South
Bank. Though the area has long been a centre
for the arts, it has been (and is being) revitalised
to such an extent that if you haven't been in a
few years, chances are you'll hardly recognise
it. The Mayor's Thames Festival in September
(*see p266*) is a sign that the river is becoming
something to celebrate once more.

The South Bank and Bankside is also one of
the few areas of the city that is truly pedestrian-
friendly (*see p78* **Walk this way**) – not only is
it possible to walk along the entire south side of
the river without seeing a car, but cutting-edge
building companies and architectural practices
such as Coin Street Community Builders (*see
p74*) have long been working hand in hand
with the local community to devise ways in
which to make the South Bank and Bankside
work not only for tourists but for the people
who live and work there. Measures include
traffic-calming schemes, the creation and
improvement of green spaces, the incorporation
of historic features into modern developments,
and community housing projects, for which the
area is renowned (*see p74* and *p80* for the **Oxo
Tower** and the **Cromwell Buildings**).

The South Bank

Lambeth Bridge to
Hungerford Bridge

Just north of Lambeth Bridge huddle the red-
brick buildings of **Lambeth Palace**, official
residence of the Archbishops of Canterbury since
the 12th century. It's closed to the public except
for the occasional fête in the grounds and on
Open House weekend (*see p266*). Next door is

Dalí Universe and the **London Eye**. *See p73.*

the **Museum of Garden History** (*see p73*)
in the old church of St Mary-at-Lambeth. St
Thomas's Hospital, containing the **Florence
Nightingale Museum** (*see p73*), stands on
one side of Westminster Bridge, but the
dominant presence is the looming bulk of the
revamped **County Hall**. The setting for the
gruesome opening scene of Hitchcock's *Frenzy*
(*see p126* **On location**) in 1972 and the home
of Ken Livingstone's Greater London Council
(1963-86), it now contains two chain hotels, the
two-floor arcade-game nirvana **Namco Station**,
the **London Aquarium** (*see p73*) and the **Dalí
Universe** (*see p73*). Behind County Hall, the
disconcertingly pristine Forum Magnum Square
is rapidly being colonised by restaurant chains
such as fish! (*see p188*) and Yo! Sushi (*see p190*).

Shakespeare's Globe Exhibition and Theatre tour

Bankside London MEMBER OF BANKSIDE MARKETING GROUP

Exhibition
Open daily
Oct – April
10am to 5pm.
May – September
(theatre season)
9am to 12 midday
Exhibition and guided
tour into the theatre.
12.30 – 4pm
Exhibition and
virtual tour.
Only closed on
24 & 25 December.
Advanced booking
essential for groups
Tel 020 7902 1500
Fax 020 7902 1515

Theatre performances
May – September
Box office
020 7401 9919

Globe Education
Workshops, lectures,
courses and evening
classes for all ages
and nationalities
Tel 020 7902 1433

Globe Restaurants
Tel 020 7902 1570

New Globe Walk
Bankside
Southwark
London SE1 9DT

Website: www.shakespeares-globe.org

Shakespeare's Globe Exhibition – ALL THE WORLD'S A STAGE – is the most exciting place in which to explore Shakespeare's theatre and the London in which he lived and worked. In the vast *Underglobe* beneath the theatre every aspect of Shakespeare's work is brought imaginatively to life using a combination of modern technology and traditional crafts. Against the historical background of Elizabethan Bankside – the city of London's playground in Shakespeare's time – the role of actor, musician and audience is explored, Elizabethan special effects are brought to life on touch screens and the secrets of period costume designs revealed. A visit to the Exhibition includes a guided tour of the Theatre

Between the **British Airways London Eye** (*see below*) and **Hungerford Bridge** (still undergoing extension work in the form of two new footbridges that will double its capacity, as well as the restoration of Brunel's original Surrey pier), there will be dramatic developments on the Jubilee Gardens site (where the main buildings of the 1951 Festival of Britain stood) as part of the revamp of the South Bank Centre (*see p74*).

British Airways London Eye

Riverside Building, next to County Hall, Westminster Bridge Road, SE1 (0870 500 0600/customer services 7654 0828/www.ba-londoneye.com). Westminster tube/Waterloo tube/rail. **Open** *Jan-Mar* 10am-7pm daily. *Apr-Jun, Oct-Dec* 9am-10pm daily. **Admission** *Jan-Mar* £8.50; £6.50 concessions. *Apr-June, Oct-Dec* £9; £7 concessions. *All year* £5 5-15s; free under-5s (must have ticket). **Credit** AmEx, MC, V. **Map** p401 M8.

After initial unpopularity, construction problems and an aborted Millennium Eve opening due to safety concerns, the Eye has won its place in the hearts of Londoners and visitors alike – to the extent that if you turn up without advance booking, especially at weekends and in school holidays, you may go away disappointed (though some tickets are usually held back for same-day sale on site). But it's worth the pain of navigating the wearisome phone booking system when you finally clamber aboard one of the 32 capsules (each of which holds 25 people) for a 30-minute ride affording views of up to 25 miles (40km) on clear days. Alternatively, book online.

Those with something to celebrate can hire a capsule with champagne, wine or Pimms and strawberries, while those looking for a more intimate experience can go for a 'Cupid's Capsule' (and if all goes well, can even marry here).

Dalí Universe

County Hall, Riverside Building, Queen's Walk, SE1 (7620 2420/www.daliuniverse.com). Waterloo tube/rail. **Open** 10am-5.30pm daily. **Admission** £8.50; £6 concessions; £5 5-15s; £22 family (2+3); free under-5s. **Credit** AmEx, DC, MC, V. **Map** p401 M8.

After the near-hysteria of the crowds besieging the London Eye (*see above*), this newish attraction is almost eerily quiet, bar the sounds of the great showman himself ranting away in almost incomprehensible French from the loudspeakers dotted around the black-walled rooms. While there's lots here for both kids and adults (the former will love Dalí's more ludic pieces, such as the lobster phone and the huge sculptures, including the spidery-legged *Space Elephant*, but should probably be steered away from the coprophilic excesses of the Casanova lithographs and works depicting bestiality), the impression one takes away is of Dalí's prolificacy rather than his talent, probably because there are no major works here (most are in the Dalí museums in his native Spain).

The works that are here, including *Spellbound*, the huge oil painting he created for the 1945 Hitchcock film, are well annotated, though, frustratingly, the videos playing silently throughout the exhibition aren't explained – were these strange, jerky films made by Dalí himself, or are they documentary footage? The shop is disappointing, with nary a surreal postcard to be seen; instead there are rare hand-signed graphics at decidedly non-souvenir prices.

Florence Nightingale Museum

St Thomas's Hospital, 2 Lambeth Palace Road, SE1 (7620 0374/www.florence-nightingale.co.uk). Westminster tube/Waterloo tube/rail. **Open** 10am-5pm Mon-Fri (last entry 4pm); 11.30am-4.30pm Sat, Sun (last entry 3.30pm). **Admission** £4.80; £3.60 5-18s, concessions; £10 family (2+2); free under-5s. **Credit** AmEx, MC, V. **Map** p401 M9.

A small museum with well-thought-out displays of personal mementoes, clothing, furniture, books, letters and portraits belonging to the famous nurse and social campaigner, as well as Crimean War relics and nursing materials. It was at St Thomas's that Nightingale set up the first nursing school in 1859. See the website or call for details of special tours, talks, temporary exhibitions and children's events.

London Aquarium

County Hall, Riverside Building, Westminster Bridge Road, SE1 (7967 8000/tours 7967 8007/www.londonaquarium.co.uk). Westminster tube/Waterloo tube/rail. **Open** 10am-6pm daily (last entry 5pm); phone for opening times during holidays. **Tours** (groups of 10 or more) phone for details. **Admission** £8.75; £6.50 concessions; £5.25 3-14s; £3.50 disabled; £25 family (2+2); free under-3s. **Credit** MC, V. **Map** p401 M9.

Easter holidays, summer vacation, half-term... these are times when you don't want to visit the London Aquarium, unless you really, really love kids and aren't that bothered about seeing any fish. The darkened corridors are awash to such a degree that you begin to wonder if you wouldn't stand a better chance of survival on the other side of the glass. To be fair to the former GLC's County Hall turned glorified goldfish bowl, it's stuffed to the gills with fish as well. Organised by geographical origin, they're well presented in big tanks and look as happy as fish ever do. There are opportunities to touch rays, among other watery creatures, while the sharks in the biggest tank are impressive to watch as they glide unblinkingly by. The circuit seems quite short and on reaching the end you wonder what you must have missed out to get round it so quickly, but kids love it and don't care how crowded it gets.

Museum of Garden History

Church of St Mary-at-Lambeth, Lambeth Palace Road, SE1 (7401 8865/www.museumgardenhistory.org). Waterloo tube/rail/C10, 507 bus. **Open** Feb mid-Dec 10.30am-5pm daily. **Admission** free; donations of £2.50 adults, £2 concessions suggested. **Credit** AmEx, MC, V. **Map** p401 L10.

The Alan Titchmarsh and Charlie Dimmock brigade will love this museum illustrating the development of the English passion for gardening, with its antique horticultural tools and photographic panels on famous garden designers and plant hunters. The tireless John Tradescant, gardener to James I and Charles I, is given particular prominence. A replica of a 17th-century knot garden has been created, using geometric shapes based on squares and whole or partial circles that incorporate the letter 'T' for Tradescant into four symmetrical positions. It also contains several dramatic examples of topiary. In the graveyard, one of the sarcophagi contains the remains of Captain Bligh, abandoned in the Pacific by his mutinous crew aboard HMS *Bounty*.

Hungerford Bridge to Blackfriars Bridge

Since its inception, the **South Bank Centre** arts complex (*see also p312*) has represented London at its most self-consciously modern. The squat concrete mass of Sir Leslie Martin's **Royal Festival Hall** – built for the Festival of Britain as a showcase for the architectural and building skills of the time and dubbed the 'people's palace' – has been hailed by many as a triumph of democratic public design, though it would be fair to say that none of the buildings in the complex are universally admired.

Things are changing, however, under a masterplan by Rick Mathers Architects. The long-term renovation of the 2,600-seat Festival Hall (*see p312*) actually began several years ago, but work scheduled for 2002-5 will bring better acoustics, the reinstatement of the original recital space, the restoration of the roof garden, new bars, cafés and backstage areas, a new staff office building, a dedicated education centre and an expanded Poetry Library. The hall is pencilled in to close for a few months in 2003, though there's the usual talk of ominous 'hitches'.

Meanwhile the stretch between the London Eye and Hungerford Bridge will be home to the BFI's **Film Centre** (comprising an enlarged National Film Theatre, the Museum of the Moving Image, a gallery, a library, an education suite and a mediatheque). David Chipperfield, the designer who was responsible for the branch of the Wagamama (*see p193*) noodle chain in Lexington Street, Soho, was awarded the commission in August 2001, but no completion date had been given as we went to press.

The **Hayward Gallery** (*see below*), derided by many as a brutalist concrete eyesore but admired by others as an elegant, sculptural modern building, is to be extended, while the building housing the Queen Elizabeth Hall and the Purcell Room is to be redeveloped. But perhaps most exciting of all is the overhaul of Sir Denys Lasdun's **Royal National Theatre** (*see p333*). In mid-2001, Trevor Nunn announced that the National's Lyttleton Theatre is to be

revitalised in an effort to lure more under-30s to see plays. This will involve the creation of two new spaces from the current 900-seat proscenium arch space: a 650-seat arena that will cut through the proscenium; and a 100-seat 'loft' carved out of the existing exhibition area, currently in the Lyttleton's circle foyer. The design allows for the proscenium to be reverted to in future years.

This stress on updating both architecture and the body of work itself (controversial new works have included, in August 2001, Mark 'Shopping & Fucking' Ravenhill's *Mother Clap's Molly House* featuring cross-dressers and gay orgies) will go hand in hand with efforts to make the South Bank more attractive to a young audience; these include inviting DJs to play, Thameside barbecues and a late-licence bar serving cheap booze.

Further east along the river, the beautifully restored **Oxo Tower Wharf** began life at the start of the 20th century as a power station for the Post Office before being bought by Oxo (who produced Oxo cubes and long eggs for pork pies here). The company incorporated its name into the design of the art deco tower to circumvent council rules against large-scale advertising. By the 1970s the building was earmarked for demolition, but local residents formed the non-profit-making Coin Street Community Builders to save it. In 1984 it purchased the tower and the swathe of derelict land between the tower and Waterloo Bridge and transformed it into a place to live, work and visit. The tower now contains flats, small crafts shops/workshops and a restaurant (*see p189*) with great views. On the ground floor there's an exhibition about the regeneration of the area (future plans include a floating Thames Lido, the 'Hothouse' community training and leisure centre and further co-operative homes).

Coin Street Builders also maintains the contrived **Gabriel's Wharf** (which, with its schmaltzy crafts shops and restaurants, is the only jarring point on the South Bank), and organises the annual Coin Street Festival, London's biggest free arts festival (*see p263*).

Hayward Gallery

Belvedere Road, SE1 (box office 7960 4242/ www.hayward-gallery.org.uk). Embankment tube/ Charing Cross or Waterloo tube/rail. **Open** *during exhibitions* 10am-6pm Mon, Thur-Sun; 10am-8pm Tue, Wed. **Admission** varies (phone for details). **Credit** AmEx, DC, MC, V. **Map** p401 M8.

One of London's finest venues for contemporary and historical art, partly because of the flexibility of its space, the Hayward can always be counted on for an intriguing mix – this year promises a retrospective of the modernist Swiss painter Paul Klee, a show by young Swedish video artist Ann-Sofi Sidén (both

17 Jan-1 Apr), an exhibition of work by American photographer Ansel Adams (early summer; dates to be confirmed) and a show devoted to the former Turner Prize winning Scottish film artist Douglas Gordon (autumn; dates to be confirmed).

Around Waterloo

A walkway links the Royal Festival Hall to **Waterloo Station**, where Eurostar trains arrive and depart from under Nicholas Grimshaw's glorious glass-roofed terminus (*see p28* **Is it terminal?**). The roundabout outside Waterloo Station was once home to a 'cardboard city' providing shelter of sorts to some of London's lost souls, but since 1999 the £20-million **BFI London IMAX Cinema** (*see p294*) has occupied the site.

Behind the station on the other side, **Lower Marsh** has a lively market on weekdays and contains a branch of the excellent Konditor & Cook café (*see p214* **Pit stops**). It leads on to the Cut, home of the Young Vic theatre (*see p338*).

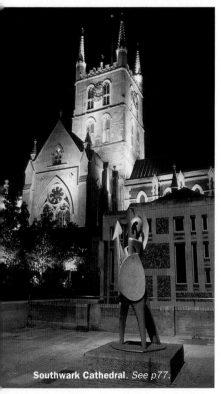

Southwark Cathedral. *See p77.*

For a less savoury aspect of Waterloo, see the surviving entrance to the London Necropolis Railway at 121 Westminster Bridge Road. From 1854, after rapid population growth and cholera epidemics caused overcrowding in city cemeteries, this small station ferried coffins and funeral parties to a cemetery set up by the London Necropolis & National Mausoleum Company in Brookwood, Woking. The station was bombed in 1941 and never rebuilt.

Bankside

With its theatres, bear-baiting pits, bawdy houses, inns and other dens of iniquity, the area between Blackfriars Bridge and London Bridge, now known as **Bankside**, was London's pleasure zone for many centuries. Far from condemning this depravity, the Church made a tidy sum from its regulation – it controlled the local brothels, among other things – and if anyone got too unruly they could always be cast into the dank depths of the Clink Prison (now the **Clink Prison Museum**; *see p77*). Next door are the remains of **Winchester Palace**, though little is left beyond the rose window of the Great Hall.

Like Battersea Power Station upriver, Bankside Power Station was designed by Sir Giles Gilbert Scott; it makes a magnificent home for the **Tate Modern**'s art collection (*see p79*). Tiny in comparison, and a reminder of the Bankside of old, is its neighbour, the reconstructed **Shakespeare's Globe** (*see p77*). Standing in its shadow is another old playhouse, the **Rose Theatre** (*see p77*), and next door is a ramshackle terrace containing the house in which Catherine of Aragon, the first wife of Henry VIII, took shelter on arriving in London in 1502, and where Christopher Wren (*see p86* **Who he?**) is said to have lived during the construction of St Paul's Cathedral. Further back from the river, Southwark Street is the new home to the idiosyncratic **Bramah Museum of Tea & Coffee** (*see p77*).

St Paul's is now linked to Bankside – and, specifically, the Tate Modern – by Norman Foster's infamous **Millennium Bridge**. Closed a few days after its inauguration because of an 'unexpected wobble', London's first new bridge in over a century was scheduled to reopen as we went to press, with a new damping system and a restriction in the number of pedestrians allowed on it at any one time. Further east is the redeveloped **Southwark Cathedral** (*see p77*).

Details of sights in the Bankside and Borough areas can be had at the **Southwark Information Centre** opposite London Bridge station (6 Tooley Street, 7403 8299, 10am-6pm Mon-Sat, 10am-5.30pm Sun; closes 4pm Nov-Mar); *see also p78* **Walk this way**.

Sightseeing

Bramah Museum of Tea & Coffee

40 Southwark Street, SE1 (7231 6197/
www.bramahmuseum.co.uk). London Bridge tube/
rail. **Open** 10am-6pm daily. **Admission** £4; £3
concessions. **Credit** AmEx, DC, MC, V. **Map** p405 S9.
Former tea taster Edward Bramah set up this
museum to chart the history of tea and coffee drinking in the early 1990s. In 2001 he moved away from
Butler's Wharf, frustrated by the disinclination to
put up signs there, and now he's further along the
river towards Bankside. The displays document
the role of tea and coffee in British society.

Clink Prison Museum

1 Clink Street, SE1 (7378 1558/www.clink.co.uk).
London Bridge tube/rail. **Open** 10am-6pm daily.
Admission £4; £3 5-15s, concessions; £9 family
(2+2). **Tours** £1 extra; hourly. **No credit cards.**
Map p404 P8.
The private prison of the successive Bishops of
Winchester, the Clink housed prostitutes, drunks,
actors and more between the 12th and 16th centuries. Given this fascinating history, it's a shame
that the exhibition devoted to it is such a shoddy
affair. The few re-creations of prison scenes have
seen better days, while the explanatory notes and
displays are shabby and unilluminating.

Golden Hinde

St Mary Overie Dock, Cathedral Street, SE1 (0870
011 8700/www.goldenhinde.co.uk). Monument
tube/London Bridge tube/rail. **Open** daily, times
vary; phone for details. **Admission** £2.50; £2.10
concessions; £1.75 4-13s; £6.50 family (2+3); free
under-4s. **Credit** MC, V. **Map** p404 P8.
This full-size reconstruction of Sir Francis Drake's
16th-century flagship is impressively shipshape considering the almost quarter century it has spent cir-
cumnavigating the world as a seaborne museum.
The five levels have been recreated in minute detail
(the diminutive proportions of the 14-cannon gun
deck and hold feel painfully real), and the kid-
friendly atmosphere on board is fleshed out by 'crew'
in Elizabethan costume. There are separate 'Living
History Experiences' (some overnight) in which participants dress in period clothes, eat Tudor fare and
learn the skills of the Elizabethan seafarer. 'Pirate
Parties' and school visits can also be arranged.

HMS Belfast

Morgan's Lane, Tooley Street, SE1 (7940 6328/
www.iwm.org.uk). London Bridge tube/rail.
Open *Mar-Oct* 10am-6pm daily (last entry 5.15pm).
Nov-Feb 10am-5pm daily (last entry 4.15pm).
Admission £5.40; £4 concessions; free under-16s
(must be accompanied by an adult). **Credit** MC, V.
Map p405 R8.
This 11,500-ton battlecruiser was built in 1938 and
played a leading role in the Normandy Landings and
supported UN forces in Korea before being decom-
missioned in 1965. Kids love exploring its seven
decks, boiler and engine rooms and massive gun turrets. Call for details of Family Learning Weekends
or to find out how to organise a children's party here.

Rose Theatre

56 Park Street, SE1 (7593 0026/
www.rosetheatre.org.uk). Cannon Street or
London Bridge tube/rail. **Open** 11am-5pm daily
(last entry 4.30pm). **Admission** £4; £3 concessions;
£2 5-15s; £10 family (2+4); free under-5s. **Credit** DC,
MC, V. **Map** p404 P8.
Everyone has heard of the Globe (*see below*), but
until excavations carried out by Museum of London
archaeologists in 1989, few knew of the Rose. In
fact, the theatre – built by Philip Henslowe and
operational from 1587 until 1606; what the Globe is
to Shakespeare, the Rose is to Christopher Marlowe
(*see p10*) – was the first playhouse to be built at
Bankside. Without it, the Globe would have ended
up somewhere else, if it had been built at all. Long
term, the Rose Theatre Trust hopes to fully exca-
vate the site, and digging is scheduled to commence
in the next two years, but funding is scarce, so for
now the space is given over to an engaging and
occasionally fascinating sound, vision and light
exhibition aimed at raising both awareness and the
financial wherewithal.

Shakespeare's Globe

21 New Globe Walk, Bankside, SE1 (7902 1500/
www.shakespeares-globe.org). Mansion House or
Southwark tube/London Bridge tube/rail. **Open**
Tours and exhibitions *May-Sept* 9am-12.30pm daily.
Oct-Apr 10am-5pm daily. **Tours** *late Sept-mid May*
half-hourly; 10am-5pm daily. **Virtual (video
screen) tours** *mid May-late Sept* 12.30-5pm
Tue-Sun. **Admission** Tours only *late Sep-mid May*
£7.50; £6 concessions; £5 5-15s; £23 family (2+3);
free under-5s. *Mid May-late Sep* £5; £4 concessions;
£3.50 5-16s; free under-5s. **Credit** AmEx, MC, V.
Map p404 O7.
The original Globe, where many of Shakespeare's
plays were first staged and which he co-owned,
burned down in 1613 during a performance of *Henry
VIII*. Nearly 400 years later, it was rebuilt not far
from its original site under the auspices of actor Sam
Wanamaker (who, sadly, didn't live to see it up and
running), using construction methods and materials
as close to the originals as possible. You can't help
but feel that Shakespeare would be pleased with the
reconstruction, which includes an impressive exhibition of memorabilia related to famous performances of his works. The centrepiece is a guided tour
of the theatre itself, but note that there are none in
the afternoon from May to September, when historically authentic performances are held (*see p334*),
though visitors still have access to the exhibition.

Southwark Cathedral

Montague Close, SE1 (7367 6700/tours 7367 6734/
www.dswark.org). London Bridge tube/rail. **Open**
8am-6pm daily (closing times vary on religious
holidays). **Tours** by arrangement; phone for details.
Services 8am, 8.15am, 12.30pm, 12.45pm, 5.30pm
Mon-Fri; 9am, 9.15am, 4pm Sat; 9am, 9.15am, 11am,
3pm Sun. **Choral Evensong** 5.30pm Tue, Fri, Sun

Sightseeing

Walk this way

While most of the north side of the Thames is choked with traffic, part of the charm of the South Bank and Bankside is its accessibility to pedestrians, which is thanks in large part to the efforts of a community working in tandem with forward-thinking design professionals to introduce environmentally sensitive but visitor-friendly facilities without compromising the character of the area.

One of these projects is the 'Station to Tate' route, devised by architects East to guide visitors from the beautiful new Southwark station to Tate Modern (*see p79*). Visitors exiting the tube are met by a strip of blue panelling and a huge arrow on the wall of a building opposite. Follow this and you'll see a blue limestone kerb that guides you to the museum; orange streetlights and bollards also mark out the route, along which pavements have been widened to make 'mats' outside pubs, and bespoke benches encourage cafés and pubs to spill out on to the pavement.

Similarly, Southwark Street (at least the Borough High Street end) has been rendered more pedestrian-friendly by a range of strategies conceived by muf architects in collaboration with local residents and schoolkids. These include pavement panels individually shaped to create an undulating kerb that acts as a traffic-calming measure (made from gravel dredged from the Thames, they also resemble the foreshore of the river) and signs to tourist attractions built into the pavement and constructed of local stone.

Up towards the Thames, the 'London Bridge Gateway & Environs' initiative, handled by Eric Parry Associates, features most dramatically a Portland stone needle that has been erected as a resolutely modern marker of what was the medieval gateway to Southwark, while cast iron light strips in the pavement mark historic openings to the river such as the line of the medieval London Bridge. Next to it, the Southwark Information Centre has been cleverly housed beneath a walkway leading to the station, and nearby benches are made from pieces of the original London Bridge that were found when the needle's foundations were being excavated. Lit from beneath, the benches seem to magically float after dark.

Back at the South Bank, the 'Spine Route' (Upper Ground, Belvedere Road and Concert Hall Approach) has been a way both of creating a coherent identity for the arts complex and improving its user-friendliness – the traffic-calmed boulevard, conceived by architects Lifschutz Davidson in 1997, has warm lighting, wide pavements, trees, specially designed street surfaces and furniture, and illuminated map boards, as well as an 'open-air art gallery' comprising 66 banners created by different artists and hung from the special streetlights. The South Bank Urban Design Strategy includes the extension of the 'Spine Route' through County Hall and St Thomas's Hospital, while the South Bank Centre's regeneration plans (*see p74*) include bringing to life these major pedestrian routes with street-level art foyers, cafés and restaurants. Indeed, upmarket chains such as Chez Gérard and Pizza Express have already started moving in.

(boys); 5.30pm Thur (girls). **Admission** *Exhibition* £3; £2.50 concessions; £1.50 5-16s; £12.50 family (5 people, max 2 children); free under-5s. **Credit** AmEx, MC, V. **Map** p404 P8.

Originally the monastic church of St Mary Overie, this building became an Anglican cathedral in 1905. The first church on the site may date from as early as the seventh century; the oldest parts of the present building are still more than 800 years old, including the Retro-Choir, where the trials of several Protestant martyrs took place during the reign of Mary Tudor (*see p11* **Who she? Bloody Mary**).

After the Reformation, the church fell into disrepair and parts of it became a bakery and a pigsty. These days, especially with the recent addition of a visitors' centre that boasts state-of-the-art displays on Southwark past and present and on London in general, including touch-screens allowing visitors to explore artefacts uncovered during recent excavations at the cathedral, it's all looking rather splendid. Among its treasures are the Stone Corpse, a grim 15th-century effigy of an emaciated cadaver in a shroud; a bronze of Shakespeare (whose brother Edmund was buried in an unknown grave here in 1607 but is commemorated in a stone in the choir); and a tablet to Sam Wanamaker, who founded Shakespeare's Globe (*see p77*). Outside, the lovely lavender-scented grounds are packed with local office-workers on sunny lunchtimes.

Tate Modern

Bankside, SE1 (7887 8000/www.tate.org.uk). Southwark tube. **Open** 10am-6pm Mon-Thur, Sun; 10am-10pm Fri, Sat. **Tours** 11am, noon, 2pm, 3pm daily. **Admission** free. *Tours* free. **Map** p401 O7.

The most eagerly awaited of the millennial projects, the Tate's modern art operation has certainly pulled in the punters, though one suspects that this is more to do with the building – a vast power station originally designed by Sir Giles Gilbert Scott (of Waterloo Bridge and the red telephone box fame) and dramatically remodelled by Swiss architects Herzog & De Meuron – than with the art itself. Indeed, many commentators have come away seriously underwhelmed, and the unconventional ordering of the works (thematically rather than chronologically, with categories such as Nude/Action/Body and History/Memory/Society) has elicited more criticism than praise.

Part of the problem may be simply that there's not that many really well-known pieces here, though there's undeniably much to divert. In October 2001 Damien Hirst's *Pharmacy* installation replaced Peter Tuschli and David Weiss's controversial *Untitled* (a trompe-l'oeil room), while the 'Subversive Objects' section of the Intelligent Object gallery includes a looped video of Buñuel and Dali's *Un Chien Andalou* of 1928, Manzoni's *Artist's Shit* of 1961 and Jeff Koons' *Vest with Aqualung* of 1985.

In 2001 the well-received temporary shows included Surrealism: Desire Unbound; this year will see shows on Andy Warhol (7 Feb-1 Apr), Finnish video artist and photographer Eija Liisa Ahtila

(30 Apr-28 July), Matisse/Picasso (11 May-18 Aug), US sculptor Donald Judd (19 Sept 2002-29 Dec) and Barnett Newman (19 Sept-5 Jan 2003). For six months of the year the vast Turbine Hall hosts works from the Unilever Series of commissions; Juan Muñoz's stunning but discomfiting lift installation will remain in place until 10 March 2002. Guided tours are available, and there are film seasons in collaboration with the NFT (*see p293*).

Whatever you feel about the art or its arrangement, this is a museum building to rival the lovely Musée d'Orsay in Paris (also a conversion, this time from a railway station), and the views over the Thames to St Paul's are fabulous. That also goes for the huge and well-stocked shop, the top-floor restaurant and the café on level 2, which won the Best Interior Design category of the *Time Out* Eating & Drinking Awards 2001.

Vinopolis, City of Wine

1 Bank End, SE1 (0870 444 4777/ www.vinopolis.co.uk). London Bridge tube/rail. **Open** 11am-9pm Mon; 11am-6pm Tue-Fri, Sun; 11am-8pm Sat (last entry 2hrs before closing). **Admission** £11.50; £5 5-18s; £10.50 concessions. £1 discount advance bookings. £2 art exhibition only. **Credit** AmEx, MC, V. **Map** p404 P8.

Vinopolis gives you an excuse to wander around drinking under the justification of learning about wine-making around the world, but it's not great value at £11.50 for five uninspired tastings (billed, cheekily, as 'complimentary', when they don't actually amount to much more than a single glassful in total). An audio-tour, available in six languages, guides you around the country displays, most of which consist of colour photos and a video, while pontificating on the types of wine produced in each region. If you're desperate for a bit more action, take the rather silly virtual Vespa trip through a Chianti vineyard or the plane tour of far-flung Australian vineyards. Extras include displays of wine-making equipment and glasses, a restaurant, a wine shop, a cheese counter and tasting courses.

Borough

Borough has a whole host of Dickensian associations – the **George** pub, London's only surviving galleried inn, is mentioned in *Little Dorrit*, as is the church of **St George-the-Martyr** (on the corner of Borough High Street and Long Lane); **White Hart Yard** housed the White Hart Inn, where Mr Pickwick meets Sam Weller in *The Pickwick Papers* (it was pulled down in 1889); and Little Dorrit herself is born in Marshalsea Prison, which used to stand a few doors away and in which Dickens' father was jailed for debt in 1824. In addition, there are Dickens-inspired street and park names. Another literary landmark, the Tabard Inn where Chaucer's pilgrims meet at the beginning of *The Canterbury Tales*, used to stand in nearby **Talbot Yard**.

Food-to-go at **Borough Market**.

Borough as a whole is enjoying something of a renaissance after a long lull. Until 1750, **London Bridge** was the only crossing point into the City, and **Borough High Street** became a stagecoach terminus. The 17th-century poet Thomas Dekker described it as 'a continued ale house with not a shop to be seen between'. Raucous Southwark Fair was held here from 1462 until its suppression by the spoilsport Corporation of London in 1763.

These days, the High Street is thriving again, with old caffs, pubs and shops alongside aromatic modern Turkish restaurants and bar chains such as the Slug & Lettuce. But the area's modern *succès fou* has been **Borough Market**, which, having hosted fruit and vegetable stalls since the 13th century, has been given a new lease of life by the Friday and Saturday gourmet food markets held here (*see also p257*). For a while there have been fears that the beautiful covered market building and unique surrounding streets, little touched this century and long popular for film sets (it's here that a certain singleton can be seen entertaining, shopping and romancing in *Bridget Jones's Diary*), may be lost to a rail improvement scheme. These fears have been lessened with the signing of a legal agreement mitigating the effect of a possible viaduct over Borough Market, but a definite decision is not expected until mid-2002. In the meantime, foodies should make sure they take advantage of the delights on offer here, which range from

a pie and mash stand and a foie gras specialist, through to wonderful delis such as De Gustibus and the acclaimed fish! restaurant and shop (*see p188*).

Several attractions are clustered around London Bridge station: the **Old Operating Theatre, Museum & Herb Garret** (*see p81*), the gory **London Dungeon** (*see below*) and **Winston Churchill's Britain at War Experience** (*see p81*). Architecture buffs should go to see the **Cromwell Buildings** at Redcross Way. This striking colonial-looking apartment block with its ironwork and plant-filled verandas is a historically significant example of the low-cost housing for which this area is renowned. Modelled after a pair of houses designed by the Prince Regent for the Great Exhibition of 1851, it was constructed in 1864 by Sir Sydney Waterlow, who had founded the Improved Industrial Dwellings Company, one of the most successful and earliest providers of low-cost housing, the previous year (in 1889 he donated Waterlow Park, part of his own estate, to the public; *see p150*).

London Dungeon

28-34 Tooley Street, SE1 (7403 7221/ www.thedungeons.com). London Bridge tube/rail. **Open** *Oct-Mar* 10.30am-6pm daily. *Apr-mid July, Sept, Oct* 10am-5.30pm daily. *Nov-Mar* 10.30am-5pm daily. *Mid July-early Sept* 10am-8pm daily. **Admission** £10.95; £9.50 students; £6.95 5-14s, concessions; £2 reduction wheelchair-users, carers free; free under-5s. **Credit** AmEx, MC, V. **Map** p405 Q8.

Creepier than the Clink Prison Museum (*see p77*) and the Chamber of Horrors at Madame Tussaud's (*see p110*) combined, the Dungeon is very good on atmosphere, with its low lighting and soundtrack of screams and moans that never lets up as you stumble through one ghoulish exhibit after another on the Plague, medieval torture, execution and disease. A recent addition is the Great Fire of London, an interactive exhibit that gives you the background on the event itself before bombarding you with smoke; you have to escape through further corridors filled with smoke and mock-ups of burning houses, then 'run the gauntlet' of fire by leaping through a revolving trommel. Evening events in the 'Deadly Diary' include a Ripper Rampage ('meet Jack the Ripper himself as he comes out after dark'), a two-week Hallowe'en festival and a 'Wicked Winter Wonderland'.

London Fire Brigade Museum

94A Southwark Bridge Road, SE1 (7587 2894/ www.london-fire.gov.uk). Borough tube. **Tours** 10.30am, 2pm Mon-Fri by appt only. **Admission** £3; £2 7-14s, concessions; free under-7s. **Credit** MC, V. **Map** p404 O9.

This small museum traces the history of firefighting from the Great Fire of London in 1666 to the present. Exhibits include old firefighting appliances. All visitors have to pre-book on guided tours, which are tailored to different needs.

Old Operating Theatre, Museum & Herb Garret

9A St Thomas's Street, SE1 (7955 4791/ www.thegarret.org.uk). London Bridge tube/rail. **Open** 10.30am-5pm daily (last entry 4.45pm). Closed 15 Dec-4 Jan. **Admission** £3.25; £2.25 concessions; £1.75 6-16s; £8 family (2+4); free under-6s. **No credit cards. Map** p405 Q8.

A relic of the days when the cure for an ingrowing toenail was amputation and when bodysnatching gangs such as the 'Borough Boys' roamed the area, the Old Operating Theatre, rediscovered in 1956, is the oldest surviving part of the original St Thomas's Hospital. Set, atmospherically, in the roof of an old medieval church (which was adjacent to the surgical ward and was extended into), it is accessed via a vertiginous wooden spiral staircase (sadly, there's no disabled access). Just inside the pungent herb garret, where medicinal herbs were once stored and are now displayed again.

When you've marvelled at the labels describing the uses of eyebright, pennyroyal, heartease ('used in love charms and for diseases of the heart') and the like and the recipes against such ills as 'mental vacancy and folly', brace yourself for the operating theatre itself. Here, an original wooden operating table has at its feet a box of sawdust designed to soak up the blood. In the eerie silence you can almost hear the screams of the unanaesthetised patients (mainly poor women operated on for teaching purposes – hence the spectator stands surrounding the table). Display cases include such delights as strangulated

hernias, leech jars, wooden nipple shields, amputation knives, massive forceps and physicians' sticks used as biting gags. Photographs of the hospital, including the female ward (now occupied by Borough High Street post office), give a real sense of its history. Call for information about lectures and summer workshops for families and children.

Winston Churchill's Britain at War Experience

64-6 Tooley Street, SE1 (7403 3171/ www.britainatwar.co.uk). London Bridge tube/rail. **Open** Apr-Sept 10am-5.30pm (last entry 5pm) daily. Oct-Mar 10am-4.30pm daily (last entry 4pm). **Admission** £5.95; £3.95 concessions; £2.95 5-16s; £14 family (2+2); free under-5s. **Credit** AmEx, MC, V. **Map** p405 Q8.

There's lots of fascinating memorabilia of London during the Blitz here, including real bombs, rare documents and photos, though overall the place is a bit shabby and home-made in feel. Topics covered here include Army Girls and other 'women at war', and rationing. Children love the atmospheric reproductions of an Anderson shelter, a GI's club and a darkened bombsite.

Tower Bridge & Bermondsey

The stretch of river from London Bridge to Tower Bridge is dominated by the **HMS Belfast** (*see p77*), the soaring, glass-roofed Hay's Galleria (a former enclosed dock that used to be visited by tea clippers from India and China and that has been turned into a naff mall crammed with Starbucks and Café Rouge outlets and tacky craft and souvenir stalls), and by the controversial new Norman Foster designed GLA building (*see p27*), which was nearing completion as we went to press and which Mayor Livingstone and his crew are scheduled to move into in July 2002, on the GLA's second birthday. Next to this, a £500-million complex, the first phase of which will be complete in 2002, will include shops, offices, a cinema, hotels, restaurants and a piazza.

This is the start of **Bermondsey**, an area that was long a focus for Christianity – **Tooley Street** was once home to no fewer than three abbots, a prior and the church of St Olave's. Its near-namesake, **St Olaf House**, a fabulous art deco 1930s warehouse, is worth a look, as is the building that will house the **Zandra Rhodes Fashion & Textile Museum** (*see p82*).

East of the spectacular Tower Bridge (*see p94*), **Butler's Wharf** is home to a trio of Sir Terence Conran restaurants and the excellent **Design Museum** (*see p82*), which Conran, the man who did much to bring good household design to the ordinary punter, helped establish. The Conran company HQ itself is just round the corner, backing on to New Concordia Wharf.

Sightseeing

Check out **St Saviour's Dock**, a muddy creek between towering warehouses, visible over a low parapet in Jamaica Road. In the 18th century, this was a notorious haunt for pirates, who were hanged at its mouth. In Dickens' day, the streets around here formed a slum called Jacob's Island, where Bill Sikes gets his come-uppance in *Oliver Twist*. Indeed, much of the area still has a Dickensian feel to it – so much so that David Lynch filmed *The Elephant Man* in Shad Thames in 1980.

But the times they are a-changing, and not all for the best. Though Bermondsey Square still has its superb antiques market (*see p231*), and though the old, listed warehouses are being sympathetically transformed into office blocks and posh flats whose names (the Vanilla & Sesame Building, Coriander Court, the Fennel Building) are evocative of their spice-storage days, much of the area is starting to feel a little fake, with its pristine cobbled streets, expensive art shops and twee delis, and the influx of chains such as Starbucks and All Bar One.

Up past the Design Museum, New Concordia Wharf is a calm marina-like backwater populated by swans and geese, with a gleaming new swing bridge in front of converted warehouses. Further up, past trendy offices affording glimpses of people hunched over laptops, is a lovely spot with old barges turned into floating gardens.

Design Museum

28 Shad Thames, SE1 (7403 6933/ www.designmuseum.org). Bermondsey or Tower Hill tube/London Bridge tube/rail/15, 78, 100 bus. **Open** 10am-5.45pm daily (last entry 5.15pm). **Admission** £5.50; £4 concessions, 5-15s; £15 family (2+2); free under-5s. **Credit** AmEx, MC, V. **Map** p405 S9.

This stark but beautiful '30s-style building is the perfect setting for this collection of innovative work across the design spectrum. The first floor holds the **Review Gallery** (dedicated to state-of-the-art innovations from round the world) and the **Temporary Gallery**, which in 2002 will host the following shows and more – the Fabulous Bouroullec Boys (1 Feb-16 June), Gio Ponti (3 May-6 Oct), Philip Treacy's hats for Isabella Blow (1 June-11 Aug), the Adventures of Aluminium (18 Oct-24 Feb 2003), and Unseen Vogue, the secret history of fashion photography (1 Nov 2002-3 Feb 2003). On the second floor, the **Collection Gallery** is devoted to the study of design for mass production, from cars, early TVs and telephones to chairs and tableware.

It's a frustrating time for the museum, which needs more room for the increasingly exciting shows it's putting on. A revamp is on the cards, but for the moment no timeframe has been established. There's one new addition, however, in the form of a 'baby' glass gallery outside on the river terrace, with displays (anything from site-specific installations to tasters of the big exhibitions inside) changing every six to eight weeks. The schedule for 2002 includes an installation by John Galliano and specially commissioned digital projects by Digit and Tomato.

The suitably stylish but misleadingly named **Blue Print Café** (it's actually a restaurant, with prices to match) shares the building and has a balcony overlooking the Thames. For snacks and coffees there's a café proper next to the tempting shop.

Zandra Rhodes Fashion & Textile Museum

83 Bermondsey Street, SE1 (7403 0222/ www.zandrarhodes.com/Museum/). London Bridge tube/rail. **Open** phone for details. **Admission** phone for details. **Map** p405 Q9.

Scheduled to open in spring 2002 (fundraising is ongoing), this striking building in the zany British fashion designer's trademark colours of orange and pink is already a local architectural landmark in its own right. Designed by Mexican architect Ricardo Legorreta and sited in a former cash-and-carry warehouse, it's a symbol of the regeneration of the area. As well as 2,000 of Rhodes's own designs and a shop selling her clothes, the museum – the first dedicated to 20th-century British fashion – will showcase British and international designers from the '50s on.

Bright young thing: the **Zandra Rhodes Fashion & Textile Museum**.

The City

A beguiling mix of secret alleyways and swooping towers, the City is not to be missed.

Maps p402-p405

The City doesn't do weekends. And during the week, when most of London's hotspots are gearing up for solid business, the City is winding down. Workdays find close on 250,000 people settling down to hard graft, helping to generate around three quarters of Britain's GNP, but by Friday night only a fraction of them will remain. Those that have chosen to live within the Square Mile shouldn't feel too marginalised, however, and neither should visitors – though pubs and shops are closed, historically the area is a goldmine, and there's no lack of things to see. Roman Londinium, for example, can be traced to this part of town. It's why the City is called the City: it's the true heart of the capital, where London originated.

Despite its economic power, the City has taken many knocks throughout its life, and not all of them fiduciary. In 1665 the Great Plague ravaged London, killing around 100,000 people. As the weather cooled and it seemed the plague might be in abeyance, along came the Great Fire of 1666, which, razing much of the City to the ground, saw off the plague for good. The loss of life was minimal (it is documented that just six people died in the fire), but the capital needed to be rebuilt. Much of Sir Christopher Wren's intensive work to that end can still be seen today (*see p86* **Who he?**).

Just under 400 years later, the City received another thumping in the Blitz, but again the Square Mile rose from the ashes to begin afresh. Perhaps it's because of these swift recoveries that the architecture of the area is such a hotch-potch of ancient and modern: the glossy glass and steel of financial might muscling up against quaint Elizabethan alehouses and conspiratorial alleyways; monotonous office façades giving way to oases of spiritual calm in the shape of the City's numerous churches.

The area is rich in other architectural treasures too. The **Lloyd's Building** (Lime Street, EC3), designed by Sir Richard Rogers (who won the contract on the back of his work on the Pompidou Centre in Paris), is a *Blade Runner*-esque monolith of externalised ducts, shafts and lifts built in high-tech concrete, steel and glass, while **Bracken House** (1 Friday Street, EC4) is worth searching out for its marriage of conservationism and invention.

Built in the '50s to house the *Financial Times* (the pink brick – Hollingsworth stone – was sought because it replicated the colour of the newspaper's pages), the building was later bought by Japanese construction giants Obiyashi Gumi. The offices, in the wings of the building, were considered of great quality, but the central bulk, which was taken up by the now-defunct hot metal presses, was deemed excess to requirements. Not that it could be simply knocked down: Bracken House was the first building in the country to gain listed status after World War II. Michael Hopkins took charge of the redesign, which had to incorporate the same colour scheme in the stones: to this end, he plundered the quarry that Richardson had used 30 years previously. On the Cannon Street side of the building, the sharp-eyed might spot the face of Winston Churchill – a great friend of Richardson's – rendered as the centrepiece to an astronomical clock.

St Andrew by the Wardrobe. *See p87.*

The look of love: Botero's **Broadgate Venus**.

Corporate culture

Imagine you're one of the corporate gods of the City, a big player with a power base the size of a country. You're so hot, the building you command your financial empires from has got enough space in it to make NASA do a double-take. Empty space says to your clients, and more importantly, your competitors, 'Hey look, we're so rich we can just fill a big room with nothing.'

But empty rooms, whether they're in your granny's parlour or part of blue chip company headquarters, are astoundingly dull to look at. So what do you put there? Art, naturally. Light them sensitively, and open-plan rooms become galleries. Deutsche Bank for one has been quick to recognise the sense in such moves. For the last 20 years it's been gobbling up German art, to the point where every floor of its 55-storey Frankfurt base boasts something to catch the eye. It's estimated that its collection runs to approximately 48,000 pieces.

The bank's sinuous London 'groundscraper' building at London Wall, built by David Walker in 1999, has continued the trend, snapping up work by Britpack artists such as Gary Hume, Damien Hirst and Rachel Whiteread, as well as Anish Kapoor. On the top floor, managers meet in rooms called The Bacon, The Freud and The Hockney.

The Lehman Brothers at 1 Broadgate have also got in on the act, boasting several Anthony Gormley sculptures in their reception area. Amassing collections of art like this is a bold, corporate statement of muscle, but it's also a tonic for the troops: staff who don't normally go to art galleries get a fix of culture every time they come through the door. And the British art scene gets a boost too. The only problem is that most of these works of art are off-limits for the average Joe... what the hell – you can always have a good nosey through the windows.

Yet for those who like to get up close and personal with their art, Broadgate is still a good bet. It might be the largest office development in Europe, but careful consideration has been paid to Mr and Ms Pedestrian. The piazza, which is used during the summer months as an arts centre hosting rock concerts, classical recitals and everything in-between, and in winter as an ice rink and for games of circular ice hockey, has some superb artworks. These include *The Broad Family* by Xavier Corbero; Fernando Botero's *Broadgate Venus*; *Fulcrum* by Richard Serra; and Jacques Lipschitz's *Bellerophon Taming Pegasus*, among many others. And unlike the Hirst at Deutsche Bank, they're accessible 24 hours a day.

Also of note is the redevelopment at Broadgate, a stunning rethink of the area that contains Liverpool Street Station. **Exchange House** in particular, with its parabolic arch echoing the arches of the train sheds over the platforms, is a testament to architectural savvy. Built on ground that is weak because it stands over the railway lines, Exchange House uses four massive plinths and the supporting structure of the arch to exert a negligible weight on its foundations.

The City is an area of continuous flux, and you'll find a lot of construction work taking place at the weekends because the place is just too darned busy throughout the week. One happy consequence of all this evolution is a more positive approach to the idea of 'mixed use', in which the new buildings and developments are not so focused on business that they ignore the pedestrian. Many of the urban facelifts now contain shops, cafés and restaurants to involve the passer-by, rather than a solemn, unwelcoming stone façade.

Unlike other districts of London, the City exists on its medieval streetplans, and away from the main drags, in the tiny passageways that thread between the grand old buildings, a real sense of dislocation can occur. You'll find that the brickwork is less grand here, but it's ingeniously coated with a glaze to reflect the miserly light – handy for the accountants who would have had to spend hours tallying figures in these cramped back rooms. This is your cue to get lost for a while in the City's secret alleyways. Chances are you'll find a peaceful tavern, a church or a length of wall from ancient times waiting for you in the shadows.

City Information Centre

St Paul's Churchyard (south side of the cathedral), EC4 (7332 1456/www.cityoflondon.gov.uk). St Paul's tube. **Open** *Apr-Sept* 9.30am-5pm daily. *Oct-Mar* 9.30am-5pm Mon-Fri; 9.30am-12.30pm Sat. **Map** p404 O6.
Information on sights, events, walks and talks within the Square Mile.

Along Fleet Street

Chancery Lane tube/Blackfriars tube/rail.

Though the newspapers turned their backs on **Fleet Street** more than a decade ago, the place will always be associated with the age of hot metal and circulation wars. Only Reuters remains, the press agency that started life in 1850 with a fleet of carrier pigeons, but the ghosts of other 'linens' pervade the street: the *Daily Telegraph* was at No.135 and the *Daily Express* at Nos.121-8, which retains its glorious glass face and art deco staircase and foyer.

Punch was based here in its infancy, the early 1840s, as well as long-dead newspapers such as the *Morning Advertiser* and the *Dispatch*.

This was the sad but inevitable demise of an industry that could not compete with the computer-based technology that replaced it, something that the aptly named Wynkyn de Worde, Caxton's apprentice and the person who introduced printing presses to Fleet Street in 1500, could not have foreseen. De Worde brought the presses to **St Bride's**, which is still referred to as the printers and journalists' church and is said to be the inspiration for the tiered wedding cake (*see p86* **Who he? Sir Christopher Wren**).

It's no coincidence that one of the arterial roads connecting Buckingham Palace to the Square Mile (or Queen to Commerce) is Fleet Street. 'Media' is the perfect word to describe the industry that was undertaken here, as the reporters mediated on the antagonism created between the two powers: the City of Westminster and the City. It was handy, for that matter, that the law courts were based nearby too. But Fleet Street was not just a haunt for the capital's hacks: it boasted plenty of literary talent too, more often than not to be found in the alehouses such as the long-gone Devil's Tavern at No.1, which entertained Pepys, Ben Jonson and Samuel Johnson, or Ye Old Cheshire Cheese (*see p219*), which was favoured by Dickens. Johnson, the father of the English dictionary, lived for a time in nearby Gough Square, which was handy for throwing out time. **Dr Johnson's House** is now open to the public (*see below*).

One of London's forgotten rivers, and its largest, the Fleet flows into the Thames at Blackfriars Bridge. Now underground, it was once a major inlet for trade. Indeed, the etymology of 'fleet' contains an Anglo-Saxon reference to 'inlet' or 'estuary'. In its heyday, the Fleet was flanked by enormous docks (located where Farringdon Street is now) that received visits from ships bearing coal, spice and fabrics. Pollution of the river at its upper reaches, however, put paid to its status as a trading post. One would presume that a whiff of the Thames today is a whole lot sweeter than it was 400 years ago.

Dr Johnson's House

17 Gough Square, off Fleet Street, EC4 (7353 3745/www.drjh.dircon.co.uk). Chancery Lane or Temple tube (both closed Sun)/Blackfriars tube/rail. **Open** *May-Sept* 11am-5.30pm Mon-Sat. *Oct-Apr* 11am-5pm Mon-Sat. *Tours* by arrangement; groups of 10 or more only. **Admission** £4; £3 concessions; £1 under-14s; free under-5s; £9 family (2+unlimited children). *Tours* free. *Evening tours* £5-£8 per head. **No credit cards. Map** p404 N6.

Sightseeing

He got around, old Dr John. He loved London as much, if not more, than he loved life if we're to take him at his word – enough, anyway, to have had 17 different residences. This one alone remains intact. He lived here from 1748 to 1759, while working on the first of his English dictionaries in the garret with the help of his six amanuenses. He also worked on his novel *Rasselas*. In 1752, following the death of his wife, his Jamaican servant Francis Barber moved into 17 Gough Square, which has been lovingly restored to its original condition. Visitors can wander through a series of panelled rooms while admiring period furniture, prints and portraits.

Around St Paul's

St Paul's tube.

When you look at the majestic dome of **St Paul's Cathedral** (*see p89*) rising out of the City's clamour, its cranes and facelifts, its traffic jams and security alerts, it's difficult not to feel a sense of peace and security. One thinks

of the Blitz, and the famous photograph by Herbert Mason of Wren's masterpiece standing firm while the surrounding buildings burned. The dome is a serene curve in a concrete jungle of angles. At night, when it is underlit, there really isn't anything in London to touch it in terms of beauty. It draws the eye. As do the two baroque towers, one of which contains the largest bell in England, 'Great Paul', which weighs 17 tonnes and is tolled daily at 1pm.

There has been a cathedral dedicated to St Paul on this site since AD 604. The current building was designed by Christopher Wren (*see p86* **Who he?**), and it isn't difficult to see why this is his masterpiece. It was begun in 1675 and took 35 years to build. Unusually for architects, Wren was still around to admire his own creation when it had been completed.

Paternoster Square, w hich was once a forbidding arena of shadowy ginnels, grim pubs and boarded-up premises, lies alongside the cathedral and is still in the process of being

Who he? Sir Christopher Wren

Of the 87 churches that were destroyed by the Great Fire of 1666, 54 were rebuilt, and of those all but three were by Sir Christopher Wren. The fact that this did not result in a monotony of style is a testament to Wren's incomparable genius, particularly when one bears in mind that he had to work on the original cramped sites.

Wren was born in 1632 in Wiltshire, the son of a high church royalist divine, and was educated at Westminster School, London, and Wadham College, Oxford. In 1657 he became Professor of Astronomy at Gresham College, London, then he returned to Oxford, where he was Savile Professor of Astronomy at Oxford from 1661 to 1673. However, he had started to be as interested in architecture and geometry as in astronomy, designing the chapel at Pembroke College, Cambridge, in 1663, the Sheldonian Theatre, Oxford, in 1664, and buildings for Trinity College, Oxford, in 1665. A year later the Great Fire provided him with his greatest career opportunity in terms of architecture, and it is for his churches and for his masterpiece **St Paul's** (*see p89*) that he has gone down in the history books, though in his own day he was also a very famous mathematician (Newton rated him among the leading geometers of his epoch), as well as an inventor of such diverse schemes as an instrument that would copy handwriting,

a process for fortifying port and a machine that was capable of knitting multiple pairs of stockings simultaneously.

Wren's City churches exhibit an extraordinary diversity of design and decoration, though many do share certain features: light interiors, painted in white and gold, clear glass windows, fine wood carving, painted altarpieces and imaginative use of ironwork. Among the best is **St Bride's** (Fleet Street, EC4, 7427 0133), completed in 1703 and one of the finest examples of the Italian style in England. The spire, at 226 feet (69 metres), is the architect's tallest; the four octagonal arcades of diminishing size are said to have been the inspiration for the first tiered wedding cake. The church was gutted in the Blitz, revealing Roman and Saxon remains, which are now displayed and labelled in the crypt, along with information on the connections between the church and the printing and newspaper publishing businesses.

St Mary Abchurch (Abchurch Yard, Abchurch Lane, EC4, 7626 0306) is a simple, Dutch-influenced red-brick construction dating from 1681-6 and concealing a splendidly rich yet light interior, largely unaltered by subsequent 'improvers' (*see below*). Beneath the shallow dome (painted by William Snow) is superb 17th-century woodwork, though the highlight is the limewood reredos (altar

scrubbed up in one of the largest redevelopments currently being undertaken in the capital. A new complex of buildings marrying classical and modern styles surrounding a beautiful monument will be unveiled to the public in spring 2003.

There's a quaint little row of shops on **Bow Lane**, while bistros, champagne bars, restaurants and shops also huddle together, vying for your attention in this cosy alleyway. Check out Porterhouse Butchers at No.6 – the sausages here are a speciality; you'll find any number of weird and wonderful variations. Further along is **St Mary Aldermary**, an attempt by Wren to hark back to the pre-Great Fire perpendicular style. Inside you'll find a little display containing oyster shells – a bit of a step up from the communion wafer, you might think, but the oysters are actually from the Thames and were a staple part of workmen's diets in the 17th and 18th centuries. Once the oysters were consumed, the shells were used as

filling material in the buildings they were erecting. The shells on display were discovered in the church tower.

Over Queen Victoria Street is **Garlick Hill**, its medieval name proving false the supposed antipathy between the English and the pungent bulb. At the bottom of the street is Wren's church of St James Garlickhythe, which has the highest roof in the City after St Paul's. Its light-filled interior remains much as it was in the 17th century, and has earned it the nickname of 'Wren's Lantern'.

South of St Paul's lies a little explored but delightful tangle of alleyways, concealing shops, pubs and the dinky Wren church of **St Andrew by the Wardrobe**. Built in 1685-95, the church's curious name dates from 1361, when the King's Wardrobe – the ceremonial clothes of the royal family – were moved to the adjoining building. Nearby, two other Wren creations, St Benet and St Nicholas Cole Abbey, are, unfortunately, usually closed. Facing the former

Hugh Howard Esq. –

screen), the only one in the City that can be attributed with certainty to the famous woodcarver Grinling Gibbons.

St Mary-le-Bow (Cheapside, EC2, 7248 5139), Wren's graceful white tower and spire (1670-3) topped by a huge dragon weathercock, is one of his greatest works. German bombers put paid to the original interior; what you see now is a reconstruction. The tradition that only those born within earshot of these church bells are true Cockneys probably dates from the 14th century, when they first rang the City's nightly curfew. The crypt of the original Norman

church survives (its arches, or 'bows', give the church its name) and is now home to **The Place Below** restaurant (*see p189*).

Arguably Wren's finest parish church, **St Stephen Walbrook** was a practice run for many of the ideas that he brought to fruition in St Paul's. Its cross-in-square plan surmounted by a central dome creates a marvellous feeling of space and light and is an ingenious use of the relatively cramped site. Although badly damaged in the Blitz, the church has been superbly restored, largely thanks to the support of Lord Palumbo, who commissioned the amorphous, Roman travertine central altar by Henry Moore. The rector, Prebendary Dr Chad Varah, founded the Samaritans here in 1953.

Sadly, many of Wren's churches were mangled by Victorian 'improvers', who preferred the dim light and stained glass of the Gothic style, and bomb damage in World War II destroyed 11 more. Today just 38 remain. St Ethelburga-the-Virgin – one of the few medieval churches to survive both the Great Fire and the Blitz – was almost completely destroyed by an IRA bomb in 1993. It is, however, to be rebuilt (at a cost of £3.6 million; to donate call 7248 3177) as a 'Centre for Reconciliation and Peace' and a world research centre investigating the role of religion in ending conflict. The time couldn't be more ripe.

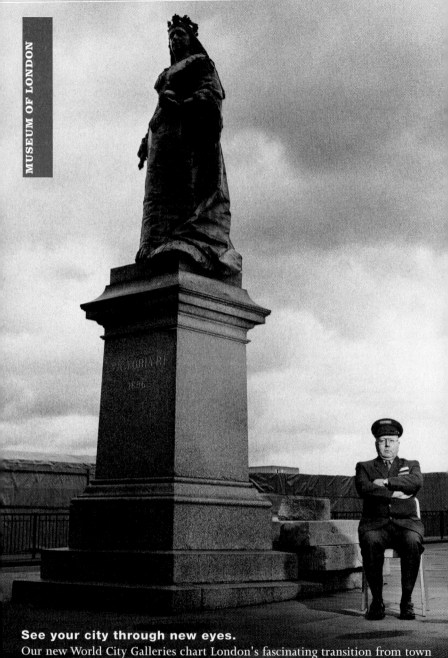

VICTORIA R
1896

See your city through new eyes.

Our new World City Galleries chart London's fascinating transition from town to thriving modern metropolis, 1789 to 1914. With over 3000 objects on display, 1000 never shown before, as well as reconstructed shops, offices and workshops. We're just a short walk from St Paul's and admission is free.

across scruffy **Queen Victoria Street** is the unexpectedly neat red-brick, 17th-century mansion of the **College of Arms** (*see below*), which still examines and records the pedigrees of those to whom such things matter.

North of Blackfriars Station is Apothecaries' Hall, one of the most charming of the livery halls (though the most interesting one is **Fishmonger's Hall**, *see p94*), and, close by on Ludgate Hill, stands the church of St Martin within Ludgate, its lead spire still visible over the surrounding buildings as Wren intended (which, alas, is more than can be said for those of most of his other churches). After reflecting on the works of God, ponder upon the sins of man round the corner in the most famous court in the land, the **Old Bailey** (*see below*), built on the site of the infamous Newgate Prison.

College of Arms

Queen Victoria Street, EC4 (7248 2762/ www.college-of-arms.gov.uk). Blackfriars tube/ rail. **Open** 10am-4pm Mon-Fri. *Tours* by arrangement 6.30pm Mon-Fri; prices vary. **Admission** free. **Map** p404 O7.

Heraldry's come on a bit since medieval times. Back then, the organisation and promotion of tournaments was the chief function of heralds. They kept things ticking over, acting as MC and scorekeeper. The knights who took part in these joustathons were recognised by the arms on their shields and the crests on their helmets. Heralds, spending so much time in the company of armour-plated competitors, soon became experts at recognising the various symbols, and became responsible for recording arms, and, eventually, for controlling their use – a practice that continues to this day within the venerable college, the present building of which dates from the 1670s. Only the wood-panelled entrance room is accessible to the public, although tours can be booked in order to view the Record Room and the artists working on the intricate certificates.

Old Bailey (Central Criminal Court)

corner of Newgate Street & Old Bailey, EC4 (7248 3277). St Paul's tube. **Open** *Public gallery* 10.30am-1pm, 2-4pm Mon-Fri. **Admission** free. No under-14s; 14-16s accompanied by adults only. **Map** p404 O6.

The Central Criminal Court – more commonly known as the Old Bailey – was built by Edward Mountford in 1907 on the site of the old Newgate Prison. The bronze figure of Justice on the copper-covered dome overlooks the area where convicts were once executed. Many notorious criminals have been tried at the Old Bailey, including Dr Crippen, Peter Sutcliffe – the Yorkshire Ripper – and Jeffrey Archer. Visitors can view trials from the public galleries, although children under 14 are not admitted. It's also a good idea not to bring bags, phones or cameras, which have been prohibited in the wake of terrorist bombings of the city in recent times. If you spot a judge

carrying a posy of flowers into court, by the way, it's not because he wants to liven the place up a bit; traditionally, the flowers masked the foul stench and the germs emanating from the prison.

St Paul's Cathedral

Ludgate Hill, EC4 (7236 4128/www.stpauls.co.uk). St Paul's tube. **Open** 9am-5.15pm Mon-Sat; services only Sun, 25 Dec. *Galleries, crypt & ambulatory* 9.30am-4pm Mon-Sat. Closed for special services, sometimes at short notice. *Tours* 11am, 11.30am, 1.30pm, 2pm Mon-Sat. **Admission** *Cathedral, crypt & gallery* £5; £2.50 6-16s; £4 concessions; free under-6s. **Audio guide** £3; £2 concessions. **Credit** *Shop* MC, V. **Map** p404 O6.

St Paul's is not all it seems. The dome you see on the outside is not the one viewed on the interior – there are two domes, one within the other, and the gap between provides the means to access the incredible galleries. The exterior **Stone Gallery** allows superb views of the Thames and its surroundings, though the best views are from the **Golden Gallery**, an exhausting but worthwhile 530 steps from ground level. Also worth visiting is the interior **Whispering Gallery**, where, purportedly, a muttered word can be understood way over on the other side (it's a bit difficult to test as the gallery is hardly ever empty of muttering visitors).

Despite its reputation for doughtiness during the German attacks on London, St Paul's received a number of direct hits, including a damaging assault on the apse. A monument to the Americans who died in Great Britain during World War II is situated there now, along with a Book of Remembrance. The only painting in the cathedral, William Holman Hunt's *Light of the World*, is on display in the North Transept. The many monuments to great Britons include one to poet John Donne in the south aisle; it was the only one to survive the Great Fire that destroyed the old cathedral. The north aisle contains a vast memorial to the Duke of Wellington, although his body is actually buried in the crypt beside the magisterial funeral carriage that transported him here. A bedfellow of Wellington in the crypt is Christopher Wren himself. The latter's memorial, at first glance, seems strangely modest, but the inscription on the stone says it all. Translated from Latin, it reads, 'If you seek his memorial, look about you.'

The cathedral is currently undergoing a good clean (it was last spruced up in the 1930s), which will take five years to complete, so be prepared to find some areas of the great building off-limits.

North to Smithfield

Barbican or St Paul's tube.

Smithfield Market was once an unusually open space – a 'smooth field' – in the middle of a bustling community. Records from as far back as 1173 refer to its use as a market selling animals, especially horses, but the large expanse of land meant that it was hankered after for other uses

Sightseeing

such as jousts and sporting events, as well as less savoury activities, including, before the gallows were moved to Tyburn, executions. Suspected witches were also killed here, along with those who did not subscribe to the ruling faith. It also hosted **Bartholomew Fair**, ostensibly a cloth fair founded by Henry I's court jester Rahere that quickly became a byword for violence and debauchery and was immortalised in a Ben Jonson play. In 1868, the fair having been banned, Sir Horace Jones built the Smithfield Market that we recognise today. The market awakes at around 3am and surrounding pubs have a special licence to open at 7am to serve the meat porters. Early birds are recommended to try the hearty breakfasts at the Fox & Anchor (*see p220*) on nearby Charterhouse Street.

The busy Rahere, as well as amusing the king, was responsible for **St Bartholomew's Hospital**. During a pilgrimage to Rome, he contracted and almost died from malaria, and vowed to build a hospital on his return to London. This he did in the shape of St Bartholomew's (affectionately referred to these days as St Bart's), following a vision of the saint, who apparently instructed him to work diligently on the project. While he was at it, Rahere threw in a priory and a church, **St Bartholomew-the-Great**, the oldest parish church in the capital (*see below*). In its grounds is **St Bartholomew's Hospital Museum** (7601 8152, 10am-4pm Tue-Fri), charting the hospital's history and containing epic biblical murals by social commentator William Hogarth, who was baptised in the church.

St Bartholomew-the-Great

West Smithfield, EC1 (7606 5171/ www.greatstbarts.com). Barbican tube/ Farringdon tube/rail. **Open** *Mid Nov-mid Feb* 8.30am-4pm Tue-Fri; 10.30am-1.30pm Sat; 8.30am-1pm, 2.30-8pm Sun. *Mid Feb-mid Nov* 8.30am-5pm Tue-Fri; 10.30am-1.30pm Sat; 8.30am-1pm, 2.30-8pm Sun. **Admission** free; donations welcome. **Map** p402 O5.

Although its nave was torn down during Henry VIII's monastic purge (it once extended the length of the churchyard to the 13th-century gateway, now the entrance from Smithfield), this is still a wonderfully evocative place; most of the Norman arches are original. Benjamin Franklin served a year as a journeyman printer in the Lady Chapel.

Around Bank

Mansion House tube/Bank tube/DLR.

A triumphant triumvirate of buildings – the **Bank of England**, the **Royal Exchange** and **Mansion House** – stake their claim to being, if not the geographical centre of the Square Mile,

then its symbolic heart. This trio of imposing buildings, made from the best Portland stone, are only let down by the architectural oddity that is at nearby **Number 1 Poultry**, which resembles the prow of a ship (perhaps the *Titanic* if the disastrous history of its construction is anything to go by). In a nutshell, it took 35 years for Lord Palumbo to redevelop the site, part of which he had inherited from his father. After a series of false starts, Palumbo commissioned one of Britain's best-known architects, James Stirling, who designed what Prince Charles rubbished as 'a 1930s wireless'. The design went through, though it was hampered by the discovery of a Roman road on the construction site. A Conran restaurant – the Coq d'Argent – and a roof terrace are a couple of the main attractions.

The Bank of England, otherwise known as 'the Old Lady of Threadneedle Street', was founded in 1694 to fund William III's war against the French. The present building is a tale of two halves: the bottom consists of Sir John Soane's elegant contribution; the top extension above the balustrade came courtesy of Sir Herbert Baker in the 1920s. As a result of the subsequent loss of the banking vaults, conservation groups were founded to ensure that important architectural works were not at risk. Replicas of the banking vaults can be found in the excellent **Bank of England Museum** (*see p91*).

The bank has issued banknotes since its inauguration and today all English notes are produced at the Bank of England Printing Works at Loughton in Essex. Each year nearly one billion notes are produced at an average unit cost of just over three pence, making the Bank one of the most cost-effective central banknote producers in Europe. Around 90 specialised inks are required for the four denominations – £5, £10, £20 and £50 – in an effort to reduce the threat of counterfeiting.

The Lord Mayor's official residence, **Mansion House** (7626 2500; group visits only, by written application to the Diary Office, Mansion House, Walbrook, EC4, at least two months in advance), was designed by George Dance and completed in 1753. It's the only private residence in the United Kingdom to have its own court of justice, which comes complete with 11 prison cells. Its magnificent pediment by Robert Taylor depicts London defeating envy and bringing plenty in its exploitation of its Empire.

The current Royal Exchange, the third on that site, was built by William Tite and opened by Queen Victoria in 1844. Within a few years its design was seen to be somewhat outmoded in the face of a Gothic revival in the 1850s.

In December 2001, after a two-year renovation, it opened as a five-star shopping complex housing the likes of Prada and Penhaligon's.

Next to the Royal Exchange, on Cornhill, keep a lookout for the statue of James Greathead who, in 1874, patented the 'Greathead Shield', a tunnelling device that enabled deep shafts to be constructed for the London tube network. Poetically, the statue incorporates a vent for one of those very same underground railways.

Further west is the centre of the City's civic life, **Guildhall** (*see below*), base of the Corporation of London, as well as an excellent library, the **Clockmakers' Company Museum** (*see below*), the church of **St Lawrence Jewry**, and the **Guildhall Art Gallery** (*see below*), housing the Corporation of London's art collection.

Next to Mansion House stands one of the City's finest churches, **St Stephen Walbrook**, the trial run for St Paul's (*see p86* **Who he?** **Sir Christopher Wren**). Nearby is the heap of stones that was the Roman **Temple of Mithras** (*see p92*). Other notable churches in the vicinity are Hawksmoor's idiosyncratic **St Mary Woolnoth** (*see p92*) at the junction of King William Street and Lombard Street and Wren's exquisite **St Mary Abchurch** off Abchurch Lane (*see p86* **Who he?**).

Bank of England Museum

entrance on Bartholomew Lane, EC2 (7601 5545/cinema bookings 7601 3985/ www.bankofengland.co.uk). Bank tube/DLR. **Open** 10am-5pm Mon-Fri. *Tours by arrangement.* **Admission** free; £1 audio guide. *Tours free.* **Map** p405 Q6.

Focusing on the restoration of the bank's Stock Office, designed by Sir John Soane in 1793, this museum provides a fascinating insight into both the history of the bank and national finances. Boasting various interactive systems and a computer-driven simulation of dealing, it makes a potentially dry subject come to life (especially when you come face to face with a stack of gold bars).

Clockmakers' Company Museum

The Clockroom, Guildhall Library, Aldermanbury, EC2 (Guildhall Library 7332 1868/Clockmakers' Company 7236 0070/www.clockmakers.org). Mansion House or St Paul's tube/Bank tube/ DLR/Moorgate tube/rail. **Open** call to check. **Admission** free. **Map** p404 P6.

The Clockmakers' Collection, which was begun in 1814 and is the oldest collection of clocks and watches in the world, was due to reopen as we went to press, after restoration work fell behind schedule. When it does, you'll be able to see more than 600 English and European watches, 30 clocks and 15 marine timekeepers, together with a number of rare horological portraits. Items of interest include a silver deck watch by Thomas Earnshaw (used by Captain George Vancouver in the discovery of the island that bears his name) and the 18th-century marine timekeeper made by John Harrison that enabled ships at sea to establish their exact position. Also on display is the watch that Sir Edmund Hillary wore when he conquered Mount Everest in 1953.

Guildhall

Gresham Street, EC2 (7606 3030/tours ext 1463/ www.corpoflondon.gov.uk). Bank tube/DLR. **Open** *May-Sept* 9.30am-5pm daily. *Oct-Apr* 9.30am-5pm Mon-Sat. Last entry 4.30pm. *Tours by arrangement; groups of 10 or more people only.* **Admission** free. **Map** p404 P6.

Guildhall has been the centre of the City's local government for more than 800 years. The stunning Great Hall fell foul of both the Great Fire and the Blitz but has been tastefully restored: banners and shields of the 100 livery companies adorn the walls and on the windows every Lord Mayor since 1189 gets a namecheck. There are also monuments to Churchill, Nelson, Wellington and the two Pitts, and legendary giants Gog and Magog dominate the walls guarding the West Gallery. Meetings of the Court of Common Council (the governing body for the Corporation of London, presided over by the Lord Mayor) take place here once a month on Thursdays at 1pm, except during August, and banquets and ceremonial events are held here too. The building alongside houses Corporation offices, the Guildhall Library and the Clockmakers' Company Museum (*see above*).

Guildhall Art Gallery

Guildhall Yard, off Gresham Street, EC2 (7332 3700/www.guildhall-art-gallery.org.uk). Mansion House or St Paul's tube/Bank tube/DLR/Moorgate tube/rail. **Open** 10am-5pm Mon-Sat (last entry 4.30pm); noon-4pm Sun (last entry 3.45pm). **Admission** £2.50; £1 concessions; free under-16s. Free to all after 3.30pm daily, all day Fri. **Credit** *over £5* MC, V. **Map** p404 P6.

The Corporation of London owns anything up to 4,000 paintings, but only 250 can be displayed at any one time. Part of the space at the Guildhall Art Gallery – enjoying a new lease of life having been closed from World War II until 1999 – is given over to rolling exhibitions in order to get some of the more obscure works before the public, though a large number of works can also be accessed via terminals throughout the building, and the website contains a

St Olave Hart Street. *See p92.*

Sightseeing

whopping 20,000 images from the collection too. The eclectic collection leans more towards historical than artistic importance.

St Mary Woolnoth

Lombard Street, EC3 (7626 9701). Bank tube/DLR. **Open** 9.30am-4.30pm Mon-Fri. **Admission** free; donations appreciated. **Map** p405 Q6.

Wulnoth, a Saxon noble, is believed to have founded this church on the site of a Roman temple to Concord. It was rebuilt many times, most recently by Hawksmoor in 1716-17, and its tiny but beautifully proportioned interior, based on the Egyptian Hall of Vitruvius, is one of the architect's finest. Edward Lloyd, in whose coffee shop Lloyd's of London was founded, was buried here in 1713. When Bank station was built between 1897 and 1900, the church was undermined, the dead removed from the vaults and lift shafts sunk directly beneath the building.

Temple of Mithras

On the raised courtyard in front of Sumitomo Bank/ Legal & General Building, Temple Court, 11 Queen Victoria Street, EC4. Mansion House tube. **Open** 24hrs daily. **Admission** free. **Map** p404 P6.

In the third century AD, the rival cults of Mithraism and Christianity were battling for supremacy. The worship of the macho Persian god Mithras appealed particularly to Roman soldiers, and the troops on the British frontier built the small temple to their champion near this spot (cAD 240-50). The reconstructed foundations aren't much to look at, but show the Roman influence on the later design of churches: rounded apse, central nave and side aisles.

Around the Tower of London

Tower Hill tube.

Though the medieval fortress of the **Tower of London** (*see p94*) is among the top five most popular tourist attractions in London, there's more to consider here than the Beefeaters and the ravens, or Sir Walter Raleigh's prison. Outside Tower Hill tube station in Wakefield Gardens you'll find part of London's **Roman wall**; though medieval brickies added several feet, it's worth a look. In fact, you can follow the course of the wall from the Tower to the **Museum of London** (*see p94*), a matter of just under two miles (three kilometres).

For those a little tired of the obvious tourist haunts – **Tower Bridge** is nearby; *see p94* – an insight into the life Samuel Pepys can be found in Seething Lane. The diarist lived here – there's a bust of him in Seething Lane Gardens – and the church where he is buried, **St Olave Hart Street** (nicknamed by Dickens 'St Ghastly Grim' on account of the leering skulls at the entrance to the cemetery) is here too. Pepys watched his beloved London burn in 1666 from **All Hallows by the Tower** (*see p93*) at the bottom of Seething Lane.

Between here and London Bridge stand two reminders of London's great days as a port: the early 19th-century **Custom House**, with a façade by Robert Smirke, and, next door, the former **Billingsgate Market** (*see p93* **Whatever happened to?**).

The lanes behind the waterfront are a rewarding hunting ground for church-spotters. **St Magnus the Martyr**, **St Mary at Hill**, **St Margaret Pattens** and **St Dunstan in the East** are all within a couple of minutes' walk of each other. The gardens of the latter are a wonderfully lush haven in which to relax after struggling to the top of the **Monument** (*see p94*). In nearby Pudding Lane, in the early hours of 2 September 1666, a fire started in a bakery that was to blaze for three days, destroying four-fifths of medieval London. Although, remarkably, only half a dozen people are thought to have died, more than 13,000 houses, 87 churches and 44 livery halls were reduced to ashes. The Lord Mayor, woken soon after the fire started, lived to regret his immediate dismissal of the danger with the words, 'Pish! A woman might piss it out.' Thankfully, the fire put paid to the City's brown rats, carriers of the Great Plague, which had wiped out 100,000 of the capital's population the previous year.

Just north-east of Monument is one of the City's most delightful surprises: **Leadenhall Market**. 'Foreigners' – meaning anyone from outside London – were allowed to sell poultry here (and, later, cheese and butter) from the 14th century. The current arcaded buildings, painted in green, maroon and cream with wonderful decorative detail, are the work of Horace Jones (architect also of Smithfield Market and Tower Bridge). Today Leadenhall remains a great place to wander, particularly around lunchtime. Reassuringly, the fresh produce stalls haven't actually been displaced – there are still fabulous cheesemongers, butchers and fishmongers here, along with restaurants and cafés. You can still see the old meat hooks lining the present-day shopfronts.

Between Leadenhall and Liverpool Street rail station there are more churches: **St Helen Bishopsgate**, off Bishopsgate (*see p94*), **St Andrew Undershaft** on St Mary Axe, **St Botolph Aldgate** (*see p94*) and **St Katharine Cree** on Leadenhall Street. The latter, one of few churches built in England during the years preceding the Civil War, is an extraordinary hybrid of classical and Gothic styles.

Near here is the oldest synagogue in the country, the superbly preserved **Bevis Marks Synagogue**, located in a courtyard off Bevis Marks; it was built in 1701 by Sephardic Jews who had managed to escape from the Inquisition in Portugal and Spain (*see p29*). This area suffered considerable damage from the IRA bombs of April 1992 and April 1993. A great deal of restoration work has been undertaken, though the tiny pre-Fire church of **St Ethelburga-the-Virgin** (built 1390) on Bishopsgate was devastated (*see p86*, **Who he? Sir Christopher Wren**).

All Hallows by the Tower

Byward Street, EC3 (7481 2928/ www.allhallowsbythetower.org.uk). Tower Hill tube.
Open *Church* 9am-5.45pm Mon-Fri; 10am-5pm Sat, Sun. **Admission** free; donations appreciated. **Audio tour** (includes admission to Undercroft Museum) suggested donation £2.50. **Map** p405 R7.
All Hallows survived the Great Fire only to be all but destroyed by Luftwaffe bombs in 1940. Though just the walls and 17th-century brick tower were left standing, post-war rebuilding has created a pleasingly light interior. A Saxon arch testifies to the church's ancient roots (seventh century). Other interesting relics include Saxon crosses, a Roman tessellated pavement, Tudor monuments, sword-rests and brasses, a superb carved limewood font cover (1682) by Grinling Gibbons, and a collection of model ships. This is a working church, so visitors should make allowances for services.

Whatever happened to?
Billingsgate fish market

For many centuries, Billingsgate market was famed for two things: the landing of fish and the foul language of its porters. Situated on the north bank of the Thames and named after a river gate in the old city wall, it officially dates back to 1698, when an Act of Parliament established a market here, but fish trading in the area may actually go back as far as 2,000 years – the Romans used a site just north and east of where London Bridge now stands for loading and unloading river-borne cargo.

In 1875 the market was moved from the waterfront to a stunning arcaded hall built by Sir Horace Jones, City Architect to the Corporation of London, but in spite of the golden fish on the top of the weathervanes (*pictured*), the building you can still see today at 16 Lower Thames Street no longer serves as the fish market, which moved to a renovated warehouse in the West India Docks in 1982. The Billingsgate bell was taken to the new market, but the clock in the centre is a fibreglass copy of the original. Though it caters mainly to hotels, restaurants and wholesalers, selling some 200 tons a day of every type of fish and seafood from herring to Caribbean parrot fish, the market is also open to the public (Trafalgar Way, E14; 7987 1118, 5-8.30am Tue-Sat).

As for the old market building, a Grade II-listed structure, that was lovingly refurbished in 1986 to plans by architect Sir Richard Rogers with the intention of providing a stunning office space for a financial institution (the cathedral-like market hall on the ground floor was converted into a dealing floor). Leased by Citibank but never occupied by them, it was finally purchased by an overseas investor in July 2001 and a new tenant is being sought for those with a cool £3.3 million a year to spare. With recession in the air, though, it looks as if this lovely building might remain unused for some time to come.

Fishmongers' Hall

London Bridge, EC4 (7626 3531/www.fishhall.co.uk).
London Bridge tube/rail. **Open** guided tour only; by
prior arrangement. **Admission** free; donations
appreciated. Charge for refreshments. **Map** p405 Q7.
The most interesting of the remaining City guilds
or livery companies (the union HQ of once-powerful
trades that no longer exist), this 18th-century hall
displays, amid a jumble of precious loot, the 12-inch
dagger used by fishmonger-mayor William
Walworth to stab Wat Tyler in the back and put
down the Peasants' Revolt of 1381.

St Botolph Aldgate

Aldgate, EC3 (7283 1670). Aldgate tube. **Open**
10am-3.30pm Mon-Fri; 9am-1pm Sun. **Admission**
free; donations appreciated. **Map** p405 R6.
The original St Botolph, built by the City's
east gate, may date back to the tenth century. The
galleried interior of the current plain brick, stone-
dressed structure (built by George Dance in 1744) is
notable for John Francis Bentley's weird if highly
original ceiling, lined with angels. Daniel Defoe was
married here in 1683.

St Helen Bishopsgate

Great St Helen's, EC3 (7283 2231/www.st-helens.
org.uk). Bank tube/DLR/Liverpool Street tube/rail.
Open 9am-5pm Mon-Fri; services only Sat, Sun.
Admission free. **Map** p405 R6.
Another survivor of the Great Fire and the Blitz,
St Helen's was badly damaged by the 1992 and
1993 IRA bombs in the City. Founded in the 13th
century, the spacious building incorporates 15th-
century Gothic arches and a 14th-century nuns'
chapel. The unusual double nave demonstrates that
this used to be two churches side by side, one
belonging to a Benedictine nunnery. St Helen's is
known as the 'Westminster Abbey of the City'
because of its splendid collection of medieval and
Tudor monuments to City dignitaries. **St Andrew
Undershaft**, nearby, and **St Olave's**, on Hart
Street, are also pre-Fire churches.

The Monument

*Monument Street, EC3 (7626 2717). Monument
tube.* **Open** 10am-5.40pm daily. **Admission** £1.50;
50p 5-15s; free under-5s. **No credit cards**.
Map p405 Q7.
The Monument is a simple Doric column, the dream-
child of Christopher Wren and Robert Hooke. Built
to commemorate London's Great Fire, it is 200ft
(61m) tall – the exact distance from the foot of the
column to the site of the bakery on Pudding Lane
where the fire broke out. For a small admission
charge, you can climb to the top; the 311 steps
require a bit of effort but your reward will be a great
view. One side of the monument contains the relief
of Charles II supervising the rebuilding of London;
the carving was done by Caius Cibber in 1672, after
he'd spent some time in jail for debt. His revenge for
that stretch was to perch the king's finger on the pert
nipple of a woman's exposed breast.

Museum of London

*150 London Wall, EC2 (7600 3699/24hr info 7600
0807/www.museumoflondon.org.uk). Barbican or St
Paul's tube/Moorgate tube/rail.* **Open** 10am-5.50pm
Mon-Sat; noon-5.50pm Sun. **Admission** free.
Credit *Shop* AmEx, MC, V. **Map** p402 P5.
The museum devoted to the history of London is,
from the beginning of 2002, undergoing a redevelopment that aims to increase gallery space, improve
access and provide a new building opposite the main
site. Work should last 18 months but the museum will
still be open for business, as it has been since 1976.
Situated on the site of a Roman fort, the museum is
well stocked and provides a thorough look at London
from prehistoric times. The Roman Gallery contains
a fascinating display on the 'Princess of the City' (*see
p154* **Who she?**), including her skeleton, facial portrait and sarcophagus. Scheduled for 2002 is a special
look at 125 years of history from the French
Revolution to the outbreak of World War I, a period
of astonishing social, economic and political change
as London emerged as the leading economic power
in Europe. Also in 2002, the museum's 25th anniversary celebrations will include a re-run of the popular
and spectacular Combat of the Gladiators and a
medieval siege; call the box office for details.

Tower Bridge Experience

*SE1 (7403 3761/www.towerbridge.org.uk). Tower
Hill tube/London Bridge tube/rail.* **Open** *Apr-Oct*
10am-6.30pm daily. *Nov-Mar* 9.30am-6pm daily.
Last entry 1hr 15min before closing. **Admission**
(includes guided tour) £6.25; £4.25 5-15s,
concessions; £18.25 family (2+2); free under-5s.
Credit AmEx, MC, V. **Map** p405 R8.
Horace Jones, the City Corporation architect, was
responsible for this City Gothic triumph of engineering,
which opened in 1894 (Jones died shortly afterwards).
Though now raised electronically, the great steam
engines used for that task until 1976 can still be
seen. The Tower Bridge Experience offers tons of
facts, entertaining displays and eye-catching anima-
tronics, including one of Horace himself. There are
also some marvellous panoramic views. If you like it
that much, you can hire parts of it out for functions;
a four-hour party in the elevated walkways, for
example, will set you back £2,500.

Tower of London

*Tower Hill, EC3 (7709 0765/www.hrp.org.uk).
Tower Hill tube/Fenchurch Street rail.* **Open**
Mar-Oct 9am-5pm Mon-Sat; 10am-5pm Sun.
Nov-Feb 10am-4pm Mon, Sun; 9am-4pm Tue-Sat.
Tours Beefeater tours (outside only, weather
permitting) free; half-hourly 9.25am-2.50pm daily.
Short talks given by yeoman warder (40min) free;
advance tickets from kiosk outside Lanthorn
Tower 3 times a day. **Admission** £11.30; £8.50
concessions; £7.50 5-15s; family £34 (2+3); free
under-5s. **Audio guides** £3. **Credit** AmEx, MC, V.
Map p405 R7.
Londoners are used to the grisly adverts on the tube
walls for this most melodramatic of tourist attractions. If those adverts are to be believed, life at the

tower when it was being used to imprison treasonous scum must have been as grim as it gets. You wouldn't be able to get through a day without some axe-happy executioner doling out the best cure for a sore throat known to man. But that might be a blessed relief when compared to getting stuck in the crowds that gather here: around 2.5 million people visit the Tower each year, so you need to get here early if you want a relatively hassle-free experience. For the bloodthirsty, **Traitor's Gate** and the **Bloody Tower** are a must: torture, murder and execution give a glimpse into what life must have been like in medieval England. The **White Tower** houses some excellent armour, and the **Waterloo Barracks** contains the world-famous **Crown Jewels**, the pick of which must be the Imperial State Crown, set with a 317-carat diamond. The free tours provide a useful introduction.

North of London Wall

Barbican or Moorgate tube/rail.

Running close to Liverpool Street Station, **London Wall** follows the northerly course of the old Roman fortifications. Part of the wall, and the remains of one of the gates into the Cripplegate Roman fort, can be seen in **St Alfage Gardens**. The area just to the north of here was levelled during the Blitz. Rather than encourage office developments, the City of London and London County Council purchased a large site in 1958 to build 'a genuine residential neighbourhood, with schools, shops, open spaces and amenities'. Unfortunately, we ended up with the **Barbican**.

In the brave new post-war world, it must have looked great on paper. This was how we would all live in the future: 6,500 state-of-the-art flats, some in blocks of 40 storeys and more, a huge arts centre with concert halls (home to the London Symphony Orchestra), a theatre (London base of the Royal Shakespeare Company), a cinema, art gallery, exhibition space, cafés and restaurants. The complex also incorporates one of the city's best museums, the **Museum of London** (*see p94*), and the **Barbican Art Gallery** (*see below*).

Frustratingly – especially considering the immense cost of the Barbican – the ideas behind it were already out of date by the time it was completed in the early 1980s. Granted, occupancy rates are high (there is little choice of residence if you want to live in the City) and the events programmes at the arts centre are usually first rate. It's just that, try as hard as you can to like the place, it doesn't seem to have any warmth or community feel.

Marooned amid the towering blocks is the only pre-war building in the vicinity – the heavily restored 16th-century church of

St Giles, where Oliver Cromwell was married and John Milton buried. The Nonconformist connection continues further north-east: **Bunhill Fields** was set aside as a cemetery during the Great Plague, though it doesn't appear to have been used at that time. Instead, because the ground was apparently never consecrated, the cemetery became popular for Nonconformist burials, gaining the name of 'the cemetery of Puritan England'. Much of the graveyard is cordoned off these days, but it's still possible to for visitors to stroll through it and take a look at the monuments to John Bunyan, Daniel Defoe and William Blake, that most unconformist of Nonconformists.

Opposite Bunhill Fields on City Road is the **Museum of Methodism** and **John Wesley's House** (*see below*). The founder of Methodism lived his last years in the Georgian house; upstairs, in 1951, Denis Thatcher married Margaret Hilda Roberts.

Barbican Art Gallery

Level 3, Barbican Centre, Silk Street, EC2 (box office 7638 8891/enquiries 7382 7105/ www.barbican.org.uk). Barbican tube/Moorgate tube/rail. **Open** 10am-6pm Mon, Tue, Thur-Sat; 10am-8pm Wed; noon-6pm Sun. **Admission** £7; £5 concessions. **Credit** AmEx, MC, V. **Map** p402 P5.
It's one thing getting to the Barbican complex – finding your way to the arts centre is something else altogether. You can try to follow the signs (there are even yellow lines on the ground to guide you), but it's probably best to ask a passer-by if you've never been here before. That said, excellent exhibitions are guaranteed for the most intrepid of EC2's explorers. One of the gallery's more populist ventures for 2002, and one that is certain to be a hit with both little kids and big kids, is 'Game On' (15 May-16 Sept), which the Barbican Art Gallery claims will be the world's largest ever gaming exhibition. There'll be the opportunity to play the best vintage games, to challenge other players in a networked area and to sample the latest 'in-development' classics of tomorrow. *Donkey Kong*, anyone?

Museum of Methodism & John Wesley's House

Wesley's Chapel, 49 City Road, Finsbury, EC1 (7253 2262). Moorgate or Old Street tube/rail. **Open** 10am-4pm Mon-Sat. *Tours* free; ad hoc arrangements on arrival. **Admission** £4; £2 concessions, under-16s; additional visits free within same month. **No credit cards. Map** p403 Q4.
John Wesley opened this chapel for worship in 1778, and in 1981 a museum of his work opened in the crypt. Highlights include the pulpit and a large oil portrait of the scene at his deathbed. His house next door has been restored to its original Georgian interior design. In the kitchen and study you can see his nightcap, preaching gown and personal experimental electric-shock machine.

Holborn & Clerkenwell

Go east for history in spades, as well as world-class nightlife.

Holborn

Maps p399 & p401

Holborn tube.

First referred to as 'Holeburnstreete' in 1249 and named after the Holebourne river, a tributary of the now-vanished Fleet, Holborn (pronounced Hó-bun) was initially a major goods route into the City. Today, though it takes something from each of its neighbouring districts (the money-mad City, commercial Covent Garden and learned Bloomsbury), it derives most of its atmosphere from the four surviving Inns of Court, which were situated here to symbolise the law's role as mediator in the historical battle for power between the City and royal Westminster.

In the Inns of Court, members of the legal profession wander safely out of touch with reality, bewigged but serious. Amble around **Lincoln's Inn** and **Gray's Inn**, and sample the joys of passing 'by unexpected ways, into its unexpected avenues, into its magnificent ample squares, its classic green recesses', as essayist Charles Lamb put it at the end of the 18th century. The alleys and open spaces of the Inns remain a haven from the fumes of central London, but most of the buildings are open by appointment only (some just for group tours).

Around Aldwych

The western flank of modern Holborn is formed by the car-filled conduit of **Kingsway**, carved out of slum-lined streets in the early 1900s in an attempt to relieve traffic congestion, and culminating in the crescent of **Aldwych**. The handsome Meridien Waldorf hotel, built here soon afterwards, and One Aldwych, one of London's most stylish hotels (*see p46*), face a trio of unashamedly imperial buildings: India House, Australia House and Bush House, once intended to be a huge trade centre and now home to the BBC's much-loved World Service.

Between here and the Thames lies **King's College**, its hideous 1960s buildings sitting uncomfortably with Robert Smirke's graceful 1829-31 originals. Infinitely easier on the eye is William Chambers' grandiose late 18th-century **Somerset House** (*see p97*), beautifully restored and now open again to the public and home to the **Courtauld Gallery**, the **Gilbert Collection** and the **Hermitage Rooms**.

The courtyard at **Somerset House**. *See p97.*

Two nearby curiosities are worth a glance. On **Temple Place** is one of a handful of still-functioning cabmen's shelters. These green-painted sheds are a legacy of the Cabmen's Shelter Fund, set up in 1874 to provide cabbies with an alternative to pubs in which to hide from the elements and get a hot meal and (non-alcoholic) drink. And around the corner on **Strand Lane** is a 'Roman' bath. Opening times are 10am-12.30pm Mon-Fri, but the interior can also be viewed through a window.

Back on the Strand are the churches of St Mary-le-Strand (James Gibbs' first public building; built 1714-17) and St Clement Danes (*see p97*). Samuel Johnson was a regular and 'solemnly devout' member of the congregation at the latter. Just north of here loom the suitably imposing neo-Gothic **Royal Courts of Justice** (*see p97*), opened in 1882 by Queen Victoria. The stress of the commission was such that the architect GE Street's crowning achievement brought him to an early grave.

The fearsome bronze griffin in the middle of the road near here marks the site of **Temple Bar** and the official boundary of the City, past which the Queen cannot stray without the Lord Mayor's permission. Just beyond is the church of **St Dunstan in the West** (*see p98*) and the 17th-century **Prince Henry's Room** (*see p97*), while just south of the Strand – and located just inside the borders of the City – are **Middle Temple** (Middle Temple Lane, EC4; call 7427 4800 for opening hours) and **Inner Temple** (Inner Temple Treasury Office, EC4; group tours of the hall, mornings only, costing £10, can be booked on 7797 8241). Built around a maze of courtyards and passageways, they're especially atmospheric when gaslit after dark.

Somerset House

Strand, WC2 (7845 4600/www.somerset-house.org.uk).
Covent Garden or Temple tube (closed Sun). **Open**
10am-6pm daily; extended opening hours for courtyard
& terrace. **Tours** phone for details. **Admission**
Courtyard & terrace free. Charge for exhibitions.
Credit *Shop* MC, V. **Map** p401 M7.

Closed to the public for almost a century, this grand
edifice was the subject of a stunning millennial
makeover. Originally a Tudor palace built by Edward
Seymour, the first Duke of Somerset and brother of
Henry VIII's third wife Jane, and later a royal and
ambassadorial residence and focus of society events,
Somerset House was demolished under King George
III, who approved the construction of William
Chambers' neo-classical design. The new building,
which took a quarter century to complete, became
home to the Navy Board, to seats of learning such as
the Royal Academy of the Arts and, eventually, to the
Inland Revenue and the Register of Births, Marriages
and Deaths. These days, the Inland Revenue remains
in the East and West wings, but the **Courtauld
Gallery**, **Gilbert Collection** and **Hermitage
Rooms** (*see below*) take up the rest. There's also a
very fine restaurant (the Admiralty; *see p200*), a café,
a river terrace, a good shop and the breathtaking
courtyard with its glorious dancing water jets and
programme of open-air events (call for details).

Courtauld Gallery

Somerset House, Strand, WC2 (7848 2526/
www.courtauld.ac.uk). **Open** 10am-6pm daily (last
entry 5.15pm), *31 Dec* 10am-4pm, *1 Jan* noon-6pm.
Tours phone for details. **Admission** £4; £3
concessions; free under-18s. Free to all 10am-2pm Mon
(not bank hols). *Annual ticket* £10. **Credit** MC, V.

Housed in the superb 18th-century **Somerset
House** (*see above*), the Courtauld represents the sum
of several donated private collections. At its heart
are the paintings of textile magnate Samuel
Courtauld, which account for the bulk of the
Impressionist and post-Impressionist works and
include the likes of Manet's *A Bar at the Folies-
Bergère*, Cézanne's *The Card Players* and Gauguin's
Nevermore. This collection was augmented largely
by Count Antoine Seilern, who gave the institute a
wealth of 14th- to 20th-century paintings, resulting
in a roomful of Rubens and a group of wonderful
early Flemish and Italian paintings.

Gilbert Collection

Somerset House, Strand, WC2 (7240 4080/
www.gilbert-collection.org.uk). **Open** 10am-6pm daily
(last entry 5.15pm), *31 Dec* 10am-4pm, *1 Jan* noon-
6pm. **Tours** phone for details. **Admission** £5; £4
concessions; free students, under-18s. Free to all after
4.30pm daily. *Annual ticket* £10. **Credit** MC, V.

London's newest museum of decorative arts is made
up of the more than 800 items that constituted the
three-pronged collection of London-born real estate
tycoon and humanitarian Sir Arthur Gilbert. Housed
in the restored, vaulted spaces are a fabulous array
of ornate gold snuff boxes, European silverware and
Italian mosaics and micromosaics.

Hermitage Rooms

Somerset House, Strand, WC2 (info 7845 4630/
Ticketmaster 7413 3398/www.hermitagerooms.co.uk).
Open 10am-6pm daily (last admission 5.15pm), *31*
Dec 10am-4pm, *1 Jan* noon-6pm. **Admission** £6; £4
concessions. **Credit** MC, V.

Open since late 2000, the Hermitage Rooms host
rotating exhibitions from the world-famous State
Hermitage Museum in St Petersburg. New exhibitions arrive every six to ten months; until 3 March
2002 French Drawings and Paintings from the
Hermitage – Poussin to Picasso shows how drawing
served both as a preparation for a painting and as an
artform in its own right for artists such as Claude,
Watteau, Greuze, Ingres, Degas, Manet, Matisse and
Picasso. For each ticket sold, £1 goes to the underfunded State Hermitage.

Prince Henry's Room

17 Fleet Street, EC4 (7936 4004). Temple tube
(closed Sun). **Open** 11am-2pm Mon-Sat. **Admission**
free; donations appreciated. **Map** p404 N6.

The oldest son of King James I of England and VI
of Scotland, Henry was just 14 when he became
Prince of Wales in 1610, the same year the house
containing this beautiful oak-panelled room,
believed to have been used by the prince's lawyers,
was built. Its magnificent plaster ceiling has the
Prince of Wales' feathers at its centre, together with
the initials PH. Henry died of typhoid at the age of
18, leaving his brother to succeed to the throne as
Charles I and eventually have his head chopped off
after a quarrel with Parliament.

The rest of the building was the Prince's Arms, a
tavern frequented by Pepys. Some of the items the
diarist left behind there, including a letter he wrote,
some framed pictures and a quill pen, are on display.

Royal Courts of Justice

Strand, WC2 (7947 6000/www.open.gov.uk).
Temple tube (closed Sun). **Open** 9.30am-1pm,
2-4.30pm Mon-Fri. No court cases during Aug
& Sept recess. **Admission** free. **Map** p399 M6.

On the premise that justice must both be done and
be *seen* to be done, anyone is free to take a pew at the
back of any of the 88 courts in this splendid Gothic
building, where the High Court presides over the
most serious civil trials in the country. Spectators can
come and go as they please, though judges don't take
too kindly to interruptions when they're passing
judgment, or when witnesses are taking oaths. Lists
in the central hall bear the names of the parties in the
cases being heard but don't give information about
the proceedings or what stage they've reached; try
asking the black-robed court ushers. No cameras or
mobile phones, and under-14s are not admitted.

St Clement Danes

Strand, WC2 (7242 8282). Temple tube (closed
Sun)/Blackfriars tube/rail. **Open** 9am-4pm Mon-Fri;
9am-3pm Sat, Sun. **Map** p399 M6.

Though almost certainly not the church that gave
rise to the nursery rhyme 'Oranges and lemons
say the bells of St Clements' (that was probably

A novel approach

If a visit to Dickens' house in Bloomsbury (*see p103*) leaves you keen to know more, you may like to take a mini-pilgrimage around some of the streets that inspired the great writer.

Walk south from the museum and along John Street, turning right into Theobalds Road. At Harpur Street make a brief detour to Dombey Street to see the road that gave Dickens the name for the main character in *Dombey and Son* (1848). Returning to Theobalds Road, walk east to Gray's Inn, where Dickens worked as a solicitor's clerk after leaving school and where Mr Pickwick's junior counsel, Mr Phunky, had his chambers.

Walk south to High Holborn, turning left into Great Turnstile, which brings you to **Lincoln's Inn Fields**, the setting for much of *Bleak House* (1853). On a guided tour of Lincoln's Inn's Old Hall and Great Hall (7405 1393), you can see how little has changed since Dickens' ferocious attack on the legal system.

Just south of the defunct Inns of Court, at 13 Portsmouth Street, is the **Old Curiosity Shop**, the supposed – though this is much disputed – inspiration behind the 1841 novel

of the same name. Dating from about 1567, it sells clothes, bags, shoes and homewares, many of them made by its Japanese owners. The constant closed sign is there to deter Dickens junkies from inundating the place.

Continue south via Sheffield Street, St Clements Lane and Houghton Street to reach Aldwych, then cut through Melbourne Place to reach Surrey Street on the other side of the Strand. From here an alley leads to the **'Roman' bath** (*see p96*) where David Copperfield took many a cold plunge.

Coming back on to the Strand, continue east, then turn right into Middle Temple Lane. **Middle Temple** is probably the best-preserved of the Inns of Court, which were familiar to Dickens from his boyhood. Even today, it is still much as it was described in *Barnaby Rudge* (1841): 'There is yet a drowsiness in its courts, and a dreamy dullness in its trees and gardens; those who pace its lanes and squares may yet hear the echoes of their footsteps on the sounding stones, and read upon its gates, in passing from the tumult of the Strand or Fleet Street, "Who enters here

St Clement Eastcheap), this Wren-designed church behaves as if it were – its bells ring out the tune three times a day (9am, noon and 3pm), and an annual Oranges and Lemons service is held for children at a local primary school. The church's name may date back to the time of Alfred the Great, when it was thought to have been used by Danes married to English women who were allowed to stay in England after their fellow countrymen were expelled. In 1941 the church burnt down in one of the last of the German air raids and in the 1950s it was restored as a memorial to allied airmen; these days it's the central church of the RAF. Outside there's a controversial statue of Arthur Harris (who is famous for the bombing of Dresden), and from time to time the bells play the *RAF March Past* and the *Dambusters' March*.

St Dunstan in the West

186A Fleet Street, EC4 (7242 6027). Chancery Lane tube. **Open** 10am-2pm Tue; 5-8pm Fri; 2-6pm Sat; 9am-2pm Sun; occasional concerts on Fri. **Admission** free; donations appreciated. **Map** p404 N6.
St Dunstan in the West was first mentioned in 1185, but the present early Gothic-revival building dates from 1831-3, when a widening of Fleet Street required a slight shift northwards. John Donne was rector here (1624-31); Izaak Walton (whose *Compleat*

Angler was published in the churchyard in 1653) held the posts of 'scavenger, questman and sidesman' (1629-44); and in 1667 a lecherous Pepys popped in to hear a sermon and unsuccessfully try to fondle a local girl ('… at last I could perceive her to take pins out of her pocket to prick me if I should touch her again'). A second girl suffered him to hold her hand 'and then withdrew'.

Around Lincoln's Inn Fields

The winding streets to the west of the courts bear the names of several of the now-defunct Inns of Chancery, such as **New Inn** and **Clement's Inn**, and are home to the one-time cradle of left-wing agitation, the LSE (London School of Economics). The broad expanse of **Lincoln's Inn Fields** is London's largest square and Holborn's focal point. On the north side of the square is **Sir John Soane's Museum** (*see p99*), and on the south side are the various **Museums of the Royal College of Surgeons** (7869 6560) with their anatomical and pathological specimens, including the skeleton of the 'Irish Giant' and the Waterloo teeth extracted from corpses on the field of battle to replace those lost by the

leaves noise behind".' It's also in Middle Temple, at Fountain Court, that Ruth Pinch meets her brother in *Martin Chuzzlewit* (1843).

Walk back up Middle Temple Lane and turn right into Fleet Street; **St Dunstan in the West** (*see p98*) will appear on your right. Dickens mentions the clock of the original church in *Barnaby Rudge*. Further along Fleet Street, on the left, is Johnson's Court, where he delivered his first published story, 'A Dinner at Poplar Walk', to the *Monthly Magazine* offices.

Wind your way up to Fetter Lane via Pemberton Row and West Harding Street and continue north. On your left you'll come to the former **Barnard's Inn**. By Dickens' day the Inn had fallen into disrepair; in *Great Expectations* (1861) he has Pip arrive at the 'dingiest collection of shabby buildings ever squeezed together in a rank corner as a club for tom cats' and live there with Herbert Pocket.

Across the road, the Prudential Assurance Company on Furnival Street marks the site of **Furnival's Inn**, a building that replaced the defunct Inn but retained its name, where Dickens started married life. Tommy Traddles lodged here in *David Copperfield* (1850). The Prudential building has a wall plaque commemorating the novelist and a bust of him in the courtyard.

Next to Furnival Street is **Staple Inn**. The stone arch beneath the 16th-century houses that conceals it leads to the nook described in *Edwin Drood* (1870) as 'one of those nooks which are legal nooks; and it contains a little Hall [...] to what obstructive purposes devoted, and at whose expense, this history knoweth not.' You can still see this 'little Hall', though it's not officially open to the public.

Cross Holborn into Brooke Street, then turn right into Greville Street. It's off here, in Bleeding Heart Yard, that Arthur Clennam became a partner in the firm of Doyce & Clennam in *Little Dorritt* (1857). Off the yard, in Ely Place, David Copperfield meets Agnes Wakefield. Coming back into Greville Street, turn right to reach Saffron Hill, the vice-sodden rookeries of which were depicted in *Oliver Twist* (1837).

For more city walks, see *Time Out Book of London Walks*, volumes 1 and 2.

living (sadly, the museums are closed from January 2002 to the end of 2003). To the east are the daunting buildings of the Inn itself.

Chancery Lane, running from the Strand to High Holborn, is home to the Public Records Office and the Law Society. At its northern end are the subterranean shops of the London Silver Vaults (7242 3844), selling everything from silver spoons to antique clocks. Around the corner, towards Holborn Circus, teeter the overhanging, half-timbered Tudor buildings of **Staple Inn**, one of the former Inns of Chancery. Across the road, by the ancient Cittie of Yorke pub, is an alley leading into the most northerly of the Inns of Court, **Gray's Inn**. The last Inn to be founded (in 1569), its Hall – group tours of which can be arranged on 7458 7800 (10am-4pm Mon-Fri) – contains a superb screen, said to be made from the wood of a galley from the Spanish Armada.

Sir John Soane's Museum

13 Lincoln's Inn Fields, WC2 (7405 2107/ www.soane.org). Holborn tube. **Open** 10am-5pm Tue-Sat; 6-9pm 1st Tue of mth. **Admission** free; donations appreciated. **Guided tours** 2.30pm Sat (£3; free concessions). **Map** p399 M5.

This eccentric but enchanting collection amassed by Sir John Soane is displayed in the house in which he lived, and the rooms remain almost exactly as they were on the day of the architect's death in 1837. Among the treasures are Cantonese chairs, ancient vases and works of art (a wall covered by Hogarth's *Rake's Progress* series opens up to reveal a stash of Piranesi drawings). The house itself, with its rooms within rooms, hidden stairways, and statues lurking in the shadows, has a feeling of mystery and magic, especially on the first Tuesday of the month, when it's lit by candles. Most spooky of all is the crypt, containing the 3,300-year-old sarcophagus of Egyptian pharaoh Seti I (Soane celebrated its purchase with a party for almost 1,000 guests and lit the burial casket from within), and a mock-Gothic 'monk's parlour' complete with human skull.

Tickets for the excellent guided tours go on sale at 2pm in the library dining room, on a first-come first-served basis. The rest of the time entry is free, but give generously as the museum is planning to extend into the house next door, which was also owned by Soane (restoration should begin in 2003).

Clerkenwell & Farringdon

Map p402

Chancery Lane or Farringdon tube.

The cosy little neighbourhood of **Clerkenwell**, which lies north and east of Holborn, has its origins in a hamlet that grew up in the 12th

Sir John Soane's Museum. *See p99.*

century around the religious foundations of the Priory of St John of Jerusalem, the long-gone St Mary's Nunnery and, from the 14th century, the Carthusian monastery of Charterhouse (now a posh OAP home). The original Clerk's Well, first mentioned in 1174 and long thought lost, was rediscovered in 1924, and can now be viewed through the window of 14-16 Farringdon Lane.

Over the centuries, a strong crafts tradition grew up in Clerkenwell, as French Huguenots and other immigrants settled to practise their trades away from the City guilds. The area was thought 'an esteemed situation for gentry' until the early 19th century, when population pressure and increasing dilapidation led to an influx of Irish, then Italian, immigrants. (Evidence of the once 10,000-strong Italian community can still be seen in St Peter's Italian Church, on Clerkenwell Road, and L Terroni & Sons, the excellent deli next door.) Radicals were also attracted; Lenin edited 17 editions of the Bolshevik paper *Iskra* from a back room (which has been preserved) in the Marx Memorial Library at 37A Clerkenwell Green. By the late 19th century the district had become a 'decidedly unsavoury and unattractive locality': prime Dickens territory (*see p98* **A novel approach**).

The fascinating enclave of **Ely Place** was once the site of the Bishop of Ely's London palace; all that remains is the delightful church of **St Etheldreda** (*see below*). The private, gated road, now lined by Georgian houses, is crown property and remains outside the jurisdiction of the City of London. Pub lovers shouldn't miss the Olde Mitre Tavern, on this site since 1546, secreted up a narrow alley off Ely Place. West of here, the long-established, no-nonsense **Leather Lane Market** sells clothes, food and pirate videos, and supports a number of cheap caffs. Running parallel is the centre of London's diamond trade, **Hatton Garden**, which doubled as a Greenwich Village street in Stanley Kubrick's *Eyes Wide Shut* (*see p290* **On Location: Kubrick's London**).

Astonishingly, it wasn't until the end of the 1980s that property developers wised up to the attractions of an area so close to the City and the West End, and Clerkenwell underwent a property boom. Along with it has come a vast improvement in the area's nightlife, which, ten or 15 years ago, was non-existent. **St John Street** is home to bloodthirsty restaurant St John (No.26; *see p197*) and hip bar Cicada (No.126; *see p219*), while Farringdon Road offers pioneering gastropub the Eagle (No.159; 7837 1353), and Hispanic eaterie Moro (*see p190*) sits nicely in Exmouth Market. Clubbers, too, are well served by the area, with Turnmills (*see p281*) and Fabric (*see p279*) in among a clutch of trendy watering holes, such as Fluid (*see 219*) and Mint (*see p220*). Actual sights are few and far between, though there's a heritage walk run by Citisights (*see p69*) and the the 16th-century **St John's Gate** and **Museum of the Order of St John** (*see below*).

Museum & Library of the Order of St John

St John's Gate, St John's Lane, EC1 (7324 4000/ www.sja.org.uk/history). Farringdon tube/rail. **Open** 9am-5pm Mon-Fri; 10am-4pm Sat. *Guided tours* 11am, 2.30pm Tue, Fri, Sat. **Admission** free; donations requested. **Map** p402 O4.
Now the headquarters of the British Order of St John, this 1504 gateway used to be the entrance to the Priory of St John of Jerusalem, founded in the 12th century. Beside it is a small museum tracing the history of the Order from the days of the crusading Knights Hospitallers to the more mundane but more useful work of today's St John Ambulance Brigade. Displays relating to the latter include examples of early ambulances, a Victorian nurse's mini-first aid kit, ceremonial attire, medals, trophies and certificates, and personal memorabilia such as the written reactions of one of the first people to enter the newly liberated Belsen camp in 1945. Oral histories cover topics ranging from first aid in the '30s Depression to the work of a welfare officer in the Gulf War.

St Etheldreda

14 Ely Place, EC1 (7405 1061). Chancery Lane tube. **Open** 7.30am-7pm daily. **Admission** free; donations appreciated. **Map** p402 N5.
Britain's oldest Catholic church (built in the 1250s) is the only surviving building of the Bishop of Ely's London residence. The simple chapel, lined with the statues of local martyrs, is London's sole remaining example (excepting parts of Westminster Abbey) of Gothic architecture from the reign of Edward I. Over the last year there's been some restoration to the stonework, and handrails have been fitted up to the top of the church and down to the crypt.

The strawberries once grown in the gardens were said to be the finest in the city (and received plaudits in Shakespeare's *Richard III*); every June the church holds a 'Strawberrie Fayre' in Ely Place. There's a good café serving hot and cold lunches.

Bloomsbury & Fitzrovia

With their artistic history and idiosyncratic attractions,
central London's backstreets have a compelling charm.

Bloomsbury

Map p399

*Chancery Lane, Holborn or Tottenham Court Road
tube/Euston or King's Cross tube/rail.*

Best known for its early 20th-century literary
associations (it was here that Virginia Woolf,
Vanessa Bell et al, aka the Bloomsbury Group,
lived and worked), Bloomsbury today derives
its transient yet genteel atmosphere from its
largely non-residential nature (it's a mixture of
academia, offices and mid-range hotels). Taking
its name from 'Blemondisberi', or 'the manor of
(William) Blemond' (he acquired the area in the
early 13th century), it was mainly rural until the
1660s, when the fourth Earl of Southampton
had Southampton (now **Bloomsbury**) **Square**
built around his house. It was followed by,
among others, Bloomsbury's only surviving
complete Georgian square, **Bedford Square**
(1775-80), and huge **Russell Square**, laid
out in 1800 and in recent years a bit of a
gay cruising spot after dark. It was being

refurbished at the time of writing and is
scheduled to reopen in March 2002, complete
with a new fountain.

Though the area had become residential
by the mid-19th century, it was never a very
fashionable district, which may explain why it
came to be colonised by large institutions such
as the **British Museum** (*see p103*) and the
University of London, whose monolithic 1930s
Senate House tower doubled as the Ministry of
Fear in the film version of Orwell's *1984*. Many
of the buildings in Bloomsbury's fine Georgian
squares contain offshoots of the university,
including the **Percival David Foundation
for Chinese Art** and the **Petrie Museum
of Egyptian Archaeology** (for both, *see
p105*), with its exhumed pot-burial and coiffured
mummy's head with eyebrows and lashes.

But the university's most macabre sight is
the body of philosopher and university co-
founder Jeremy Bentham, displayed in a glass
case (as he requested in his will) in a hallway of
the South Cloister at University College London
(Gower Street). Now clad in Bentham's old

Lamb's Conduit Street has a laid-back appeal. *See p103.*

clothes, stuffed with straw, wool, cotton and moth-repelling lavender and topped with a wax head (the skull is kept in a safe), the body was illegally dissected (only executed murderers could be cut up at the time) at Webb Street School of Anatomy in Borough after Bentham's death in 1832. For years it attended board of governors meetings and it's still wheeled out for the annual Bentham Dinner. There are a few display cases relating to Bentham's career, plus some grim but fascinating photos documenting the creation of his 'auto icon'.

Further east are some of Bloomsbury's most charming corners, including pedestrianised **Woburn Walk** (off Upper Woburn Place), with its bow-windowed shops and cafés, the pioneering housing development of Brunswick Square, which boasts both the **Renoir** cinema (*see p289*) and **Skoob** second-hand bookshop (*see p233*), **Marchmont Street** with its eateries and shops, the pleasant kids' park of **Coram's Fields** (*see p272*), the fine pubs on up-and-coming **Lamb's Conduit Street** (including the Lamb; *see p220*) and **Dickens' House** on Doughty Street (*see below*).

British Museum

Great Russell Street, WC1 (7636 1555/recorded info 7323 8783/disabled info 7637 7384/minicom 7323 8920/www.thebritishmuseum.ac.uk). Holborn, Russell Square or Tottenham Court Road tube. **Open** *Galleries* 10am-5.30pm Mon-Wed, Sat, Sun; 10am-

jeremy Bentham's 'auto icon'. *See p101.*

8.30pm Thur, Fri. *Great Court* 9am-6pm Mon; 9am-9pm Tue, Wed, Sun; 9am-11pm Thur-Sat. *Highlights tours (90min)* 10.30am, 1.30pm, 2.30pm, 3.30pm. *Focus tours (60min)* 11.30am, 12.30pm. **Admission** free; donations appreciated. *Temporary exhibitions* prices vary; phone for details. *Highlights tours* £7; £4 concessions, 11-16s; under-10s free. *Focus tours* £5; £3 concessions, 11-16s; under-10s free. **Map** p399 K5.
The mighty British Museum began life as royal physician Dr Hans Sloane's 'cabinet of curiosities', a miscellany of books, paintings, classical antiquities and stuffed animals that he bequeathed to the nation in 1753. Over the next century, the plunder of empire, including the Elgin Marbles, overwhelmed the storage space, and in 1847 Robert Smirke designed the present impressive neo-classical edifice. Modern-day logistical problems, which stemmed from the presence of the **British Library** (*see p105*) at the heart of the ever-expanding and enormously popular museum, began to be tackled as its 250th anniversary (in 2003) loomed. In 1998, after long delays, the library moved to Euston Road, freeing up 40% of the space. In late 2000 the stunning, glass-roofed **Queen Elizabeth II Great Court**, the largest covered public space in Europe, was unveiled, with cafés and restaurants and longer opening hours than the galleries.
At its centre is the restored **Reading Room**, which is now open to the public (it houses a library dedicated to world civilisation, funded by the late philanthropist publisher Paul Hamlyn, plus a state-of-the art multimedia centre that allows you to tour the facilities and plan your visit). In addition, the space for temporary exhibits was doubled, and in March 2001 the **Sainsbury African Galleries** returned ethnography to the museum after a 30-year absence – this will be completed in 2003 with the opening of the **Wellcome Gallery of Ethnography**. Also due in 2003 is the reopening of the restored **King's Library**, which specialises in the history and evolution of museums, while a new **British Museum Study Centre** is in the pipeline.
Don't try to see everything – you can't. Focus on specific areas of interest with the help of a souvenir guide (£6), try one of the four suggested tours on the £2.50 leaflets, book a 90-minute tour at the information desk (£7) or join a free 'Eye Openers' tour concentrating on one aspect of the collections. Visitors in a real rush should make a beeline for the peat-preserved Lindow Man (Celtic Europe, Room 50), the Sutton Hoo Ship Burial (Middle Ages, Room 41) and the Rosetta Stone (Egyptian Sculpture, Room 4). Temporary exhibitions worth looking out for in 2002 include Unknown Amazon (until April) and Agatha Christie & Archaeology (until March).

Dickens' House

48 Doughty Street, WC1 (7405 2127/ www.dickensmuseum.com). Chancery Lane or Russell Square tube. **Open** 10am-5pm Mon-Sat. *Tours* by arrangement. **Admission** £4; £3 concessions; £2 5-15s; £9 family. *Tours* free. **Credit** *Shop* AmEx, MC, V. **Map** p399 M4.

A little peace of London

Tucked away in deepest Bloomsbury, tranquil Tavistock Square has become, over the past 35 years, an unofficial peace garden and focus for peace-related events. Its curious history began back in 1953, when Pandit Nehru, the first prime minister of India, planted a copper beech to mark his visit to the square after St Pancras Borough Council donated the centre of it for a statue of Mahatma Gandhi. Gandhi had visited the area on more than one occasion to talk to students at the Indian YMCA at the top of Gower Street (now in Fitzroy Square). The statue (*pictured*), created by Polish-born sculptor Fredda Brilliant, was finally unveiled in 1968 by the then PM Harold Wilson, while students took over the square in a non-violent protest against the hypocrisy of the British Government.

The peace theme was reprised by the planting of a cherry tree in memory of the victims of Hiroshima by the Mayor of Camden in 1967. On 6 August each year it becomes a shrine to the victims of the atomic bombs dropped on Japan during World War II, with CND placards and bunches of flowers placed around its base and origami birds hung from its branches.

More than two decades later, in 1986, a field maple was planted in the square by the League of Jewish Women to mark the United Nations International Year of Peace, and in 1994, on International Conscientious Objectors Day, Michael Tippett, the president of the Peace Pledge Union, unveiled a massive piece of 450 million-year-old volcanic slate commemorating the struggle of objectors past and present. Every 15 May it provides a focus for Objectors Day activities Most recently, in 1997, a Friendship Tree (a maidenhair or gingko bilboa) dedicated to the 'poetic genius of WB Yeats' was planted by the High Commissioner for India.

The focal point of the square, the Gandhi statue, is particulary splendid early in the morning, when sticks of burning incense are often placed on it. A candle is kept alight in a glass jar at its base, and some of the orange and yellow chrysanthemums from the surrounding flowerbeds are placed on the great leader's feet. You might even see students from the nearby School of Oriental and Asian Studies (SOAS) practising t'ai chi

on the grass. At other times, peace groups hold readings, demos, meditation and bell-ringing sessions.

The park (7974 1693) is open from 7.30am until dusk daily. If you get infected by the peace bug, turn your visit into a mini-walk by starting at the Quaker Friends House just north of Tavistock Square at 173-7 Euston Road (7663 1135/www.quaker.org.uk) and ending at the statue of Tiruvalluvar just behind the SOAS building, at the top of Woburn Square. The Quakers are a pacifist bunch who strive to 'work through quiet processes for a world where peaceful means bring about just settlements'; worship meetings are held on Sundays at 11am (open to all), and there's a library (1-5pm Mon, Tue, Thur, Fri; 10am-5pm Wed) and bookshop (10am-5pm Tue-Fri). To look round the building and use the buffet, you need to call in advance (7663 1000). Tiruvalluvar was a weaver sage who wrote the *Tirrukkural*, a 2,200-year-old South Indian Dravidian treatise on ethical living through non-violence, dharma ('right behaviour'), asceticism and vegetarianism. Gandhi called the *Tirrukkural* 'a treasure of wisdom'.

Dickens' two-and-a-half-year stay in this Georgian terraced house, the sole survivor among his many London residences, coincided with a period of great productivity – *The Pickwick Papers*, *Oliver Twist* and *Nicholas Nickleby* were all written here. Though only the drawing room has been restored to its original state, the house is packed with Dickens memorabilia. In 2002 (Apr-Dec), a special exhibition, Bleak House – the View from Gormenghast, will celebrate both the 150th anniversary of the publication of *Bleak House* and the centenary of the Dickens Fellowship, which founded the museum. It will include rare character portraits from a little-known edition illustrated by *Gormenghast* author Mervyn Peake. On Wednesday nights (May-Sept) the one-man 'Sparkler of Albion' shows bring the author and his characters to life.

Percival David Foundation of Chinese Art

53 Gordon Square, WC1 (7387 3909/ www.pdfmuseum.ac.uk). Euston Square, Goodge Street or Russell Square tube/Euston tube/rail. **Open** 10.30am-5pm Mon-Fri. **Admission** free; donations appreciated. **Map** p399 K4.

The best collection of Chinese ceramics outside China, plus an extensive library of East Asian and Western books on Chinese art and culture. The permanent collection – 1,700 pieces dating mainly from the 10th to 18th centuries – is on the first and second floors; temporary shows are on the ground floor. Under-14s must be accompanied by an adult.

Petrie Museum of Egyptian Archaeology

University College London, Malet Place, WC1 (7679 2884/www.petrie.ucl.ac.uk). Goodge Street tube. **Open** 1-5pm Tue-Fri; 10am-1pm Sat. **Admission** free; donations appreciated. **Map** p399 K4.

Housing about 80,000 objects, the Petrie is one of the world's greatest collections of Egyptian and Sudanese archaeology. It started life as a teaching resource for the Professor of Egyptian Archaeology and Philology, a position created by the bequest of Victorian Egyptologist Amelia Edwards (1831-92), but it was mainly thanks to the first professor, William Flinders Petrie, that it grew to its present international stature. The horde includes the world's oldest piece of clothing (from 2800 BC). While planning a new building (about five years away), the museum has secured government funding to place its entire collection on the web by March 2002.

St George Bloomsbury

Bloomsbury Way, WC1 (7405 3044). Holborn or Tottenham Court Road tube. **Open** 9.30am-5.30pm Mon-Fri; 10am-12.30pm Sun. **Map** p399 L5.

A classical portico leads from the smoke-blackened exterior of this episcopal Hawksmoor church (1716-31) into its genteelly flaking interior. In October 2001 the World Monument Fund put the church on its list of threatened monuments, eliciting interest from both prestigious institutions and a private donor,

and raising hopes that a £2.5 million restoration will go ahead in 2002. There are some summer concerts, and opera singers often perform at Sunday services.

St Pancras Parish Church

Euston Road, NW1 (7388 1461). Euston tube/rail. **Open** phone for details & access. **Services** 8am, 10am, 6pm Sun; 1.15pm Wed. *Recital* 1.15pm Thur. **Admission** free.

Built in 1822 at a cost of £89,296, this was the most expensive church since St Paul's (*see p89*). Its spectacular exterior (the doorway of which provides shelter for many of the area's homeless people) was inspired by the Ionic Temple of Erectheum in Athens and its main features, the Caryatid porches, are used as entrances to the burial vaults.

Somers Town

On the other side of **Euston Road** from Bloomsbury, this area, parts of which were once bordered by a moat, is largely composed of council estates. It's on the north side of Euston Road that you'll find both the controversial new **British Library** (*see below*) and the much-loved **St Pancras Station**, a glorious Victorian glass-and-iron train shed fronted by Sir George Gilbert Scott's exuberant, high Gothic Midland Grand Hotel, currently known as **St Pancras Chambers** (*see p106*).

Across St Pancras Road, the eyesore of **King's Cross Station** is well suited to this seedy area given over to drug dealing and prostitution. There's been much talk of regeneration of the area over the last few years, but as yet its only real draws are the Scala nightclub (*see p281*), and further north, on the fringes of Somers Town, the fascinating **St Pancras Gardens** (*p106*). The stretch between the two was being razed for the Channel Tunnel Rail Link as we went to press, and the six gasholders had been dismantled, though the three listed ones will be rebuilt in the future (*see p40*).

British Library

96 Euston Road, NW1 (7412 7332/www.bl.uk). Euston Square tube/Euston or King's Cross tube/rail. **Open** 9.30am-6pm Mon, Wed-Fri; 9.30am-8pm Tue; 9.30am-5pm Sat; 11am-5pm Sun. **Admission** free; donations appreciated. **Map** p399 K3.

Love it or hate it (Prince Charles, that great scourge of modern architects, likened it to a 'secret police building', while MP Gerald Kaufman described it as 'a Babylonian ziggurat seen through a funfair distorting mirror'), this imposing red-brick building is here to stay – and so it should be, after a 36-year gestation (including 15 years of construction). Inside, it's the displays that will hold your attention, especially the John Ritblat Gallery, a permanent showcase of the best of the library's vast collection of rare and historic items, including the Lindisfarne Gospels

Who she? Jean Rhys

Born in the West Indies to a Welsh doctor father and a Dominican Creole mother, the young Jean Rhys acquired a sense of otherness that was to remain without her throughout her life and that invested her fiction with its powerful blend of dislocation and desolation. The locales she chose for her short stories and novels reflect this feeling of unrootedness – as her one-time lover Ford Madox Ford wrote in his preface to her collection *The Left Bank*, 'I should like to call attention to her profound knowledge of the life of the Left Bank – of many of the Left Banks of the world. For something mournful – and certainly hard up! – attaches to almost all uses of the word left. The left hand has not the cunning of the right: and every city has its left bank. London has, round Bloomsbury...'

Rhys first washed up in Bloomsbury in 1909, after a short-lived sojourn at a Cambridge boarding school at the age of 16, and in the area's melancholy squares and streets full of bedsits and cheap hotels she found a reflection of her own state of mind. Accepted, to her surprise, at the Academy of Dramatic Art (now the Royal Academy of Dramatic Art) on Gower Street, she lived in a boarding house in Upper Bedford Place, and though her acting training was cut short when her father died, obliging her to join a touring musical company, she returned to Bloomsbury again and again in her fiction.

In her story 'Till September Petronella', Petronella Gray, a typical Rhys lost soul 'walking the tightrope' between survival (usually achieved through humiliating means, such as asking former lovers for money) and poverty, inhabits a bedsit in Torrington Square and idolises a French girl, Estelle, who lives downstairs. 'When I went into her room,' she says wistfully, 'it didn't seem like a Bloomsbury bedsitting room – and when it comes to Bloomsbury bed-sitting rooms I know what I'm talking about.' When Estelle leaves, Petronella's depression is lifted by a trip to the country with some wealthy artists, but finally humiliated by them as 'a ghastly cross between a barmaid and a chorus-girl', she returns to sit in her room, sleepless, and wait for the clock of nearby Church of St Christ the King to strike.

These days Torrington Square has been more or less subsumed by the University of London and seems eminently respectable,

(c700), the Magna Carta (1215), literary manuscripts from Chaucer to Heaney, and a collection of scribbled Beatles lyrics. There's also a hands-on gallery about the history of book production; a stamp exhibition; and the Pearson Gallery for temporary exhibitions, including, until 7 April 2002, Lie of the Land: the Secret Life of Maps.

Call for times and prices of guided tours, some of which feature a visit to one of the Reading Rooms (for information about Readers' Tickets call 7412 7677), and details of events, discussions and lectures.

St Pancras Chambers

St Pancras Station, Euston Road, NW1 (7304 3927). King's Cross tube/rail. **Open** 11.30am-3.30pm Mon-Fri; *guided tours* call for details. **Admission** free; *guided tours* £9. **No credit cards. Map** p399 L3. This small exhibition about the long-deserted Midland Grand Hotel (*see p28* **Is it terminal?**) is limited to a few displays on its history. To see the famous, and fabulous, interior before the building is converted into posh flats and a hotel (work is pencilled in to begin in about two years), call to put your name down for one of the sporadic weekday tours.

St Pancras Gardens

St Pancras Road, NW1 (7974 1693). King's Cross tube/rail. **Open** 7am-dusk daily; events (eg birds of prey displays) phone for details. **Map** p399 K2.

After more than a decade of neglect, this glorious churchyard was restored in 2000-1 with funding from the Heritage Lottery Fund and Camden Council. St Pancras Old Church, set on one of the oldest sites of Christian worship in London (it may date back to the early fourth century), has been ruined and rebuilt several times since medieval times, and was used as a barracks and stable for Cromwell's troops in the Civil War. But it's the gardens themselves that enthral, containing as they do the tomb of writer William Godwin and his first wife, early feminist Mary Wollstonecraft (it was over her grave that her daughter, also called Mary, and the poet Shelley professed their love for each other), and the Soane family tomb, the mausoleum of which was designed by Sir John himself (it's central dome influenced Sir Giles Gilbert Scott's design of the K2 and subsequent phone boxes). Most stunning of all is the Hardy tree, so-called because novelist Thomas Hardy, then a trainee architect, had to exhume human remains here in the 1860s, when the Midland Railway Line was built over part of the churchyard; he left some of the gravestones propped against an ash and the tree grew up through them, so that wood and stone fused. The churchyard, which features in *A Tale of Two Cities* as a spot where bodysnatcher Jerry Cruncher is known to 'fish', is also the final resting place of one of Dickens' schoolmasters from his Camden youth.

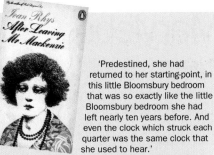

though a literary connection remains in the form of a blue plaque to poet Christina Rossetti, who lived at No.30 from 1876 to 1894, and who is mentioned in Rhys's story 'The Day They Burned the Books' ('by a flicker in Mrs Sawyer's eyes I knew that worse than men who wrote books were women who wrote books').

In the novel *Good Morning Midnight* (1939), the narrator Sasha Jensen, sent to Paris to dry out by a concerned friend, lies in her bath in a squalid hotel and thinks of 'the other room... the one just off the Gray's Inn Road,' where she was 'as usual trying to drink myself to death' when she wasn't taking 'little health-strolls' around nearby Mecklenburgh Square.

But it is in an earlier novel, *After Leaving Mr Mackenzie* (1930), that Bloomsbury takes on its greatest force in conveying the state of mind of the protagonist. Julia Martin returns from Paris after cheques from her former lover dry up, checking into a cheap hotel at '33 Arkwright Gardens, WC' (this time a fictional location).

'Predestined, she had returned to her starting-point, in this little Bloomsbury bedroom that was so exactly like the little Bloomsbury bedroom she had left nearly ten years before. And even the clock which struck each quarter was the same clock that she used to hear.'

Leaving the hotel, Julia stops to buy violets from the flower-seller on the corner of Woburn Square, hoping he will recognise her, but is repulsed by his cold, glassy gaze. Carrying on along Torrington Place towards Tottenham Court Road, she hallucinates her own ghost emerging from the fog, a bunch of violets in her hand, 'And she had the feeling that, like the old man, it looked at her coldly, without recognising her.'

Rhys didn't receive critical acclaim until the late 1960s, when she published the novel widely regarded as her masterpiece, *Wide Sargasso Sea*. Thankfully for fans of her strange, sad fiction, this led to the reissue of her early stories and novels. In 1978 she was made a CBE, and she died the following year, in Exeter.

Fitzrovia

Maps p398 & p399

Goodge Street, Great Portland Street, Oxford Circus, Tottenham Court Road or Warren Street tube.

For a long time the haunt of down-at-heel artists and writers, who came here to drink away their talent in pubs such as the Fitzroy Tavern on **Charlotte Street**, Fitzrovia was so-called after lovely Fitzroy Square in its north-western corner (named after Henry Fitzroy, the son of Charles II, and later the Earl of Euston). Today it's a relatively quiet backwater – tourists tend not to stray north of Oxford Street, though the booming restaurant scene has made up for the decline in the quality of the watering holes.

Beyond **Pollock's Toy Museum**, **All Saints** (for both, *see below*), and the BT Tower (closed to the public since a bomb attack in 1971, though there have been whispers about a revamp of the old revolving restaurant), sights are few. Yet the area has a certain neglected charm, provided you avoid scruffy **Tottenham Court Road**. Barely a century ago, this was a quiet rural road lined by cow sheds; now it's the place for electronic goods and computers, and classy furniture and household wares.

All Saints

Margaret Street, W1 (7636 1788/ www.ucl.ac.uk/~ucgbmxd/allss.htm). Oxford Circus tube. **Open** 7am-7pm daily. **Services** 8am, 11am, 5.15pm, 6pm Sun; phone for details of other days. **Map** p398 J5.

Designed by William Butterfield around the time that Ruskin's *Stones of Venice* was published, this Victorian church embodies Ruskinian principles. It's noted for its structural polychromy (the use of highly coloured materials rather than surface decoration). Its organ, being rebuilt at the time of writing, should be back in use on All Saints Day (1 Nov) 2002.

Pollock's Toy Museum

1 Scala Street (entrance on Whitfield Street), W1 (7636 3452/www.pollocksweb.co.uk). Goodge Street tube. **Open** 10am-5pm Mon-Sat. **Admission** £3; £1.50 3-18s; free under-3s. **Credit** *Shop* MC, V. **Map** p398 J5.

This lovingly run museum, which has its origins in a 'Theatrical Print Warehouse' inherited by Benjamin Pollock in the 1870s, is home to a collection of thousands of children's toys from the last two centuries (and a few older pieces), including teddy bears, clockwork tin railways, old board games, Action Men, and folk toys from around the world. The shop (*see p260*) sells playing cards, jigsaws, marbles, magic sets, puppets and more. Toy theatre performances can be booked for a minimum of ten kids.

Sightseeing

Marylebone

Having shaken free of its disreputable past, Marylebone
is now one of London's most civilised enclaves.

Maps p395 & p398

*Baker Street, Bond Street, Edgware Road, Great
Portland Street, Marble Arch, Oxford Circus or
Regent's Park tube.*

Hemmed in by the noisy thoroughfares of
Oxford Street, Edgware Road, Marylebone
Road and Great Portland Street, Marylebone
was once made up of two ancient manors,
Lileston (Lisson) and Tyburn (named after a
stream that flowed through the area). By the
14th century these manors were violent and
disreputable (indeed, Tyburn was the site of
a famous gallows from 1388 to 1783; the site
is marked by a plaque on the traffic island at
Marble Arch), and after frequent ransacking of
the parish church (which stood on what is now
Oxford Street; large numbers of human bones
were found marking the spot), a second was
built about halfway up what has since become
Marylebone High Street, opposite the long-gone
manor house. It was named St Mary by the
Bourne, which came to designate the entire
area, eventually being shortened to Marylebone.

Though nothing remains of the first two
parish churches, you can see the foundations of
the third (which was demolished after damage
sustained during World War II) towards the top
of the high street, in the **Memorial Garden
of Rest**. Connected with many well known
figures (Francis Bacon married here in 1606,
William Hogarth painted the interior in 1735,
Lord Byron was baptised here in 1788, and
Lord Nelson worshipped here), the garden is
a lovely place to sit and take stock of the huge
range of places to visit in this increasingly hip
area, with its compact shops, restaurants and
pubs centred around **Marylebone Lane** and
Marylebone High Street.

Away from the shopping hub, Marylebone
is a sedate world of orderly Georgian squares
and streets. In the 16th century, its northern half
– now Regent's Park – became a royal hunting
ground, while the southern section was bought
up by the Portman family. Two centuries later,
the Portmans developed many of the elegant
streets and squares that lend much of this
relatively unvisited part of the city its dignified
air. One of these squares, **Manchester
Square**, is home to the **Wallace Collection**
(*see p109*). Behind it is the glorious church of
St James's Spanish Place (*see below*).

Nearby **Harley Street** and **Wimpole
Street** have been renowned since the mid
19th century for their medical establishments
(*see p110* **Pill Island**). It was from No.50 that
Elizabeth Barrett eloped with fellow poet Robert
Browning in 1846; they were secretly married at
the fourth **St Marylebone Parish Church**, on
Marylebone Road. Dickens lived next door to the
church at 1 Devonshire Terrace (demolished in
1959). Across the road, the **Royal Academy of
Music** (*see p315*), founded in 1822 and designed
by Nash, has a stunning new glass recital
building and a new museum.

Portland Place, leading up to Regent's
Park, was the glory of 18th-century London.
Though many of its houses have been rebuilt,
its spacious proportions have been maintained.
Where it links at **Langham Place** with Nash's
Regent Street is the BBC's HQ, Broadcasting
House. Next door is Nash's church **All Souls**
(1822-4), with its slender spire. Over the road is
the Langham Hilton, the first of London's grand
hotels (it opened in 1865), while further north is
the splendidly solid **RIBA** (*see p300*).

North of Marylebone Road, the landscape
changes with the ugly '50s and '60s housing
developments of Lisson Grove. One treasure
is the plush Landmark Hotel, which opened
as the Great Central Hotel in 1899 and was
the last significant Victorian hotel to be built
in the golden age of steam. After closing in
1939, it was used as offices and, in wartime,
was requisitioned for convalescing officers
and soldiers on leave. In 1986 it was bought
by a Japanese firm and reinstated as a hotel.

Slightly further west, **Church Street**, while
a little rough around the edges, is a popular
local food and general market that is rapidly
gentrifying at its eastern end – Alfie's Antiques
Market (*see p231*) and the clutch of designer
homewares shops that have sprung up round it
are being touted as the new Portobello.

St James's Spanish Place

*Spanish Place, 22 George Street, W1 (7935 0943/
www.spanishplace.hemscott.net). Baker Street or
Bond Street tube.* **Open** 7am-7.30pm daily.
Services 7.15am, 12.30pm, 6pm Mon-Fri; 10am,
6pm Sat; 10.30am, noon, 6pm Sun. **Admission** free.
This early Gothic Roman Catholic church derives its
name from an Iberian connection dating back to the
restoration of Charles II, when a Spanish embassy

Church Street market. See p108.

of medieval swordsmanship. Café Bagatelle serves good Modern British food in the stunning glass-roofed Sculpture Garden.

Regent's Park

Regent's Park (7486 7905, open 5am-30min before dusk daily), laid out in 1817-28 by John Nash (and named for his faithful patron), is central London's most well-mannered park. Originally part of Middlesex Forest, it's lively in summer, with a boating lake, tennis courts, three playgrounds, music, a café and an open-air theatre (*see p338*). The **Outer Circle**, the main road running around the park, is bordered to the south by Marylebone Road and Nash's sublimely proportioned Park Crescent, completed in 1818 and originally intended to be a full circus. To the west of the park is the London Central Mosque, built in 1978 to service the spiritual needs of some of the city's many Muslims, whose shops, cafés and restaurants are a feature of nearby **Edgware Road** and **Bayswater** (*see p178*). To the east are the splendid Palladian mansions of **Cumberland Terrace** (also by Nash; it's hard to believe that after World War II they'd become so rundown that the Crown Commissioners considered demolishing them), while the north edge of the park offers up **London Zoo** (*see p110*).

At 18 Park Square East (now home to the Prince's Trust, Prince Charles's charity for underprivileged 14- to 30-year-olds), you'll see the word Diorama in large letters at the top of the building; dioramas (large pictures fusing photography to metal to create spectacular scenes) were invented by Bouton and Daguerre (of the Daguerreotype fame). The London diorama was designed by Augustus Pugin in 1823 at a cost of £10,000 but was a commercial failure and was sold various times from 1848 on – the last time, with 16 pictures, for £3,000. It was converted into a Baptist chapel but later used as an arts centre.

Just below Regent's Park are **Madame Tussaud's** (*see p110*) and the **London Planetarium** (*see below*). Nearby Baker Street, which is as alienating as Jerry Rafferty described it in his 1978 hit ('it's got so many people but it's got no soul'), is home to the **Sherlock Holmes Museum** (*see p110*).

London Planetarium

Marylebone Road, NW1 (0870 400 3000/ www.madame-tussauds.com). Baker Street tube. **Open** *June-Aug* 10am-5pm daily; *Sept-May* 12.30-5pm Mon-Fri; 10am-5pm Sat, Sun. **Admission** £7; £4.85 5-15s; £5.60 concessions. Under-5s not admitted. *Combined ticket with Madame Tussaud's* £14.45; £9.95 5-15s; £11.30 concessions; £49 family (2+2 or 3+1). **Credit** AmEx, MC, V. **Map** p398 G4.

was re-established in London, first in Ormond Street, then in Manchester Square. In 1791, just after the repeal of laws affecting Catholic worship, a chapel was built on the corner of Spanish Place and Charles Street (now George Street). Most of the holy objects in today's church came from this older building, which was mentioned by Thackeray in *Vanity Fair*. Official Spanish links ceased in 1827 but some items, including Alfonso XIII's standard, remain.

The present church opened in 1890, directly opposite the first. Its Lady Chapel was designed by JF Bentley, architect of Westminster Cathedral. It was at St James's that 19-year-old Vivian Hartley, later known as Vivien Leigh, wed barrister Leigh Holman in 1932. The funeral of Russian choreographer Vaslav Nijinsky also took place here in 1950.

Wallace Collection

Hertford House, Manchester Square, W1 (7935 0687/www.the-wallace-collection.org.uk). Bond Street tube. **Open** 10am-5pm Mon-Sat; noon-5pm Sun. **Admission** free. **No credit cards. Map** p398 G5. Revamped for its centenary in 2000, this sumptuously restored late 18th-century house belonged to Sir Richard Wallace, who, as the illegitimate heir of the Marquis of Hertford, inherited the furniture, paintings and Sèvres porcelain that the latter, a great francophile, bought for safekeeping after the Revolution. Highlights include a Minton-tiled smoking room, rooms full of armour and weaponry and works by Titian, Velázquez, Gainsborough and Sir Joshua Reynolds. Franz Hals' *Laughing Cavalier* and Fragonard's *The Swing*, with its pink-cheeked lovers and complicit nymphs and statues, stand out.

Lectures have included Antonia Fraser on Marie Antoinette (whose desk is here), and there are art classes and periodic events such as demonstrations

Sightseeing

The main event at the child-oriented planetarium is a fairly basic 20-minute star show projected on to a screen on the dome's ceiling. The film plays every 40 minutes, so if you just miss one you have to wait in the lobby, which, though it's done up to look space age (with models of planets and astronauts, a zero-gravity weighing machine and other gravity-inspired games, and a poorly stocked shop), has little to hold kids' attention. Book ahead to avoid queues.

London Zoo

Regent's Park, NW1 (7722 3333/ *www.londonzoo.co.uk). Baker Street or Camden* *Town tube then 274, C2 bus.* **Open** *Nov-Mar* 10am-4pm daily; *Apr-Oct* 10am-5.30pm daily. **Admission** £10; £7 3-14s; £8.50 concessions; free under-3s. **Credit** AmEx, MC, V. **Map** p398 G2.

In accordance with modern sensibilities, London Zoo, which celebrated its 175th birthday in 2001, lays heavy stress on its breeding programmes (of the more than 600 species that live here, 150 are on the International Union for the Conservation of Nature's Red List of the world's most threatened species), yet it still manages to entertain. You'll need at least a day to make the most of it (printed guides are available at the front desk). Popular attractions include feeding times, reptile handling and the Web of Life exhibition in the Millennium Conservation Centre where biodiversity is both explained and celebrated. Elsewhere, the penguins parading like city gents in their famous modernist pool designed by Tecton and Lubetkin are perennial favourites, as is the children's petting zoo.

If you come in spring and summer, or on a winter weekend, you can reach the zoo by canalboat from Little Venice or Camden Lock (London Waterbus Company, 7482 2550); this has the advantage of allowing you to circumvent the queues at the zoo.

Madame Tussaud's

Marylebone Road, NW1 (7935 6861/ *www.madame-tussauds.com). Baker Street tube.* **Open** *May-Sept* 9.30am-5.30pm daily. *Oct-June* 10am-5.30pm Mon-Fri; 9.30am-5.30pm Sat, Sun. Times vary during school holidays; phone for details. **Admission** £12; £9.50 concessions; £8.50 5-15s; £39 family (2+2 or 3+1; timed tickets only). *Combined ticket with Planetarium* £14.45; £11.30 concessions; £10 5-15s; £49 family (2+2 or 3+1; timed tickets only). **Credit** AmEx, MC, V. **Map** p398 G4.

Madame Tussaud's is constantly besieged by tourists, though a new hotline giving visitors timed entry is intended to eradicate the queues. There's no reason you'd want to come here unless you have children in tow, but sadly even they are likely to be more charmed by the idea of Tussaud's than the reality – once they've stuck their fingers up Pierce Brosnan's nose and peeked up Darcey Bussell's tutu, they're clamouring for the Chamber of Horrors, where waxen guts spill out of bloody corpses and royal heads sit on spikes. The Horrors aren't quite as horrifying as

Pill Island

Worlds away from the horrors of bloodletting and amputation, genteel Marylebone has always nurtured a more civilised, progressive (not to mention elite) approach to medicine, with Harley Street and Wimpole Street particularly well known for their private dentists and doctors, including plastic surgeons catering to the rich and famous.

Harley Street came into being in the early 18th century, when Robert Harley, the first Earl of Oxford, developed this then-rural area of Marylebone. The street remained residential until the middle of the 19th century, when the Institute of Sick Governesses moved from nearby Chandos Street to 1 Harley Street, with Florence Nightingale as superintendent. From then on, frock-coated private doctors and consultants, including some of the most celebrated practitioners of their day, began moving here, using ground-floor dining rooms and libraries as their waiting and consulting rooms while they themselves lived 'above the shop'.

In the 1940s, a decade after being dubbed Pill Island, the area saw larger establishments, with up to a dozen physicians at one address, replace consulting rooms in family houses. Demand for premises grew so high that

they once they were, however, and incite scoffs and giggles from those who've seen the far creepier London Dungeon (*see p80*).

Additions to the main collection such as Ken Livingstone and Alan Titchmarsh are hardly going to set the kids alight: you'd be better off making for the new 'Superstars' section, where you'll find a motley crew including Samuel L Jackson, Chris Tarrant and David Beckham. Geri Halliwell is due soon – contain yourselves.

Sherlock Holmes Museum

221B Baker Street, NW1 (7935 8866/ *www.sherlock-holmes.co.uk). Baker Street tube.* **Open** 9.30am-6pm daily. **Admission** £6; £4 under-16s. **Credit** AmEx, DC, MC, V. **Map** p398 G4.

This attempt to reconstruct the home of the fictional detective, including his study complete with deerstalker, magnifying glass, pipe, violin, notebook and disguises, would be fine were it not for the rather ludicrous pretence that Sherlock Holmes actually existed and lived at 221B Baker Street. The organisers have gone so far as to summon up a handwritten diary by Doctor Watson and a Blue Heritage

Harley Street house numbering extends beyond the famous road itself into some side streets. In the 1960s the number of private medical practitioners here peaked at about 2,000; it's now settled at about 1,500.

Of Marylebone's esteemed medical societies, the Royal Society of Medicine at 1 Wimpole Street is not open to the public, but the British Dental Association at No.64 (7935 0875) offers guided tours (by appointment) and has two reconstructed surgeries complete with original furniture and equipment.

Elsewhere in Marylebone, the Royal College of Nursing in another elegant building (once home to Herbert Asquith, British PM from 1908 to 1915) in nearby Cavendish Square, became a residential club for nurses in 1922. Further north, near Regent's Park, the Royal College of Obstetricians and Gynaecologists (27 Sussex Place; 7772 6200) has instruments dating from the 16th century, including the obstetric forceps invented by Peter Chamberlen (1601-83), 'physician ordinary' to James I, Charles I and Charles II.

Most interesting to architecture lovers is the Royal College of Physicians on the other side of the park, at 11 St Andrew's Place (7935 1174). The much-admired modernist pavilion was created by Sir Denys Lasdun, best known for the Royal National Theatre (*see p74*), in 1960-4 and provides a home for the country's oldest medical society. You need permission to get in (as well as the stunning rooms there's a small collection of instruments and other medical curiosities), but it's worth coming along just to view the magnificent exterior (*pictured*).

For other peeks into London's medical history, visit the Science Museum's Wellcome Wing (*see p140*); the Museum of the Order of St John (*see p100*); the Alexander Fleming Laboratory Museum (*see p178*), and the Old Operating Theatre (*see p81*). Also, Barber-Surgeons' Hall (7653 6666) is available for hire and makes a gruesome party venue – as well as cutting hair and shaving beards, barber-surgeons performed operations, extracted teeth, lanced boils, set fractures and let blood, only rarely with medical training. Some displays of equipment, such as bleeding bowls and lancets, serve as reminders of this gory trade.

Plaque outside. Scant info about the displays, which include wax models depicting scenes from the stories, makes the experience even more disorienting.

Diehard fans would do better to visit the Sherlock Holmes Collection of books, journals, photos, film-scripts and more round the corner at Marylebone Library (7641 1039, by appointment only).

Oxford Street & Marylebone High Street

Discreet Marylebone hits snooty Mayfair at **Oxford Street**, with **Marble Arch**, another Nash creation, marking its western extent. This wholly unremarkable monument was intended as the entrance to Buckingham Palace but, discovered to be too puny, was moved to this site in 1851.

London's most famous shopping street is a scruffy canyon filled with tacky stalls and high street chains; Selfridges (*see p236*) is one of its few redeeming features. More original shops can be found on **Marylebone High Street**, which has undergone a renaissance over the past few years. This is largely down to Sir Terence Conran, who opened a branch of the Conran Shop (No.55; *see p255*) and a fine restaurant, Orrery (*see p193*), in a former Victorian stables here. Other retailers were quick to follow suit, including Aveda (Nos.28-9; *see p253*) and Space.NK (No.83A, *see p254*), and food and drink destinations have multiplied. 'Old favourites' include the child-friendly Giraffe (6-8 Blandford Street, *see p274*) and smart Italian Ibla (89 Marylebone High Street, *see p192*), while Peter Gordon's Providores & Tapa Room (109 Marylebone High Street, *see p193*) is a new arrival.

But the boom, sadly, has a downside – some of the long-established independent shops (which still include a bookshop, fishmonger and bespoke shoemaker) are being usurped by voracious chains such as Prêt-à-Manger, Starbucks and Gap, little by little depriving the area of what has hitherto constituted its charm – its individuality.

Mayfair & St James's

Alternately genteel and tacky, swanky and low-key,
Mayfair and St James's are worth a closer look.

Mayfair

Map p400

Bond Street, Green Park, Hyde Park Corner, Marble Arch, Oxford Circus or Piccadilly Circus tube.
Situated in the very heart of London, Mayfair has belonged to the Grosvenor family since 1677 and derived its name from the annual fair that was held in, you guessed it, May. The tradition ran until the 18th century, when the local toffs forced its closure because they felt it was lowering the tone of the area.

Roughly speaking, Mayfair is wedged between Oxford Street, Regent Street, Piccadilly and Park Lane. Its expansive, handsome architecture means that it acts as a magnet to the wealthy, and the highest echelons of society have enjoyed its clubs, restaurants and shops and its immaculate squares and parks for the best part of three centuries. This is a seriously moneyed district, but don't let the broad Georgian thoroughfares, purring Jags and Beemers, and swanky shopfronts put you off.

Mayfair's location means it's a short walk to pretty much any of the major draws in the capital. As far as shopping is concerned, you can either slum it in **Oxford Street** or polish your credit card for **Bond Street** and **Piccadilly**, as well as some interesting little retreats such as **Burlington Arcade** and **Shepherd Market**. There's also a fine, arty cinema in the shape of the **Mayfair Curzon** (*see p290*) with its fabulous interior. Sightseeing too is a cut above: Mayfair and St James's aces include the new **Handel House Museum** (*see p113*) and the **Wellington Arch** (*see p115*), open to visitors for the first time in its history. There are also some seriously plush hotels that are out of reach of most pockets, including Claridge's, the Connaught and the daddy of them all, the **Ritz** (*see p53*). If you're feeling a bit flush, book ahead to enjoy a Ritz cream tea to die for.

Three large squares dominate the north of Mayfair: Hanover, Berkeley and the immense Grosvenor, which contains the US Embassy. A statue of Franklin D Roosevelt stands in the centre of the square, and Grosvenor Chapel on

Glory days: the newly restored **Wellington Arch** is now open to the public. *See p115.*

South Audley Street enjoys a healthy turn-out of American expats. To the east lies Mayfair's commercial spread, which includes **Savile Row**, world renowned for its tailoring, and the jewellery, art, antiques and clothing found on New and Old Bond streets. Get your hankies ready because you'll be weeping at the prices. Two of London's best-known auction houses are found on New Bond Street – Phillips and Sotheby's – while near the corner of New Bond Street and Grafton Street is a bizarre street bench upon which sit statues of Roosevelt and Churchill, for all the world like two seedy tramps waiting for spare change with which to purchase their next can of soup.

Talking of which, at the southern end of New Bond Street is the **Faraday Museum** (*see below*) celebrating the achievements of the man dubbed the 'father of electricity'.

Faraday Museum

Royal Institution, 21 Albemarle Street, W1 (7409 2992/www.ri.ac.uk). Green Park tube. **Open** 9am-5pm Mon-Fri. *Tours* by arrangement. **Admission** £1. *Tours* £5. **No credit cards. Map** p400 J7.
This small museum in the building in which Michael Faraday was professor features a re-creation of the lab where he discovered the laws of electromagnetics. While you're at the Royal Institution, ask to see the prized possession, which isn't on public display: a silver cup presented to Humphry Davy by Tsar Alexander I in 1825 in gratitude for what Davy's famous lamp had done for the miners of Russia.

Handel House Museum

25 Brook Street (entrance at rear), W1 (7495 1685/ www.handelhouse.org). Bond Street tube. **Open** 10am-6pm Tue, Wed, Fri, Sat; 10am-8pm Thur; noon-6pm Sun. **Admission** £4.50; £3.50 concessions; £2 children. **No credit cards. Map** p400 J7.
On Brook Street you'll find two blue plaques stating that, in differing periods, two influential tunesmiths were neighbours here: George Frideric Handel (*see p312* **Who he?**) and Jimi Hendrix. After a long period of restoration work on the house, the Handel House Museum finally opened in November 2001. This is the first museum devoted to a composer in London, and it offers rare access to beautifully restored Georgian interiors where key works such as *Messiah* were composed. Also on display are some beautiful pieces of art and re-creations of the rooms in which Handel lived. Two harpsichords that mirror the kind of instruments Handel would have used in his house are played frequently during opening hours.

Piccadilly Circus

It was probably a hell of a lot more dangerous, but hands up those who preferred it when the Eros fountain was a proper traffic island. The pedestrianisation of one section of the death race that Piccadilly Circus is famous for has not really improved things at the convergence of some of the busiest streets in the city. Despite the presence of the bewinged, matchmaking cherub, there's certainly nolove lost between the horn-bent taxi drivers and kamikaze cyclists, pedal-to-the-metal bus drivers or 'please God' pedestrians.

Piccadilly Circus is so named for the stiff collars that were the sartorial speciality of tailor Robert Baker, who lived nearby in the 17th century. The gaudy neon advertising hoardings that overlook the maelstrom have been a fixture since 1910, as have, it would seem, the slices of pizza on sale at the grim cafés at various corners. On the plus side, there's Tower Records, which is open at ungodly hours for CD-loving insomniacs (*see p257*), and a monster Waterstone's bookshop with lifts, a café and – who'd have thought it? – customer loos (*see p232*).

The **Trocadero** (1 Piccadilly Circus, 7439 1711/www.troc.co.uk; 10am-midnight daily) lies nearby, a so-called entertainment zone filled with various American-influenced fast-food joints, amusement arcades, cinema screens and the ubiquitous, iniquitous tourist shops where you can buy 'London by night' postcards and other abject tat.

Regent Street

Connecting Piccadilly Circus to Oxford Circus to the north and Pall Mall to the south, Regent Street is a broad, curving boulevard that was conceived by John Nash in the early 1800s to clear away the slums and improve transport. The grandeur of the sweeping road is impressive, but the shops let it down somewhat, though some of the names along here – **Liberty** (*see p236*) and **Hamleys** (*see p260*) – have been here since its inception.

Piccadilly & Green Park

Piccadilly heads west out of town, bypassing Green Park on the way to Hyde Park Corner. Fortnum and Mason's quintessentially British department store is, along with the Ritz hotel (*see p53*), the jewel in Piccadilly's crown, though for the shopper who prefers a more serene setting, the streets leading off this arterial road bring plenty of choice. **Burlington Arcade**, which runs down the side of Burlington House, home to the **Royal Academy of Arts**, opened in 1819 (*see p114*); Regency laws state that whistling, the raising of umbrellas and running in the arcade are punishable offences. Somewhat less quaint is the arcade's history as a brothel. The first-floor windows above the shopfronts once housed

Sightseeing

prostitutes to tempt the impulse buyer. Nearby **Haymarket** was probably the reason for such behaviour, as it was, in the 1860s, hooker central – a fact not lost on miserablist writer Fyodor Dostoyevsky, who noted, 'It is the district where at night the prostitutes gather in their thousands.'

Green Park is, perhaps surprisingly, considering its privileged address, the least pretentious of the parks in central London. It doesn't boast the views or the diversity of birds of St James's Park (*see p130*), and it doesn't lay claim to the same amount of land as Hyde Park (*see p136*), but for all that, it's a nice little retreat to relax in when you've had your fill of exhaust fumes and concrete. Once part of the meadowland surrounding St James's Palace, it was enclosed by Henry VIII and made into a Royal Park by Charles II. Queen's Walk from Green Park tube to Buckingham Palace is especially pleasant in the autumn, with the path a riot of colourful fallen leaves. The original gas lamps are still in place too.

At the far end of Piccadilly, at Hyde Park Corner, you'll find **Apsley House** (*see below*) with its Duke of Wellington memorabilia and the stunning **Wellington Arch** (*see p115*), now open to the public for the first time after a £1.5-million restoration by English Heritage.

Screen classic: Mayfair's **Curzon**. *See p112.*

Apsley House: The Wellington Museum

149 Piccadilly, W1 (7499 5676/www.vam.ac.uk). Hyde Park Corner tube. **Open** 11am-5pm Tue-Sun. **Admission** £4.50 (includes audio-guide); £3 concessions; free under-18s. *Tours* £2.50 per person (min 10); by arrangement. **Credit** AmEx, DC, MC, V. **Map** p400 G8.

Known, rather grandly, as No.1 London due to its being the first building one encountered during a visit to London from the village of Kensington, Apsley House was built by Robert Adam in the 1770s and was the London residence of the Duke of Wellington from 1817 to 1852 – the year of his death. Though his descendants still live here, some of the rooms are open to the public and contain interesting trinkets. Goya's Wellington portrait shows the Iron Duke (so called for the iron shutters he installed in his house after rioters broke his windows in protest at his Reform Bill) entering Madrid, hot on the heels of his defeat of the French in 1812. An X-ray of the painting in 1966 showed that Wellington's head had been brushed in over that of Joseph Bonaparte, Napoleon's elder brother – Goya had been working on the portrait when he found out that Wellington had been victorious and having jumped the gun, decided to curry favour with a quick repair job.

Royal Academy of Arts

Burlington House, Piccadilly, W1 (7300 8000/ www.royalacademy.org.uk). Green Park or Piccadilly Circus tube. **Open** 10am-6pm Mon-Thur, Sat, Sun; 10am-8.30pm Fri. *Tours* times vary. **Admission** varies. *Tours* free. **Credit** AmEx, MC, V. **Map** p400 J7.

Britain's first art school (it opened in 1768) has a permanent collection, but only a fraction of it is on show at any one time; make an appointment with the curator to see the rest. That said, the temporary exhibitions enjoy the most visits of any London gallery and booking is advisable. Exhibits in 2002 will include Paris: Capital of the Arts 1900-68 (26 Jan-12 Apr), featuring work by the great figures of the modern movement (Picasso, Matisse, Léger and Duchamp) and showing how artists as diverse as Kandinsky, Brancusi and Giacometti were also drawn to the dynamism of the French capital.

St James's Church Piccadilly

197 Piccadilly, W1 (7734 4511/www.st-james-piccadilly.org). Piccadilly Circus tube. **Open** 8am-7pm daily (phone for details of evening events). **Map** p400 J7.

This charming church, which was consecrated in 1684, is the only one the prolific Sir Christopher Wren (*see p86* **Who he?**) built on an entirely new site. It was also one of the architect's favourites: 'I think it may be found beautiful and convenient,' he said. Aside from providing a ministry, it stages an array of concerts (*see p311*), lectures (it's the home of the Blake Society) and markets: an antiques market takes place in the churchyard every Tuesday, with an arts and crafts fair following suit from Wednesday to Saturday.

James Bond's Mayfair

London was made for 007, and he for it. Although he could fit in anywhere on earth (except, if you consider the films, for Roger Moore in *Live and Let Die*, plodding around Harlem in that God-awful safari suit), London was the city that sustained him, in fact as well as fiction, and although, according to Ian Fleming's books, he used to live in a flat in one of those rather lovely squares off the King's Road in Chelsea, it was in suave Mayfair – where else? – that he, and his creator, spent much of their time.

Ian Fleming was born in Mayfair in 1908, at 27 Green Street, and later in his life bought a flat in Hay's Mews. John Barry, the composer of many Bond soundtracks, lived in Mayfair, as did Cubby Broccoli, one of the two producers to bring 007 to the screen, who had a house on Green Street. It was in a Mayfair barber shop, Kurt's, that Broccoli first clapped eyes on George Lazenby in 1966.

'I looked across to the next chair and saw some handsome character with a strong jaw, great physique and a lot of self-assurance,' he said. 'I remember thinking what a good Bond he would make.' Judge for yourself by watching *On Her Majesty's Secret Service*, Lazenby's one appearance as Bond.

The books themselves contain various references to Mayfair. In the novella 'The Property of a Lady', Bond is briefed to identify a top Soviet agent in London. His work takes him to Sotheby's on New Bond Street, where a Fabergé egg is being auctioned, but he drops by at 138 Regent Street first to brush up on his knowledge of Fabergé, courtesy of a Mr A Kenneth Snowman – who actually exists, and who accompanies Bond to the auction itself. Snowman's shop, Wartski's (named after his maternal grandmother), is now on Grafton Street, near, poetically enough, New Bond Street.

Ladies' man: **George Lazenby** as 007.

Australian spy and aviator Sidney Cotton could claim some responsibility for the gadgetry that passes through Q branch into James Bond's pockets, and perhaps some of the English spy's characteristics. He, like Bond, was debonair and good-looking, with a certain arrogance and a disdain for authority. Fleming became friends with him and visited him in his Mayfair flat, where they would sit up late discussing items for 007's kit bag.

Fleming's enjoyment of a good lunch, which he often took at the Connaught (Carlos Place, W1, 7499 7070), has rubbed off on some of the Bond 'descendants': Roger Moore's son Geoffrey co-owns the restaurant Hush at 8 Lancashire Court, W1 (7659 1500). It shouldn't come as any surprise to learn that vodka martinis feature on the cocktail menu.

Wellington Arch

Hyde Park Corner, W1 (7930 2726/www.english-heritage.co.uk). Hyde Park Corner tube. **Open** *Apr-Sept* 10am-6pm Wed-Sun; *Oct* 10am-5pm Wed-Sun; *Nov-Mar* 10am-4pm Wed-Sun. **Admission** £2.50; £1.90 concessions; £1.30 5-16s; free under-5s. **Credit** MC, V.

The Wellington Arch has suffered a number of indignities since its construction in the 1820s, in the wake of public clamour to build memorials marking Britain's triumph over Napoleonic France. Initially topped by a giant statue of the Duke of Wellington astride a horse, it was moved in 1882 from its original position as a grand entrance to London to its current home at Hyde Park Corner because of a road-widening scheme. The statue was taken down at the same time and replaced in 1912 by the stunning *Quadriga*, which is the largest bronze sculpture in England. Designed by the 25-year-old Decimus Burton, the arch has been in the care of English Heritage since 1999, which has restored it and opened it to the public for the first time. Inside are three floors of exhibits about the history of the arch and some of its uses: it was

Sightseeing

London's smallest police station at one point, and during the war an air raid siren was fixed to one of the chariot's wheels. Views from the balcony take in the Houses of Parliament, the London Eye and Buckingham Palace, although these are obscured by trees in summer.

St James's

Maps p400 & p401

Green Park or Piccadilly Circus tube.

Not many visitors – nor many Londoners, for that matter – venture too far into St James's, which takes as its borders Piccadilly, Haymarket, the Mall and Green Park. And, it's safe to say, that's just the way its habituées like it. If anything, St James's is even posher than Mayfair, its comrade in swank north of Piccadilly. This is a London that has remained unchanged for decades, perhaps even centuries: charming in its way, but unreconstructed and snooty with it.

Much of the snootiness can be found among the gentlemen's clubs of the area. Not that you'll be allowed in, of course: these temples to self-importance are more exclusive than a year's worth of Sun covers. The clubs, most of them on **St James's Street** and **Pall Mall**, evolved from 17th-century coffee houses as meeting places for the gentry, though most date only from the 19th century. Ultra-aristocratic White's (Prince Charles had his stag party here), at 37 St James's Street, is the oldest (founded in 1693); while Brook's (60 St James's Street) boasts a list of past members that includes William Pitt and Horace Walpole; the 1832 Reform Act spawned both the 'radical' Reform Club (104 Pall Mall) and the reactionary, right-wing Carlton Club (69 St James's Street).

The material needs of the venerable gents of St James's are met by the anachronistic shops and restaurants of **Jermyn** (which is pronounced 'jér-mun') **Street** and **St James's Street**. If you ignore the fact that well-to-do

Whatever happened to?
The Playboy Club

In the late 1950s the Playboy rabbit head was a trademark as recognisable as the McDonald's arches are today. *Playboy* magazine, which offered intelligent articles, interviews and fiction alongside its 'tasteful' photographs of beautiful women, possessed a certain cachet, and when the first Playboy Club opened in Chicago in February 1960, it drew the kind of crowd that *Playboy* was eager to represent: independent, solvent and with good taste. In the last three months of 1961, more than 132,000 people visited the Chicago club, making it the busiest nightclub in the world.

Dozens more clubs opened around the world, attracting in excess of a million members, and the Playboy Bunny became the icon of the sexual revolution. Yet times change fast, and by the end of the '60s the sophisticated lounge nightclub scene the Playboy clubs promoted, complete with jazz bands, comedians and singers, was declining in popularity. Also, a glut of imitators had diluted the market.

By the time London's Playboy & Casino Club opened at 45 Park Lane in 1966, complete with Bunny Girl croupiers, few of the established clubs were making a profit, and by the 1970s all the clubs except London

were on the ropes. Indeed, profits from the gambling that took place at the Park Lane venue were able to balance the losses made on the American clubs, which didn't have casinos, making London the fulcrum of the Playboy Club network.

Run by Victor Lownes, a friend and business partner of Playboy chief Hugh Hefner, the London club had its grand unveiling in June 1966, attracting stars of the calibre of Dustin Hoffman, Woody Allen and Julie Christie to celebrate the arrival of Bunnies in Britain. Despite the uncomfortable Bunny Girl outfits, there was certainly no shortage of candidates for the role among London's young office workers, secretaries and nurses eager for their slice of 'Swinging London' – the job brought with it wages of £35 a week, which was big money at the time, especially when supplemented by lavish tips – and a chance to mingle with celebs such as John Wayne, Tony Curtis and Sean Connery.

By the 1980s, however, the Playboy Bunny had become anachronistic and faintly ridiculous. What had once been daring and stylish was now, at its best, 'cute'. Fear that the members, who paid a hefty annual

Sightseeing

tourists make up most of the clientele these days, you'll find it's still a thrill to see the lovingly crafted quality of the goods and the time-warp shopfronts, among them cigar retailer JJ Fox (19 St James's Street) and upmarket cobbler John Lobb (No.6).

Around the corner is the Queen Mum's gaff at Clarence House on **Stableyard Road**. Its architect, John Nash, was also responsible for the remodelling of **St James's Palace** in the early 19th century. Built by Henry VIII on the site of St James's Hospital, the palace was one of the principal royal residences for more than 300 years and is still used by Prince Charles and various minor royals; indeed, tradition still dictates that foreign ambassadors to the UK are officially known as 'Ambassador(s) to the Court of St James'. Although the palace is closed to the public, it's possible to explore Friary Court on **Marlborough Road** and attend the Sunday services at the Chapel Royal (October to Good Friday; 8.30am, 11.30am). It was here that

Charles I took holy communion on the morning of his execution, and that Victoria and Albert (among many other royals) were married.

Two other notable St James's mansions stand nearby and overlook Green Park. The neo-classical Lancaster House was rebuilt in the 1820s by Benjamin Dean Wyatt for Frederick, Duke of York, and much impressed Queen Victoria with its splendour. Closed to the public, it's now used mainly for government receptions and conferences. A little further north, on **St James's Place**, is beautiful, 18th-century **Spencer House** (*see p118*), ancestral townhouse of Princess Diana's family and now open as a museum and art gallery.

Across Marlborough Road lies the Queen's Chapel, which was the first classical church to be built in England. Designed by Inigo Jones in the 1620s for Charles I's intended bride of the time, the Infanta of Castile, the chapel now stands in the grounds of Marlborough House and is only open to the public during Sunday services (Easter to July;

subscription, would start seeking legal advice if the clubs were to close was enough of a spur to keep the clubs going, but there no longer existed the whiff of exclusivity – the entertainment the 'keyholders' found at Playboy Clubs could be found at any upmarket bar. People too were changing: going to a cocktail lounge for dinner and a show wasn't enough; they wanted somewhere to dance and flirt. The Bunnies had become mere waitresses in funny uniforms. It was an age of *Deep Throat* and *The Devil in Miss Jones*. Sex was going hardcore and Playboy just wasn't that kind of rabbit.

It still seemed feasible that the larger clubs in major cities could afford to stay afloat, but when London's flagship club hit trouble, in the shape of a casino war against Ladbrokes, the writing was on the cards. Ladbrokes had had its nose put out of joint by the success of Playboy, but it got its own back by appealing to the gaming commission that Playboy had broken British gaming laws by allowing its gamblers credit – a practice that was in contravention of the gaming charter. As a result, Playboy London closed in 1981, and the building in which it was situated was sold off to Prince Jefri Bolkiah, younger brother of the Sultan of Brunei. Plans have recently been announced to turn it into a small and very exclusive 'apart-hotel'.

Twenty years later, however, and those bunnies are poking their heads above ground once more. Playboy has launched an online casino at PlayboyCasino.com (ironically, it is Ladbrokes that has provided the software for the site). There are distant rumours of a new casino in London too, so if the online version goes well it might not be too long before you're placing your bets with a woman in a pair of floppy ears.

The splendid Palm Room at **Spencer House**, ancestral London home of Princess Di's clan.

8.30am, 11.30am). The house itself was built by Sir Christopher Wren (*see p86* **Who he?**) and his son for Queen Anne's bosom buddy, Sarah, Duchess of Marlborough.

Reached from the west via King Street or the Mall, **St James's Square** was the most fashionable address in London for the 50 years after it was laid out in the 1670s: some seven dukes and seven earls were residents by the 1720s. The Prince Regent was attending a ball at No.16 in 1815 when a bloodied and dirty major arrived to announce the victory at Waterloo; the hostess was 'much annoyed with the Battle of Waterloo as it spoilt her party'. Alas, no private houses survive on the square today, though among the current occupants is the prestigious London Library, in the north-west corner. This private library was founded by Thomas Carlyle in 1841 in a demonstration of his disgust at the inefficiency of the British Library (a sentiment that many would have recognised until recent times).

Further east, overlooking the Mall, is **Carlton House Terrace**, which was built by Nash in 1827-32 on the site of Carlton House. When the Prince Regent came to the throne as

George IV, he decided his home was not ostentatious enough for his elevated station and levelled what Horace Walpole had once described as 'the most perfect palace' in Europe. No.6 Carlton House Terrace, now occupied by the Royal Society, was the Germany Embassy during the Nazi era; its interior was designed by Albert Speer, Hitler's architect.

Spencer House

27 St James's Place, SW1 (7499 8620/ www.spencerhouse.co.uk). Green Park tube. **Open** House *Feb-July, Sept-Dec* 11.45am-4.45pm Sun. Last entry 4.45pm. Restored gardens *specific days, spring, summer;* phone or check website. **Admission** *Tour only* £6; £5 10-16s. No under-10s. **Map** p400 J8.

Open to the public only on Sunday, and then by compulsory one-hour guided tour, this is one of the capital's most splendid Palladian mansions. Visitors are shown eight restored state rooms, which are now used mainly for corporate entertaining. Apart from its being the ancestral London house of Princess Diana's family, the most notable features of Spencer House are the extravagant murals of the Painted Room, the beautiful painted ceiling in the Great Room, and the collection of 18th-century paintings.

Soho & Leicester Square

Long a centre for entertainment and cheap eats,
Soho remains one of London's most lively and authentic areas.

Soho

Maps p398-p401

*Leicester Square, Oxford Circus, Piccadilly Circus
or Tottenham Court Road tube.*

With very few sights in the normal sense of the
word, bohemian Soho is actually an attraction
in its own right – the kind of place you need to
wander around to get the feel of, it's the perfect
locale for the urban *flâneur* looking for the
weirdest and most wonderful that London
has to offer. All human life is here, in all its
contradictions – the media types who work,
drink and snort here co-exist with council estate
and housing association residents, prostitutes,
market traders, dealers, tailors, struggling
artists and legions of homeless people who have
colonised the area's doorways and alleys.

Soho is home to about 5,000 people, which
is part of the reason why it hasn't suffered
the tourist-led bastardisation of its neighbour,
Covent Garden (*see p123*). Anyway, there's
little developers could do with these narrow
streets, mean buildings and scant greenery

– all a far cry from the Middle Ages, when the
area was used for farming, before becoming
a hunting ground for London's aristocracy in
the 16th and 17th centuries. It wasn't until the
last quarter of the 17th century that it became
residential, when, post-Great Fire, the City
became too crowded. Many of the properties
erected to cope with the overflow in the late
1600s were the work of builder Richard Frith,
who lent his name to Frith Street.

Among the first residents were Greek
Christians (hence Greek Street) fleeing
Ottoman persecution, and a larger wave of
French Protestants (Huguenots) forced out
of France by Louis XIV. However, despite the
speed with which its pastoral history became
swallowed up, the area's name at least retained
some of its past identity: when the huntsmen
who once frequented it spied their intended
target, they would shout 'So-ho!'

Many early, well-to-do residents left their
Soho Square mansions for Mayfair in the
early 18th century. In their place came artists,
writers, radicals and more foreign immigrants,
particularly Italians. John Galsworthy, in *The*

New Year celebrations draw the crowds to **Chinatown**. *See p122.*

Whatever happened to?
The Colony Club

'It was a place where people could go and lose their inhibitions,' said artist and legendary boozer Francis Bacon (*pictured*) of the Colony Room Club, the private drinking establishment set up on Dean Street by Muriel Belcher in 1948. With her Jamaican girlfriend Carmel, Belcher had run away from Birmingham (and her domineering father, a wealthy Jewish impresario) and washed up in wartime London, where she ran the Music Box in Leicester Square. When she got enough money together, she set up a tiny two-room club with a 3-11pm drinking licence that appealed to hard-drinking artists curtailed by laws obliging pubs to close in the afternoon. She also realised the power of the pink pound three decades before everyone else, creating an ambience in which gays could feel safe.

When Francis Bacon, still a struggling young artist, began frequenting the club, Belcher quickly found out about his circle of influential friends (including Lucien Freud, Frank Auerbach and Patrick Caulfield) and shrewdly agreed to pay him £10 a week, plus free drinks in perpetuity, if he brought them to the Colony. Soon, pretty much the whole of the 'School of London' had made the place their local.

Though Muriel always said 'I know fuck all about art', she and Bacon struck up an immediate affinity beyond their financial arrangement, with the artist calling Muriel 'mother' and she referring to him as her daughter. Each was drawn to the other's outrageous, campy streak. 'Muriel was a benevolent witch, who managed to draw in all London's talent up those filthy stairs,' says jazz musician George Melly, who met his wife at the Colony. 'She was like a great cook, working with the ingredients of people and drink. And she loved money.'

Belcher reigned campily over the assembly from a mock-leopardskin 'perch', vetting everyone who walked in and performing a ritual kiss of welcome if they passed the test. She established a cult of rudeness, unleashing torrents of verbal abuse to test the resilience of newcomers, but was also warm and affectionate ('cunty' and 'Mary' were her favourite terms of endearment) and even raised funds for a local school. It's a testament to her wit and charisma that even now, more than 20 years after her death, many of the older clientele still call the club Muriel's.

After a rocky period and threatened closure, the Colony has now been colonised by a new generation of art stars attracted by its seedy, nicotine-stained charm and jumble of artworks adorning the green walls, including a Michael Andrews mural and a more recent Gavin Turk blue plaque. Among current luminaries are YBAs Damien Hirst (whose son Connor became an honorary lifetime member after a visit at the age of eight days), Tracey Emin, Marc Quinn and

Forsyte Saga, summed up the Soho of the 19th century as 'untidy, full of Greeks, Ishmaelites, cats, Italians, tomatoes, restaurants, organs, coloured stuffs, queer names…'

As the resident population dropped in the 20th century, the area became known for its entertainments (legal and otherwise) and cheap restaurants. Jazz came to Soho in the 1950s – the late Ronnie Scott opened his jazz club on Gerrard Street in 1959, moving it to Frith Street six years later (*see p322*) – while the '60s saw lots of pop and rock history in the making: the 2 i's Coffee Bar at 59 Old Compton Street, now a Dôme brasserie, was crammed with hopefuls after Adam Faith and Cliff Richard were discovered here in the late '50s; the now-defunct Bricklayer's Arms on Broadwick Street was the setting for the first meeting of the Rolling Stones after Brian Jones put out an ad for a blues band; and the Marquee Club, which has three locations including 90 Wardour Street (now part of Mezzo), hosted early gigs by Hendrix, the Byrds and Pink Floyd. Meanwhile, the sex industry for which the area has been renowned since the mid-19th century, when it became a centre of prostitution, expanded in the 1960s and further still during the sleazy 1970s.

However, Soho began to turn the corner in the '80s and '90s, spurred on by a boom in gay business (the so-called 'pink pound'). Pubs such as the Golden Lion on Dean Street had long been the haunt of gay servicemen (as well as writer Noel Coward and murderer Dennis Nilsen, who picked up some of his victims in it), but the gay cafés, bars and shops (including the Admiral Duncan, the victim of a homophobic bomb attack

Sarah Lucas; in fact, young artists make up two thirds of the membership selection committee.

Yet the Colony's enduring popularity can be put down not only to its exclusivity but to the unique bohemian atmosphere that Muriel Belcher created and that has somehow withstood the passage of time: those lucky enough to gain entry will find no cocktails, draught beer, coffee, tea or ciabatta sandwiches here. Says Melly, 'People are nostalgic about the idea of old Soho, and the Colony is the last of the lot.'

And Muriel herself lives on here – from a window arch hangs her patent leather bag and lacquered walking stick, while from the many photos of her that adorn the wall she continues to preside over the great institution that she set up more than half a century ago.

in summer 1999; see p304) that appeared along Old Compton Street injected some much-needed vitality into a district that had become the sole province of dirty old men.

That Soho is now more popular than ever is a cause for both celebration and concern. Old Compton Street and surrounds are the closest London gets to a 24-hour culture; Bar Italia (see p215 **Pit stops**), a Soho institution, offers authentic Italian coffee all through the night and was even immortalised in a Pulp song of the same name ('There's only one place we can go, it's round the corner in Soho, where all the broken people go'). Yet the chains are moving in, bringing with them those faint hearts who used to find Soho too grimy, and many residents have been complaining that their district is being turned into a noisy nightlife theme park.

The heart of Soho

The core of Soho is **Old Compton Street** and its surrounding streets. Here is Soho at its most heterodox and lively: gay bars, off-licences, delis, heaving boozers, pâtisseries and cheap to chic restaurants. The most evocative way to enter Soho, however, is via the arch of the Pillars of Hercules pub leading from Manette Street to Greek Street. The sense of passing through a portal into a different world has entranced many Soho neophytes in the past. Just north of here is shady **Soho Square**, built on land once known as Soho Fields and initially known as King Square (a weather-beaten statue of the king in question, Charles II, stands in the centre). In summer, office workers munch their sandwiches on the grass, while, around the square's edge, London's one remaining French Protestant church and St Patrick's Catholic church provide spiritual nourishment.

The short streets leading down from here to Old Compton Street are brimful of eateries and historical associations. Casanova and Thomas de Quincey lodged on **Greek Street**, the street on which Josiah Wedgwood had his London showroom. Restaurants L'Escargot Marco Pierre White (No.48; see p196) and the Hungarian Gay Hussar (No.2) have survived the years, as has the Coach & Horses pub (No.29; see p221). Somewhat more recent is private members' club Soho House (No.40), a rival to the Groucho (see below).

Neighbouring **Frith Street** has been home to John Constable, Mozart and William Hazlitt (at No.6, in what is now one of London's most charming hotels; see p55). Over Bar Italia (see above) are the rooms where John Logie Baird first demonstrated the wonder of TV. The Vietnamese cuisine of Saigon (No.45; see p199) adds to the multicultural feel of the block.

Dean Street, meanwhile, is the site of such famed drinking haunts as the French House (No.49; unofficial HQ of De Gaulle and the Free French during World War II; see p223); the Colony Club (No.41), presided over by the fearsome Muriel Belcher and second home to Francis Bacon and assorted literary and artistic layabouts from the 1950s on (see p120 **Whatever happened to?**); and the Groucho Club (No.44), a focus for today's arts and media crowd, including actor Keith Allen and artist Damien Hirst. It's over Quo Vadis (No.28), the restaurant that Hirst co-founded with chef Marco Pierre White, that Karl Marx and his family lived in two cramped rooms from 1851 to 1856.

West of here, work begins to get an equal billing with play. **Wardour Street** has long associations with the film industry and remains home to several film production companies. At

Sightseeing

the street's southern end is the churchyard of St Anne. Only the early 19th-century tower of the church survived the Blitz, but it's worth a look to read the memorial slabs of William Hazlitt and Theodore, King of Corsica, who died broke.

At the eastern end of **Brewer Street**, sex shops, shows and clip joints dominate (though the City Gates Church Christian Fellowship, tucked away on Greens Court, attempts to provide a more wholesome alternative). Leading south to Shaftesbury Avenue is **Rupert Street** market, majoring in clothes, jewellery and CDs, while to the north is another one of Soho's portals, the tiny arch of Walkers Court. It leads past Paul Raymond's Revuebar into **Berwick Street**, home to several great record and CD shops – not for nothing is it featured on the cover of Oasis's *(What's the Story) Morning Glory?* – and central London's only surviving fruit and veg market (*see p257*).

Branching off west is **Broadwick Street**, birthplace of William Blake and centre of a severe cholera outbreak in 1854. Local doctor John Snow became convinced that the disease was being transmitted by polluted water and had the street's water pump chained up. That Snow was proved correct led to a breakthrough in epidemiology. The doctor is commemorated by a handleless replica water pump and in the name of the street's pub (appropriate, this, as the only locals who survived the outbreak were those who drank beer rather than water).

West Soho

The area west of Berwick Street is considerably less interesting than the eastern half of Soho. Sure, Brewer Street is dotted with interesting shops – among them the Vintage Magazine Store (Nos.39-43, 7439 8525) and Anything Left-Handed (No.57, 7437 3910) – while Windmill Street is not without its sleazy charm, but much of west Soho is given over to flats and offices and has little of interest for the visitor.

Still, proof that change can be a good thing arrives on **Carnaby Street** and its surrounding thoroughfares. Hip in the 1960s – it was the epicentre of Swingin' London – it then degenerated into consumer hell, and became overrun with shops selling, for want of a better phrase, total crap. However, though Carnaby Street itself still reeks a little of tourist tat, many of the character-sapping enterprises have bitten the dust and been replaced by hipper retailers, and the area has turned itself around. **Newburgh Street**, in particular, is now home to some great fashion shops, while both **Foubert's Place** and the bar- and restaurant-dominated **Kingly Street** have more to offer than at any time for years.

Chinatown

Map p401
Leicester Square or Piccadilly Circus tube.

Shaftesbury Avenue, extending from New Oxford Street to Piccadilly Circus, was driven through slums in the 1880s. Over the next 20 years, seven theatres were built along the street; six still stand, and Shaftesbury Avenue is the heart of Theatreland. It also has a brilliantly revamped cinema in the form of the Curzon Soho (*see p290*) and a handful of Chinese opticians, herbalists, restaurants and travel agents that mark it out as the northern edge of Chinatown, which extends down to Leicester Square.

In the 1950s many Chinese – mainly from Hong Kong and London's original Chinatown in Limehouse – were drawn to **Gerrard Street** and **Lisle Street** by cheap rents. Today the ersatz oriental gates, stone lions and pagoda-topped phone booths suggest a Chinese theme park, yet Chinatown is in fact a close-knit residential and working enclave: beyond the many restaurants (for a selection, *see p199*), few concessions are made to tourism. How long this will remain the case is in some doubt, however: rent hikes may begin to force residents out over the coming year. Join in the Chinese New Year celebrations before it's too late (*see p262*).

Leicester Square

Map p401
Leicester Square or Piccadilly Circus tube.

Leading from Lisle Street to Leicester Square is Leicester Place, home to one of London's cheapest but most comfortable cinemas, the Prince Charles (*see p293*) and the French Catholic church of Notre Dame de France, which contains some murals by Jean Cocteau.

Leicester Square itself is one of the city's great tourist meeting points. It started out as a chic aristo hangout in the 17th and 18th centuries, when Leicester House fronted the north side, but the attractions of the theatre and the flesh had taken over by the mid 19th century. Over the years it became neglected and rundown to the point where the area's only visitors were tourists who didn't know any better, film-goers drawn by the big cinemas in the square – which today include the Empire, the Warner Village West End multiplex, and a pair of Odeons that hold most of London's glitzy premières (for all, *see p290-1*) – and winos.

However, Westminster Council tarted the place up in the mid-1990s, and today the cambered square is a far nicer space, albeit one that's done few favours by the undistinguished buildings around it and the abysmal buskers.

Covent Garden
& St Giles's

Loved by shoppers but reviled by many Londoners, Covent Garden
has many low-key charms behind its touristy façade.

Neal Street, one of **Covent Garden**'s offbeat shopping streets. *See p127.*

Covent Garden

Maps p399 & p401

*Covent Garden, Leicester Square, Temple or
Tottenham Court Road tube.*

Say the name 'Covent Garden' to your average
punter, and like as not they'll assume you're
talking about the area's pedestrianised piazza
(*see p125*), where gift shops, market stalls and
street entertainers vie for visitors' attention.
The heavily touristy nature of the area – it's
hellishly busy most weekends, especially in
summer – the influx of chain restaurants and
shops, and the assorted street entertainers are
not to everyone's taste, yet Covent Garden
works: even those Londoners who can't stand
the place appreciate the need for it.

Of course, there's more to Covent Garden
than shops and stalls, and time spent exploring
its manifold historic and theatrical associations
will be time well rewarded. Its name is a
corruption of the 'convent garden' of the Abbey
of St Paul at Westminster, which originally
stood on the site. In the 1630s would-be
property speculator the Earl of Bedford asked
Inigo Jones to develop the centre of Covent
Garden into an area 'fitte for the habitacions
of *Gentlemen* and men of ability'. Influenced
by the Italian neo-classicism of Palladio, Jones
designed the bluff, no-nonsense church of
St Paul's (*see p125*); its main entrance
facing on to the square beneath the portico
has never been used, as William Laud, the
bishop of London, insisted that the altar be
in its traditional place against the east wall.

Nowadays the redundant portico provides a stage-like area where jugglers and other street entertainers perform.

London's first planned square was an immediate hit with the well-to-do, but as the fruit and vegetable market, founded in 1656, grew to uncomfortable proportions, and newer, more exclusive developments sprung up further west, Covent Garden's reputation slumped. Coffee houses, taverns, Turkish baths and brothels thrived: John Cleland's archetypal tart-with-a-heart, Fanny Hill, lodged here for a while. Later, the area's grandiose Victorian gin palaces acted as 'the lighthouses which guided the thirsty soul on the road to ruin'.

Yet, throughout these years, Covent Garden remained a fashionable venue for theatre and opera (as celebrated at the **Theatre Museum**; *see below*). From the time the first **Royal Opera House** (*see p310*) opened in Bow Lane in 1732, London's beau monde has gingerly picked its way through the filth and rotting vegetables to enjoy the glittering pleasures of the stage. The Theatre Royal in Drury Lane was the other main attraction; it was here that David Garrick revolutionised English theatre. With the Royal Opera House, the area's theatrical reputation has been maintained to this day; and though the fruit and veg market has long gone (in 1974, to a new site in Battersea), the piazza remains a shopping hub thanks to redevelopment led by the now-defunct Greater London Council (*see p25* **Who he? Ken Livingstone**).

Covent Garden Piazza

One of London's few extensive pedestrianised public spaces, the piazza does have more than its fair share of shops and stalls dispensing cheap tat (particularly in **Jubilee Market** on the south side), but jewellery fans will find plenty to satisfy among the **Apple Market** stalls in the market building. The jewel in the piazza's crown, however, is the stunning (and expensively redeveloped) **Royal Opera House**, which you can pop into for drinks, snacks, full meals and tours (for more, *see p307*). **London's Transport Museum** (*see below*) is also a don't-miss, particularly if you have little ones to keep entertained.

London's Transport Museum

Covent Garden Piazza, WC2 (7379 6344/ www.ltmuseum.co.uk). Covent Garden tube. **Open** 10am-6pm Mon-Thur, Sat, Sun; 11am-6pm Fri. Last entry 5.15pm. **Admission** £5.95; £3.95 concessions; free under-16s when accompanied by an adult. **Credit** MC, V. **Map** p401 L6.

A model for hands-on museums everywhere, the LTM is hard to fault (if only the tube worked as well; *see p70* **Rumblings**). A thoroughgoing

exploration of the ways London life has been shaped by public transport since the 1820s, it features everything from old buses that both kids and adults love clambering over and a video of the emotional gathering to commemorate central London's last tram journey, to mobile displays of modern developments such as the Docklands Light Railway and the new Croydon tramlink. School groups predominate, and there are plenty of fathers and sons wandering around (you can see mothers taking a break in the adjoining Aroma coffee shop), but no one can fail to be won over by the interactive facilities, from the low-tech (a Funbus soft play area for tots) to the dynamic (a tube simulator). In July 2001 a new learning centre opened, while a massive refurbishment (pencilled in for 2003 and expected to entail the closure of the museum for 18 months) will create rooms for displays on taxis and watercraft. Real geeks and trainspotters will want to visit the Acton Town depot, which has 370,000 additional exhibits; see the website for details of the occasional open days.

St Paul's Covent Garden

Bedford Street, WC2 (7836 5221). Covent Garden or Leicester Square tube. **Open** 9am-4.30pm Mon-Fri; 9am-12.30pm Sun. **Admission** free; donations appreciated. **Map** p401 L7.

Known as 'the Actors' Church' because of its long-standing association with Covent Garden's Theatreland (lining its interior walls are memorials to a galaxy of stars, from Ivor Novello to Hattie Jacques), this plain Tuscan pastiche of a church was designed by Inigo Jones as part of a square commissioned by the Earl of Bedford in 1631. Pepys' diary of 1662 contains the first recorded sighting of a Punch and Judy show under its portico, a fact commemorated in the Covent Garden May Fayre & Puppet Festival (*see p263*); it's also under the portico that George Bernard Shaw based the first scene of *Pygmalion*. Shortly after Pepys' visit, in 1665, the first known victim of the Great Plague, Margaret Ponteous, was buried in St Paul's churchyard.

Theatre Museum

Tavistock Street (entrance Russell Street), WC2 (7943 4700/www.theatremuseum.org). Covent Garden tube. **Open** 10am-6pm Tue-Sun. Last entry 5.30pm. **Admission** £4.50; £2.50 concessions; free under-16s, over-60s. **Credit** AmEx, MC, V. **Map** p401 L6.

This magical realm is the kind of place that's best enjoyed with kids, at whom much of it is aimed: there are make-up and dress-up sessions (free with entry; call for times), plus puppets in everything from paper to metal and imaginative interactive gizmos such as the 'silver trail', along which you can play with anything that's marked in silver. For adults there's a whistlestop tour of 400 years of stage life, both thematic and by actors and theatre, dance and opera companies. Among the curiosities are old costumes, a reconstructed dressing-room, and a skull given to Sarah Bernhardt by Victor Hugo. There's also a display on the restoration of London's

Sightseeing

art deco Savoy Theatre (*see p127*). Running on into 2002 is Let Paul Robeson Sing!, an exhibition on the life and career of the black actor and singer (to Sept); for children the main gallery continues its look behind the scenes at the Royal National Theatre's production of *Wind in the Willows*.

Elsewhere in Covent Garden

East of the piazza, in **Bow Street**, stands the Magistrates' Courts. During the 1750s and 1760s the courts were presided over by novelist and barrister Henry Fielding, and his blind half-brother John ('the blind beak'), who was said to be able to recognise 3,000 thieves by their voices alone. It was Henry who, horrified by the lawlessness and danger of Georgian London, established the Bow Street Runners, precursors of the modern police force. Nearby, on Great Queen Street, is the HQ of the United Grand Lodge of England, the **Freemasons' Hall** (*see below*), while further along is Browns members-only club (No.4; 7831 0802), formerly the New Romantic

On location: Hitchcock's *Frenzy*

Perhaps his most controversial picture, the brutally violent and sexually explicit *Frenzy* is the only Hitchcock film to have garnered an X certificate, yet it also has a strangely anachronistic feel: Richard Blaney, the ex-RAF hero played by Jon Finch, comes complete with trademark moustache and clipped, frightfully posh accent, for instance. But it's not just the characters' behaviour and speech that seems out of date: the London in which the film is set (ostensibly 1972, the year it was made) also feels older, which might be explained by the fact that *Frenzy* is not just another thriller – it's also Hitchcock's valentine to the city in which he grew up but that he hadn't used as a location for 20 years. As one of the film's stars, Anna Massey, explained, 'He came from a '40s London. That's what he remembered and that's what he created in a way'.

The film's opening sequence – a sweeping shot along the Thames on a beautiful day as Tower Bridge is raised, to the pomp and ceremony of a British brass band – sets us up for an upbeat talk by an MP outside County Hall, who is promising his listeners that the Thames will be free of pollution. Cue naked body washing up on the riverbank, the latest victim of the Necktie Murderer. What follows is a motif fans of Hitchcock won't be slow to pick up on: a case of mistaken identity.

The real killer, Bob Rusk (played by Barry Foster) lives and works as a fruit trader in Covent Garden. For Hitchcock, this was an area bursting with personal associations: he'd come here with his father, who sold wholesale veg, and as a child he'd accompanied his parents to theatres in Drury Lane. Meanwhile, Rusk's bachelor pad at 3 Henrietta Street (the building, the ground floor of which was occupied by Duckworth & Co in the film, is now owned by a book distributor) once belonged to the writer Clemence Dane, whose novel formed the basis for Hitchcock's 1930 film *Murder*, and there's a blue plaque to Ivor Novello, who starred in *The Lodger* (Hitchcock's second, silent film, made in 1926), at 11 Aldwych, where the actor once had a flat.

The two pubs featured in the film, the Globe on Bow Street and the Nell of Old Drury on Catherine Street, still exist, while the fruit and veg market itself was a primary location, particularly in the astonishing scene where the camera follows the killer as he leads the ill-fated Babs, played by Massey, up the stairs to his flat, then recoils and pulls back into the market. Despite the gory nature of *Frenzy*, the real traders are said to have been very excited that Hitchcock wanted to film their operations centre, since it was about to be closed and shunted off south of the river, after serving as London's vegetable market since the 17th century. Indeed, this is one of the many fascinating aspects of this complex film – its portrait of a long-gone slice of authentic London life.

For more on Hitchcock in London, *see p163*.

club Blitz, from which Visage frontman Steve Strange turned away Mick Jagger for 'not being cool enough'.

Connoisseurs of London pubs shouldn't miss the Lamb & Flag (*see p223*) at 33 Rose Street. Built in 1623, it's one of central London's few surviving wooden-framed buildings. Another delightful echo of the past is **Goodwin's Court**, a tiny alley running between St Martin's Lane and Bedfordbury, which contains a row of bow-fronted 17th-century houses still lit by clockwork-operated gas street lighting.

However, most locals journey to Covent Garden for hip clothes shops; **Floral Street** offers rich pickings for clubbers, while more mainstream chains are represented on parallel **Long Acre**. Pedestrianised **Neal Street**, the site of the shortlived but influential **Roxy**, which in 1976 hosted gigs by X Ray Spex, the Sex Pistols, the Clash and the Damned (at No.41), is agreeably offbeat – everything from kites to oriental tea sets can be had here. **Neal's Yard** (off Shorts Gardens), a hippie haven of health food and natural remedies, is a reminder of the 'alternative' scene that did so much, through its mass squats and demonstrations, to stop the brutal redevelopment of Covent Garden after the market moved to Battersea in 1974.

The consumer heaven continues up **Shorts Gardens** and **Earlham Street** to **Seven Dials**, a one-time hangout for criminals and now a quaint little junction.

Freemasons' Hall

Great Queen Street, WC2 (7831 9811/ www.grandlodge-england.org). Covent Garden or Holborn tube. **Open** call for details of weekday tours. **Admission** free. **Map** p399 L6.

Of the 20 or so temples in this monumental art deco edifice, which is undergoing constant renovation, the centrepiece is the Grand Temple with its beautiful carved doors, superb mosaic ceiling and stained-glass windows. Though the Masons are notorious for their secretiveness, the hall can be seen during the week, when there are five guided tours a day (call for details), and at the annual Open House weekend (*see p268*, **Grand Openings**). There are also occasional big band concerts.

The Strand

Skirting the southern edge of Covent Garden, the **Strand** was, until Victoria Embankment was constructed in the 1860s, a muddy riverside bridle path. Built to link the City with Westminster and lined with the palatial homes of the aristocracy from the 13th century, it turns southwards at **Charing Cross**. In front of the railway station is an 1863 monument commemorating the original cross, erected near

here by the sorrowful Edward I to mark the passing of the funeral procession of his queen, Eleanor, in 1290.

The Strand became as notorious for pickpockets and prostitution as Covent Garden (Boswell recalled how '… last night … I met a monstrous big whore in the Strand, whom I had a great curiosity to lubricate'), but within 100 years Disraeli thought it the finest street in Europe. The building of the grand **Savoy Hotel** enhanced this reputation, but the adjoining Savoy Theatre actually predates the hotel by eight years: it was built by Richard D'Oyly Carte to host Gilbert and Sullivan operas (though it was reconstructed in its current art deco form in 1929, and restored in 1990 after a devastating fire; see *p125* **Theatre Museum**).

Today's Strand, brimming with traffic and lined with offices, shops, theatres, and the odd pub and restaurant, is a harsh and rather forlorn place, an impression that's heavily reinforced by the many homeless people who bed down in its doorways.

The Embankment

From the Strand, pedestrianised Villiers Street leads past Terry Farrell's monster-toy-brick **Embankment Place** and the characterful Gordon's wine bar (*see p223*) to **Embankment Gardens** and Embankment tube station. All that remains of grand York House, which stood here from the 13th to the 17th century, is **York Watergate** on Watergate Walk, which once let on to the Thames.

Across from the gardens, sandwiched between the river and the Embankment's constant traffic, is **Cleopatra's Needle**. Nothing to do with Cleopatra, this 60-foot (19-metre) granite obelisk dates from around 1475 BC. Presented to Britain by Egypt in 1819, it didn't make the long journey here until 1878. Buried under the needle are various objects including, bizarrely, photographs of 12 of the best-looking English women of the day. The sphinxes at the base were replaced facing the wrong way after being cleaned in the early 20th century.

Walk over Hungerford Bridge (to which two new footbridges were being added as we went to press) towards the South Bank Centre to enjoy one of the best views of London's riverscape, particularly at night. The huge white New Adelphi building, with its giant clock, stands on the site of the Adam brothers' celebrated Adelphi, built in 1768-72. This terrace of 11 houses over arches and vaults was more of an architectural than commercial success, but it was mindless vandalism that the whole thing was pulled down in 1936.

Centre Point, designed by Richard Seifert.

St Giles's

This curious little pocket of London, which doesn't really form part of the clear-cut areas that surround it (Covent Garden, Soho and Fitzrovia), has a tawdry history. A leper hospital was established here by Queen Matilda, wife of Henry I, in 1101, when St Giles's was still a small village outside London. The hospital was dissolved by Henry VIII in 1539 but its chapel became the new parish church, **St Giles-in-the-Fields**; this was rebuilt in 1630, then replaced by a new church constructed in 1730-4, after St George Bloomsbury (*see p105*) was built, creating a new parish carved out of the ancient parish of St Giles's.

As well as being the parish where the Great Plague started, in 1665, it was here that prisoners on their way to be executed at the Tyburn gallows, which stood at Marble Arch from the 14th to the 18th century, were allowed to stop for one last drink (paid for by the churchwardens) in the Angel pub on **St Giles High Street** – something to think about as you sup a pint there.

The 19th century saw St Giles's nosedive further with the emergence of the Rookeries: a small area bordered by St Giles High Street, Bainbridge Street and Dyott Street and overrun with criminals, prostitutes and vagrants. These days a hostel for the homeless sits underneath Centre Point, the tall building on the corner of **Charing Cross Road** and New Oxford Street, and the top stretch of Charing Cross Road and the streets behind it are frequented by drug users, dealers and petty criminals.

Take particular care if you're walking the streets around **Denmark Street**, which you may want to do if you're a music buff: currently home to many instrument and sheet music shops and informally known as 'Tin Pan Alley', it has a colourful musical history: Gioconda la Café (dubbed 'musicians' café') was once the greasy spoon where the Small Faces signed up for their first recording, and where Bowie was introduced to his first band, the Lower Third. At No.4, now the Helter Skelter music bookshop, was Regents Sound Studios, where the Stones laid down *Not Fade Away* and the Kinks recorded their first demo; while at No.6, now a guitar shop, the Sex Pistols wrote *Anarchy in the UK* in a dingy ground-floor room, and Bananarama squatted while living on benefit.

The remainder of the Charing Cross Road – south of Denmark Street – is more pleasant, at least for bibliophiles. It's long been dominated by bookshops: the modern Borders (No.120) faces up to the idiosyncratic Foyles, which celebrates its centenary in two years (for both, *see p232*). Further down Charing Cross Road, south of Shaftesbury Avenue, second-hand and specialist book stores dominate.

St Giles-in-the-Fields

St Giles High Street, WC2 (7240 2532/www.giles-in-the-fields.org). Tottenham Court Road tube. **Open** 9am-4pm Mon-Fri; open for services Sun, call for details. **Admission** free; donations appreciated. **Map** p399 K6.
There's been a house of prayer on this site for just over 900 years, though this Palladian building, designed by Henry Flitcroft (who went on to design Woburn Abbey), dates back to the early 1700s. Particularly worthy of attention is the pulpit from the chapel in nearby West Street when John and Charles Wesley preached in the 18th century. Note also the allegorical medieval 'Pelican in her piety' image above the alter, in which a mother bird feeds her young with her own blood. There are few remaining tombstones in the churchyard, which doesn't merit a visit, especially given the dubious nature of the area. Call for details of lunchtime recitals.

Westminster

It may draw its lifeblood from history and politics, but Westminster is also a must-see for art fans.

All change for **Trafalgar Square**.

Maps p400 & p401

Embankment, Piccadilly Circus, Pimlico, St James's Park or Westminster tube/Charing Cross or Victoria tube/rail.

Westminster has been at the centre of matters both royal and religious for the best part of 1,000 years, since Edward the Confessor built his 'West Minster' and palace on marshy Thorney Island in the 11th century, while its political heart began beating in the 1300s, when the first Parliament met in the abbey.

The area has some arresting Gothic architecture, though in the summer it can be difficult to see due to the sheer volume of visitors. The architectural highlight of recent times, however, is more readily accessible: Westminster tube station, for so long an ugly thing to be ignored, has been transformed as part of the extensive Jubilee line renovation. Visit it to see how a tube station ought to be built. *See also p268* **Grand openings**.

Trafalgar Square

Has anybody ever really enjoyed buying a tub of bird food in order to incite an armada of bewinged vermin into dive-bombing them? Possibly, but the fact is that pigeons carry more diseases than your average sewer rat, and the ban on feeding them here has meant that the square is cleaner and more attractive. But the dwindling numbers of our foul, feathered friends have also resulted in **Trafalgar Square**, which was laid out on the site of the demolished King's Mews 170 years ago, looking even more like a giant roundabout than before. Sir Edwin Landseer's magnificent lions are a focal point for tourists with their cameras and intrepid climbers, while Nelson stands on his column staring down Whitehall as if seeking a nicer spot.

But all this will change if Ken Livingstone (*see p25* **Who he?**) has his way. The only venue over which the Mayor exercises control, the square played host to the South Africa Freedom Day concert in 2001 and looks set to become a focal point for celebrations promoting London's ethnic diversity (*see p33* **The melting pot**). Livingstone's initiatives are part of the World Squares for All masterplan by Norman Foster & Partners, phase one of which, scheduled for completion in 2003 or 2004, includes the pedestrianisation of the north side of the square. The opening of a hip new Hilton hotel, the Trafalgar (*see p53*), has also upped the area's kudos.

At present, however, the most interesting aspect of the square is the fourth plinth. Built in 1841, it was intended for a statue of William IV, but a lack of funds put paid to that idea. Arguments have raged for the past 150 years as to which monarch or idol should be resurrected, and the plinth remained vacant until a commission set up in 1999 to consider its long-term use concluded that it should showcase contemporary artworks, both British and international, on a rotating basis. The current exhibition, which runs until May 2002, has consisted of three very different works. The first was *Ecce Homo*, a life-sized statue of Christ by Mark Wallinger; it was followed by Bill Woodrow's *Regardless of History*, a strange but eye-catching fusion of a face, a tree and a book. The final piece is Rachel Whiteread's *Monument*, an inverted cast of the plinth in perspex. Whiteread's stunning *House*, a cast of the interior of an East End terraced house, was torn down by the local council not long after its completion in 1993; justice may be partially served if the impressive *Monument* were to become a permanent fixture in Trafalgar Square, of which it already seems an integral part (even the dastardly pigeons seem to like it).

By contrast, the low-key, low-rise buildings on the north side of the square, which were built in 1832-8, don't seem a grand enough home for the **National Gallery** (*see below*). The adjoining **National Portrait Gallery** (*see below*) can be accessed around the corner on Charing Cross Road. A more impressive structure, on the north-east corner of the square, is James Gibbs's perky church of **St Martin-in-the-Fields** (*see p131*).

National Gallery

Trafalgar Square, WC2 (info line 7747 2885/ www.nationalgallery.org.uk). Leicester Square tube/Charing Cross tube/rail. **Open** 10am-6pm Mon, Tue, Thur-Sun; 10am-9pm Wed. *Micro Gallery* 10am-5.30pm Mon, Tue, Thur-Sun; 10am-8.30pm Wed. *Sainsbury Wing* 10am-6pm Mon, Tue, Thur-Sun; 10am-9pm Wed. *Tours* free; times vary; check info line. **Admission** free; temporary exhibitions prices vary. **Credit** *Shop* MC, V. **Map** p401 K7.

The National Gallery was founded in 1824 with just 38 pictures – a far cry from its position today as one of the world's greatest museums of western European painting. There are paintings from as far back as the 13th century here, but before you go charging in to ogle the Canalettos and Constables, courtesy of a number of audio-guides or guided talks (there's even a Micro Gallery where a computer will devise a tour for you or print out your favourite paintings), have a look at what you're stepping on – the entrance foyer is a mass of mosaics courtesy of a Russian called Boris Anrep, who took his admiration of pavement chalk artists to astonishing lengths, completing 50 in all between 1928 and 1952. You're stepping on the noses of such luminaries as Winston Churchill, Virginia Woolf, Greta Garbo and, bizarrely, TS Eliot regarding the Loch Ness Monster.

Temporary exhibitions for 2002 include Aelbert Cuyp (13 Feb-12 May), one of the most important Dutch painters of the 17th century; Baroque Painting in Genoa (13 Mar-16 June), the first major display in Britain of 17th-century paintings from one of the richest and most cosmopolitan cities of northern Italy, including work by both native painters and foreign artists such as Rubens and Van Dyck; Fabric of Vision: Dress and Drapery in Painting (19 June-8 Sept), examining the role played by costume and drapery in works by artists from the Middle Ages to the 20th century, including Tintoretto, Delacroix and Picasso. Also scheduled is Madame de Pompadour:

Some residents of **St James's Park**. *See p131.*

Images of a Mistress (16 Oct 2002-12 Jan 2003), which explores how the mistress of Louis XV manipulated her image for social and political reasons.

National Portrait Gallery

2 St Martin's Place, WC2 (7306 0055/ www.npg.org.uk). Leicester Square tube/Charing Cross tube/rail. **Open** 10am-6pm Mon-Wed, Sat, Sun; 10am-9pm Thur, Fri. *Tours* Aug free; times vary. **Admission** free; selected exhibitions £5; £3 concessions. **Credit** AmEx, MC, V. **Map** p401 K7.

The NPG might have a host of po-faced subjects on its walls, but by god has it fought to slough off that stuffy image. A restaurant, imaginatively called Portrait, allows views across Westminster, while a swanky escalator whisks you to the main collection at the top of the Ondaatje Wing, where the great and the good stare you down from across the ages. Highlights include Marcus Gheeraerts's portrait of Queen Elizabeth I standing astride England, and some of the smaller exhibits such as the miniature of Thomas Cromwell by Hans Holbein.

If you think the Duke of Monmouth looks a bit green around the gills, there's a reason for that. James Scott, the duke in question, was one of 13 children fathered by Charles II. Favourite to succeed his father to the throne, James positioned himself against the Catholic James II and mustered an army to defeat this usurper to the throne, but in 1685 he was captured and taken to Tower Hill, where it took the notorious bungling executioner Jack Ketch four attempts to separate James's head from his body. Later, somebody mentioned that the Duke of

Monmouth had been a royal – after a fashion – but that no portrait of him existed, so the Royal Surgeon stitched him together and plonked him down in front of William Wissing, who had 24 hours to complete the portrait before his subject went off. Now you know what that fluffy white cravat was for.

Look out in 2002 for Mario Testino: Portraits, the first ever gallery exhibition of the photographer better known for his work in fashion photography. Featuring more than 150 portraits selected by Testino himself, the exhibit will include Robbie Williams, John Galliano, Gwyneth Paltrow, Kate Moss and Princess Diana.

St Martin-in-the-Fields

Trafalgar Square, WC2 (7766 1100/Brass Rubbing Centre 7930 9306/box office evening concerts 7839 8362/www.stmartin-in-the-fields.org). Leicester Square tube/Charing Cross tube/rail. **Admission** free. *Brass rubbing* £2.90-£15 (special rates for groups and families). *Evening concerts* £6-£16 (7.30pm Thur-Sat).* **Open** *Church* 8am-6pm daily. *Brass Rubbing Centre* 10am-6pm Mon-Sat; noon-6pm Sun. **Credit** MC, V. **Map** p401 L7.
A church has stood on this site since the 13th century, 'in the fields' between Westminster and the City. Inside, dark woodwork and ornate Italian plasterwork greet visitors to this parish church for Buckingham Palace (note the royal box to the left of the gallery). For details of free lunchtime concerts, *see p311.* There's also a café, an art gallery, a gift shop and the London Brass Rubbing Centre.

St James's Park & surrounds

From Trafalgar Square, the grand processional route of the **Mall** (home of the **ICA Gallery**; *see p132*) passes under Admiralty Arch and past St James's Park to the Victoria Memorial in front of **Buckingham Palace** (*see below*). which, up close, seems rather small, squat and unimposing. More satisfying is a wander round the carriages of the **Royal Mews** behind the palace, or a stroll in **St James's Park**.

In the 17th century Charles II had the deer park of St James's Palace converted into a garden by French landscape gardener Le Nôtre; and St James's Park was landscaped further by John Nash in the early 19th century. The view of Buckingham Palace from the bridge over the lake is wonderful, particularly at night when the palace is floodlit. The lake itself is now a sanctuary for wildfowl, among them pelicans (fed at 3pm daily) and Australian black swans. There's a playground at the Buckingham Palace end, and a café. Many Londoners rate St James's as the loveliest and most intimate of the capital's central parks. It's certainly much improved since the days of James Boswell – Dr Johnson's lusty biographer – who enjoyed a rather different species of fauna during his walks there in the mid 1700s: 'At night, Erskine

[Andrew Erskine, Boswell's close friend] and I strolled through the streets and St James's Park. We were accosted there by several ladies of the town. Erskine was very humorous and said some very wild things to them. There was one in a red cloak of a good buxom person and comely face whom I marked as a future piece, in case of exigency.'

On the south side of the park, the Wellington Barracks, home of the Foot Guards, contains the **Guards' Museum** (*see below*). Nearby are the fully intact Georgian terraces of Queen Anne's Gate and Old Queen Street.

Buckingham Palace & Royal Mews

SW1 (7930 4832/recorded info 7799 2331/ credit card bookings 7321 2233/Royal Mews 7839 1377/www.royalresidences.com). Green Park or St James's Park tube/Victoria tube/rail. **Open** State Rooms *early Aug-Sept* 9.30am-4.15pm daily. Royal Mews *Oct-July* noon-4pm. *Aug-Sept* 10.30am-4.30pm Mon-Thur. Last entry 30min before closing. **Admission** £11; £5.50 5-17s; £9 concessions; £27.50 family (2+2); free under-5s. *Royal Mews* £4.60; £2.60 5-17s; £3.60 concessions; £11.80 family (2+2); free under-5s. **Credit** AmEx, MC, V. **Map** p400 H9.
Although Buckingham House, as it once was known, was built in 1703 for the Duke of Buckingham, it was purchased by George III and converted into a palace by his son George VI. It didn't become a royal residence until 1837, though, when Queen Victoria moved in. In August and September, while the Windsors are off on their hols, the State Apartments – the rooms used for banquets and investitures – are open to the public. Unless you're really into upmarket knick-knacks, the only real items of interest are the artworks dotted about the place; the Queen's Gallery, featuring highlights of Her Maj's art collection, is scheduled to reopen in May 2002 after remodelling.

Around the corner, on Buckingham Palace Road, the Royal Mews is home to the royal carriages that are rolled out for the Royals to wag their hands from on very important occasions. The Coronation Coach, the Glass Coach, the immaculately groomed horses and the sleek black landaus make the Mews one of the capital's better-value collections. Top banana, though, goes to Her Majesty's State Coach, a breathtaking double-gilded affair built in 1761. The Mews is closed during Royal Ascot and on state occasions.

Guards' Museum

Wellington Barracks, Birdcage Walk, SW1 (7414 3271). St James's Park tube. **Open** 10am-4pm daily (last entry 3.30pm). **Admission** £2; £1 concessions; free under-16s; £4 family (2 + unlimited children). **Credit** *Shop* AmEx, MC, V. **Map** p400 J9.
The British Army has five Guards regiments, whose history is recorded by this small museum founded in the 17th century under Charles II. It contains mainly uniforms and oil paintings, viewed to an accompaniment of martial music, but also houses a collection of curios, including the Guards' oldest medal (awarded by Cromwell to officers of

Sightseeing

The Black Museum

New Scotland Yard contains a secret – well, quite a few secrets, and many of them grisly. In a large room on the first floor resides the Black Museum or, as it's more officially known, the Crime Museum. Between these walls sits evidence from the most notorious British crimes committed over the last 150 years. Some of the trinkets on display belonged to felons who together form a rogues' gallery of some of the most nefarious villains ever to terrorise these shores, among them Dr Crippen (*pictured*), the Kray Twins, John Christie, Dennis Nilsen and the daddy of them all, Jack the Ripper. Case files, weapons and death masks from the hanged convicts can all be viewed here.

Six years after the Prisoner's Property Act (1869) authorised the police to retain certain items of prisoners' property for instructional purposes, an Inspector Neame established the crime museum with the help of his assistant, PC Randall, who became the 'curator' (all subsequent curators have been police officers too) responsible for looking after the exhibits. The displays were principally for the use of furthering the education of young police officers in the ways and means of crime detection and prevention.

The real crime here is that members of the public are not allowed to visit the museum. That said, some high-profile ghouls have been given special permission to ogle the artefacts over the years: royal rubberneckers George V and Edward VII enjoyed a visit, as did Harry

Houdini, Stan Laurel, Oliver Hardy and Sir Arthur Conan Doyle. We have a bitter *Observer* journalist to thank for the current moniker by which the museum is known: he christened it the Black Museum after being refused entry in 1877.

This particular crime scene has altered since its foundation. Its first address was at Old Scotland Yard, off Whitehall. In 1890 the Metropolitan Police moved to New Scotland Yard on Victoria Embankment and took the Black Museum with it. During both world wars the museum was closed, but it flourished once more in 1968 when the Met moved to its current HQ on Broadway, SW1.

his New Model Army at the Battle of Dunbar in 1651) and a bottle of Iraqi whisky that was captured in the Gulf War. The Guards can be seen in ceremonial action performing the change of guard at St James's Palace and at Buckingham Palace (*see p264* **Frequent events**).

ICA Gallery

The Mall, SW1 (box office 7930 3647/membership enquiries 7766 1439/www.ica.org.uk). Piccadilly Circus tube/Charing Cross tube/rail. **Open** *Galleries* noon-7.30pm daily. **Membership** *Daily* £1.50, £1 concessions Mon-Fri; £2.50, £1.50 concessions Sat, Sun; free under-14s. *Annual* £25; £15 concessions. **Credit** AmEx, DC, MC, V. **Map** p401 K8.

At its opening in 1948, art historian and anarchist Herbert Read promised that the ICA (Institute of Contemporary Arts) would be different from other art museums. And to this day, he's been right: the ICA maintains a reputation as a challenging arena in which to witness all forms of artistic expression,

and many leading artists had their first London exhibitions at the ICA, including Moore, Picasso and Max Ernst. Yet as well as highlighting the importance of more established artists from abroad, it has a fine track record in promoting young artists from these shores: Damien Hirst, Helen Chadwick, Gary Hume and the Chapman brothers all had early exposure here. With its spaces separated by a lengthy corridor and a couple of flights of stairs, the ICA has a somewhat ramshackle feel, but the shows frequently provoke reaction and debate. A feature of programming in recent years has been the inclusion of contemporary architects such as Future Systems, Rem Koolhaas and Zaha Hadid.

Exhibitions for 2002 include the Swedish artist Annika Larsson (8 Feb-10 Mar), LA-based artist and writer Frances Stark (23 May-14 July) and Dutch artists Jeroen De Rijke and Willem De Rooij (23 May-14 July). Also, in spring 2002 (29 Mar-5 May), the ICA and Beck's will present a major exhibition and art prize designed to promote contemporary artists.

Whitehall to Parliament Square

From Trafalgar Square the long, gentle curve of **Whitehall** takes you into the heart of political Britain. Lined up along the street, many of the big ministries maintain at least the façade of heart-of-the-empire solidity. Halfway down the street, the Horse Guards building (try to pass by when the mounted scarlet-clad guards are changing; *see p264*) faces the **Banqueting House** (*see below*), central London's first classical-style building. Near here is Edwin Lutyens's ascetically plain memorial to the dead of both world wars, the **Cenotaph**, and, on **Downing Street**, the anonymous official homes of the prime minister and chancellor of the exchequer (closed off by iron security gates since 1990). At the end of King Charles Street sit the **Cabinet War Rooms** (*see below*), the operations centre used by Churchill and his Cabinet during World War II air raids.

Parliament Square was laid out in 1868 and the architecture here is on a grand scale. **Westminster Central Hall**, with its great black dome, was built on the site of the old Royal Aquarium in 1905-11 and is used for conferences (the first assembly of the United Nations was held there in 1946) as well as for Methodist church services. Following a lengthy facelift, **Westminster Abbey** (*see p134*) is now resplendent in its original pristine white. But despite its present air of respectability, the area around it was a den of iniquity at the back end of the 19th century. Thieves were much in evidence, possibly because the abbey was known to be a sanctuary for criminals. Memorials within are manifold: look out for William Shakespeare, Charles Dickens and Oscar Wilde, granted a plot after years of umming and aahing regarding his gross indecency scandal. Similarly shaped to the abbey but much smaller, **St Margaret's Westminster** (*see p134*) stands in the shadow of the abbey, like a promising child next to an indulgent parent. Both Samuel Pepys and Winston Churchill were married here.

Few buildings in London genuinely dazzle, but the **Houses of Parliament** (*see below*) are an exception. Built between 1834 and 1858 by Charles Barry and fancifully decorated by Augustus Pugin, their Disneyland Gothic chutzpah simultaneously raises a smile, a gasp and, perhaps, a chuckle. Although formally still known as the Palace of Westminster, the only surviving part of the medieval royal palace is **Westminster Hall** (and the **Jewel Tower**, just south of Westminster Abbey; *see p134*).

Parliament's clock tower, popularly known as **Big Ben** (though it's the name of the bell rather than the tower itself), seems rather stumpy when viewed close up, especially with the London Eye (*see p73*) leering down above it from the other side of the river. The tower originally contained a small prison cell; Emmeline Pankhurst, in 1902, was its last occupant. A statue of the suffragette stands in **Victoria Tower Gardens**, by the river on the south side of Parliament. Here too is a cast of Rodin's glum-looking *Burghers of Calais* and a splendid Gothic revival drinking fountain. In the shadow of Big Ben, at the end of Westminster Bridge, stands a statue of Boudicca and her daughters gesticulating ambiguously towards Parliament.

Banqueting House

Whitehall, SW1 (7930 4179/www.hrp.org.uk). Westminster tube/Charing Cross tube/rail. **Open** 10am-5pm Mon-Sat (last entry 4.30pm); sometimes closes at short notice; phone to check. **Admission** £3.90; £2.30 5-15s; £3.10 concessions; free under-5s. **Credit** MC, V. **Map** p401 L8.

The only surviving part of the original Whitehall Palace (which was destroyed by fire in 1698), Inigo Jones's classically inspired Banqueting House (1619-22) was the first building in central London in the classical Renaissance style. There's a video and small exhibition in the undercroft, but the chief glory is the first-floor hall, designed for court ceremonials and magnificently adorned with ceiling paintings by Rubens (1635) – Charles I commissioned the Flemish artist and diplomat to glorify his less than glamorous father James I and celebrate the divine right of the Stuart kings. A bust over the entrance commemorates the fact that Charles was beheaded outside this building in 1649.

Cabinet War Rooms

Clive Steps, King Charles Street, SW1 (7930 6961/www.iwm.org.uk). St James's Park or Westminster tube. **Open** *Oct-Mar* 10am-6pm daily. *Apr-Sept* 9.30am-6pm daily. Last entry 5.15pm. **Admission** £5; £3.90 OAPs, students; £2-£2.70 concessions; free under-15s. **Credit** AmEx, MC, V. **Map** p401 K9.

The secret underground HQ of Churchill's World War II Cabinet has been preserved largely as it was left when it closed down on 16 August 1945. Every book, chart and pin in the Map Room occupies the same space now as it did on VJ day, and Churchill's bedroom (apparently so unwelcoming that he preferred to catch up on his sleep at the bomb-damaged Savoy) still contains the BBC microphones with which he addressed the nation. Other highlights include the Transatlantic Telephone Room and a collection of Churchill's private papers and speeches.

Houses of Parliament

Parliament Square, SW1 (Commons info 7219 4272/Lords info 7219 3107/tours 7344 9966/ www.parliament.uk). Westminster tube. **Open** (when in session) *House of Commons Visitors' Gallery* 2.30-10pm Mon-Wed; 11.30am-7.30pm Thur; 9.30am-3pm Fri. *House of Lords Visitors' Gallery* from 2.30pm Mon-Wed; from 3pm Thur; from 11am Fri. *Tours* summer recess only; phone for details. **Admission** *Public gallery* free. *Tours* £3.50; free under-2s. **Map** p401 L9.

The first Parliament was held here in 1275, but Westminster did not become Parliament's permanent home until 1532, when Henry VIII upped sticks to Whitehall. Parliament was originally housed in the choir stalls of St Stephen's Chapel, where members sat facing each other from opposite sides; the tradition continues today. The only remaining parts of the original palace are Westminster Hall, with its hammer-beam roof, and the Jewel Tower; the rest burned down in a fire (1834) and was rebuilt in neo-Gothic style by Charles Barry and Augustus Pugin. There are 1,000 rooms, 100 staircases, 11 courtyards, eight bars and six restaurants; none of them is open to the public, but anyone can watch the Commons or Lords in session from the visitors' galleries. The best spectacle, however, is Prime Minister's Question Time at 3pm on Wednesdays, for which you need advance tickets (available through your MP or embassy). There's no minimum age but children must at least be able to sign their name in the visitors' book.

Parliament goes into recess at Christmas, Easter and summer, at which times the galleries are open only for pre-booked guided tours (which are not free; call for details of how to book).

Jewel Tower

Abingdon Street, SW1 (7222 2219/www.english-heritage.org.uk). Westminster tube. **Open** *Apr-Sept* 10am-6pm daily. *Oct* 10am-5pm daily. *Nov-Mar* 10am-4pm daily. Last entry 30min before closing. **Admission** £1.60; 80p 5-16s; £1.20 concessions; free under-5s. **Credit** MC, V. **Map** p401 L9.

Together with Westminster Hall, this moated tower is a relic from the medieval Palace of Westminster. Built in 1365-6 to house Edward III's booty (*not* the Crown Jewels, as the notice outside would have it), it stored House of Lords records from 1621 to 1864. Today it has an informative exhibition that includes a lively video on Parliament past and present.

St Margaret's Church, Westminster Abbey

Parliament Square, SW1 (7222 5152/ www.westminster-abbey.org). St James's Park or Westminster tube. **Open** 9.30am-4.30pm Mon-Fri; 9.30am-2.45pm Sat; 2-5pm Sun (times might change at short notice due to services). Last entry 1hr before closing. **Services** 11am Sun; phone to check. **Admission** free. **Map** p401 K9.

Founded in the 12th century but rebuilt in 1486-1523 and restored many times since, this historic church is dwarfed by the adjacent abbey. The impressive east window (1509) with its richly coloured Flemish glass commemorates the marriage of Henry VIII and Catherine of Aragon. Later windows celebrate Britain's first printer, William Caxton, buried here in 1491; explorer Sir Walter Raleigh, executed in Old Palace Yard; and writer John Milton (1608-74), who married his second wife here.

Westminster Abbey

Dean's Yard, SW1 (7222 5152/tours 7222 7110/www.westminster-abbey.org). St James's Park or Westminster tube. **Open** *Nave & royal chapels* 9.30am-4.45pm Mon-Fri; 9am-2.45pm Sat. *Chapter House* Nov-Mar 10am-4pm daily. Apr-Sept 9.30am-5pm daily. Oct 10am-5pm. *Pyx Chamber & Abbey Museum* 10.30am-4pm daily. *College Garden* Apr-Sept 10am-6pm Tue-Thur. Oct-Mar 10am-4pm Tue-Thur. Last entry 1hr before closing. **Admission** *Nave & royal chapels* £6; £2 11-15s; £3 11-15s; £3 concessions; £12 family (2+3); free under-11s with paying adult. *Chapter House, Pyx Chamber & Abbey Museum* £2.50; £1 with main entrance ticket; free with £2 audio-guide. **Credit** MC, V. **Map** p401 K9.

Westminster Abbey has been bound up with British royalty since Edward the Confessor built his church to St Peter (consecrated in 1065) on the site of the Saxon original. With two exceptions, every king and queen of England since William the Conqueror (1066) has been crowned here, and many are also buried here: the royal chapels and tombs include Edward the Confessor's shrine and the Coronation Chair (1296). Of the original abbey, only the Pyx Chamber (the one-time royal treasury) and the Norman Undercroft remain; the Gothic nave and choir were rebuilt by Henry III in the 13th century; the Henry VII Chapel, with its spectacular fan vaulting, was added in 1503-12; and Hawksmoor's west towers completed the building in 1745.

The interior is cluttered with monuments to statesmen, scientists, musicians and poets. The centrepiece of the octagonal Chapter House is its 13th-century tiled floor, while the Little Cloister surrounding a pretty garden offers respite from the crowds, especially during the free lunchtime concerts (call for details). Worth a look, too, are the statues of ten 20th-century Christian martyrs in 15th-century niches over the west door. Come as early or late as possible or on midweek afternoons to avoid the tour groups.

Millbank

Millbank runs along the river from Parliament to Vauxhall Bridge. Just off here **St John's Smith Square**, built as a church in 1713-28 by Thomas Archer, is now a venue for classical music (*see p313*). This exuberant baroque fantasy has not been without its detractors: most famously, Dickens thought it 'a very hideous church with four towers at the corners, generally resembling some petrified monster, frightful and gigantic, on its back with its legs in the air'.

By the river, just north of Vauxhall Bridge, stood the Millbank Penitentiary, an attempt to build a model prison based on the ideas of Jeremy Bentham (*see p101*). But it was a grim place that lasted only 70 years before being replaced by the rather more enlightened Tate Gallery, now **Tate Britain** (*see p135*). Overshadowing the Tate is the 387-foot

(240-metre) **Millbank Tower** while, over the river, the giant toy-town-building-block bulk of **Vauxhall Cross** is the strangely conspicuous HQ of the internal security service, MI6 (*see p30* **Love 'em or hate 'em?**).

Tate Britain

Millbank, SW1 (7887 8000/www.tate.org.uk). Pimlico tube/C10, 77A, 88 bus. **Open** 10am-5.50pm daily. *Tours* free; 11.30am, 2.30pm, 3.30pm Mon-Fri. **Admission** free; *special exhibitions* prices vary. **Credit** MC, V. **Map** p401 K11.

After the sailing of the Tate's international modern art collection downriver to Tate Modern (*see p79*; there are shuttle buses and boats between the two sites), the Millbank gallery stretched out a little to better accommodate its collection of British art from the 16th century to the present day. The Clore Gallery extension, meanwhile, continues to house the Turner bequest. The obvious overlap between the two Tates is modern and contemporary British art, and the galleries will undoubtedly play swapsies with works as and when needs arise.

On 1 November 2001 the launch of Tate Britain, which began in March 2000, was complete. Announced in 1997 – the 100th birthday of the Tate Gallery, as it was previously known – the Centenary Development project has provided Tate Britain with ten new and five refurbished galleries, as well as the dramatic new Manton Entrance on Atterbury Street providing visitors with full access, new information points, a cloakroom, toilets and a shop. Keeping pace with the physical transformation of Tate Britain, the project also embraces progress in the provision of digital information about the Tate Collection: as we went to press, it was hoped that the entire British Collection would be online by the start of 2002.

Exhibitions for 2002 include Hamish Fulton (14 Mar-2 June), an exhibition bringing together new and recent work by the artist who first came to prominence in the late 1960s as one of a number of artists engaged in creating both a new kind of landscape art and exploring new forms of sculpture; Lucian Freud (20 June-15 Sept), the largest retrospective to date of the work of one of the greatest living realist painters; and Gainsborough (17 Oct-12 Jan), with a special focus on his continuing significance for British culture.

Victoria & Pimlico

Victoria Street, stretching from Parliament Square to Victoria Station, links political London with backpackers' London. **Victoria Coach Station** is a short distance away in **Buckingham Palace Road**; **Belgrave Road** provides an almost unbroken line of cheap and fairly grim hotels. The area has seldom made the same for long. In the 18th and early 19th centuries, it was dominated by the Grosvenor Canal, but in the 1850s much of this was buried under the new Victoria Station. A century later,

many of the shops and offices along Victoria Street were pulled down and replaced by the anonymous blocks that now line it.

Westminster Cathedral (*see below*) always comes as a pleasant surprise, coming into view only when you draw level with it. Built between 1896 and 1903, its interior has never been finished. Further down Victoria Street is the grey concrete monstrosity that is the **Department of Trade and Industry** HQ.

Continuing along Victoria Street, you come to **Christchurch Gardens**, burial site of Thomas ('Colonel') Blood, the 17th-century rogue who nearly got away with stealing the Crown Jewels. A memorial is dedicated to the suffragettes, who held their first meetings at **Caxton Hall**, visible on the far side of the gardens. **New Scotland Yard** with its famous revolving sign is in Broadway; *see p132* **The Black Museum**. Strutton Ground, on the other side of Victoria Street, is home to a small market. At the other end, Richard Rogers' glorious **Channel Four Building** on the corner of Chadwick Street and Horseferry Road is worth a look.

Pimlico fills the triangle of land formed by Chelsea Bridge, Ebury Street, Vauxhall Bridge Road and the river. Thomas Cubitt built elegant streets and squares here in the 1830s, as he had in Belgravia, albeit on a less grand scale. The cluster of small shops and restaurants around Warwick Way forms the heart of Pimlico, but Belgrave Road, with its rows of solid, dazzling white terraces, is its backbone. Nearby are many dignified, beautifully maintained townhouses.

Westminster Cathedral

Victoria Street, SW1 (7798 9055/tours 7798 9064/www.westminstercathedral.org.uk). Victoria tube/rail. **Open** 7am-7pm Mon-Fri, Sun; 8am-7pm Sat. **Admission** free; donations appreciated. *Campanile* £2; £1 concessions; £5 family (2+2). *Audio-guide* £2.50; £1.50 concessions. **Map** p400 J10.

A delightfully bizarre neo-Byzantine confection with candy-striped stone and brick bands, Britain's premier Catholic cathedral was begun in 1895 and completed in 1903 by John Francis Bentle. The site on which it was built, originally known as Bulinga Fen and forming part of the marsh around Westminster, was reclaimed by the Benedictine monks who owned Westminster Abbey and subsequently used as a market and fairground. After the Reformation, the land was used in turn as a maze, a pleasure garden, a ring for bull-baiting, and as the location for a prison, before being acquired by the Church in 1884.

Recent construction work has resulted in a new piazza at the front of the cathedral. The columns and mosaics (which are made from more than 100 kinds of marble) are magnificent; Eric Gill's sculptures of the Stations of the Cross (1914-18) are world-renowned; and the view from the 273-foot (83-metre) Campanile Bell Tower is superb.

Knightsbridge & South Kensington

Looking for an absolutely fabulous time? Upper-crust Knightsbridge and South Ken have shops, museums and green spaces galore.

Knightsbridge

Maps p395-p397, p400
Knightsbridge or South Kensington tube.

Posh Knightsbridge was once a village notorious for its taverns and its highwaymen, but these days most people who come here are only too pleased to be parted from their cash, as the area is something of a shopping mecca. Indeed, two of London's best-known department stores can be found here: **Harrods** (*see p235*) and the infinitely hipper **Harvey Nichols** (*see p236*), with its buzzy Fifth Floor Café.

The smaller shops along **Brompton Road** and its attendant avenues are no less exclusive. Jewellery found in the window displays here isn't cheapened by a price tag; the people who can afford this stuff don't need to know how much it costs. **Beauchamp Place** (pronounced bee-chum and a favourite

haunt of the late Princess Diana) is packed with bijou boutiques, antique shops and old-fashioned awnings that hark back to a less complicated time. Nearby **Walton Street** possesses a disorientingly Mediterranean feel, with its brightly painted walls and colourful plants. The galleries along it are worth a nosey, as are the other backstreets, which feature some peaceful squares and gardens.

Hyde Park & Kensington Gardens

Maps p394 & p395
High Street Kensington, Hyde Park Corner, Knightsbridge, Lancaster Gate, Marble Arch or Queensway tube.

At one-and-a-half miles (2.25 kilometres) in length and around a mile (1.5 kilometres) in width, Hyde Park (5am-midnight daily; 7298

The Grade II-listed **Michelin Building** is heaven for foodies and design lovers. *See p138.*

Sightseeing

2100/www.royalparks.gov.uk) is the largest of London's royal parks and the first to have been opened to the public, in the early 17th century. It developed a reputation as a fashionable place to be seen in – if you could dodge the highwaymen and duellists, that is. In the 1730s Queen Caroline, the Charlie Dimmock of her day, dammed the Westbourne river – now, like the Tyburn and the Fleet, part of the capital's hidden waterways – to create the Serpentine.

In 1851 the Great Exhibition took place at Joseph Paxton's Crystal Palace, then situated in Hyde Park. Six million people visited it in just six months, eager to see the 'works and industry of all nations', but despite this success, in 1854 the palace was dismantled and rebuilt in south-east London, where it remained until it was destroyed by fire in 1936.

Every morning you can watch soliders of the Household Cavalry emerge from their barracks to ride through the park to Horse Guards Road for the **Changing of the Guard** (*see p264* **Frequent events**), while on royal anniversaries and other special occasions a 41-gun salute is fired in the park, opposite the Dorchester Hotel (*see p51*) in Park Lane. For those more interested in verbal firepower, Speakers' Corner near Marble Arch has been a hotbed of bile and guile more or less every Sunday since 1872, when the Parks and Gardens Act established it as a free-speech platorm (it's now the world's oldest). Be sure to bring your soapbox if you have something you want to get off your chest.

Merging into Hyde Park is **Kensington Gardens** (7298 2100/www.royalparks.gov.uk). Open from dawn till dusk daily, these are part of **Kensington Palace** (*see below*), which has been a royal residence since William III's asthma precipitated a search for a more lung-friendly abode in 1689. Worth investigating is the sunken garden, the Orangery built for Queen Anne, and the **Serpentine Gallery** (*see below*), which is free to enter and hosts excellent exhibitions on a regular basis.

If you have kids with you, don't miss, in the north of the gardens, the new **Diana, Princess of Wales Memorial Playground** (*see below*). Situated not far from the **Elfin Oak**, a gnarled, partly hollow stump taken from Richmond Park and carved with the figures of elves, fairies and animals, the playground will eventually be part of a seven-mile (10.5-kilometre) commemorative walk designed to remember the life of the princess, who lived at Kensington Palace up until her untimely death. Indeed, in mid 2001 it was decided that a memorial fountain to Diana will be erected on the shore of the Serpentine Lake, close to the Lido (*see p324* **In the swim**).

Diana, Princess of Wales Memorial Playground

near Black Lion Gate, Broad Walk, Kensington Gardens, W8 (7298 2117/recorded info 7298 2141). Bayswater or Queensway tube. **Open** 10am-8pm (or 1hr before dusk if earlier) daily. **Admission** free (adults must be accompanied by a child except 9.30-10am daily).

Alongside standard play equipment such as swings, slides and climbing frames, this innovative new £1.7-million playground, dedicated to the memory of the woman many once thought was destined to be the next queen, boasts a pirate ship, teepees, totem poles carved by Native American Indians, and, in the beach cove, sand-blasted concrete with tiny footprints and imprints of fossils. The Tree House Encampment, which is also suitable for wheelchair users, has 'tree-phones' allowing kids to communicate across the playground, while the Movement & Musical Garden has various interactive instruments.

The playground was built on the site of an earlier one funded by JM Barrie, whose *Peter Pan in Kensington Gardens* was published in 1906 (hence the Peter Pan statue close to the Long Water back over towards Hyde Park). Barrie lived nearby and took a daily stroll in the gardens. In homage to this historical link, images from 1930s illustrations of *Peter Pan* are etched into the glass in the Home Under the Ground, which houses the toilets and the playground attendant's office.

Kensington Palace

W8 (7937 9561/www.hrp.org.uk). Baywater, High Street Kensington or Queensway tube. **Open** 10am-5pm (last entry) daily. **Admission** (includes audioguide) £8.80; £6.30 5-15s; £6.90 concessions; £26.10 family (2+3). **Credit** AmEx, MC, V. **Map** p394 B8.

The birthplace, in 1819, of Queen Victoria and the last home of Princess Diana, Kensington Palace has known many royal residents since William and Mary moved here from Whitehall in 1689. Indeed, a number of royals lived here up until George III became king and relocated to Buckingham House, which was renamed Buckingham Palace (*see p131*). Initially a modest Jacobean mansion, Kensington Palace was spruced up by Sir Christopher Wren (*see p86* **Who he?**) and Nicholas Hawksmoor (and later, William Kent) to its present glory. Tours of the State Departments are available, including the room where Queen Victoria was baptised and the King's Gallery with its fine 17th-century paintings. The royal ceremonial dress collection can be found here too, allowing you to check out some of Liz's clobber.

Serpentine Gallery

Kensington Gardens (near Albert Memorial), W2 (7402 6075/www.serpentinegallery.org). Lancaster Gate or South Kensington tube. **Open** 10am-6pm daily. *Tours* free; 3pm Sat. **Admission** free. **Map** p395 D8.

Housed in a Grade II-listed tea pavilion with French windows looking out on to the surrounding Kensington Gardens, the Serpentine Gallery was

Sightseeing

founded in 1970 and has established itself as a gallery of international repute. Its exhibits have included work by Man Ray, Henry Moore, Andy Warhol, Bridget Riley, Damien Hirst and Rachel Whiteread, to name but a few. The gallery attracts hundreds of thousands of visitors a year, organises up to seven exhibitions annually and is the only publicly funded gallery in London to consistently maintain free admission. The first exhibition of 2002 will present the work of Richard Artschwager, one of the key artistic figures of post-war American art and a contemporary of Roy Lichtenstein, Jasper Johns, Walter De Maria and Malcolm Morley.

Belgravia & Brompton

Maps p397 & p400
Hyde Park Corner, Knightsbridge, Sloane Square or South Kensington tube.

East of Sloane Street, west of Grosvenor Place and north of Eaton Square lies **Belgravia**. Until it was developed by Lord Grosvenor and Thomas Cubitt in the 1820s, the area comprised open fields and was popular as a site for duels. As soon as the first grand stucco houses were raised, Belgravia established a reputation as a highly exclusive, largely residential district. It remains so today, although the judgement of Disraeli that Belgravia was 'monotonous… and so contrived as to be at the same time insipid and tawdry' might be echoed by anyone who has found themselves lost in this curiously characterless embassy land. Characterful relief is provided by the Grenadier pub in Old Barrack Yard, off Wilton Row, once frequented by the Duke of Wellington and said to be haunted by the ghost of one of his officers, beaten to death for cheating at cards.

The area known as **Brompton**, meanwhile, sits west of Belgravia, bounded approximately by Sloane Street, King's Road, Sloane Avenue and Brompton Road. The area is very similar to Belgravia, and, outside of the **London Oratory** (*see below*), provides little in the way of sights, unless jealously ogling the beautiful houses of local rich folk is your idea of fun.

London Oratory
Thurloe Place, Brompton Road, SW7 (7808 0900). South Kensington tube. **Open** 6.30am-8pm daily. **Admission** free; donations appreciated. **Map** p397 E10.
The second largest Catholic church in the city – only Westminster Cathedral tops it – the London Oratory is an awesome, daunting spectacle whether you're a believer or not. Built in 1880-4 to the designs of little-known architect Herbert Gribble after an open competition, and known to most Londoners as the Brompton Oratory, it's a shameless attempt to imitate a florid Italian baroque church, both outside and in; indeed, many of the ornate internal decorations

predate the building, including Mazzuoli's late 17th-century statues of the apostles, which previously stood in Siena Cathedral. All in all, it's an anachronistic but fascinating place in which to spend a half-hour or so, both from architectural and sociological perspectives. During the Cold War, the church was used by the KGB as a dead letter box.

South Kensington

Maps p396 & p397
Gloucester Road or South Kensington tube.

It's all down to Prince Albert that we have such a trailblazing museum quarter in South Kensington, which was the beneficiary of the £186,000 profit from the 1851 Great Exhibition, plus the same again from the government coffers. Albert sanctioned the purchase of 35 hectares (87 acres) for the building of institutions to further the influence of science and art in Britain. Though he died before the scheme was completed, his legacy has been a great success, bringing into being Imperial College, the Royal Geographical Society, the Royal College of Art, the Royal College of Music plus the crowd-pleasers: the **Science Museum**, the **Natural History Museum** and the **Victoria & Albert Museum** (for all three, *see p140*).

Albert's sterling work was commemorated by the construction of the **Royal Albert Hall** (venue for the annual 'Proms' concerts; *see p265 and p313*) and the freshly restored Albert Memorial opposite in Hyde Park. The latter was finally unveiled by the Queen in October 1998 after a decade-long restoration programme. Designed by Sir George Gilbert Scott and finished in 1872, it centres around a gilded Albert holding a copy of the catalogue of the 1851 Great Exhibition. It's hard to believe that the modest German Prince, who explicitly said, 'I would rather not be made the prominent feature of such a monument', would have approved of the finished product, or the fact that its restoration cost £11 million (£3 million under budget, and completed a year earlier than expected). Guided tours of the memorial can be booked on 7495 0916 or www.tourguides.co.uk; they allow you to get closer to the memorial and examine, in particular, the superbly crafted and wonderfully detailed marble frieze of 168 leading literary and artistic figures.

The well-to-do residential area of South Kensington stretches down to meet Chelsea somewhere around Fulham Road. Near its northern end, at No.81, stands the unique, exuberant, art nouveau **Michelin Building**, which was designed by Espinasse for the tyre manufacturers in 1905. It now houses book publishers, the beautiful if pricey **Bibendum**

On location: Polanski's *Repulsion*

Rosemary's Baby might be the better known of Roman Polanski's 'haunted house' films of the 1960s, but *Repulsion*, his first English-language movie, was the one that kick-started the Polish-born director's career in the west, earning him top prizes at film festivals in Venice and Berlin.

When Polanski came to London in 1964, the year he wrote the script, he spoke virtually no English. He spent a lot of time immersing himself in London life, including its women, whom he managed to proposition despite the language barrier. He considered his young French star, the then-unknown Catherine Deneuve, a bedpost notch in the making, but his Jekyll and Hyde behaviour both on set and off it, at his Knightsbridge flat, infuriated her.

The film sparked a great deal of controversy on its release in 1965, with its depictions of violent murders and rapes, but it increased Polanksi's standing in the film industry, earning him comparisons with Hitchcock. *Repulsion* is rumoured to have been heavily influenced by the behaviour of a young actress called Flora, with whom Polanski fell in love while studying at Lodz film school.

Unaware that she had stabbed her two previous lovers, he was only saved from being knifed in bed by the fact that she liked to chant before attacking, which woke him up.

Repulsion was shot in a South Kensington that's remained surprisingly unchanged since 1965. Dino's, where the increasingly disturbed Carole Ledoux (Deneuve) tries to eat a plate of fish and chips, continues to do brisk trade; it's right by South Ken tube station, which is clearly visible as Carole walks from her flat just a few streets away in Earl's Court (at 15 Kensington Mansions, Trebovir Road) to work, avoiding the attentions of workmen en route. Madame Denise's, a beauty parlour at 31 Thurloe Place, is still a place to get your nails buffed, though not as thoroughly as Carole liked to do it, one likes to hope. The Hoop & Toy on Thurloe Street, meanwhile, is the pub in which Colin, Carole's would-be boyfriend (played by John Fraser), drinks with his friends, trying to deal with the headache that Deneuve is causing him and that she cures so effectively later in the film, back at her flat, where her full-scale breakdown finally occurs.

restaurant and Sir Terence Conran's design shrine, the **Conran Shop** (*see p255*). Fulham Road, lined with swish antique shops, bars and restaurants, continues down to Chelsea's football ground, **Stamford Bridge** (*see p327*), and on through Fulham towards Putney Bridge.

Natural History Museum

Cromwell Road, SW7 (7942 5000/www.nhm.ac.uk).
South Kensington tube. **Open** 10am-5.50pm Mon-Sat;
11am-5.50pm Sun. *Tours* free, hourly; 11am-4pm
daily. **Admission** £9; £4.50 concessions; free OAPs,
under-16s. **Free** for all after 4.30pm Mon-Fri; after
5pm Sat, Sun, public hols. **Credit** AmEx, MC, V.
Map p397 D10.

You could count the number of items in the magnificent Natural History Museum on the fingers of one hand – if you had 68 million fingers. This quite astonishing collection (not all of it on show at the same time) means that it isn't the place for a quick half-hour visit. Even devoting a whole day to it would leave you unfulfilled. But for sheer size and spectacle, it takes some beating. From the moment you enter via the main Cromwell Road entrance and are confronted with the famous diplodocus, you know you're in a special place, and you'll find there's enough here to keep even the most distracted child amused. The most popular exhibits are in the **Life Galleries**, where the Dinosaurs, Creepy-Crawlies and Mammals exhibits are always busy. The **Earth Galleries**, which you can get straight into from the Exhibition Road entrance, deal with Mother Nature when she's got her gloves off, with fascinating displays on volcanoes and earthquakes. There's also a survey of the planet's natural rocks and minerals.

Part of the new **Darwin Centre**, which is devoted to the museum's zoological resources, should be open to the public by summer 2002. Phase two is still in development and it will be a good few years yet before its entomological and botanical exhibits are ready to greet visitors.

Science Museum

Exhibition Road, SW7 (7942 4454/4455/
www.sciencemuseum.org.uk). South Kensington tube.
Open 10am-6pm daily. **Admission** £7.95; £4.95
students; free under-16s, concessions. Free for all
after 4.30pm daily. **Credit** AmEx, MC, V.
Map p397 D9.

Spread over seven floors, the Science Museum palpably crackles with educational exhibits. The main attractions here include Stephenson's Rocket, a V2 missile and the Apollo 10 command module. As well as many other interesting and entertaining showpieces, there are interactive displays such as the Launch Pad, a technological adventure playground, and Flight Lab, where would-be pilots can try out their skills on a flight simulator. The Wellcome Wing, which opened just two years ago, is a high-tech extension containing news on recent developments in science, as well as interactive games and an IMAX cinema (*see p294*).

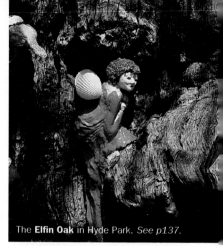

The **Elfin Oak** in Hyde Park. *See p137.*

Victoria & Albert Museum (V&A)

Cromwell Road, SW7 (7942 2000/www.vam.ac.uk).
South Kensington tube. **Open** 10am-5.45pm Mon,
Tue, Thur-Sun; 10am-10pm Wed. *Tours* daily;
phone for details. **Admission** £5; free concessions.
Free for all after 4.30pm daily. £15 season ticket.
Credit AmEx, MC, V. **Map** p397 E10.

The V&A was founded in 1852 as a Museum of Manufactures, to inspire and educate British manufacturers and designers by building on the success of the Great Exhibition of the previous year. In 1857 it moved from Marlborough House in the centre of town to the fields of Brompton, where it was renamed the Victoria & South Kensington Museum. In 1899 it was renamed the Victoria and Albert Museum after the widowed Queen Victoria, who, on her last public appearance, laid the foundation stone.

The V&A houses the world's greatest collection of decorative arts as well as the national sculpture collection. Admission is just £5, but it's handy to know that entry is free after 4.30pm. A free guide (you'll need it) helps you find your way around the labyrinthine displays. There are 145 galleries to see, but you'd be wise to choose a section or two and deliberate over them rather than try to rush around and see everything the museum has to offer.

The galleries reflect centuries of achievement in such varied fields as ceramics, sculpture, furniture making, jewellery, metalwork, textiles and dress, from Britain, Europe and Asia. The museum also contains the national collections of furniture, sculpture, glass, ceramics, watercolours, portrait miniatures and photography. Around four million objects are held by the museum, including the finest collection of Italian Renaissance sculpture outside Italy.

In November 2001 the British Galleries, which tell the story of Britain's rise from a minor island in 1500 to a major world power and cultural authority in 1900, reopened after a massive modernisation programme. But those eager to see Daniel Libeskind's Spiral, which will form the V&A's contemporary wing, will have to wait until 2004, the scheduled completion date.

Chelsea

The former capital of chic still has plenty to charm visitors.

Maps p396 & p397
Sloane Square or South Kensington tube.

The good old days might be gone – it's no longer one of three private roads out of the capital used by royalty; the hungry artistic community of the 19th century has dissipated; the fashion mavericks and rock stars of the '60s and '70s have grown old, and the Sloane Rangers of the '80s have shoved awf (perhaps not such a bad thing) – but Chelsea is still a major draw. After all, there must be something in a place that gave its name to both a boot and a bun. Its football team, based at the cash-haemorrhaging Chelsea Village at Stamford Bridge, is still fashionable, albeit in a continental way, and the shopping is still strong here, with the **King's Road** full of all the high-street regulars plus a few snazzy extras. **Sloane Square**, at its north-east end, contains the upmarket department store Peter Jones, which in turn faces the **Royal Court** theatre (*see p332*), where many of George Bernard Shaw's plays were premiered.

The ghost of Sex – Vivienne Westwood's '70s clothes shop that is widely credited as the place where the punk look was born – exists in the shape of World's End at No.430, still owned by Westwood and notable for its sloping floor and clock that goes backwards. Antique shops such as Antiquarius (*see p231*) also maintain a strong presence in Chelsea, while Sir Terence Conran has increased his empire in the form of the Bluebird gastrodome consisting of a restaurant, café, shop and food hall (*see p251*) in a former Grade II listed garage.

By the river

Chelsea Harbour's swift development from industrial wasteland into a prestigious mixed-use area containing opulent apartments, the Conrad International London hotel (*see p62* **Rock hotels**), office space, high-class shops and restaurants and a marina took just two and a half years. However, and in spite of its popularity with the rich and famous, including

All that glitters: the **Albert Bridge** by night. *See p142.*

The annual Chelsea Flower Show is held in the grounds of the **Royal Hospital Chelsea**. *See p143.*

the late Princess of Wales, and Michael Caine (who had an ill-fated joint restaurant venture, The Canteen, here with Marco Pierre White for a while), it's a bit of a ghost town.

Many writers and painters have enjoyed Chelsea's charms in the past, especially Cheyne Walk parallel to the river, which has entertained a fair share of artists and has blue plaques in abundance. Pre-Raphaelite painter Rosetti lived at No.16 with a muster of peacocks whose cries probably had his neighbours seething; George Eliot lived at No.4; JMW Turner lived at No.119; and Ian Fleming spent some time at Carlyle Mansions, which has also housed Henry James and TS Eliot over the years. Hilaire Belloc, Mrs Gaskill and James McNeill Whistler also lived on Cheyne Walk, and Oscar Wilde lived on Tite Street, in a house he had to abandon after his arrest for gross indecency at the Cadogan Hotel. **Carlyle's House** (*see p143*) on Cheyne Row belonged to Victorian historian Thomas Carlyle.

The saint and statesman Thomas More – an early resident of Chelsea – was placed in the Tower of London (*see p94*) by King Henry VIII in 1535 for refusing to swear to the Act of Succession and the Oath of Supremacy, an act of treason that brought about his beheading. His final words on the scaffold were 'The King's good servant, but God's First.' Although his manor house has long gone – it stood on an area of land that is now the site of Beaufort Street, and parts of the original orchard wall can still be seen bordering the

gardens of the houses on the west side of Paultons Square – L Cubitt Bevis' statue of the 'man for all seasons' can be seen contemplating Chelsea Embankment outside **Chelsea Old Church**, where the statesman built his own chapel (*see p143*). It's from the Embankment that the stunning **Albert Bridge** arches over the Thames to Battersea.

Along Royal Hospital Road you'll find the **Chelsea Physic Garden** (*see p143*), where rock and herb gardens were cultivated in an attempt to measure their restorative properties. Further along is the **National Army Museum**, which contains military insight from Agincourt on (*see p143*), and next door to that is the **Royal Hospital** itself (*see p143*), which is home to the fabulous red-coated Chelsea Pensioners and protector of war veterans since the days of Charles II.

Part of the hospital's ground were once the location of **Ranelagh Gardens**, celebrated during the 18th century as a favourite haunt of pleasure-seeking toffs ('You can't set your foot without treading on a Prince, or Duke of Cumberland,' as Horace Walpole wrote). Canaletto's painting of the gardens, where the eight-year-old Mozart gave a concert in 1764 – hangs in the National Gallery.

It's worth bearing in mind that most of this area is poorly served by the tube, so unless you're prepared for a long walk from the station at Sloane Square, take a bus.

Carlyle's House

24 Cheyne Row, SW3 (7352 7087/
www.nationaltrust.org.uk). Sloane Square tube/11, 19,
22, 39, 45, 49, 219 bus. **Open** *Apr-Oct* 11am-5pm
Wed-Sun. **Admission** £3.50; £1.75 5s-16s.
Map p397 E12.

In the care of the National Trust since 1930, this
house was lived in by the great Victorian scholar
from 1834 until his death in 1881. Jane, his wife,
had a strong influence in the tasteful Victorian
decor and the furniture, portraits and books, which
are all still in place. Virginia Woolf, a friend of
Carlyle's and a visitor to Cheyne Row, made several references to him in her essays and novels, and
the house itself might have served as the model for
the Hilberrys' house in *Night and Day*. What struck
her especially was the lack of running water. 'They
were Scots,' she reported in her essay for *Good
Housekeeping*, 'fanatical about cleanliness.' She
also described the house as a battlefield: 'the scene
of labour, effort and perpetual struggle.'

Chelsea Old Church

Cheyne Walk, Old Church Street, SW3
(7352 5627/www.domini.co.uk/chelsea-old-church).
Sloane Square tube/11, 19, 22, 49, 319 bus.
Open 2-5pm Tue-Fri; 8am-1pm, 2-7pm Sun.
Admission free; donations appreciated.
Map p397 E12.

All Saints, as this church is known, dates back to
the 13th century. The chapel on the south side was
rebuilt in 1528 by Thomas More for use as his private chapel. The church was damaged by bombing
in 1941 and for nine years the congregation worshipped in a ward of the Royal Hospital, but in 1950
the More Chapel, with extensions, was reopened for
service. There are monuments to local families such
as the Lawrences and the Cheynes, as well as local
resident Henry James. Rumour has it that heir-
obsessed King Henry VIII wed Jane Seymour in this
church before the state ceremony.

Chelsea Physic Garden

66 Royal Hospital Road (entrance in Swan Walk),
SW3 (7352 5646/www.cpgarden.demon.co.uk).
Sloane Square tube/11, 19, 22, 239, 319 bus.
Open *Apr-late Oct* noon-5pm Wed; 2-6pm Sun.
Tours 1.30pm, 3.30pm (check blackboard to confirm).
Admission £4; £2 5-16s, concessions (not incl
OAPs). *Tours* free. **Credit** *shop only* MC, V.
Map p397 F12.

Established in 1673 by the Worshipful Society of
the Apothecaries of London, Chelsea Physic
Garden's main objective was to provide medical
students with the means to study plants used in
healing. Sir Hans Sloane helped to develop the garden in the early 18th century (the garden at the time
was described as being three acres, one rood and
35 perches, plus greenhouse, stoves and barge-
houses) and the grounds are still used today for
research and education. Although the opening
hours are limited, guided tours can be arranged;
during these you'll be allowed to see such features

as a garden demonstrating the history of medicinal plants; one of the oldest rock gardens in Europe,
dating back to 1773; and greenhouses containing
the types of yams from which modern contraceptives and steroids were synthesised.

National Army Museum

Royal Hospital Road, SW3 (7730 0717/
www.national-army-museum.ac.uk). Sloane Square
tube/11, 19, 239 bus. **Open** 10am-5.30pm daily.
Admission free. **Map** p397 F12.

The only museum to be dedicated to the history of
the British Army over the past 500 years, the
National Army Museum includes exhibits such as
Redcoats taking in the archers of Agincourt (1415)
to the redcoats of the American Revolution in 1792;
the Victorian Soldier, which studies the history of
the British Army and its influence across the globe
between 1816 and 1914; The Road to Waterloo,
which features a huge model of the famous battle
complete with 75,000 toy soldiers; and From World
War to Cold War covering World Wars I and II and
the period up to 1964, including the Korean War,
with a reconstruction of a World War I trench.
Finally, a special exhibition, Ashes and Blood, deals
with the history of the British Army in South Africa
from 1795 to 1914 and includes extensive displays
on the Zulu and Boer Wars, with items such as a
Boer 'Wanted' notice for Winston Churchill and
boxes of chocolate that were sent by Queen Victoria
as gifts to her troops. Also on display is a grisly
scene recreating the loss of the Earl of Uxbridge's
leg following the battle of Waterloo. The limb was
damaged so badly it had to be amputated and the
surgeon's instruments are there for all to see.
Apparently Uxbridge recorded a running commentary of the operation for his wife and was sufficiently
sanguine about the whole experience to have his
biography entitled *One Leg*.

Royal Hospital Chelsea

Royal Hospital Road, SW3 (7730 5282). Sloane
Square tube/11, 19, 22, 137, 211, 239 bus.
Open *Museum, chapel & hall* 10am-noon, 2-4pm
Mon-Sat; *May-Sept also* 2-4pm Sun. **Admission** free.
Map p397 F12.

After being inspired by Louis XIV's splendid Hôtel
des Invalides in Paris, King Charles II made up his
mind that he wanted the same kind of thing for
his own veteran soldiers, and commissioned Sir
Christopher Wren (*see p86* **Who he?**) to come up
with something really special. Carlyle reckoned
that he did, describing the hospital as 'quiet and
dignified and the work of a gentleman.' Today,
approximately 400 former servicemen call this
place home, and they are considered such a national treasure that a statue depicting a Chelsea pen-
sioner in uniform was unveiled at the hospital as
part of the millennium celebrations. Each May, the
grounds of the hospital play host to the famous
Chelsea Flower Show (*see p263*), while the museum possesses a fine collection of medals and
records dating back to its inception.

North London

For market lovers, culture vultures and outdoor types, London has more than its fair share of northern lights.

Camden

Camden Town or Chalk Farm tube.

Stretching, approximately, from the statue of Victorian politician Richard Cobden at **Mornington Crescent** to the borders of **Chalk Farm**, via **Camden High Street**, Camden Town started to get built up with cheap lodging houses from 1816, when the Regent's Canal and, later, the railway were laid out. It soon became known for its rough characters. Dickens moved here in 1822, when he was ten; the four-room house at 16 Bayham Street (no longer extant, but commemorated by a plaque) is reputed to have been the model for the Crachits' house in *A Christmas Carol*.

Irish and, after 1945, Greek Cypriots migrated to Camden; traces of the latter are still visible in the scattered tavernas and Greek cafés, and the Greek Orthodox church near the Royal Veterinary College (founded in 1791) on **Royal College Street**. Until the late 1960s,

Pod-u-like: **Lord's** NatWest media centre. *See p145.*

this was still a slum area; a surge in property prices, coupled with Camden's popularity as a (relatively) cheap bohemian hangout – the struggling actors in the film *Withnail & I* live here – brought the place into new repute. Then the professional classes and media celebs such as Alan Bennett moved in, renovating houses in some of Camden's lovely crescents. The influx of money shows itself in buildings such as Nicholas Grimshaw's high-tech Sainsbury's supermarket on **Camden Road**, where Bennett can sometimes be seen stocking up.

But to say that Camden is not to everyone's taste is a gross understatement. On a weekday it's a drab high street awash with litter and framed by a host of unremarkable shops and takeaway food vendors; at night you'll find a spreadeagled selection of pubs and clubs with little in common save an NW1 postcode. It's at the weekend, when Camden's enormously popular market (*see p256*) reaches fever pitch, that you'll see it, perversely, both at its best and worst. Some of the goods on sale are worth the trip, particularly the collectibles in the Stables market and the homewares in the main Market Hall at Camden Lock, but there's far too much hippie, ethnicky nonsense on offer, much of it overpriced. When you're stuck in a horrible crush here on a Sunday afternoon, bearings lost and will to live rapidly evaporating, it's hard not to come to the conclusion that Camden has become what Carnaby Street was a decade ago: an area defeated by its own popularity and erstwhile hipness.

That said, there are other sides to Camden than the market. The **Jewish Museum** (*see below*) on Albert Street, just off **Parkway**, is a gem; and a reflection, along with many of the restaurants and bars, of the area's cultural diversity. To these ends, try the Caribbean fare at the Mango Room (*see p207*) or top-notch pub food at the Engineer (65 Gloucester Avenue, NW1, 7722 0950). If it's a scorcher outside, cool down with a sorbet or ice-cream at Marine Ices (8 Haverstock Hill, NW3, 7482 9003), a north London institution; while on chilly nights the Jazz Café (*see p322*) is a welcoming refuge.

Close by, on **Chalk Farm Road**, the Roundhouse (8963 0940) was built as a turning point for trams but became a music venue graced by legends such as Pink Floyd, Hendrix and the Doors during its heyday in the '60s. These days it's a multipurpose venue used for everything from exhibitions and plays to circuses and gigs. Towards the end of 2002 it's scheduled to close for two years while the maze of tunnels beneath it – the 'undercroft' – is converted into a creative arts centre.

Jewish Museum, Camden
129-31 Albert Street, NW1 (7284 1997/ www.jewmusm.ort.org). Camden Town tube. **Open** 10am-4pm Mon-Thur; 10am-5pm Sun. **Admission** £3.50; £2.50 OAPs; £1.50 5-16s, concessions; free under-5s. **Credit** MC, V.
This colourful museum provides a fascinating insight into one of Britain's oldest immigrant communities (*see p14* **Jewish London**). The focus here (the other branch of the museum is in Finchley, at the Sternberg Centre, 80 East End Road, N3; 8349 1143) is on the history of Jews in Britain. Eighteenth-century oil paintings, artefacts from a tailor's 'sweatshop', silver and chinaware, and photographs and passports from 19th-century immigrants evocatively convey the different facets of Jewish life in Britain over the last 600 years. The museum also has one of the finest collections of Jewish ceremonial art in the world, including a collection of silver Hanukka candlesticks, spice boxes and an amazing 16th-century Italian synagogue ark, which was brought to Britain in the 19th century by an Englishman who had picked it up while doing his European Grand Tour. A series of audio-visual programmes provides information on Jewish festivals and Jewish life, and there are regular temporary exhibitions. The first exhibition of 2002 explores the history of the Spanish and Portuguese Jewish community in Britain.

Around Camden
North of Camden, green relief comes in the form of charming **Primrose Hill** and, at the edge of Hampstead Heath, **Gospel Oak**. As Camden has grown, it seems to have swallowed its neighbours. Fat cat retail outlets have moved in, causing small shops in neighbouring areas to suffer. **Kentish Town** has become a series of bargain stores and cheap eateries, linking Camden to **Highgate** and **Tufnell Park**. There have been, nevertheless, benefits from the social elevation of its southern neighbour, such as the ceaseless conversions of traditional London boozers into modern gastropubs. Travel along Highgate Road, past one of London's busiest music venues, the **Forum** (*see p317*), for nosh and a pint at the **Vine** or the **Bull & Last** (No.86 and No.168 respectively).

South and east of Camden, **Camley Street Natural Park** offers bucolic charm amid the railway sheds and gas works. The **Regent's Canal**, which runs along one side of the park, opened in 1820 to provide a working waterway

to link east and west London; the nearby **Canal Museum** (*see below*) is there for those who want to know more. These days, the transportation of industrial materials along the canal has largely ceased. The towpath provides an attractive walk from Little Venice through Primrose Hill to Camden, or you can take a short trip on the canal in an open barge.

London Canal Museum
12-13 New Wharf Road, King's Cross, N1 (7713 0836/www.canalmuseum.org.uk). King's Cross tube/rail. **Open** 10am-4.30pm Tue-Sun. **Admission** £2.50; £1.25 8-16s, concessions; free under-8s. **Credit** MC, V. **Map** p399 L2.
Documenting the history of London's canals and the lives of the families who worked on it, this museum is housed in a former ice warehouse built in 1862 for Swiss immigrant Carlo Gatti. Gatti made his name in Britain as an ice-cream maker, and the museum also traces the history of the ice trade, featuring a huge Victorian ice well that was used to store ice imported from Norway and brought by ship and then barge to be stored here. There's also archive footage of the early canals and a barge cabin to explore.

St John's Wood
St John's Wood or Swiss Cottage tube.
This wealthy enclave west of Regent's Park contains the world's most famous cricket ground, **Lord's** (*see p326*), together with its **MCC Museum** (*see below*). From here, **Grove End Road** leads into **Abbey Road**, made famous by the Beatles when it was still called EMI Studios (No.3). The zebra crossing outside is always busy with Japanese and American tourists scrawling their names on the wall. Further north is the former paint factory that's now home to the **Saatchi Gallery** (*see p146*).

Lord's Tour & MCC Museum
Marylebone Cricket Club, Lord's, St John's Wood Road, NW8 (7432 1033/www.lords.org). St John's Wood tube/13, 46, 82, 113, 274 bus. **Open** *Tours* (phone for availability) *Oct-Mar* noon, 2pm daily. *Apr-Sept* 10am, noon, 2pm daily. **Admission** *Tours* £6.50; £5 concessions; £4.50 5-15s; free under-5s. **Credit** MC, V.
Looking like a cross between a digital alarm clock and an alien starship, Lord's NatWest Media Centre dominates the grounds of this most traditional of British institutions. The centre, which opened in 1999, has been hailed as one of the best examples of modern architecture in London, and along with the innovative PVC 'tented' roof of the Mound Stand has propelled the grounds to the forefront of modern design landmarks. Guided tours of the grounds include a chance to view the grounds from the Mound, a wander through the pavilion, the visitors' dressing room and the Long Room, and a tour of the museum. The collection of battered bats,

photographs, blazers and paintings in the latter is delightfully anecdotal and will engage even those who had no prior interest in the game.

Saatchi Gallery

98A Boundary Road, NW8 (info 7624 8299/7328 8299). St John's Wood or Swiss Cottage tube. **Open** *During exhibitions* noon-6pm Thur-Sun; phone to check exhibition dates. **Admission** £5; £3 12-16s, concessions; free under-12s. **Credit** MC, V.

This gallery has never shied from flinging a pot of paint in the public's face, as John Ruskin once said of Whistler. These days it's more likely to be an in-yer-face unmade bed – the gallery is synonymous with the Britart scene of the 1990s, which propelled the careers of Tracey Emin, Damien Hirst, Sarah Lucas et al into fast and fabulous orbit. The vast whitewashed warehouse space shows a rotating selection from ad-man Charles Saatchi's latest shopping sprees, which have recently had more of a European emphasis. Richard Wilson's *20:50*, an installation in sump oil and galvanised steel, is the only permanent piece of art and alone makes a visit worthwhile.

Hampstead

Golders Green or Hampstead tube/Hampstead Heath rail.

Villagey Hampstead has long been popular with the literati and chattering classes. Pope and Gay took the waters here during its brief time as a spa; Wilkie Collins, Thackeray and Dickens drank at Jack Straw's Castle on **North End Way**; and Keats strolled on the heath with Coleridge and Wordsworth. Happily,

Hampstead's hilly geography has prevented the sort of urbanisation that Camden has suffered, and it remains, together with **Highgate**, a haven for much of London's (moneyed) intelligentsia and literary bigwigs.

Hampstead tube stands at the top of the steep High Street, lined with opulent but unexciting shops and bars. Running north, and further uphill, from here is **Heath Street**. Don't miss Louis Pâtisserie (No.32) for tea and sticky mittel-European cakes. Just off the southern end of Heath Street is **Church Row**, one of Hampstead's most beautiful streets, with twin lines of higgeldy-piggeldy terraces leading down to **St John at Hampstead**, where painter John Constable and his wife lie at rest in the sylvan graveyard. Close by, on **Holly Hill**, is Hampstead's nicest pub, the Hollybush (*see p225*); while another minute's climb brings you to **Fenton House** (*see p147*) with its fine porcelain and paintings.

The celestially inclined might like to gaze skyward at the nearby **Hampstead Scientific Society Observatory** (Lower Terrace, 8346 1056). On Hampstead's southern fringes is the house where Sigmund Freud lived the last year of his life, having fled Nazi persecution in Vienna in 1938 (now the **Freud Museum**; *see p148*). Nearby is **Camden Arts Centre** (*see p147*), with its eclectic programme of exhibitions.

East of Heath Street a maze of attractive streets shelters **Burgh House** on New End Square (a Queen Anne house that now houses a small museum) and **2 Willow Road** (*see*

Local colour at **Green Lanes**. *See p152.*

Noble rot

Until last year one of north London's most important and influential modernist buildings, the Grade I-listed, white stucco Isokon Flats, lay abandoned, dilapidated and incongruous amid the red-brick Edwardian villas of Lawn Road, Belsize Park, just south of Hampstead Heath. Commissioned in the early '30s by mass furniture producer Jack 'Plywood' Pritchard as an experiment in 'existenz minimum', the reinforced concrete apartment block was designed along Corbusian lines by Canadian architect Wells Coates. Intended as a kind of hotel for single professionals, it had 36 rather basic studio flats; residents were expected to eat and relax together in spacious communal areas, which included the fashionable Isobar and a clubroom, designed by emigré architect Marcel Breuer.

The Isokon was quick to attract illustrious tenants, including Agatha Christie, Henry Moore and modernists such as Walter Gropius and Laszlo Moholy-Nagay fleeing fascist Europe, as well as Pritchard and his family.

The rot began to set in during the 1970s, when Camden Council bought the block and repair work started to lag behind. Tenants complained about poor sound-proofing and

heating, and about the tiny kitchenettes. In 1998 the council, faced with a renovation bill of £1 million, decided to sell up. But despite much interest from architecture buffs, no one came forward to stump up the cash, probably because of the council's stipulation that the building continue to be used for housing. As the months went by, vandalism and decay pushed repair costs up by another million.

Just as the Isokon seemed destined to be lost for ever, Notting Hill Housing Group stepped in to save the day, purchasing the block and setting up the Isokon Trust to safeguard its future. Renovation work was due to begin as we went to press, with 25 flats developed into affordable housing for key workers such as nurses, and the remaining 11 being sold on the open market.

p148), a house built by emigré architect Ernö Goldfinger for himself in the 1930s (*see p182* **Who he?**). Nearby, off Keats Grove, is **Keats' House** (*see p148*), where he did most of his best work. Around the corner, on South Hill Park, Ruth Ellis shot her former boyfriend outside the Magdala pub in 1955 (look for the bullet holes in the wall), becoming the last woman to be hanged in Britain.

Camden Arts Centre

Arkwright Road, corner of Finchley Road, NW3 (7435 2643/www.camdenartscentre.org). Finchley Road tube/Finchley Road & Frognal rail. **Open** 11am-7pm Tue-Thur; 11am-5.30pm Fri-Sun. **Admission** free. **Credit** *Shop* MC, V.
This innovative venue mixes visual art with performance in imaginative and arresting ways. There are also regular talks by artists, usually in conjunction with current exhibitions, and open studios held by the artist-in-residence. The spring season (15 Feb-14 Apr) features retrospective photo-text works by Douglas Huebler, an American conceptual artist, and new drawings, sculptures and photographs by David Shrigley. There will also be a series of contemporary performance works by British-based artists to run concurrently with these exhibitions.

The centre will close for refurbishment from July 2002 to June 2003, but a series of off-site projects will run during this period; call for details.

Fenton House

3 Hampstead Grove, NW3 (7435 3471/info 01494 755563/www.nationaltrust.org.uk). Hampstead tube. **Open** *Mar* 2-5pm Sat, Sun. *Apr-Oct* 2-5pm Wed-Fri; 11am-5pm Sat, Sun. Last entry 4.30pm. *Bank hols* 11am-5pm. *Tours* £10; phone for details. **Admission** £4.40; £2.20 5-15s; free under-5s. *Joint ticket with 2 Willow Road £6.30.* **No credit cards.**
Dainty satinwood furniture and pottery poodles adorn this pretty William and Mary house dating from 1693. One of the earliest houses in Hampstead, it features the Benton Fletcher Collection of early keyboard instruments, which are played during the summer at fortnightly concerts (call for details). Another notable feature is the four attic rooms, which have retained the atmosphere of a 17th-century property with impressive views over London. The house re-opens on 2 March 2002 after a winter break; if you can't wait that long join one of the architectural walking tours that begin with Ernö Goldfinger's 1930s house at 2 Willow Road (*see p148*) and go back in time through Georgian and Edwardian Hampstead to end up at Fenton House. For tickets (£6) call 01494 755572.

Freud Museum

*20 Maresfield Gardens, NW3 (7435 2002/
www.freud.org.uk). Finchley Road tube/Finchley
Road & Frognal rail.* **Open** noon-5pm Wed-Sun.
Admission £4; £2 concessions; free under-12s.
Credit MC, V.
Freud lived here with his daughter Anna for the last
year of his life after fleeing Nazi Austria in 1938.
Following Anna's death in 1986, and according to
her wishes, the house became a museum. Freud's
study, a reproduction of the one he left behind in
Vienna, is crammed with his enormous collection of
ancient antiquities and statuettes, as well as books
on every aspect of the mind, archaeology and
ancient history. Upstairs, there's some fascinating
footage of Freud and his family, as well as a collection devoted to the belongings of Anna, who
became an eminent child analyst. Commentary to
the exhibits is made up of extracts from Freud's
writing, which although interesting, offer little
insight into the life of the great man, and are only
of use to the earnest psychology students flitting
round the place taking notes.

Keats' House

*Keats Grove, NW3 (7435 2062/
www.keatshouse.org.uk). Hampstead Heath rail/
Hampstead tube/24, 46, 168 bus.* **Open** *Easter-Oct*
noon-5pm Tue-Sun. *Nov-Easter* 10am-4pm Tue-Sun.
Tours 3pm Sat, Sun. **Admission** £3; £1.50
concessions; free under-16s. **Credit** (over £5) MC, V.

Though a small plum tree has replaced the original
tree under which Keats penned *Ode to a Nightingale*,
this is still hallowed ground. A lavender-lined path
leads you to the front door of the revered Romantic
poet, who lived here from 1818 to 1820 and wrote
many of his best-loved poems in the house's secluded environs. Inside is a trove of personal effects,
including a copy of the original letter written by
Keats to girl-next-door sweetheart Fanny Brawne –
there are also two locks of her hair kept in a display
case, along with a brief testimony to her hair's vitality. Other cabinets contain original manuscripts, and
visitors can nose around the poet's bedroom, living
room and kitchen. A tour of the house, which may
close for a couple of months towards the end of 2002
(call for details), is included in the admission price.

2 Willow Road

*2 Willow Road, NW3 (7435 6166/www.nationaltrust.
org.uk). Hampstead tube/Hampstead Heath rail.*
Open *Mar* noon-5pm Sat (tours 12.30pm, 3.30pm).
Last entry 4pm. *28 Mar-3 Nov (*by tour only*) every
45min 12.15-4pm Thur-Sat. *9 Nov-14 Dec* noon-5pm
Sat. Closed 15 Dec 2002-end Feb 2003. **Admission**
£4.40; £2.20 5-15s; free under-5s. *Joint ticket with
Fenton House* £6.30. **No credit cards**.
A significant example of pre-war modernism (indeed,
it's been acquired by the National Trust), 2 Willow
Road was designed and built by anglophile Austro-
Hungarian architect Ernö Goldfinger (*see p182* **Who
he?**) in 1939 as part of a terrace of three houses. An

The melting pot: Turkish London

Of the several waves of immigration that
laid the foundations for London's Turkish
community, the first took place in the early
1940s, when Turkish Cypriots came to Britain
in search of better economic opportunities,
arriving by boat with British passports (Cyprus
is a British colony) at Dover. Many settled in
Newington Green, which by the 1970s had
become known as Little Cyprus.

It was following the military coup in
mainland Turkey in 1980 that Turkish
immigrants began arriving in large numbers,
settling close to the established Turkish
Cypriot community as well as in nearby
Dalston, Stoke Newington, Haringay and
Islington. In the 1980s Turkish Kurds fleeing
Turkey for political and economic reasons
began to put down roots in Dalston.

Today the early Turkish Cypriot immigrants
are an assimilated and integrated part of
London, while the more recent Turkish and
Kurdish communities often remain tight-knit
groups, despite their growing success in the
restaurant and supermarket businesses.

Where to go
The **Rio Cinema** in Dalston (*see p292*) hosts
an annual Turkish Film Festival in December,
featuring films from up-and-coming, as well as
more established, directors. A recent addition
to the season is the Kurdish Film Festival in
November; phone for details.

Where to shop
Yashar Halim (495 Green Lanes, N4, 8340
8090), one of the oldest and most famous
Turkish supermarkets in the capital, has a
bakery with a wide range of Turkish bread,
including corec (with sesame seeds) and
pitta, as well as various loaves made with
cheese and spinach. The newer **Turkish
Food Centre** (363 Fore Street, N9, 8807
6766) is a sort of Turkish mini-Tesco selling
an enormous variety of Turkish food.

Traditional jewellery, such as the blue
stone 'eye' amulets often given to babies
as good luck charms, can be bought at
Erbiller Jewellery (449 Green Lanes, N4,
8340 4004). **Vitrine** (386 Green Lanes, N4,

inspiration to lovers of modern architecture and modern art alike (it contains a collection amassed by Goldfinger and his artist-wife Ursula Blackwell, including works by Max Ernst, Marcel Duchamp, Bridget Riley and others), the house retains its original fixtures and fittings, including some of Ernö's prototype furniture. A video and guided tour supply the necessary background detail.

Hampstead Heath

A stroll across Hampstead Heath's rolling woodland and meadows could almost make you believe you were in the middle of the countryside. Take your kite up to **Parliament Hill** and catch the stunning view over the city, or explore the renovated pergola of the **Hill Garden** across the road from the Old Bull & Bush pub. Then there are the famous ponds (*see p324* **In the swim**), which attract sunbathers and swimmers in summer and a few diehard health fanatics in the winter.

If you're after culture, **Kenwood House** (*see below*) boasts an impressive collection of paintings (and its Brew House restaurant serves one of the best breakfasts in London). There are also lakeside concerts on Saturdays in the summer at Kenwood, and band concerts on summer Sunday afternoons on **Golders Hill Park** and Parliament Hill. Funfairs are held at the upper and lower ends of the heath on bank holidays (*see p265* **Frequent events**). On the edges of the heath, two historic pubs, Jack Straw's Castle and the Spaniards Inn, offer beer and decent nosh. You can pick up a diary of events at information points on the heath.

Kenwood House/Iveagh Bequest

Kenwood House, Hampstead Lane, NW3 (8348 1286/www.english-heritage.org). Hampstead tube/ Golders Green tube then 210 bus. **Open** *Apr-Sept* 10am-6pm Mon, Tue, Thur, Sat, Sun; 10.30am-6pm Wed, Fri. *Oct* 10am-5pm Mon, Tue, Thur, Sat, Sun; 10.30am-5pm Wed, Fri. *Nov-Mar* 10am-4pm Mon, Tue, Thur, Sat, Sun; 10.30am-4pm Wed, Fri. *Tours* by appointment only. **Admission** free; donations appreciated. *Tours* £3.50; £2.50 concessions; £1.50 under-16s. **No credit cards**.
This splendid neo-classical house contains a wonderful collection of paintings, including works by Rembrandt, Vermeer, Turner, Gainsborough and Reynolds. Robert Adam remodelled the house in 1764-73, transforming the original brick building into a majestic villa for Lord Mansfield – the richly decorated library is stunning. Kenwood remained in the Mansfield family until 1922; when developers attempted to buy the estate, the house and grounds were saved for the public by the 1st Earl of Iveagh, a brewing magnate, who bequeathed the estate to the nation in 1928. Check out the dining room for the crème de la crème of Lord Iveagh's Old Masters: Vermeer's *The Guitar Player* takes pride of place,

Sightseeing

7503 6737), a café-bookshop, specialises in self-help, mind/body books and fiction in both Turkish and English.

What to eat

Istanbul Iskembecisi (9 Stoke Newington Road, N16, 7254 7291) is the place to try traditional Turkish tripe (*iskembe*), garlic, yoghurt and chilli-oil soup, said to be essential in avoiding raki-induced hangovers. Iskembe is an acquired taste, however, so those of a less adventurous nature might want to stick to the spicy kebab specialities at **Mangal II** (4 Stoke Newington Road, N16, 7254 7888). For Turkish-Cypriot food you should try **Eyva** (279 Green Lanes, N4, 8880 2260), which specialises in takeaway mezzes.

Where to drink

The Turkish beverage of choice is raki, an ouzo-type drink that is best consumed mixed with three parts of water. Head for **Turku Café Bar** (79 Stoke Newington Road, N16, 7923 1961), where a saz (mandolin-type

Turkish delights at **Yashar Halim**.

instrument) player entertains drinkers most nights of the week. There are numerous other Turkish bars and clubs stretched along Stoke Newington Road.

Pondlife at **Hampstead Heath**. *See p149.*

but don't miss Rembrandt's self-portrait in the corner. More recent claims to fame include a starring role in *Notting Hill*. Also look out for one of Kenwood's hidden treasures, the exquisitely restored Romany Buckland Caravan in a small building near the Coach House restaurant.

Highgate

Archway or Highgate tube.

East of Hampstead Heath, perched on a hill of its own, graceful Highgate gets its name from a tollgate that used to stand on the site of the **Gate House** pub on the High Street; dinky shops now predominate. There are fine views from the top of **Highgate Hill**, at the foot of which legend has it that Dick Whittington, about to quit town, heard the Bow bells peal out 'Turn again Whittington, thrice Lord Mayor of London Town'. The 'event' is commemorated on the Whittington Stone near the eponymous hospital.

North of Highgate tube station, **Highgate Wood** (*see below*) and **Queen's Wood** offer shady walks. Highgate's best-known sight is **Highgate Cemetery** (*see below*). Adjoining this is beautiful **Waterlow Park** (7272 2825), which was donated to Londoners by low-cost housing pioneer Sir Sydney Waterlow in 1889 (*see p80*). It has ponds, a mini-aviary, tennis courts, a putting green and a garden café in 16th-century Lauderdale House.

Further down Swain's Lane you can peep through the Gothic entrance to **Holly Village**, a private village that was built in 1865. Hornsey Lane, on the other side of Highgate Hill, leads you to the **Archway** (or 'Suicide Bridge'), a Victorian viaduct offering vertiginous views of the City and East End.

Highgate Cemetery

Swain's Lane, N6 (8340 1834). Archway tube/C11, 271 bus. **Open** *East Cemetery Apr-Oct 10am-5pm Mon-Fri; 11am-5pm Sat, Sun. Nov-Mar 10am-4pm Mon-Fri; 11am-4pm Sat, Sun. West Cemetery tours Apr-Oct noon, 2pm, 4pm Mon-Fri; 11am, noon, 1pm, 2pm, 3pm, 4pm Sat, Sun, bank hols. Nov-Mar 11am, noon, 1pm, 2pm, 3pm Sat, Sun.* **Admission** *East Cemetery £2. West Cemetery tours £3; £1 8-16s* (reduced rate for 1st child in group only, other children pay full rate). No children under 8 admitted. *Camera fee £1.* No camcorders permitted. **No credit cards.**

It's a case of celeb-spotting with a twist at this romantic and leafy resting place for Victorian Britain's best and brightest. With its dramatic tombs of towering angels and curling roses, it's a must for devotees of the high Victorian style of commemorating the dead. Karl Marx and George Eliot on the East Side may be the most famous, but the West Side, which can only be viewed on a tour, is breathtakingly beautiful: long pathways wind through tall tombs and gloomy catacombs, and some of the funerary architecture is remarkably elaborate. Poet Christina Rossetti and chemist Michael Faraday can be found on the West Side among striking statues and sarcophagi. Burials still take place (the cemetery is then closed).

Highgate Wood

8444 1505. Highgate tube. **Open** *Woods dawn-dusk daily; Oshobasho Café 8.30am-6pm (dusk if earlier) Tue-Sun, bank hol Mon.* **Admission** free.

A short walk from Highgate tube station are the bosky environs of Highgate Wood, which has a nature trail, a great kid's playground, and plenty of open space for picnics and ball games. Alternatively, just mingle with the couples, children and dog walkers along the tranquil paths. The woods are worth visiting for Oshobasho Café alone, where you can tuck into healthy veggie fare or coffee and cakes on the leafy terrace. It's the perfect urban retreat.

Islington

Map p402

Angel tube or Highbury & Islington tube/rail.

Islington's fortunes have ebbed and flowed: Henry VIII owned several houses here and liked to hunt nearby, and in the 19th century it was known for its smart shopping streets, theatres and music halls, but its fortunes plummeted in the early 20th century and it became rundown. These days it's decidedly of two parts. Like so much of London, its Georgian squares and Victorian terraces have been gentrified in the past 25 years, and rising property prices have pushed out some of the poorer population. The middle classes are served by antique shops, bijou restaurants, an independent cinema (the Screen on the Green; *see p291*), music at the Victorian Union Chapel (*see p322*), and theatre at the King's Head (*see p338*) and, until a long refurb forced it to vacate its Islington premises for a time, the Almeida (*see p337*). It's all too easy to forget that Islington and its chic Canonbury and Highbury neighbours are close to ramshackle housing projects such as **Essex Road**'s Marquess Estate.

Islington is best taken at a stroll. Start at Angel tube station, and walk along **Upper Street**, past the glass façade of the Business Design Centre and the adjacent Hilton hotel, along the side of the triangular Green and up to Highbury. This way, you'll take in the shops and allow yourself a bite to eat at restaurants as varied as Alsatian eaterie Tartuf (88 Upper Street, 7288 0954) and Modern European spot Granita (*see p207*).

But before striking out for **Highbury** and beyond, make sure you sample the architectural delights of Regency **Canonbury Square** and **Compton Terrace**, both well-maintained pieces of architectural history. The square, once home to George Orwell (No.27) and Evelyn Waugh (No.17A), houses the **Canonbury Tower**, which affords great views (call 7359 6888 to arrange admission). This is Islington's oldest monument, with possibly Roman foundations. Also on the square is the dedicated **Estorick Collection of Modern Italian Art** (*see below*).

Highbury Fields, at the north end of Upper Street, was where 200,000 Londoners fled to escape the Great Fire of 1666. Beyond here, on the way to Finsbury Park, lies compact Highbury Stadium, where the **Arsenal Tour** (*see below*) lets fans get up close and personal with their favourite team.

The Arsenal Tour

Arsenal Stadium, Avenell Road, N5 (7704 4000/ www.arsenal.co.uk). Arsenal tube. **Tours** *Advance bookings only* 11am, 2pm Mon-Fri. **Admission** £4; £2 concessions, under-16s. **Credit** *Shop* MC, V.
Ah, the roar of the crowd, the thrill of the terraces… For the ultimate Arsenal experience, a tour of Highbury Stadium is unmissable. The tour packs in visits to the boardrooms, directors' areas, press rooms, marble halls and players' tunnels, while the stadium, a listed art deco building, provides the necessary aesthetic dimension for those too other-worldly to appreciate the inherent aesthetic of the 'beautiful game'. Entry to the museum is included in the price, providing access to Britain's largest collection of a single club's memorabilia. It's enough to make a Gunners fan weep.

Estorick Collection of Modern Italian Art

39A Canonbury Square, N1 (7704 9522/ www.estorickcollection.com). Highbury & Islington tube/rail/271 bus. **Open** 11am-6pm Wed-Sat; noon-5pm Sun. **Admission** £3.50; £2.50 concessions; free students with valid NUS card. **No credit cards.**

Situated in a beautiful Georgian townhouse in north London's Little Italy, this gallery features Eric and Salome Estorick's amazing collection of Italian Futurist paintings, photos and sculptures. Estorick was a US political scientist, writer and art collector who started collecting 40 years after the short-lived Futurist movement launched itself in 1910. His acquisitions include Balla's *Hand of the Violinist* and Boccioni's *Modern Idol*, as well as pieces by Carra, Marinetti, Russolo and Severini. The museum has the clout to exhibit work from major Italian museums and often holds temporary shows relating to Italian modern art. The gallery also houses a library with more than 2,000 books on modern Italian art, a shop, and a café with alfresco seating. Temporary exhibitions in 2002 include Pasta: Italian Culture on a Plate (26 June-15 Sept).

Dalston & Stoke Newington

Dalston: Dalston Kingsland rail/30, 38, 56, 67, 149, 242, 243, 277 bus. Stoke Newington: Stoke Newington rail/73 bus.

Bishopsgate in the City passes through Shoreditch and becomes Kingsland High Street, otherwise known as the A10, the busy main road that runs out through Dalston, Stoke Newington, past the Hassidic enclave of Stamford Hill, via Tottenham and out of London altogether. Though scruffy and, at times, intimidating, **Dalston** is a vibrant place

The heavenly **Union Chapel**. *See p150.*

Sightseeing

with kosher shops and bustling market stalls selling Afro-Caribbean vegetables. Lots of the small cafés and late-night restaurants reflect the Turkish influx into the area (*see p148* **The melting pot: Turkish London**).

Middle-class house buyers started moving in to **Stoke Newington** in a big way after 1980. Green spaces can be found at **Clissold Park** (*see below*) and the rambling old boneyard of **Abney Park Cemetery**. Attractive, villagey Stoke Newington Church Street has a number of good restaurants: **Rasa** (No.55), famed for its superlative vegetarian south Indian cooking, was joined by **Rasa Travancore** (No.56) in 2001, offering Syrian Christian cuisine (*see p212*, **Who he? Sivadas Sreedharan**), while further up, trendy café **Blue Legume** (No.101) has a great laid-back vibe. For shoppers there's a liberal peppering of second-hand bookstores and the joyful anarchy of **Cookson's Junk Yard** (121 Marton Road, 7254 9941).

Clissold Park

Stoke Newington Church Street, N16 (7923 3660/ tennis courts 8806 2542/café 7923 3703). Bus 73. **Open** *Park 7.30am-dusk daily. Café 10am-dusk daily.* Named after a local 19th-century curate, Clissold House and Park actually date back to much earlier times; the nearby Queen Elizabeth Walk refers to a visit made by the young Elizabeth I. One of the park's more bizarre modern-day claims to fame is that one-time Baader Meinhof member Astrid Proll worked here for a time while she was on the run in the late 1970s (she was employed, under an assumed name, as a park warden). Nowadays, the only exotic species you're likely to find are the inhabitants of the small zoo, though the tennis courts, lake and tea rooms do offer an escape of a much more refined kind.

Further north

Moving towards the northern perimeter of London, dull suburban streets are enlivened by the immigrant communities that have made them their home. **Golders Green, Hendon** (where the impressive **Royal Air Force Museum** is located; *see below*) and **Finchley** have large Jewish communities. Finchley is home to London's second **Jewish Museum** to go with the one in Camden (*see p144*). Golders Green is also the focus of a growing population of Chinese and Japanese City workers. There's been a Jewish cemetery on Hoop Lane since 1895; cellist Jacqueline du Pré is buried here, while **Golders Green Crematorium** has consumed hundreds of notable bodies, including those of TS Eliot, Marc Bolan and Anna Pavlova.

Tottenham and **Haringey** retain a strong Greek Cypriot and Turkish Cypriot identity. Both areas are fun for the sweet-toothed

wanting to try a few honey-soaked pastries or the not-so-sweet-toothed drawn by the fabulous kebab shops of Green Lanes. **Cricklewood**'s Indian population has also contributed a marvellous array of shops, stocking all kinds of sugary goodies. **Muswell Hill**'s prime attraction is the glant glasshouse of **Alexandra Palace** (*see below*).

Alexandra Park & Palace

Alexandra Palace Way, N22 (park 8444 7696/ info 8365 2121/boating 8889 9089/ www.alexandrapalace.com). Wood Green tube/ Alexandra Palace rail/W3, W7, 84A, 144, 144A bus. **Open** *Park 24hrs daily (admission free). Palace times & admission prices vary depending on exhibitions.* Alexandra Palace, or Ally Pally as it's fondly known, has had a bit of a rum deal as historic landmarks go. Hailed as 'the People's Palace' when it opened in 1873, with the aim of providing affordable entertainment facilities to all, it burned to the ground 16 days later. Although it was rebuilt and went on to become the site of the first TV broadcasts by the BBC, it suffered a similar fate in 1980, when a fire swept through the building, razing it to the ground for a second time. Dramatic history aside, the palace offers one of the best panoramas of London, and its grounds provide a multitude of attractions including an outdoor ice rink (*see p325*), a boating lake, playgrounds and a pitch-and-putt course. Its entertainment and exhibition centre also hosts fairs and events, ranging from the annual Motor Show (9-10 Mar) to the Afro Hair & Beauty Show (2-3 June). There are also bank holiday funfairs (*see p265* **Frequent events**) and a free and very popular fireworks display on Bonfire Night (*see p267*).

Royal Air Force Museum Hendon

Grahame Park Way, NW9 (8205 2266/ www.rafmuseum.org.uk). Colindale tube/Mill Hill Broadway rail/32, 226, 292, 303 bus. **Open** 10am-6pm daily. *Tours* daily; times vary, phone for details. **Admission** £7.50; £4.90 concessions; free under-16s accompanied by an adult, OAPs, registered disabled. *Tours* free. **Credit** MC, V.
Billed as the birthplace of aviation in Britain, Hendon Aerodrome houses more than 70 aircraft, together with aviation memorabilia and artefacts that span the first 100 years of flight history. The main hangar displays the planes themselves: from early World War I planes such as the FE2 to the impressive Halifax and Lancaster bombers of World War II, which in turn are dwarfed by the high-tech might of the Cold War era Valiants and Vulcans. There's an interactive show about the Battle of Britain, an authentic chapel used by troops during the Falklands War, and, for *Top Gun* wannabes, the chance to literally put yourself in the pilot's seat with the help of a Red Arrows flight simulator or the 'touch and try' Jet Provost cockpit in the interactive gallery. The 'Landmark' building, a Grade II-listed aircraft hangar that will be used as an additional interactive centre, is expected to open in 2003.

East London

Have a butcher's at one of London's most colourful quarters.

Whitechapel & Spitalfields

Maps 10 & 12

Aldgate, Aldgate East, Shoreditch or Whitechapel tube.

Whitechapel has always been eclipsed by the City. Its situation, on the main route from London to Essex, ensured that it became a suburb in its own right, but it has never enjoyed the cachet of its neighbour. The bell-founders and other tradesmen too noisy to be tolerated in the City were corralled here in their droves, and the Whitechapel Bell Foundry (established 1570) and Gunmakers' Company Proof House still survive in **Fieldgate Street** and **Commercial Road** respectively. By Victorian times, the area was ravaged by poverty and became a virulent breeding ground for crime, in particular prostitution. The image of 19th-century Whitechapel supplied by Charles Booth ('its streets full of bullying and selling, the poor living on the poor') vividly depicts the kind of decayed morality and miserable living conditions that allowed Jack the Ripper to dispatch his victims undetected.

Inevitably, low rents attracted a steady influx of immigrants, whose multicultural influence has enriched the area over the last few centuries. First, it was French Protestant refugees, the Huguenots, in the early 18th century; then Irish and Germans in the early 19th century and Jewish refugees from eastern Europe from 1880 to 1914; and then, as the Jews prospered and moved north, Indians and Bangladeshis, who between the 1950s and 1970s took over textile businesses on Commercial Street and Commercial Road.

The best way to enter the heart of the East End is to take the 15 bus through the City and get off at **Aldgate East** at the stop between Goulston Street and Old Castle Street (keep an eye out for Tubby Isaacs' jellied eel stall – established 1919 – by the Aldgate Exchange pub). **Commercial Street**, which sweeps off to the left through Spitalfields towards **Shoreditch**, is largely a wide swathe of Victorian warehouses. Halfway up it is the covered **Spitalfields Market** (*see p249*). An organic market is now held where the old fruit and veg market (established in 1682) left off, surrounded by traders who enjoy a thriving weekend trade in books, music, clothes,

household accessories and arts and crafts (there are more than 300 stalls on a Sunday). The western part of the market (now surrounded by hoardings) has been earmarked for development, but the market itself is scheduled to remain, despite local fears to the contrary.

After dark this stretch of Commercial Street – highlighted by Hawksmoor's **Christ Church Spitalfields** (*see p154*) opposite – has a Hell's Kitchen look about it, with prostitutes standing along the kerb. The sex trade, though, has a considerable history in the area, much like the nearby Ten Bells pub, where the Ripper met several of his prostitute victims before butchering them on nearby streets. Today, the pub gains regular custom from the many Ripper walking tours that stop in every night, and, ironically, from an array of strippers who draw an early evening clientele of City gents.

Fournier Street, which runs alongside Christ Church to link Commercial Street with Brick Lane, is altogether more respectable: a reminder of the Huguenots, whose skill at silk weaving brought them prosperity in the East End. Their tall houses, with distinctive shutters and ornate, jutting porches, line the street. You can see inside one at **19 Princelet Street**, a rare Grade II-listed, unrestored silk merchant's home built in 1719, with a hidden synagogue added in 1869. It's currently awaiting major repairs, after which it will open as a museum of immigration; until then call to get details of the occasional openings, or to book a group visit (7247 5352/www.19princeletstreet.org.uk). Similar houses can be found in nearby **Elder Street** and **Folgate Street**, where the unique, recreated Georgian residence, **Dennis Severs' House** (*see p154*), is distinguished by the flickering gas flames over its front door.

For a quirky area tour, try Janet Cardiff's 'The Missing Voice (Case Study B)', available from **Whitechapel Library** (77 Whitechapel High Street; call 7713 1402). Provided you leave ID as a deposit, the library will lend you a CD Walkman with Cardiff's recorded voice leading you through the streets of the East End. Rather than a conventional guided tour, she has constructed a narrative that is part detective story, part urban guide, part film-noir. 'Have you ever had the urge to take off somewhere and not tell anyone?' she asks. Well, now you can.

Sightseeing

Christ Church Spitalfields

corner of Commercial Street & Fournier Street, E1 (7247 7202). Aldgate East tube/Liverpool Street tube/rail/67 bus. **Open** *Services* 10.30am Sun; phone for details of other times. **Map** p403 S5.

The ubiquitous Hawksmoor was responsible for this long-standing church, built in 1714 as a place of worship for the Huguenot silk weavers and still an impressive sight after dark. Having fallen into disrepair, the church was due for a programme of restoration as we went to press. Work is unlikely to begin before March 2002, so call to check for opening times after that date.

Dennis Severs' House

18 Folgate Street, E1 (7247 4013/ www.dennissevershouse.co.uk). Liverpool Street tube/rail. **Open** noon-2pm Mon; Mon evenings (times vary, phone to book); 2-5pm 1st Sun of mth. **Admission** £7 Mon afternoon, Sun; £10 Mon eve. **No credit cards. Map** p403 R5.

Provided you park your disbelief at the door (and the zealous staff will ensure you do), you may just have a memorable time at Dennis Severs' House. It defies categorisation; no longer a private house, nor, strictly speaking, a museum or an art installation, this once rundown silk weaver's house has been restored as an historical time capsule, furnished by the eccentric Mr Severs (who died in 1999) with original objects and furniture found in local markets. The interior is arranged as a 'still-life drama' encapsulating interiors from the early 18th century to Victorian times – unfinished glasses of port stand on the table before a crackling hearth, the beds look like they've been slept in, books lie open on a chair and cooking smells linger in the air. The idea is to wander around the house and just take it all in. And remember: no talking and, most definitely, no mobile phones.

Brick Lane

Traditionally, **Brick Lane**'s two main attractions were its plethora of cheap curry restaurants and Brick Lane Market (*see p256*). Many of the former are, alas, uninspiring these days, though a notable exception is Sweet &

Who she? Princess of the City

In 1999, during the course of excavations investigating the remains of Spitalfields' medieval hospital, priory and cemetery of St Mary Spital (which stood on the site of the present-day Spital Square), archaeologists stumbled across part of an even older burial ground – a Roman one this time. Its focal point was a huge, lidded stone sarcophagus within which, as a metal detector scan revealed, lay something metal. In the soil around the sarcophagus, a unique glass vessel and jet ornaments hinted that the occupant of the tomb might be female.

These suspicions proved well founded when, prising the box open, the archaeologists found an inner lead coffin containing, in turn, the perfectly preserved skeleton of a young, slender female who came to be known to those involved in piecing together her story as the Princess of the City. The life history that emerged from the reconstructive work was that of a high-born woman brought up in a warm, Mediterranean land such as Spain, southern France or Italy (shown by analysis of her teeth, which had oxygen isotopes locked into them). Objects that she took with her to the grave 1,600 years ago (including expensive glass vessels that would probably have contained perfumed oil) indicate that she was pagan rather than Christian, while

minute fragments of Chinese silk decorated with fine gold threads woven in Syria, the remains of a pillow of bay leaves on which her head had been lain, and the highly decorated nature of the lead coffin bespeak a life of fabulous wealth and luxury. Seemingly part of one of Britain's most important Roman families, she died in her early 20s, probably from an infectious disease.

In parallel with this biographical reconstruction, the Princess was brought back to life through a clay facial portrait carried out by a medical artist. Said Liz Barham of the Museum of London, where the facial portrait, along with the sarcophagus, coffin and skeleton (*pictured*), is on permanent display in the Roman Gallery (*see p94*): 'It was strange seeing her face for the first time. She has very strong features.'

The privileged life of this young Roman woman contrasts sharply with another major find of the 12-month dig: among the medieval remains that were uncovered more than seven feet (two metres) below the surface were part of the priory church, a stone pulpit, a chapel with a bone-filled basement, and the medieval charnel house and cemetery, among whose 8,600-plus burials was a disabled young Christian man who was one of 30 victims of a 13th-century epidemic found in a burial pit.

Spicy (No.40). Brick Lane's Jewish heritage survives in the 24-hour Beigel Bake (No.159), while the Pride of Spitalfields in Heneage Street is one of the few good old-fashioned pubs remaining in this area. Several younger, trendier brasseries, restaurants and bars have taken root around the manor, the best known being the Vibe Bar (91 Brick Lane) and Les Trois Garçons restaurant (*see p208*). These additions reflect the changing face of Brick Lane's social mix as it moves into the 21st century. Hip folk have been coming to catch the latest in designer furniture, clothing and art since the Truman Brewery opened up to entrepreneurs cut from a savvier, artier pattern than their '80s forebears.

Whitechapel Road

Fieldgate Street, running behind the huge East London Mosque, is worth a detour for a look at the grim, derelict, Victorian bulk of Tower House, built as a hostel for the homeless. Stalin

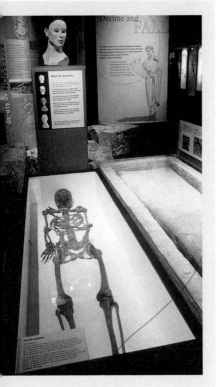

and Lenin stayed here while attending the Fifth Congress of the Russian Social Democratic Labour Party in nearby Fulbourne Street. The Elephant Man, Joseph Merrick, was exhibited at what is now the Bombay Saree House, before Sir Frederick Treves, a surgeon at the **Royal London Hospital** opposite, spotted him and provided a home for him in the hospital buildings. The hospital is topped by a helipad and contains a museum with a section on Merrick plus a general rundown on the history of medicine and the hospital itself (*see p155*).

Crime has always thrived in this area. George Cornell was shot dead by Ronnie Kray in May 1966 at the Blind Beggar pub (No.337), while **Sidney Street**, which leads off Whitechapel Road opposite Cambridge Heath Road, was the site of a famous siege on 3 January 1911. Several anarchists barricaded themselves into a house and took potshots at the police and soldiers outside before the house caught fire. Two charred bodies were recovered but the gang's leader, a Russian enigmatically named Peter the Painter, was never found.

For decades, the alley at **Wood's Buildings** (down the side of the Bombay Saree House, across Whitechapel Road from the Royal London Hospital) led to what was arguably the most desolate spot in the whole of the East End: an almost-forgotten tract of land dominated by a huge, ruined Victorian school. It was here that Jack the Ripper claimed his first victim. The school may now have been converted into luxury flats, but the view back along the alley towards Whitechapel Road is still tinglingly Dickensian. However, be aware that the old East End is disappearing with alarming rapidity: catch it while you can.

Back towards the City, the art nouveau **Whitechapel Art Gallery** (*see p156*) on Whitechapel High Street specialises in contemporary art. The lobby of Whitechapel Public Library is adorned with a painted-tile depiction of the hay market that was held in the High Street for 300 years until its abolition in 1928. A modest clothing market continues to do well further along Whitechapel Road.

Royal London Hospital Archives & Museum
St Philip's Church, Newark Street, E1 (7377 7608). Whitechapel tube. **Open** 10am-4.30pm Mon-Fri. **Admission** free.
Closed until its relaunch in January 2002, with new and improved exhibits, the Archives & Museum have a section devoted to the tragic figure of Joseph Merrick, the Elephant Man, who was among the patients here. Other exhibits deal with the development of healthcare in the East End from the 18th century, as well as the history of the hospital, and

Sightseeing

nursing and medicine in general, including a section on heroic nurse Edith Cavell, executed by the Germans in 1915 for helping Allied soldiers to escape from occupied Belgium.

Whitechapel Art Gallery

80-82 Whitechapel High Street, E1 (7522 7888/ recorded info 7522 7878/www.whitechapel.org). Aldgate East tube/15, 25, 253 bus. **Open** 11am-5pm Tue, Thur, Fri; 11am-8pm Wed; 11am-6pm Sat, Sun. *Tours* 2.30pm Sun. **Admission** free. *Tours* free. **Map** p405 S6.

Combining its large ground-floor gallery and skylit upper gallery with an eye for provocative talent, the Whitechapel remains one of London's best exhibition spaces. Over the years it has maintained a continually challenging programme; recent years have seen themed shows such as 2000's Protest & Survive, and major one-person exhibitions on artists such as Rosemarie Trockel and Jeff Wall. This year the gallery will showcase the work of American photographer Nan Goldin (21 Jan-31 Mar) and will host a retrospective of the Brazilian artist Helio Oiticica (26 Apr-23 June), alongside the work of grown-up Britartist Liam Gillick.

Shoreditch & Hoxton

Map p403

Old Street tube/rail.

The intersection of two Roman roads (**Old Street**, running east–west, and **Kingsland Road**, running north–south) marked the beginnings of **Shoreditch**. Not quite the City or the East End, the place seems uncertain of its identity, and its main focal point, around Old Street station, is dour. But it has seen more cheerful times. James Burbage founded London's first theatre on the corner of **Great Eastern Street** and **New Inn Yard**. Called, simply, the Theatre, it lasted barely 20 years before decamping to Southwark and becoming the Globe (*see p77*). The same year, 1598, Ben Jonson, then Britain's foremost playwright after Shakespeare, fought actor Gabriel Spencer at Hoxton Fields (now **Hoxton Square**) and killed him. As he was a clergyman, Jonson escaped the gallows, but he had his left thumb branded.

Hoxton is the section of Shoreditch north of Old Street and west of Kingsland Road. From Victorian times until the outbreak of World War II, it was known chiefly for its overcrowded slums and its music halls. Both features have since disappeared under unappealing blocks of flats, but an influx of artists, musicians and other bohemian types in recent years has given the area an unexpected if arrogant chic. Centred around **Hoxton Square**, former home of the now-defunct Lux Cinema, are some cool bars

(*see p218*) and many 'trying really very hard to be cool' bars, plus a few decent restaurants including the Real Greek, *see p211*), yet shops and other basic facilities remain conspicuous by their absence and the whole area is still pretty unpleasant. The nearby **Geffrye Museum** (*see below*) looks at the history of interior design.

Geffrye Museum

Kingsland Road, E2 (7739 9893/recorded info 7739 8543/www.geffrye-museum.org.uk). Liverpool Street tube/rail, then 149, 242 bus/Old Street tube/rail, then 243 bus. **Open** 10am-5pm Tue-Sat; noon-5pm Sun, bank hol Mon. **Admission** free; donations appreciated. Under-8s must be accompanied by an adult. **Map** p403 R3.

These beautiful almshouses, built in 1715, were converted into a museum of furniture and interior design in 1914 and are now one of London's most fascinating and beguiling museums. A series of rooms, reconstructed in period style, amounts to an informative and atmospheric voyage through the ages of British domestic interiors from the Elizabethan era to the present day; not least in winter, when the rooms are charmingly garnished with period Christmas decorations. The 20th-century rooms and exhibits are displayed in a 1998 extension to the almshouses, with Edwardian, 1930s and 1960s living rooms and a 1990s loft conversion arranged in a loop around a sinuous, skeletal staircase leading down to the **Geffrye Design Centre**, a showcase gallery for contemporary designers and makers based locally in the East End, educational art rooms, and a cosy temporary exhibition gallery, which in 2002 will offer up Cutting Edge: a History of British Cutlery & Place Settings (26 Mar-2 June) and Onetree (25 June-1 Sept), an exhibition designed to demonstrate the value of woodlands by distributing different parts of a single oak tree to 70 artists and exhibiting their various creations.

A bright, airy restaurant separating the old and new sections of the museum looks out over the walled herb garden, which provides a pleasant 'outdoor room' in fine weather to go alongside the series of period garden rooms that opened in 1999. Family Sundays, held once a month, are popular for picnics on the front lawns and child-friendly activities. All in all, a delightful enterprise.

Bethnal Green & Hackney

Bethnal Green tube/rail/Hackney Central or Hackney Downs rail.

Known in Victorian times as the poorest area of London, **Bethnal Green** was targeted with wholesale slum clearance and the building of huge council estates during the 20th century but remains impoverished. The **Bethnal Green Museum of Childhood** (*see p157*), originally the east London branch of the V&A, opened in 1872. Almost as ancient is the art

Sightseeing

deco inlaid Anglo-Italian caff E Pellicci (332 Bethnal Green Road), run by the friendly Pellicci family for a century and now open again after a fire.

Hackney, to the north, was originally an extended village, popular in the 15th and 16th centuries with merchants who wanted to live near, but not too near, to the City. Hackney's oldest house, **Sutton House** (*see p158*), dates from this period. In his diary entry for 11 June 1664, Pepys records that he went 'with my wyfe only to take ayre, it being very warm and pleasant, to Bowe and Old Ford; and thence to Hackney. There… played at shuffle board, ate cream and good cherries'. The rural idyll continued until the 19th century, when the area's market gardens were buried under terraced houses and workshops, themselves to be replaced by housing estates after World War II.

Hackney is best approached selectively. **Columbia Road** (*see p257*) and **Ridley Road** have fine markets; the former also has pottery shops specialising in terracotta. **Mare Street** offers the **Hackney Empire** (8985 2424/www.hackneyempire.co.uk), in its heyday one of London's great music halls and still a popular theatre. Dedicated fund-raising and generous contributions have ensured that the Empire reached its £15million target for restoration. The grand re-opening is scheduled for late

2002 – meanwhile, a skeleton programme is maintained next door at the Hackney Empire Bullion Room (call the main number for details).

Hackney Central Hall opposite was built as a Methodist meeting hall in 1907; in 2001 it reopened as Ocean, a music venue (*see p317*). A Technology & Learning Centre, due to open in April 2002, is being built on the south side of the Town Hall Square, incorporating a Central Library, shops, restaurants, offices, and a new site for the Hackney Museum (8986 6914/www.hackney.gov.uk/hackneymuseum), which will chart the history of immigration and settlement in the area over the last 1,500 years through interactive displays and activities.

Bethnal Green Museum of Childhood

Cambridge Heath Road, E2 (8983 5200/recorded info 8980 2415/www.museumofchildhood.org.uk). Bethnal Green tube/rail. **Open** 10am-5.50pm Mon-Thur, Sat, Sun. **Admission** free; donations welcome. Under-8s must be accompanied by an adult.

A strange concept perhaps, but one that works – this museum offers a mixture of the nostalgic and the bizarre in its exhaustive array of dolls, trains and puppets. The best of the lot are the enormous, elaborate, multi-levelled dolls' houses, which are astonishing to behold. Evidently, children had the gift of imagination before television was invented to take it all away. Displayed in large glass cases, the dolls – some of which are centuries old – are interesting, albeit in a slightly macabre way. Some have mature faces and are dressed in fantastic costumes, while

Roll over Chucky, it's the **Bethnal Green Museum of Childhood**.

others are naked and hang forlornly from cupboard walls. Many displays are probably more interesting for nostalgic adults, but the kids can be usefully deposited in the soft play area (weekends and school holidays only; £2) or distracted by the roaming art cart (weekends and school holidays only).

Sutton House

2 & 4 Homerton High Street, E9 (8986 2264/ www.nationaltrust.org.uk). Bethnal Green tube then 253, 106, D6 bus/Hackney Central rail. **Open** Historic rooms *Jan-4 Feb 2002* 11.30am-5.30pm Wed, Sun, bank hol Mon. Last entry 5pm. *From 5 Feb 2002* 2-5pm Fri, Sun, bank hol Mon, 4 June (Jubilee Day). **Admission** £2.10; 50p 5-16s; £4.80 family (2+2); free under-5s. *Tours* free. **Credit** MC, V.
The oldest house in the East End, this National Trust-owned red-brick Tudor mansion was built in 1535 for Henry VIII's first secretary of state. It opened as a community centre in the late 1980s after a fierce debate over its future that led to the superb restoration now on view. There are Tudor, Jacobean and Georgian interiors, as well as the Edwardian chapel and medieval foundations in the cellar. It also boasts what is possibly London's oldest loo: a

16th-century 'garderobe'. There's even a protected wall of graffiti, believed to have been done by squatters in the early '80s. The café and shop are open all year, and on the fourth Sunday of the month (excluding January) there are free 'discovery days' with guided tours and workshops on various aspects of Tudor life (phone for details).

Docklands

Assorted stops on the Docklands Light Railway.

The cradle of London, **Docklands** stretches east from Tower Bridge to the Isle of Dogs and beyond, containing in its landscape myriad insights into British history. As the British Empire expanded in the 18th and 19th centuries, so did the traffic along the Thames, as ships arrived laden with goods from all corners of the globe. Different docks were built to specialise in various types of cargo: rum and hardwood at West India Docks on the **Isle of Dogs**; wool, sugar and rubber at **St Katharine's Dock** by Tower Bridge;

The melting pot: Vietnamese London

The Vietnamese community began coming to Britain in the mid 1970s, many of them arriving as 'boat people' after the end of the Vietnam War. Although they were originally dispersed all over Britain, the largest number were housed in Hackney, where housing was cheap and where there was a tradition of supporting immigrant communities. As the community there grew and developed, many of those who were sent to other parts of Britain eventually gravitated to Hackney, and today it has the largest concentration of Vietnamese immigrants in the UK.

Vietnamese businesses, especially restaurants and supermarkets, can be found clustered along Mare Street, E8, and Kingsland Road, E2. Centres such as An Viet House have been set up to offer support to the community, and recently the Hai Duong project was established to foster cultural and business links between the Vietnamese in Hackney and the town of Hai Duong in Vietnam.

Where to shop

Ten kilogram sacks of fragrant rice line the front of **Huong-Nam Supermarket** (185-7 Mare Street, 8985 8050), which offers Vietnamese goods as well as some Chinese and Thai fare. In the chill cabinets there are all manner of

fresh goods, while a whole wall is dedicated to varieties of dried noodles. There's also a freezer bursting with fish, meat, dim sum and specialist Vietnamese imports. Goods flown in from Vietnam are labelled in French or Vietnamese, and there is little English either written or spoken in the shop.

Other supermarkets along this strip include **Vietnam Supermarket** (No.193A, no phone), which has good lychees, and **London Star Night** (No.203-13; no phone), which has a huge stock of CDs, videos, teas and Asian sweets, while beautiful jade Buddhas and other traditional Vietnamese jewellery can be found at **Kim Hiep** (No.263, no phone).

Where to eat and drink

Green Papaya (191 Mare Street, 8985 5486) does a mean banana flower salad, as well as other traditional fare such as grilled tilapia. It also has a lovely garden patio that's lit up with fairy lanterns on summer evenings. **Huong-Viet** (12-14 Englefield Road, N1, 7249 0877), based in An Viet House, serves up delicious *banh xeo* (traditional pancakes) alongside numerous varieties of *pho* (soup, with the light lemony beef stock that is a staple of Vietnamese cuisine). There are also numerous informal café-style eateries along Kingsland Road, most notably Viet Hoa (*see p211*).

ivory, coffee and cocoa at London Docks in **Wapping**. During World War II the docks suffered heavy bombing (in particular 57 consecutive nights of firebombing), but by the 1950s they had again reached full capacity.

But the recovery was to be short-lived: the abrupt collapse of the Empire sparked a series of crippling strikes. Above all, the introduction of deep-water container ships led to the closure, one by one, of all of London's docks from Tower Bridge to Barking Creek between 1967 and 1984. From March 2002, the **Museum in Docklands** (*see p161*) will chart the history of the docks and the Port of London.

Since then efforts have been made to spruce up the area. In 1981 the Conservative government set up the London Docklands Development Corporation (LDDC) with a brief to regenerate the eight-and-a-half square miles (2,200 hectares) of derelict land by building new offices and homes and attracting new businesses. Accused from the outset of favouring wealthy outsiders over the needs of local people, the LDDC came

badly unstuck in the recession of the early 1990s, when developers found themselves with brand-new buildings and no one to move into them. Since then the situation has improved: the population of Docklands had increased from 39,400 in 1981 to 77,000 by the time the organisation ceased operation in March 1998. Its responsibilities have been taken over by other new bodies.

Docklands remains one of the most fascinating areas of London to visit, with its stark contrasts of old and new architecture, its rich pockets of history and picturesque wharves. And the Docklands Light Railway (DLR), combined with the Jubilee line, mean it's more accessible than ever before.

St Katharine's

Just east of Tower Bridge on the north bank of the Thames, St Katharine's once housed more than 1,000 cottages, a brewery and the 12th-century church of St Katharine, all of which were demolished (without compensation) to

Mare Street is a focal point for London's Vietnamese community.

make way for a grandiose new docklands development scheme in 1828. **St Katharine's Dock**, which was built over the old settlement, remained open until 1968, re-emerging in 1973 as the first of the Docklands redevelopments. **St Katharine's Haven**, now a yacht marina, houses a squadron of russet-sailed, century-old barges in one corner of the dock, while the restaurants, cafés and pubs around the rest of the dock pull in tourists by the coachload.

Wapping

In 1598 London historian John Stowe saw **Wapping High Street** as a 'filthy strait passage, with alleys of small tenements or cottages… built and inhabited by sailors' victuallers'. Today it's a quiet thoroughfare hemmed in on either side by warehouses (those in **Wapping Wall** are the most spectacular) and new flats.

The river at Wapping, to the east of St Katharine's, brims with history. Until well into the 19th century convicted pirates were taken at low tide to **Execution Dock** (near the River Police station, at Wapping New Stairs), hanged, and left there in chains until three tides had washed over them. The Captain Kidd pub (108 Wapping High Street) commemorates one of the most famous recipients of this brand of rough justice: Kidd had been dispatched by the government to capture pirates in the Indian Ocean but decided to become one himself.

Another historic pub, the Town of Ramsgate (62 Wapping High Street), is where bloodthirsty Judge Jeffreys, who sent scores of pirates to Execution Dock, was himself captured as he tried to escape to Hamburg disguised as a sailor (he died in the Tower of London). 'Colonel' Blood was also caught here after attempting to steal the Crown Jewels in 1671. Dating from 1520, the Prospect of Whitby (*see p227*) is the oldest and most famous of the Wapping riverside pubs, but beware the coach parties; Pepys, Dickens, Whistler and Turner were regulars. The White Swan & Cuckoo (on the corner of Wapping Lane and Prusom Street) lacks a riverside view but is friendly and serves good food.

The streets north of the **Highway** are working-class tenements with a colourful past. A large mural at St George's Town Hall on **Cable Street** commemorates the battle between local people and fascist blackshirts, led by Sir Oswald Mosely, on 4 October 1936. The march, meant to intimidate the local Jewish population, was abandoned and the blackshirts were never seen in such numbers again in the East End. The church of St George-in-the-East,

just off the Highway on **Cannon Street Road**, was built in 1714-29 to the designs of Nicholas Hawksmoor. Although the interior was rebuilt after the Blitz, the exterior and monumental tower are typical of the architect.

Limehouse

Sandwiched between Wapping and the Isle of Dogs, Limehouse was named after the medieval lime kilns that once stood there. But, as with Wapping, its prosperity came from the sea: a 1610 census revealed that half the working population were mariners, and Limehouse later became a centre for shipbuilding. The straw-coloured **Sail Makers' & Ship Chandlers' Building** still stands at 11 West India Dock Road.

The importance of Limehouse is reflected in the immense size of **St Anne's Limehouse** (corner of Commercial Road and Three Colt Street). Built between 1712 and 1724 in what were then open fields, this is probably Hawksmoor's most dramatic creation. The clock tower is the second highest in Britain after the one in which Big Ben is housed, and the church is the only non-HM ship in the world to have permission to fly the white ensign year round.

Britain's first wave of Chinese immigrants, mainly seamen, settled in Limehouse in the 19th century. Their influence survives in some of the street names (**Ming Street**, **Canton Street**) and in the few Chinese restaurants that remain around **West India Dock Road**. In Victorian times Limehouse was notorious for its gambling and drug dens (Oscar Wilde's Dorian Gray comes here to buy opium) and it features in stories by Sax Rohmer (creator of oriental villain Fu Manchu) and Sir Arthur Conan Doyle. Dickens knew Limehouse well: he regularly visited his godfather in Newell Street and used the tiny, dark and still superb Grapes (*see p227*) as the model for the Six Jolly Fellowship Porters in *Our Mutual Friend* (1865).

Isle of Dogs

Bristling with cranes and the skeletons of yet more high-rise office blocks, the Isle of Dogs has seen Docklands redevelopment at its most intense. The 800-foot (244-metre) rocket-shaped focal point, **Canary Wharf**, was designed by Cesar Pelli and remains the tallest building in the UK; since it was erected in 1991 it has dominated the London skyline The only pity is that owing to fear of IRA attack – a bomb at South Quay in February 1996 killed two people and caused a huge amount of damage – the public can't enjoy the view from the top. Still, the sight of the tower through the glass-domed roof of Canary Wharf DLR station is spectacular and almost makes up for the disappointment at not being able to ride the elevator to the top.

There's little about the Isle that isn't subject to dispute. Some insist that it isn't an island at all but a peninsula (though the main section of West India Docks effectively splits it in two), and no one can agree on whether 'Dogs' refers to the royal kennels that were once kept here or whether it's a corruption of the dykes that were built by Flemish engineers in the 19th century. Above all, argument continues to rage over whether the Isle of Dogs is a crucible of economic progress or a giant adventure playground for big business.

The best way to see Docklands is from the overhead Docklands Light Railway (DLR). At the undeveloped southern end of the Isle is Mudchute City Farm, a big hit with kids. **Island Gardens**, at the very tip, offers an unparalleled view across the Thames towards Greenwich. Alternatively, you could arrive in one of the most expensive (and expensive) stations in the world; the Foster-designed **Canary Wharf** station, resplendent in glass and steel, is said to be as long as Canary Wharf Tower itself is high. Nearby, at West India Quay, is the new **Museum in Docklands** (*see below*), due to open in spring 2002.

Museum in Docklands

Warehouse No.1, West India Quay, Hertsmere Road, Docklands, E14. (7001 9800/ www.museumindocklands.org.uk). West India Quay DLR. **Open** *From Mar 2002; hours subject to change* 10am-6pm Mon-Sat; noon-6pm Sun. **Admission** phone for details. **Credit** MC, V. Located in a Grade I-listed warehouse and scheduled to open in March 2002, this £16.5-million museum will chart the history of the Port of London and Docklands with an array of multimedia presentations, including reconstructed scenes, engravings and arte-facts. Tracing the history of the docks chronologically, the galleries will detail Roman trading activities, the medieval port, colonial expansion and the success of the East India Company, Thames ship-building, and 20th-century decline and regeneration.

Mile End, Bow & Stratford

Bow Church, Bow Road or Mile End tube/Stratford tube/DLR/rail.

Mostly common land until the 16th century, **Mile End** experienced a minor population explosion in the 1800s as industrialisation took hold. The area never really suffered the ravages of poverty endured by neighbouring Whitechapel and Bethnal Green; nevertheless,

it was here that the **Trinity Almshouses** were built in 1695 (near the junction with Cambridge Heath Road) for '28 decayed masters and commanders of ships'. Look out for the model galleons, on either side of the entrance. In the 1860s William Booth founded the Salvation Army in Mile End.

To the south-west, **Mile End Park** borders Copperfield Road, home to the **Ragged School Museum** (*see p162*) and **Matt's Gallery** (*see p299*). The park was undergoing a dramatic transformation as we went to press; around £12 million of funds from the Millennium Commission, with match funding from a range of sponsors, has paved the way for it to be remodelled by architects and planners Tibbalds TM2, incorporating CZWG's award-winning bridge over Mile End Road. To date, a go-kart track plus the landscaping of two major tranches of land, the Art Park and the Ecology Park, have been completed. These energy-efficient, turf-covered buildings will be used as educational facilities and temporary exhibition spaces. The final phase of development, a children's park at the extreme south end of the site and a play arena at the northern tip, are scheduled for completion in autumn/winter 2002.

To the north of Mile End, **Victoria Park** (8533 2057) is a welcome slice of green stretching towards Hackney. Fringed by the Hertford Union Canal, it's a useful detour for those weary of Hackney's plains of cement. At the main Sewardstone Road entrance look out for the deranged-looking Dogs of Alcibiades, which have stood here since 1912. The park's large ponds and tearooms give it an atmosphere reminiscent of Regent's Park.

Bow, to the east, has played a major role in the growth of London. In the 12th century the narrow Roman bridge over the River Lea at Old Ford was supplemented by a new bridge downriver. Its bow shape gave the whole area its name. Grain was transported by boat from Hertfordshire and unloaded at mills along the river. In the 19th century new factories sprang up, notably the Bryant & May match factory, scene of a bitter but ultimately successful match-girls' strike in 1888. A quarter of a century later, Bow struck another blow for women's rights when Sylvia Pankhurst, sister of Emmeline, launched the East London Federation of Suffragettes.

Stratford ('street by the ford') was formed north of the 12th-century bridgehead. A wealthy Cistercian monastery, Stratford Langthorne Abbey, helped put it on the map. The abbey was dissolved by Henry VIII in 1538, but by then Stratford's prosperity was ensured, thanks to the development of early industries such as gunpowder manufacture. In the mid 19th century, much of the area was covered by railway lines and marshalling yards, and it remains a busy transport nexus, boasting a railway, tube and DLR station and a decidedly odd-looking bus station.

Modern Stratford has a busy, well-defined centre, focused on Broadway, where an obelisk commemorates 19th-century philanthropist Samuel Gurney. Look for the distinctive green dome and globe of the Transport & General Workers Union building in **West Ham Lane**, then head through the big indoor shopping centre to **Gerry Raffles Square**. Here the Stratford Picture House faces the venerable Theatre Royal Stratford East (*see p338*), which re-opened in December 2001 with a new neighbour: Stratford Circus (*see p287*), a slick new arts centre that host performances by the likes of the Cholmondeleys and the Featherstonehaughs during 2002.

Ragged School Museum

48-50 Copperfield Road, E3 (8980 6405/ www.raggedschoolmuseum.org.uk). Mile End tube. **Open** 10am-5pm Wed, Thur; 2-5pm 1st Sun of mth. *Tours* by arrangement; phone for details. **Admission** free; donations appreciated.
Ragged schools were a Victorian invention designed to educate poor children; this sparse, rather limited but nonetheless compelling museum is designed to inform the public about these archaic institutions, as well as commemorating the development of east London. A ground-floor exhibit explains the history of the Tower Hamlets that eventually become the eastern boroughs; the first floor is devoted to a recreation of a Victorian ragged school classroom; and the top floor is designed like a 19th-century home. The Standing on Common Ground: Ocean View exhibition (to 20 Mar 2002) offers a photographic record of the culturally diverse inhabitants of the nearby Ocean Estate.

Walthamstow

Walthamstow tube/rail.

The name comes from the Old English word 'Wilcumestowe': a place where guests are welcome. It's a description that still applies today: Walthamstow is noticeably friendly. Its borders are ancient ones: **Epping Forest** (*see p354*) to the north, **Walthamstow Marshes** to the west. The first settlers lived here in the Bronze Age, when the whole area was thickly forested. In medieval times, much of the forest was cleared and replaced by farmland. Even now, most of its largely working-class population has been spared the tenements and tower blocks that litter other parts of east London.

Walthamstow has two main thoroughfares. The narrow **High Street** contains the longest and, after Brixton, most varied market in London. **Walthamstow Market** stretches for more than a mile and is lined by inexpensive shops. The second thoroughfare is undulating **Hoe Street**, consisting of a drab selection of kebab shops and mini-marts, although the Dhaka Tandoori (No.103) is rather good.

Lloyd Park contains the Waltham Forest Theatre and a variety of imported water birds. The aviary and manicured bowling green, frequented by white-clad elderly locals, make it particularly pleasant on a sunny summer's afternoon. The 18th-century building with its back imperiously turned to the park is the **William Morris Gallery** (*see p163*). From here, a short walk up Forest Road will be amply rewarded by a dramatic view of the art nouveau **Walthamstow Town Hall**, one of the most startling pieces of municipal architecture in London. Its beautiful proportions, green and gold clock tower and circular reflecting pool have graced many a film and TV production; indeed, in pre-glasnost days, it was frequently called to stand in for Moscow or Leningrad.

The area's oldest buildings are the well-concealed enclave of **Walthamstow Village**. Vestry Road is the site of the **Vestry House Museum** (*see below*) and the Monoux Almshouses, built in 1795 and 'endowed for ever... for the use of six decayed tradesmen's widows of this parish and no other'. Nearby St Mary's Church has a modest but tranquil interior. Timbered **Ancient House**, opposite the churchyard, was once a farmhouse. Restored in 1934, it sags like an unsuccessful fruit cake. The Village continues along Orford Road, with its Italian restaurants and cosy pub. Further north, just across the A406, lies **Walthamstow Stadium**, one of London's best-known greyhound racing tracks (*see p328*).

Vestry House Museum

Vestry Road, E17 (8509 1917/www.lbwf.gov.uk). Walthamstow Central tube/rail. **Open** 10am-1pm, 2-5.30pm Mon-Fri; 10am-1pm, 2-5pm Sat. *Tours* groups only, by arrangement. **Admission** free.
This pint-sized museum was once a 19th-century police station (as evidenced by the still operational cell, into which visitors can be locked – at their request, of course). The main exhibition concentrates on the social history of the area, incorporating some fascinating photographs, plus the original 1834 model of Frederick Bremer's motor car (this was Britain's first ever combustion engine car). It does seem strange, however, that there's nothing about Britain's first powered flight, which was conducted by A V Roe over Walthamstow Marshes in 1909. Still, the costume and toy sections are well worth a look.

It's a dog's life at **Walthamstow Stadium**. *See p162.*

Sightseeing

William Morris Gallery

Lloyd Park, Forest Road, E17 (8527 3782/ www.lbwf.gov.uk/wmg). Walthamstow Central tube/rail. **Open** 10am-1pm, 2-5pm Tue-Sat; 1st Sun of mth. *Tours* phone for details. **Admission** free. **Credit** MC, V.

Opened to the public more than 50 years ago, this was the childhood home of influential late-Victorian designer, craftsman and socialist William Morris. In four rooms on the ground floor Morris's biography is expounded through his work and political writings. Upstairs are galleries devoted to his associates – Burne-Jones, Philip Webb and Ernest Gimson – who assisted in contributing to the considerable popularity Morris's style retains today. From April 2002 there will also be a temporary exhibition of photographs (by Frederick Evans) and drawings (by Edmund Hort New) of Kelmscott Manor, Morris's Oxfordshire home.

Leyton & Leytonstone

Leyton or Leytonstone tube.

Badly bombed in World War II, **Leyton** was redeveloped somewhat haphazardly and it lacks the cohesion and charm of neighbouring Walthamstow. Much of the land originally consisted of marshy, fertile farmland, and during the 18th century the area was best known for its market gardening. Inevitable of mid 19th-century industrialisation led to much of the marshland being covered by railways and gas works, and to a downturn in the area's fortunes as the population swelled with low-paid railway workers. The

proliferation of discount supermarkets and second-hand furniture and electrical shops testifies to the fact that Leyton remains one of London's poorest areas.

Leytonstone, to the east of Leyton, took its name from a milestone on the Roman road from the City to Epping Forest. The petrol station on the corner of Leytonstone High Road is on the site of a greengrocer's shop where Alfred Hitchcock spent his early childhood. There are also some striking murals in Leytonstone tube depicting various scenes from his films.

Further east

There's little to interest the visitor beyond Blackwall. Much of **Canning Town** was flattened by German bombers, and ugly post-war housing estates did nothing to revive its fortunes. Neighbouring **Newham** fared even worse: the collapse of a tower block, Ronan Point, in 1968 caused several deaths. **Beckton**, to the east, has been more fortunate, with better-than-average new housing. South of Beckton, **London City Airport** was opened in 1987, using the long, narrow quay between Royal Albert Dock and George V Dock as a runway for short-haul airliners.

Near the Thames Barrier is London's first new park construction in recent history, **Thames Barrier Park** (North Woolwich Road, E16). Its tea pavilion, together with its playground and fountains, make it particularly popular with families.

South London

Look past the North/South divide to discover the delights of this historically rich and culturally diverse area.

Charlton, Woolwich & Eltham

Little more than 200 years ago, a journey along the Old Dover Road over **Shooters Hill** to Charlton was an arduous – not to say dangerous – one. The road was steep and bumpy, and the wild countryside hid many a fearsome highwayman (the famous Dick Turpin among them) lying in wait for easy prey. But ruthless as the robbers may have been, the law was equally hard on those who were caught: convicted highwaymen could expect to be hanged at a gallows at the bottom of Shooters Hill and have their bodies displayed on a gibbet at the summit. In 1661 Samuel Pepys recorded that he 'rode under a man that hangs at Shooters Hill, and a filthy sight it was to see how the flesh is shrunk from his bones'.

Charlton village itself originally grew up around the Jacobean manor **Charlton House** (*see below*) but is now a relatively unremarkable London suburb. **Maryon Park**, used in Antonioni's film *Blow-Up*, is a pleasant place for a stroll, while the nearby **Thames Barrier** (*see p165*), which stretches between Silvertown on the north bank and Woolwich on the south, has an entertaining visitor centre that explains its role in protecting London from flooding.

Woolwich attracts fewer visitors than its more glamorous neighbour Greenwich, though it has plenty to offer, including a good shopping centre. The character of Woolwich has been shaped by military and naval associations. Woolwich Arsenal was established in Tudor times as the country's main source of munitions. Over the centuries the arsenal spread to colossal proportions: at its peak, in World War I, the site stretched 32 miles (52 kilometres) along the river and employed 72,000 people. When the arsenal closed down in 1967, the land was used to build a monstrous concrete housing estate, **Thamesmead**. **Woolwich Garrison**, historic home of the Royal Artillery, remains, and has the longest Georgian façade in the country. It's best seen from Woolwich Common or Grand Depot Road, where the remains of the **Royal Garrison Church of St George** have been left as consecrated ground after being hit by a flying bomb in 1944 (the end walls and altar still stand). Military aficionados will enjoy the new artillery museum, **Firepower** (*see p165*).

Henry VIII established the Royal Dockyard at Woolwich in 1512, initially so his new flagship, the *Great Harry*, could be built there. It moved to Chatham in 1869. Downstream from the Woolwich Ferry terminal, the stretch of river known as Gallions Reach was the scene of the Thames' worst-ever shipping accident in 1878, when a crowded pleasure steamer, the *Princess Alice*, was struck broadside by a collier, with the loss of about 700 lives.

The **Woolwich Ferry** has existed since the 14th century; the old paddle steamers were replaced by diesels as late as 1963. (There is also a foot tunnel.) Today the seating area outside the Waterfront Leisure Centre, next to the terminal, is a fine spot to watch a great river at work. Railway enthusiasts might like to take the ferry across the river to the **North Woolwich Old Station Museum** (*see p165*).

Despite being despoiled by numerous bleak housing estates, there are a surprising number of pleasant green spaces in this part of south-east London, many of them connected by the excellent **Green Chain Walk** (call 8921 5028 for maps, or log on to www.greenchain.com). It takes in wonderful ancient woodlands such as **Oxleas Wood** (easily accessible from Falconwood rail station), a couple of miles south of Woolwich. A mile and a half south-west of here is the beautifully restored art deco **Eltham Palace** (*see below*).

Charlton House

Charlton Road, SE7 (8856 3951). Charlton rail/53, 54, 380, 442 bus. **Open** 9am-11pm Mon-Fri; 9am-5.30pm Sat. **Admission** free.
The finest Jacobean house in London, and possibly the country, red-brick Charlton House was built in 1612 as a retirement gift for Adam Newton, tutor to James I's son Prince Henry. It's not known for sure who the architect was, though John Thorpe is the most likely contender. The orangery, on the other hand, is almost certainly the work of Inigo Jones. Though the house's current existence as a community centre and public library is undoubtedly useful, it seems a shame that no more effort has been made to restore the interior of this beautiful building.

Eltham Palace

Court Yard, off Court Road, Eltham, SE9 (8294 2577/www.english-heritage.org.uk). Eltham rail. **Open** *Apr-Sept* 10am-6pm Wed-Fri, Sun. *Oct* 10am-5pm Wed-Fri, Sun. *Nov-Mar* 10am-4pm Wed-Fri,

Sun. **Admission** *House & grounds (incl. audio tour)* £6.20; £4.70 students, OAPs; £3/10 5-15s; free under-5s. *Grounds only* £3.60; £2.70 concessions; £1.80 5-16s; free under-5s. **Credit** MC, V.

Built on the site of an extensive royal palace, modern Eltham Palace is a wonderful homage to 1930s art deco: the meticulously restored interior is a joy. Stephen Courtauld, a member of the textile family and patron of the arts (*see also p97*, Courtauld Gallery), acquired the site in the mid-1930s and, with the aid of architects and designers, built this fabulous country home. The interior plays with geometry, line and contrasts of light and dark, from the deep wooden veneers to the truly modern concrete and glass dome in the light-filled entrance hall. Sadly, all that remains of the ancient royal residence that was finally abandoned in the mid-1600s is the impressive 15th-century great hall – the second largest of its kind in England – which was cleverly incorporated into the modern building. Note that it's closed from 24 December 2002 to 4 March 2003.

Firepower

Royal Arsenal, Woolwich, SE18 (8855 7755/ www.firepower.org.uk). Woolwich Arsenal rail. **Open** 10am-5pm daily (last entry 4pm). **Admission** £6.50; £5.50 concessions; £4.40 5-16s; £18 family (2+2 or 1+3); free under-5s. **Credit** MC, V.

Replacing the old Museum of Artillery, this £15-million attraction charts the dramatic history of the Royal Regiment of Artillery. The museum is centred around 'Field of Fire', a multimedia presentation that aims to recreate the experiences of artillery gunners in the 20th century, from World War I to Bosnia. The Gunnery Hall features a series of static displays illustrating the development of artillery weapons in the 20th century, while the interactive Real Weapon gallery allows visitors to learn the principles of targeting. All in all, there's much more to Firepower than the ragged uniforms and massed medals of its staid predecessor.

North Woolwich Old Station Museum

Pier Road, E16 (7474 7244). Beckton DLR/North Woolwich, Woolwich Arsenal or Woolwich Dockyard rail, then foot tunnel to North Woolwich Pier. **Open** *Jan-Nov* 1-5pm Sat, Sun. *School hols* 1-5pm daily. **Admission** free.

Trainspotters will want to make the pilgrimage to this otherwise charmless part of London, where this museum displays trains, tickets, station signs and a 1920s ticket office. It's at its best on the first Sunday of each month during summer, when the Coffee Pot and Pickett steam engines chug up and down.

Thames Barrier Visitors' Centre

1 Unity Way, SE18 (8305 4188/www.environment-agency.gov.uk). North Greenwich tube/Charlton rail/riverboats to & from Greenwich Pier (8305 0300) & Westminster Pier (7930 3373)/177, 180 bus. **Open** *Apr-Sept* 10.30am-4.30pm daily. *Oct-Mar* 11am-3.30pm daily. **Admission** £1; 75p concessions; 50p 5-16s; free under-5s. **Credit** MC, V.

Succeeding where King Canute failed, and costing a cool £535 million when it was completed in 1982, the Thames Barrier is London's first line of defence against devastating surge tides and one of the world's modern engineering marvels. Stretching like sci-fi sentinels across the river at Woolwich Reach, south-east London, the barrier's nine piers anchor massive steel gates that are raised from the riverbed several times a year in order to avert flooding in London's low-lying areas. The fascinating Visitors' Centre on the south bank features a variety of interactive exhibits explaining how the barrier was built and how it does its job. The barrier is raised for a test each month (in addition to a full yearly test; *see p266*); it's worth timing a visit to see it in action.

Greenwich & Blackheath

Greenwich is one of south London's biggest attractions. Today it's best known for its maritime associations, but for many years it was the playground of the Tudor royals. Henry VIII and his daughters Mary I and Elizabeth I were born here, and Greenwich Palace, perfectly positioned for hunting on the undulating land around, was Henry's favourite residence.

After the Tudors, the palace fell on hard times. Under Oliver Cromwell, it became first a biscuit factory, then a prison. In 1660, however,

A saucy stallholder at **Greenwich Market**. *See p166.*

Sightseeing

the newly restored monarch Charles II embarked on an ambitious scheme to return Greenwich to its former glory. Work began on a new palace, but only one riverside wing was ever built. William and Mary, who succeeded Charles, preferred the royal palaces located at Hampton Court and Kensington. They ordered Sir Christopher Wren (*see p86* **Who he?**) to design another wing for the unfinished building, to create the Royal Naval Hospital. Better known today as the **Old Royal Naval College** (the Navy moved out in 1998; *see p168*), this is the great edifice you see from the river today, split down the centre to allow an unobscured view of **Queen's House** (*see p168*) behind, now part of the **National Maritime Museum** (*see p167*). Maritime Greenwich was designated a UNESCO World Heritage Site in 1997.

The nicest way to arrive at Greenwich is by river to Greenwich Pier, where you'll disembark in the shadow of the **Cutty Sark** (*see p167*). The **Greenwich Tourist Information**

Centre (0870 608 2000), based in Pepys House beside the *Cutty Sark*, provides full details on sights and transport in the area. On the other side of the ship, **Greenwich Reach** is a leisure and retail complex slated for completion in 2004; it'll include a cinema, restaurants, flats and London's first central cruise-liner terminal.

The centre of Greenwich is a busy, traffic-ridden place. Visitors flood in every weekend to peruse the arts and crafts stalls of sprawling **Greenwich Market** (*see p256*). The church of **St Alfege Greenwich** (1712-18) on Greenwich High Road takes its name from the Archbishop of Canterbury, who was martyred on the site by marauding Vikings in 1012, after courageously refusing to sanction a demand for ransom that would have secured his release. The church is normally open to visitors at weekends.

A Thames-side walkway by the *Cutty Sark* takes you past the riverside front of the Old Royal Naval College to the Trafalgar Tavern (*see p229*), built directly on to the river and a

Who he? Raymond Chandler

You wouldn't immediately associate LA's king of noir with a leafy London suburb, but Raymond Chandler spent 17 years in London, and studied at Dulwich College from 1900 to 1905. Had he not, one of the most well-known and best-loved private detectives in fiction would have gone by another name – Philip Marlowe owes his identity to Marlowe House, where the young Chandler received his formal education.

Chandler invested in his work a pathos for his downtrodden detective and a panache for bitingly sharp dialogue that is echoed today in a genre that, consciously or not, owes a great debt to a man who wrote such killer lines as 'From thirty feet away she looked like a lot of class. From ten feet away she looked like something made up to be seen from thirty feet away.' (*The High Window*)

It's probable that the headmaster of Dulwich College at the time, AH Gilkes, a novelist in his own right, had some bearing on Chandler's decision to concentrate on fiction. But Chandler wasn't the only one to benefit from Gilkes' guidance: PG Wodehouse, the creator of Jeeves and Wooster, was there from 1894 to 1900, and CS Forrester, who invented Horatio Hornblower, attended in 1915 and 1916.

Though Chandler moved back to the United States, he retained his connection with London, reporting for the *Daily Express*

between 1908 and 1912. But his real passion was for literature and, until he hit the big time with his first Marlowe novel, *The Big Sleep*, in 1939, he churned out short stories for the burgeoning pulp magazines. This stint of writing was financially unrewarding but proved to be invaluable for the development of his work.

Britain's own master thriller writer of the same period, Ian Fleming (*see p115* **James Bond's Mayfair**), met Chandler in 1958 for a radio discussion that was recorded by the BBC. Chandler, whose star was on the wane at this time, nevertheless exerted some influence over Fleming, and imparted a little wisdom regarding the subject of being knocked unconscious, believing that victims of a coshing will, more often than not, vomit upon recovery. In the next James Bond novel, 007 did precisely that.

In that same year, Chandler spent some time in Swan Walk, Chelsea, where he wrote the first chapters of another Marlowe novel, *Poodle Springs*. He never completed the book (it was finished by crime writer Robert B Parker many years later) because his health, weakened by years of hard boozing, was deteriorating. He died in Los Angeles in March 1959.

Those interested in finding out more about Raymond Chandler should try Tom Hiney's outstanding biography.

favourite of literary buddies Thackeray, Dickens and Collins (Dickens set the wedding feast in *Our Mutual Friend* here). Tiny **Crane Street**, on the far side of the pub, leads you to the bizarre, white, castellated Trinity Hospital, which, since 1617, has been home to '21 retired gentlemen of Greenwich'. The path continues as far as the Cutty Sark Tavern, dating from 1695. Seats outside the pub afford a view of the still-active wharfs downstream.

The remains of 20 Saxon grave mounds and a Roman temple may have been identified within its precincts, but the beautiful riverside **Greenwich Park** (8858 2608) is more famous for its Tudor and Stuart history. Henry VIII was born at Greenwich Palace, and it remained his favourite residence. In 1616 James I commissioned Inigo Jones to rebuild the Tudor palace; the result was **Queen's House** (*see p168*), England's first Palladian villa. In the 1660s this was redesigned by André Le Nôtre, who landscaped Versailles. Charles II's plan for a new palace was later adapted to become the **Old Royal Naval College** (*see p168*).

Crowning the hill at the top of Greenwich park are the **Royal Observatory** (*see p168*) and Flamsteed House, both designed by Sir Christopher Wren (*see p86* **Who he?**). Temporally speaking, this is the centre of the planet: Greenwich Mean Time, introduced in 1890, sets the world's clocks. Visitors can straddle the Greenwich Meridian Line and stand in the eastern and western hemispheres of the world simultaneously. Each day since 1833 the red time-ball on the north-eastern turret of the observatory has dropped at 1pm as a signal to shipmasters on the river to adjust their chronometers. At the southern end of the park stands the 18th-century **Ranger's House** (*see p168*), a beautiful edifice housing, from May 2002, the equally stunning Wernher collection of paintings and sculpture.

To avoid the long hike up the hill, take the Shuttle Bus (8859 1096), a royal blue minibus that meets the boats at Greenwich Pier and transports visitors up through Greenwich Park, stopping at the National Maritime Museum and the Royal Observatory. Tickets for the hop-on, hop-off service are valid all day and cost £1.50 for adults and 50p for children.

A long road, **Maze Hill**, runs south from Trafalgar Road, forming the eastern boundary of Greenwich Park. At the top of the hill, at the corner of Maze Hill and Westcombe Park Road, is a castle-like house built by architect-playwright John Vanbrugh, who lived here from 1719 to 1726. From here, the view back towards the Old Royal Naval College and the City is superb. On Croom's Hill, west of the park, is the **Fan Museum** (*see below*).

Back north and sticking out into the Thames, Greenwich Peninsula is notorious as the site of the **Dome**. While it seems certain that history will not be kind to the Millennium Experience, the future of the Dome itself is less assured. Proposals for its future use have ranged from a business park to a sports stadium, but as we went to press, no real plan had emerged.

Cutty Sark

King William Walk, SE10 (8858 3445/ www.cuttysark.org.uk). Cutty Sark DLR/Greenwich DLR/rail. **Open** 10am-5pm daily (last entry 4.30pm). **Admission** £3.50; £2.50 concessions; £8.50 family (2+2); free under-5s. *Combined ticket with National Maritime Museum & Royal Observatory* £12; £9.60 concessions; £2.50 under-16s. **Credit** MC, V.

Hercules Linton's 1869 vessel was once one of the fastest ships on the ocean; today its claim to fame is as the world's only surviving tea and wool clipper. The beautifully restored decks and crew's quarters can be explored, while the lower decks house an extensive exhibition charting the history of the *Cutty Sark* and her days as a trading vessel, plus a variety of maritime relics, including paintings, models and – another record – the world's largest collection of carved and painted figureheads. Low-tech hands-on exhibits such as a knot-tying board and a hammock keep younger visitors entertained. On summer weekends there are shanty singers and costume storytelling sessions reliving life aboard the ship.

Fan Museum

12 Crooms Hill, SE10 (8305 1441/www.fan-museum. org). Cutty Sark DLR/Greenwich DLR/rail. **Open** 11am-5pm Tue-Sat; noon-5pm Sun. **Admission** £3.50; £2.50 concessions; free under-7s. Free OAPs, disabled 2-5pm Tue. **Credit** MC, V.

Housed in two converted Georgian townhouses, this unexpectedly compelling museum is one of only two permanent exhibitions of hand-held folding fans in the world. To avoid damage to their elasticity, the fans need to be periodically rested, so only a fraction of the huge collection is on view at any one time.

National Maritime Museum

Romney Road, SE10 (8858 4422/info 8312 6565/ www.nmm.ac.uk). Cutty Sark DLR/Greenwich DLR/ rail. **Open** 10am-5pm daily. **Admission** £7.50; £6 concessions; free under-16s, OAPs. *Combined ticket with Cutty Sark & Royal Observatory* £12; £9.60 concessions; £2.50 under-16s, OAPs. **Credit** AmEx, MC, V.

This thoroughly modern visitor attraction seems to get bigger and better with every visit. Its well-designed interior arranges themed exhibitions round three sides of the vast central atrium, Neptune Court, to give the museum an unusually open, airy feel, while the galleries themselves successfully combine traditional exhibits with interactive elements so as to be entertaining and educational in equal measure. The galleries are not meant to be seen in any particular order, so it's probably best to ignore the bewildering colour-coded floor plan.

On level one, the **Explorers** gallery examines pioneering sea travel, from early Polynesian and Viking voyages to the vain, imperialist drive of later European exploration. **Passengers** looks at the more passive participants in marine expeditions, concentrating on the mass migration of the early 20th century, while **Maritime London** brings old prints and lithographs together with video installations to help reconstruct London's nautical past and explore the city's current role as the financial hub of the shipping industry. Next door, **Rank & Style** looks at the way in which climate and class affect Naval uniform styles. Upstairs, **Seapower** concentrates on the Navy and sea trade in the 20th century, from World War I to the Gulf War, while in the next gallery, **Trade & Empire** is an examination of some of the less glorious episodes in Britain's maritime history.

Level three is home to **All Hands** and **The Bridge**, two hands-on, interactive galleries in which younger visitors can learn to send a distress signal using Morse code, flags or radio, or try their hands at steering a Viking longboat, a paddle steamer and a modern passenger ferry. The **Nelson Gallery**, a comprehensive monument to this country's most celebrated naval hero, and the 17th- and 18th-century models in the **Ship of War** exhibition, are just as popular with both adults and kids. From March to September 2002 an exhibition will explore the origins of tattooing in Polynesia and its gradual acceptance into western culture, largely through its popularity among sailors.

Old Royal Naval College

King William Walk, SE10 (8269 4747/ www.greenwichfoundation.org.uk). Cutty Sark DLR/ Greenwich DLR/rail. **Open** 10am-5pm daily (last entry 4.15pm). **Admission** £3; £2 concessions; free accompanied under-16s. Free for all from 3.30pm daily; free to all all day Sun. **Credit** MC, V.

One of the finest examples of monumental classical architecture in the country, Wren's spectacular riverside buildings were begun in 1696. The college is split in two to give an unimpeded view of **Queen's House** (*see below*) from the river, and vice versa. Originally a grand almshouse for former Royal Navy seamen, the building was adapted for use as a Naval college in 1873, but after 125 years in residence the Navy vacated the buildings in 1998 and the University of Greenwich took up residence. The spectacular Painted Hall (which was decorated by James Thornhill in 1708-27) and the chapel are open to the public, and there's a space for temporary exhibitions.

Ranger's House

Chesterfield Walk, SE10 (8853 0035/www.english-heritage.org.uk). Blackheath rail or Greenwich DLR/rail. **Open** from 5 March 2002; call for details. **Admission** £4.50; call for concessions details.

As the name suggests, this lovely 18th-century red-brick villa was once home to the Greenwich park ranger; more recently it's been used to display a collection of Jacobean and Stuart portraits. Major redevelopment over the past year, funded by English Heritage, have converted it into the new home for the Wernher Collection of paintings, sculpture, jewellery, furniture and crafts dating from 3BC to the 19th century, viewable from late spring on.

Queen's House

Romney Road, SE10 (8312 6565/www.nmm.ac.uk). Cutty Sark DLR/Greenwich DLR/rail. **Open** 10am-5pm daily. **Admission** £1; free under-16s, OAPs. **Credit** AmEx, DC, MC, V.

Designed by Inigo Jones in 1616 for James I's wife, Anne of Denmark, the Queen's House was one of the first truly classical buildings in Britain. Formerly decorated in period style, the building was recently refurbished, reopening in April 2001 as an annexe of the National Maritime Museum. It currently houses **A Sea of Faces**, a permanent exhibition of more than 130 portraits of sea captains and shipwrights from the 17th century to the present day – including work by the likes of Reynolds, Gainsborough and Hogarth – and **Maritime Greenwich**, an exhibition examining the area and its associated personalities.

Royal Observatory

Greenwich Park, SE10 (8312 6565/ www.rog.nmm.ac.uk). Cutty Sark DLR/Greenwich DLR/rail. **Open** 10am-5pm daily. **Admission** £6; £4.80 concessions; free under-16s, OAPs. *Combined ticket with Cutty Sark & National Maritime Museum £12; £9.60 concessions; £2.50 under-16s, OAPs.* **Credit** AmEx, DC, MC, V.

Founded in 1675, when Charles II appointed the first Astronomer Royal, John Flamsteed, and charged him with the task of finding out 'the so much desired longitude of places for the perfecting of the art of navigation', the Royal Observatory devotes several galleries to the search for a means of determining longitude at sea. The rest of the museum includes exhibits on the development of more accurate timepieces and an extensive history of the buildings as a working observatory, including the Octagon Room, a faithful restoration of Sir Christopher Wren's original interior design for Flamsteed House.

Blackheath

Maze Hill brings you to the edge of windswept **Blackheath**. Blackheath Village, on the far side of the heath, exudes middle-class values. **The Paragon**, a beautiful crescent of prestigious colonnaded houses on the edge of the heath, was built in the late 18th century with the express purpose of attracting the right sort of people to the area at a time when it was still struggling to lose its reputation as a no-go area plagued by highwaymen. Allowed to fall into disrepair in the 1920s and 1930s, and badly bombed during World War II, the crescent has since been restored to its original state.

Rotherhithe

West of Greenwich, the Thames curves past **Deptford**, once home to the Royal Naval Docks, to **Rotherhithe**. Samuel Pepys knew Rotherhithe as Redriffe, though both names probably derive from the Anglo-Saxon words 'redhra' and 'hyth': 'mariner's haven'. Though there's little to attract mariners these days, the river bank at Rotherhithe remains a pleasant haven, with superb views across the river and one of the best riverside pubs in London, the Mayflower (*see p229*), which dates from 1550 and was built on piles so it stands directly over the river. It was given its present name when *The Mayflower* docked here in 1620 before

heading to America. Its captain, Christopher Jones, is buried in the church of **St Mary's Rotherhithe** (*see below*).

St Mary's Rotherhithe

*St Marychurch Street, SE16 (7231 2465).
Rotherhithe tube.* **Open** 7am-6pm Mon-Thur; 8am-6pm Sat, Sun. **Admission** free.
Local sailors and watermen built this beautiful parish church in 1715. Sadly, acts of burglary and vandalism in the 20th century mean the interior can now only be viewed through glass, under the watchful eye of a video camera. Still, the communion table in the Lady Chapel is worth attention: it's made from timber salvaged from the warship *Fighting Temeraire*, the subject of a Turner painting in the National Gallery.

Whatever happened to? Bedlam

The Bethlehem Royal Hospital was set up in Bishopsgate in 1247 by the Sheriff of London as a priory with an attached care facility intended to provide relief for the poor suffering from any ailment and for those without lodging (hence its name; Bethlehem means 'house of bread' in Hebrew), and it wasn't until the 14th century that it began to take in 'distracted' patients, as they were euphemistically known. Over time, Bethlehem was shortened to Bedlam, and the presence of mental patients at the hospital eventually gave rise to the use of the word to mean madhouse. In 1547, when the priory was dissolved, the Mayor and Corporation of London purchased the hospital from Henry VIII and it became a fully fledged lunatic asylum.

In 1675-6 Bedlam moved to a beautiful new building in Moorfield, with two statues at the entrance called *Melancholy* and *Madness*, modelled after inmates (one of whom is reputed to have been Cromwell's porter). It was at this point that the asylum began to exploit the public's morbid fascination with mental illness by charging up to 100,000 visitors a year a penny each to come and ogle the inmates, who were treated with considerable brutality, as seen in part of Hogarth's *Rake's Progress* of 1735 (*pictured*).

Lined up in cells arranged in galleries, the patients continued to be treated as zoo animals until 1770, when concerns were voiced about the effects on their 'tranquility' of treating them as 'sport and diversion'. By this time the work of John Howard and the madness of King George III had changed public perceptions of pyschiatric illness and whipping had been outlawed. After 1851

the hospital was under regular government inspection and was praised for its high standards, with the criminal patients being sent to Broadmoor from 1864 onwards.

By that time it had moved again, to Lambeth in 1815. In 1930 patients were taken to yet another premises, this time in Addington in Surrey, but these days the Bethlehem Royal Hospital can be found in Beckenham, Kent. The original site is now occupied by Liverpool Street station, while the Lambeth building, minus its wings, which were demolished, has housed the Imperial War Museum (*see p172*) since 1936.

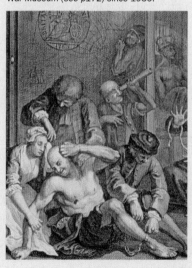

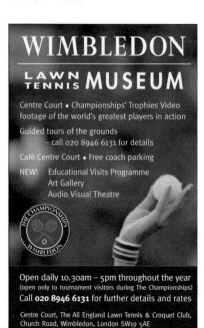

Camberwell, Peckham & Dulwich

Standing at the busy junction of Camberwell Road and Denmark Hill, on what is still laughingly called 'Camberwell Green', it's hard to believe that as recently as the mid-19th century **Camberwell** was a pretty country village. It's now as bustling and traffic-ridden an area as south London has to offer, though traces of its idyllic past remain: **Camberwell Grove**, a steep hill lined with tall Georgian houses is a particularly picturesque slice of the old town, while **St Giles Church**, with its 210-foot (72-metre) spire, is a typically grandiose, early Victorian structure by Sir George Gilbert Scott of St Pancras Station fame (*see p28* **Is it terminal?**). If you're looking for something a little more modern, one of Camberwell's numerous bars should fit the bill: Redstar (319 Camberwell Road) is an especially hip hangout.

Similarly, nearby **Peckham**, while no longer one of London's prettier areas, was formerly a stopping place for cattle drovers on their way to market. As a child, William Blake saw a vision of angels on the Rye, and in her novel *The Ballad of Peckham Rye* (1960), Muriel Spark refers, without irony, to 'the dusky scope of the Rye's broad lyrical acres'. The Victorian terraces that feature in the novel are now mostly gone, replaced by monolithic council estates and tower blocks, though the bleakness is alleviated by the prize-winning **Peckham Library** (*see p32*).

West of here, long **Lordship Lane** is the main thoroughfare through more sedate **Dulwich**. **Dulwich Park**, with its dramatic view of the Crystal Palace TV transmitter (in **Crystal Palace Park**), and adjoining **Dulwich Village** lie at the southern tip of Lordship Lane. Dotted with modern sculpture, the grounds of **Dulwich Picture Gallery** (*see below*) are a pleasant place in which to sit. The rarefied atmosphere of the Village, with its distinctive dark brick, is as great a contrast to Peckham as you could imagine.

Heading south out of the Village, College Road is lined with fine detached houses. At **Dulwich Common**, palatial, red-brick **Dulwich College** greets you, serene in its verdant grounds. Old boys include PG Wodehouse and Raymond Chandler (*see p166* **Who he?**). Close by is the marvellously eccentric **Horniman Museum** (*see below*).

Built to house the 1851 Great Exhibition, the all-glass **Crystal Palace** was originally erected in Hyde Park (*see p136*) but was moved to Sydenham after the Exhibition closed, and used for exhibitions, plays and concerts. The extensive grounds contained an amusement park and, dotted here and there, a number of striking life-sized models of dinosaurs. In 1936 the Crystal Palace caught fire and burned to the ground; the small but informative **Crystal Palace Museum** (8676 0700, open 11am-5pm Sun, bank hols only), housed in the old engineering school where John Logie Baird invented TV, chronicles the history of the palace. The model dinosaurs, which survived the blaze and are now classified as listed buildings, are a reminder of how quirky the whole place once was. Views from the park – which also contains the **National Sports Centre** (*see p330*) – are breathtaking.

Dulwich Picture Gallery

Gallery Road, SE21 (8693 5254/ www.dulwichpicturegallery.org.uk). North Dulwich or West Dulwich rail. **Open** 10am-5pm Tue-Fri; 11am-5pm Sat, Sun, bank hol Mon. **Admission** £4; £3 concessions; free under-16s. Free to all Fri. **Credit** MC, V.

Designed by Sir John Soane in 1811, the lovely Dulwich Picture Gallery was revamped in 2000 to great acclaim by Rick Mather Architects, who are currently masterminding the South Bank redevelopment (*see p74*). The modern extension includes a café, educational facilities and extra space for temporary exhibitions, which in 2002 include a display of the furniture collection of 18th-century author William Beckford (6 Feb-14 Apr); 'Inspired by Italy', the work of influential 17th-century Dutch landscape artists Both and Berchem (22 May-26 Aug); and a retrospective of paintings by 19th-century artist David Wilkie (11 Sept-1 Dec).

Horniman Museum

100 London Road, SE23 (8699 1872/ www.horniman.demon.co.uk). Forest Hill rail/63, 122, 176, 185, 312, 352, P4 bus. **Open** 10.30am-5.30pm Mon-Sat; 2-5.30pm Sun. **Admission** free; donations appreciated. **Credit** *Shop* MC, V.

Founded by 19th-century tea merchant Frederick Horniman, this gloriously idiosyncratic museum is worth the trip. The heart of the collection is the natural history hall, where an immense stuffed walrus presides over an eclectic display of other specimens. Equally interesting is the recently revamped **Living Waters Aquarium**, which demonstrates the life in a river on its way to the sea. But the most popular gallery is **African Worlds**, a large space devoted to African art and sculpture, including several Egyptian mummies and a spectacular 20ft high (6.1m) tribal mask. In summer, the formal sunken gardens with their fine views are an added attraction, as is the small zoo containing farmyard animals.

A major redevelopment programme taking place throughout 2001 will see a new world cultures gallery, a hands-on gallery, a new temporary exhibition space, a shop and café open in spring 2002. There'll also be new space for the vast musical instruments collection in autumn 2002.

Sightseeing

Stockwell, Kennington & Vauxhall

The settlements at **Stockwell** date back to medieval times, when a manor house stood on the site of present-day Stockwell Gardens, but like so many regions of south London, it remained a country village until the feverish house- and railway-building of the 1840s. Today South Lambeth Common, on which cattle used to graze, is no more than a scrap of grass outside Stockwell tube station bearing a clock tower and war memorial.

St Mark's Church, between Prima Road and Camberwell New Road, was built in 1824 on the site of a gallows; many of the Jacobites who fought in the 1745 rebellion were hanged, drawn and quartered here. Nearby **Kennington Park** was originally Kennington Common; in the 18th and 19th centuries, preachers – among them John Wesley – addressed large audiences here. The nearby **Foster's Oval** (*see p327*) is the home of Surrey County Cricket Club.

Head north on Kennington Road towards Lambeth to reach the **Imperial War Museum** (*see below*) or turn onto Kennington Lane to explore some of south London's most delightful streets: **Cardigan Street**, **Courtney Street** and **Courtney Square** are lined with clean, neat, light-brown terraced houses dating from 1914. The unexpected glimpse of the Palace of Westminster from Cardigan Road is a reminder of how close the area is to central London.

Lying between Kennington and the Thames, **Vauxhall** offers little of interest, although the area bounded by Tyers Street, Goding Street and Glasshouse Walk was once an 18th-century pleasure park, **Vauxhall Gardens**.

Imperial War Museum

Lambeth Road, SE1 (7416 5000/www.iwm.org.uk). Lambeth North tube/Elephant & Castle tube/rail. **Open** 10am-6pm daily. **Admission** £6.50; £3.25-£4.50 concessions; free under-16s, OAPs. Free to all 4.30-6pm daily. **Credit** MC, V. **Map** p404 N10.
It's ironic indeed that the national museum of war and conflict is housed in the city's most famous lunatic asylum, Bedlam (*see p169* **Whatever happened to?**); a rotating clock-hand in the basement symbolising the cost of war in terms of human lives illustrates this particular form of madness, with a body count of more than 100 million.

Entering the vast atrium you're confronted with an impressive display of the hardware of war, including a modern Polaris missile and a rather more primitive Sopwith Camel bi-plane. The lower ground floor holds the excellent permanent exhibition on the history of warfare in the 20th century, including the popular 'experiences': the Blitz and the Trench, which do a good job of bringing history to life.

Secret War, on the first floor, attempts to shed light on the clandestine world of espionage from 1909 to the present day. Exhibits range from Brezhnev's uniform to an original German 'Enigma' encrypting machine. The second floor is devoted to art collections, including the huge *Gassed,* painted in 1919 by John Singer Sargent, and works by CRW Nevinson and Stanley Spencer. Meanwhile, the museum's new £17-million, five-storey extension houses a two-floor permanent exhibition on the Holocaust; documents, artefacts, photographs and survivors' testimonies comprise a truly moving display.

Temporary exhibitions for 2002 include 'Voices from Korea' examining the experiences of soldiers and civilians during the Korean War (1950-53).

Brixton

Though it's existed for more than 1,000 years, there really was very little of interest to say about Brixton until it began to expand in the mid-19th century. During the 1860s and 1890s, railways and trams were built to link the previously sleepy settlement to the heart of London, and by the turn of the century the character of Brixton had altered: large houses built 100 years earlier were turned into flats and boarding houses popular with theatre people.

Brixton's ethnic identity changed dramatically during the 1940s and 1950s with the arrival of immigrants from the West Indies (*see p174* **The melting pot: Caribbean London**). A generation later, economic decline and hostility between the black community and the police led to the famous riots of 1981, 1985 and 1995. Today, however, the mood in Brixton is largely upbeat. Problems, particularly drug-related (the recent relaxation of laws regarding possession of marijuana has seen an increase in the number of people openly smoking it on the streets, which is still an offence) certainly remain, contributing to a volatile edge that results in occasional flare-ups. The most recent of these was in July 2001, when violence erupted after police shot a man dead after mistaking his novelty cigarette lighter for a real firearm. But Brixton's edge is also part of its charm: it boasts some of London's best nightlife and has a vibrant, cosmopolitan feel.

By day Brixton buzzes with shoppers, but it's after trading finishes that things really hot up: cinema-goers congregate outside the Ritzy (*see p292*), and drinking and dancing joints such as the Dogstar and the Bug Bar (for both *see p282*) start to fill. There's plenty more noise, chaos and colour in evidence in **Brixton Market** (*see p256*), which sprawls between Electric Avenue and Brixton Station Road. More serene attractions include **Brockwell Park**, 15 minutes' walk from the tube, with its recently restored 1930s lido (*see p324* **In the swim**).

Clapham

One of south London's more upmarket areas, **Clapham** has the rare advantage of boasting two centres: **Clapham Junction**, technically part of Battersea, and **Clapham Common**. Though the former was once no more than a country crossroads, after the arrival of the railways it became the bustling hub of the city's transport system, and the station is still one of the busiest in the world.

Northcote Road, which runs south from Clapham Junction, is awash with shops, bars and restaurants, while **Battersea Rise**, leading towards the common, is an arty stretch with a similarly huge array of eateries. The road eventually becomes **Clapham Common North Side**, boasting parades of tall, stately houses with great views of the common, which is somewhere between a park and a wild place; its bleak atmosphere has never been more vividly evoked than in Graham Greene's *The End of the Affair*. By day, it's popular with joggers and footballers; after dark, parts of it become gay cruising grounds.

The streets around the north end of the common have poshed up with fine bars and restaurants, perhaps in an attempt to compete with villagey **Clapham Old Town**, just north-east of the common. At its central point attractive 18th-century pubs face on to an approximate square bounded by the Pavement.

Holy Trinity Church, on the edge of the common, was known in the 19th century as the HQ of the Clapham Sect, a group of wealthy Anglicans – among them William Wilberforce, the anti-slavery campaigner – who advocated 'muscular Christianity'. The church was rebuilt after being hit by a V2 in 1945.

Battersea

Battersea derives its name from a small Saxon settlement, Batrices Ege (Badric's Island), that stood here more than 1,000 years ago. For centuries it was best known as a centre for market gardening, but it underwent a transformation in the early19th century, when scores of factories sprang up, and a dense network of railway lines was laid.

Battersea is best approached by rail. The journey from Victoria Station grants you a great view of Sir Giles Gilbert Scott's **Battersea Power Station** (built 1929-33 and closed in 1983), which has been subject to innumerable development plans in recent years. In late 2000 planning permission was finally granted to convert the power station into a vast riverside business and entertainment complex including 700 hotel rooms, a 2,000-seat theatre,

Kew Gardens' Palm House. *See p174.*

See p174.

a multiplex cinema office space and residential accommodation, but no definite completion date has yet been set.

Battersea has long been a favourite spot among artists and writers: the old **Battersea Bridge** was the subject of Whistler's moody *Nocturnes*; Turner used to paint the river from **St Mary's Battersea**. **Battersea Park** (8871 7530), meanwhile, has a bloody history: in 1671 Colonel Blood hid in reeds near what is now the boating lake, waiting to shoot King Charles II as he bathed (though his nerve ultimately failed him); and in 1829 the Duke of Wellington fought a pistol duel here with Lord Winchilsea, who had accused him of treason for introducing the Catholic Emancipation Bill. The park's most famous feature, **Festival Gardens**, created for the 1951 Festival of Britain, was recently the subject of a £12-million restoration, along with the sub-tropical gardens and the elegant Thameside promenade. The Peace Pagoda by the Thames was built by Japanese monks and nuns in 1985 to commemorate Hiroshima Day.

Putney, Barnes, Mortlake & Kew

When Thomas Cromwell and scores of other Tudor courtiers bought homes in the village and travelled to their jobs in the royal palaces around west London, **Putney** effectively became London's first suburb. It's stayed true to its heritage: away from the busy High Street it's a peaceful spot, especially west of the bridge along the Embankment, with its ubiquitous canoe trailers hitched to Land Rovers. The annual **Boat Race** (*see p262*) starts from here.

(*see p262*)

Strike inland and you'll eventually come to **Mortlake**. On the way, the main road, Queen's Ride, crosses a railway line at **Barnes Common**; on the western side of the bridge there's a spindly tree invariably decorated with flowers and other offerings to Marc Bolan, who was killed when his car collided with the tree in 1977. Since May 2000, Barnes has also been the setting for the **WWT Wetland Centre** (*see p175*), a unique mosaic of wetland habitats.

Kew is synonymous with the **Royal Botanic Gardens** (known as Kew Gardens; *see below*), the world's principal botanical research centre. Just north of the Kew Road entrance is the old-fashioned Maids of Honour tea shop (288 Kew Road). **Kew Green**, with its cricket ground surrounded by pubs, and elegant **St Anne's Church**, built in 1714, is also worth a visit.

Royal Botanic Gardens

Kew, Richmond, Surrey (8332 5022/recorded info 8940 1171/www.rbgkew.org.uk). Kew Gardens tube/rail/Kew Bridge rail/riverboat to Kew Pier.

Open *end Mar-Aug* 9.30am-6.30pm Mon-Fri; 9.30am-7pm Sat, Sun. *Sept, Oct* 9.30am-5.30pm daily. *End Oct-end Mar* 9.30am-3.45pm daily. **Admission** £6.50; £4.50 concessions; free under-17s. **Credit** MC, V.

Developed in the 17th and 18th centuries in the grounds of the 17th-century Dutch-style **Kew Palace** (closed for restoration until at least early 2004), and landscaped by 'Capability' Brown, the world-famous Kew Gardens now cover 120 hectares (300 acres) and are filled with every imaginable variety of tree, shrub and flower. In the late 18th century botanists collected specimens from all continents to be planted at Kew to form the basis of its extraordinary botanical collections. It's now a world-renowned centre for horticultural research and boasts the world's largest collection of orchids. A good option for first-time visitors is to take the 'Kew Explorer' road train from its stop by the Victoria Gate for a 35-minute tour. It stops at all the main sights and a ticket (£2.50; £1.50 concessions) can be used to hop on and off throughout the day.

Among the highlights are the immense glasshouses, the most famous of which is the steamy **Palm House** (Decimus Burton and Richard Turner, 1848),

The melting pot: Caribbean London

Following World War II, Britain looked to her overseas colonies as a way of rebuilding the country's workforce, and it was in 1948 that the first wave of Caribbean immigrants arrived in Britain on the *Empire Windrush*. Lambeth Council offered cheap housing to the immigrants in areas such as Clapham and Stockwell – initially they were housed in an air raid shelter on Clapham Common – and many of them were hired to work in Brixton as conductors on London Transport buses. As a result, the focus of the Caribbean community began to grow up around the market there. Lucille Harris, a *Windrush* passenger who lived near Brixton Market, remembers that Brixton then had 'hardly any buildings standing as far as you can look it, bomb and burn outright through and through.'

The community quickly grew, and by the 1970s was established as a vibrant part of the area's identity. However, in the late 1970s racial tension began to surface between the local community and police, leading to the first Brixton riots of 1981, which left 299 police and 65 civilians injured and much property destroyed. The Scarman Report that followed the riots highlighted the breakdown in communication between the police and community leaders as being at the core of the problem, and policing methods in the area were forced to change.

Today, despite some gentrification and the influx of other cultures to the area, Brixton still boasts a strong and significant Caribbean presence. For a history of the Caribbean community in the area, the **Black Cultural Archives** (378 Coldharbour Lane, SW9; 7738 4591) are a must. Apart from providing information on all aspects of black history, the centre also hosts exhibitions and has an excellent bookshop.

Present-day community issues are explored artistically at **Brixton Art Gallery** (35 Brixton Station Road, SW9; 7733 6957), an innovative space featuring sculpture, painting and moving-image works that draw on the rich multicultural mix of the area. Local artists are highlighted, and there are strong community links. The **Oval House Theatre** (52-54 Kennington Oval, SE11; 7582 7680) is also a good place to catch up on a culturally diverse programme of events, often exploring issues of racism and multicultural identity.

Where to go

Brixton Market (*see p256*) specialises in all manner of West Indian fare. Stalls spill over with green coconuts, yams, plantain and breadfruit; while flying fish and halal meat are sold alongside wigs and Bob Marley bootlegs. Don't miss the mouthwateringly enticing Caribbean bakery in the Granville Arcade.

the finest surviving glass-and-iron structure in the country. The **Temperate House**, meanwhile, is the largest ornamental glasshouse in the world. The specimens, which are arranged geographically, include the largest indoor plant in the world, the Chilean wine-palm.

In addition to the glasshouses, don't miss the **Marianne North Gallery**, which displays paintings by this extraordinary Victorian artist and traveller; the **Great Pagoda** by William Chambers (1762) near the Lion Gate; and the **Japanese Gateway & Landscape**. Opposite the Palm House, Museum No.1 houses the **Plants & People** exhibition exploring humankind's reliance on plants. There are cafés, restaurants and shops around the gardens, though to enjoy Kew at its best you should wander along pathways away from the obvious tourist attractions, enjoying the views from the **Riverside Walk** or the seclusion of the woods at the south-west end.

Highlights in 2002 include Beauty in Danger: Orchids at the End (9 Feb-10 Mar), featuring more than 100,000 orchids from around the world, and Summer Swing (16-20 July), an outdoor jazz festival.

WWT Wetland Centre

Queen Elizabeth's Walk, SW13 (8409 4400/ www.wetlandcentre.org.uk). Hammersmith tube, then 283 bus/Barnes rail/33, 72 bus. **Open** *Mar-Oct* 9.30am-6pm daily (last entry 5pm). *Nov-Feb* 9.30am-5pm daily (last entry 4pm). **Admission** £6.75; £5.50 concessions; £4 4-16s; £17.50 family (2+2); free under-4s. **Credit** MC, V.

Created from scratch on the site of four redundant Thames Water reservoirs by the Wildfowl and Wetlands Trust (WWT), this 105-acre (422-hectare) complex of lakes, reedbeds, ponds, grasslands and mudflats attracts an abundance of birds and other wildlife. Serious birdwatchers will twitch with delight at the prospect of observing more than 130 species of birds ducking and diving in the wild reserve, while the two wetland exhibition areas boast interactive displays that are great for kids. CCTV screens and hides are dotted around the complex to allow vistors a closer look at their feathered friends. The Peter Scott Visitors' Centre houses a children's discovery centre, a gallery, a shop and a café, and the glass-fronted Observatory looks out over the main lake.

Where to shop

Reggae is everywhere in Brixton. **Blacker Dread** (40b, Coldharbour Lane SW9; 7274 4476) specialises in Jamaican and US reggae imports, **Supertone Records** (110 Acre Lane, SW2; 7737 7761) in Jamaican reggae imports covering roots, revival and dub. Once you've got the tunes, **Weatherman Shop** (57 Atlantic Road; no phone) is the place to kit yourself out with an array of hats, jewellery and other essential rasta-style accessories.

The vibrant **Juice Bar** (407 Coldharbour Lane, SW9; 7737 5528), also known as The Souls of Black Folk, is Britain's only black-issues second-hand bookshop; subjects stocked range from biographies of black sports stars to the works of James Baldwin and Chinua Achebe. It also has a fair number of English-language books from Africa and the Caribbean, a few rare first editions and some new books. The venue is something of a community focal point, with poetry readings, comedy shows and a buzzy café-bar that serves coffee, fresh juices and smoothies, such as the delicious Brixton Riot. Food includes organic and vegetarian options.

Where to eat

Traditional West Indian eateries include **Bamboula** (12 Acre Lane, SW2; 7737 6633), which serves home-style Jamaican

fare such as curried goat, swordfish and rice and peas; and the tiny **Bushman Kitchen Caribbean Kiosk** (36 Brixton Station Road; no phone), which offers similar takeaway sustenance. **My Father's Place** (336 Coldharbour Lane, SW9; 7737 3255) is another option, serving traditional West Indian and Jamaican fare such as jerk chicken and assorted curries.

Where to drink and dance

The rather swanky **Brixtonian Havana Club** (*see p229*) offers Cuban music and salsa dancing and sells more than 300 types of rum, including the Cuban speciality Anejo, which costs £6 a pop. Caribbean cuisine (cassava fritters, codfish, curry chicken) is also served here. The **Effra** (38a Kellett Road, SW2; 7274 4180), which features jazz, is another local watering hole that's well worth a visit.

Wimbledon

Just as most people think of Kew for its gardens, most equate **Wimbledon** with its summer tennis tournament *(see p330)*. But the truth is that the glamour of Wimbledon fortnight is short-lived, and the rest of the year Wimbledon is a pretty uneventful suburb. The main drag, **Wimbledon Broadway**, is dominated by the huge **Centre Court** shopping centre, and, further east, **Wimbledon Theatre**, an entertaining example of Edwardian architecture at its most feverish.

Beyond lies the other main attraction, **Wimbledon Common**, a huge, partially wooded expanse crisscrossed with paths and horse tracks. The windmill towards the north-east corner dates from 1817; Baden-Powell wrote part of *Scouting for Boys* while living in it in 1908. The museum it now houses is closed in winter, though the tearoom is open year round. **Putney Vale Cemetery**, in the north-east corner of the common (accessible from Roehampton Vale), is one of London's largest graveyards and is the final resting place of Lillie Langtry.

On the east side of the common, the disused **Bluegate Gravel Pit** forms an idyllic lake. If you cross Parkside and go down Calonne Road, you'll discover Wimbledon's biggest surprise: a fully fledged Thai Buddhist temple, the **Buddhapadipa Temple** (1-6pm Sat; 8.30-10.30am, 12.30-6pm Sun). Close by is the All England Lawn Tennis Club and the **Wimbledon Lawn Tennis Museum** *(see below)*. Next door, **Wimbledon Park** has public tennis courts and a large boating lake.

Wimbledon Lawn Tennis Museum

Centre Court, All England Lawn Tennis Club, Church Road, SW19 (8946 6131/www.wimbledon. org/museum). Southfields tube/39, 93, 200 bus. **Open** 10.30am-5pm daily; spectators only during championships. **Admission** £5; £4.25 concessions; £3.50 5-16s; free under-5s. **Credit** MC, V.
A well-designed museum tracing the history of the game from the lawns of Victorian England to the multi-million-pound sport of today. Displays include a mock-up of an Edwardian tennis party, a section on tennis since 1968 and an array of personal memorabilia, such as some of Pat Cash's headbands.

Richmond

Though it's now plagued with heavy traffic and the roar of low-flying jets approaching Heathrow, it's still not difficult to envisage **Richmond** as the bustling English country town it once was. Until the early 16th century, the whole area was called Sheen; but Richmond received its new name when Henry VII acquired the local manor house and named it after his earldom in Yorkshire. Elizabeth I spent the last few summers of her life at Richmond and died here in 1603. Richmond Palace fell into neglect in subsequent centuries, and all that now remains is a gateway on **Richmond Green**: best reached from alley-like **Brewer's Lane**, with its rows of pubs and antique shops. The church of **St Mary Magdalene**, in Paradise Road, is worth a look for its combination of architectural styles dating from 1507 to 1904.

The **Museum of Richmond** *(see p177)* is housed in the old Victorian town hall, but the best reason to come to this part of London is to enjoy the Great Outdoors: with the exception of Epping Forest, **Richmond Park** is the last vestige of the great oak forests that surrounded London until medieval times, and is ideal for rambling, cycling and riding. It is also home to much wildlife, most famously herds of red and fallow deer. Notable buildings in the park include **Pembroke Lodge** (now a café), the childhood home of philosopher Bertrand Russell, and **White Lodge**, a fine Palladian villa. During your rambles, don't miss the exquisite **Isabella Plantation**, a woodland haven landscaped with a stream, ponds and spectacular floral displays.

Elsewhere, enjoy the impressive view from the top of **Richmond Hill**, with the nearby **Terrace Gardens** descending steeply towards the river. If the river isn't flooding, follow its course towards **Petersham** and **Ham**. The Thames is at its most tranquil here and, in the early morning and evening, **Petersham Meadows** are impossibly pastoral: brown cattle grazing on water meadows beside the misty river.

The **Peace Pagoda** in Battersea Park. *See p173.*

Museum of Richmond

Old Town Hall, Whittaker Avenue, Richmond,
Surrey (8332 1141/www.museumofrichmond.com).
Richmond tube/rail. **Open** *May-Sept* 11am-5pm
Tue-Sat; 1-4pm Sun. *Nov-Apr* 11am-5pm Tue-Sat.
Admission £2; £1 concessions; free under-16s.
No credit cards.
The focus may be on Richmond's popularity as a
royal resort, but this museum also traces the area's
history from its role as a prehistoric settlement to
life in the town during World War II.

Further south

A delightful walk or bike ride south along the
Thames from Richmond takes you close to a
clutch of fine country villas: **Marble Hill**
House, **Orleans House** and **Ham House**
(for all, *see below*). Past **Twickenham** (home
to the **Museum of Rugby**; *see below*) the river
reaches Horace Walpole's idiosyncratic home,
Strawberry Hill, the busy shopping centre
of **Kingston** and curves around to **Hampton**
Court Palace (*see below*).

Ham House

Ham, Richmond, Surrey (8940 1950/
www.nationaltrust.org.uk). Richmond tube/rail, then
371 bus. **Open** *House* Apr-Oct 1-5pm Mon-Wed, Sat,
Sun. *Gardens* 11am-6pm/dusk Mon-Wed, Sat, Sun.
Admission £6; £3 5-15s; £15 family. **Credit** AmEx, MC, V.
Built in 1610 and extended during the 1670s, Ham
is most famous for its lavish interiors and exquisite
furniture and paintings. From the house, water
meadows lead down to the Thames, while the formal gardens are being restored to their original state.
'The wilderness' is in fact a carefully planted, almost
maze-like section, divided into garden rooms.

Hampton Court Palace

East Molesey, Surrey (8781 9500/www.hrp.org.uk).
Hampton Court rail/riverboat from Westminster or
Richmond to Hampton Court Pier (Apr-Oct). **Open**
Palace Apr-Oct 10.15am-6pm Mon; 9.30am-6pm Tue-
Sun. Nov-Mar 10.15am-4.30pm Mon; 9.30am-4.30pm
Tue-Sun (last entry 45min before closing). *Park*
dawn-dusk daily. **Admission** *Palace, courtyard,*
cloister & maze £10.80; £7.20 5-15s; £8.30
concessions; £32.20 family (max 5 people); free under
5s. *Maze only* £2.50; £1.60 5-15s. **Credit** AmEx, MC, V.
Expensive but essential, Hampton Court Palace's
interiors and gardens make for one of London's most
fascinating days out. In 1514 Cardinal Wolsey started to build up Hampton Court as his country seat.
After his fall from favour in 1529, Henry VIII took
over the palace, adding the fabulous vaulted ceiling
of the Chapel Royal, which took 100 men nine
months to complete. In the 1690s William and Mary
commissioned Sir Christopher Wren (*see p86* **Who**
he?) to rebuild the State Apartments in classical
Renaissance style (the King's Apartments, badly
damaged by fire in 1986, have been restored).

There are six bite-size tours. Highlights include
Henry VIII's hammer-beam-roofed **Great Hall**, the
Renaissance Picture Gallery and the **Tudor**
Kitchens, where period-dressed minions make
16th-century dishes and chat to visitors. Elsewhere,
there's foolery several times a day in **Clock Court**.
In the extensive gardens look out for the famous
maze and the **Great Vine**. The world's oldest
known vine was probably planted by 'Capability'
Brown around 1770 and still produces an annual
crop of 500-700lbs (230-320kg) of black grapes, sold
to visitors. Various special events, including cos-
tumed guided tours of the royal apartments and presentations on court life in Tudor and Stuart times,
take place daily in the house and gardens.

Marble Hill House

Richmond Road, Twickenham, Middx (8892 5115/
www.english-heritage.org.uk). Richmond tube/rail/
St Margaret's rail/33, 90, 290, H22, R70 bus.
Open *Apr-Oct* 10am-6pm daily. *Nov-Mar* 10am-4pm
Wed-Sun. **Admission** £3.30; £2.50 concessions;
£1.70 5-15s; free under 5s. **Credit** MC, V.
Set in acres of parkland beside the Thames, this is a
perfect Palladian villa. It was built in 1724-9 for
Henrietta Howard, the mistress of George II, and later
occupied by Mrs Fitzherbert, George IV's secret wife.
Cube Hall has beautiful moulded decoration, and the
house has been immaculately restored with Georgian
furnishings and paintings. There are concerts in the
park on Sunday evenings in summer (*see p313*).

Museum of Rugby/
Twickenham Stadium

Gate K, Twickenham Rugby Stadium, Rugby Road,
Twickenham, Middx (8892 8877/www.rfu.com).
Hounslow East tube, then 281 bus/Twickenham rail.
Open *Museum* 10am-5pm Tue-Sat; 2-5pm Sun (last
entry 4.30pm). *Tours* 10.30am, noon, 1.30pm, 3pm
Tue-Sat; 3pm Sun. **Admission** Combined ticket £6;
£4 concessions; £19 family. **Credit** MC, V.
This carefully collated and imaginatively presented
museum explores the history and folklore of rugby
union. Rugby tots will enjoy the interactive exhibits,
including a real scrum machine, while old-timers can
listen to early radio commentary and muse on the
days when players still wore bow ties. The highlight
is the excellent stadium tour.

Orleans House Gallery

Riverside, Twickenham, Middx (8892 0221/
www.richmond.gov.uk/depts/opps/leisure/arts/orleans
house). St Margaret's rail. **Open** *Apr-Sept* 1-5.30pm
Tue-Sat; 2-5.30pm Sun. *Oct-Mar* 1-4.30pm Tue-Sat;
2-4.30pm Sun. **Admission** free.
Orleans House derives its name from one-time resident Louis Philippe, the exiled Duke of Orléans,
though it was built in 1710 for James Johnston,
William III's secretary of state for Scotland. Much
of the building was demolished in 1926, with the
notable exception of the Octagon Room, an eight-
sided turret designed by James Gibbs. This room
and a later gallery have been open to the public as
exhibition venues since 1972.

Sightseeing

West London

From gritty, up-and-coming Paddington via ever-hip Notting Hill
to the leafy 'burbs, west London defies easy categorisation.

Sightseeing

Paddington & Bayswater

Maps p394 & p395

*Bayswater, Lancaster Gate or Queensway tube/
Paddington tube/rail.*

Just north of Hyde Park, Paddington derives
its name from the ancient Anglo-Saxon
chieftain Padda but is best known for its train
station with its magnificent iron girder roof,
designed by Isambard Kingdom Brunel in 1851
(*see p28* **Is it terminal?**). It was the building
of the station, along with the Grand Junction
Canal (1801), that precipitated the population
boom in Paddington and Bayswater in the
mid 19th century: the area was previously
considered off limits residentially thanks to the
Tyburn gallows near present-day Marble Arch.

In the early 20th century there was another
slump when the district became synonymous
with prostitution and poverty, and it can't be
denied that Paddington and Bayswater still
have somewhat of a neglected, seedy edge:
many of their white stuccoed houses are
either cheap hotels or have been carved up into
warrens of bedsits. Still, the last two or three
years have seen a bit of a boom, largely thanks
to the Heathrow Express (*see p356*), which
now provides a fast link from the airport into
Paddington, and more upmarket establishments
have started to move in, including the minimalist
Hempel hotel (*see p61*). The old Great Western
Hotel is nearing the end of its transformation
into a plush Hilton, while the massive, ongoing
redevelopment of **Paddington Basin**, which is
responsible for the mesh of cranes that dominate
the skyline, is transforming the old Canal Basin
and Goods Yard into a complex of expensive
flats and offices. Such moves can't fail to haul
the area up by the scruff of its neck, as designer
bars and restaurants begin to flood in.

For the moment, though, Paddington remains
predominantly a zone of cheap hotels, hostels,
and tourist-oriented restaurants offering set
menus to people who don't stop to consider
that London might have more to offer than
steakhouses and dodgy trattorias. In terms of
attractions, there's only really the **Alexander
Fleming Laboratory Museum** (*see below*).

Queensway, in the heart of Bayswater, is
also by and large a tacky tourist trap, though
there are some decent eateries, particularly

Chinese restaurants such as Mandarin Kitchen
(*see p216*) and Royal China (*see p207* **The
best dim sum**), while Whiteley's mall –
a former department store and one of Hitler's
favourite buildings – has a wide range of
shops and an eight-screen cinema (*see p292*).

A left turn at the north end of Queensway
opens up the richer pickings of trendy
Westbourne Grove, where there are
some excellent Middle Eastern and African
eateries, including the Sudanese Mandola (*see
p216*), increasing numbers of hip shops such
as SPAce.NK (*see p253*), and the Westbourne,
a relative newcomer to the 'designer hotel'
scene (*see p62*). The Grove's western end,
towards Portobello Road and Notting Hill, is
markedly posher, with delis, antique shops and,
particularly on Ledbury Road (which bisects
Westbourne Grove), cool clothes boutiques.

Alexander Fleming
Laboratory Museum

*St Mary's Hospital, Praed Street, W2 (7725 6528).
Paddington tube/rail/7, 15, 27, 36 bus.* **Open** 10am-
1pm Mon-Thur. By appointment 2-5pm Mon-Thur;
10am-5pm Fri. **Admission** £2; £1 concessions,
children. **No credit cards. Map** p395 D5.
Alexander Fleming made his momentous chance discovery of penicillin in this very room on 3 September
1928, when a Petri dish of bacteria became contam-
inated with a mysterious mould. His laboratory has
now been recreated, while displays and a video offer
insights into both his life and the role of penicillin in
the fight against disease.

Maida Vale & Kilburn

*Kilburn, Kilburn Park, Maida Vale or Warwick
Avenue tube.*

North of the roaring but atmospheric Westway
(*see p39*) lies much of Edgware Road, as well
as Maida Vale and Kilburn. **Edgware Road**
follows the course of ancient Watling Street, a
traffic-clogged thoroughfare redeemed only by
some of London's best kebab shops and Middle
Eastern cafés. Fans of old London should also
try the Regent Milk Bar, an unreconstructed
1950s ice-cream parlour (No.362, 7723 8669).

Maida Vale, named after the British
victory against the French at the Battle of
Maida in southern Italy in 1806, is an affluent
area characterised by Edwardian purpose-built

flats, and prettified immeasurably by the locks around **Little Venice**. You can walk from here along the canals to **London Zoo**, or even take a boat there (*see p110*). **Kilburn High Road** is well known for its pubs, patronised primarily by Irish expats. Kilburn is also a good place for bargain shopping, and its mainly Afro-Caribbean and Irish populations are well served by one of London's more enterprising local arts complexes, the Tricycle (*see p338*).

Notting Hill

Map p394
Notting Hill Gate or Westbourne Park tube.

There was little but piggeries in this area until a wave of white stuccoed buildings mapped out Notting Hill in the early and mid 1800s. After a period of prosperity, however, the district's fortunes declined again in the 20th century; it was solidly white and working class until the '50s, when an influx of West Indian immigrants were forced to live in hideous properties owned by notorious slum landlord Peter Rachman. Riots, incited by white racists, followed in 1958, and it was only in the late 1980s that the area flourished once more.

Despite its sickly-sweet depiction in the Hugh Grant and Julia Roberts movie named after it and the concomitant increase in the number of tourists, Notting Hill is still one of London's best places for a weekend stroll. **Notting Hill Gate** itself is little more than a busy through road, although it does boast two cinemas: the Gate and the Notting Hill Coronet (for both, *see p292*), the latter being one of the last cinemas in London where you can smoke. Around the corner on Pembridge Road above the Prince Albert pub is the tiny Gate Theatre (*see p338*), one of the best pub-theatres in town.

But when people talk about Notting Hill they really mean **Portobello Road**. This narrow, snaking thoroughfare, most famed for its market (*see p256*) and antique shops, forms the spine of the neighbourhood. There are cafés, bars, restaurants, curiosity shops and delis, many of which have been patronised by the same people for decades, the newly revamped Electric Cinema (*see p293* **Electric dreams**) and, towards its northern end, a huge flea market with modish second-hand clothes, shoes and accessories on Fridays and Saturdays.

At the north end of Portobello Road, **Golborne Road** is a great place to buy Portuguese and Moroccan groceries and pâtisseries. The other main feature of Golborne Road is Trellick Tower, built in 1973 by Ernö Goldfinger (*see p182* **Who he?**) and seen as a hideous carbuncle by some and by others as a seminal piece of modern architecture.

Urban construct: **Paddington** is being transformed. *See p178.*

Sightseeing

Just east of Portobello Road, the Westbourne Park area is scruffy but perennially hip, especially around All Saint's Road, which has been colonised by quirky little boutiques over the last few years. It's also home to interesting restaurants such as Bali Sugar (*see p216*), and trendy bars such as Babushka (7727 9250), now specialising in vodka but in a previous incarnation the decidedly sleazy Black Cap pub from which Richard E Grant and Paul McGann are obliged to beat a very hasty retreat in the famous 'perfumed ponce' scene in the film *Withnail and I*.

Up at the top of Ladbroke Grove, meanwhile, Kensal Green Cemetery on Harrow Road, opened in 1833, is a huge and beautiful resting place for many a famous Londoner, including Thackeray, Trollope and Brunel. Parts of *Look Back in Anger* were shot here back in 1959.

Kensington & Holland Park

Maps p394-p397
High Street Kensington or Holland Park tube.

No doubt to the delight of its heritage-conscious upper-class residents, Kensington is mentioned in the Domesday Book of 1086. In the 17th century the district grew up around Holland House (1606) and Campden House (1612) and was described by one historian in 1705 as a place 'inhabited by gentry and persons of note, with an abundance of shopkeepers and artificers'. This is still the case with both aspects of Kensington in evidence around the **High Street**. A lively mix of chain stores and individual shops stretches along the busy main road while the nearby streets and squares are lined by large townhouses. The most famous of the squares, **Kensington Square**, sports a

The melting pot: Punjabi London

London's Indian community began arriving in west London from the Punjab and Gujarat regions of India in the early 1970s, as did Pakistanis and Sri Lankans. With their proximity to Heathrow and surplus of low-skilled jobs in service and manufacturing industries, areas such as Wembley, Neasden and Southall were natural magnets for immigrants looking for work. The original arrivals quickly established themselves as successful retailers and restaurant owners, and in the mid '70s the community expanded to include a large proportion of East African Indians fleeing political repression. Today the area's cosmopolitan base has widened further with the arrival of Afghans and Somalis.

Southall, which is only 20 minutes by train from Paddington, remains the centre of the Punjabi community, with its Broadway often

dubbed 'Little Punjab'. The area's colourful market and nearby temples make it a fascinating and vibrant destination.

What to see:
The marble pinnacles and domes of the **Shri Swaminarayan Mandir** temple rise incongruously in a landscape otherwise dominated by grim post-war towers and nearby estates. The temple, the first ever traditional Hindu temple built in Europe, is popular with Sikhs, Hindus and Muslims. In 2002 the area will also see the opening of the biggest Sikh temple outside of India.

For more earthly delights, spend some time in **Southall Market** (there's a car park off the High Street, opposite North Road). This is the nearest thing you'll get to a proper Indian market outside the country itself: on Tuesdays there's a live fowl market, where little birds in tiny cages are passed over the heads of the crowd; the meat market on Wednesdays is followed by a live horse auction at 1pm; on Saturdays the market is taken over by endless rows of sari fabrics as well as men's suits in the brightest of colours. There are also stalls selling Bollywood film music, Islamic stalls selling Mecca souvenirs, and Hindu stalls with plastic statuettes and posters of the gods.

If the market leaves you flagging somewhat, plonk yourself down at the **Himalaya Palace Cinema**, the only cinema in Britain with a Chinese façade. It's also

generous display of plaques denoting residents of distinction, such as Thackeray (No.16) and John Stuart Mill (No.18).

Kensington Square is just behind the art deco splendour of Barker's department store (built 1905-13). Next door, on the sixth floor of the former Derry & Toms, is the Roof Gardens (*see p281*), one of London's most stunning venues. Over the road from here, at the foot of **Kensington Church Street**, is the church of St Mary Abbots, distinguished by the tallest steeple in London (250 feet, or 85 metres) and the secluded gardens to its rear.

Further west is **Holland Park**, one of London's most romantic parks. Beautiful woods and formal gardens surround the reconstructed Jacobean **Holland House**, named after an early owner, Sir Henry, Earl of Holland. The house suffered serious bomb damage during World War II and only the ground floor and arcades

survived; the restored east wing contains the most dramatically sited youth hostel in town (*see p65*), while the summer ballroom has been converted into a stylish contemporary restaurant, the Belvedere. Open-air theatre and opera under an elegant canopy are staged in the park during the summer (*see p338*), and for children there's an adventure playground with tree-walks and rope swings, while tame rabbits, squirrels and peacocks patrol the grounds. The Kyoto Japanese Garden provides a tranquil retreat from the action.

Among the historic houses worth a visit are **Leighton House** (*see p182*), the 19th-century home of the painter Lord Leighton, and Linley Sambourne House, home of Edward Linley Sambourne, cartoonist for the satirical magazine *Punch*, which is scheduled to reopen in autumn 2002; phone the curator of Leighton House for details.

the place to come for Bollywood movies – there's a large and regularly rotating list of films on offer (*see p294*).

Where to shop

The colourful and tempting **Royal Sweets** (92 The Broadway; 8574 0832) offers a huge range of Asian sweets, including *ras malai*, *angir*, *barfi* and *halwa*. In the summer stock up on *kulfi* in the classic mango and pistachio flavours, and various sorbets.

Southall has a massive range of clothing, accessory and jewellery shops, with everything from designer bindis to traditional *salwar kameez* on offer. **Bina Musical Stores** (31-3 The Green, 8843 1411) specialises in Indian instruments such as tablas and sitars.

Where to eat

For old-fashioned-style Punjabi and northern Indian fare, head for veteran eaterie **Brilliant** (72-6 Western Road, 8574 1928), which numbers Prince Charles among its diners. **Madhu's Brilliant** (39 South Road, 8574 1897) and **Balti & Tandoori World** (185-7 The Broadway, 8867 9991) are popular too.

There are also numerous cafés serving cheaper eats in less formal settings: **Rita's Samosa Centre** and **Giftos Lahore Karahi**, both on the Broadway, are a good start.

Where to drink

Situated on South Road, **The Glassy Junction** (No.97, 8574 1626) is the only place in the country where you can buy

alcohol with rupees, although sterling is also accepted, of course. A large variety of Indian beers (try a Lal Toofan), live bhangra concerts and the amazing glitzy decor make this a brilliant alternative to yet another night down the pub.

Leighton House

12 Holland Park Road, W14 (7602 3316/
www.rbkc.gov.uk/leightonhousemuseum). High Street
Kensington tube. **Open** 11am-5.30pm Mon, Wed-Sun.
Tours by appointment noon Wed, Thur. **Admission**
free; donations appreciated. *Tours* £3 per person
(min group of 15). **No credit cards**.
Situated on the edge of Holland Park, this stunning
19th-century building is the one-time residence and
studio of Frederic, Lord Leighton (1830-96), an eminent Victorian artist; hanging in the midst of its
sumptuous interiors are paintings and drawings by
both Leighton himself (among them *The Death of
Brunelleschi* and *Clytemnestra From The Battlements
Of Argos*) and some of his contemporaries, such as
John Everett Millais and Edward Burne-Jones. The
house was designed in 1864 by Leighton in collaboration with the architect George Aitchison, and the
pair continued to improve and extend it until shortly
before Leighton's death. In addition to the permanent
displays and temporary exhibitions, there's a busy
programme of talks and recitals; call for details or
check out the informative website.

Earl's Court & Fulham

Maps p396 & p397
Earl's Court, Fulham Broadway or
West Brompton tube.

Earl's Court changed from hamlet to built-up
urban area with the arrival of the Metropolitan
Railway in 1860, and from 1914 many of its
imposing houses were subdivided into flats.
It remains a district where many have lived
but few have settled. Once known as Kangaroo
Valley thanks to the number of Antipodean
trekkers staying in its bedsits and budget hotels,
it's always had a seedy reputation. In the late
'70s and '80s it became the gay centre of London,
with the action centring most famously on the
Coleherne pub. One of England's more famous
dominatrixes, Lindy St Clair ('Miss Whiplash'),
set up parlour on Eardley Crescent until
bankrupted by the Inland Revenue. Freddie
Mercury also lived around here, at Garden

Who he? Ernö Goldfinger

Born in Budapest in 1902, architect Ernö
Goldfinger ended his days in London in 1987,
in the house at 2 Willow Road, Hampstead
(*see p148*) that represented the fruition
of his dream to build a home and studio in
accordance with his avant-garde principles,
which were rooted in a bold use of form,
colour and materials, including reinforced
concrete, and a holistic approach to design.

Goldfinger trained at the Ecole des Beaux
Arts in Paris in 1921 and four years later
joined the atelier of progressive architect
Auguste Perret in 1925. In the '30s he
returned to Hungary but fled it with the
onset of World War II, settling in Hampstead
and almost immediately incurring the wrath
of many of its more conservative residents
by tearing down some cottages to build three
modernist homes on Willow Road. What his
critics overlooked was the regard for London's
Georgian architecture that was inherent in
the buildings: architecture writer Sir Nikolaus
Pevsner pointed out that the Goldfinger
houses represented 'the contemporary style
in an uncompromising form; yet [go] infinitely
better with the Georgian past of Hampstead
than anything Victorian.'

You can see from the thought that went
into his own house, with its fitted furniture,
integral garage and subtle detailing, that
Goldfinger was a social visionary who truly
cared about where, and how, people lived:

he even moved into one of his buildings,
the Balfron Tower in Poplar, for a while
to check that it functioned in the way he
intended. But his most infamous work is
west London's Trellick Tower, reviled in some
quarters but now a modern icon that has
appeared in countless TV ads and on T-shirts
and clocks – it even featured in a Blur song,
Best Days ('Trellick Tower's been calling').

Situated just off Golborne Road with its
funky shops and stalls spilling over from
Portobello Market, the now Grade II-listed,
31-storey building was completed in 1972,
by which time architectural opinion had
turned against tower blocks. Writer Ian
Fleming hated the building so much he
actually named one of the Bond villains
after him. Unrepentant, Goldfinger declared,
'The only trouble with high rises is that we
don't build high enough.'

The building's early years seemed to
back up the critics' objections: a spate of
burglaries, rapes and suicides led it to be
dubbed 'the tower of terror', and it inspired
a JG Ballard novel, the dystopian *High Rise*
in which different floors wage war against
one another. However, the formation of a
residents' association improved security and
maintenance, and these days the building is
regarded with pride by many Londoners. With
its separate lift shaft, it looks particularly
dramatic lit up at night as you drive into or out

Lodge, 1 Logan Place, and Earl's Court retains a strong gay vibe. The area is more widely known as the site of the **Exhibition Centre**, used as an internment camp in World War II.

The pleasantly laid-out **Brompton Cemetery** is sometimes exploited for sexual encounters (the proximity to graves presumably sharpening the experience), although an unmolested stroll in search of the grave of Emmeline Pankhurst is perfectly possible. The peace is only broken on Saturday afternoons when Chelsea FC are playing at home: the massive bulk of their Stamford Bridge stadium overlooks the tombs.

Neighbouring **Parsons Green** and **Fulham** are home to a more established and affluent population with aspirations of Chelsea living. Parsons Green is centred around a small green that once – of course – supported a parsonage. It was considered the aristocratic part of Fulham even in 1705, when Bowack said it was inhabited by 'Gentry and persons of Quality'.

Despite the proximity of Hurlingham Sports Club and the Queen's (Tennis & Rackets) Club, which hosts the Stella Artois pre-Wimbledon tournament, you can enter **Fulham Palace** (*see below*) without a massive bank balance. Next door, Bishop's Park offers pretty river walks.

Fulham Palace

Bishop's Avenue, off Fulham Palace Road, SW6 (7736 3233). Putney Bridge tube/74, 220 bus. **Open** Museum *Mar-Oct* 2-5pm Wed-Sun. *Nov-Feb* 1-4pm Thur-Sun. **Admission** *Museum* £1; 50p concessions; free under-16s if accompanied by adult. *Tours* £3; free under-16s. **No credit cards**.
The official residence of the Bishops of London from 704 until 1973, Fulham Palace is now a chaos of periods and architectural styles; the oldest part dates from 1480, the most recent, William Butterfield's neo-Gothic chapel, from 1866. There's a quirky museum tracing its history, but to see the palace interior you need to join one of the informative Sunday tours, held twice a month in summer and monthly in winter. The beautiful grounds are open daily.

of London along the Westway. It's also a much sought-after address among architecture buffs, many of whom are eager to snap up the flats with their small but crucial design details such as cedar panelled balconies and light switches that sit flush with the door frames (some also have stunning 280° views).

Lee Boland, who chairs the residents' association, bore witness to the architect's ongoing obsession with how his buildings worked for their inhabitants: 'I met Mr Goldfinger in the lift once,' she said. 'I didn't know who he was but he kept asking me about the faults and what I liked and didn't like. I said I liked everything, except the designer hadn't put a broom cupboard in the kitchen. "Bloody women," he said. "Never satisfied".'

But would-be purchasers will find that it's not that easy to get into this once-detested block: most of the 217 flats are reserved for people in housing need, including refugees, and not many of the tenants have chosen to buy, meaning that few flats are sold on. Nor can interested visitors just walk in off the street: tight security means you'll have to wait until the next Open House Weekend (*see p268* **Grand openings**) to get a peek at how the émigré architect made of tower-block living something inspirational.

The **Trellick Tower**: Goldfinger's masterpiece.

Sightseeing

Shepherd's Bush & Hammersmith

Goldhawk Road, Hammersmith or Shepherd's Bush tube.

The approach to **Shepherd's Bush** from Holland Park Avenue is marked by Shepherd's Bush roundabout, with the Thames Water Tower springing out of its centre. The tower, which looks like a state-of-the-art toilet cistern, is a surge pipe for London's underground ring main. Designed by students at the Royal College of Art, it doubles as a huge barometer. **Shepherd's Bush Common** once formed the centre of what was, 150 years ago, a 'pleasant village'. Now, however, the common is a scruffy traffic island.

But all is not gloom in W12, for this is the site of one of London's most prestigious new-writing theatres, the Bush (*see p337*), and to two great music venues, the Shepherd's Bush Empire (*see p317*) and Bush Hall (*see p310*). Shepherd's Bush market, between **Shepherd's Bush** and **Goldhawk Road** tubes, is one of west London's busiest and, unlike Portobello Road, is very much geared to the local (Afro-Caribbean) population.

Shepherd's Bush and neighbouring White City are home to the **BBC Television Centre**, where you can take a backstage tour (*see below*). Nearby **Loftus Road** is the turf of Queens Park Rangers FC. The wide open spaces of Wormwood Scrubs to the north are marred by one of London's most famous and forbidding Victorian jails, but less than a mile down Goldhawk Road is **Ravenscourt Park**, a much more agreeable space with an adventure playground and a number of tennis courts.

South of Shepherd's Bush, Hammersmith is less depressing than its neighbour but is still best known for its huge traffic interchange and the stone-clad corporate monstrosity of the **Broadway Centre**. The district is not, however, without its more notable architectural landmarks. There's the **Olympia Exhibition Centre** on Hammersmith Road and the brown, ship-shaped curiosity called the London Ark, the city's first energy-saving, eco-friendly building (which, ironically, leans across one of the city's least eco-friendly roadways, the A4). Knobbly Hammersmith Bridge, built in 1824, was London's first suspension bridge; Lower Mall, running along the river from the bridge, is a pleasant spot for a stroll or a pint at one of several riverside pubs, of which the Dove (*see p230*) is the pick.

Nor is Hammersmith without culture. On the main shopping route of **King Street** stands the Lyric theatre (*see p338*), while the Riverside Studios (*see p286*) on **Crisp Road** is a three-theatre contemporary arts centre with a gallery and a repertory cinema.

BBC Television Centre Backstage Tours

*Wood Lane, W12 (0870 603 0304/www.bbc.co.uk/tours). White City tube. **Tours** by appointment only; regularly Mon-Sat; phone for details. **Admission** Tours £7.95; £6.95 concessions; £5.95 10-16s; £21.95 family (2+2 or 1+3). No under-10s. **Credit** MC, V.*

The world's most famous TV studios are responsible for thousands of shows a year, from *Blue Peter* to *Crimewatch UK*. A typical backstage tour will allow you glimpses into the news centre, various studios and a production gallery, but no two tours are ever the same because this is a working TV centre (hence the ban on children under ten). Tours, which must be pre-booked and last an hour and a half (wear comfy shoes, as there's a lot of walking involved), can be combined with being in the audience of a BBC show; call for details.

Chiswick

Turnham Green tube/Chiswick rail.

A leafy suburb coveted by BBC execs, actors and minor celebs, Chiswick is in a world of its own. Turning your back on the tarmacked swoops of Hammersmith and walking west by the river from Hammersmith Bridge, **Chiswick Mall** gives off a different vibe. Lining this mile-long riverside stretch is an assortment of grand 17th- to 19th-century townhouses with flowery, wrought-iron verandas. The nearby Fuller's Griffin Brewery on Chiswick Lane South has stood on the same site since the 17th century and offers tours that include a full tasting session (8996 2063; pre-booked tours at 11am, noon, 1pm, 2pm Mon, Wed-Fri; £5). Chiswick Mall ends at the church of St Nicholas. Only the ragstone tower of the 15th-century building remains; the rest of the church is 19th century. Gravestones commemorate local painters Hogarth and Whistler, but they're buried elsewhere.

Other Chiswick attractions include Palladian **Chiswick House** (*see below*) and **Hogarth's House** (*see p185*). Further west is the **Kew Bridge Steam Museum**, and next door is the **Musical Museum** (for both, *see p185*). South of here, overlooking Kew Gardens from the opposite side of the river, is **Syon House** (*see p185*). A cutesy riverside promenade, just east of Kew Bridge on the north side of the river, runs by the mini-village of Strand-on-the-Green, and takes in three of the best pubs in the area.

Chiswick House

Burlington Lane, W4 (8995 0508/www.english-heritage.org.uk). Turnham Green tube then E3 bus to Edensor Road/Chiswick rail/Hammersmith tube/

rail then 190 bus. **Open** *Apr-Sept* 10am-6pm daily. *Oct* 10am-5pm daily. *Nov-Mar* 10am-4pm Wed-Sun. Last entry 30min before closing. Closed 1-16 Jan. **Admission** *includes audio-guide* £3.30; £2.50 concessions; £1.70 5-16s; free under-5s. **Credit** MC, V.
The first and finest 18th-century Palladian villa in Britain, Chiswick House was designed by the third Earl of Burlington as a temple to hospitality: the glamorous events hosted by the Burlington dynasty attracted the cream of London society, from artists to politicians. It was Lord Burlington's passion for the fine arts that made the interiors here such a feast for the eyes: keen to create a house and garden of a kind found in ancient Rome, he employed William Kent to design sumptuous interiors to contrast with the restrained exterior. The extraordinary Domed Saloon is lit from the drum by windows derived from the Roman baths of Diocletian. The classical Italianate gardens with their temples, statues and lake are no less spectacular. Part of *The Servant*, which starred James Fox and Dirk Bogarde, was filmed here at Chiswick House in 1963.

Hogarth's House

Hogarth Lane, Great West Road, W4 (8994 6757). Turnham Green tube/Chiswick rail. **Open** *Apr-Oct* 1-5pm Tue-Fri; 1-6pm Sat, Sun. *Nov, Dec, Feb, Mar* 1-4pm Tue-Fri; 1-5pm Sat, Sun. **Admission** free; donations appreciated. **No credit cards**.
This early 18th-century house was the country retreat of painter, engraver and social commentator William Hogarth. Fully restored in 1997, for the 300th anniversary of Hogarth's birth, it now functions as a gallery displaying most of his well-known engravings, including *Gin Lane*, *Marriage à la Mode*,

Harlot's Progress and a copy of *Rake's Progress*, part of which depicts a scene in Bedlam lunatic asylum (*see p169* **Whatever happened to?**).

Kew Bridge Steam Museum

Green Dragon Lane, Brentford, Middx (8568 4757). Gunnersbury tube/Kew Bridge rail/65, 237, 267, 391 bus. **Open** 11am-5pm daily. **Admission** *Mon-Fri* £3; £1 5-15s; £2 concessions; £7 family (2+3); free under-5s. *Sat, Sun* £4; £2 5-15s; £3 concessions; £10.50 family (2+3); free under-5s. **Credit** MC, V.
This museum of water supply, housed in a Victorian riverside pumping station, looks at London's use and abuse of the world's most precious commodity. The highlight, or low point, depending on your take on it, is a walk-through sewer experience. On weekends at 3pm one of the biggest working steam engines in the world, a Cornish beam engine built in 1845 for use in the tin mines, stirs into motion.

Musical Museum

368 High Street, Brentford, Middx (8560 8108). **Open** *Apr-Oct* 2-5pm Sat, Sun; *summer hols also* 2-4pm Wed. **Admission** £3.20; £2.50 concessions; free under-3s. **No credit cards**.
Visitors to this interesting little museum, one of west London's best-kept secrets, can discover the world of automatic musical instruments during an hour-and-a-half demonstration.

Syon House

Syon Park, Brentford, Middx (8560 0883/ www.syonpark.co.uk). Gunnersbury tube/rail then 237, 267 bus. **Open** House *late Mar-early Nov* 11am-5pm Wed, Thur, Sun, bank hol Mon. Last entry

Stairway to heaven: the **Shri Swaminarayan Mandir temple**. *See p186.*

4.15pm. *Tours* by arrangement. **Admission** *House & Gardens (includes audio-guide)* £6.95; £6.50 concessions; £5.95 5-15s; £15 family (2+2); free under-5s. *Gardens only* £3.50; £2.50 concessions, 5-15s; £8 family (2+2); free under-5s. *Tours* free. **Credit** AmEx, MC, V.

The London home of the Duke of Northumberland – it's been in the family for 400 years – Syon House was built on the site of a medieval abbey dedicated to the Bridgettine order (founded by Swedish mystic St Bridget) and is named after Mount Zion in the Holy Land. Brutally dissolved by Henry VIII, the monastery was remodelled as a house by 1517, though in 1547 it seems to have got its revenge when Henry's coffin, brought here en route to Windsor, burst open in the night, allowing the dogs to slobber on his remains. The fine Robert Adam neo-classical interior was created in 1761 for the 1st Duke of Northumberland. Among the many paintings on display inside are works by Gainsborough, Reynolds and Van Dyck. The gardens, which afford views of Kew Gardens (*see p174*) across the river, were modelled by 'Capability' Brown and now house a 19th-century conservatory, a miniature steam train, a garden centre, the London Butterfly House and the Aquatic Experience (all have separate admission charges beyond entry to the house and gardens).

Further west

A couple of miles west of Chiswick is the suburb of **Ealing**, famous for Ealing Studios with its distinctive brand of anarchic comedy. The oldest site of continuous film production in Britain and the country's first studio built for sound, Ealing is undergoing a £70-million conversion to a state-of-the art facility geared to the digital age. Work, which is expected to be complete by 2004 and includes the renovation of the three original sound stages, is being carried out in phases so the studio can continue with TV and film production.

The area is a one-stop option for shopping (the Broadway Centre lies at its heart) and eating and drinking, plus it boasts a large selection of museums and parks. Especially worth a visit is **Walpole Park**, home to Pitshanger Manor (*see below*) and the annual Ealing Jazz Festival. Further west still, in the middle of gigantic Osterley Park, is **Osterley House** (*see below*), another Robert Adam revamp.

Just north of here are the colour and curries of **Southall**, which, like many previously sleepy parts of west London, has been given a new lease of life by Indian immigrants. The mainly Punjabi community (*see p180* **The melting pot: Punjabi London**) offers a great opportunity to sample authentic north Indian cuisine in the cheap restaurants that line the Broadway. Visit on a Sunday, when the locals stroll among the market stalls and sari stores.

To the north, **Wembley** has been similarly enlivened by the mainly Gujarati community, although this district is better known as the home of the famous stadium. Plans to replace the 78-year-old structure were in limbo as we went to press, with some senior FA figures saying that the England team should continue playing international games at different venues around the country instead of at a national stadium.

Nearby **Neasden** is another piece of sprawling suburbia, once satirised by the Monty Python team but now most famous for the multi-billion-rupee **Shri Swaminarayan Mandir** temple that was built here by a Hindu sect, replicating the Akshardam outside Ahmedabad in Gujarat, western India. Constructed in 1995, it required 5,000 tons of marble and limestone and the work of around 1,500 sculptors for an enterprise unprecedented in this country since cathedral-building in the Middle Ages. Visitors are welcome, but dress discreetly. *See also p180* **The melting pot: Punjabi London**.

Osterley House

Osterley Park, off Jersey Road, Isleworth, Middx (8232 5050/recorded info 01494 755566/ www.nationaltrust.org.uk). Osterley tube. **Open** *Park* 9am-dusk daily. *House end Mar-early Nov* 1-4.30pm Wed-Sun (closed Good Friday). **Admission** *House* £4.30; £2.15 5-15s; £10.50 family. Now a National Trust property, Osterley House was built for Sir Thomas Gresham (the founder of the Royal Exchange; *see p90*) in 1576 but transformed by Robert Adam in 1761. His revamp is most prominent in the imposing colonnade of white pillars in front of the courtyard of the house's red-brick body. The splendid state rooms are worth a visit in themselves, but the still-used Tudor stables and the vast parkland walks add to Osterley's allure.

Pitshanger Manor & Gallery

Walpole Park, Mattock Lane, Ealing, W5 (8567 1227/www.ealing.gov.uk/pitshanger). Ealing Broadway tube/rail. **Open** 10am-5pm Tue-Sat. Closed bank hols. *Tours* by arrangement. **Admission** free. Set in the beautiful surrounds of Walpole Park, Pitshanger Manor was largely rebuilt by Sir John Soane (for Sir John Soane's Museum, *see p99*), who transformed it into an idiosyncratic Regency villa, retaining only a wing designed in 1768 by George Dance the Younger. Painstakingly restored, the interior offers up the contrast between Soane's decorative schemes in his library, breakfast room and bedchamber and the formal rooms in the Dance wing, with their elaborate plasterwork. Tours include a short video, *A Day in the Death of John Soane*, that looks at Soane's use of Pitshanger to entertain friends and clients. The adjacent Gallery, which opened in 1996, is the biggest contemporary art gallery in west London.

Eat, Drink, Shop

Restaurants

Food, glorious food: British cooking – in all its guises – is going from strength to strength.

London's myriad restaurants are not only a reflection of the cosmopolitan nature of the city but, more significantly, of its population's continually evolving interest in cuisines of all types and nationalities.

As a nation, the British have traditionally cultivated a magpie approach to food, happily incorporating everything from curries and kebabs to pizzas into the gamut of their national diet. A trip to any of the vibrant centres of Indian London (Wembley, Southall or Tooting, say) would be richly rewarded (though Brick Lane has become known as a prime spot for an authentic curry, these days a decent meal there has become rarer than pork phall in Karachi).

Similarly, for those who want to get their teeth into a decent pizza, **Pizza Express** (check www.pizzaexpress.co.uk for branches) remains the best of the chains. Other good bets within central London include **Condotti** (4 Mill Street, Mayfair, W1, 7499 1308), **Pizza on the Park** (11-13 Knightsbridge, SW1, 7235 5273), the **Soho Pizzeria** (16-18 Beak Street, Soho, W1, 7434 2480), **Purple Sage** (90-92 Wigmore Street, Marylebone, W1, 7486 1912), **Spiga** (84-6 Wardour Street, Soho, W1, 7734 3444) and **La Spighetta** (43 Blandford Street, Marylebone, W1, 7486 7340).

DOS AND DON'TS

For most people, eating out in London is an informal affair. It's very rare that a restaurant enforces a dress code, although the pricier the restaurant, the smarter the clientele tend to be. But then, you're either the kind of person who dines at La Tante Claire (*see p203*) or you're not.

Not all London restaurants insist on reservations, but it certainly doesn't do any harm to make them; we'd suggest booking ahead if at all possible. While some London eateries are entirely non-smoking and others allow smoking anywhere, the most common arrangement in all but the smallest operations is for staff to set aside sections of the restaurant for smokers. If you're passionate either way, be sure to mention it when you book.

Restaurants are one of the few areas of British life where tipping is standard practice; ten to 15 per cent is usual. Some places add service automatically, so double-check the bill or you may tip twice. Be wary of places that

include service in the bill but then leave the the space for gratuities empty on your credit card slip. And always try and tip in cash, as some restaurants don't pass on credit card tips to their table staff.

We've listed a range of main course prices for all the restaurants in this section, except for those places that only serve set menu meals; where that's the case, we've listed those prices instead. But bear in mind that restaurants can (and often do) change their menus at any time without giving notice, so these prices should only be used as guidelines.

For the best places to eat with the kids, *see p274*, and for the best places to live it up, *see p202*. Aside from the options listed below, vegetarians might like to try **Roussillon** (*see p205*), **Mandola** (*see p215*) and **Sri Siam** (*see p199*). In addition, most Thai and Turkish places have fine meat-free ranges.

For more information on all aspects of eating out in London, buy the annual *Time Out Eating & Drinking Guide* (£9.99).

South Bank & Bankside

Fish

fish!

3B Belvedere Road, SE1 (7234 3333). Waterloo tube/rail. **Open** 11.30am-10.30pm Mon-Sat; noon-10pm Sun. **Main courses** £8.50-£16.95. **Credit** AmEx, DC, JCB, MC, V. **Map** p401 L9.
Despite the irritating exclamation mark, fish! is a friendly, airy and light restaurant. There are usually a couple of meat dishes and one vegetarian on the menu, but it would be madness to ignore the multitude of excellent fish options.
Branches: throughout the city.

Livebait

41-5 The Cut, SE1 (7928 7211). Southwark tube/ Waterloo tube/rail. **Open** noon-3pm, 5.30-11.30pm Mon-Sat. **Main courses** £12.95-£28. **Credit** AmEx, DC, MC, JCB, V. **Map** p404 N8.
This branch of Livebait (there are six in London) sports the trademark fish-shop chic of checked tiles and Formica tables. The menu includes inventive, tasty dishes such as asparagus- and mushroom-stuffed squid with red pepper coulis and chorizo.
Branches: 21 Wellington Street, WC2 (7836 7161); 175 Westbourne Grove, W11 (7727 4321).

Modern European

Oxo Tower Restaurant & Brasserie
*Oxo Tower Wharf, Barge House Street, SE1
(7803 3888). Blackfriars or Waterloo tube/rail.*
Open *Brasserie* noon-3.30pm, 5.30-11.30pm
Mon-Sat; 6-10.30pm Sun. *Restaurant* noon-3pm,
6-11pm Mon-Fri; noon-3.30pm, 6-11pm Sat;
noon-3.30pm, 5.30-11pm Sun. **Main courses**
Brasserie £7-£17. *Restaurant* £11-£25.
Credit AmEx, DC, MC, V. **Map** p404 N7.
The view is fabulous and the cooking generally
excellent in both the brasserie and the restaurant.
The former probably offers better value for money,
although you'll probably want to keep your distance
from the rather intrusive pianist.

The People's Palace
*Level 3, Royal Festival Hall, SE1 (7928 9999/
www.peoplespalace.co.uk). Waterloo tube/rail.* **Open**
noon-3pm, 5.30-11pm daily. **Main courses** £12.50-
£17. **Credit** AmEx, DC, MC, V. **Map** p401 M8.
It's easy to wander almost accidentally into this
restaurant (and diners have to wander bemused out
again to find the loos). The room is spacious with
vast windows framing a splendid view over the
river. They're fitted with blinds that dip and rise
with the glare. There's often room if you turn up on
spec but book ahead to be sure of a window seat.
Good, Modern European cooking.

Cigala: minimal decor,
maximal praise. *See p190.*

Other

Baltic
*74 Blackfriars Road, SE1 (7928 1111). Southwark
tube.* **Open** noon-3pm, 6-11pm Mon-Sat; noon-3pm,
6-10.30pm Sun. **Main courses** £11-£12.50. **Credit**
AmEx, MC, V. **Map** p404 N8.
Occupying a Grade II-listed building, Baltic includes
a sleek, modern bar (ideal for a vodka rendezvous)
with dark concrete floor and white walls, and a huge
atrium-roofed dining room. Food consists of Polish-
based cuisine taken to a higher level.

Tas
*33 The Cut, Bankside, SE1 (7928 2111).
Waterloo tube/rail.* **Open** noon-11.30pm Mon-Sat;
noon-10.30pm Sun. **Main courses** £4.65-£14.45.
Credit AmEx, MC, V. **Map** p404 N8.
Tas successfully adds a dose of chic into the Turkish
restaurant formula. Staff serve some excellent food
with charm and panache. The room is airy, light and
devoid of knick-knacks.

The City

Mediterranean

Eyre Brothers
*70 Leonard Street, EC2 (7613 5346). Old Street
tube/rail.* **Open** noon-3pm, 6.30-11pm Mon-Sat. **Main
courses** £13-£23. **Credit** MC, V. **Map** p403 Q4.
This slick, glamorous restaurant is located in a 'characterful' street of warehouses, with only a wall of
plate glass to announce it. The kitchen runs the
length of the back wall, while partitions divide the
room into bite-sized portions. The fairly brief menu
offers accomplished Mediterranean cooking.

Oriental

K-10
*20 Copthall Avenue, EC2 (7562 8510/www.k10.net).
Liverpool Street or Moorgate tube/rail.* **Open**
11.30am-3pm, 5-10pm Mon-Fri. **Main courses** £1-
£3.50. **Credit** AmEx, DC, JCB, MC, V. **Map** p405 Q6.
Expect good kaiten-zushi at this long basement
room with its faux-slate flooring and bare white
walls. The menu is contemporary and affordable.

Vegetarian & organic

The Place Below
*St Mary-le-Bow, Cheapside, EC2 (7329 0789/
www.theplacebelow.co.uk). St Paul's tube/Bank
tube/DLR.* **Open** 7.30-10.30am, 11.30am-2.30pm Mon-
Fri. **Main courses** £7. **Credit** MC, V. **Map** p404 P6.
This popular café in the crypt of St Mary-le-Bow
church (which also hosts art, music and talks) is a
welcome alternative to the City's usual brand of
pinstriped watering holes. Expect snacky food and
soups to eat in or take away.

Eat, Drink, Shop

Quiet Revolution

49 Old Street, EC1 (7253 5556/
www.quietrevolution.co.uk). Old Street tube/rail.
Open 9am-10pm Mon-Fri; 10am-4pm Sat, Sun. **Main
courses** £3.95-£10.95. **Credit** MC, V. **Map** p402 P4.
Neither quiet nor revolutionary, this large and minimalist Old Street eaterie offers a welcome choice of
(mainly) vegetarian and (totally) organic food, but
the occasional meat dish does rear its head. There's
a branch in Aveda (*see p253*) in Marylebone.

Holborn & Clerkenwell

French

Club Gascon

*57 West Smithfield, EC1 (7796 0600). Barbican
tube/Farringdon tube/rail.* **Open** noon-2pm, 7-11pm
Mon-Fri; 7-10.30pm Sat. **Main courses** *Tapas* £2.50-
£15. **Credit** MC, V. **Map** p402 O5.
Cooking of quality and charm, focused on the produce and recipes of southwestern France and served
in tapas-sized portions, is the secret to this restaurant's enduring popularity. To experience it at its
best, indulge in the £30 five-course set menu. The
youthful Miyake-dressed waiting staff earn every
penny of the service charge.

Modern European

Bank Aldwych

1 Kingsway, WC2 (7379 9797/
*www.bankrestaurant.co.uk). Covent Garden or Holborn
tube.* **Open** 7.30-11.30am, noon-3pm, 5-11.30pm Mon-
Fri; 11.30am-3.30pm, 5-11.30pm Sat; 11.30am-3.30pm,
5.30-10pm Sun. **Main courses** £8.95-£19.50. **Credit**
AmEx, DC, MC, V. **Map** p399 M6.
Of all the ex-banks that now proliferate as eateries,
this has achieved the transition with the most
panache and confidence. Clever design and excellent
food are among its main assets.

Smiths of Smithfield

67-77 Charterhouse Street, EC1 (7236 6666/
www.smithsofsmithfield.co.uk). Farringdon tube/rail.
Open *Bar* 7am-5pm Mon-Fri; 10.30am-5pm Sat, Sun.
Dining Room noon-2.30pm, 6-10.30pm Mon-Sat.
Main courses £9.50-£11.50. **Credit** AmEx, DC,
MC, V. **Map** p402 O5.
The Smiths complex – ground-floor bar/café, first-
floor cocktail bar, and two restaurants on the next
two floors – has been a big hit in Smithfield, and
rightly so. A guaranteed good night out – but only
for the young at heart.

Oriental

Yo! Sushi/Yo! Below

*95 Farringdon Road, EC1 (Yo! Sushi 7841 0785/
Yo! Below 7841 0790). Farringdon tube/rail.*
Open *Yo! Sushi* noon-11pm Mon-Sat; noon-10pm
Sun; *Yo! Below* noon-11pm Mon-Wed; noon-1am

Thur, Fri; 5.30pm-1am Sat. **Main courses** *Yo!
Sushi* £1.50-£3.50. *Yo! Below* £6.50-£7. **Credit**
AmEx, JCB, MC, V. **Map** p402 N4.
One of the newer outposts of the ever-expanding
empire, this branch also combines a Yo! Sushi with
a Yo! Below – but this time with tarot-card readers,
'the largest bed in the world' (said to fit 60) and
serve-yourself saké piped to the tables.
Branches: throughout the city.

Spanish

Cigala

*54 Lamb's Conduit Street, WC1 (7405 1717).
Holborn or Russell Square tube.* **Open** noon-3pm,
6-10.45pm Mon-Fri; 12.30-3.30pm, 6.10.45pm Sat;
12.30-3.30pm Sun. **Main courses** £11-£22.
Credit AmEx, DC, JCB, MC, V. **Map** p399 M5.
Opened in 2001, this fashionably minimal restaurant
attracted rave reviews in its first few months,
though in our opinion it has yet to mature into a
good all-rounder. Serving more closely Spanish-
inspired food than Moro (it was set up by former
Moro partner Jake Hodges), it's strong on starters
such as revuelto con gambas (scrambled egg with
prawns) and on modern Spanish wines.

Gaudí

63 Clerkenwell Road, EC1 (7608 3220/
*www.turnmills.co.uk/gaudi). Farringdon tube/rail/55,
243 bus.* **Open** noon-2.30pm Mon-Fri; noon-2.30pm,
7-10.30pm Sat. **Main courses** £16-£17.25. **Credit**
AmEx, DC, MC, V. **Map** p402 N4.
Food at Gaudí is rooted in traditional Spanish cooking, yet in terms of ingredients, cooking style and
presentation, it's modern, well constructed and formal. The interior pays homage to the restaurant's
namesake, with swirly wrought-iron banisters and
wavy, brightly tiled walls.

Moro

*34-6 Exmouth Market, EC1 (7833 8336).
Farringdon tube/rail.* **Open** *Bar* 12.30-10.30pm
Mon-Fri; 7-10.30pm Sat. *Restaurant* 12.30-2.30pm,
7-10.30pm Mon-Fri; 7-10.30pm Sat. **Main courses**
£10.50-£14.50. **Credit** AmEx, MC, V. **Map** p402 N4.
Getting a table at this deservedly revered restaurant
is difficult. The food (it's traditional Spanish incorporating influences from North Africa and the
Middle East) remains of a consistently high standard and the atmosphere is unpretentious. Service
is informal but proficient.

Bloomsbury & Fitzrovia

Indian

Rasa Samudra

5 Charlotte Street, W1 (7637 0222/
www.rasarestaurants.com). Goodge Street tube.
Open noon-2.45pm, 6-10.45pm Mon-Sat; 6-10.45pm
Sun. **Main courses** £8.95-£12.50. **Credit** AmEx,
MC, V. **Map** p398 J5.

A classy Fitzrovia branch of the small Rasa chain (*see p212* **Who he? Sivadas Sreedharan**), Rasa Samudra adds glorious Keralan seafood cuisine to the Nair vegetarian dishes that are offered by the other branches. The decor is very stylish, with comfortable red chairs, pink walls and linen with a hint of saffron yellow.
Branches: 55 & 56 Stoke Newington Church Street, N16 (7249 0344/1340); 16 Dering Street, W1 (7629 1346).

Italian

Passione
10 Charlotte Street, W1 (7636 2833/www. passione.com). Goodge Street tube. **Open** 12.30-2.15pm, 7-10.15pm Mon-Fri; 7-10.30pm Sat. **Main courses** £9-£18. **Credit** AmEx, DC, JCB, MC, V. **Map** p398 J5.
Despite his appearances on *The Naked Chef*, Passione maestro Gennaro doesn't need any celeb endorsements when his food is this good. The menu changes frequently, and includes familiar standards, as well as more intriguing dishes. A little pricey, perhaps, but undeniably lovely.

Modern European

Pied à Terre
34 Charlotte Street, W1 (7636 1178). Goodge Street or Tottenham Court Road tube. **Open** 12.15-2.30pm, 7-11pm Mon-Fri; 7-11pm Sat. **Set lunch** £19.50 two courses; £23 three courses. **Set dinner** £39.50 two courses; £50 three courses; £65 eight courses. **Credit** AmEx, DC, MC, V. **Map** p398 J5.
Small and simply but stylishly decorated, Pied à Terre is a true gourmet's retreat. Luxurious ingredients do not dominate the menu as they do in other expensive restaurants; instead the emphasis is on novel unions of flavour assuredly combined. Intelligent, attentive staff complete the picture.

Oriental

Archipelago
110 Whitfield Street, W1 (7383 3346). Goodge Street or Warren Street tube. **Open** noon-2.30pm, 6-11.15pm Mon-Fri; 6-11.15pm Sat. **Set lunch** £26.50 three courses. **Set dinner** £32.50 two courses; £38.50 three courses. **Credit** AmEx, JCB, MC, V. **Map** p398 J4.
The menu is a wonderland of weird and wonderful ingredients (chocolate-covered scorpions lurk among the desserts) to complement the kooky bohemian decor. But beneath the shock-value swagger, you'll find some seriously tasty food.

Han Kang
16 Hanway Street, W1 (7637 1985). Tottenham Court Road tube. **Open** noon-3pm, 6-11pm Mon-Sat. **Main courses** £5-£28 (for two). **Credit** MC, V. **Map** p399 K5.

Fine settings in a fine setting at the **Criterion**. *See p195.*

Hidden away, this long-established little Korean restaurant looks more classy from the outside than from within, but the full menu offers plenty of well-executed dishes. If you're only after a quickish bite, go for one of the ten lunch specials.

Silks & Spice
23 Foley Street, W1 (7636 2718). Goodge Street or Oxford Circus tube. **Open** noon-11pm Mon-Fri; 5.30-11pm Sat; 5.30-10.30pm Sun. **Main courses** £5.95-£21. **Credit** AmEx, MC, V. **Map** p398 J5.
Despite its rather gloomy and cluttered interior, the Foley Street branch of this Thai-Malaysian offers a reliable (and lengthy) selection of noodle, rice, soupy and salady faves, plus more adventurous specials. The spicing is uncompromising.
Branches: throughout the city.

Marylebone

Fish & chips

Sea Shell
49-51 Lisson Grove, NW1 (7224 9000). Marylebone tube/rail. **Open** noon-2.30pm, 5-10.30pm Mon-Fri; noon-10.30pm Sat. **Main courses** £6.75-£16. **Credit** AmEx, JCB, MC, V. **Map** p395 E4.

Eat, Drink, Shop

Not exactly glowing with charm (it's neat, tidy and rather inert), Sea Shell inspires loyalty in everyone from Marylebone locals and pinstriped commuters to pensioners and cabbies (Tom Jones has even been known to pop in to the adjoining fish and chip shop). The snow-white haddock is encased in ethereal groundnut oil batter, the chips are fat and vinegary, and the mushy peas among the best we've eaten.

Indian

Porte des Indes

32 Bryanston Street, W1 (7224 0055/www. blueelephant.com). Marble Arch tube. **Open** noon-2.30pm, 7-11.30pm Mon-Fri; 7-11.30pm Sat; noon-3pm, 7-10.30pm Sun. **Main courses** £7.95-£15. **Credit** AmEx, DC, JCB, MC, V. **Map** p395 F6.
Porte des Indes' setting (a former Edwardian ballroom with sweeping marble staircase, red wood floor and large domed skylight) has few equals. Pondicherry, a former French colony in south-east India, provides the culinary theme.

Italian

Ibla

89 Marylebone High Street, W1 (7224 3799). Baker Street or Regent's Park tube. **Open** noon-2.30pm, 7-10.15pm Mon-Fri; 7-10.15pm Sat. **Set lunch** £15 two courses; £18 three courses. **Set meal** £30 three courses; £35 four courses. **Credit** AmEx, DC, MC, V. **Map** p398 G5.
Ibla's quirky interior – one room painted shiny olive green, the other a luscious chilli-pepper red – is as polished as a Chinese lacquered box. Chef Stefano Frigerio likes to take a risk or two, so expect some leftfield dishes alongside more conventional offerings.

Middle Eastern

Fairuz

3 Blandford Street, W1 (7486 8108/8182). Baker Street or Bond Street tube. **Open** noon-11.30pm Mon-Sat; noon-10.30pm Sun. **Main courses** £9-£12. **Credit** AmEx, DC, MC, V. **Map** p398 G5.

Look who's cooking

Rock 'n' roll must be spinning in its grave – or should that be gravy? – because the new rock 'n' roll is cooking, and the new rock stars are the chefs. It's become difficult to turn on the television these days without seeing an earnest face staring at you over a pan of sautéd pancetta, and Jamie Oliver is not so much a celebrity chef as a walking £ sign.

The loveable Mockney rogue has rocketed to stardom on the back of his *Naked Chef* series and is a ubiquitous presence in the British media, with lucrative book deals, television work and a barrage of Sainsbury's ads (though his contract for this ends in March 2002). **Monte's** (164 Sloane Street, SW1, 7235 0555), at which he is a consultant (he very rarely cooks there), has proved something of a disappointment. Your average punter can only get lunch there – you can have dinner if you're a member of the club – and prices are high for cooking that can seem uninspired. It serves as a warning for those other showbiz panhandlers to stick to what they're best at.

All those food programmes showing us how to debone a chicken or deglaze a pan are making galloping gourmets of many of us. That may be why the number of restaurant-goers in the capital is falling, though stiff prices, breathtaking wine

mark-ups and arrogant service could also be partly to blame. That said, the abrasive but nonetheless affable Gordon Ramsay (*pictured*), who baulks at the label of celebrity chef, seems to be bucking the trend. This ex-footballer is almost as well known for his temper as his terrines, but he is undoubtedly the capital's best chef. And he has been given yet more room to showcase his talents, this time at the restaurant at Claridge's hotel, now called **Gordon Ramsay at Claridge's** (55 Brook Street, W1, 7499 0099). He'll be dividing his time between that and his eponymous eaterie in Chelsea (*see p205*).

Other celebrity chefs with their own restaurants include Antony Worrall Thompson (**Wiz**, 123A Clarendon Road, W11, 7229 1500); Gary Rhodes (**Rhodes in the Square**, Dolphin Square, Chichester Street, SW1, 7798 6767; and **City Rhodes**, 1 New Street Square, EC4, 7583 1313); and Marco Pierre White (among others **Mirabelle**, 56 Curzon Street, W1, 7499 4636; and the **Criterion**, *see p195*).

But the chances of your dinner actually being prepared by the celebrity owner are high only at Gordon Ramsay's, though Gary Rhodes does occasionally get his chef's whites dirty when he's in town. Presumably the others are all in make-up.

This intimate, rustic-style space makes a mellow setting in which to enjoy some lovingly prepared classics of Lebanese cuisine served in more than decently sized portions. You may even get to hear the music of Lebanese diva Fairuz, after whom the restaurant is named.

Maroush

21 Edgware Road, W1 (7723 0773/www. maroush.com). Marble Arch tube. **Open** noon-2am daily. **Main courses** £12.50. **Minimum** £48 per diner if occupying table after 10.30pm. **Credit** AmEx, DC, MC, V. **Map** p395 F6.

On the ground floor, this flagship of the Maroush chain has a long bar and tables for casual eating; in the dimly lit basement, you'll find an international group of diners intent on a big night out. The steep post-10.30pm charge is in place because this branch puts on late-night live music and belly dancing. The dress code is smart casual.

Branches: 38 Beauchamp Place, SW3 (7581 5434); 62 Seymour Street, W1 (7724 5024); 68 Edgware Road, W2 (7224 9339).

Patogh

8 Crawford Place, W1 (7262 4015). Edgware Road tube. **Open** 1pm-midnight daily. **Main courses** £5-£9.50. **No credit cards. Map** p395 E5.

Patogh is tiny, with just five or six tables on the ground floor and an upstairs of similarly intimate proportions. From the charcoal grill come great organic kebabs, and, from the traditional clay oven, bicycle wheel-sized hot discs of flatbread.

Modern European

Orrery

55 Marylebone High Street, W1 (7616 8000/ www.orrery.co.uk). Baker Street or Regent's Park tube. **Open** noon-3pm, 7-11pm daily. **Main courses** £14.50-£26. **Credit** AmEx, DC, JCB, MC, V. **Map** p398 G4.

This slender fillet of elegant skylit space houses the Conran group's smallest – and finest – restaurant. The food can be breathtaking, from conception down to the smallest detail of execution, while service is flawless, precise and smiling. It may be expensive, but this is one of the best restaurants in London. Try Sundays for reasonably priced set lunch and dinner menus.

Oriental

Wagamama

101A Wigmore Street, W1 (7409 0111/www. wagamama.com). Bond Street or Marble Arch tube. **Open** noon-11pm Mon-Sat; 12.30-10.30pm Sun. **Main courses** £4.85-£7.35. **Credit** AmEx, DC, JCB, MC, V. **Map** p398 G6.

Wagamama isn't exactly the venue to propose in – the communal tables are always packed – but it does offer fairly priced, well-portioned, consistently good noodle-oriented tucker. A healthy, discerning alternative to fast food.

Branches: throughout the city.

Other

Original Tajines

7A Dorset Street, W1 (7935 1545). Baker Street tube. **Open** 12.30-3pm, 6-11pm Mon-Fri; 6-11pm Sat. **Main courses** £8.95-£11. **Credit** MC, V. **Map** p398 G5.

Original Tajines has a conservatory-like atmosphere (peach walls, tiled tables and floors) with restrained North African touches. The Moroccan food and wine are both of a high quality, attracting a mixed crowd of locals and tourists.

Providores & Tapa Room

109 Marylebone High Street, W1 (7935 6175/ www.theprovidores.co.uk). Baker Street or Bond Street tube. **Open** *Providores* noon-2.45pm, 6-10.45pm Mon-Sat; noon-2.45pm, 6-10pm Sun; *Tapa Room* 9-11.30am, noon-10.30pm Mon-Fri; 10am-3pm, 4-10.30pm Sat; 10am-3pm, 4-10pm Sun.

The richly imaginative **Archipelago**. *See p191.*

Main courses *Providores* £11-£15, *Tapa Room* £1.50-£9. Cover £1.50 (lunch Sat, Sun). **Credit** AmEx, MC, V. **Map** p398 G5.

The ground-floor Tapa Room is a sassy, absurdly busy café with a no-bookings policy that serves a kind of global tapas menu. Providores is the smarter, bookable restaurant on the first floor. Expect anything from breakfast's boiled eggs with Vegemite soldiers to the full global taste explosion.

Six-13

19 Wigmore Street, W1 (7629 6133/www.six13.com). Bond Street tube. **Open** noon-3pm, 5.30-11pm Mon-Thur, Sun; 11.30am-3.30pm Fri (summer only; 11.30am-1pm winter); 8-11pm Sat (winter only). **Main courses** £11-£20. **Credit** AmEx, DC, MC, V. **Map** p398 G5.

'Kosher fusion' is the description given to the food at Six-13, London's first restaurant to offer observant Jews a taste of more modern (gastronomic, even) cooking. The wine list includes an impressive array of kosher bottles, while attractive art deco-ish decor and smooth service are added bonuses.

Mayfair & St James's

British

1837

Brown's Hotel, 33 Albemarle Street, W1 (7408 1837/www.brownshotel.com). Green Park tube. **Open** 6.30-10.30am, noon-2.30pm, 7-10pm Mon-Fri; 7.30-11.30am, 7-10pm Sat; 7.30-11.30am Sun. **Main courses** *Set lunch* £20 two courses, £25 three courses, £29 five courses. *Set meal* £37 grazing menu; £80 chef's selection incl glass of wine with each course. **Credit** AmEx, DC, JCB, MC, V. **Map** p400 G7.

Superb service, genuinely lovely food and the understated glamour of the place make 1837 a good (and good-value) romantic destination. It strives not to rest on the laurels of its reputation, and a recent meal yielded such masterful dishes as crisply seared Atlantic sea bass with parsley coulis. Voted Best Hotel Restaurant at the *Time Out* Eating & Drinking Awards 2001.

French

The Criterion

224 Piccadilly, W1 (7930 0488). Piccadilly Circus tube. **Open** noon-2.30pm, 5.30-11.30pm Mon-Sat; 5.30-10.30pm Sun. **Main courses** £13.75-£25. **Credit** AmEx, DC, MC, V. **Map** p401 K7.

The Criterion's dining room is impressively furnished with a burnished gold ceiling, some exotic neo-classical paintings and plenty of marble. The French, classical cooking can be worthy of these grand surroundings. It's particularly popular with expense-accounters, at whom the wine list seems largely aimed, though there are a few more reasonably priced bottles in each category.

Indian

Tamarind

20 Queen Street, W1 (7629 3561/www.tamarind restaurant.com). Green Park tube. **Open** noon-3pm, 6-11.30pm Mon-Fri; 6-11.30pm Sat; noon-2.30pm, 6-10.30pm Sun. **Main courses** £10.50-£28.60. **Credit** AmEx, DC, JCB, MC, V. **Map** p400 H7.

The excellent menu at this large, expensive, strikingly designed basement restaurant is strong on tandoori and north-west Indian dishes yet ranges across the subcontinent. Pan-fried aubergine steaks filled with paneer, peppers and herbs were a perfectly executed highlight of a recent visit. One of only two of London's Indian restaurants to have been awarded a Michelin Star.

Italian

Cecconi's

5A Burlington Gardens, W1 (7434 1500). Green Park tube. **Open** noon-3pm, 7-11pm daily. **Main courses** £12-£23. **Credit** AmEx, DC, JCB, MC, V. **Map** p400 J7.

After a massive refurb, Cecconi's has an urbane, clubby, cigar-lounge feel, with sexy leather seating, low lighting and acres of white linen. The stylish bar serves a mean selection of cocktails, and the restaurant produces accomplished interpretations of traditional northern Italian cuisine.

Modern European

Quaglino's

16 Bury Street, SW1 (7930 6767/www.conran.com). Green Park or Piccadilly Circus tube. **Open** *Bar* 11.30am-1am Mon-Thur; 11.30am-2am Fri, Sat; noon-11pm Sun. *Restaurant* noon-2.30pm, 5.30pm-midnight Mon-Thur; noon-2.30pm, 5.30pm-1am Fri, Sat; noon-2.30pm, 5.30-11pm Sun. **Main courses** £13.50-£18.50. **Credit** AmEx, DC, JCB, MC, V. **Map** p400 J7.

This huge basement dining hall set in an old hotel ballroom is best enjoyed in a group: its grandeur reliably confers a sense of occasion. The service has been known to be a bit sloppy but the food's still good, and the large shellfish bar at the far end of the room sells well-priced oysters.

Oriental

Kaya

42 Albemarle Street, W1 (7499 0622/0633). Green Park or Piccadilly Circus tube. **Open** noon-3pm, 6-11pm Mon-Sat; 6-11pm Sun. **Main courses** £7.50-£17. **Credit** AmEx, DC, JCB, MC, V. **Map** p400 J7.

Kaya isn't the sort of restaurant you'd come to for a knees-up – the decor is plain and simple (beige walls with Korean prints), the atmosphere hushed, and the staff diffident and attentive. That said, the upmarket Korean food is good.

Eat, Drink, Shop

Flights of fancy at **Nobu**.

Matsuri

15 Bury Street, SW1 (7839 1101/www.matsuri-restaurant.com). Green Park or Piccadilly Circus tube. **Open** noon-2.30pm, 6-10.30pm Mon-Sat. **Main courses** £10-£28. **Credit** AmEx, DC, JCB, MC, V. **Map** p400 J7.

Matsuri is old school Japanese, with high prices, a central location and an emphasis on excellent service. Most of the restaurant is given over to teppanyaki, but the sushi counter, which is run by two friendly *itamae-san*, is also worth a punt.

Nobu

Metropolitan Hotel, 19 Old Park Lane, W1 (7447 4747). Hyde Park Corner tube. **Open** noon-2.15pm, 6-10.15pm Mon-Thur; noon-2.15pm, 6-11pm Fri, Sat; 6-9.30pm Sun. **Main courses** £5-£27.50. **Credit** AmEx, DC, MC, V. **Map** p400 H8.

As buzzy as ever, Nobu remains one of the capital's sexiest and sassiest destination restaurants – in spite of its inconvenient booking system and occasional lapses in service standards. The food – Japanese with Latin American flourishes – remains both inventive and very tasty, and the superb cocktails and sakes are worth a mention too.

Oriental

Dorchester Hotel, 55 Park Lane, W1 (7317 6328). Hyde Park Corner or Marble Arch tube. **Open** noon-2.30pm, 7-11pm Mon-Fri; 7-11pm Sat. **Main courses** £17.50-£29. **Credit** AmEx, DC, JCB, MC, V. **Map** p400 G7.

The private dining rooms at the Oriental are among the loveliest in London: orientalist fantasies decorated respectively in the Chinese, Thai and Indian styles. By comparison, the rather low-ceilinged main dining area is disappointing, although it's perfectly smart and comfortable. The cooking is high-class, westernised Chinese food.

Other

Gaucho Grill

19 Swallow Street, W1 (7734 4040). Piccadilly Circus tube. **Open** noon-3pm, 5-11pm Mon-Fri; noon-11pm Sat; noon-10.30pm Sun. **Main courses** £7.50-£32.50. **Credit** AmEx, DC, MC, V. **Map** p400 J7.

Part of a well-liked group of Latin American steakhouses, this branch of the Gaucho Grill is a secluded cellar restaurant with whitewashed walls, dark-wood tables and cowhide-upholstered seating. The steaks here are sensational, although non-carnivorous options are always available.
Branches: 12 Gracechurch Street, EC3 (7626 5180); 64 Heath Street, NW3 (7431 8222).

Momo

25 Heddon Street, W1 (7434 4040). Oxford Circus or Piccadilly Circus tube. **Open** noon-2.30pm, 7-11pm Mon-Sat; noon-2.30pm, 6.30-10.30pm Sun. **Main courses** £9.75-£17.50. **Credit** AmEx, DC, MC, V. **Map** p400 J7.

A magnificent ground-floor restaurant filled with gorgeous carpets, lanterns and antiques, Momo offers ambitious and mostly excellent Moroccan cuisine. The wine list is cosmopolitan, with plenty of choice for around £20. For more buzz, go at night.

Sofra Bistro

18 Shepherd Market, W1 (7493 3320). Green Park tube. **Open** noon-midnight daily. **Main courses** £6.95-£15.95. **Credit** AmEx, MC, V. **Map** p400 H8.

One of three Sofras in London, this Mayfair branch offers pretty good Turkish food at bargain prices, but in surroundings that have suffered a bit from the restaurant's popularity. Still, tasty food at great prices (for the location) make it worth a visit.
Branches: 1 St Christopher's Place, W1 (7224 4080); 36 Tavistock Street, WC2 (7240 3773).

Soho & Chinatown

French

L'Escargot Marco Pierre White

48 Greek Street, W1 (7437 2679/www.whitestar line.org.uk). Leicester Square or Tottenham Court Road tube. **Open** *Ground floor* 12.15-2.15pm, 6-11.30pm Mon-Fri; 6-11.30pm Sat. *Picasso*

Room noon-2.15pm, 7-11pm Tue-Fri; 7-11pm
Sat. **Main courses** *Ground floor* £12.95-£17.95.
Set lunch *Picasso Room* £20.50 two courses;
£25.50 three courses. **Set meal** *Picasso Room*
£42 three courses. **Credit** AmEx, DC, JCB, MC,
V. **Map** p399 K6.
The introduction of a new chef at L'Escargot has
given the ground-floor operation of this Greek
Street old-timer a new lease of life. The standard of
cooking here is excellent, with the cuisine taking
some original twists and turns around well-chosen
classic themes. Up on the first floor you'll find the
more formal restaurant.

Indian

Masala Zone
9 Marshall Street, W1 (7287 9966/www.
realindianfood.com). Oxford Circus tube.
Open noon-3pm, 5.30-11pm Mon-Sat; noon-3pm
Sun. **Main courses** £5-£9.50. **Credit** MC, V.
Map p398 J6.

It may occupy an oppressive-looking concrete
bunker, but Masala Zone's interior mixes appealing modern industrial design with enchanting
Indian tribal art to wonderful effect. The cooking
itself consists of high-quality, low-priced dishes
that are ideal for both a quick workaday lunch or
for post-work refuelling.

Italian

Vasco & Piero's Pavilion
15 Poland Street, W1 (7437 8774/www.vascos
food.com). Oxford Circus or Tottenham Court Road
tube. **Open** noon-3pm, 6-11pm Mon-Fri; 7-11pm Sat.
Main courses £9.50-£15.50. **Credit** AmEx, DC,
JCB, MC, V. **Map** p398 J6.
This reliable old Soho stager has recently had a mild
makeover, but its large number of regular punters
aren't going to be upset by the newly ochre walls
punctuated by gentle watercolours. The simple
Umbrian food remains as good as ever, and is fine-
ly tuned to the different seasons.

Best of British

Contemporary British cuisine is becoming
harder to define. In one sense it's a culinary
chimera that has profited immeasurably
from the cultural diversity of modern Britain,
yet at the same time, quintessential British
cuisine of the 'Sunday roast' variety has
also evolved radically in the last decade.
Innovative interpretations of traditional
recipes and ingredients have reinstated
many forgotten dishes on London's menus
(Fergus Henderson, the chef at **St John**
restaurant, being one of the most notable
pioneers of this process; *see below*). With
this in mind, we've compiled a selection of
London's best British restaurants, from the
priciest to the most humble, to give the truest
reflection of our nation's gastro profile.

To begin at the beginning, **Rules** (35
Maiden Lane, WC2, 7836 5314) is London's
oldest restaurant and still one of the best
places to sample classic British fare (game
is a forte). The same is true of **Simpson's-in-
the-Strand** (100 Strand, WC2, 7836 9112),
where the legendary roast trollies are stocked
daily with expertly cooked joints.

More modern examples of British cooking
are **Alfred** (245 Shaftesbury Avenue, WC2,
7240 2566) and **Lindsay House** (21 Romilly
Street, W1, 7439 0450), both of which
serve up fresh, inspired examples of Modern
British cuisine. Those who want to dig a
little deeper might consider trying Fergus

Henderson's adventurous self-styled 'nose
to tail eating' at **St John** (26 St John Street,
EC1, 7251 0848/4998).

For something simpler but just as
satisfying, try the **Quality Chop House**
(94 Farringdon Road, EC1, 7837 5093),
or get your fill of the huge variety of sausages
at **Stanleys** (6 Little Portland Street, W1,
7462 0099). Otherwise, to try recipes by
a big-name British chef, you can visit either
of Gary Rhodes' restaurants (*see p192*
Look who's cooking).

Moving down the scale to good old fish and
chips, one of the best places to sample a
nice bit of battered marine life is **Geales** (2
Farmer Street, W8, 7727 7528), set among
the pastel-coloured houses of Notting Hill.
More central and of equally good quality is
the **North Sea Fish Restaurant** (7-8 Leigh
Street, WC1, 7387 5892).

If you want to go cheaper still, you should
pay a visit to one of the proper London pie
and mash shops, the fast-fading purveyors
of sustenance to London's hungry and
thriftiest workers. Michaele Manze opened
his shop, **Manze's** (87 Tower Bridge Road,
SE1, 7407 2985) back in 1892, in the days
when the pies were still filled with eels
caught in the Thames Estuary. These days,
mince is the preferred filling, served along
with a wedge of mash and a ladle of liquor
(parsley-based gravy).

Oriental

Busaba Eathai
106-10 Wardour Street, W1 (7255 8686).
Piccadilly Circus tube. **Open** noon-11pm Mon-Thur;
noon-11.30pm Fri, Sat; noon-10pm Sun. **Main**
courses £5.50-£8.50. **Credit** AmEx, JCB, MC, V.
Map p398 J6.
This funky Thai diner has a warm and modern dark
wood interior, illuminated by pendant lights that
hang low over the square communal tables.
The food is excellent (we rate the green curry as
one of the best in town) and the fruit juices and
smoothies are also superb.

Golden Harvest
17 Lisle Street, WC2 (7287 3822). Leicester Square or
Piccadilly Circus tube. **Open** noon-12.45am Mon-Thur,
Sun; noon-1.45am Fri, Sat. **Main courses** £3.95-£18.
Minimum £7.50 per person from 6pm. **Credit** MC, V.
Map p401 K7.
Golden Harvest is a nice place with friendly staff
and generally fine seafood (the restaurant also
owns the Chinatown fishmonger's in Newport
Place). The two dining floors are simply furnished
but clean and bright.

Kulu Kulu
76 Brewer Street, W1 (7734 7316). Piccadilly
Circus tube. **Open** noon-2.30pm, 5-10pm Mon-Fri;
noon-3.45pm, 5-10pm Sat. **Main courses** £1.20-£3.
Credit JCB, MC, V. **Map** p400 J7.
With its authentic, no-nonsense trappings – from the
traditional patterns on the plates to the stubby, grey,
vinyl-covered rotating stools – Kulu Kulu could
have been transplanted straight from a Tokyo sidestreet. Sushi here is excellent, and the plate rates are
some of the lowest in town.

Melati
21 Great Windmill Street, W1 (7437 2745).
Piccadilly Circus tube. **Open** noon-11.30pm
Mon-Thur, Sun; noon-12.30am Fri, Sat. **Main**
courses £5.95-£7.85. **Credit** AmEx, JCB, MC, V.
Map p401 K7.
Hidden away among the strip bars and sex joints,
Melati is a real Soho institution. The raffia-furnished
dining room tends to fill up in the early evening,
and the extensive menu offers Indonesian and
Malay specialities, plus an excellent-value range
of meal-in-one dishes.

Mr Kong
21 Lisle Street, WC2 (7437 7341/9679).
Leicester Square or Piccadilly Circus tube. **Open**
noon-2.45am daily. **Main courses** £5-£26.
Minimum £7 after 5pm. **Credit** AmEx, DC, JCB,
MC, V. **Map** p401 K7.
The specials list at Mr Kong offers many wonderful
dishes that all too often don't make it on to English-
language menus. We loved the braised belly pork
with yam in hot-pot. There are three dining rooms:
the best of them on the first floor. It's not always
open, but it's worth enquiring.

Tiny treasure **Patogh**. *See p193.*

New Diamond
23 Lisle Street, WC2 (7437 2517/7221). Leicester
Square tube. **Open** noon-3am daily. **Main courses**
£5.80-£22. **Minimum** £10 (from 5pm). **Credit**
AmEx, DC, MC, V. **Map** p401 K7.
Clean, light walls decorated by a few pieces of
Chinese artwork together with trendy spotlighting
make New Diamond a hip contender among
Chinatown's restaurants. The menu is adventurous.

Ramen Seto
19 Kingly Street, W1 (7434 0309). Oxford
Circus tube. **Open** noon-3pm, 6-10pm Mon-Sat.
Main courses £4.50-£6.80. **Credit** JCB, MC, V.
Map p398 J6.
Excellent value, this pocket-sized eat-in and take-
away joint dispenses a standard range of Japanese
cuisine with calm and warmth.

Saigon
45 Frith Street, W1 (7437 7109). Leicester Square
tube. **Open** noon-11.30pm Mon-Sat. **Main courses**
£3-£13.75. **Credit** AmEx, DC, MC, V. **Map** p399 K6.
This oasis of calm in the heart of Soho looks as if it's
leapt from the pages of a Vietnamese Tourist Board
brochure. The food has a reputation for being consistently good if not always dazzling.

Sri Thai Soho
16 Old Compton Street, W1 (7434 3544).
Leicester Square tube. **Open** noon-3pm, 6-11pm
Mon-Sat; 6-10.30pm Sun. **Main courses** £7.50-
£10.95. **Credit** AmEx, DC, MC, V. **Map** p399 K6.

Eat, Drink, Shop

With a great location in the heart of Old Compton Street's pink promenade, Sri Thai Soho is a deceptively large place with unusually cool styling for a Thai restaurant. The menu, put together, by Ken Hom, generally delivers in terms of quality (as you'd expect for these prices).
Branches: 85 London Wall, EC2 (7628 5772); Bucklersbury House, 3 Queen Victoria Street, EC4 (7628 5772).

Modern European

Alastair Little
49 Frith Street, W1 (7734 5183). Tottenham Court Road tube. **Open** noon-3pm, 6-11pm Mon-Fri; 6-11pm Sat; noon-3.30pm Sun. **Main courses** £16-£18. **Credit** AmEx, DC, JCB, MC, V. **Map** p399 K6.
Alastair Little and his chefs succeed in enhancing flavours without unnecessary flourishes. The daily changing menu is both imaginative and impressive – rump of lamb with buttered spring greens was a perfect, simple dish. Relaxed but sophisticated.
Branch: 136A Lancaster Road, W11 (7243 2220).

Sugar Club
21 Warwick Street, W1 (7437 7776/ www.thesugarclub.co.uk). Oxford Circus or Piccadilly Circus tube. **Open** noon-3pm, 6-10.30pm Mon-Sat; 12.30-3pm, 6-10.30pm Sun. **Main courses** £12-£20. **Credit** AmEx, DC, JCB, MC, V. **Map** p400 J7.
There are never any problems with the 'wow' factor here. Digesting the exotic menu requires a leap of faith (and much translation by the staff), but whatever you think of globetrotting, eclectic cuisine, the Sugar Club manages to pull off fabulous feats of culinary fantasy that are worth checking out.

Teatro
93-107 Shaftesbury Avenue, W1 (7494 3040/ www.teatro.co.uk). Leicester Square tube. **Open** noon-3pm, 6-11.45pm Mon-Fri; 6-11.45pm Sat. **Main courses** £12.50-£17. **Credit** AmEx, DC, MC, V. **Map** p399 K6.
A narrow, curving corridor leading to the first-floor dining room offers seductive glimpses of Teatro's louche private bar. The restaurant itself is an evenly proportioned room of muted colours flecked with bright, bold canvases. The cooking can be a bit too stagey but when it's good, it's very good.

Vegetarian & organic

Mildred's
58 Greek Street, W1 (7494 1634). Leicester Square or Tottenham Court Road tube. **Open** noon-11pm Mon-Sat. **Main courses** £5.30-£6.50. **No credit cards. Map** p399 K6.
The crowd packing this small, basic but jolly café know they can rely on substantial portions of decent veggie fare, including an energising 'detox salad'. The less virtuous will also be pleased to hear that the place is licensed.

Covent Garden & St Giles's

Belgian

Belgo Centraal
50 Earlham Street, WC2 (7813 2233/www.belgo-restaurants.com). Covent Garden tube. **Open** noon-10.30pm Mon, Sun; noon-11.30pm Tue-Sat. **Main courses** £8.95-£18.95. **Credit** AmEx, DC, JCB, MC, V. **Map** p399 L6.
The lift at Belgo Centraal is still tirelessly cranking up and down, ferrying hungry hordes towards pots of mussels and bottles of beer. The vast halls now seem a bit gimmicky, but there's still no better place to get mussels, chips and beer in central London.
Branches: 72 Chalk Farm Road, NW1 (7267 0718); 124 Ladbroke Grove, W10 (8982 8400).

Fish

J Sheekey
28-32 St Martin's Court, WC2 (7240 2565). Leicester Square tube. **Open** noon-3pm, 5.30pm-midnight Mon-Sat; noon-3.30pm, 5.30pm-midnight Sun. **Main courses** £9.75-£24.50. **Credit** AmEx, DC, MC, V. **Map** p401 K7.
Encompassing four small rooms, this is a discreet and intimate restaurant with soft oak-panelled walls and plush upholstery. The menu is market-fresh, and the speciality fish pie is exceptional. If you can't secure a table at the Ivy, this fine sister restaurant is a great alternative.

Fish & chips

Rock & Sole Plaice
47 Endell Street, WC2 (7836 3785). Covent Garden tube. **Open** 11.30am-10pm Mon-Sat; 11.30am-9pm Sun. **Main courses** £7-£13. **Credit** JCB, MC, V. **Map** p399 L6.
This is a classy central chippie with a downstairs dining room and lots of sloping outdoor tables beneath a fine array of hanging baskets. Our latest visit found the fish – haddock and rock salmon – to be the freshest we've tasted for some time. Mushy peas are the real thing, too.

French

The Admiralty
Somerset House, The Strand, WC2 (7845 4646/ www.gruppo.co.uk). Embankment or Temple tube/ Charing Cross tube/rail. **Open** noon-2.45pm, 6-10.45pm Mon-Sat; noon-2.45pm Sun. **Main courses** £17.50-£23.50. **Credit** AmEx, DC, JCB, MC, V. **Map** p401 L7.
Situated in the lovely Somerset House (*see p97*), the Admiralty was the deserving winner of the *Time Out* Best New Restaurant award in 2001. Set up by Oliver Peyton, responsible for several great London restaurants, and designed by Andy Martin

The lush and lovely **Momo**. *See p196.*

and jeweller Solange Azagury Partridge, it's as breathtaking as the building in which it's set; rich colours are enhanced by beautiful chandeliers and a few stuffed animals. But the food doesn't pale into insignificance, with Morgan Meunier's sophisticated but ungimmicky dishes establishing expectations that are more than met.

Modern European

The Ivy
1 West Street, WC2 (7836 4751). Covent Garden or Leicester Square tube. **Open** noon-3pm, 5.30pm-midnight Mon-Sat; noon-3.30pm, 5.30pm-midnight Sun. **Main courses** £8.75-£21.75. **Credit** AmEx, DC, JCB, MC, V. **Map** p399 K6.
If you ever get over the booking hurdle (do it six months in advance even for an unfashionable slot) and actually step inside theatreland's favourite restaurant, you'll find a long and flexible menu (weekly specials slot in among a constant list of salads, soups, seafood, roasts, grills and so on), plus plenty of celebs for rubbernecking. Deeply glam.

Oriental

Thai Pot
1 Bedfordbury, WC2 (7379 4580/www.thaipot. co.uk). Covent Garden tube/Charing Cross tube/rail. **Open** noon-3pm, 5.30-11.15pm Mon-Sat. **Main courses** £6.50-£10. **Credit** AmEx, DC, MC, V. **Map** p401 L7.

Noisy and bustling, Thai Pot has high ceilings adorned with plaster mouldings and walls rag-rolled cream on blue, hung with black and white photos. The excellent menu contains a useful guideline (little chilli symbols) as to the spiciness of each dish. The steamed dumplings are recommended.
Branches: 5 Princes Street, W1 (7499 3333); 21-3 Cockspur Street, SW1 (7839 4000).

Vegetarian & organic

Food For Thought
31 Neal Street, WC2 (7836 9072/0239). Covent Garden tube. **Open** 9.30-11.30am, noon-8.30pm Mon-Sat; noon-5pm Sun. **Main courses** £2.50-£5.80. **Minimum** £2.50 (noon-3pm, 6-7.30pm). **No credit cards. Map** p399 L6.
This pioneering veggie wholefood joint might not deliver any surprises, but the perennial queues on its narrow stairs are testament to its enduring appeal. Intimate and handy Neal Street's shopping.

World Food Café
Neal's Yard Dining Room, First floor, 14 Neal's Yard, WC2 (7379 0298). Covent Garden or Leicester Square tube. **Open** 11.30am-3.45pm Mon-Fri; 11.30am-5pm Sat. **Main courses** £4.55-£7.95. **Minimum** £5 (noon-2pm Mon-Fri; 11.30am-5pm Sat). **Credit** MC, V. **Map** p399 L6.
The beautifully light, high-ceilinged room with its view across Neal's Yard wins you over before you even begin with the food. But when you do, things only get better. The juices and lassis are also superb.

Going for broke

True story. In summer 2001 a small party of businessmen spent £44,000 on a meal at Pétrus restaurant in St James's. This is a shade more than the average London diner might consider blowing on food and fine wine, but the need for a splurge comes to us all now and again. Next time you feel like slipping into a fancy frock or getting some soup stains on your favourite tie, bear in mind some of the following restaurants.

But first, a few pointers. Most of these restaurants have set menus (lunch and dinner) that can dramatically reduce the cost of a meal (while, of course, limiting your choice). For a three-course set menu, expect to pay anything up to £35 at lunch and £65 in the evening. In terms of wine, the choice is usually vast, and you'll need to hunt around the list for the cheaper bottles (don't expect much help from the sommelier). Lastly, be aware that booking a table can be an infernally convoluted experience, with diners often having to comply with time slots dictated by the restaurant.

Perhaps the best known of London's high-rolling dining rooms are **La Tante Claire** (see p203) and **Gordon Ramsay** (see p205). Both Ramsay and Pierre Koffmann (La Tante Claire) are highly accomplished cooks and continue to produce superlative food. Fish lovers should head for **One-O-one** (101 William Street, SW1, 7290 7101), where meticulously sourced and expertly cooked seafood is the main thrust of the menu.

John Burton-Race at the Landmark (222 Marylebone Road, NW1, 7631 8000) is the first London venture of the former chef at L'Ortolan in Berkshire, while **Le Gavroche** (43 Upper Brook Street, W1, 7408 0881) has a little more history behind it, plus the added bonus of Michel Roux manning the stoves. Further west, the sunny **Aix en Provence** (129 Holland Park Avenue, W11, 7221 5411) has replaced the former Room at the Halcyon; in the kitchen Nigel Davies is turning out some highly impressive food.

A calmer, more sophisticated spot than the **Capital** (22-4 Basil Street, SW3, 7589 5171) is hard to imagine; Eric Chavot's menu continues to impress. In Chelsea, **Aubergine** (11 Park Walk, SW10, 7352 3449) is still home to some incendiary cooking, though the decor is as dull as ever. If you're feeling really flush, **Mju** (The Millennium Knightsbridge, 17 Sloane Street, SW1, 7201 6330; pictured) provides fabulous French-Japanese food.

Westminster

British

Shepherd's

Marsham Court, Marsham Street, SW1 (7834 9552). Pimlico or Westminster tube. **Open** 12.30-2.45pm, 6.30-11pm Mon-Fri. **Main courses** £18.50. **Credit** AmEx, DC, JCB, MC, V. **Map** p401 K10.

Behind a relatively anonymous exterior, Shepherd's continues unabated in its role as quality caterer to Westminster's political animals (expect to see a mix of ministers, backbenchers, journos and the occasional peer). The yellow walls display august prints and cartoons, while the food itself is reliably good.

Indian

The Cinnamon Club

The Old Westminster Library, Great Smith Street, SW1 (7222 2555/www.cinnamonclub.com). St James's Park tube. **Open** 7.30-10am, noon-3pm, 6-10.30pm Mon-Fri; 6-10.30pm Sat; noon-4pm Sun. **Set lunch** £15 two courses; £18 three courses. **Credit** MC, V. **Map** p401 K9.

This former library (books still line the gallery) has a slightly sombre feel and can get noisy with guffawing besuited men, but the cooking – inventive Indianis – masterfully spiced and presented. Don't miss the ambrosial desserts.

Quilon

St James's Court Hotel, 41 Buckingham Gate, SW1 (7821 1899). St James's Park tube. **Open** noon-2.30pm, 6-11pm Mon-Fri; 6-11pm Sat. **Main courses** £11.50-£19.95. **Credit** AmEx, DC, MC, V. **Map** p400 J9.

Pronounced 'Koy-lon', this is an upmarket Keralan restaurant serving a short but enticing menu (scallops in a potato basket and chicken chilli fry are sample dishes). The accomplished cooking – along with attentive, unobtrusive service and spacious, serene surroundings – make for a civilised meal worthy of a special celebration.

Knightsbridge & South Kensington

Indian

Zaika

1 Kensington High Street, W8 (7795 6533). High Street Kensington tube. **Open** noon-2.30pm, 6.30-10.30pm Mon-Fri, Sun; 6.30-10.30pm Sat. **Main courses** £9.95-£21.50. **Credit** AmEx, MC, V. **Map** p394 C8.

Although relocated from Fulham to L'Anis' old site, Vineet Bhatia's Zaika has retained its staff, class and innovative menu. The decor is an impressive marriage of old and new, the cooking imaginative and sometimes exceptional.

Modern European

The Fifth Floor

Harvey Nichols, SW1 (7235 5250). Knightsbridge tube. **Open** *Bar* 11am-11pm Mon-Sat; noon-6pm Sun. *Restaurant* noon-3pm, 6-11pm Mon-Fri; noon-3.30pm, 6-11pm Sat; noon-3.30pm Sun. **Main courses** £16-£24. **Credit** AmEx, DC, JCB, MC, V. **Map** p397 F9.

This airy, light restaurant at the top of Harvey Nichols has well-spaced tables that offer a more inviting alternative to the frantic pace of the in-store café and sushi bar. Standards in the kitchen are high and the wine list has some great wines by the glass. Views on two sides – over the shop and street – facilitate some A-grade peoplewatching. Staff are attentive without being fawning.

La Tante Claire

The Berkeley, Wilton Place, SW1 (7823 2003). Knightsbridge tube. **Open** 12.30-2pm, 7-11pm Mon-Fri; 7-11pm Sat. **Main courses** £23-£35. **Minimum** £50 dinner. **Credit** AmEx, DC, MC, V. **Map** p400 G8.

The decor here is light and almost feminine, while the food displays a phenomenal lightness and fuss-free brilliance that's rarely bettered in London. The wine list offers a whole spectrum of goodies to suit all pockets, and sommeliers expertly offer just as much advice as is needed.

Oriental

Vong

The Berkeley, Wilton Place, SW1 (7235 1010/ www.jean-georges.com). Hyde Park Corner or Knightsbridge tube. **Open** noon-2.30pm, 6-11.30pm Mon-Fri; 11.30am-2pm, 6-11.30pm Sat; 11.30am-2pm, 6-10.30pm Sun. **Main courses** £16-£32. **Credit** AmEx, DC, JCB, MC, V. **Map** p400 G8.

Vong's dining room is a sunken recess of vaguely oriental opulence; its helpful staff seem knowledgeable about the excellent French/Thai fusion dishes on the menu and the wine list. Even if you're not dining on expenses (which many customers are), this is worth a visit.

Spanish

Cambio de Tercio

163 Old Brompton Road, SW5 (7244 8970). Gloucester Road tube. **Open** 12.30-2.30pm, 7-11.30pm Mon-Sat; 12.30-2.30pm, 7-11pm Sun. **Main courses** £13.50-£15.50. **Credit** AmEx, MC, V. **Map** p396 C11.

Without any major hype, Cambio de Tercio has become a showcase for some of the best sophisticated modern Spanish cuisine in London. Striking but well-balanced flavours, memorable sauces and expertly sourced ingredients are trademarks. The decor is stylish despite occasional cod Spanishery, and service is very attentive.

Belgravia & Pimlico

British

Boisdale

15 Eccleston Street, SW1 (7730 6922/www.boisdale. co.uk). Victoria tube/rail. **Open** *Bar* 8am-midnight daily. *Restaurant* noon-2.30pm, 7-11pm Mon-Fri; 7-11pm Sat. **Main courses** £15-£21.50. **Credit** AmEx, DC, MC, V. **Map** p400 H10.
This Scottish-inspired restaurant has a small front dining room, a covered open space, a cosy back bar, and a large open-plan restaurant/bar where jazz is played. The restaurant is excellent but it's worth a visit just for the superior bar menu and jazz.

French

Roussillon

16 St Barnabas Street, SW1 (7730 5550/ www.roussillon.co.uk). Sloane Square tube. **Open** noon-2.30pm, 6.30-10.30pm Mon-Fri; 6.30-10.30pm Sat. **Set lunch** £15 two courses; £18 three courses. **Set dinner** £29 two courses; £35 three courses; £35 (vegetarian), £42 four courses; £50 seven courses. **Credit** AmEx, JCB, MC, V. **Map** p400 G11.
The cooking here is exquisite, especially when it comes to vegetables, yet portions are tiny. The setting – two smart rooms – is pleasant, and if you can track down an affordable bottle of wine on the list, you should be in for a memorable meal.

Italian

Zafferano

15 Lowndes Street, SW1 (7235 5800). Knightsbridge tube. **Open** noon-2.30pm, 7-11pm Mon-Sat; noon-2.30pm, 7-10.30pm Sun. **Set lunch** *Mon-Fri* £19.50 two courses; £23.50 three courses. **Set meal** (dinner, Sat-Sun lunch) £29.50 two courses; £35.50 three courses; £39.50 four courses. **Credit** AmEx, DC, MC, V. **Map** p397 F9.
Pure class and deservedly busy, Zafferano easily outstrips rivals such as the River Café and Assaggi (*see p215*) by the unassuming elegance of its service. The cooking, too, is delightful. Prices are competitive, particularly at lunch.

Oriental

Hunan

51 Pimlico Road, SW1 (7730 5712). Sloane Square tube. **Open** noon-2.30pm, 6-11pm Mon-Sat. **Main courses** £7-£28. **Credit** AmEx, MC, V. **Map** p400 G11.
Hunan, named after the central Chinese province that is famed (like Sichuan) for its spicy and fragrant food, is a breath of fresh air in the stifling Cantonese atmosphere of London's Chinese dining, offering dishes you won't find anywhere else in the city.

Nahm

Halkin Hotel, Halkin Street, SW1 (7333 1234). Hyde Park Corner tube. **Open** noon-2.30pm, 7-10.30pm Mon-Fri; 7-10.30pm Sat, Sun. **Main courses** £24-£29. **Set lunch** £23 three courses. **Set dinner** £47 five courses. **Credit** AmEx, DC, JCB, MC, V. **Map** p400 G9.
Chef David Thompson runs this excellent operation, capturing the styles and flavours of Thai cooking perfectly. Though the menu is confusing and the prices hard to swallow, this is easily the best Thai food in Britain, and the setting is elegant.

Chelsea

Indian

Vama

438 King's Road, SW10 (7351 4118/www.vama. co.uk). Sloane Square tube then 11, 22, 211 bus. **Open** 12.30-3pm, 6.30-11.30pm Mon-Sat; 12.30-3pm, 6.30-10.30pm Sun. **Main courses** £6.35-£18.50. **Credit** AmEx, JCB, MC, V. **Map** p397 D12.
Vama is a cut above the numerous other Indian restaurants on this stretch of the King's Road. The decor (beiges, browns and chunky wood furniture) is stylish, the food delicious and the service friendly, efficient and unflappable.

Modern European

Bibendum

Michelin House, 81 Fulham Road, SW3 (7581 5817/www.bibendum.co.uk). South Kensington tube. **Open** noon-2.30pm, 7-11pm Mon-Fri; 12.30-3pm, 7-11pm Sat; 12.30-3pm, 7-10.30pm Sun. **Main courses** £15.50-£26.50. **Credit** AmEx, DC, MC, V. **Map** p397 E10.
Lunch is a fine time to enjoy this Conran flagship. The surroundings – in the restored Michelin House – are as handsome as ever, but over-formal service, steeply priced food and a largely corporate clientele add starch to proceedings in the evenings.

Gordon Ramsay

68-9 Royal Hospital Road, SW3 (7352 4441/3334). Sloane Square tube. **Open** noon-2pm, 6.45-11pm Mon-Fri. **Set lunch** £35 three courses. **Set dinner** £65 three courses (from à la carte menu); £80 seven courses. **Credit** AmEx, DC, MC, V. **Map** p397 F12.
There's a new sense of lightness and informality chez Ramsay, but booking times are still as rigid and prices are, of course, high. That said, the cooking here is world class, with excellent ingredients. *See p192* **Look who's cooking**.

Oriental

Itsu

118 Draycott Avenue, SW3 (7584 5522/ www.itsu.com). South Kensington tube/49 bus. *Bar* **Open** 6pm-midnight Mon-Sat; 6-10pm Sun.

Eat, Drink, Shop

Restaurant **Open** noon-11pm Mon-Sat; noon-10pm Sun. **Main courses** £2.50-£4.50. **Credit** AmEx, MC, V. **Map** p397 E10.

Someone has to keep the Sloanes in sushi, and this stylish, spacious restaurant seems to be making a handsome living from doing just that. Like its clientele, Itsu's sushi is modish and well turned out, featuring luxurious ingredients.

Other

Cactus Blue

86 Fulham Road, SW3 (7823 7858/ www.cactusblue.com). South Kensington tube. **Bar Open** 5.30-11.45pm Mon-Fri; noon-11pm Sat; noon-10.30pm Sun. *Restaurant* **Open** 5.30-11.45pm Mon-Fri; noon-11.45pm Sat; noon-11pm Sun. **Main courses** £9.95-£14.95. **Credit** AmEx, DC, MC, V. **Map** p397 D11.

With its spacious, cool interior and modern-day Western theme, Cactus Blue is a slightly bizarre but happy meld of west Texas and west London. The cooking imaginative and well executed but it doesn't cost a packet, ensuring that the place is always crowded. The cocktail list probably helps too.

Nikita's

65 Ifield Road, SW10 (7352 6326). Earl's Court or West Brompton tube. **Open** 7.30-10.30pm Tue-Sat. **Main courses** £9.50-£14.95. **Credit** AmEx, JCB, MC, V. **Map** p396 C12.

Nikita's small bar is an atmospheric spot for a rendezvous, with a great line-up of vodkas. The basement dining room is a more mellow affair, with its twilight lighting and Byzantine motifs. Food (borscht, blinis, stroganoff and the like) can be spot on and the staff know how to look after you.

North London

Mediterranean

Halepi

48-50 Belsize Lane, Belsize Park, NW3 (7431 5855). Belsize Park or Swiss Cottage tube. **Open** 6-11pm Mon-Fri; noon-3pm, 6-11pm Sat; noon-11pm Sun. **Main courses** £7.90-£24. **Credit** AmEx, DC, JCB, MC, V.

A basket of loose bulghur wheat sits by the door at this popular restaurant, forming part of the arty,

The best dim sum

The Cantonese term 'dim sum' means something approximating 'to touch the heart' and is used to refer to the vast array of dumplings and other titbits that southern Chinese people like to eat with their tea for breakfast or at lunchtime. London's many Chinese restaurants provide some of the best opportunities in the world to sample dim sum. It's the perfect chance for novices to build upon their appreciation of Chinese food, and it's virtually impossible to rack up a bill of more than £15 per head. Why not risk £2 for a taste of steamed chicken's feet in black bean sauce, or a cold coconut soup with drifting tapioca pearls.

Dim sum is served from midday through the afternoon (never after 6pm); any restaurants offering so-called dim sum on evening menus are just referring to a few lonely dumplings provided as starters, not to the whole 'yum cha' tea ritual). Weekend dim sum lunches are noisy, boisterous occasions, so they are great for children, but note that adventurous toddlers and hot dumpling trollies are not a happy combination, and that vegetarians are likely to be very limited in terms of choice, as most snacks contain meat or seafood.

For a guide to the snacks you're likely to encounter in dim sum restaurants, see the *Time Out Eating & Drinking Guide 2002*.

New World

1 Gerrard Place, Chinatown, W1, 7734 0396). Leicester Square or Piccadilly Circus. **Open** 11am-11.45pm Mon-Sat; 11am-11pm Sun. Dim sum 11am-6pm daily. **Main courses** £4.35-£8.80, £1.70-£3.50 dim sum. **Credit** AmEx, DC, JCB, MC, V. **Map** p401 K7.

This cheerful restaurant is one of only two places in London to serve dim sum Hong Kong-style, from circulating trollies.

Golden Dragon

28-9 Gerrard Street, Chinatown, W1 (7734 2763). Leicester Square or Piccadilly Circus tube. **Open** noon-11.30pm Mon-Thur; noon-midnight Fri, Sat; 11am-11pm Sun. Dim sum noon-5pm Mon-Sat; 11am-5pm Sun. **Main courses** £6-£25, £1.90-£3.50 dim sum. Minimum £10. **Credit** AmEx, DC, MC, V. **Map** p401 K7.

Dim sum at this huge Chinatown restaurant is thought by many to be among the best in town.

Hakkasan

8 Hanway Place, Fitzrovia, W1 (7907 1888). Tottenham Court Road tube. **Open** noon-2.30pm, 6-11.30pm Mon-Fri; noon-4.30pm, 6-11.30pm Sat, Sun. **Main courses** £5.90-£40, £3.50-£16 dim sum. **Credit** AmEx, MC, V. **Map** p399 K5.

rarefied decor. The food is tasty and authentically Greek, with such dishes as pork stew with kolokassi (taro root) featuring on the menu.

Iznik

19 Highbury Park, Highbury, N5 (7354 5697).
Highbury & Islington tube/rail/4, 19, 236 bus.
Open 10am-4pm, 6.30pm-midnight Mon-Fri;
6.30pm-midnight Sat, Sun. **Main courses**
£7.25-£9.50. **Credit** MC, V.
Iznik continues to set high standards for northern Turkish food. The Ottoman-inspired menu delivers strong, accomplished flavours; the room (decorated with Iznik and Beykoz-style ceramics) is pretty and clean; and service is personal and efficient. Full of well-behaved Arsenal fans before home games.

Modern European

Granita

127 Upper Street, Islington, N1 (7226 3222). Angel
tube/Highbury & Islington tube/rail. **Open** 6.30-
10.30pm Tue; 12.30-2.30pm, 6.30-10.30pm Wed-Sat;
12.30-3pm, 6.30-10.30pm Sun. **Main courses**
£11.50-£15. **Credit** MC, V. **Map** p402 O3.

Genre-bender **Hakkasan**.

The latest brainchild of Alan Yau, the creator of the much admired and imitated Wagamama (*see p193*), Hakkasan has wowed the critics

Granita on a Saturday night is just a little too noisy. The bare floor and tables and general minimal decor mean that, even without background music, the volume sounds like it's on high. The food, however, is generally way ahead of most restaurants in N1.

Other

Afghan Kitchen

35 Islington Green, Islington, N1 (7359 8019).
Angel tube. **Open** noon-3.30pm, 5.30-11pm Tue-Sat.
Main courses £4.50-£6. **No credit cards**.
Map p402 O2.
This popular bare-walled Islington staple is very small, with two communal wooden tables downstairs and four upstairs, so expect to queue. The unchanging and limited menu offers tasty dishes.

Mango Room

10 Kentish Town Road, Camden, NW1 (7482
5065). Camden Town tube. **Open** 6pm-midnight
Mon; noon-3pm, 6pm-midnight Tue-Sun. **Main**
courses £9-£12. **Credit** MC, V.
Despite its rather seamy location, Mango Room is the next best thing to a fortnight in the Caribbean with its fabulous decor and funky Chinese food. Dim sum such as sesame-scattered triangular pastries filled with venison instead of pork are superb.

Harbour City

46 Gerrard Street, Chinatown, W1 (7439
7859). Leicester Square or Piccadilly Circus
tube. **Open** noon-11.30pm Mon-Thur; noon-
midnight Fri, Sat; 10.30am-10.30pm Sun.
Dim sum noon-5pm Mon-Sat; 11am-5pm Sun.
Main courses £4.50- £18, £1.80-£2.80 dim
sum. Minimum £5. **Credit** AmEx, DC, MC, V.
Map p401 K7.
Comparatively quiet for a Chinatown restaurant, Harbour City has delightful dim sum. Of the three dining rooms, the nicest is on the bright, airy first floor.

Royal China

13 Queensway, Bayswater, W2 (7221
2535). Queensway tube. **Open** noon-11pm
Mon-Thur; noon-11.30pm Fri, Sat; 11am-
10pm Sun. Dim sum noon-5pm Mon-Sat;
11am-5pm Sun. **Main courses** £6-£9,
£1.90-£2.70 dim sum. **Credit** AmEx, DC,
MC, V. **Map** p394 C7.
Fantastic dim sum are served at this original branch, which resembles a large, black, shiny lacquered box. *See also p211.*

Eat, Drink, Shop

Itsu delivers sushi and style. *See p205.*

Two's company

You know the kind of place: candles dripping wax on the tables, romantic corners and window seats, conversation burbling gently in the background. Yep, that'll be the bistro. It's the ultimate cliché in the book of lurve, home to first dates, torrid affairs and golden weddings, as well as the preserve of intense young men with complicated beards or girlfriends getting together for some gossip. But when it's done well, the neighbourhood bistro is hard to beat. Listed below are some of London's finest.

Andrew Edmunds (46 Lexington Street, W1, 7437 5708) is a discreet little Soho bistro with a simple, dimly lit wooden interior enlivened by bunches of flowers and a menu of excellent Modern European cooking. Further west, **Julie's** (135-7 Portland Road, W11, 7229 8331) sits modestly on a quiet Holland Park corner, which it shares with the restaurant of the same name.

Another cosy, intimate spot is **Odette's Wine Bar** at the bottom of Primrose Hill (130 Regent's Park Road, NW1, 7722 5388), where every inch of the cellar wall space is occupied by paintings, prints and photos. Alternatively, for some highly authentic Breton bistro action, head down to Richmond to **Chez Lindsay** (11 Hill Rise, Richmond, Surrey, 8948 7473), which does excellent galettes, crêpes and seafood dishes.

Also down south are **Gastro** (67 Venn Street, SW4, 7627 0222) and **Le Chardon** (65 Lordship Lane, SE22, 8299 1921) – both are classic examples of popular local *bistros du coin*. Closer to the centre of things are the quaint little **Bar du Marché** opposite hectic Berwick Street market (19 Berwick Street, W1, 7734 4606) and, towards the City, **Les Trois Garçons** (1 Club Row, E1, 7613 1924; *pictured*), where eccentric decor and listed pub premises are a delightful culture clash.

For a perfect date, combine a visit to the Mile End stalwart **Frocks** (95 Lauriston Road, E9, 8986 3161) with a stroll in nearby Victoria Park, or drop in on the Columbia Road flower market on a Sunday morning before settling into the snug interior or on to the gorgeous patio of **Perennial** (110-112 Columbia Road, E2, 7739 4556).

– its slightly 'rough around the edges' but vibrantly coloured interior is a blast of sunshine. The menu offers high-quality West Indian cuisine.

Singapore Garden
83 Fairfax Road, Belsize Park, NW6 (7624 8233). Swiss Cottage tube/South Hampstead rail. **Open** noon-2.45pm, 6-10.45pm Mon-Thur, Sun; noon-2.45pm, 6-11.15pm Fri, Sat. **Main courses** £5.50-£27.50. **Minimum** £10. **Credit** AmEx, DC, JCB, MC, V. **Map** p395 F5.
Situated down a quiet west London sidestreet, this well-established restaurant attracts an affluent, multicultural crowd. The cream walls, bright oil paintings and jazz soundtrack create a cool backdrop for the lively and authentic Singaporean food.

Solly's
148A Golders Green Road, Golders Green, NW11 (ground floor & takeaway 8455 2121/first floor 8455 0004). Golders Green tube. **Open** *Ground floor* 11am-11pm Mon-Thur, Sun; 11am-3pm Fri; 1hr after Sabbath-1am Sat. *First floor* 6.30-11.30pm Mon-Thur; noon-11pm Sun; winter also 1hr after Sabbath-11pm Sat. **Main courses** £8.50-£15. **Credit** AmEx, MC, V.
Sadly, Solly died early in 2001, but such is the smooth operation of this well-established place that customers still crowd the downstairs bar and casual dining area during the day. The menu of quality Jewish food is the same in both venues.

Vegetarian & organic

Heartstone
106 Parkway, Camden, NW1 (7485 7744). Camden Town tube. **Open** 8am-9.30pm Tue-Sat; 10am-4pm Sun. **Main courses** £8.50-£15. **Credit** MC, V.
The menu at this sparklingly new mauve-tinted café, which was the winner of the Best Organic Restaurant category in the *Time Out* 2001 Eating & Drinking Awards, runs the gamut from innovatively flavoured salads through to a classy version of omelette and chips, and marinated chicken with tahini and red root coleslaw. Reasonable prices and a friendly atmosphere are added bonuses.

East London

Indian

Café Spice Namaste
16 Prescot Street, Whitechapel, E1 (7488 9242). Aldgate East or Tower Hill tube/Tower Gateway DLR. **Open** noon-3pm, 6.15-10.30pm Mon-Fri; 6.30-10.30pm Sat. **Main courses** £9.95-£15.95. **Credit** AmEx, DC, JCB, MC, V. **Map** p405 S7.
This former magistrate's court has two large dining rooms decked out in striking peach, cyan and magenta banners, separated by a central bar and

Eat, Drink, Shop

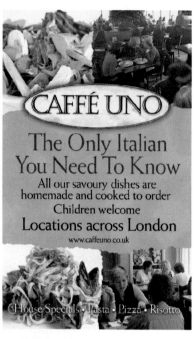

reception area. The excellent menu is forever pushing against the boundaries of what's deemed acceptable for an 'Indian' restaurant, as well as nosing out regional specialities. The highly professional staff know – and clearly love – their stuff.

Mediterranean

The Real Greek
15 Hoxton Market, Hoxton, N1 (7739 8212/ www.therealgreek.co.uk). Old Street tube/rail/26, 48, 55, 149, 242 bus. **Open** noon-3pm, 5.30-10.30pm Mon-Sat. **Main courses** £9-£16.90. **Credit** MC, V. **Map** p403 R3.
This was the restaurant that featured in the climactic fighting scene in the film of *Bridget Jones's Diary*. The superb modern Greek food here is not only tasty but fun and inventive (though prone at times to a touch too much experimentation). If you're used to thinking that Greek means kebabs, you'll find the prices are a touch high.

Oriental

Green Papaya
191 Mare Street, Hackney, E8 (8985 5486). Bethnal Green tube/rail/48, 55, D6, 253, 277 bus. **Open** 11am-midnight Mon-Sat; 11am-11.30pm Sun. **Main courses** £4.50-£8. **Credit** MC, V.
Green Papaya has a relaxed charm, enhanced by a large garden with heaters, lively groups of Vietnamese regulars and helpful but unobtrusive service. The menu, a mix of North and South Vietnamese dishes, is unusual and alluring. The prawn and sweet potato fritters and the barbecued chicken with satay sauce keep us coming back, along with an exceptionally good banoffi pie.

Royal China
30 Westferry Circus, Canary Wharf, E14 (7719 0888). Canary Wharf tube/DLR/Westferry DLR. **Open** noon-11pm Mon-Thur; noon-11.30pm Fri, Sat; 11am-10pm Sun; (dim sum) noon-5pm daily. **Main courses** £6-£40, dim sum £1.90. **Credit** AmEx, DC, JCB, MC, V.
This latest branch of the expanding Royal China empire has a fabulous riverside location, with plate-glass windows offering views of the broad sweep of the Thames. The atmosphere is generally brisk and cheerful, the food impeccable.
Branches: 40 Baker Street, W1 (7487 4688); 3 Chelverton Road, SW15 (8788 0907); 13 Queensway W2 (7221 2535); 68 Queen's Grove, NW8 (7586 4280).

Viet Hoa
70-72 Kingsland Road, Shoreditch, E2 (7729 8293). Old Street tube/26, 48, 55, 67, 149, 242, 243 bus. **Open** noon-3.30pm, 5.30-11pm daily. **Main courses** £2.15-£6.90. **Credit** MC, V. **Map** p403 R3.
This popular café continues to pack in a huge influx of non-Vietnamese Hoxton and Shoreditch hipsters alongside a smattering of Vietnamese families.

Expect checked tablecloths and spacious canteen seating upstairs, waiters in bow-ties and waistcoats downstairs. Food is more than decent, though we have found the service sluggish on occasion.

Other

Arkansas Café
Unit 12, Old Spitalfields Market, 107 Commercial Street, Spitalfields, E1 (7377 6999). Aldgate East tube/Liverpool Street tube/rail. **Open** noon-2.30pm Mon-Fri; noon-4pm Sun; dinner by arrangement. **Main courses** £3.50-£13.50. **Credit** DC, MC, V. **Map** p403 R5.
Meat lovers are in paradise at this quirky place in the midst of Old Spitalfields Market. Sit on broken old chairs or a church pew and tuck into fabulously juicy barbecued steak, chicken or even a whole pig (evenings only, with advance notice).

Little Georgia
2 Broadway Market, London Fields, E8 (7249 9070). Bethnal Green tube then 106 bus/26, 48, 55, 236 bus. **Open** 6.30-10pm Tue-Thur; 6.30-10.30pm Fri, Sat; 1-3pm Sun. **Main courses** £8-£12. **Credit** MC, JCB, V.
Huge windows, claret walls and varnished floorboards give a pleasing impression of space in a dining room that also incorporates all the trappings one might expect in a Georgian restaurant. The fine traditional cooking keeps the regulars loyal in this newly buzzing neighbourhood.

South London

French

Chez Bruce
2 Bellevue Road, Wandsworth Common, SW17 (8672 0114). Wandsworth Common rail. **Open** noon-2pm, 7-10.30pm Mon-Thur; noon-2pm, 6.30-10.30pm Fri; 12.30-2.30pm, 6.30-10.30pm Sat; 12.30-3pm Sun. **Set lunch** (Mon-Sat) £21.50 three courses; (Sun) £25 three courses. **Set dinner** £30 three courses. **Credit** AmEx, DC, JCB, MC, V.
Great global wines, honestly priced and simply presented, and Bruce Poole's sensational (mainly French) cooking are two good reasons to come here. For those in need of further encouragement, the rustic dining room is relaxed and convivial.

Indian

Kastoori
188 Upper Tooting Road, Tooting, SW17 (8767 7027). Tooting Broadway tube. **Open** 6-10.30pm Mon, Tue; 12.30-2.30pm, 6-10.30pm Wed-Sun. **Main courses** £3.95-£5.95. **Credit** MC, V.
Despite its lurid decor, Kastoori has been a mainstay of Tooting's restaurant scene for more than a decade. The food is a 'pure vegetarian' mix of Gujarati and East African Asian cuisine.

Eat, Drink, Shop

Italian

Enoteca Turi

*28 Putney High Street, Putney, SW15 (8785
4449). East Putney or Putney Bridge tube/Putney
rail/14 bus.* **Open** 12.30-2.30pm, 7-11pm Mon-Fri;
7-11pm Sat. **Main courses** £9.50-£13.50. **Credit**
AmEx, DC, MC, V.

This bright modern restaurant would sit perfectly
well in the West End but has the advantage of
Putney prices. The pleasing seasonal menu is supplemented by a list of daily specials, and there's a
lengthy, helpfully annotated wine list.

Modern European

The Glasshouse

*14 Station Parade, Kew, Surrey (8940 6777).
Kew Gardens tube/rail.* **Open** noon-2.30pm,
7-10.30pm Mon-Thur; noon-2.30pm, 6.30-10.30pm
Fri, Sat; 12.30-2.45pm, 7.30-10pm Sun. **Set lunch**
£19.50 three courses; (Sun) £23.50 three courses. **Set
dinner** £27.50 three courses. **Credit** AmEx, MC, V.

Bright and airy thanks to its wide, windowed
frontage and its clever lighting, the Glasshouse
manages to combine modern elegance with a high

standard of traditional style and service. The food
runs to such extravagances as juicy roast foie gras
with fig and port tatin.

Other

Brixtonian Havana Club

*11 Beehive Place, Brixton, SW9 (7924 9262/
www.brixtonian.co.uk). Brixton tube/rail.* **Open**
Bar noon-2am daily. *Restaurant* noon-3pm,
7-10.30pm Mon-Thur, Sun; noon-3pm, 7-11pm Fri,
Sat. **Main courses** £12.50. **Credit** MC, V.

A smart loft conversion with bare brickwork, wood-
en beams and painted glass. The menu combines
Caribbean heritage (focusing on a particular island
each month) with global influences. Lots of rums.

Canyon

*Riverside, near Richmond Bridge, Richmond, Surrey
(8948 2944). Richmond tube/rail.* **Open** noon-4pm,
6-11pm Mon-Fri; 11am-4pm, 6-11pm Sat, Sun.
Main courses £9-£16. **Credit** AmEx, MC, V.

The riverside location makes Canyon one of the best
spots in London for alfresco dining, while the modernist building, with its pebble garden, is like a little slice of California. The adventurous modern
American menu (brunch at weekends) is impressive.

Who he? Sivadas Sreedharan

The aromas of coconut and chilli waft
delicately through the air, smiling waiters
glide graciously through the rooms with cups
of chai in hand, and Indian music tinkles
softly in the background. Rasa Samudra (*see
p190*), the colourful and welcoming Keralan
restaurant on Charlotte Street, is something
of a London institution.

'Living in London now is like living in a
different country compared to when I first
came here a decade ago,' says Rasa's 36-
year-old owner Sivadas Sreedharan (or Das,
as he's known). Das arrived in London from
Kerala in southern India in 1991 and opened
his first restaurant, specialising in South
Indian vegetarian cuisine, in Stoke Newington
in 1994. Since then, he says, 'Londoners
have gone from being indifferent to being
tremendously interested in and helpful
towards outsiders. On the whole, different
religions and races co-exist here and racial
issues are not so divisive.'

Although Das worked in a hotel in Delhi
before coming to London, he still felt very
much a 'village boy' when he arrived. 'I had
a complete culture shock; Asian culture was
only just starting to flourish here, and people
had very fixed ideas about Indian food and

culture. But it's been increasingly easy to do
what I want here. Education about different
cultures and acceptance of ethnic groups
have helped. Food also has a strong part to
play in promoting intercultural relationships.'

In addition to owning four restaurants
(Rasa, Rasa W1, Rasa Samudra and
Rasa Travancore; call 7249 0344 or see
www.rasarestaurants.com for details), Das is
the author of two books and makes frequent
TV appearances. He's also behind the annual
Kerala Food Festival, held in London, and
hopes to open a cooking school here, as well
as new restaurants in New York in the future.

Does the man never rest? Only, it seems,
to indulge in his other great passion – cricket.
'My favourite place in London is Lord's cricket
ground,' he says. 'I like England winning,
except when India are playing.' He's also
a big fan of London's markets, especially New
Spitalfields Market, where he used to go once
a week at 3am to pick up fresh produce from
all over the world.

'If you wanted, you could find lots to
complain about living in London, but the
beautiful things far outnumber any of them,'
says Das with a benign smile.

The Lavender

171 Lavender Hill, Clapham, SW11 (7978 5242).
Clapham Junction rail. **Open** 10am-3pm, 7-11pm
Mon-Fri; 10.30am-4pm, 7-11pm Sat; 10.30am-4pm,
7-10.30pm Sun. **Main courses** £7-£10.50.
Credit AmEx, MC, V.
Offering friendly service, a relaxing vibe and good
food at affordable prices, this is everything a local
restaurant should be. The surroundings are charmingly understated and unpretentious, and portions
are very big and, on the whole, very tasty.
Branches: 112 Vauxhall Walk, SE11 (7735 4440); 24
Clapham Road, SW9 (7793 0770); 61 The Cut, SE1
(7928 8645).

O Cantinho de Portugal

135-137 Stockwell Road, Stockwell, SW9 (7924
0218). Stockwell tube/Brixton tube/rail/2, 322,
345 bus. **Open** *Bar* 11am-11pm daily. *Restaurant*
noon-midnight daily. **Main courses** £4-£9.
Credit MC, V.
Large, loud and warmly welcoming, Cantinho is an
enjoyably kitsch haven from the grime of Stockwell
Road. The menu is dominated by standard
Portuguese fare – fish, shellfish and pork – plus one
or two stray dishes that would seem more at home
on a British menu from the '70s.

West London

Indian

Gifto's Lahore Karahi

162-4 The Broadway, Southall, Middx (8813 8669/
www.gifto.com). Southall rail/207 bus. **Open** noon-
11.30pm Mon-Thur; noon-midnight Fri-Sun. **Main
courses** £2.50-£8.90. **Credit** AmEx, JCB, MC, V.
Enlarged and transformed, Gifto's has confirmed its
dominance of Southall. Its huge ground-floor dining
room has a new minimalism, while the fine menu of
Punjabi classics – tandooris, karahis and pungent
stews such as nihari and paya – has been joined by
a short list of Bombay-style snacks.

Karahi King

213 East Lane, North Wembley, Middx (8904
2760/4994). North Wembley tube/245 bus. **Open**
noon-midnight daily. **Main courses** £3.50-£12.
No credit cards.
Expansive, light and modish, Karahi King is more
congenial than its drab exterior might suggest.
Wielding wok-like utensils over fierce flames, the
cooks produce Punjabi (by way of East Africa)
karahi and tandoori cooking of rare excellence.

Eat, Drink, Shop

Keen canteen **Mandalay**. *See p215.*

Pit stops

The good news for those without the time, wallet or inclination for a big lunch while out enjoying London is that it is better supplied with quality cafés (from trad to trendy), coffee shops, soup bars and lunch stops than ever.

The South Bank & Bankside

Konditor & Cook *10 Stoney Street, Borough, SE1 (7407 5100). London Bridge tube/rail.* **Open** 8.30am-6.30pm Mon-Fri; 10.30am-2.30pm Sat. **No credit cards. Map** p404 P8.
There's a perfectionist at the heart of this slick bakery/café, where the amazing cakes and pastries are all made with free-range eggs and organic butter. Tables are cramped.
Southwark Cathedral Refectory *Southwark Cathedral, Montague Close, SE1 (7407 5740). London Bridge tube/rail.* **Open** 10am-5pm daily. **Credit** DC, MC, V. **Map** p404 P8.
A great location and impressive food make this a useful place to take a cake break from the nearby attractions of the Tate Modern or Borough Market.
Tate Modern Café: Level 2 *Second Floor, Tate Modern, Sumner Street, SE1 (7401 5014). London Bridge tube/rail.* **Open** 10am-

3pm daily; 10am-3pm, 6.30-9.30pm Fri, Sat. **Credit** AmEx, DC, MC, V. **Map** p404 O7.
Award-winning design from Herzog & de Meuron (it scooped the Best Interior Design category at the *Time Out* Eating & Drinking Awards 2001), plus panoramic views of St Paul's and the London Eye and decent brasserie food, ensure that this café remains perennially busy.

The City

See also **The Place Below** *(p189),* **Arkansas Café** *(p209) and* **Quiet Revolution** *(p190).*

Holborn & Clerkenwell

Goodfellas *50 Lamb's Conduit Street, WC1 (7405 7088). Holborn tube.* **Open** 8am-6.30pm Mon-Fri; 10am-5pm Sat. **Map** p399 M4.
Punters queue out of the door for a Goodfellas lunchtime hot buffet. The salad bar is also always worth a visit.

Bloomsbury & Fitzrovia

October Gallery Café *24 Old Gloucester Street, WC1 (7242 7367). Holborn tube.* **Open** 12.30-2.30pm Tue-Fri, Sun. **Map** p399 L5.

Italian

Assaggi

*The Chepstow, 39 Chepstow Place, Notting Hill, W2
(7792 5501). Notting Hill Gate tube.* **Open** 12.30-
2.30pm, 7.30-11pm Mon-Fri; 1-2.30pm, 7.30-11pm Sat.
Main courses £15.95-£18.75. **Credit** AmEx, DC,
MC, JCB, V. **Map** p394 B6.

Apart from the obstructive booking policy, occasionally aggressive service and refusal to cook beef
more than medium-rare, Assaggi is worth a visit for
its interesting seasonal menu, which ranges from
plain good to excellent. The room is a nice blend of
upstairs-in-a-pub (which it is) and unpretentious
modernisms; the wines are pleasingly priced.

Rosmarino

*1 Blenheim Terrace, St John's Wood, NW8 (7328
5014). St John's Wood tube.* **Open** noon-2.30pm,
7-10.30pm Mon-Fri; noon-3pm, 7-10.30pm Sat;
noon-3pm, 7-10pm Sun. **Main courses** (Mon-Fri
lunch only) £9.50-£13.50. **Set meals** (dinner, Sat
& Sun lunch) £22.50 two courses, £27 three courses,
£30 four courses. **Credit** AmEx, MC, V.

High standards, soothing minimalist decor, leisure-
ly yet attentive service, a tempting menu (including
daring desserts) and fair prices combined to make
Rosmarino the winner of the *Time Out* Best Local
Restaurant award in 2001.

Modern European

Clarke's

*124 Kensington Church Street, Kensington,
W8 (7221 9225). Notting Hill Gate tube.* **Open**
12.30-2pm, 7-10pm Mon-Fri. **Main courses** (lunch
only) £14. **Credit** AmEx, DC, JCB, MC, V.
Map p394 B7.

Sally Clarke was a pioneer of the 'don't mess with
the best ingredients' school of Californian cooking,
and her simple Kensington restaurant can always
be counted on for good food. Lunch offers more
flexibility than the no-choice dinner menu, but the
ingredients are consistently top-notch.

Oriental

Mandalay

*444 Edgware Road, Paddington, W2 (7258 3696/
www.bcity.com/mandalay). Edgware Road tube.*
Open noon-2.30pm, 6-10.30pm Mon-Sat. **Main
courses** £3.90-£6.90. **Credit** AmEx, DC, JCB, MC,
V. **Map** p395 E4.

Don't come here expecting a glam night out – this is
a rather homely looking, canteen-style restaurant.
However, if you're interested in decent, good-value
Burmese food served by charming staff, book a table
and join the crowds of existing fans.

Cake heaven: **Pâtisserie Valerie**.

This Victorian school building has a peaceful
atmosphere that verges on the monastic.
There are some tables in the courtyard.

Marylebone

De Gustibus *53 Blandford Street, W1
(7486 6608). Baker Street or Bond Street
tube.* **Open** 7am-7pm Mon-Fri. **No credit
cards**. **Map** p398 G5.

A neat little café with large front windows,
De Gustibus offers a choice of imaginative
made-to-order sandwiches, along with some
more substantial dishes.

Pâtisserie Valerie at Sagne *105
Marylebone High Street, W1 (7935 6240).
Baker Street or Bond Street tube.* **Open**
7.30am-7pm Mon-Fri; 8am-7pm Sat;
9am-6pm Sun. **Credit** AmEx, DC, MC, V.
Map p398 G5.

A cut above the coffee chain competition
on Marylebone High Street, this popular
café-pâtisserie is the genuine article.

Mayfair & St James's

Victory Café *Basement, Gray's Antiques
Market, South Molton Lane, W1 (7495
6860). Bond Street tube.* **Open** 10am-5.30pm
Mon-Fri. **No credit cards**. **Map** p398 H6.

This post-war triumph of a café has
resolutely retro decor, but there are no
austerity measures on the decent menu.

Soho

For dim sum, *see p206*. See also
Mildred's *(p200)*, **Kulu Kulu** *(p199)*
and **Ramen Seto** *(p199)*.

Mandarin Kitchen

14-16 Queensway, Bayswater, W2 (7727 9012).
Bayswater or Queensway tube. **Open** noon-11.30pm
daily. **Main courses** £5.90-£25. **Credit** AmEx, DC,
JCB, MC, V. **Map** p394 C6.
This specialist seafood restaurant is a favourite
haunt both among discerning Cantonese and
London's European chefs. You may have to queue
for a while, even if you've booked a table. The service is notoriously brusque.

Tawana

3 Westbourne Grove, Bayswater, W2 (7229 3785).
Bayswater, Queensway or Royal Oak tube. **Open**
noon-3pm, 6-11pm daily. **Main courses** £5.25-
£17.95. **Credit** AmEx, DC, MC, V. **Map** p394 B6.
Tawana has an elegant colonial style , with its cool
white walls, bamboo furniture, potted palms, and
tables dressed with miniature orchids and celadon
crockery. Service can be slightly uneven but the
cooking is flawless.

Other

Bali Sugar

33A All Saints Road, Notting Hill, W11 (7221
4477/www.thesugarclub.co.uk). Westbourne Park
tube. **Open** 12.30-3pm, 6.30-11pm daily. **Main**
courses £12.50-£17.80. **Credit** AmEx, DC, MC, V.

Atypically for an All Saints Road restaurant, Bali
Sugar is fancy rather than funky. The menu follows
suit, offering accomplished, globetrotting dishes
featuring exotic ingredients. The cooking can be
overly ambitious but the wine list is always reliable.

Mandola

139-41 Westbourne Grove, Notting Hill, W11
(7229 4734). Notting Hill Gate tube/23 bus.
Open noon-11.30pm Mon-Sat; noon-10.30pm Sun.
Main courses £6.50-£10.50. **Credit** MC, V.
Map p394 A6.
This perennially popular Sudanese restaurant has
a discreetly lit dark wood interior and an intoxicatingly convivial atmosphere. Food, with the likes
of chicken tava (marinated in garlic) with spring
onions and sweet peppers, doesn't disappoint.

Rodizio Rico

111 Westbourne Grove, Bayswater, W2 (7792 4035).
Bayswater or Notting Hill Gate tube. **Open** 6.30-11.30pm
Mon-Fri; 12.30-4.30pm, 6.30-11.30pm Sat; 1-11.30pm
Sun. **Main courses** £11.50 (vegetarian); £17.70 two
courses. **Credit** AmEx, MC, V. **Map** p394 B6.
The gutsy grills and hacienda-style decor of this
Brazilian all-you-can-eat carvery provide a welcome
taste of summer whatever the London weather is
doing. Drink fruity Brahma beer or South American
wines, or cut loose with a caipirinha.

▶ ## Pit stops (continued)

Bar Italia *22 Frith Street, W1 (7437 4520).*
Leicester Square or Tottenham Court Road
tube. **Open** 24 hours daily; closed 3am-6am
Sun. **No credit cards. Map** p398 K6.
Nighthawks, posers, preeners and office
workers unite at this Soho institution.
EAT *16A Soho Square, W1 (7222 7200).*
Tottenham Court Road tube. **Open** 7am-5pm
Mon-Fri; 10am-6pm Sat. **Map** p399 K6.
Excellent sarnies, wraps, salads and soups to
be consumed either in the small mezzanine
dining area or in Soho Square.

Maison Bertaux *28 Greek Street, W1 (7437*
6007). Leicester Square, Piccadilly Circus or
Tottenham Court Road tube. **Open** 9am-8pm
daily. **Map** p399 K6.
The window display at this quintessentially
French café-pâtisserie situated in the heart
of Soho is enough to crack all but the most
determined dieter.
Pâtisserie Valerie *44 Old Compton Street,*
W1 (7437 3466). Leicester Square or
Tottenham Court Road tube. **Open** 7.30am-
8pm Mon-Fri; 8am-8pm Sat; 9.30am-7pm
Sun. **Map** p399 K6.
Pâtisserie Valerie is continually busy with
lunchtime punters after something savoury,
or with the weak-willed sneaking an afternoon
treat or looking for a birthday cake to take
back to the office.
Star Café *22 Great Chapel Street, W1*
(7437 8778). Tottenham Court Road tube.
Open 7am-4pm Mon-Fri. **Map** p399 K6.
Great sarnies at lunchtime, substantial
pasta dishes and an excellent breakfast
menu make the Star a glittering fixture in
London's café firmament.

De Gustibus. See *p215.*

Springbok Grill

42 Devonshire Road, Chiswick, W4 (8742 3149/ www.springbokcafecuisine.com). Turnham Green tube. **Open** 6.30-11pm Mon-Sat. **Main courses** £9.50-£23.50. **Credit** DC, MC, V.

There's an odd disjuncture between the interior design (café-style terracotta walls with turquoise vinyl tables) and the style of cooking (neat mounds of food on huge zebra-patterned plates) at this authentic South African outpost. But the ambience is relaxed, despite an open kitchen that exposes the means of production with breathaking honesty, and the food more than competent.

Polish

Patio

5 Goldhawk Road, Shepherd's Bush, W12 (8743 5194). Goldhawk Road or Shepherd's Bush tube. **Open** noon-3pm, 6-11.30pm Mon-Fri; 6-11.30pm Sat, Sun. **Main courses** £7.50-£8.90. **Credit** AmEx, DC, JCB, MC, V.

Something of a west London institution, Patio's cosy drawing-room clutter of mirrors, credenza and stately piano has been the scene of many a good night out. The set menu is a superb (and cheap) introduction to Polish cuisine; a shot of vodka is thrown in to get things going. And they do.

Wódka

12 St Alban's Grove, Kensington, W8 (7937 6513/www.wodka.co.uk). Gloucester Road or High Street Kensington tube. **Open** 12.30-2.30pm, 7-11.15pm Mon-Fri; 7-11.15pm Sat, Sun. **Main courses** £10.50-£13.90. **Credit** AmEx, DC, MC, V. **Map** p396 C9.

A spare modern interior sets the tone for Wódka's contemporary take on classic Polish cuisine, though there are impressive flower arrangements and period details such as wall tiles. The food is tasty and the service friendly and smiling.

Vegetarian & organic

The Gate

51 Queen Caroline Street, Hammersmith, W6 (8748 6932/www.gateveg.co.uk). Hammersmith tube. **Open** noon-3pm, 6-10.45pm Mon-Fri; 6-10.45pm Sat. **Main courses** £7.50-£10.50. **Credit** AmEx, DC, MC, V.

Without question the best vegetarian restaurant in town, this is also one of London's most enjoyable eating experiences – of any kind. The Gate scores seriously high in all the categories that matter: environment, service, presentation, quality of ingredients and, of course, taste. The best place in town to tame a carnivore without pain.

A fairly well-kept secret (it's never too crowded), this gallery café combines a central location with decent grub.

Knightsbridge & South Kensington

Gloriette Pâtisserie *128 Brompton Road, SW3 (7589 4750). Knightsbridge tube.* **Open** 7am-8.30pm Mon-Fri; 7am-7pm Sat; 9am-6pm Sun. **Credit** AmEx, MC, V. **Map** p397 E9. With its array of gorgeous continental cakes, chocolates and fresh coffees and its easy-going vibe, Gloriette is the perfect place in which to relax and indulge.

Westminster

Café in the Crypt *Crypt of St Martin-in-the-Fields, Duncannon Street, WC2 (7839 4342). Charing Cross tube/rail.* **Open** Coffee bar 10am-8pm Mon-Wed; 10am-10.30pm Thur-Sat; noon-8pm Sun. *Buffet* noon-3.15pm, 5-7.30pm daily; 8.30-10.30pm Thur-Sat. **Map** p401 K7. Situated in the cool crypt of the famous Trafalgar Square church, this café offers appealing decor and grub ranging from soups to casseroles.

Covent Garden & St Giles's

See also **Rock & Soul Plaice** (*p200*), **World Food Café** (*p201*) and **Food for Thought** (*p201*).

Neal's Yard Beach Café *13 Neal's Yard, WC2 (7240 1168). Covent Garden tube.* **Open** 10am-7.30pm daily. **Map** p399 L6. A vibrant pit stop for snacks and some of the creamiest milkshakes in town.

Photographers' Gallery Café *5 Great Newport Street (7831 1772). Leicester Square tube.* **Open** 11am-6pm daily. **Map** p401 K6.

Eat, Drink, Shop

Pubs & Bars

The absinthe to Zinfandel of London drinking.

It may once have been the case that the bright young things of London were prepared to part with their beer money in exchange for just some ordinary pint in some ordinary boozer, but those days are gone. Now the majority of under-30s gravitate towards the slicker designs, more imaginative drinks and (often) later opening hours (*see p226* **After hours**) of the capital's bars, choosing DJs over pub quizmasters and distressed mirrors in place of dartboards. And everything from hip style bars to formulaic chains have sprung up to meet the demand.

Naturally, the good, honest hostelry still has its place (despite the tendency of big breweries to rip out the guts of characterful pubs and install prosthetic interiors). So whether you're after a few slow ales or a Knicker Dropper Glory, you'll find no shortage of opportunities to wet your whistle.

Get wired at **Cynthia's Robotic Bar**.

The South Bank & Bankside

Anchor Bankside
34 Park Street, SE1 (7407 1577). London Bridge tube/rail. **Open** 11am-11pm Mon-Sat; noon-10.30pm Sun. **Credit** AmEx, DC, MC, V. **Map** p404 P8.
Dating back to 1775, this Thames-side boozer has numerous bars and crannies (including the Johnson Room, where the great man wrote parts of his dictionary), plus oak beams and rattling staircases.

Auberge
1 Sandell Street, off Waterloo Road, SE1 (7633 0610). Waterloo tube/rail. **Open** noon-midnight Mon-Fri; noon-11pm Sat. **Credit** AmEx, DC, MC, V. **Map** p404 N8.
A busy bar stocked with Belgian beers and top-notch wines, not to mention serviceable French grub (steak frites, croque monsieur and the like). Customers tend to be on the well-heeled side.

Cynthia's Robotic Bar
4 Tooley Street, SE1 (7403 6777/ www.cynbar.co.uk). London Bridge tube/rail. **Open** 5pm-6am Mon-Sat; 8pm-3am Sun. **Credit** AmEx, DC, MC, V. **Map** p405 Q8.
For those not overenamoured of pubs and in search of something more than a little bit kitsch, Cynthia's, with its mirrored caverns and LED bar decorations, could be the answer. Cocktails such as Space Benders and Full Thrust are dispensed by robots Cynthia and Rasta.

Market Porter
9 Stoney Street, SE1 (7407 2495). London Bridge tube/rail. **Open** 6-8.30am, 11am-11pm Mon-Fri; noon-11pm Sat; noon-10.30pm Sun. **Credit** AmEx, MC, V. **Map** p404 P8.
A modern makeover has chased away some of its nostalgic appeal, but the Porter remains one of London's finest pubs. There's a wide and imaginative selection of real ales and an equally diverse (and appreciative) clientele.

Royal Oak
44 Tabard Street, SE1 (7357 7173). Borough tube/ London Bridge tube/rail. **Open** 11am-11pm Mon-Fri. **Credit** MC, V. **Map** p404 P9.
Recently restored (the mahogany gleams once again, the etched glass sparkles like new), this is a strong candidate for London's best pub. The full range of Harvey's cask-conditioned canon is on offer, from Mild to Old, including seasonal brews.

Vinopolis Wine Wharf

*Stoney Street, SE1 (7940 8335/
www.vinopolis.co.uk). London Bridge tube/rail.*
Open 11am-11pm Mon-Sat. **Credit** AmEx, MC, V.
As you might expect from the bar at London's only
wine-themed attraction, Wine Wharf's got a great
wine list (even if the stuff is served in annoying
plastic holders). Bricks and metal betray the area's
industrial past and clocks showing times in some of
the world's wine regions add touches of personality.

The City

Black Friar

*174 Queen Victoria Street, EC4 (7236 5474).
Blackfriars tube/rail.* **Open** 11.30am-11pm Mon-Fri.
Credit AmEx, MC, V. **Map** p404 O6.
An extraordinary wedge-shaped pub with an art
nouveau façade, and Edwardian marble, mosaics
and pillared fireplaces inside. There's also some
decent beer and, more often than not, a sizeable
crowd of City suits on hand to enjoy it.

Jamaica Wine House

*St Michael's Alley, off Cornhill, EC3 (7626 9496).
Bank tube/DLR.* **Open** 11am-11pm Mon-Fri.
Credit AmEx, DC, MC, V. **Map** p405 Q6.
London's first coffee house, this premises was
rebuilt after the Great Fire and converted into a pub
at the end of the 19th century, hence the nicely aged
mahogany interior. Despite the wine house moniker
and theming, you'll find the beer's better.

Tsunami

*1 St Katherine's Way, E1 (7488 4791/www.tsunami-
events.com). Tower Hill tube.* **Open** 11am-11pm Mon-
Fri; 6-11pm Sat. **Credit** AmEx, DC, JCB, MC, V.
Map p405 S7.
Unsurprisingly, decor here features a wave-shaped
bar and a picture of a massive tidal wave. Still,
Tsunami's a good bet for a slick night of cocktail
quaffing; choose from a list of 80 and let the black-
clad staff do the rest.

Twentyfour

*Level 24, Tower 42, 25 Old Broad Street, EC2 (7877
2424/www.twenty-four.co.uk). Bank tube/DLR/
Liverpool Street tube/rail.* **Open** 11am-11pm Mon-
Fri. **Credit** AmEx, DC, JCB, MC, V. **Map** p402 N5.
A heady mix of alcohol and altitude, Twentyfour is
situated in the Tower 42 skyscraper. Suede-covered
pouffes, easy chairs and a killer wine and cocktail
list all take second place to the view.

Ye Olde Cheshire Cheese

*145 Fleet Street, EC4 (7353 6170). Blackfriars
tube/rail.* **Open** 11.30am-11pm Mon-Fri; noon-3pm,
6-11pm Sat; noon-3pm Sun. **Credit** AmEx, DC, JCB,
MC, V. **Map** p404 N6.
It might look closed but it probably isn't; a dark
frontage conceals the unprepossessing alleyway
entrance. Inside, it's a warren of wooden settles, bare
boards and sawdust, known to Dickens, Thackeray
and Johnson. Perfect for an historical pint.

Storming cocktails at **Tsunami**.

Holborn & Clerkenwell

Bleeding Heart Tavern

*Bleeding Heart Yard, off Greville Street, EC1
(7242 8238). Chancery Lane tube/Farringdon
tube/rail.* **Open** noon-11pm Mon-Fri. **Credit** AmEx,
DC, MC, V. **Map** p402 N5.
With its gory past safely behind it, this City yard
plays host to claret of a different kind. The wine list
is extensive, the surroundings are warm and comfortable, and the food is modern, French and tasty.

Cicada

*132-136 St John Street, EC1 (7608 1550/
www.cicada.nu). Farringdon tube/rail.* **Open**
noon-11pm Mon-Fri; 6-11pm Sat. **Credit** AmEx,
DC, MC, V. **Map** p402 O5.
Cicada has all the classic EC1 credentials: busy open-
plan bar; heavily stylised restaurant area with open
kitchen; and pan-Asian food. Avoid knocking-off
time and the throngs of thirsty office bods.

Fluid

*40 Charterhouse Street, EC1 (7253 3444/
www.fluidbar.com). Barbican tube/Farringdon
tube/rail.* **Open** noon-midnight Mon-Wed; noon-2am
Thur, Fri; 7pm-2am Sat. **Credit** AmEx, DC, MC, V.
Map p402 O5.
Japanese theming, slinky tunes and laid-back leather
sofas make Fluid a favourite among clubbers and
fashionistas. Snacks of the likes of miso soup, and
crisp, cool beers complete the picture.

Eat, Drink, Shop

Jamaica Wine House, a polished operation. *See p219.*

Fox & Anchor

115 Charterhouse Street, EC1 (7253 5075).
Farringdon tube/rail. **Open** 7am-3pm Mon, Tue;
7am-9pm Wed-Fri. **Credit** AmEx, MC, V.
Map p402 O5.
Tucked up a side street just off Smithfield and
easily missed, the Fox & Anchor is a gem. In def-
erence to the hungry market workers, it opens at
7am to serve up huge, artery-clogging breakfasts,
and the well-preserved Edwardian bar is also a
great bet for a few slow ales.

Jerusalem Tavern

55 Britton Street, EC1 (7490 4281/
www.stpetersbrewery.co.uk). Farringdon tube/rail.
Open 11am-11pm Mon-Fri. **Credit** AmEx, MC, V.
Map p402 O5.
This small, intimate tavern looks as if it's been preserved from the days of the Young Pretender. The
sole London outpost of St Peter's Brewery out in
Suffolk, Jerusalem Tavern also has half a dozen of
its great beers on draught.

Mint

182-6 St John Street, EC1 (7253 8368/
www.mintbar.co.uk). Farringdon tube/rail.
Open 11am-midnight Mon-Fri; 6pm-midnight Sat.
Credit AmEx, DC, MC, V. **Map** p402 O5.
Ultra-modern with a curvy glass bar and funky
lighting, Mint knocks up decent cocktails for the
designers and dot.commers who tend to haunt the
place, though wine buffs will have a lot to get
enthusiastic about as well.

Na Zdrowie

11 Little Turnstile, WC1 (7831 9679). Holborn
tube. **Open** noon-11.30pm Mon-Fri; 6-11.30pm Sat.
Credit MC, V. **Map** p399 M5.
Large cubic seats double up as drinks tables among
the mirror mosaic and metalwork of this sassy
Polish vodka bar. There's also decent borschty fodder to soak up the shots.

Bloomsbury & Fitzrovia

Bradley's Spanish Bar

42-4 Hanway Street, W1 (7636 0359). Tottenham
Court Road tube. **Open** noon-11pm Mon-Sat;
3-10.30pm Sun. **Credit** MC, V. **Map** p399 K6.
Bradley's jukebox is a must-hear and the draught
San Miguel is ideal for taking the edge off a London
summer thirst. The backstreet location has helped
it remain a locals' favourite.

Duke of York

7 Roger Street, WC1 (7242 7230). Chancery Lane
or Russell Square tube. **Open** noon-11pm Mon-Fri;
6-11pm Sat. **Credit** MC, V. **Map** p399 M4.
Looking like a pastiche of a '50s bar, the Duke has
become one of this area's trendier hangouts. The
British food is inventive.

The Lamb

94 Lamb's Conduit Street, WC1 (7405 0713).
Holborn or Russell Square tube. **Open** 11am-11pm
Mon-Sat; noon-4pm, 7-10.30pm Sun. **Credit** AmEx,
MC, V. **Map** p399 M4.

One of London's most celebrated pubs, and rightly so, the Lamb is a central London flagship for Wandsworth's Young's brewery. The decor is carefully restored Victorian, with three wood-panelled drinking areas, and there's also a no-smoking bar for those who value their lungs.

Marylebone

Dover Castle
43 Weymouth Mews, W1 (7580 4412).
Great Portland Street or Regent's Park tube.
Open 11.30am-11pm Mon-Fri; noon-11pm Sat.
Credit MC, V. **Map** p398 H5.
Despite its classy West End mews location, the Dover Castle is incredibly cheap, and consequently always busy with the well informed, sunk in old-fashioned leather chairs and sofas.

Match
37-8 Margaret Street, W1 (7499 3443). Oxford Circus tube. **Open** 11am-midnight Mon-Sat.
Credit AmEx, DC, MC, V. **Map** p398 J5.
Just a short walk from the maelstrom of Oxford Circus, Match is a little bit of Hoxton come west. There's a DJ cockpit to spur on the starry-eyed big-nighters and amazing cocktails.

Windsor Castle
29 Crawford Place, W1 (7723 4371). Edgware Road tube. **Open** 11am-11pm Mon-Sat; noon-10.30pm Sun.
Credit MC, V. **Map** p395 F5.
The Windsor looks like a cluttered souvenir shop, with all manner of Brit memorabilia dotted about, plus a selection of traditional beers (Bass, Hancock's HB and Guinness) available to help wash down the incongruous Thai grub.

Mayfair & St James's

For hotel bars, *see p224* **Smooth operators**.

Che
23 St James's Street, SW1 (7747 9380/
www.chelondon.co.uk). Green Park tube. **Open**
11am-11pm Mon-Fri; 5-11pm Sat. **Credit** AmEx,
DC, MC, V. **Map** p400 J8.
The eponymous Ernesto must be spinning in his mausoleum at having this exclusive bar themed in his 'honour', but any non-revolutionaries with money to burn flock to its huge, wall-length humidor and its well-stocked bar.

Trader Vic's
Hilton Hotel, Park Lane, W1 (7493 8000 ext 420).
Green Park or Hyde Park Corner tube. **Open** 5pm-1am Mon-Thur; 5pm-3am Fri, Sat; 5-10.30pm Sun.
Credit AmEx, DC, MC, V. **Map** p400 G8.
As theme bars go, Trader Vic's is a joyous exercise in high camp (boasting bamboo ceilings with pufferfish and coral, hula music and girls togged out in silky flower-print dresses). And their list of over-the-top cocktails is suitably vast.

Soho & Leicester Square

Alphabet
61-3 Beak Street, W1 (7439 2190). Leicester Square tube. **Open** noon-11pm Mon-Fri; 4-11pm Sat. **Credit** AmEx, MC, V. **Map** p400 J6.
Smarter bars there certainly are, but for Soho loafing Alphabet's still hard to beat. There's a covetable leather sofa by the window, but if that's already been nabbed squeeze on to the artily mismatched chairs around the zinc-topped tables. The basement bar is busier and louder.

Coach & Horses
29 Greek Street, W1 (7437 5920). Leicester Square tube. **Open** 11am-11pm Mon-Sat; noon-10.30pm Sun.
Credit MC, V. **Map** p399 K6.
So Jeffrey Bernard drank himself to death here – big deal. The real point is that the Coach & Horses, with its rickety Formica tables, last resort sandwiches and larger than life landlord, is what Soho drinking dens are all about.

Cork & Bottle
44-6 Cranbourn Street, WC2 (7734 6592/
www.donhewitsonlondonwinebars.com).
Leicester Square tube. **Open** 11am-midnight Mon-Sat; noon-10.30pm Sun. **Credit** AmEx, DC, MC, V. **Map** p401 K7.
A nondescript doorway is all that's visible at street level of this cosy underground burrow. There's a big, juicy wine list, along with blackboards and flyers announcing assorter bin ends, wines of the month, and the like.

The best Pubs & bars

For a game of pool
Elbow Room (*see p225*).

For a trip back in time
Black Friar (*see p219*).

For superior pub grub
Fire Stables (*see p229*).

For a boogie
The Plug (*see p229*).

For speciality beers
Bierodrome (*see p225*).

For an honest pint
Pride of Spitalfields (*see p227*).

For utter camp
Trader Vic's (*see left*).

For the so-hip-it-hurts factor
Westbourne (*see p230*).

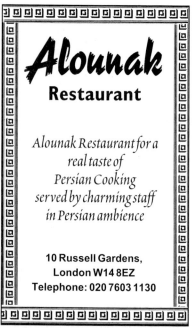
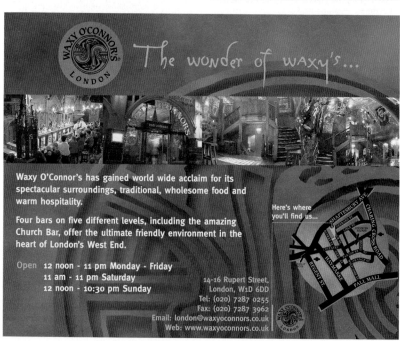

French House

49 Dean Street, W1 (7437 2799). Leicester Square tube. **Open** noon-11pm Mon-Sat; noon-10.30pm Sun. **Credit** AmEx, DC, MC, V. **Map** p399 K6.

The restaurant above the pub room has gone, but this Soho institution remains. During the war, it was a meeting place for the French Resistance, and in continued opposition to British boorishness, staff still refuse to serve pints (halves only). How quaint.

Lab

12 Old Compton Street, W1 (7437 7820). Leicester Square or Tottenham Court Road tube. **Open** noon-midnight Mon-Sat; 4-10.30pm Sun. **Credit** AmEx, MC, V. **Map** p399 K6.

The cocktail list at this Soho bar is as weighty as your average computer manual, but fortunately, it's much more comprehensible and makes for lip-smacking reading. Sit at the space-age bar to watch the mixology at work.

Covent Garden & St Giles's

Angel

61 St Giles High Street, WC2 (7240 2876). Tottenham Court Road tube. **Open** 11.30am-11pm Mon-Fri; noon-11pm Sat; noon-10.30pm Sun. **Credit** MC, V. **Map** p399 K6.

The Angel has been nicely converted, with many Victorian features left intact (though there's only room for about six in the tiny saloon bar). Beers run the gamut from Old Brewery Bitter to Ayingerbräu.

Detroit

35 Earlham Street, WC2 (7240 2662/www.detroit-bar.com). Covent Garden or Leicester Square tube. **Open** 5pm-midnight Mon-Sat. **Credit** AmEx, DC, MC, V. **Map** p399 L6.

A funkily orchestrated take on troglodytic bar life, Detroit gives the impression of having been tunnelled out of the earth – think mud-brown walls and burrow-like nooks. The cheerful bar staff and perky cocktails provide the requisite sunshine.

Freedom Brewing Company

41 Earlham Street, WC2 (7240 0606/ www.freedombrew.com). Covent Garden or Leicester Square tube. **Open** noon-11pm Mon-Sat; noon-10.30pm Sun. **Credit** AmEx, MC, V. **Map** p399 L6.

One of the capital's most successful microbreweries, Freedom is a modernist take on the beer hall (whitewashed brick vaulting, old iron columns, spacey lighting), and has interesting bar snacks to match.

Gordon's

47 Villiers Street, WC2 (7930 1408). Covent Garden or Embankment tube/Charing Cross tube/rail. **Open** 11am-11pm Mon-Sat; noon-10pm Sun. **Credit** MC, V. **Map** p401 L7.

Large on atmosphere, light on spring-cleaning, and perennially busy, this cult London wine bar is reminiscent of the bar that time forgot somewhere in deepest rural France. Wine is the only way to go and value is exceptional for central London.

Lamb & Flag

33 Rose Street, WC2 (7497 9504). Covent Garden tube. **Open** 11am-11pm Mon-Thur; 11am-10.45pm Fri, Sat; noon-10.30pm Sun. **No credit cards**. **Map** p401 L7.

If historic pubs are your thing and provided you can stand crowds and you like real ale, this'll be right down your alley. Built in 1623, it's one of London's last wooden-framed buildings.

Westminster

Boisdale

15 Eccleston Street, SW1 (7730 6922/ www.boisdale.co.uk). Victoria tube/rail. **Open** *Back Bar* noon-11pm Mon-Fri. *Macdonald Bar* noon-1am Mon-Fri; 7pm-1am Sat. **Credit** AmEx, DC, MC, V. **Map** p400 H10.

Boisdale's cosy back bar and open-plan restaurant/bar (where live jazz features regularly) are becoming popular local hangouts. The restaurant is also a respected purveyor of fine British food.

Red Lion

48 Parliament Street, SW1 (7930 5826). Westminster tube. **Open** 11am-11pm Mon-Sat; noon-7pm Sun. **Credit** MC, V. **Map** p401 L9.

There's been a tavern here since 1434, but this incarnation has existed since 1900, hence the mahogany and etched glass fittings. The silent TV screens are tuned to the BBC Parliamentary Channel, which gives a good indication of who the regulars are.

Knightsbridge & South Kensington

Grenadier

18 Wilton Row, SW1 (7235 3074). Knightsbridge tube. **Open** noon-11pm Mon-Sat; noon-10.30pm Sun. **Credit** AmEx, DC, MC, V. **Map** p400 G9.

As worn and comforting as a pair of retired general's slippers, the Grenadier is a cosy mix of stripped flooring, candy-striped wallpaper and military knick-knacks. Apparently, it's Chris Evans' favourite pub, but don't let that put you off.

Nag's Head

53 Kinnerton Street, SW1 (7235 1135). Hyde Park Corner tube. **Open** 11am-11pm Mon-Sat; noon-10.30pm Sun. **No credit cards**. **Map** p400 G9.

Perhaps the floor of this pint-sized saloon has been raised, or the bar lowered, but the net result is that staff address your navel. Still, the superbly eccentric decor and the diminutive downstairs snug make this one of SW1's most civilised watering holes.

Chelsea

Builder's Arms

13 Britten Street, SW3 (7349 9040). Sloane Square tube. **Open** 11am-11pm Mon-Sat; noon-10.30pm Sun. **Credit** MC, V. **Map** p397 E11.

The conservative decor (ottomans, still lifes, leather sofas) is enlivened with the odd dissident touch, such as the large painting of Salvador Dalí staring piercingly at the customers. The drinks list is varied (with some 30-odd wines), and the nosh, in keeping with the locale, is posh.

Lots Road Pub & Dining Room
114 Lots Road, SW10 (7352 6645). Fulham Broadway or Sloane Square tube then 11, 19, 22 bus. **Open** 11am-11pm Mon-Sat; 11am-10.30pm Sun. **Credit** AmEx, MC, V. **Map** p396 C13.
The interior comprises cream walls, dark wood settles, leather armchairs and views of Chelsea Harbour. There are hand-pumped bitters (Brakspear and Courage Directors), a decent wine list and excellent food from the open kitchen.

Phene Arms
9 Phene Street, SW3 (7352 3294). Sloane Square or South Kensington tube. **Open** 11am-11pm Mon-Sat; noon-10.30pm Sun. **Credit** AmEx, DC, MC, V. **Map** p397 E12.
The most convivial pub in Chelsea, the Phene Arms has a central bar that comes complete with wrought-iron fittings and cheesy red lanterns, while the garden is lively practically all year round, thanks to the outdoor heaters.

North London

25 Canonbury Lane
25 Canonbury Lane, Islington, N1 (7226 0955). Highbury & Islington tube/rail. **Open** 5-11.30pm Mon-Thur; 4-11.30pm Fri; noon-11.30pm Sat; noon-11pm Sun. **Credit** MC, V.
A warm and homely mishmash of dark wood floor, red, duck-egg blue and gold colours, antique fittings and frescoes. Drinks centre on cocktails.

The Albion
10 Thornhill Road, Barnsbury, N1 (7607 7450). Angel tube. **Open** 11am-11pm Mon-Sat; noon-10.30pm Sun. **Credit** AmEx, DC, MC, V. **Map** p402 N1.
A little piece of rustic charm in non-rustic N1. The hunting/fishing decor feels a bit contrived, but the interior is genuinely Georgian.

Bar Vinyl
6 Inverness Street, Camden, NW1 (7681 7898). Camden Town tube. **Open** 11am-11pm Mon-Sat; 11am-10.30pm Sun. **Credit** AmEx, DC, MC, V.
The most Camdenesque of Camden bars, this is a long, sparse box of a room with a bar slowly curving along one wall and limited seating at the back. Music is loud and the bar food basic.

Smooth operators

There are days when your local boozer or throbbing DJ bar just won't do it, when you need to be transported away from your humdrum cares and concerns into a soothing fantasy world of low lighting, leather seating, exotic nibbles and outrageously expensive cocktails. On days like these, only hotel bars – formerly the province of expense account business travellers and gullible tourists but reinvented over the past few years to appeal to a younger, more chic market – will do, and to hell with the cost.

For history in spades and a slightly faded opulence, you can do no better than the Savoy's **American Bar** (Strand, WC2, 7836 4343), which will appeal to all but the most jaded of lounge lizards. You may not spot Peter Ustinov and Omar Sharif among the clientele these days, but settle into a sofa, have the waiter bring you a cigar, order some aged scotch, and create a little smoke-wreathed glamour world of your own. **The Library Bar** at the Lanesborough Hotel (1 Lanesborough Place, Hyde Park Corner, SW1, 7259 5599) is also sumptuous and traditional, with a gentlemen's club vibe and book-lined shelves. But punters don't come here for the decor so much as for the

fabulous Martinis concocted by bar manager Salvatore Calabrese, who is also a world expert on vintage cognacs (the 'Liquid History' collection he has built up here includes some of the world's oldest and rarest Grande Champagne cognacs)

For swish surroundings without such a heavy, wood-panelled feel, there's **Claridge's Bar** (55 Brook Street, W1, 7629 8860), which is nothing if not discreet, from its barely noticeable entrance to the starchy maître d' and deco classicism of the interior. The bar was gorgeously revamped by hip designer David Collins to celebrate the hotel's centenary in 1998 and is an oasis of calm and good taste. Collins, who designed many of London's glammest restaurants, including Mirabelle, is also behind the Berkeley Hotel's sumptuous new **Blue Bar** (1 Wilton Place, SW1, 7235 6000), painted in a striking hue dubbed by the designer 'Lutyens Blue' and kitted out with pale lilac leather chairs. Staff are discreet but friendly, and the Martinis are outstanding. London drinking doesn't get much more relaxing than this.

Those preferring something a little more trashy should aim for the dizzying heights of **Windows** (7208 4021) at the Park Lane

Pubs & Bars

Bierodrome
173-4 Upper Street, Islington, N1 (7226 5835/ www.belgo-restaurants.co.uk). Angel tube/Highbury & Islington tube/rail. **Open** noon-midnight daily. **Credit** AmEx, MC, V. **Map** p402 O1.
A huge range of beers and heavy, fish- and meat-based Belgian food. The staff are cheerful, despite – or perhaps because of – their bizarre *Texas Chainsaw Massacre*-style leather tunics.

The Clifton
96 Clifton Hill, St John's Wood, NW8 (7372 3427). St John's Wood tube. **Open** 11am-11pm Mon-Sat; noon-10.30pm Sun. **Credit** AmEx, MC, V.
Blending in perfectly with the surrounding houses, the Clifton can be hard to spot (except in summer, when its outside tables are packed to overflowing). Inside is all manner of carved wood, a Gothic-looking bar, ornate fireplaces and snug corners.

Duke of Cambridge
30 St Peter Street, Islington, N1 (7359 3066/ www.singhboulton.co.uk/duke). Angel tube. **Open** 5-11pm Mon; noon-11pm Tue-Sat; noon-10.30pm Sun. **Credit** AmEx, MC, V. **Map** p402 O2.
The original organic pub, the Duke offers a patio for fairweather visitors and a cool, expansive bar. If you get peckish, the food is excellent.

Elbow Room
135 Finchley Road, Swiss Cottage, NW3 (7586 9888). Swiss Cottage tube. **Open** noon-midnight Mon-Fri; noon-1am Fri-Sat; noon-10.30pm Sun. **Admission** £2 after 9pm, £5 after 10pm Fri, Sat. **Credit** MC, V.
It might look unimpressive from the outside, but if you fancy a few bevvies, a decent burger and a few frames of pool, look no further.

The Flask
14 Flask Walk, Hampstead, NW3 (7435 4580). Hampstead tube. **Open** 11am-11pm Mon-Sat; noon-10.30pm Sun. **Credit** MC, V.
Not to be confused with the similarly named boozer located across the heath, this high-ceilinged pub situated at the bottom of a pretty pedestrianised lane off the high street boasts two bars, public and saloon, plus a restaurant.

Hollybush
22 Holly Mount, Hampstead, NW3 (7435 2892). Hampstead tube. **Open** 11am-11pm Mon-Sat; noon-10.30pm Sun. **Credit** MC, V.
One of the oldest and most picturesque drinking haunts in the area, the Hollybush is well hidden up a tiny backstreet. It has four bars, low ceilings, wood and plaster walls and a real coal fire that is great for toe-warming after winter walks.

Mood indigo: the Berkeley's **Blue Bar**.

Hilton. The decor may be uninspired, the cocktails unexceptional and the pianist an '80s throwback, but who cares when the views over Hyde Park from the floor-to-ceiling windows of the 28th floor are as breathtaking as this? Equally showy but targeted at a more fashionable, post-work crowd is **Rockwell**, the flagship bar of the Hilton's new Trafalgar Hotel (2 Spring Gardens, SW1, 7870 2959; *see also p53*). Bourbon cocktails are the speciality here and the modish American bar food is pretty good too.

For something more muted, you'll need to head back to the Park Lane Hilton, where basement bar **Zeta** (7208 4067) counteracts the kitsch of its neighbour Trader Vic's (*see p221*) with an orientally minimalist approach, including staff kitted out like hip priests. It serves fancy 'bar bites' such as Canadian crab, as well as excellent and (for a hotel bar) reasonably priced cocktails. While no one will swallow the line implied by the 'new testament' section of the menu involving fresh juices and healthy additives with regular liqueurs – that you can get smashed and do yourself good at the same time – there's no denying that a little luxury every now and then is the perfect tonic for a weary soul.

For more hotel bar reviews, see *Time Out Pubs & Bars* 2001/02.

Eat, Drink, Shop

After hours

British licensing laws are as draconian as ever, and you'll find that London landlords can clear the house at closing time quicker than Bernard Manning in a mosque. But don't despair: you can still have a few hours of fun before stumbling into a cab. Here's where to do it in central London.

AKA
18 West Central Street, WC1 (7836 0110). **Open** 6-11pm Mon; 6pm-3am Wed-Fri; 7pm-7am Sat; varies Sun, phone for details.

Atlantic Bar & Grill
20 Glasshouse, W1 (7734 4888). **Open** noon-3am Mon-Fri; 6pm-3am Sat.

Bar Code
3-4 Archer Street, W1 (7734 3342). **Open** 1pm-1am Mon-Sat; 1-10.30pm Sun.

Blues Bistro & Bar
42-3 Dean Street, W1 (7494 1966). **Open** noon-midnight Mon-Thur; noon-1am Fri; 5.30pm-1am Sat; 5pm-midnight Sun.

Café Bohème
13-17 Old Compton Street, W1 (7734 0623). **Open** 8am-3am Mon-Sat; 8am-midnight Sun.

Corney & Barrow
116 St Martin's Lane, WC2 (7655 9800). **Open** noon-midnight Mon-Wed; noon-2am Thur-Sat.

Denim
4A Upper St Martin's Lane, WC2 (7497 0376). **Open** 5pm-1am Mon-Sat; 5-11.30pm Sun.

Down Mexico Way
25 Swallow Street, W1 (7437 9895). **Open** 5pm-3am Mon-Sat.

The Edge
11 Soho Square, W1 (7439 1313). **Open** noon-1am Mon-Sat; noon-10.30pm Sun.

Garlic & Shots
14 Frith Street, W1 (7734 9505). **Open** 5pm-midnight Mon-Wed; 6pm-1am Thur-Sat; 5-11pm Sun.

Havana
17 Hanover Square, W1 (7629 2552). **Open** 5pm-2am Mon-Thur; 5pm-3am Fri, Sat; 6pm-1am Sun.

The Langley
5 Langley Street, WC2 (7836 5005). **Open** 4.30pm-1am Mon-Sat; 2-10.30pm Sun.

Mash
19-21 Great Portland Street, W1 (7637 5555). **Open** 7.30am-2am Mon-Sat.

Oxygen Bar
17-18 Irving Street, WC2 (7930 0907). **Open** 2pm-2am Mon-Thur; 2pm-3am Fri, Sat; 2-10pm Sun.

Saint
8 Great Newport Street, WC2 (7240 1551). **Open** 5pm-1am Mon; 5pm-2am Tue-Thur; 5pm-3am Fri; 7pm-3am Sat.

Sak
49 Greek Street, W1 (7439 4159). **Open** 5.30pm-2am Mon, Tue; 5.30pm-3am Wed-Sat.

The Spot
29-30 Maiden Lane, WC2 (7379 5900). **Open** noon-1am Mon-Sat; 6pm-1am Sun.

10 Room
10 Air Street, W1 (7734 9990). **Open** 5.30pm-3am Mon-Fri; 8pm-3am Sat.

Two Thirty Club
23 Romilly Street, W1 (7734 2323). **Open** 5.30pm-midnight Tue-Fri; 6pm-midnight Sun.

Village Soho
81 Wardour Street, W1 (7434 2124). **Open** 4pm-1am Mon-Sat; 3-10.30pm Sun.

West Central
29-30 Lisle Street, WC2 (7479 7980). **Open** basement bar 10.30pm-2am Mon-Thur; 10.30pm-3am Fri, Sat.

Windows
Hilton Hotel, Park Lane, W1 (7208 4021). **Open** 5.30pm-2am Mon-Sat.

Yo! Below
52 Poland Street, W1 (7439 3660). **Open** 5pm-midnight Mon-Thur; 5pm-1am Fri, Sat; 5.30-10.30pm Sun.

Zeta
35 Hertford Street, W1 (7208 4067). **Open** 4pm-2am Mon, Tue; 4pm-3am Wed-Sat.

Lansdowne

90 Gloucester Avenue, Primrose Hill, NW1
(7483 0409). Camden Town or Chalk Farm tube.
Open noon-11pm Mon-Sat; noon-10.30pm Sun.
Credit MC, V.
Famous for attracting various glitterati, the
Lansdowne also draws plenty of ordinary folk to its
smoky, tightly packed bar. The smart upstairs
restaurant is a better bet than the bar food.

Medicine Bar

181 Upper Street, Islington, N1 (7704 9536/1070).
Angel tube/Highbury & Islington tube/rail. **Open**
5pm-midnight Mon-Thur; 3pm-2am Fri; noon-2am
Sat; noon-10.30pm Sun. **Credit** MC, V. **Map** p402 O1.
Despite bearing all the hallmarks of super-hipness,
there's a warm, pubby feel to the Medicine Bar.
Maybe it's the ornate wooden back bar, which was
carved in an era when a pub was a pub. The excellent music is strictly 2002.

Shakespeare

57 Allen Road, Stoke Newington, N16 (7254 4190).
Bus 73. **Open** 5-11pm Mon-Fri; noon-11pm Sat;
noon-10.30pm Sun. **No credit cards**.
The large wooden bar and church pew seating are
enlivened by colourful French drinking posters at
what many consider to be N16's best pub. The fab
jukebox ranges from Mingus to Madchester.

East London

Cantaloupe

35-42 Charlotte Road, Shoreditch, EC2 (7613 4411/
www.cantaloupe.co.uk). Old Street tube/rail. **Open**
11am-midnight Mon-Fri; noon-midnight Sat; noon-
10.30pm Sun. **Credit** AmEx, MC, V. **Map** p403 R4.
The first rough-edged former warehouse to inject
life into Shoreditch's bar/restaurant scene,
Cantaloupe still attracts a huge crowd. There's a
raised restaurant area.

Grapes

76 Narrow Street, Limehouse, E14 (7987 4396).
West Ferry DLR. **Open** noon-3pm, 5.30-11pm
Mon-Fri; 11am-11pm Sat; 11am-10.30pm Sun.
Credit AmEx, DC, MC, V.
This superb little pub steeped in Dickensian charm
is a real treat in summer if you can find space on the
small riverside deck. Mobile phones are banned, and
there's no music to disturb the convivial hubbub.
Excellent fish and chips are served.

Great Eastern Dining Room

54-6 Great Eastern Street, Shoreditch, EC2
(7613 4545/www.greateasterndining.co.uk).
Old Street tube/rail. **Open** noon-midnight Mon-Fri;
6pm-midnight Sat. **Credit** AmEx, DC, MC, V.
Map p403 R4.
Young creatives still populate this dark, high-
ceilinged bar and restaurant, though on Saturday
nights there's a preponderance of barely legal teens.
The Italian food is hit and miss.

Life's a beach at **Sand**. *See p229.*

Home

100-106 Leonard Street, Shoreditch, EC2 (7684
8618/www.homebar.co.uk). Old Street tube/rail.
Open noon-midnight Mon-Fri; 6pm-midnight Sat.
Credit AmEx, DC, MC, V. **Map** p403 Q4.
Not the trailblazer it once was, this slick bar is still
worth a visit, if only for a Home Lush (Absolut and
Chambord crowned with champagne), as well as
decent DJs and staff most bars can only dream of.

The Light

233 Shoreditch High Street, E1 (7247 8989).
Shoreditch tube/Liverpool Street tube/rail. **Open**
12.30pm-midnight Mon-Wed; 12.30pm-2am Thur, Fri;
6.30pm-2am Sat; 12.30-10.30pm Sun. **Credit** AmEx,
MC, V. Map p403 R5.
A former electricity generating station that's been
given a stunning makeover, and is full of space and
light. A first-floor lounge bar has DJs and a small
terrace with a view over the city.

Pride of Spitalfields

3 Heneage Street, Spitalfields, E1 (7247 8933).
Aldgate East tube. **Open** 11am-11pm Mon-Sat; noon-
10.30pm Sun. **Credit** AmEx, MC, V. **Map** p403 S5.
A genial family-run pub with a mixed crowd, from
businessmen and medical students to builders and
OAPs. The beer's good, and well under £2 a pint.

Prospect of Whitby

57 Wapping Wall, Wapping, E1 (7481 1095).
Wapping tube. **Open** 11.30am-11pm Mon-Sat;
noon-10.30pm Sun. **Credit** AmEx, DC, MC, V.

Eat, Drink, Shop

Sosho: silly name, great cocktails.

Built in 1520 and last remodelled in 1777, this historic pub has aged gracefully. The pewter-topped counter, stone-flagged floors, giant timbers and pebbled windows have all been preserved. Enjoy the river views but beware the weekend coach parties.

Shoreditch Electricity Showrooms
39A Hoxton Square, Hoxton, N1 (7739 6934). Old Street tube/rail. **Open** noon-11pm Mon-Wed; noon-midnight Thur; noon-1am Fri, Sat; noon-10.30pm Sun. **Credit** AmEx, MC, V. **Map** p403 R3.
Hanging on to a corner of its main square, the SES is very much part of Hoxton's resurgence – and something of a cliché these days. But anywhere that serves boar, quail and haddock, and draught Kirin at £2.65 a pint, can't be all bad.

Sosho
2 Tabernacle Street, Shoreditch, EC2 (7920 0701). Moorgate or Old Street tube/rail. **Open** 11am-midnight Mon-Wed; 11am-2am Thur, Fri; 7pm-2am Sat. **Admission** £3-£9 after 9pm Fri; £5-£7 after 8pm Sat. **Credit** AmEx, DC, JCB, MC, V.
Peerlessly discerning (and winner of the 2001 *Time Out* Best Bar award), Sosho, like its sibling Match (*see p221*), comes into its own as soon as the cocktail shaker appears, wielded by bar tenders of rare

dexterity. The spacious lounge is decorated with glam touches, while DJs mix it up as confidently as their colleagues working the bar above.

291
291 Hackney Road, Bethnal Green, E2 (7613 5676/ www.291gallery.com). Liverpool Street or Old Street tube/rail/26, 48, 55 bus. **Open** 6.30pm-midnight Tue, Wed, Thur; 6.30pm-2am Fri, Sat. **Credit** MC, V.
A mix of brasserie, bar, art centre and performance space, 291 is friendly and atmospheric. Food is inventive, but bottled beers or draught Hoegaarden are preferable to the hit-and-miss cocktails.

South London

Bread & Roses
68 Clapham Manor Street, Clapham, SW4 (7498 1779). Clapham Common or Clapham North tube. **Open** 11am-11pm Mon-Sat; noon-10.30pm Sun. **Credit** MC, V.
An excellent, spacious hostelry with a minimalist interior that somehow manages to retain a traditional pub atmosphere. There's good beer, music, poetry and comedy events, and a tasty, affordable African buffet on Sundays.

Brixtonian Havana Club

11 Beehive Place, Brixton, SW9 (7924 9262/
www.brixtonian.co.uk). Brixton tube/rail. **Open** noon-
1am Mon-Wed; noon-2am Thur-Sat; noon-midnight
Sun. **Credit** MC, V.
Rum connoisseurs can't get enough of this place,
which stocks more than 300 varieties. The relaxed
vibe matches the Caribbean flavours; evening entertainment ranges from DJ sets to open-mic sessions.

Dogstar

389 Coldharbour Lane, Brixton, SW9 (7733 7515/
www.dogstarbar.co.uk). Brixton tube/rail. **Open**
noon-3am Mon-Thur, Sun; noon-4am Fri, Sat.
Credit AmEx, MC, V.
Where the Brixton revival began, offering late bev-
erages and loud sounds to twentysomethings bored
with the prices and pretensions of the West End.

Drawing Room

103 Lavender Hill, Battersea, SW11 (7350 2564).
Clapham Junction rail. **Open** 6pm-midnight Mon-Fri;
10.30am-midnight Sat; 10.30am-11pm Sun. **Credit**
MC, V.
Locals have a soft spot for this old favourite, despite
– or maybe because of – its erratic service, unpredictable food and increasingly shabby surroundings. Go for the mismatched crockery, chintzy
tablecloths, mad clocks and laid-back vibe.

Fire Stables

*27-9 Church Road, SW19 (8946 3197). Wimbledon
tube/rail then 200, 93 bus.* **Open** 10am-11pm Mon-
Sat; 10am-10.30pm Sun. **Credit** AmEx, MC, V.
It used to be a dire boozer called the Castle, but these
days the Fire Stables is an upmarket bar with fantastic cooking. The deserving winner of the *Time
Out* 2001 Best Gastropub award.

Mayflower

*117 Rotherhithe Street, Rotherhithe, SE16
(7237 4088). Rotherhithe tube/188, P11, P13 bus.*
Open noon-11pm Mon-Sat; noon-10.30pm Sun.
Credit AmEx, DC, MC, V.
A historic seafaring inn with rackety wooden floors,
small wood-partitioned areas and narrow settles (the
timbers are reputed to have come from *The
Mayflower* ship). Greene King bitters are on offer,
plus a short but varied wine list.

The Plug

90 Stockwell Road, Stockwell, SW9 (7274 3879/
www.theplug.co.uk). Stockwell tube. **Open** noon-
midnight Mon-Thur, Sun; noon-3am Fri, Sat.
Credit MC, V.
A glimpse of what Brixton used to be like. This is
the place to sink liquor fast and dance in the same
fashion, aided by special drinks of ludicrous strength
and DJs who can get the crowd going.

Sand

*156 Clapham Park Road, Clapham, SW4 (7622
3022/www.sandbarrestaurant.co.uk). Clapham
Common tube.* **Open** 5pm-2am Mon-Sat; 5pm-1am
Sun. **Credit** MC, V.

The decor's easy on the eye, the listening (Sinatra,
Bacharach) easy on the ear, and candles, spotlights
and intimate (and usually reserved) alcoves make it
all very cosy. Add DJs at weekends, miniature
movies and the obligatory sharp Antipodean staff.

Time

*7A College Approach, Greenwich, SE10 (8305
9767/www.timerestaurant.com). Cutty Sark DLR/
Greenwich rail.* **Open** noon-11pm Mon-Sat;
noon-10.30pm Sun. **Credit** AmEx, MC, V.
Once a Victorian music hall, funky Time now manages an odd combination-look that mixes original
features with comfortable sofas, weekend DJs and
ever-changing contemporary art on the walls.

Trafalgar Tavern

*Park Row, Greenwich, SE10 (8858 2437/
www.trafalgartavern.co.uk). Cutty Sark DLR/
Greenwich or Maze Hill rail.* **Open** 11.30am-11pm
Mon-Sat; noon-10.30pm Sun. **Credit** MC, V.
This historic pub on the site of the Old George Inn
was built in 1837 as a tribute to naval hero Horatio
Nelson. There's mahogany panelling, stone fire-
places and the like, plus a riverside terrace.

West London

Albertine

1 Wood Lane, Shepherd's Bush, W12 (8743 9593).
Shepherd's Bush tube. **Open** noon-11pm Mon-Fri;
6.30-11pm Sat. **Credit** MC, V.
It's not about gimmicks at Albertine, it's purely
about wine. The friendly owner is usually on hand
to help navigate the lengthy selection.

Anglesea Arms

*35 Wingate Road, Hammersmith, W6 (8749
1291). Goldhawk Road or Ravenscourt Park tube.*
Open 11am-11pm Mon-Sat; noon-10.30pm Sun.
Credit MC, V.
The Anglesea Arms has tables out front (weather
permitting), a bar and a dining room, all of which fill
up quickly, so arrive early. The draught Hoegaarden
with a slice of lemon is great on a hot day.

Archery Tavern

4 Bathurst Street, Paddington, W2 (7402 4916).
Lancaster Gate tube. **Open** 11am-11pm Mon-Sat;
noon-10.30pm Sun. **Credit** AmEx, MC, V.
Map p395 D6.
This genteel pub sticks to the most traditional for-
mulae – plates on the walls, bunches of dried hops
and regulars who commandeer their favourite seat
and ask the staff (by name) to turn the music down.

Churchill Arms

*119 Kensington Church Street, Kensington, W8
(7727 4242). High Street Kensington or Notting Hill
Gate tube.* **Open** 11am-11pm Mon-Sat; noon-10.30pm
Sun. **Credit** MC, V. **Map** p394 B8.
Lepidopterists will want to check out the boxed butterflies on display at the back of this pub; others can
sink a few ales and tuck into good, cheap Thai food.

Eat, Drink, Shop

How the udder half live: **The Cow**.

The Cow

*89 Westbourne Park Road, Notting Hill, W2
(7221 0021). Royal Oak tube or Westbourne Park.*
Open noon-11pm Mon-Sat; noon-10.30pm Sun.
Credit AmEx, MC, V. **Map** p394 B5.
An informal, pretty Guinness and oyster bar serving sumptuous plates of fish and pints of prawns to the trendily scruffy of west London.

Dove

*19 Upper Mall, Hammersmith, W6 (8748 5405).
Hammersmith tube.* **Open** 11am-11pm Mon-Sat;
noon-10.30pm Sun. **Credit** AmEx, MC, V.
More than 300 years old and gloriously dishevelled,
the Dove has three small split-level rooms around a
central bar and a pretty ivy-clad riverside terrace.

Jacs

*48 Lonsdale Road, Notting Hill, W11 (7792 2838).
Notting Hill Gate tube.* **Open** 6-11pm Tue-Sat;
7-10.30pm Sun. **Credit** MC, V. **Map** p394 A6.
This underground speakeasy has dubious decor but
is actually a pretty cool gaff with occasional DJs.

Westbourne

*101 Westbourne Park Villas, Notting Hill, W2 (7221
1332). Royal Oak tube.* **Open** 5-11pm Mon; noon-
11pm Tue-Fri; 11am-11pm Sat; 11am-10.30pm Sun.
Credit AmEx, DC, MC, V. **Map** p394 B5.

The only way to get an outside table here at this terminally hip pub is to turn up when it's chucking it
down. A good range of wines and beers, as well as
smoothies, make it worth the squeeze.

White Horse

*1-3 Parsons Green, Fulham, SW6 (7736 2115/
www.whitehorsesw6.com). Parsons Green tube.*
Open 11am-11pm Mon-Sat; 11am-10.30pm Sun.
Credit AmEx, MC, V.
This imposing multi-bar Victorian boozer has been
pleasantly modernised and comfortably decked out
with sofas and chunky wooden furniture. More than
100 fine wines are stocked, plus real ale and every
available Trappist brew.

White Swan

*Riverside, Twickenham, Middx (8892 2166/
www.massivepub.com). Twickenham rail.* **Open**
Apr-Sept 11am-11pm Mon-Sat; noon-10.30pm Sun.
Oct-Mar 11am-3pm, 5.30-11pm Mon-Thur; 11am-
11pm Fri, Sat; noon-10.30pm Sun. **Credit** MC, V.
This characterful riverside pub with more than
three centuries of history attracts pub connoisseurs
from miles around. Raised to avoid flooding, the
White Swan overlooks Eel Pie Island, the one time
1960s rock hangout and still a last refuge for keepers of 'alternative culture'.

Eat, Drink, Shop

Shops & Services

London may be the best for high street chains and department stores, but smaller independent shops still constitute much of its appeal.

For most major UK and global chains you needn't stray much further than **Oxford Street** and **Regent Street**, though at weekends you'll be fighting for space with half of London. Other popular shopping areas include **Covent Garden** and **King's Road**, both of which offer high fashion as well as quirkier independent shops. **Knightsbridge** draws the crowds with high-class department stores Harrods (*see p235*) and Harvey Nichols (*see p236*).

For further shop listings and reviews, the *Time Out Shopping Guide* is available in most good bookshops and newsagents. For information on consumer rights, *see p363*.

LATE OPENING

Stores in central London are open late one night a week (usually until 7pm or 8pm). Those in the West End (Oxford Street to Covent Garden) are open until late on Thursdays, while Wednesday is late opening in the chi-chi Chelsea/Knightsbridge/Kensington triangle. In addition, some shops are open on Sundays, especially in the weeks leading up to Christmas.

Antiques

Camden Market, **Greenwich Market** and **Portobello Road Market** (for all, *see p256*) have antiques stalls.

Alfie's Antiques Market

13-25 Church Street, Marylebone, NW8 (7723 6066/www.ealfies.com). Edgware Road tube/ Marylebone tube/rail. **Open** 10am-6pm Tue-Sat. **Credit** varies. **Map** p395 E4.
One of the best antiques centres to visit as a starting point – whether you're just beginning to collect, or looking for something specific. With around 150 dealers, there's plenty to look at. What you won't find is the exclusive and snobbish attitude common in some London centres; the downside is the whole place can feel a bit shabby. It's particularly good for Arts and Crafts furniture, old advertising, 20th-century glass and ceramics and vintage clothes (*see p258* **Thrifty business** and *p245* **Who she? Sparkle Moore**).

Antiquarius

131-41 King's Road, Chelsea, SW3 (7351 5353). South Kensington or Sloane Square tube/19, 22, 319 bus. **Open** 10am-6pm Mon-Sat. **Credit** varies. **Map** p397 F11.

The sheer number of dealers at Antiquarius, many of them specialists, means that most people will find something of interest. Strengths here include French art deco, clocks, textiles, jewellery and small *objets de vertu*.

Bermondsey (New Caledonian) Market

Bermondsey Square, Bermondsey, SE1. Bermondsey tube. **Open** 5am-2pm Fri (starts closing around noon). **Map** p405 Q10.
This is a mecca for serious collectors, with dealers from all over the South-East. Most good stuff goes by 9am, so get here early.

Camden Passage

Camden Passage, off Upper Street, Camden, N1 (7359 0190). Angel tube. **Open** Arcade & shops 10am-4pm Tue, Thur, Fri; 8am-5pm Wed, Sat. *Market* 7am-2pm Wed; 8am-5pm Sat. **Credit** varies. **Map** p402 O2.
This narrow street lined with antiques shops holds a twice-weekly market. There are four arcades nearby; the most northerly, the Georgian Village, houses specialists in art nouveau, ceramics and commemorative wares. The Mall, in a former tramshed, has furniture shops in the basement and small shops on the ground floor, with Decodence (Bakelite and early plastics) not to be missed. The other two arcades – Angel and Pierrepont – hold more diversity, and there are usually some exciting outdoor stalls: some run by professional dealers, others bric-a-brac spread out on the pavement.

Grays Antiques Market & Grays in the Mews

58 Davies Street & 1-7 Davies Mews, Mayfair, W1 (7629 7034/www.emews.com or www.egrays.com). Bond Street tube. **Open** 10am-6pm Mon-Fri (book emporium also open 10am-6pm Sat). **Credit** varies. **Map** p398 H6.
The main market, which is housed in an old Victorian plumbing factory, has a fine selection of stalls, with a heavy emphasis on jewellery. Grays in the Mews is more of a mixed bag, with antiquities, toys, Bohemian glassware, prints, watercolours, antiquarian books, specialist dolls and a range of golfing memorabilia.

Bookshops

The big bookstore chains – **Waterstone's**, **Books Etc** and **Borders** – have branches all over London; the largest are listed below.

General

Books Etc

263 High Holborn, Holborn, WC1 (7404 0261). Holborn tube. **Open** 9am-7pm Mon-Fri. **Credit** AmEx, MC, V. **Map** p399 K6.
This extremely popular shop, part of the Borders empire (*see below*), has a good general stock.

Borders

203 Oxford Street, Soho, W1 (7292 1600/ www.borders.com). Oxford Circus tube. **Open** 8am-11pm Mon-Sat; noon-6pm Sun. **Credit** AmEx, MC, V. **Map** p398 J6.
An impressive general stock of books, music and videos, plus lots of US import titles by writers the UK has yet to wake up to.

Foyles

113-19 Charing Cross Road, Soho, WC2 (7437 5660/www.foyles.co.uk). Tottenham Court Road tube. **Open** 9.30am-8pm Mon-Sat; noon-6pm Sun. **Credit** AmEx, MC, V. **Map** p399 K6.
This quirky, old-fashioned establishment is entering the modern world after the death of fearsome London bookselling doyenne Christina Foyle. The paperback fiction is no longer shelved by publisher, – a weird anachronism that made it nearly impossible to find what you wanted.

Waterstone's

203-6 Piccadilly, St James's, W1 (7851 2400/ www.waterstones.co.uk). Piccadilly Circus tube. **Open** 10am-11pm Mon-Sat; noon-6pm Sun. **Credit** AmEx, DC, MC, V. **Map** p400 J7.
The arrival of Waterstone's in the high street changed bookselling in this country for good, mostly for the better. This flagship store, Europe's biggest bookshop, is a great environment in which to browse a wide selection of titles (you can even sit and read books at your leisure) and attend author signings and readings. There's a gallery space, an event room, cafés and bars, and even a restaurant.

Specialist

Books for Cooks

4 Blenheim Crescent, Notting Hill, W11 (7221 1992/www.booksforcooks.com). Ladbroke Grove tube. **Open** 10am-6pm Mon-Sat. **Credit** AmEx, DC, MC, V.
Recipe books and books about food from every conceivable part of the globe. The test kitchen is booked up two weeks ahead for weekdays and six weeks ahead for Saturdays.

Children's Book Centre

237 Kensington High Street, Kensington, W8 (7937 7497/www.childrensbookcentre.co.uk). High Street Kensington tube. **Open** 9.30am-6.30pm Mon, Wed, Fri, Sat; 9.30am-6pm Tue; 9.30am-7pm Thur; noon-6pm Sun. **Credit** AmEx, MC, V. **Map** p396 A9.

Get bitten by the travel bug at **Daunt Books**.

In addition to its 20,000 titles for ages 0-13, the Children's Book Centre carries activity games, puzzles, videos, cassettes and character toys.

Cinema Bookshop

13-14 Great Russell Street, Fitzrovia, WC1 (7637 0206). Tottenham Court Road tube. **Open** 10.30am-5.30pm Mon-Sat. **Credit** MC, V. **Map** p399 K5.
For three decades Fred Zentner has been selling all manner of film-related material out of these tiny premises. The shop deals in new and out-of-print books, covering everything 'from pre-cinema to yesterday's director', as well as stills, lobby cards and other paraphernalia.

Daunt Books

83-4 Marylebone High Street, Marylebone, W1 (7224 2295). Baker Street or Bond Street tube. **Open** 9am-7.30pm Mon-Sat; 11am-6pm Sun. **Credit** MC, V. **Map** p398 G5.
Having undergone recent expansion, Daunt now has a wider general selection augmenting its outstanding stock of travel titles. A strong contender for most beautiful retail interior in London, if not the world. **Branch**: 193 Haverstock Hill, Belsize Park, NW3 (7794 4006).

Edward Stanford

12-14 Long Acre, Covent Garden, WC2 (7836 1321/ www.stanfords.co.uk). Covent Garden or Leicester Square tube. **Open** 9am-7.30pm Mon-Fri; 10am-7pm Sat; noon-6pm Sun. **Credit** MC, V. **Map** p401 L6.
Your first stop for maps and globes, Stanford also does more general travel literature and tons of guides. The basement is devoted to maps and guides to the British Isles.

Forbidden Planet

*71-5 New Oxford Street, St Giles's, WC1
(7836 4179). Tottenham Court Road tube.*
Open 10am-6pm Mon-Wed, Sat; 10am-7pm
Thur, Fri. **Credit** AmEx, MC, V. **Map** p399 L5.
This is where to come for SF (never sci-fi, please, not
to real fans) from US publishers and UK specialist
presses, in particular. The basement selection also
extends to slipstream fiction. The ground floor is
packed with comics, videos, magazines and models.

Gay's the Word

*66 Marchmont Street, Bloomsbury, WC1 (7278
7654/www.gaystheword.co.uk). Russell Square
tube.* **Open** 10am-6.30pm Mon-Sat; 2-6pm Sun.
Credit AmEx, DC, MC, V. **Map** p399 L4.
The biggest gay and lesbian bookshop in Britain
has been a reassuring presence on this lovely
neighbourhood street since 1979. Books are shelved
by genre – fiction, travel, counselling, biography,
second-hand, sex manuals – and there are magazines and cards, too.

Grant & Cutler

*55-7 Great Marlborough Street, Soho, W1
(7734 2012/www.grantandcutler.com). Oxford Circus
tube.* **Open** 9am-6pm Mon-Wed, Fri;
9am-7pm Thur; 9am-5.30pm Sat. **Credit** MC, V.
Map p398 J6.

The best Shops

For a bookish browse
Waterstone's. *See p232.*

For an art fix
The Pineal Eye. *See p239.*

For cheap chic
H&M; Zara. *See p239.*

For money-back guarantees
John Lewis. *See p236.*

For everything-under-one-roof
Selfridges. *See p236.*

For body modification
Into You. *See p248.*

For an uplifting experience
Rigby & Peller. *See p246.*

For a girl's best friend
Tiffany & Co. *See p248.*

For your daily bread
& Clarke's. *See p250.*

For writing home
Paperchase. *See p253.*

The *ne plus ultra* of foreign-language booksellers,
Grant & Cutler is stuffed to the gills with books,
cassettes, CDs, videos and software packages in up
to 200 different languages.

Murder One

*71-3 Charing Cross Road, Soho, WC2 (7734 3483/
www.murderone.co.uk). Leicester Square tube.*
Open 10am-7pm Mon-Wed; 10am-8pm Thur-Sat.
Credit AmEx, MC, V. **Map** p401 K6.
Maxim Jakubowski's centre-of-operations covers
numerous genres, including crime and mystery,
horror, SF and fantasy, and romance.

Silver Moon Women's Bookshop

*64-8 Charing Cross Road, Covent Garden,
WC2 (7836 7906/www.silvermoonbookshop.co.uk).
Leicester Square tube.* **Open** 9.30am-7.30pm Mon-Fri;
10am-6.30pm Sat; noon-6pm Sun. **Credit** AmEx, MC,
V. **Map** p401 K6.
'Europe's largest women's bookshop,' states the
sign, and we don't doubt it. Two floors of books
about women's issues and books by women.

Talking Books Shop

*11 Wigmore Street, Marylebone, W1 (7491 4117/
www.talkingbooks.co.uk). Bond Street tube.*
Open 9.30am-5.30pm Mon-Fri; 10am-5pm Sat.
Credit AmEx, MC, V. **Map** p398 G6.
Spoken-word cassettes and CDs, including radio
comedy, classic drama and audiobooks.

Zwemmer Media Arts

*80 Charing Cross Road, Covent Garden, WC2 (7240
4157/www.zwemmer.com). Leicester Square tube.*
Open 10am-6.30pm Mon-Wed, Fri; 10am-7pm
Thur; 10am-6.30pm Sat. **Credit** AmEx, DC, MC, V.
Map p401 K6.
Tight for space but with friendly staff, Zwemmer
Media specialises in photography and cinema.
Branches: The Art Shop 24 Litchfield Street,
Covent Garden, WC2 (7240 4158); **The Design
Shop** 72 Charing Cross Road, Covent Garden,
WC2 (7240 1559); **Whitechapel Art Gallery
Bookshop** 80 Whitechapel High Street,
Whitechapel, E1 (7247 6924); **Barbican Theatre
Bookshop** Barbican Centre, Silk Street, The City,
EC2 (7382 7007).

Antiquarian/second-hand

The **Riverside Walk Market** (10am-5pm
Sat, Sun and irregular weekdays) on the South
Bank (*see p74*) under Waterloo Bridge has
cheap paperbacks. Another fertile hunting
ground in terms of second-hand bookshops
is Charing Cross Road, WC2.

Skoob Russell Square

*10 Brunswick Centre, off Bernard Street,
Bloomsbury, WC1 (7278 8760/www.skoob.com).
Russell Square.* **Open** 10.30am-7.30pm Mon-Sat;
noon-5pm Sun. **Credit** AmEx, MC, V. **Map** p399 L4.
One of London's most comprehensive second-hand
bookshops, Skoob caters for students, academics

Eat, Drink, Shop

PANDORA

Dress Agency/Consignment Shop
Armani to Zikha

"Have you ever wondered how some women always manage to look smartly dressed. Natural style, money to burn?"

They have discovered the secret of second hand clothes shopping.

PANDORA,
London's leading Dress Agency.
Approximately 5,000 items; huge collection;
· suits · dresses · hats · shoes · accessories
All the top designer labels, all in perfect condition.

**16-22 Cheval Place,
Knightsbridge,
London SW7 1ES
Open 9am-6pm
Mon-Sat
Tel (020) 7589 5289**

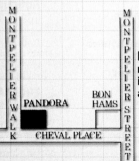

PANDORA is a minute from Harrods – ideal for buyers and sellers

and those with special interests. Prices are low and students are given a discount. The video and DVD section is getting pretty extensive, too.

Ulysses

40 Museum Street, Bloomsbury, WC1 (7831 1600). Holborn or Tottenham Court Road tube. **Open** 10.30am-6pm Mon-Sat. **Credit** AmEx, DC, MC, V. **Map** p399 L5.

Probably London's best place for 20th-century first editions, fiction in particular. Most books are kept in cabinets, but you can browse through shelves of the slightly less valuable stuff. There are trestles of cheapies outside, along with rare children's books, biography, philosophy, poetry and prints.

Unsworths Booksellers

12 Bloomsbury Street, Bloomsbury, WC1 (7436 9836/www.unsworths.com). Tottenham Court Road tube. **Open** 10am-8pm Mon-Sat; noon-8pm Sun. **Credit** AmEx, DC, MC, V. **Map** p399 K5.

A large, breezy shop with a good line in remaindered titles – recent books, both European and US editions, come in at 50% of the publishers' price. The proximity to University College London means that academic subjects are well represented.

Department stores

Fortnum & Mason

181 Piccadilly, St James's, W1 (7734 8040/ www.fortnumandmason.co.uk). Green Park or Piccadilly Circus tube. **Open** 10am-6.30pm Mon-Sat. **Credit** AmEx, DC, MC, V. **Map** p400 J7.

Traditionally dressed assistants and stately surroundings make this store a favourite of foreign visitors who want a taste of ye olde England. The ground-floor food hall is legendary, though the prices reflect the constant tourist flow. The interiors department is straight out of *Country Life*, while fashion is very much of the grown-up ilk, with names such as Yves Saint Laurent and Jean Muir for the ladies and Barbour for the country gent. Once you've ordered your hamper from the basement, soak up the atmosphere in the Salmon & Champagne Bar.

Harrods

87-135 Brompton Road, Knightsbridge, SW1 (7730 1234/www.harrods.com). Knightsbridge tube. **Open** 10am-7pm Mon-Sat. **Credit** AmEx, DC, MC, V. **Map** p397 F9.

The famous food halls, the striking decor and the legendary sales make Harrods a must-visit store of the theme-park genre, though the dress requirements (no rucksacks or ripped jeans) and the £1 charge to use the toilets bespeak snobbery rather than style. It's worth coming for the revamped homewares department alone: the 'Modern Living' area features furniture by Hulsta, Flexiform and Former, while the 'Contemporary Gallery' has the hip feel of Jerry's Home Store. For cosmetics junkies there's the pricey skincare ranges of Crème de la Mer and Prada, and the leather-clad Défilé range, while for the boys there are two newish men's departments: the Bodyzone men's grooming area and the men's shoe department, with designs by Gucci, Prada and Dolce & Gabbana. The 60-plus fashion concessions are – surprise! – mainly at the chic end of the market.

Feast your eyes or feed your face at **Harrods**' legendary food halls.

Harvey Nichols

109-25 Knightsbridge, Knightsbridge, SW1 (7235 5000/www.harveynichols.com). Knightsbridge tube. **Open** 10am-7pm Mon, Tue, Sat; 10am-8pm Wed-Fri; noon-6pm Sun. **Credit** AmEx, DC, MC, V. **Map** p397 F9.

High fashion for style junkies from the likes of Loewe, Hussein Chalayan and Luella Bartley, as well as old favourites Joseph, Versace and Alberta Ferretti. Top Brit designers Alexander McQueen and Stella McCartney (for Chloé) are on the first floor among all the other catwalk favourites. The ground-floor beauty hall has undergone a makeover, and while all the traditional and niche brands remain, there's a greater emphasis on a holistic approach to beauty, with organic products from Dr Hauschka and Everest Hill Aromas among the additions. The food hall on the fifth floor goes from strength to strength, with a strong range of sleekly packaged products and a great selection of fresh produce – the prices are as steep as you'd expect, but at least your cupboards will look as stylish as your wardrobe.

John Lewis

278-306 Oxford Street, Marylebone, W1 (7629 7711/www.johnlewis.co.uk). Bond Street or Oxford Circus tube. **Open** 9.30am-7pm Mon-Wed, Fri, Sat; 9.30am-8pm. **Credit** MC, V. **Map** p398 H6.

John Lewis outdoes nearby rivals for its family-friendly layout and products, and excels in a number of areas. The basement kitchen department is crammed with useful and stylish cookware and electrical goods, while the famous haberdashery section is extensive and the staff's helpfulness is impressive, even by John Lewis's standards. The other high point is the top-floor electrical department, where the range of products, knowledgeable assistants, low prices and impressive guarantees make for one of the best places in town to buy TVs, stereos, phones and computers – the only drawback is that everyone knows this, and so a queuing system for assistance has been instituted. The fashion departments, though uninspired, are no-nonsense places in which to kit yourself out for the office or casual weekends. All products are covered by the 'never knowingly undersold' policy.

Branches: Brent Cross Shopping Centre, Brent Cross, NW4 (8202 6535); **Peter Jones** Sloane Square, Chelsea, SW1 (7730 3434); Wood Street, Kingston, Surrey (8547 3000).

Liberty

210-20 Regent Street, Soho, W1 (7734 1234/www.liberty.co.uk). Oxford Circus tube. **Open** 10am-6.30pm Mon-Wed; 10am-8pm Thur; 10am-7pm Fri, Sat; noon-6pm Sun. **Credit** AmEx, DC, MC, V. **Map** p398 J6.

After a rocky period, Liberty has been modernising of late; more glitzy brands are promised in both the menswear and womenswear departments, as well as in interiors. The mock-Tudor façade combined with the crafty and heavily patterned accessories and Liberty's own printed fabrics mean the shop still

Selfridges: stately but funky.

has an old-fashioned air, but there are enough cutting-edge offerings (such as the Designers Guild concession) to keep the store on the stylish side of traditional. Particular strong points are jewellery by the likes of Wright & Teague and Slim Barrett, the sumptuous silks in the haberdashery department, the rug department, and the linens, throws and cushions. Furniture is also anything but run-of-the-mill.

Marks & Spencer

458 Oxford Street, Marylebone, W1 (7935 7954/www.marks-and-spencer.com). Bond Street or Marble Arch tube. **Open** 9am-9pm Mon-Fri; 8.30am-7.30pm Sat; noon-6pm Sun. **Credit** AmEx, MC, V. **Map** p398 G6.

Marks & Sparks has had a well-publicised hard time of late, and these days it's the food that attracts the most customers. In 2001 it redesigned 25 shops throughout the UK; the new format aims to make the stores more attractive to customers, as do attempts to provide more stylish clobber (at the risk of alienating some of the more traditional clientele), but only time will tell how the old favourite will cope with the 21st century.

Branches: throughout the city.

Selfridges

400 Oxford Street, Marylebone, W1 (7629 1234/www.selfridges.com). Bond Street or Marble Arch tube. **Open** 10am-7pm Mon-Wed; 10am-8pm Thur, Fri; 9.30am-7pm Sat; noon-6pm Sun. **Credit** AmEx, DC, MC, V. **Map** p398 G6.

Under the auspices of Vittorio Radice (*see p246* **Who he?**), Selfridges has risen from a long slumber to become London's funkiest department store. Recent innovations have included the introduction of a new selection of men's and women's fashion running from streetwear through to formalwear; newcomers include Fake London, Ann Demeulemeester, Fake Genius, Matthew Williamson, Yohji Yamamoto and Viktor & Rolf. Home design, which often features in the fabulous window displays, is also worth a look. The food hall and first-floor beauty hall are other strong points.

Electronics

Tottenham Court Road, W1, has a glut of electronics and computer shops. It's best to know what you're after and shop around for the best prices: staff are notoriously pushy.

Computers & games

Two other good stockists of games are **Virgin Megastore** and **HMV** (for both, *see p257*).

Apple Centre
78 New Oxford Street, Bloomsbury, WC1 (7692 9990/www.square2.co.uk). Tottenham Court Road tube. **Open** 9am-5.30pm Mon-Wed, Fri; 9am-6.30pm Thur. **Credit** MC, V. **Map** p399 L5.
A central mecca for all things Mac, this comprehensively stocked store is the leading authority on Apple computers and their applications.

Computer Exchange
32 Rathbone Place, Fitzrovia, W1 (7636 2666/ www.cex.co.uk). Tottenham Court Road tube. **Open** 10am-7pm daily. **Credit** MC, V. **Map** p399 K5.
A fantastic part-exchange emporium dealing in second-hand games in just about every format, which, depending on their condition, can cost as little as £1. The store also holds a select line of imported Japanese and US titles and is often first with some incredible pre-release stuff. The really good stuff is downstairs in the unrivalled retro section, which charts the development of gaming since the '70s and includes a huge number of old computers, consoles and games.

Gultronics
52 Tottenham Court Road, Fitzrovia, W1 (7637 1619/www.gultronics.co.uk). Tottenham Court Road tube. **Open** 9am-6pm Mon-Wed, Fri, Sat; 9am-7pm Thur. **Credit** AmEx, MC, V. **Map** p399 K5.
A wide variety of PCs, from top-spec speedmongers to a fine line of laptops that starts at £680 and goes up to around £3,000. Regular special offers ensure there's always a bargain or two to be had. **Branches**: throughout the city.

Hi-fi

Hi-Fi Experience
227 Tottenham Court Road, Fitzrovia, W1 (7580 3535/www.hifilondon.co.uk). Goodge Street or Tottenham Court Road tube. **Open** 10am-7pm Mon-Fri; 9am-6pm Sat. **Credit** AmEx, DC, MC, V. **Map** p399 K5.

Staff here can be patronising but the stock continues to impress, with lines from the likes of Bang & Olufsen and a good selection of home cinema equipment. Eight demo rooms are available in which to put them the goods to the test.

Richer Sounds
2 London Bridge Walk, Borough, SE1 (7403 1201/www.richersounds.com). London Bridge tube/rail. **Open** 10am-6pm Mon-Wed, Fri; 10am-7pm Thur; 10am-5pm Sat. **Credit** MC, V. **Map** p405 Q8.
A good selection of quality separates – from names such as Technics, Arcam and Marantz – at some of the most competitive prices in the capital. Check the website for a list of offers.
Branches: throughout the city.

Photography

Jessops
63-9 New Oxford Street, St Giles's, WC1 (7240 6077/www.jessops.com). Tottenham Court Road tube. **Open** 9am-6pm Mon-Wed, Sat; 9am-8pm Thur; 9am-7pm Fri; 11am-5pm Sun. **Credit** AmEx, DC, MC, V. **Map** p399 L5.
The largest of 14 London branches, this shop has a huge choice of cameras, accessories and materials (including cheaper own-brand stuff). There's a vast array of 35mm, APS, medium-format and digital wares for both the amateur and professional markets, plus a growing portfolio of digital services.
Branches: throughout the city.

Snappy Snaps
23 Garrick Street, Covent Garden, WC2 (7836 3040). Leicester Square tube. **Open** 8.30am-6pm Mon-Fri; noon-5pm Sat. **Credit** MC, V. **Map** p401 L7.
An outstanding high street film processing chain offering the full gamut of developing services.
Branches: throughout the city.

Fashion

For vintage and retro clothing shops, *see p258* **Thrifty business**.

Boutiques

Aime
32 Ledbury Road, Notting Hill, W11 (7221 7070). Notting Hill Gate or Westbourne Park tube. **Open** 10.30am-7pm Mon-Sat. **Credit** MC, V. **Map** p394 A6.
This shop is a little piece of France in a trendy part of London. Owned by two half-French, half-Cambodian sisters, it sells clothes exclusively by French designers such as Barbara Bui, Christophe Lemaire and Les Prairies de Paris. There's also a selection of classic French fabric and leather bags by Ursule Beaugeste, shoes by Isabel Marant and Christophe Lemaire, some tempting homewares, and French music and books.

Eat, Drink, Shop

Browns

23-27 South Molton Street, Mayfair, W1 (7514 0000/www.brownsfashion.com). Bond Street tube. **Open** 10am-6.30pm Mon-Wed, Fri, Sat; 10am-7pm Thur. **Credit** AmEx, MC, V. **Map** p398 H6.

The Browns empire sets the tone for South Molton Street, with menswear, womenswear and homewares on one side of the road, the more youthful Browns Focus right opposite and the bargain-hunter's paradise, Labels for Less, five doors down. Designers stocked at Browns include Alexander McQueen, Matthew Williamson, Chloé, Miu Miu and Prada Sport, while Browns Focus prides itself on a selection of the most cutting-edge contemporary fashions, as well as some of the most innovative jewellery around.

Koh Samui

65 Monmouth Street, Covent Garden, WC2 (7240 4280). Covent Garden or Leicester Square tube. **Open** 10am-6.30pm Mon-Wed, Fri, Sat; 10am-7pm Thur; 11am-5.30pm Sun. **Credit** AmEx, MC, V. **Map** p399 L6.

Other boutiques stock the same designers, but Koh Samui always seems to choose the best pieces. It boasts a wonderful mix of established labels and up-and-coming talent and is never afraid to take a chance on the more avant-garde. Current British favourites include Julien Macdonald, Matthew Williamson, Luella Bartley and Elspeth Gibson. **Branch:** 28 Lowndes Street, Chelsea, SW1 (7838 9292).

The Pineal Eye

49 Broadwick Street, Soho, W1 (7434 2567). Oxford Circus tube. **Open** 11am-7pm Mon-Fri; noon-7pm Sat. **Credit** AmEx, MC, V. **Map** p398 J6.

On the ground floor, new artists and designers exhibit their work, which is often in the form of installation, while the basement showcases one-off pieces and special designerwear items. Labels stocked are global and include Lutz, Adam Entwistle, Dior Menswear, Andre Walker and Olivier Theyskens. Art magazines, jewellery and shoes are also sold.

Tokio

309 Brompton Road, Kensington, SW3 (7823 7310). South Kensington tube. **Open** 10am-6.30pm Mon-Sat. **Credit** AmEx, MC, V. **Map** p397 E10.

Keen on tailoring, colour and design, Tokio is good at offering something that's unusual yet wearable. Often the first store to discover new designers and select the pieces from established collections that other boutiques overlook, Tokio stocks Tracey Frith, Anthony Symonds, Boyd, Clements Ribeiro, Jessica Ogden, Maurizio Pecoraro and more, plus footwear by Diego Dolcini and Marc Jacobs and a range of jewellery and bags.
Branch: 197 Westbourne Grove, W11 (7792 2515).

Whistles

12 St Christopher's Place, Marylebone, W1 (7487 4484). Bond Street tube. **Open** 10am-6pm Mon-Wed, Fri, Sat; 10am-7pm Thur; noon-5pm Sun. **Credit** AmEx, MC, V. **Map** p398 H6.

All Whistles branches stock a core range but vary when it comes to the independent designer pieces. St Christopher's Place is by far the largest and best stocked, though from recent inspection sister stores are hot on its heels. Whistles' superb own range sits well beside such labels as Rozae Nichols, Martine Sitbon, Claudette and Dries van Noten. Accessories are always key, with shoes by Rodolphe Menudier, bags by Ally Capellino and stunning geometric print silk hats, bags and halter-neck tops by Ginka.
Branches: throughout the city.

Budget

H&M

261-71 Regent Street, Marylebone, W1 (7493 4004/ www.hm.com). Oxford Circus tube. **Open** 10am-7pm Mon-Wed, Sat; 10am-8pm Thur, Fri; noon-6pm Sun. **Credit** AmEx, MC, V. **Map** p400 J7.

This Swedish chain keeps up a constant flow of bang-up-to-the-minute trends. Quality isn't a forte here, but who's complaining at these prices? H&M won the Best Menswear category in the *Time Out* Retail Awards 2001.
Branches: throughout the city.

Miss Selfridge

214 Oxford Street, Marylebone, W1 (7434 0405). Oxford Circus tube. **Open** 9am-8pm Mon-Wed, Fri, Sat; 9am-8pm Thur; noon-6pm Sun. **Credit** AmEx, MC, V. **Map** p398 G6.

From the people who brought you Selfridges (*see p236*), this funky chain for trendy young things won't break the bank.
Branches: throughout the city.

Top Shop/Top Man

214 Oxford Street, Marylebone, W1 (7636 7700/ www.topshop.co.uk). Oxford Circus tube. **Open** 9am-8pm Mon-Wed, Fri, Sat; 9am-9pm Thur; noon-6pm Sun. **Credit** AmEx, DC, MC, V. **Map** p398 J6.

The leader of the budget pack, the world's biggest fashion store offers rails of bargain streetwear, clubwear and catwalk knock-offs, plus a café and a men's and women's hairdressers.
Branches: throughout the city.

Zara

118 Regent Street, Mayfair, W1 (7534 9500/ www.inditex.com). Piccadilly Circus tube. **Open** 10am-7pm Mon-Wed, Fri, Sat; 10am-8pm Thur; noon-6pm Sun. **Credit** AmEx, DC, MC, V. **Map** p400 J7.

Like its Spanish confrère Mango (*see p242*), the hugely successful Zara has clothes that convey designer quality and style without the price. Unlike H&M (*see above*), stock tends to be chic and classic rather than throwaway trendy. As an added bonus, Zara was voted Best New Shop in the *Time Out* Retail Awards 2001.
Branches: 242-8 Oxford Street, Marylebone, W1 (7318 2700); 48-52 Kensington High Street, Kensington, W11 (7368 4680).

Children

See also p260 **Cheeky Monkeys**.

Daisy & Tom

181 King's Road, Chelsea, SW3 (7352 5000).
Sloane Square tube then 11, 19, 22 bus/49 bus.
Open 10am-6pm Mon, Tue, Thur-Sat; 10am-7pm
Wed; noon-6pm Sun. **Credit** AmEx, MC, V.
Map p397 E12.
This children's department store stocks toys, games,
books and kids' clothing.

Jigsaw Junior

97 Fulham Road, Chelsea, SW3 (7823 8915/
www.jigsaw-junior.com). South Kensington tube.
Open 10am-6.30pm Mon-Sat; noon-6pm Sun.
Credit AmEx, MC, V. **Map** p397 D11.
The junior line offers floral dresses and fashion-
conscious denim and khakis for lucky young ladies
with moneyed parents.
Branches: throughout the city.

Trotters

34 King's Road, Chelsea, SW3 (7259 9620/
www.trotters.co.uk). Sloane Square tube.
Open 9am-6.30pm Mon, Tue, Thur-Sat; 9am-7pm
Wed; 10am-6pm Sun. **Credit** AmEx, MC, V.
Map p397 F11.

Spanish chic at **Zara**. *See p239*.

Shops by area

For designer clothes by area, *see p241*. For
second-hand clothes, homewares and books
by area, *see p258* **Thrifty Business**.

The South Bank & Bankside

Borough Market (Markets, p257); **Konditor
& Cook** (Food & drink, p250).

The City

Petticoat Lane Market (Markets, *p256*);
Timothy Everest (Fashion accessories &
services, *p250*); **YHA Adventure Shop**
(Sport, *p260*).

Holborn & Clerkenwell

Antoni & Alison (Fashion accessories &
services, *p247*); **Books Etc** (Bookshops,
p232); **Into You** (Fashion accessories &
services p248); **Lesley Craze Gallery/Craze 2**
(Fashion accessories & services, *p248*);
Woodhams at One Aldwych (Florists, *p250*).

Bloomsbury & Fitzrovia

Apple Centre (Electronics, *p237*); **Cinema
Bookshop** (Bookshops, *p232*); **Computer
Exchange** (Electronics, *p237*); **Gay's the
Word** (Bookshops, *p233*); **Gultronics**
(Electronics, *p237*); **Habitat** (Homewares,

p255); **Heal's** (Homewares, *p255*); **Hi-Fi
Experience** (Electronics, *p237*); **HMV** (Music
shops, *p257*); **Michael's Shoe Care** (Fashion
accessories & services, *p247*); **Paperchase**
(Gifts & stationery, *p253*); **Purves & Purves**
(Homewares, *p255*); **Skoob** (Bookshops,
p233); **Ulysses** (Bookshops, *p235*);
Unsworths Booksellers (Bookshops, *p235*;
Virgin Megastore (Music stores, *p257*).

Marylebone

Alfie's Antiques Market (Antiques, *p231*);
Aveda Institute (Health & beauty, *p253*);
Bliss (Pharmacies, *p260*); **Danish Express**
(Fashion accessories & services, *p247*);
Daunt Books (Bookshops, *p232*);
Divertimenti (Homewares, *p255*);
French & Teague (Marylebone, Fashion,
p246); **John Lewis** (Department stores,
p236); **H&M** (Fashion, *p239*); **Marks &
Spencer** (Department stores, *p236*); **Miss
Selfridge** (Fashion, *p239*); **Mulberry** (Fashion
accessories & services, *p248*); **Niketown**
(Sport, *p260*); **Osprey** (Fashion accessories
& services, *p48*); **Selfridges** (Department
stores, *p246*); **Shellys** (Fashion accessories
& services, *p249*); **Talking Books Shop**

A great range of trendy kids' clothes and shoes (Diesel jeans, Oilily dresses), plus a hairdresser and a children's library. The clothes for under-11s are upmarket and fun. Toys include the Galt range, Dr Seuss games and wooden toys.
Branch: 127 Kensington High Street, Kensington, W8 (7937 9373).

Designer

London's high-falutin', high-end, high-fashion clothing emporia tend to be concentrated in and around two main areas: Mayfair and Chelsea/South Kensington/Knightsbridge; below is a basic list. Most shops are open 10am-6pm Monday to Saturday, with many Knightsbridge and South Kensington stores staying open until 7pm on Wednesday and the West End shops opening until 7pm on Thursday. If you're looking for a wide range of labels under one roof, try Harrods (*see p235*), Harvey Nichols, Liberty or Selfridges (for all, *see p236*).

Chelsea, SW3
Sloane Square tube.
King's Road: Joseph (sale shop), World's End (Vivienne Westwood).

Knightsbridge, SW1, SW7
Knightsbridge tube.
Sloane Street: Alberta Ferretti, Armani, Chanel, Christian Dior, Gucci, Hermès, MaxMara, Tommy Hilfiger.

Mayfair, W1
Bond Street tube.
Avery Row: Paul Smith (sale shop).
Brook Street: Comme des Garçons, Pleats Please (Issey Miyake).
Conduit Street: Alexander McQueen, Issey Miyake, Moschino, Krizia, Vivienne Westwood, Yohji Yamamoto.
Davies Street: Vivienne Westwood.
New Bond Street: Burberry, Calvin Klein, Donna Karan, Collezioni Armani, Emporio Armani, Fenwick, Louis Vuitton, Miu Miu, Nicole Farhi, Ralph Lauren, Tommy Hilfiger, Yves Saint Laurent.
Old Bond Street: Anna Molinari Blumarine, Dolce & Gabbana, DKNY, Gianni Versace, Joseph, Prada.

South Kensington, SW1, SW3
South Kensington tube.
Brompton Road: Emporio Armani, Issey Miyake, Betty Jackson, Paul Costelloe.
Draycott Avenue: Betsey Johnson, Galerie Gaultier.
Fulham Road: Voyage.
Sloane Avenue: Paul Smith.

(Bookshops, *p233*); **Toni & Guy** (Health & beauty, *p254*); **Top Shop/Top Man** (Fashion, *p239*); **Villandry** (Food & drink, *p251*), **Whistles** (Fashion, *p239*).

Mayfair & St James's
Angela Hale (Fashion accessories & services, *p247*); **Black Market** (Music shops, *p257*); **Browns** (Fashion, *p239*); **Buckingham Dry Cleaners** (Fashion accessories & services, *p247*); **Electrum Gallery** (Fashion accessories & services, *p247*); **Fortnum & Mason** (Department stores, *p235*); **Godiva** (Food & drink, *p251*); **Grays Antiques Market & Grays in the Mews** (Antiques, *p231*); **Hamleys** (Toys & games, *p260*); **Harold Moores Records** (Music shops, *p257*); **Jigsaw** (Fashion, *p242*); **John Lobb** (Fashion, *p248*); **Lillywhite's** (Sport, *p260*); **Ozwald Boateng** (Fashion accessories & services, *p249*); **The Pen Shop** (Gifts & stationery, *p253*); **The Refinery** (Health & beauty, *p253*); **Tiffany & Co** (Fashion accessories & services, *p248*); **Tower Records** (Music shops, *p257*); **Vidal Sassoon** (Health & beauty, *p254*); **Vision Express** (Opticians, *p255*);

Waterstone's (Bookshops, *p232*); **Wright & Teague** (Fashion accessories & services, *p236*); **Zara** (Fashion, *p239*).

Soho
Agent Provocateur (Fashion, *p246*); **Algerian Coffee Stores** (Food & drink, *p250*); **American Retro** (Fashion accessories & services, *p247*); **Berwick Street Market** (Markets, *p257*); **Bond International** (Fashion, *p243*); **Borders** (Bookshops, *p232*); **Daddy Kool** (Music shops, *p257*); **Fish** (Health & beauty, *p254*); **Foyles** (Bookshops, *p232*); **Grant & Cutler** (Bookshops, *p233*); **Liberty** (Department stores, *p236*); **Milroy's of Soho** (Food & drink, *p251*); **Mr CD** (Music shops, *p257*); **Muji** (Homewares, *p255*); **Murder One** (Bookshops, *p233*); **Pâtisserie Valerie** (Food & drink, *p250*); **The Pineal Eye** (Fashion, *p239*); **Reckless Records** (Music shops, *p257*); **Selectadisc** (Music shops, *p257*); **Shop** (Fashion, *p245*); **Sister Ray** (Music shops, *p257*).

Covent Garden & St Giles's
Accessorize (Fashion accessories & services, *p247*); **Camper** (Fashion accessories &

Mid-range

French Connection

99-103 Long Acre, Covent Garden, WC2 (7379 6560/www.frenchconnection.com). Covent Garden tube. **Open** 10.30am-7pm Mon-Wed, Fri, Sat; 11am-8pm Thur; noon-6pm Sun. **Credit** AmEx, DC, JCB, MC, V. **Map** p401 L6.
Savvy street-chic that is still ahead of most of the competition in terms of style and quality.
Branches: throughout the city.

Gap

30-31 Long Acre, Covent Garden, WC2 (7379 0779/ www.gap.com). Covent Garden tube. **Open** 10am-7pm Mon-Wed, Sat; 10am-8pm Thur; 10am-7.30pm Fri; noon-6pm Sun. **Credit** AmEx, MC, V. **Map** p401 L6.
The joint winner (along with Top Shop; *see p239*) of the Best High Street Store category of the *Time Out* Retail Awards 2001, this US brand has all but achieved world domination.
Branches: throughout the city.

Jigsaw

126-7 New Bond Street, Mayfair, W1 (7491 4484/www.jigsaw-online.com). Bond Street tube. **Open** 10am-6.30pm Mon-Wed, Fri, Sat; 10am-7.30pm Thur; noon-6pm Sun. **Credit** AmEx, MC, V. **Map** p398 H6.
Hip, wearable, sexy and cute are the words that best decribe Jigsaw's style – on top of which, it really does have some of the best trousers in London, in a range of great fabrics.
Branches: throughout the city.

Karen Millen

22-3 James Street, Covent Garden, WC2 (7836 5355/www.karenmillen.co.uk). Covent Garden tube. **Open** 10.30am-7.30pm Mon-Wed, Fri, Sat; 10am-8pm Thur; noon-6pm Sun. **Credit** AmEx, DC, MC, V. **Map** p399 K6.
A clubber's delight, this shop has a sparkly air, with lots of diamanté, sequins, silky knits and figure-hugging dresses beaded and ruffled to within an inch of their lives.
Branches: throughout the city.

Kookaï

Unit 13, The Market, Covent Garden, WC2 (7379 1318/www.kookai.co.uk). Covent Garden tube. **Open** 10am-7pm Mon-Wed, Fri, Sat; 10am-8pm Thur; noon-6pm Sun. **Credit** AmEx, DC, MC, V. **Map** p401 L7.
If you're a young fashion maven without the bank balance to support high-fashion prices, you can't go far wrong at Kookai. Designs are young, hip and in the Prada mode.
Branches: throughout the city.

▶ Shops by area (continued)

services, *p248*; **Carhartt** (Fashion, *p243*); **Carluccio's** (Food & drink, *p251*); **Charles Worthington** (Health & beauty, *p254*); **Diesel** (Fashion, *p243*); **Dr Marten Department Store** (Fashion accessories & services, *p248*); **Duffer of St George** (Fashion, *p245*); **Edward Stanford** (Bookshops, *p232*); **Forbidden Planet** (Bookshops, *p233*); **French Connection** (Fashion, *p242*); **Gap** (Fashion, *p242*); **Jessops** (Electronics, *p237*); **Koh Samui** (Fashion, *p239*); **Lush** (Health & beauty, *p254*); **Karen Millen** (Fashion, *p242*), **Kirk Originals** (Health & beauty, *p254*); **Kookaï** (Fashion, *p242*); **Mango** (Fashion, *p243*); **MDC Classic Music** (Music shops, *p258*); **Natural Shoe Store** (Fashion accessories & services, *p248*); **Neal Street East** (Gifts & stationery, *p253*); **Neal's Yard Dairy** (Food & drink, *p250*); **Neal's Yard Remedies** (Health & beauty, *p254*); **Oasis** (Fashion, *p243*); **Office** (Fashion accessories & services, *p248*); **Ray's Jazz** (Music shops, *p259*); **The Sanctuary** (Health & beauty, *p253*); **Silver Moon Women's Bookshop** (Bookshops, *p233*); **Snappy Snaps** (Electronics, *p237*); **Space.NK** (Health & beauty, *p254*); **Stephen Jones** (Fashion accessories & services, *p247*); **The Tea House** (Food & drink, *p250*); **Ted Baker** (Fashion, *p243*); **R Twining & Co** (Food & drink, *p250*); **Wild Bunch** (Florists, *p250*); **Zwemmer Media Arts** (Bookshops, *p233*).

Knightsbridge & South Kensington

Harrods (Department stores, *p235*); **Harvey Nichols** (Department stores, *p236*); **High & Mighty** (Fashion, *p247*); **Rigby & Peller** (Fashion, *p246*); **Tokio** (Fashion, *p239*).

Chelsea

Antiquarius (Antiques, *p231*); **Benjamin Pollock's Toy Shop** (Toys & games, *p260*); **Bluebird** (Food & drink, *p251*); **The Conran Shop** (Homewares, *p255*); **Daisy & Tom** (Fashion, *p239*); **Designers Guild** (Homewares, *p255*); **Holding Company** (Homewares, *p255*); **Jigsaw Junior** (Fashion, *p240*); **Jimmy Choo** (Fashion, *p248*); **Jo Malone** (Health & beauty, *p254*); **Manolo Blahnik** (Fashion, *p248*); **Patrick Cox** (Fashion accessories & services, *p248*); **Rococo** (Food & drink, *p251*); **Trotters** (Fashion, *p240*).

Mango

8-12 Neal Street, Covent Garden, WC2 (7240 6099/www.mangoshop.com). Covent Garden tube.
Open 10am-7pm Mon-Wed, Fri, Sat; 10am-8pm Thur; noon-6pm Sun. **Credit** AmEx, DC, MC, V. **Map** p396 B9.
Up-to-the-minute designs in great fabrics sold in stylish shops at nice prices.

Oasis

13 James Street, Covent Garden, WC2 (7240 7445/ www.oasis-stores.com). Covent Garden tube.
Open 10am-7pm Mon-Wed, Fri-Sun; 10am-8pm Thur; **Credit** AmEx, DC, JCB, MC, V. **Map** p401 L6.
Funky and affordable, with constantly revolving fashion based on key catwalk trends that have been remodelled for the high street.
Branches: throughout the city.

Ted Baker

1-4 Langley Court, Covent Garden, WC2 (7497 8862/www.tedbaker.co.uk). Covent Garden tube.
Open 10am-7pm Mon-Wed, Fri; 10am-7.30pm Thur; 10am-6.30pm Sat; noon-5pm Sun. **Credit** AmEx, DC, MC, V. **Map** p401 L6.
Hip, youthful menswear and womenswear with a semi-designer status and prices to match. There's also a concession on the ground floor of Selfridges.
Branch: 7 Foubert's Place, Soho, W1 (7437 5619).

Street

Bond International

17 Newburgh Street, Soho, W1 (7437 0079/ www.bondinternational.com). Oxford Circus tube.
Open 10.30am-6.30pm Mon-Sat. **Credit** AmEx, MC, V. **Map** p398 J6.
Bare floorboards, graffitied walls, pounding beats and rails packed with baggy b-boy threads. Favourite labels include Silas, Oeuf, Stüssy and Zoo.

Carhartt

56 Neal Street, Covent Garden, WC2 (7836 5659/ www.thecarharttstore.co.uk). Covent Garden tube.
Open 11am-6.30pm Mon-Wed, Fri, Sat; 11am-7pm Thur; noon-5pm Sun. **Credit** MC, V. **Map** p399 L6.
This stylish, functional workwear is a staple brand among London's young trendies.
Branch: 13 Newburgh Street, Soho, W1 (7287 6411).

Diesel

43 Earlham Street, Covent Garden, WC2 (7497 5543/www.diesel.com). Covent Garden tube.
Open 10am-7pm Mon-Wed, Fri, Sat; 10am-8pm Thur; noon-6pm Sun. **Credit** AmEx, JCB, MC, V. **Map** p399 L6.
Good for its high-quality denimwear and stylish separates, this three-storey flagship store also stocks all the latest lines in bags, luggage and

Eat, Drink, Shop

North London

Camden Market (Camden, Markets, *p256*); **Camden Passage** (Islington, Antiques, *p231*); **Fresh & Wild** (Camden, Organic London, *p249*); **Skate Attack** (Kentish Town, Sport, *p260*);

East London

Brick Lane Market (Spitalfields, Markets, *p256*); **Columbia Road Flower Market** (Bethnal Green, Markets, *p257*); **eat my handbag bitch** (Spitalfields, Homewares, *p255*; **Fred Bare** (Spitalfields, Fashion accessories & services, *p247*); **Spitalfields Market** (Spitalfields, Organic London, *p249*), **Spitalfields Organics** (Spitalfields, Organic London, *p249*).

South London

Bermondsey Market (Bermondsey, Antiques, *p231*); **Brixton Market** (Brixton, Markets, *p256*); **Greenwich Market** (Greenwich, Markets, *p256*); **Richer Sounds** (Borough, Electronics, *p237*).

West London

Aime (Notting Hill, Fashion, *p237*); **& Clarke's** (Kensington, Food & drink, *p250*); **Bill Amberg** (Notting Hill, Fashion accessories & services, *p248*); **Books for Cooks** (Notting Hill, Bookshops, *p232*); **Boots** (Bayswater, Pharmacies, *p260*); **Cheeky Monkeys** (Ladbroke Grove, Toys & games, *p260*); **Children's Book Centre** (Kensington, Bookshops, *p232*); **Crabtree & Evelyn** (Kensington, Health & beauty, *p254*); **The Dispensary** (Notting Hill, Fashion, *p245*); **Early Learning Centre** (Hammersmith, Toys & games, *p260*); **The Green Room** (Kensington, Health & beauty, *p253*); **Honest Jon's** (Ladbroke Grove, Music shops, *p258*); **Intoxica!** (Ladbroke Grove, Music shops, *p258*); **Planet Organic** (Bayswater, Organic London, *p249*); **Portobello Road Market** (Notting Hill, Markets, *p256*); **Rough Trade** (Notting Hill, Music shops, *p259*); **SPAce.NK** (Notting Hill, Health & beauty, *p253*); **Urban Outfitters** (Kensington, Fashion, *p246*); **Wild at Heart** (Notting Hill, Florists, *p250*); **Zafash** (Earl's Court, Pharmacies, *p260*).

beachwear. Funky accessories such as watches and key holders are also available here, as is a limited children's clothing range.

The Dispensary

9 Newburgh Street, Soho, W1 (7287 8145/ www.thedispensary.net). Oxford Circus or Piccadilly Circus tube. **Open** 10.30am-6.30pm Mon-Sat; noon-5pm Sun. **Credit** AmEx, MC, V. **Map** p398 J6.

An ultra-trendy but sometimes pricey store that combines relatively mainstream street styles with some rather more unexpected finds. The staff can sometimes be a bit snooty. This Soho branch sells womenswear only.

Branches: *Mens- & womenswear* 25 Pembridge Road, Notting Hill, W11 (7221 9290), 200 Kensington Park Road, Notting Hill, W11 (7727 8797); *Menswear* 15 Newburgh Street, Soho, W1 (7734 4095).

Duffer of St George

29 Shorts Gardens, Covent Garden, WC2 (7379 4660/www.dufferofstgeorge.com). Covent Garden or Leicester Square tube. **Open** 10.30am-7pm Mon-Fri; 10.30am-6.30pm Sat; 1-5pm Sun. **Credit** AmEx, DC, MC, V. **Map** p399 L6.

Duffer's own-brand clothes are as hip as ever and its choice of labels right on the nail: Clements Ribeiro, Pringle knitwear, vintage Levi's and Evisu.
Branches: 34 Shorts Gardens, Covent Garden, WC2 (7836 3722); 31 Savile Row, Mayfair, W1 (7734 3666).

Shop

4 Brewer Street (basement), Soho, W1 (7437 1259/ www.shopgirlstore.com). Leicester Square or Piccadilly Circus tube. **Open** 10.30am-6.30pm Mon-Fri; 11am-6.30pm Sat. **Credit** AmEx, JCB, MC, V. **Map** p400 J7.

Who she? Sparkle Moore

Toweringly tall, with a mane of peroxide blonde hair, scarlet lips and a nipped-at-the-waist 1950s circle skirt, Sparkle Moore is difficult to miss. But the native New Yorker's penchant for retro style is more than just a way of dressing – it's a way of life.

Moore's shop **The Girl Can't Help It** in Church Street's Alfie's Antiques Market (*see p231*) is an exuberant celebration of '40s and '50s Hollywood glamour. Frequent customers include designers such as Stella McCartney and Dolce & Gabbana and stars such as Nicole Kidman and Kylie Minogue. The tiny interior overflows with Gilda-esque gowns, pinklewicker stilettoes, raunchy pin-up postcards and silver-plated cigarette cases. Her north London home, meanwhile, is kitted out like a Hollywood starlet's pad and is a retro collector's paradise.

'I was always interested in London because of the dynamic music and fashion scenes,' says Moore, who set up home here in 1998. 'In the 1960s I came here to listen to music, then in the 1970s I became tour manager with Johnny Thunders & the Heartbreakers and was here all the time.'

Inspired from an early age by her aunt and uncle's interest in rock 'n' roll and her mother's fascination with Elvis, Moore began collecting kitsch Americana and set up a shop selling retro clothes and accessories in New York's Soho in 1980.

London was a natural next step. 'I was drawn to the diversity and creativity of London,' says Moore. 'I felt immediately accepted here – coming from a big Italian family I had the affinity of a European with the outgoingness of an American. But I miss the things I first came here for – some things are disappearing, such as a certain level of politeness. On the other hand you can now get nearly all the things here that I originally missed from home, like packs of ice for drinks!'

Moore also missed New York's cocktail bars and was disappointed that there were so few places to drink socially apart from pubs. Taking matters into her own hands, she organised a series of club nights, More Than Vegas and Blue Martini, that featured cocktails, DJs, dancing and a distinctly retro vibe. 'But these days there's no shortage of places to go for cocktails' she explains. Moore and her Dutch boyfriend Jasja, who runs **Cad van Swankster**, the men's clothing and accessories part of the business venture, sip their cocktails of choice at Trader Vic's at the Hilton Park Lane, the Centurion and the Lanesborough's Library Bar.

'But I'll give you a tip,' says Moore. 'The best cocktails in London are at the Savoy's American Bar.' Spoken like a true expat.

For more on London hotel bars, *see p224* **Smooth operators**.

Eat, Drink, Shop

The perfect Soho store: nothing but a door with a neon sign above it advertises Shop's presence at street level, then it's down a strip-joint style staircase and into the small showroom dominated by kitsch '70s decor and blaxploitation imagery. The stock won't disappoint, either: this is the home of the funky, retro Hysteric Glamour range as well as sexy Shopgirl lingerie.

Urban Outfitters

36-8 Kensington High Street, Kensington, W8 (7761 1001/www.urban.com). High Street Kensington tube. **Open** 10am-7pm Mon-Wed, Fri, Sat; 10am-8pm Thur; noon-6pm Sun. **Credit** AmEx, JCB, MC, V. **Map** p396 A9.

It's easy to while away an hour here, selecting the best in streetwear, browsing through the funkiest new gadgets and checking out the newest sounds at Carbon Concession. Women's labels include Fake Genius, Erotokritos and Claudie Pierlot.

Underwear

Marks & Spencer (*see p236*) is very well known for its range of good-quality and affordable undies.

Agent Provocateur

6 Broadwick Street, Soho, W1 (7439 0229/ www.agentprovocateur.com). Oxford Circus tube. **Open** 11am-7pm Mon-Sat. **Credit** AmEx, MC, V. **Map** p398 J6.

AP has a feel that's somewhere between *Playboy* centrefold and 1950s Miss World. **Branch**: 16 Pont Street, SW1 (7235 0229).

Rigby & Peller

2 Hans Road, Kensington, SW3 (7589 9293/ www.rigbyandpeller.com). Knightsbridge tube. **Open** 9.30am-6pm Mon, Tue, Thur-Sat; 9.30am-7pm Wed. **Credit** AmEx, MC, V. **Map** p397 F9.

R&P might look down at heel but the doorman and the royal warrants prove this place means business. A personal service is offered for off-the-peg made-to-measure bras or outerwear such as bustiers.

Unusual sizes

French & Teague

41 Great Castle Street, Marylebone, W1 (7255 2277/ www.sixteen47.com). Oxford Circus tube. **Open** 10am-6pm Mon-Wed, Fri, Sat; 10am-7pm Thur. **Credit** MC, V. **Map** p398 J6.

Who he? Vittorio Radice

The man who put the oomph into **Selfridges**, one of London's most esteemed department stores (*see p236*), Vittorio Radice came to London from Milan 11 years ago. He spent six years at Habitat, revamping the furniture store and giving it a much-needed facelift, before taking over as Chief Executive at Selfridges.

'There is a rooted vitality in London which is what drew me here,' says Radice. 'Over the last ten years London has been at the centre of a fantastic revolution in fashion, music and, in particular, art, which took off with the Brit Art scene around 1993. But there has also been a transformation in hotels, which have become sleeker and more contemporary, and with restaurants, which have moved towards simpler cuisine. There are great restaurants opening all the time – you can even find good Italian food here now!'

Radice's enthusiasm for the energy he finds here is reflected in his transformation of Selfridges from a staid and solidly reliable

upmarket department store into a hip and buzzy place to shop, with an emphasis on new designers and young fashion (it won the Best Department Store category in the *Time Out* Retail Awards 2001).

'London is definitely the place for ideas and creativity,' he says. 'I love the atmosphere of places like Covent Garden, and shops such as the new Maharishi which has opened there. But I like the cultural side of the city too and visit the Barbican and the Royal Festival Hall to hear world music. London is totally multi-ethnic and multi-religious – every country in the world is represented here.'

Despite the threat of recession, Radice has no plans to leave London anytime soon. 'My family and I were welcomed from day one, and I felt I blended in here immediately. People were very welcoming and willing to help me. We moan about London, but we should be aware that the grass is actually greenest here – and that's not just from the weather!'

Diffusion – chic day- and eveningwear in sizes 16-47 – is the successful clothing range founded by comic Dawn French and designer Helen Teague.

High & Mighty

81-3 Knightsbridge, Knightsbridge, SW1 (7589 7454/www.highandmighty.co.uk). Knightsbridge tube. **Open** 10am-6.30pm Mon-Fri; 10am-6pm Sat. **Credit** AmEx, DC, JCB, MC, V. **Map** p397 F9.

An extensive and well-priced range of clothing for big and/or tall men.
Branches: 145-7 Edgware Road, Paddington, W2 (7723 8754); The Plaza, 120 Oxford Street, Fitzrovia, W1 (7436 4861).

Fashion accessories & services

General

Accessorize

Unit 22, The Market, Covent Garden, WC2 (7240 2107/www.accessorize.co.uk). Covent Garden tube. **Open** 9am-8pm Mon-Sat; 11am-7pm Sun. **Credit** AmEx, DC, MC, V. **Map** p401 L6.

Keenly priced items for glamming up any outfit.
Branches: throughout the city.

American Retro

35 Old Compton Street, Soho, W1 (7734 3477/ www.americanretro.com). Leicester Square tube. **Open** 10.30am-7.30pm Mon-Fri; 10.15am-7pm Sat. **Credit** AmEx, DC, MC, V. **Map** p399 K6.

If you dig urban street style, the androgynous look and a Philippe Starck lifestyle, American Retro will feel like a second home.

Antoni & Alison

43 Rosebery Avenue, Clerkenwell, EC1 (7833 2002/ www.antoniandalison.co.uk). Farringdon tube/rail/19, 38, 341 bus. **Open** 10.30am-6.30pm Mon-Fri; noon-4pm Sat. **Credit** AmEx, MC, V. **Map** p402 N4.

What started as a groovy T-shirt collection has grown into a range of must-have accessories.

Dry cleaning, laundries & repairs

Buckingham Dry Cleaners

83 Duke Street, Mayfair, W1 (7499 1253/ www.buckinghamdrycleaners.com). Bond Street tube. **Open** 8am-6pm Mon-Fri; 9.30am-12.30pm Sat. **Credit** AmEx, JCB, MC, V. **Map** p398 G6.

Unbeatable for quality of cleaning and service.

Danish Express

16 Hinde Street, Marylebone, W1 (7935 6306). Bond Street tube. **Open** 8.30am-5.30pm Mon-Fri; 9.30am-12.30pm Sat. **Credit** AmEx, DC, MC, V. **Map** p398 G5.

Danish Express has a same-day service on items received before 10am, and attractive prices to boot.
Branch: **Janet's Hand Laundry** 281A Finchley Road, Golders Green, NW3 (7435 6131).

Michael's Shoe Care

7 Southampton Row, Bloomsbury, WC1 (7405 7436). Holborn tube. **Open** 8am-6.30pm Mon-Fri. **Credit** AmEx, DC, JCB, MC, V. **Map** p399 M5.

Michael's carries out a range of shoe repairs, including reheeling and shoe-dyeing, as well as fixing scarves, brollies and briefcases.
Branches: throughout the city.

Hats

Fred Bare

14 Lamb Street, Spitalfields, E1 (7247 9004). Liverpool Street tube/rail. **Open** 10am-5pm Mon-Fri, Sun. **Credit** DC, JCB, MC, V. **Map** p400 J7.

This trendy hat shop offers an alluring mix of cosy pull-ons and daywear hats.
Branch: 118 Columbia Road, Bethnal Green, E2 (7729 6962).

Stephen Jones

36 Great Queen Street, Covent Garden, WC2 (7242 0770). Covent Garden or Holborn tube. **Open** 11am-6pm Mon-Wed, Fri; 11am-7pm Thur; also by appointment. **Credit** AmEx, DC, MC, V. **Map** p400 J7.

For cutting-edge, crafted fashion statements, few can rival Jones. Prices start at £70.

Jewellery

Angela Hale

5 The Royal Arcade, 28 Old Bond Street, Mayfair, W1 (7495 1920/www.angelahale.co.uk). Green Park tube. **Open** 10am-6pm Mon-Sat. **Credit** AmEx, MC, V. **Map** p400 J7.

Angela Hale does striking jewellery that is inspired by Victorian and art deco designs but has a distinctly contemporary feel.

Electrum Gallery

21 South Molton Street, Mayfair, W1 (7629 6325). Bond Street tube. **Open** 10am-6pm Mon-Fri; 10am-5pm Sat. **Credit** AmEx, DC, JCB, MC, V. **Map** p398 H6.

This Mayfair gallery offers two floors full of exciting jewellery collections.

florence-b

37A Neal Street, Covent Garden, W1 (7240 6332). Covent Garden tube. **Open** 11am-7pm Mon-Sat; noon-6pm Sun. **Credit** MC, V. **Map** p399 L6.

Showcases between 20 and 30 designers with original, eye-catching styles.
Branches: 188A King's Road, Chelsea, SW3 (7352 4401); 25A Old Compton Street, Soho, W1 (7287 3789).

Frontiers

37 & 39 Pembridge Road, Notting Hill, W11 (7727 6132). Notting Hill Gate tube. **Open** 11am-6.30pm Mon-Sat; noon-4.30pm Sun. **Credit** MC, V. **Map** p394 A7.

From antique and tribal jewellery from Asia and North Africa to delicate Indian silver jewellery, plus terracotta and glazed pots.

Eat, Drink, Shop

Into You

144 St John Street, Finsbury, EC1 (7253 5085/
www.into-you.co.uk). Angel tube/Farringdon tube/
rail. **Open** noon-7pm Mon-Sat. **Credit** MC, V.
Map p402 O3.

A top-notch tattoo and piercing outfit with five
artists offering classic designs and expert piercing.

Lesley Craze Gallery/Craze 2

34-5 Clerkenwell Green, Clerkenwell, EC1 (Lesley
Craze Gallery 7608 0393/Craze 2 7251 0381/
www.lesleycrazegallery.co.uk). Farringdon tube/rail.
Open 10am-5.30pm Mon-Sat. **Credit** AmEx, MC, V.
Map p402 N4.

This gallery/shop is divided into two: Lesley Craze
Gallery displays precious metal pieces by up to 100
designers, while Craze 2 works in mixed media.

Tiffany & Co

25 Old Bond Street, Mayfair, W1 (7409 2790/
www.tiffany.com). Green Park tube. **Open** 10am-6pm
Mon-Fri; 10am-5.30pm Sat. **Credit** AmEx, JCB,
MC, V. **Map** p400 J7.

Seriously romantic and seriously pricey, but if
you've seen the film, you'll know that all but the
most depleted of wallets can afford some kind of
Tiffany trinket. Also sold in Harrods (*see p235*).
Branch: The Courtyard, Royal Exchange,
EC3 (7495 3511).

Wright & Teague

1A Grafton Street, Mayfair, W1 (7629 2777/
www.wrightandteague.com). Green Park tube.
Open 10am-6pm Mon-Wed, Fri, Sat; 10am-7pm
Thur. **Credit** AmEx, MC, V. **Map** p400 J7.

Gary Wright and Sheila Teague started out 25 years
ago and were possibly the first designers since the
Victorians to engrave their jewellery with such
phrases as 'a symbol of my love' and 'cherish'. The
hearts, crosses and pendants for men and women
are made up in silver, gold and platinum.

Leather goods

Bill Amberg

10 Chepstow Road, Notting Hill, W2 (7727 3560/
www.billamberg.com). Notting Hill Gate or
Westbourne Park tube. **Open** 10am-6pm Mon-Wed,
Fri, Sat; 10am-7pm Thur. **Credit** AmEx, MC, V.
Map p394 A5.

Timeless designs with universal appeal. Bags are the
mainstay of Amberg's business, but he also makes
home accessories and furniture (by commission).

Mulberry

11-12 Gees Court, St Christopher's Place,
Marylebone, W1 (7493 2546/www.mulberry.com).
Bond Street tube. **Open** 10am-6pm Mon-Wed, Fri,
Sat; 10am-7pm Thur. **Credit** AmEx, DC, JCB, MC, V.
Map p398 H6.

Purveyors of the classic landed gentry look,
Mulberry offers quintessentially English clothing,
homewares, leather luggage and accessories.
Branches: throughout the city.

Osprey

11 St Christopher's Place, Marylebone, W1 (7935
2824). Bond Street tube. **Open** 11am-6pm Tue, Wed,
Fri, Sat; 11am-7pm Thur. **Credit** AmEx, MC, V.
Map p398 H6.

Somewhere between high street and designer,
Osprey carries a range of reasonably priced, handmade leather bags and accessories.

Shoes

If you really want to treat your feet, try two
of the biggest names in fashion shoes: **Jimmy
Choo** (169 Draycott Avenue, SW3, 7235 0242)
and **Manolo Blahnik** (49-51 Old Church
Street, SW3, 7352 3863). For something rather
more trad, try **John Lobb** (*see p117*).

Camper

39 Floral Street, Covent Garden, WC2 (7379
8678/www.camper.es). Covent Garden tube.
Open 10.30am-7pm Mon-Sat; noon-6pm Sun.
Credit AmEx, DC, MC, V. **Map** p401 L6.

Camper has stylish, fashionable shoes from Majorca.
Branches: 8-11 Arcade, 28 Old Bond Street,
Mayfair, W1 (7629 2722); 35 Brompton Road,
Knightsbridge, SW3 (7584 5439).

Dr Marten Department Store

1-4 King Street, Covent Garden, WC2 (7497 1460/
www.drmartens.com). Covent Garden tube. **Open**
10am-7pm Mon-Wed, Fri, Sat; 10.30am-8pm Thur;
noon-6pm Sun. **Credit** AmEx, MC, V. **Map** p401 L7.

World-famous, hard-as-nails footwear and clothing
at DM's Covent Garden megastore.

Natural Shoe Store

21 Neal Street, Covent Garden, WC2 (7836 5254/
www.naturesko.com). Covent Garden tube. **Open**
10am-6pm Mon, Tue; 10am-7pm Wed-Fri; 10am-
6.30pm Sat; noon-5.30pm Sun. **Credit** AmEx, DC,
MC, V. **Map** p399 L6.

Environmentally friendly and cruelty-free shoes in
a range of styles. Vegan shoes are also available.
Branch: 325 King's Road, Chelsea, SW3 (7351 3721).

Office

57 Neal Street, Covent Garden, WC2 (7379 1896/
www.officelondon.co.uk). Covent Garden tube.
Open 10.30am-7.30pm Mon-Wed, Fri, Sat;
10.30am-8pm Thur; 10am-7pm Sat; noon-6pm Sun.
Credit AmEx, JCB, MC, V. **Map** p399 L6.

The Office chain offers a range of fashionable
footwear for all occasions, from the smart and
sober to the impossibly trendy.
Branches: throughout the city.

Patrick Cox

129 Sloane Street, Chelsea, SW1 (7730 8886).
Sloane Square tube. **Open** 10am-6pm Mon,
Tue, Thur-Sat; 10am-7pm Wed; 11am-5pm Sun.
Credit AmEx, MC, V. **Map** p397 F10.

The ever-cool Cox produces a range of mainly 1960s-
inspired styles, but he's still best known for his
stylish 'wannabe' loafers.

Eat, Drink, Shop

Shellys

266-70 Regent Street, Marylebone, W1 (7287 0939/www.shellys.co.uk). Oxford Circus tube. **Open** 10am-7pm Mon-Wed, Fri; 10am-8pm Thur; 10am-7pm Sat; noon-6pm Sun. **Credit** AmEx, DC, JCB, MC, V. **Map** p398 J6.

Shellys, which has about 14 branches around town, offers a huge selection of reasonably priced if not top-quality shoes, boots and trainers for both sexes, ranging from the casual and functional to the glam and impractical (big heels and lots of straps). **Branches**: throughout the city.

Tailors

Since the mid 19th century, Savile Row, W1, has been the traditional home of men's tailoring and many of London's finest tailors are still there.

Ozwald Boateng

9 Vigo Street, Mayfair, W1 (7437 0620). Piccadilly Circus tube. **Open** 10am-6pm Mon-Sat. **Credit** AmEx, MC, V. **Map** p400 J7.

The Anglo-Ghanaian Boateng's trademarks are his bright colours and clean, lean lines.

Organic London

With food scare after food scare making many of us think more about what we're putting in our mouths, and complementary medicine having become many people's first port of call when struck down by minor ailments, London's organic retailing has gone from hippy niche market to burgeoning industry, as evidenced by the rising popularity of farmers' markets (*see p257*) and the growth of **Fresh & Wild** (*pictured*) into an organic mini-empire.

The latter (for branches call the main branch at 49 Parkway, Camden, NW1, on 7428 7575 or see www.freshandwild.com) has expanded rapidly, with new stores in Clapham Junction, Soho and Stoke Newington, without losing its character and charm. The vision behind the chain is fantastic: its aisles are packed with more than 5,000 organic foods and natural remedies, many sourced from local suppliers. You can bag your own muesli, weigh dried fruit and nuts by the scoop, or browse through two aisles dedicated to organic baby products. There are even organic beers, wines and ciders and pet food.

Planet Organic (42 Westbourne Grove, Bayswater, W2, 7221 7171/ www.planetorganic.com) has had a more restrained growth, but the opening of a second branch in central London (22 Torrington Place, Fitzrovia, WC1, 7436 1929) is testimony to the vast inroads made by the organic industry into our daily habits. Dedicated to striking the balance between quality and affordability, Planet Organic is the green version of supermarket shopping, with an almost entirely organic stock. The enormous range more than compensates for the lack of intimacy; the organic meat, fish and cheese counters are a beauty to behold, and the comprehensive booze section even features organic champagne for that special occasion. Added attractions include occasional in-store massages in the homeopathic section, where qualified, informative staff are available for advice on specific ailments. The bicycle home delivery service is especially popular.

Further afield, Spitalfields, E1, has both **Spitalfields Organics** (103A Commercial Street, 7377 8909), with hundreds of health foods, organic cosmetics and bodycare products, plus some vitamins and supplements, and **Spitalfields Market** (65 Brushfield Street, 7377 1496), which on Fridays and, particularly, Sundays (crafts and antiques stalls are set up through the week) comes alive with a dozen or so organic producers selling relishes, pickles, herbs and spices, breads and cakes, and fruit and vegetables.

In terms of supermarkets offering organic produce, they don't come much better than **Waitrose** (199 Finchley Road, NW3, 7624 0453 or see www.waitrose.com for branches), the deserved winner of the Best Food Shop category in the *Time Out* Retail Awards 2001.

Eat, Drink, Shop

Timothy Everest

32 Elder Street, The City, E1 (7377 5770).
Liverpool Street tube/rail. **Open** 9am-6pm Mon-Fri;
9.30am-3pm Sat; also by appointment. **Credit**
AmEx, DC, MC, V. **Map** p403 R5.

Tailor to Posh and Becks and designer of a range of
suits for Marks & Spencer's Autograph label (*see*
p236), Everest keeps a close eye on trends but can
still make a perfectly good traditionally cut suit.

Florists

Wild at Heart

49A Ledbury Road, Notting Hill, W11 (7727 3095).
Notting Hill Gate or Westbourne Park tube. **Open**
8.30am-7pm Mon-Sat. **Credit** AmEx, JCB, MC, V.
Map p394 A6.

Hot pinks, strong scents and lime-green flowers
housed in an architectural masterpiece.
Branch: Great Eastern Hotel, Liverpool Street, The
City, EC2 (7618 5350).

Wild Bunch

17 Earlham Street, Covent Garden, WC2 (7497
1200). Covent Garden tube. **Open** 9.30am-7.30pm
Mon-Sat. **Credit** AmEx, MC, V. **Map** p399 K6.

An unassuming stall with everything you would
find in the most fancy flower shops and more.

Woodhams at One Aldwych

1 Aldwych, Holborn, WC1 (7300 0777/
www.woodhams.co.uk). Covent Garden or Temple
tube/Charing Cross tube/rail. **Open** 10am-6pm
Mon-Fri; 10am-5pm Sat. **Credit** AmEx, MC, V.
Map p401 M6.

A gleaming, perfumed shrine to the ultra-modern
school of flower arranging.

Food & drink

For department-store food halls, *see p235-7*.

Bakeries & pâtisseries

For other café-pâtisseries, *see p214* **Pit stops**.

& Clarke's

122 Kensington Church Street, Kensington, W8
(7229 2190/www.sallyclarke.com). Notting Hill Gate
tube. **Open** 8am-8pm Mon-Fri; 9am-4pm Sat.
Credit AmEx, MC, V. **Map** p399 B8.

Considered by some to be the best bakery in town,
this supplies not just the public but high-class
London shops and restaurants too. It also does
delicious cakes, pâtisseries and deli fare.

Konditor & Cook

22 Cornwall Road, South Bank, SE1 (7261 0456).
Waterloo tube/rail/27 bus. **Open** 7.30am-6.30pm
Mon-Fri; 8.30am-2.30pm Sat. **Credit** JCB, MC, V.
Map p404 N8.

Well known among sweet-toothed Londoners as
the shop that managed to put the pzazz into pas-
try, Konditor & Cook continues to bake up a storm

in the heart of trendy SE1. The goodies on offer
from other producers include great bread from
& Clarke's (*see above*).
Branches: 46 Gray's Inn Road, Bloomsbury, WC1,
(7404 6300); 10 Stoney Street, Bankside, SE1 (7407
5100); 66 The Cut, South Bank, SE1 (7620 2700).

Pâtisserie Valerie

44 Old Compton Street, Soho, W1 (7437 3466/
www.patisserievalerie.co.uk). Piccadilly Circus or
Tottenham Court Road tube. **Open** 7.30am-8pm
Mon-Fri; 8am-8pm Sat; 9.30am-7pm Sun. **Credit**
AmEx, DC, JCB, MC, V. **Map** p399 K6.

Of the many French pâtisseries in Soho, Valerie is
undoubtedly the most famous. Dating back to the
1920s, it has all the hallmarks of a classic cake shop,
with shining windows and cabinets full of goodies.
Branches: throughout the city.

Cheese shops

Neal's Yard Dairy

17 Shorts Gardens, Covent Garden, WC2 (7240
5700). Covent Garden tube. **Open** 9am-7pm Mon-
Sat. **Credit** MC, V. **Map** p399 L6.

One of London's finest cheesemongers, Neal's Yard
continues to showcase the best cheeses from the
British Isles. Stock is regularly rotated. The staff are
laid-back and knowledgeable, and encourage customers to taste before buying.
Branch: 6 Park Street, Bankside, SE1 (7378 8195).

Coffee & tea

Algerian Coffee Stores

52 Old Compton Street, Soho, W1 (7437 2480/
www.algcoffee.co.uk). Leicester Square or Piccadilly
Circus tube. **Open** 9am-7pm Mon-Sat. **Credit** AmEx,
MC, V. **Map** p399 K6.

The aroma that hits your nose when you walk into
this long-established Soho shop is a mixture of the
50 or so coffee blends that it imports from just about
everywhere in the world. Add exotic teas and novelty coffees, plus a range of quality pre-packaged
confectionery and biscuits, and you see why this is
one of the most popular coffee stores in town.

The Tea House

15A Neal Street, Covent Garden, WC2 (7240 7539).
Covent Garden tube. **Open** 10am-7pm Mon, Wed, Sat;
10am-7.30pm Thur; 10.30am-7pm Fri; noon-6pm Sun.
Credit AmEx, JCB, MC, V. **Map** p399 L6.

A good selection of around 60 teas from every
corner of the tea-producing world.

R Twining & Co

216 Strand, Covent Garden, WC2 (7353 3511/
www.twinings.com). Temple tube/Charing
Cross tube/rail. **Open** 9.30am-4.45pm Mon-Fri.
Credit AmEx, DC, MC, V. **Map** p399 M6.

Established on this site way back in 1706,
Twining's is the oldest company to have traded
continuously under the same name, from the same

premises, and under the control of the same family, in this country, and very probably in the world. As well as the teashop, where you can sample some of the goodies that are on offer in the shop, there's also a small museum in which you can learn all about the firm's history.

Confectioners

Godiva
247 Regent Street, Mayfair, W1 (7495 2845/ www.godiva.com). Oxford Circus tube. **Open** 9.30am-7pm Mon-Sat; noon-6pm Sun. **Credit** AmEx, DC, JCB, MC, V. **Map** p398 J6.
Butter, cream and hazelnut paste give Godiva's famous confectionery its characteristically smooth texture. Make no mistake – this is an adult range: truffles, pralines and palets (which consist of chocolate paste wrapped up in a crispy chocolate shell) come in extremely grown-up flavours such as red wine and black tea.
Branches: throughout the city.

Rococo
321 King's Road, Chelsea, SW3 (7352 5857/ www.rococochocolates.com). Sloane Square tube. **Open** 10am-6.30pm Mon-Sat; noon-5pm Sun. **Credit** AmEx, JCB, MC, V. **Map** p397 D12.
Rococo is a mecca for chocolate worshippers the world over. The deliriously messy house truffles contain Valrhona's manjari, which is the rarest chocolate in the world, while budding confectioners can buy the raw material in the form of Valrhona grand cru bars.

Oriental goodies at **Neal Street East**, *p253*.

Delicatessens

Bluebird
350 King's Road, Chelsea, SW3 (7559 1000/ www.conran.com). Sloane Square tube then 11, 19, 22, 49, 211, 319, 345 bus. **Open** 9am-8pm Mon-Wed; 9am-9pm Thur-Sat; 10am-6pm Sun. **Credit** AmEx, DC, JCB, MC, V. **Map** p397 D12.
Sir Terence Conran's gourmet food hall, created from the shell of the Grade II-listed Bluebird Garage, is a bright, clean-cut place that also contains a florist, a café and the Bluebird restaurant.

Carluccio's
28A Neal Street, Covent Garden, WC2 (7240 1487/ www.carluccios.com). Covent Garden tube. **Open** 11am-7pm Mon-Sat; noon-6pm Sun. **Credit** AmEx, MC, V. **Map** p399 L6.
As you'd expect from Mr Mushroom, his shop stocks a good selection of seasonal wild funghi, as well as frighteningly expensive black and white truffles. Most of the stock bears the Carluccio name, from spaghetti to olive oils. There are also focaccia sandwiches and delicious tarts, cakes and quiches.
Branches: throughout the city.

Villandry
170 Great Portland Street, Marylebone, W1 (7631 3131/www.villandry.com). Great Portland Street tube. **Open** 8.30am-10pm Mon-Sat; 9am-4pm Sun. **Credit** AmEx, JCB, MC, V. **Map** p398 H5.
The large plate glass frontage tempts people in with a lovely array of cakes, pastries and bread. Inside are fine cheeses, wines, vegetables and other treats from around the world.

Wines & spirits

For everyday use, **Oddbins**, with branches all over London (see www.oddbins.co.uk), is hard to beat, though supermarkets such as Sainsbury's and Safeway have vastly improved their alcohol selections in recent years.

Gerry's
74 Old Compton Street, Soho, W1 (7734 4215). Leicester Square or Tottenham Court Road tube. **Open** 9am-6.30pm Mon-Fri; 9am-5.30pm Sat. **No credit cards**. **Map** p399 K6.
Gerry's shelves are crammed with just about every spirit and obscure liqueur you can imagine, and then some. Vodka is a speciality, with more than 100 varieties stocked. If you don't see it, ask.

Milroy's of Soho
3 Greek Street, Soho, W1 (7437 9311/ www.milroys.co.uk). Tottenham Court Road tube. **Open** 11am-7pm Mon, Tue; 11am-11pm Wed-Sat. **Credit** AmEx, DC, MC, V. **Map** p399 K6.
The most famous whisky specialist in London. Milroy's has a huge selection of whiskies from Scotland, Ireland and America. Service is expert and friendly. Around 600 of the 700 whiskies are available by the glass in the downstairs bar.

Eat, Drink, Shop

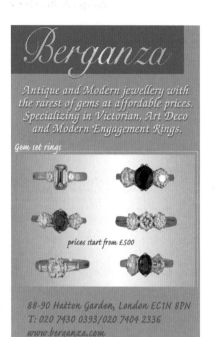

Gifts & stationery

Most of London's large museums have excellent gift shops, in particular **London's Transport Museum** (*see p125*), the **British Museum** (*see p103*), the **V&A** (*see p140*) and the **Tate Modern** (*see p79*).

Neal Street East

5 Neal Street, Covent Garden, WC2 (7240 0135). Covent Garden tube. **Open** 11am-7pm Mon-Wed; 10am-7.30pm Thur; 10am-7pm Fri, Sat; noon-6pm Sun. **Credit** AmEx, MC, V. **Map** p399 L6.
London's leading ethnic emporium has a massive range of oriental and South American goods, including clothing, jewellery, books, homewares, kitchen ware, and cards and gifts.
Branch: 39 Shelton Street, WC2 (7379 1595).

Paperchase

213-15 Tottenham Court Road, Fitzrovia, W1 (7467 6200). Goodge Street tube. **Open** 9.30am-7pm Mon, Wed, Fri, Sat; 10am-7pm Tue; 9.30am-8pm Thur; noon-6pm Sun. **Credit** AmEx, MC, V. **Map** p399 K5.
This three-floor flagship branch has a vast selection of notebooks, writing books, pens, cards and the like, plus an extensive art materials department.
Branches: throughout the city.

The Pen Shop

199 Regent Street, Mayfair, W1 (7734 4088/ www.penshop.co.uk). Oxford Circus tube. **Open** 9.30am-6pm Mon, Tue, Fri, Sat; 10am-6pm Wed; 9.30am-7pm Thur. **Credit** AmEx, DC, JCB, MC, V. **Map** p400 J7.
Pens by Lamt, Waterman, Cross, Shaeffer and Parker, plus Yard O Led's distinctive silver pens and Mont Blanc's chic black models.

Make room in your schedule for **SPAce.NK**.

Branches: 10 West Mall, Liverpool Street Station, The City, EC2 (7628 4416); 88 Brompton Road, Knightsbridge, SW3 (7581 4559).

Health & beauty

Beauty services

The Green Room

21 Earl's Court Road, Kensington, W8 (7937 6595). High Street Kensington tube. **Open** 9am-9pm Mon-Thur; 9am-6pm Fri, Sat; 10am-5pm Sun. **Credit** AmEx, MC, V. **Map** p396 A9.
The Body Shop continues its 'beauty without cruelty' ethos at its Green Room salons, where friendly staff undertake a range of 'natural'-based therapies.
Branches: throughout the city.

The Refinery

60 Brook Street, Mayfair, W1 (7409 2001/ www.the-refinery.com). Bond Street tube. **Open** 10am-7pm Mon, Tue; 10am-9pm Wed-Fri; 9am-6pm Sat; 11am-5pm Sun. **Credit** AmEx, MC, V. **Map** p398 H6.
In the newly hip world of men's grooming, London's cosmopolitan gents think nothing of booking themselves in for an Enzymatic Body Wrap or facial. The salon's anti-urban detox treatments are just the antidote to a hard day at the office. There's also a selection of 15-minute 'Pit Stop' treatments.
Branch: 38 Bishopsgate, The City, EC2.

The Sanctuary

12 Floral Street, Covent Garden, WC2 (08700 630300/www.thesanctuary.co.uk). Covent Garden tube. **Open** *Day members* 9.30am-6pm Mon-Fri, Sun; 9.30am-8pm Sat. *Evening members* 5pm-10pm Wed-Fri. **Credit** AmEx, DC, JCB, MC, V. **Map** p401 L6.
Frolic like a Grecian maiden among white stucco, green foliage and whirlpools at this gorgeous women-only spa. Treatments ranging from seaweed wraps and hydrotherapy baths to facials are available.

SPAce.NK

127-31 Westbourne Grove, Notting Hill, W11 (7727 8002/www.spacenk.com). Notting Hill Gate tube. **Open** 10am-7pm Mon, Fri; 9am-9pm Tue-Thur; 9am-7pm Sat; 10am-5pm Sun. **Credit** AmEx, JCB, MC, V. **Map** p394 B6.
The ugly name (the 'ce' is silent) belies a beautiful, serene operation offering all manner of pamperings.

Cosmetics & herbalists

Aveda Institute

28-9 Marylebone High Street, Marylebone, W1 (7224 3157/www.aveda.com). Baker Street or Bond Street tube. **Open** 9.30am-7pm Mon-Fri; 9am-6pm Sat. **Credit** AmEx, JCB, MC, V. **Map** p398 G5.
At the forefront of holistic skincare, Aveda's lotions and potions are made with 97% natural ingredients. It's not cheap, but you get what you pay for.
Branches: throughout the city.

Eat, Drink, Shop

Crabtree & Evelyn

*6 Kensington Church Street, Kensington, W8
(7937 9335/www.crabtree-evelyn.com). High Street
Kensington tube.* **Open** 10am-6pm Mon-Wed, Fri,
Sat; 10am-7pm Thur; 11am-5pm Sun. **Credit** AmEx,
MC, V. **Map** p394 B8.
Crabtree & Evelyn is famous for its upmarket fem-
inine toiletries and gifts beautifully packaged in
old-fashioned, bijou boxes and bottles.
Branches: throughout the city.

Jo Malone

*150 Sloane Street, Chelsea, SW1 (7730 2100/
www.jomalone.co.uk). Sloane Square tube.* **Open**
10am-6pm Mon-Tue, Fri, Sat; 10am-7pm Wed, Thur.
Credit AmEx, MC, V. **Map** p397 E10.
Skincare products don't come more chic than these
highly covetable goodies.
Branches 24 Threadneedle Street, The City, EC3
(7444 1999).

Lush

*Units 11, The Market, Covent Garden, WC2
(7240 4570/www.lush.co.uk). Covent Garden tube.*
Open 10am-7pm Mon-Sat; noon-6pm Sun.
Credit AmEx, MC, V. **Map** p401 L7.
Cheese-like slabs of natural soap, fruity scents and
food-themed bath-treats.
Branches: 123 King's Road, Chelsea, SW3 (7376
8348); 40 Carnaby Street, Soho, W1 (7287 5874);
Unit 42, Lower Concourse, Victoria Station, Pimlico,
SW1 (7630 9927); 1-3 Quadrant Arcade, 80-82 Regent
Street, Mayfair, W1 (7434 9927).

Neal's Yard Remedies

*15 Neal's Yard, Covent Garden, WC2 (7379 7222/
www.nealsyardremedies.com). Covent Garden tube.*
Open 10am-7pm Mon-Sat; 11am-5pm Sun. **Credit**
AmEx, MC, V. **Map** p399 L6.
Legendary for its alternative health and beauty
products, this tiny store is crammed with trademark
blue bottles filled with wonderful-smelling skin, hair
and bath concoctions.
Branches: throughout the city.

Pure Beauty

*19-20 Long Acre, Covent Garden, WC2
(7836 4127). Covent Garden tube.* **Open**
10am-8pm Mon-Fri, 10am-7pm Sat, noon-6pm Sun.
Credit MC, V. **Map** p401 L6.
The first of a new gang of stand-alone beauty stores
by Boots (*see p260*), this targets those who want to
splash out yet remains accessible. Brands include
the new Barefoot Doctor range and Clarins alongside Boots' own Botanics products.
Branches: 151-151A Oxford Street, Soho, W1 (0845
129 6604); 14 Canada Place, Canary Wharf Shopping
Centre, Docklands, E14 (0845 129 6603).

Space.NK

*4 Thomas Neal Centre, 37 Earlham Street, Covent
Garden, WC2 (7379 7030/www.spacenk.co.uk).
Covent Garden tube.* **Open** 10am-7pm Mon-Wed,
Fri, Sat; 10am-7.30pm Thur; noon-5pm Sun.
Credit AmEx, JCB, MC, V. **Map** p399 L6.

The place for cutting-edge cosmetics. Prices match
the calibre of the products.
Branches: throughout the city.

Hairdressers

Charles Worthington

*34 Great Queen Street, Covent Garden, WC2 (7831
5303/www.charlesworthington.co.uk). Covent Garden
tube.* **Open** 8am-9pm Mon-Thur; 10.15am-7pm Fri;
8am-6pm Sat. **Credit** AmEx, MC, V. **Map** p399 L6.
Every first-time visitor to a Charles Worthington
salon receives a Client Service Guarantee brochure
– such is the confidence in the highly trained staff
here. While a cut and finish with award-winning
Charles will set you back £200, the same with a
graduate stylist is a snip at £25.

Fish

*30 D'Arblay Street, Soho, W1 (7494 2398/
www.fishweb.co.uk). Oxford Circus or Tottenham
Court Road tube.* **Open** 10am-7pm Mon-Wed, Fri;
10am-8pm Thur; 10am-5pm Sat. **Credit** JCB, MC, V.
Map p399 K6.
Fish is a unique and cosmopolitan little salon that
has its finger firmly on the pulse of current hair-
cutting and colouring trends.

Toni & Guy

*8 Marylebone High Street, Marylebone, W1 (7935
7900/www.toniandguy.co.uk). Bond Street tube.*
Open 10am-5.30pm Mon, Tue; 10am-6.30pm
Wed-Fri; 9am-5.30pm Sat. **Credit** AmEx, DC,
MC, V. **Map** p398 G5.
For high-fashion styles at affordable prices look no
further. The salons have a professional but friendly
atmosphere and are popular with both sexes.
Branches: throughout the city.

Vidal Sassoon

*60 South Molton Street, Mayfair, W1 (7491 8848/
www.vidalsassoon.co.uk). Bond Street tube.*
Open 10.30am-6pm Mon-Wed; 10.30am-6.45pm
Thur; 10.30am-5.15pm Fri; 9am-5.15pm Sat.
Credit AmEx, MC, V. **Map** p398 H6.
Since the '60s Vidal Sassoon has been synonymous
with dramatic blunt cuts, and the salons are still
good for those with straight hair. Prices for a cut
and blow dry vary between salons (here they start
at £45 for a stylist).
Branches: throughout the city.

Opticians

Kirk Originals

*29 Floral Street, Covent Garden, WC2 (7240 5055/
www.kirkoriginals.com). Covent Garden tube.*
Open 10.30am-6.30pm Mon-Wed, Fri, Sat;
10.30am-7pm Thur. **Credit** MC, V. **Map** p399 L6.
Kirk makes frames in limited editions of between
two and 250 (numbered) copies, so when you buy
here you know you're getting a true original.
Designs are witty and retro.

Vision Express
263-5 Oxford Street, Mayfair, W1 (7409 7880/
www.visionexpress.co.uk). Oxford Circus tube.
Open 9.30am-8pm Mon-Sat; noon-6pm Sun.
Credit AmEx, MC, V. **Map** p398 H6.
Twenty-minute eye tests and glasses within an hour.
Branches: throughout the city.

Homewares

For second-hand furniture and home
accessories, *see p258* **Thrifty business**.

The Conran Shop
Michelin House, 81 Fulham Road, Chelsea, SW3
(7589 7401/www.conran.com). South Kensington
tube. **Open** 10am-6pm Mon, Tue, Fri; 10am-7pm
Wed, Thur; 10am-6.30pm Sat; noon-6pm Sun.
Credit AmEx, MC, V. **Map** p398 G5.
A one-stop shop for clean, stylish design, this was
voted Best Interiors Shop in the *Time Out* Retail
Awards 2001. Each product is selected by Conran
himself, which results in a consistently good range of
lighting, kitchen, bathroom and furniture products,
as well as the vast choice of top quality accessories,
from silverware to leather goods and bedlinen.
Branch: 55 Marylebone High Street, Marylebone,
W1 (7723 2223).

Designers Guild
267-71 & 275-7 King's Road, Chelsea, SW3 (7351
5775/www.designersguild.com). Sloane Square tube
then 11, 19, 22 bus. **Open** 9.30am-5.30pm Mon, Tue;
10am-6pm Wed-Sat; noon-5pm Sun (nos.267-71 only).
Credit AmEx, MC, V. **Map** p397 E10.
Three floors of modernist furniture and accessories,
tableware and bedlinen, plus an espresso bar.

Divertimenti
45-7 Wigmore Street, Marylebone, W1 (7935 0689/
www.divertimenti.co.uk). Bond Street tube. **Open**
9.30am-6pm Mon-Wed, Fri; 9.30am-7pm Thur;
10am-6pm Sat; noon-5.30pm Sun. **Credit** AmEx,
DC, MC, V. **Map** p398 G6.
A huge range of seriously cool cookware available
in a central location just behind Selfridges.
Branch: 139-41 Fulham Road, Chelsea, SW3
(7581 8065).

Purves & Purves: time for a clean sweep.

eat my handbag bitch
6 Dray Walk, Old Truman Brewery, 91-5
Brick Lane, Spitalfields, E1 (7375 3100/
www.eatmyhandbagbitch.co.uk). Aldgate East
tube/Liverpool Street tube/rail. **Open** 11am-7pm
Mon-Sat. **Credit** AmEx, MC, V. **Map** p403 S5.
Despite the name, this is actually a rather serious if
incredibly fashionable modern design shop. There's
a concession in Selfridges (see p236).

Habitat
196 Tottenham Court Road, Fitzrovia, W1
(7631 3880/www.habitat.net). Goodge Street tube.
Open 10am-6pm Mon-Wed; 10am-8pm Thur;
10am-6.30pm Fri; 9.30am-6.30pm Sat; noon-6pm Sun.
Credit AmEx, MC, V. **Map** p398 J4.
The high street gateway to modern interior design.
The ever-expanding firm produces a desirable
catalogue each month, as well as new seasonal furniture ranges. Innovations in seating, home office
products and kitchens sit alongside retro classics.
Branches: throughout the city.

Heal's
196 Tottenham Court Road, Fitzrovia, W1
(7636 1666/www.heals.co.uk). Goodge Street tube.
Open 10am-6pm Mon-Wed; 10am-8pm Thur;
10am-6.30pm Fri; 9.30am-6.30pm Sat; noon-6pm Sun.
Credit AmEx, DC, MC, V. **Map** p399 K5.
A high street store for well-heeled customers, Heal's
offers a more exclusive (and more expensive) take
on modern furniture than neighbouring Habitat.
Designs range from one-offs and limited editions to
reissued retro classics and contemporary pieces.
Branch: 234 King's Road, Chelsea, SW3 (7349 8411).

Holding Company
241-5 King's Road, Chelsea, SW3 (7352 1600/
www.theholdingcompany.co.uk). Sloane Square tube
then 11, 19, 22 bus. **Open** 10am-6pm Mon, Tue,
Thur, Fri; 10am-7pm Wed, Sat; noon-6pm Sun.
Credit AmEx, JCB, MC, V. **Map** p397 D12.
The Holding Company provides clever solutions to
the universal problem of modern living: clutter.

Muji
187 Oxford Street, Soho, W1 (7437 7503/
http://207.97.150.242). Oxford Circus tube.
Open 10am-7pm Mon-Wed, Sat; 10am-8pm Thur;
10am-7.30pm Fri; noon-6pm Sun. **Credit** AmEx, DC,
JCB, MC, V. **Map** p399 K6.
The Japanese 'no brand goods' store offers a
range of stylish accessories, from cardboard and
polypropylene storage to kitchen and tableware.
Branches: throughout the city.

Purves & Purves
220-24 Tottenham Court Road, Fitzrovia, W1
(7580 8223/www.purves.co.uk). Goodge Street tube.
Open 9.30am-6pm Mon, Wed, Fri, Sat; 10am-6pm
Tue; 9.30am-7.30pm Thur; 11.30am-5.30pm Sun.
Credit AmEx, JCB, MC, V. **Map** p398 J4.
Famous for its pricey vivid-coloured sofas and
chairs, Purve & Purves appeals to both the moneyed shopper and the fashionista on the lookout for

Eat, Drink, Shop

a new trend. Sofas, rugs and a wide range of (mainly kitchen) accessories are the staple products. You'll find names such as Philippe Starck, Ron Arad and B&B Italia.
Branch: Canada Place, Canary Wharf Shopping Centre, Docklands, E14 (7719 1169).

Markets

General

Brick Lane Market

Brick Lane (north of railway bridge), Cygnet Street, Sclater Street, E1; Bacon Street, Cheshire Street, Chilton Street, E2. Aldgate East or Shoreditch tube/ Liverpool Street tube/rail. **Open** 8am-1pm Sun. **Map** p403 S5.
The Spitalfields area has undergone huge gentrification over the last few years, resulting in this chaotic, uncontrolled market becoming a lot more ordered. That notwithstanding, you'll still find a massive range of goods on sale at this sprawling, ever-entertaining East End institution, including meat, fruit and veg, electrical goods, tools, bicycles, clothing, jewellery and household goods. A trip here is a quintessential Sunday morning out in London: make sure not to miss it.

Brixton Market

Electric Avenue, Pope's Road, Brixton Station Road, Brixton, SW9. Brixton tube/rail. **Open** 8am-6pm Mon, Tue, Thur-Sat; 8am-3pm Wed.
Running down Electric Avenue into two shopping arcades on either side of Atlantic Road, this thriving multicultural market has a community feel. African and Caribbean produce and other exotic staples can be found, along with traditional fruit and veg and fish. There are also record stalls, second-hand clothes and bric-a-brac. *See also p176* **Caribbean London**.

Camden Market

(7284 2084). Camden Town or Chalk Farm tube. **Camden Market** *Camden High Street, junction with Buck Street, NW1.* **Open** 9am-5.30pm Thur-Sun. **Camden Lock Market** *Camden Lock Place, off Chalk Farm Road, NW1.* **Open** 10am-6pm Sat, Sun. *Indoor stalls* 10am-6pm Tue-Sun. **Stables Market** *off Chalk Farm Road, opposite junction with Hartland Road, NW1.* **Open** 8am-6pm Sat, Sun. **Camden Canal Market** *off Chalk Farm Road, south of junction with Castle Haven Road, NW1.* **Open** 10am-6pm Sat, Sun. **Electric Market** **Camden** *High Street, south of junction with Dewsbury Terrace, NW1.* **Open** 9am-5.30pm Sun.
London's fourth-biggest tourist attraction stopped being cutting edge a long time ago, and has for the past decade contented itself with selling manufactured rebellion to those happy to find youth culture represented in such unequivocal terms. Street fashion and retro clothes dominate the main market, while Camden Lock maintains its crafts heritage. It's usually busy and, at times, claustrophobic.

Columbia Road Market. *See p257.*

Greenwich Market

Cutty Sark DLR/Greenwich DLR/rail. **Antiques Market** *Greenwich High Road, SE10.* **Open** 9am-5pm Sat, Sun. **Central Market** *off Stockwell Street, SE10.* **Open** *Outdoor* 7am-6pm Sat; 7am-5pm Sun. *Indoor (Village Market)* 10am-5pm Fri, Sat; 10am-6pm Sun. **Crafts Market** *College Approach, SE10.* **Open** *Antiques* 7.30am-5pm Thur. *General* 9.30am-5.30pm Fri-Sun. **Food Market** *off Stockwell Street, SE10.* **Open** 10am-4pm Sat.
Still going strong, Greenwich is less frenetic than Camden and Portobello and generally cheaper. The covered section that makes up Greenwich Market proper is filled with arts and crafts that range from personal craftsmanship to uninspired tat. The nearby Village Market is funkier, with interesting second-hand clothing stalls, lots of records and books, and some great '50s, '60s and '70s furniture. Sundays here are another London tradition.

Petticoat Lane Market

Middlesex Street & around, The City, E1. Liverpool Street tube/rail. **Open** 9am-2pm Sun. *Wentworth Street* also 10am-2.30pm Mon-Fri. **Map** p405 R6.
While Brick Lane gets hip and Spitalfields Market appeals to the ecological intentions of London's liberals, nearby Petticoat Lane remains resolutely traditional, and as East End as they come. But although much is unremarkable, there's a hell of a lot of it, and almost every type of consumer durable can be found at a very low price. Up on Cutler Street are gold and silver jewellery traders, a leftover from the gold and coin mart that used to operate here.

Portobello Road Market

Portobello Road, Notting Hill, W10, W11; Golborne Road, W10. Ladbroke Grove, Notting Hill Gate or Westbourne Park tube. **Open** *Antiques Market* 4am-6pm Sat. *General Market* 8am-6pm Mon-Wed; 9am-1pm Thur; 7am-7pm Fri, Sat. *Organic Market* 11am-6pm Thur. *Clothes & Bric-a-Brac Market* 7am-4pm Fri; 8am-5pm Sat; 9am-4pm Sun. *Golborne Road Market* 9am-5pm Mon-Sat. **Map** p394 A6.
Though now even more of a tourist attraction since the release of *Notting Hill*, Portobello still hasn't gone the way of Camden and given in to tackiness. There's something for everyone at this lengthy street mart; the choice of antiques is huge, though prices have always been high, and you'll also find some of west London's cheapest fruit, veg and flowers. But it's probably most famous for its new and vintage clothes stalls (*see also p258* **Thrifty business**).

Flowers

Columbia Road Flower Market
Columbia Road (between Gosset Street & the Royal Oak pub), Bethnal Green, E2. Old Street tube/rail/ 26, 48, 55 bus. **Open** 8am-1pm Sun. **Map** p403 S3.
Without question the prettiest street market in town, Columbia Road offers flowers, shrubs, bedding plants and other horticultural delights spread in all directions. Roundabout shops stock flowers and lots of garden accessories.

Food

For information on London's increasingly popular farmers' markets, call 01225 787914 or see www.farmersmarkets.net. For Spitalfields organic market, *see p249* **Organic London**.

Berwick Street Market
Berwick Street & Rupert Street, Soho, W1. Leicester Square or Piccadilly Circus tube. **Open** 8am-6pm Mon-Sat. **Map** p398 J6.
The best and cheapest selection of fruit and vegetables in central London can be found here, in one of the last parts of Soho with a genuinely seedy feel. There are also very good cheese, fish, bread, and herb and spice stalls.

Borough Market
8 Southwark Street, between Borough High Street, Bedale Street, Winchester Walk & Stoney Street, Borough, South Bank, SE1 (7407 1002/ www.boroughmarket.org.uk). London Bridge tube/rail. **Open** noon-6pm Fri; 9am-4pm Sat. **Map** p404 P8.
This superb farmers' market, nicknamed London's Larder, is the most exciting food market in the city, and it's going from strength to strength in the face of wrangles over a proposed train link (*see p80*). There are some good cut flowers, as well as quality coffees, fruit, veg and meat. A number of traders specialise in organic produce.

Music shops

Megastores

HMV
150 Oxford Street, Fitzrovia, W1 (7631 3423/ www.hmv.co.uk). Oxford Circus tube. **Open** 9am-8pm Mon-Sat; noon-6pm Sun. **Credit** AmEx, JCB, DC, MC, V. **Map** p398 J6.
This behemoth of a music shop has three floors that are crammed with CDs, books, games and DVDs. Every musical genre has its own dedicated department, though some are clearly more dedicated than others. These days there's a bigger range of vinyl, especially in the underground dance and hip hop section.
Branches: 360 Oxford Street, Mayfair, W1 (7514 3600); Trocadero, 18 Coventry Street, St James's, W1 (7439 0447); 42-44 King Street, Covent Garden, WC2 (7379 8935).

Tower Records
1 Piccadilly Circus, Mayfair, W1 (7439 2500/ www.towerrecords.co.uk). Piccadilly Circus tube. **Open** 9am-midnight Mon-Fri; 8.30am-midnight Sat; noon-6pm Sun. **Credit** AmEx, DC, JCB, MC, V. **Map** p400 J7.
This enormous flagship store sells a little of everything, and a lot of most things. The stock is mainly made up of CDs, but there's an adequate selection of dance vinyl and new LPs. The massive jazz section holds a wealth of international releases, and the folk, world, classical and opera departments are big. The range of videos and DVDs is equally impressive, and along with a nice line in boxed sets the store has books, magazines and computer games aplenty.
Branches: 62-4 Kensington High Street, Kensington, W8 (7938 3511); 162 Camden High Street, Camden, N1 (7424 2800); Unit 001B, Whiteley's Shopping Centre, Bayswater, W2 (7229 4550).

Virgin Megastore
14-16 Oxford Street, Fitzrovia, W1 (7631 1234/ www.virgin.com). Tottenham Court Road tube. **Open** 9.30am-9pm Mon-Sat; noon-6pm Sun. **Credit** AmEx, DC, JCB, MC, V. **Map** p399 K6.
In keeping with current tastes and trends this shop – the biggest and most brazen of the megastores – combines typically frenetic mainstream sections (a manic dance 12in area; a massive Top 40 display) with good ranges of classical, jazz and opera. Those in search of rock and indie are well catered for, and along with good lines of soul and funk there's a floor dedicated to videos and DVDs, plus a packed games department and numerous rock books and mags.
Branches: 225-9 Piccadilly, St James's, W1 (7930 4208); King's Walk Shopping Centre, King's Road, Chelsea, SW3 (7591 0957); 213-219 Camden High Street, Camden, NW1 (7482 5307).

Specialist music shops

Soho's Berwick Street is a music mecca – **Selectadisc** (no.34) and **Sister Ray** (no.94) are particularly strong on indie, **Reckless Records** (no.30) is good for mainstream, there's Jamaican music at **Daddy Kool** (no.12) and general cut-price CDs at **Mr CD** (no.80).

Black Market
25 D'Arblay Street, Soho, W1 (7437 0478/ www.blackmarket.com). Oxford Circus tube. **Open** 11am-7pm Mon-Sat. **Credit** AmEx, MC, V. **Map** p399 K6.
A tiny corridor, with nodding DJs behind the counter. Strong on imported house and drum 'n' bass.

Harold Moores Records
2 Great Marlborough Street, Soho, W1 (7437 1576/www.hmrecords.co.uk). Oxford Circus tube. **Open** 10am-6.30pm Mon-Sat; noon-6.30pm Sun. **Credit** MC, V. **Map** p398 J6.
Harold Moores has a breathtaking range of classical music both in the upstairs CD section and downstairs, where you can browse through around

60,000 mint-condition second-hand LPs, including strong lines of early and chamber music, opera, historical and nostalgia. A fine line of classical music videos is also available.

Honest Jon's
276 & 278 Portobello Road, Ladbroke Grove, W10 (8969 9822/www.honestjons.co.uk). Ladbroke Grove tube. **Open** 10am-6pm Mon-Sat; 11am-5pm Sun. **Credit** AmEx, DC, JCB, MC, V. **Map** p394 A6.
These two popular adjoining shops offer the very best in jazz, soul, funk, Latin and reggae on both CD and vinyl. Prices are honest indeed, even when it comes to the rarer records.

Intoxica!
231 Portobello Road, Ladbroke Grove, W11 (7229 8010/www.intoxica.co.uk). Ladbroke Grove tube. **Open** 10.30am-6.30pm Mon-Fri; 10am-6.30pm Sat; noon-5pm Sun. **Credit** AmEx, DC, JCB, MC, V. **Map** p394 A6.
Considered by many to be the best second-hand record shop in London, Intoxica! is particularly strong on '60s and '70s rock, funk and soul, garage, rockabilly, ska, punk and new wave.

MDC Classic Music
437 Strand, Covent Garden, WC2 (7240 2157/ www.mdcmusic.co.uk). Charing Cross tube/rail. **Open** 9am-7pm Mon-Sat; noon-6pm Sun. **Credit** AmEx, MC, V. **Map** p401 L7.

Eat, Drink, Shop

Thrifty business

The future of the planet may very well depend on it, but recycling is something Londoners seem to have in their blood, if the number of second-hand, charity and junk stores in the capital is anything to go by. We point dedicated followers of second-hand fashion, whether it be clothes or homewares, in the direction of the most fertile hunting grounds.

Marylebone, W1, NW1 & NW8
If the first words that come into your head when you hear the name Marylebone are 'posh' and 'genteel', you may be surprised to find the area among our top areas for thrifty shopping. Moneyed though most of its inhabitants may be, however, the area has something a little jaded and careworn about it, and, largely overlooked until recently in favour of the more commercial Oxford Street, its disused shop spaces have provided inexpensive premises for second-hand and charity stores.

Having upped and come over the past five years or so, Marylebone High Street's excellent array of charity shops has started to dwindle of late, as the chains have moved in and rents have soared. You'll still find Oxfam, Cancer Research, Sue Ryder and the Geranium Shop for the Blind, but shops are tending to shift around with bewildering frequency as newer shops take over the prime spots, so you might have to ask other shopkeepers to point you in the right direction.

Otherwise, you'll find dress agencies **Charon** (74 Marylebone Lane, W1, 7486 2901) and **Catwalk** (52 Blandford Street, W1, 7935 1052), the nearly new designer menswear store **L'Homme Designer Exchange** (50 Blandford Street, W1,

7224 3266), the excellent **Century** (68 Marylebone High Street, W1, 7487 5100) with its vintage American furniture, and the delightful **Sixty6** (66 Marylebone High Street, W1, 7224 6066), with its gorgeous girlie frocks and 20th-century design classics, including Murano glassware.

North of Marylebone Road, the grittier Church Street is home at its western end to a large and thriving food and general market, while its eastern end is rapidly being colonised by small shops offering one-off treasures. **Alfie's Antiques Market** (13-25 Church Street, NW8; *see also p231*), a long-stander, paved the way; current highlights here include **Persiflage** (7724 7366), specialising in vintage hats, **Peter Pinnington Tin Tin Collectables** (7258 1305), with its fabulous clothes and handbags, **The Girl Can't Help It/Cad van Swankster** (7724 8984; *see also p245* **Who she? Sparkle Moore**), **Huxtables Old Advertising** (7724 2200) with its antique grocery tins and bottles, **S Brunswick House & Garden** (7724 9097), with its old garden furniture and accessories, **Paolo Bonino** (07767 498766), which is full of '60s and '70s homewares, and Italian 20th-century specialist **Vincenzo Caffarella** (7724 3701).

Across the road you'll find the extraordinary **Gallery of Antique Costume & Textiles** (2 Church Street, 7723 9981), with its exotic fabrics and clothing, most of it geared at collectors. For books, step round the corner to Bell Street to the chaotic yet mellow **Archive Bookstore** (no.83, 7402 8212), which specialises in music but also has more general stock, and **Stephen Foster Books** (no.96, 7724 0876), with its fine selection of art, design and fashion tomes.

If it's out now in the classical market, you'll get it here. MDC is quite commercially minded, specialising in mainstream artists, popular classics and West End musicals. Prices are very low.

Branches: throughout the city.

Ray's Jazz Shop

180 Shaftesbury Avenue, WC2 (7240 3969). Leicester Square tube. **Open** 10am-6.30pm Mon-Sat; 2-5.30pm Sun. **Credit** MC, V. **Map** p399 L6.

The grandfather of London jazz shops, Ray's offers a great selection of CDs, LPs and books, all of them helpfully categorised (there's even a 'Rare as Hen's Teeth' section), as well as a consistently reliable range of Miles and Coltrane back catalogues. You can happily count on everything stocked here being reasonably priced. Downstairs you'll find Ray's Folk and Blues Basement.

Rough Trade

130 Talbot Road, Notting Hill, W11 (7229 8541/ www.roughtrade.com). Ladbroke Grove or Notting Hill Gate tube. **Open** 10am-6.30pm Mon-Sat; 1-5pm Sun. **Credit** AmEx, JCB, MC, V. **Map** p394 A5.

An infamous and highly influential purveyor of all things alternative, Rough Trade specialises in underground releases, mainstream oddities and classic reissues on vinyl and CD. In terms of risk-taking, these guys are second to none, and their off-the-wall imports of Japanese thrash and death

Exotica from the **Gallery of Antique Costume & Textiles**.

Portobello, W10 & W11

It's no surprise that second-hand shops have colonised Portobello Road and its surrounding streets, hoping to feed off the custom of the famous market, the covered section of which (Portobello Green) still attracts the fashion pack in search of inspiration for upcoming catwalk shows. For many people this is still London's number one second-hand destination, and in spite of the increasing number of tourists attracted to the market in the wake of the Hugh Grant and Julia Roberts cheesefest *Notting Hill*, there are still bargains to be found.

Vintage clothes junkies are sure to find something to please among the vast choice of shops, which include **The Antique Clothing Shop** (282 Portobello Road, 8964 4830),

295 Portobello Road (no phone), **Skins** (232 Portobello Road, 7221 4203), **Still** (61D Lancaster Road, 7243 2932), **Stuart Craig** (Admiral Vernon Antiques Arcade, 141-9 Portobello Road, 7221 8662), **Ember** (206 Portobello Road, no phone), **One of a Kind** (253 Portobello Road, 7792 5284), **Rellik** (8 Golborne Road, 8962 0089), **Sheila Cook Textiles** (283 Westbourne Grove, 7792 8001), **Vent** (178A Westbourne Grove, no phone), **Dolly Diamond** (51 Pembridge Road, 7792 2479), **Retro Man** (32 Pembridge Road, 7598 2233) and **Retro Woman** (34 Pembridge Road, 7792 1715). Slightly further afield, **Virginia** (91 Portland Road, 7727 9908) has sublimely romantic vintage pieces, while at the opposite end of the spectrum **The 1920s-70s Crazy Clothes Connection** (134 Lancaster Road, 7221 3989) has some delightfully trashy party pieces.

Those in search of something a little different for their pad will find interesting pieces at **Les Couilles du Chien** (65 Golborne Road, 8968 0099), literally 'the dog's bollocks', **Bazar** (82 Golborne Road, 8969 6262), **307** (307 Portobello Road, 8969 0621), the trio of lighting specialists at 194, 196 and 198 Westbourne Grove, **Jones Lighting**, **The Facade** and **Le Paul Bert** (7229 6866/7727 2159/7727 8708), **Solaris @ Millio Interiors** (170 Westbourne Grove, 7229 8100), **Visto** (41 Pembridge Road, 7243 4392) and **Retro Home** (20 Pembridge Road, 7221 2055). For books, try the stylish **Simon Finch Rare Books** (61A Ledbury Road, 7792 3303) and the **Portobello Bookshop** (328 Portobello Road, 8964 3166).

For more on the Marylebone and Portobello areas, see the Marylebone and West London sightseeing chapters respectively.

Eat, Drink, Shop

metal seem like clear indications of insanity. Or is it genius? That the store is still going strong after 25 years suggests the latter.

Branch: 16 Neal's Yard, Covent Garden, WC2 (7240 0105).

Pharmacies (late-night)

For details of emergency health services in the capital, *see p365*.

Bliss Chemist
5-6 Marble Arch, Marylebone, W1 (7723 6116). Marble Arch tube. **Open** 9am-midnight daily. **Credit** AmEx, MC, V. **Map** p395 F6.

Boots
75 Queensway, Bayswater, W2 (7229 9266/ www.boots.co.uk). Baywater or Queensway tube. **Open** 9am-10pm Mon-Sat; 2-10pm Sun. **Credit** MC, V. **Map** p394 C6.
Branches: throughout the city (not late-night).

Zafash
233-5 Old Brompton Road, Earl's Court, SW5 (7373 2798/www.doctors24hour.com). Earl's Court tube. **Open** 24hrs daily. **Credit** AmEx, MC, V. **Map** p396 B11.

Sport & adventure

Lillywhite's
24-36 Lower Regent Street, St James's, SW1 (7930 3181). Piccadilly Circus tube. **Open** 10am-7pm Mon-Wed, Fri; 10am-8pm Thur; 10am-6pm Sat; noon-6pm Sun. **Credit** AmEx, DC, JCB, MC, V. **Map** p401 K7.

The mother of all sports stores, Lillywhite's covers all the major sports, with football, tennis, skiing, diving and outdoor pursuits particularly well represented. As well as sportswear from Nike, Adidas and the rest, it also carries new ranges from Tommy Hilfiger, Ralph Lauren, DKNY and SMTC. The fitness department has rowing machines and the usual torture devices.

Niketown
236 Oxford Street, Marylebone, W1 (7612 0800/ www.nike.com). Oxford Circus tube. **Open** 10am-7pm Mon-Wed; 10am-8pm Thur-Sat; noon-6pm Sun. **Credit** AmEx, JCB, MC, V. **Map** p398 J6.

Three storeys of sports gear and streetwear, including more trainers than you can shake a stick at, from the giant multinational Nike. This is a themed shopping experience for those who can stomach modern-day logo overload.

Skate Attack
72 Chase Side, Southgate, N14 (8886 7979/ www.skateattack.com). Southgate tube. **Open** 9.30am-6pm Mon-Sat. **Credit** AmEx, MC, V.

The largest skate shop in Europe holds everything a skater could need, from beginners' in-line skates to professional ice hockey boots.

YHA Adventure Shop
16-18 Ludgate Hill, The City, EC4 (7329 4578/ www.yhaadventure.com). St Paul's tube. **Open** 9am-6.30pm Mon, Tue, Fri; 9am-7.30pm Wed, Thur; 9am-6pm Sat; 11am-5pm Sun. **Credit** AmEx, DC, JCB, MC, V. **Map** p401 L7.

The Youth Hostel Association's shop has a fine range of walking and camping gear.
Branches: 174 Kensington High Street, Kensington, W8 (7938 2948); 120 Victoria Street, SW1 (7233 6500).

Toys & games

It's also worth trying the toy and game departments in **Harrods** (*see p235*), **John Lewis** and **Selfridges** (for both, *see p236*). For computer games, *see p237*. For young children, *see p239* **Daisy & Tom**.

Benjamin Pollock's Toy Shop
44 The Market, Covent Garden, WC2 (7379 7866/ www.pollocks-coventgarden.co.uk). Covent Garden tube. **Open** 10.30am-6pm Mon-Sat; noon-5pm Sun. **Credit** AmEx, JCB, MC, V. **Map** p401 L7.

This delightful Covent Garden shop specialises in quaint, old-fashioned toys and games (*see p107*).

Cheeky Monkeys
202 Kensington Park Road, Ladbroke Grove, W11 (7792 9022/www.cheekymonkeys.com). Ladbroke Grove tube. **Open** 9.30am-5.30pm Mon-Fri; 10am-5.30pm Sat. **Credit** MC, V. **Map** p394 A6.

Copious and lavish dressing-up outfits, plus traditional toys, plastic novelties and baby gifts.
Branches: 24 Abbeville Road, Clapham, SW4 (8673 5215); 1 Bennett Court, Bellevue Road, Wandsworth, SW17 (8672 2025); 94 New King's Road, Parsons Green, SW6 (7731 3031); 38 Cross Street, Islington, N1 (7288 1948).

Early Learning Centre
Unit 7, King's Mall, Hammersmith, W6 (8741 2469/www.elc.co.uk). Hammersmith tube. **Open** 9am-5.30pm Mon-Sat; 11am-5pm Sun. **Credit** AmEx, MC, V.

The place for safe but fun educational toys and games for young children.
Branches: throughout the city.

Hamleys
188-96 Regent Street, Mayfair, W1 (8752 2278/ www.hamleys.com). Oxford Circus tube. **Open** 10am-8pm Mon-Fri; 9.30am-8pm Sat; 11am-5pm Sun. **Credit** AmEx, DC, MC, V. **Map** p400 J7.

'The world's most famous toyshop' is either a dream or a complete nightmare, depending on which way you look at it. Chaotic, it's always struggling to maintain the image that it's created for itself over the years. The stock, spread over five floors, is comprehensive, with electronic games and consoles, hobbies, models, board games, dolls and bears in plentiful supply.
Branch: Unit 3, The Market, Covent Garden, WC2 (7240 4646).

Arts & Entertainment

By Season

From the solemn to the plain silly, London's social calendar is brimming.

If the first thing that comes into your head when you think of London is celebrations, commemorations, historic contests and archaic rituals, think again – though royal and governmental events are very much part of its roster of annual events (especially this year, which sees the 50th anniversary of the Queen's accession to the throne; *see p263*), this is also a city with a great sense of humour and fun, and a healthy appreciation of the ridiculous.

We've focused on the best of London's regular annual events; scores more are advertised in the national press and in *Time Out* magazine. For some events you need to book in advance, some charge admission on the day/night, while others are free; it's a good idea to phone and check. All the dates given below were correct at the time of going to press, but always double-check nearer the time.

Details of other cultural festivals are listed elsewhere in the book. For **dance**, *see p288* **Festivals**; for **film**, *see p294*; for Mardi Gras, *see p306* **Whatever happened to? Gay Pride**; and for **music**, *see p313* and *p318*. Also, many of the big museums and galleries, such as the **National Gallery** (*see p130*) and the **British Museum** (*see p103*), often hold talks, discussions and other events; call them for details. For public holidays in the UK, *see p376*.

January-March 2002

London International Boat Show

Earl's Court Exhibition Centre, Warwick Road, Earl's Court, SW5 (01784 472222/ www.bigblue.org.uk). Earl's Court tube. **Map** p396 A11. **Date** 3-13 Jan 2002.
A huge crowd-puller featuring all things nautical.

London International Mime Festival

various venues (7637 5661/www.mimefest.co.uk). **Date** 12-27 Jan 2002.
Those whose knowledge of mime stops at Marcel Marceau should check out this visual theatre festival, which includes animation, puppetry and more.

Great Spitalfields Pancake Day Race

Spitalfields Market, entrance on Commercial Street or Brushfield Street, Spitalfields, E1 (7375 0441). Liverpool Street tube/rail. **Map** p403 R5. **Date** 12 Feb 2002.
Would-be tossers should call several days in advance to take part in this madcap spectacle.

Chinese New Year Festival

around Gerrard Street, Chinatown, W1 (7439 3822/ www.chinatown-online.co.uk). Leicester Square or Piccadilly Circus tube. **Map** p401 K7. **Date** 17 Feb 2002; phone for confirmation.
One of London's most thrilling festivals: you can't help but get caught up in the surging crowds that follow the 'dragons' as they snake their way through the streets, gathering gifts of money and food.

Ideal Home Show

Earl's Court Exhibition Centre, Warwick Road, Earl's Court, SW5 (box office 0870 606 6080/groups 0870 241 0272/www.idealhomeshow.co.uk). Earl's Court tube. **Map** p396 A11. **Date** 7 Mar-1 Apr 2002.
Britain's biggest consumer show has everything from kitchen utensils to full-scale houses.

Chelsea Antiques Fair

Chelsea Old Town Hall, King's Road, Chelsea, SW3 (01444 482514/www.penman-fairs.co.uk). Sloane Square tube. **Open** 11am-8pm Mon-Fri; 11am-7pm Sat; 11am-5pm Sun. **Admission** £5; free under-18s. **Credit** MC, V. **Map** p397 E12. **Date** 15-24 Mar 2002.
Held twice a year (also held 13-22 Sept 2002), this is good for both idle browsers and serious collectors.

St Patrick's Day

Date 17 Mar 2002.
London has the third biggest Irish population of any city. While you won't find extravagant, organised events, there's plenty of boisterous Irish jubilation and heavenly nectar to be had in Kilburn (NW6).

Head of the River Race

Thames, from Mortlake, SW14, to Putney, SW15 (01932 220401/www.horr.co.uk). Mortlake rail (start), Hammersmith tube (mid point) or Putney Bridge tube (finish). **Date** 23 Mar 2002.
As impressive as the Oxford & Cambridge race (*see below*) but less well known, this takes place over the same 4¼-mile (6.8km) course, in the opposite direction. To get a good view of the 400-plus crews (best spots are Hammersmith Bridge or at the finish line at Putney), pitch up about half an hour before the 9.45am start from Mortlake.

Oxford & Cambridge Boat Race

Thames, from Putney, SW15, to Mortlake, SW1 (www.theboatrace.org). Putney Bridge tube (start), Hammersmith tube (mid point) or Mortlake rail (finish). **Date** 30 Mar 2002.
The 148th boat race contested by Oxford and Cambridge universities gets underway at 3.07pm. Huge crowds line the course from Putney to Mortlake, with the riverside pubs in Mortlake and Hammersmith the most popular vantage points.

The **London-Brighton Car Run**. *See p267.*

April-June 2002

London Harness Horse Parade
Battersea Park, Albert Bridge Road, Battersea, SW11 (01733 234451). Battersea Park or Queenstown Road rail/97, 137 bus. **Date** 1 Apr 2002.
A traditional Easter Monday parade of working nags with their various commercial and private carriages.

London Marathon
Greenwich Park to Westminster Bridge via the Isle of Dogs, Victoria Embankment & St James's Park (7620 4117/hotline 7902 0189/www.london-marathon.co.uk). **Date** 14 Apr 2002.
The world's biggest road race attracts some 35,000 starters. Would-be runners must apply by the previous October to be entered in the ballot.

Museums & Galleries Month 2002
various venues (7233 9796/www.may2002.org.uk). **Date** 1 May-4 June 2002.
Special events, activities, exhibitions and welcome days by museums and galleries around the country.

Covent Garden May Fayre & Puppet Festival
St Paul's Church Garden, Covent Garden, WC2 (7375 0441). Covent Garden tube. **Map** p401 L7. **Date** 12 May 2002.
Puppetry galore from 10.30am to 5.30pm, in commemoration of the first recorded sighting of Mr Punch in England by Samuel Pepys in 1662 – and it's free. *See also p267,* Punch & Judy Festival.

Chelsea Flower Show
grounds of Royal Hospital, Royal Hospital Road, Chelsea, SW3 (recorded info 7649 1885/ www.rhs.org.uk). Sloane Square tube. **Map** p397 F12. **Date** 21-24 May 2002.
This riverside gardening extravaganza is famous around the world. Only Royal Horticultural Society members are allowed in on the first two days.

Victoria Embankment Gardens Summer Events
Victoria Embankment Gardens, Villiers Street, Westminster, WC2 (7375 0441/ info@alternativearts.co.uk). Embankment tube. **Map** p399 L7. **Date** 26 May-21 July 2002.
A series of free open-air events taking place by the river, including an Open Air Dance Festival (1-2 June), the Move It Mime Festival (9 June), the Midsummer Poetry Festival (23 June) and the Summer Season of Street Theatre (July). Phone for details of individual events.

Coin Street Festival
various venues on the South Bank, SW1 (7401 2255/ www.coinstreetfestival.org). Southwark tube/Waterloo tube/rail or Blackfriars rail. **Date** June-Sept 2002 (phone for details).
London's biggest free festival of music, dance and performance, now in its 11th year, lasts all summer long. Events, which include lunchtime concerts, and Community Celebration, take place on the South Bank (*see p71*) between the Royal National Theatre and Tate Modern.

London Wildlife Week
various locations (7261 0447/ www.wildlondon.org.uk). **Date** 1st wk June 2002.
The free seasonal activities taking place at 60-plus nature reserves and urban woodland areas in Greater London as part of this week-long event include wildlife watches (of creatures ranging from butterflies to bats), guided walks, fruit-picking, picnics, an Apple Day (apple-bobbing, kids' games, storytelling) and Fungal Forays.

Golden Jubilee Weekend
Various venues (Golden Jubilee Office 0845 000 2002/www.goldenjubilee.gov.uk). **Date** 1-4 June 2002.
This weekend forms the main focus of the Queen's Golden Jubilee celebrations, which are taking place throughout the year and include a regional tour, Windsor Horse Show, London String of Pearls (in which some of the capital's most famous landmarks are open to the public, many for the first time, for tours, exhibitions and performances), and the construction of a new footbridge, the Jubilee Bridge, over the Thames. The double bank holiday weekend will include pop and classical concerts in Buckingham Palace Gardens, fireworks, a pageant in The Mall, and a service at St Paul's. As more plans/events are confirmed they will be updated on the website; see also www.londontouristboard.com for information nearer the time.

Derby Day
Epsom Downs Racecourse, Epsom Downs, Surrey (01372 470047/www.epsomderby.co.uk). Epsom Town Centre or Tattenham Corner rail then shuttle bus. **Date** 8 June 2002.
Carnivalesque in atmosphere, this is the most important flat race of the season. You'll have to fork out some if you want comfort and a good view. *See also p328* **Epsom**.

Arts & Entertainment

Frequent events

Ceremony of the Keys

*Tower of London, The City, EC3 (7709 0765/
www.hrp.org.uk). Tower Hill tube.* **Date** daily.
Maximum *Apr-Oct* party of 7. *Nov-Mar* party
of 15. **Map** p405 R7.

Dating back 700 years, the ceremony of
locking the entrances to the Tower of London
starts at 9.53pm every evening (the public
need to assemble at the West Gate by 9pm).
It's all over by 10pm, when the last post is
sounded. To watch, you have to apply in
writing for free tickets, giving a choice of
three dates (Ceremony of the Keys Office,
HM Tower of London, EC3 4AB) with a
stamped self-addressed envelope (UK only,
international stamps are not accepted) at
least two months in advance.

Changing of the Guard

*Buckingham Palace, Horse Guards & St
James's Palace, SW1 (infoline 0906 866
3344/www.royal.gov.uk). Green Park or
St James's Park tube/Victoria tube/rail.*

The **Tower of London**: don't get locked up.

Ceremonies
Buckingham Palace Apr-Aug 11.15am daily.
Sept-Mar alternate days (may be cancelled
in very wet weather). **Map** p400 H9. *Horse
Guards* 11am Mon-Sat; 10am Sun.
Map p401 K8.

London Garden Squares Day

*various venues (7839 3969/
www.londongardenstrust.org.uk).* **Date** 9 June 2002.
This chilled-out and eminently civilised annual event
(this year is the fifth) includes, alongside the chance
to discover normally inaccessible green oases all over
London (from Japanese gardens to secret 'children
only' play areas), live jazz, choral concerts, cream
teas, Pimms tastings and Scottish dancing.

Beating Retreat

*Horse Guards Parade, Whitehall, Westminster, SW1
(7414 2271). Westminster tube/Charing Cross
tube/rail.* **Map** p401 K8. **Date** 11, 12 June 2002.
For those who like their pomp and circumstance,
there's no better event than this colourful musical
ceremony, which begins at 7pm. The 'Retreat' is
beaten on drums by the Mounted Bands of the
Household Cavalry and the Massed Bands of the
Guards Division.

Royal Academy Summer Exhibition

*Royal Academy, Burlington House, Piccadilly,
Mayfair, W1 (7300 8000/www.royalacademy.org.uk).
Green Park or Piccadilly Circus tube.*
Map p400 J7. **Date** 11 June-19 Aug 2002.
A wildly mixed annual showcase of around 10,000
works that have been submitted by artists of all
styles and standards, from members of the
Academy to enthusiastic amateurs, for inclusion in
the Summer Exhibition. A panel of eminent
Academicians boils the choice down to approxi-
mately 1,000 entries for display.

Trooping the Colour

*Horse Guards Parade, Whitehall, Westminster,
SW1 (7414 2479). Westminster tube/
Charing Cross tube/rail.* **Map** p401 K8.
Date 15 June 2002.
There's no rest for the Queen even on her official
birthday (she was actually born on 21 April): at
10.45am she makes the 15-minute journey from
Buckingham Palace to Horse Guards Parade, then
hurries back to the palace balcony to watch a
midday Royal Air Force flypast before a gun salute
is fired in Green Park. Huge crowds gather on The
Mall to egg her on.

Royal Ascot

*Ascot Racecourse, Ascot, Berkshire (01344 622211/
www.ascot-authority.co.uk). Ascot rail.* **Date** 18-21
June 2002.
It's big hats at the ready for this society bash mas-
querading as a sporting event, held at the best flat
racing course in the country. Tickets are most in
demand for Ladies' Day (20 June), when the Queen
drops by. *See also p328.*

Architecture Week

*various venues (7973 6469/
www.architectureweek.org.uk).* **Date** 21-30 June 2002.
The sixth annual Architecture week encompasses
a huge range of previews, tours, lectures, exhibitions and installations designed to fuel public
debate about the urban environment. Major venues
such as the British Museum (*see p103*) and Tate
Modern (*see p79*) are involved.

Arts & Entertainment

Every other day the new guard (usually one of the five regiments of Foot Guards in their scarlet coats and bearskin hats) line up in the forecourt of Wellington Barracks, Birdcage Walk, from 10.45am; at 11.27am they march, accompanied by their regimental band, to Buckingham Palace for the changing of the sentries, who stand guard in the palace forecourt. At Horse Guards in Whitehall (which is the official entrance to the royal palaces), it's the Household Cavalry who mount the guard (10am-4pm daily); they ride to Whitehall via The Mall from Hyde Park for the daily changeover.

Funfairs
Alexandra Park *Muswell Hill, N22 (8365 2121/www.alexandrapalace.com). Wood Green tube/Alexandra Palace rail/W3 bus.* **Dates** selected public holidays (*see p376*); phone for details.
Hampstead Heath *NW3 (7485 4491 for a leaflet detailing events in the park). Belsize*

Park or Hampstead tube/Gospel Oak or Hampstead Heath rail/24, C11 bus. **Dates** selected public holidays (*see p376*); phone for details.

Gun Salutes
Hyde Park, W2, & Tower of London, EC3. **Dates** 6 Feb (Accession Day); 21 Apr (Queen's birthday); 2 June (Coronation Day); 10 June (Trooping the Colour, *see p264*); 4 Aug (Queen Mother's birthday); State Opening of Parliament (*see p267*). If the date falls on a Sun, salutes are fired the following Mon. **Map** p405 R7.
On royal occasions cannons are primed for gun salutes. The King's Troop of the Royal Horse Artillery makes a mounted charge through Hyde Park, sets up the guns and fires a 41-gun salute (at noon, except for the State Opening of Parliament) opposite the Dorchester Hotel. Not to be outdone, the Honourable Artillery Company fires a 62-gun salute at the Tower of London at 1pm.

Covent Garden Flower Festival
Covent Garden Market, Covent Garden, WC2 (7735 1518/www.cgff.co.uk). Covent Garden tube. **Map** p401 L7. **Date** last wk of June; call for confirmation.
Installations, demonstrations, floral fashion shows, giant fruit and street performers, all free to the public, in the sixth annual flower show on the Piazza.

Wimbledon Lawn Tennis Championships
PO Box 98, Church Road, Wimbledon, SW19 (8944 1066/recorded info 8946 2244/www.wimbledon.org). Southfields tube/Wimbledon tube/rail. **Date** 24 June-7 July 2002.
Dazzling whites and strawberries and cream; just pray it doesn't rain. *See also p330.*

City of London Festival
venues in & around the City, EC2 (info 7377 0540/box office 7638 8891/www.colf.org). **Date** 24 June-11 July 2002.
Celebrating its 40th birthday in 2002, this mainly classical, jazz and world music festival takes place in some of the City's finest buildings.

July-September 2002

Henley Royal Regatta
Henley Reach, Henley-on-Thames, Oxfordshire (01491 572153/www.hrr.co.uk). Henley-on-Thames rail. **Date** 3-7 July 2002.
First held in 1839 and now a five-day affair, this regatta is about as posh as you get.

Greenwich & Docklands International Festival
various venues near the Thames at Greenwich & Docklands (8305 1818/www.festival.org). **Date** 5-13 July 2002.
A host of theatrical and musical events by the river.

Soho Festival
St Anne's Gardens & part of Wardour Street, W1 (7439 4303/www.thesohosociety.org.uk). Tottenham Court Road tube. **Map** p401 K7. **Date** 14 July 2002 (call to check).
The famous Waiter's Race, a spaghetti-eating competition and an alpine horn blowing contest bring locals and visitors together in aid of the Soho Society.

Swan Upping on the Thames
various points along the Thames (7236 1863/ 7197/www.royal.gov.uk/faq/swans.htm). **Date** 15-19 July 2002.
An archaic ceremony in which groups of herdsmen round up, divide up and mark all the cygnets on the Thames as belonging to the Queen, the Vintners' or the Dyers' livery companies. The route and departure time change daily; phone for details.

BBC Sir Henry Wood Promenade Concerts
Royal Albert Hall, Kensington Gore, South Kensington, SW7 (box office 7589 8212/ www.bbc.co.uk/proms). Gloucester Road, Knightsbridge or South Kensington tube/9, 10, 52 bus. **Map** p397 D9. **Date** 19 July-14 Sept 2002.

Famed for its jingoistic Last Night, this huge music festival includes more than 70 mostly classical concerts. The range of composer and repertoire is impressive. *See also p313.*

Respect Festival

7983 4274/www.respectfestival.org.uk. **Date** probably 3rd Sat in July (call for details).
Events in the United States on 11 September 2001 strengthened Mayor Livingstone's commitment to bring back the free anti-rascist music and entertainment festival that first took place in July 2001 in Finsbury Park in north London. Organisers were tendering for a new park as we went to press, and no acts had been selected.

South East Marine Week

various locations throughout the South-east (7261 0447/www.wildlondon.org.uk). **Date** 3-11 Aug 2002.
Fifty free events to introduce people to marine life, including a beach party at Hammersmith foreshore (involving a welly-throwing contest, marine art and sculptures, netting for fish and river-dipping), 'Born to be Tidal' arts events in front of Tate Modern (*see p79*), pirate boat trips from King's Cross and wildlife walks along Greenwich waterfront.

Great British Beer Festival

Olympia, Hammersmith Road, Kensington, W14 (01727 867201/www.camra.org.uk). Kensington (Olympia) tube/rail. **Date** 6-10 Aug 2002.
In excess of 300 traditional British ales and ciders, plus a range of international beers, are on offer at this CAMRA (Campaign for Real Ale) beer orgy.

Notting Hill Carnival

Notting Hill, W10, W11 (8964 0544/ www.thecarnival.tv). Ladbroke Grove, Notting Hill or Westbourne Park tube. **Date** 25, 26 Aug 2002.
Europe's biggest street party draws more than a million revellers on the Sunday and Monday of August Bank Holiday weekend, so you'll be lucky if you get near the main drag to see the costume parade, live music and sound systems close up, though there is talk of rerouting this year to improve crowd safety. Bad press (muggings, pickpocketing, a couple of murders in 2000) and terrible loos don't deter the crowds.

Annual Thames Barrier Full Tidal Closure

Thames Barrier Info & Learning Centre, 1 Unity Way, Woolwich, SE18 (8305 4188). Charlton rail. **Date** Sept (depends on tides; call for details).
See the engineering marvel of the Thames Barrier (*see p165*), built in 1982 as the first line of defence against surge tides, go through its yearly full test.

Great River Race

Thames, from Ham House, Richmond, Surrey, to Island Gardens, Greenwich, E14 (8398 9057/ www.greatriverrace.co.uk). **Date** 7 Sept 2002.
The Great River Race sees more than 250 'traditional' boats, from Chinese dragon boats and shallops to Viking longboats and Cornish gigs, vie over a 22-mile (35km) 'marathon' course, hoping to win the UK Traditional Boat Championship. The event kicks off at 3.30pm.

Brick Lane Festival

Brick Lane Market, Brick Lane, E1 (7655 0906/ www.bricklanefestival.org). Aldgate East tube. **Map** p404 S5/6. **Date** 8 Sept 2002.
This annual celebration of Spitalfields' multicultural communities, both past and present, involves food, music (from Caribbean DJs to Asian drumming bands), dance and performance, rickshaw rides, stilt-walkers, clowns and jugglers. A main stage showcases top world music acts, while a children's area has funfair rides, inflatables and workshops.

Regent Street Festival

Regent Street, W1 (7491 4429/www.regent-street.co.uk). Oxford Circus or Piccadilly Circus tube. **Map** p399 J6. **Date** 8 Sept 2002.
The third annual festival kicks off at noon, with a celebrity opening from a stage at the junction of Regent Street and New Burlington Street. Attractions will include dodgems, carousels, a big wheel and other fairground attractions, and, for kids, theatre, street entertainers and storytelling. There'll be live pop, rock, classical music and jazz too.

The Mayor's Thames Festival

between Waterloo Bridge & Blackfriars Bridge (7928 8998/www.thamesfestival.org). Blackfriars tube/rail/Waterloo tube/rail. **Date** 14, 15 Sept 2002.
The Thames Festival weekend of events celebrating London's river became the Mayor's Thames Festival in 2001. Among the treats on offer are a sandcastle competition, wandering musicians, a river clean-up and exhibition of weird river rubbish, a lantern procession and a firework finale. There are also food and crafts stalls.

London Open House

various venues in London (0900 160 0061/ www.londonopenhouse.org). **Date** 21, 22 Sept 2002.
For architecture buffs and snoopers, this unique event allows free access to buildings of architectural and cultural interest that are normally closed to the public (*see p268* **Grand openings**).

Shake your batty at the **Notting Hill Carnival**.

Horseman's Sunday
Church of St John & St Michael, Hyde Park Crescent, Paddington, W2 (7262 1732). Edgware Road tube/Paddington tube/rail. **Map** p395 E6.
Date 22 Sept 2002.
A surreal event in which a horseback vicar blesses more than 100 horses before they all trot through Hyde Park. The ceremony dates back to 1969, when local riding stables feared closure and held an open-air service to protest.

Soho Jazz & Heritage Festival
various venues (7434 3995/www.sohojazzfestival.co.uk). Oxford Circus, Leicester Square or Piccadilly Circus tube. **Date** Sept/Oct 2002 (call for details).
Hours of (mostly free) live jazz for Soho residents and visitors. The 17th annual festival takes place in a variety of well-known jazz venues, including the 100 Club, Ronnie Scott's, Mezzo and Pizza Express (*see also p322* **Jazz venues**), plus smaller bars, clubs and restaurants.

October-December 2002

Punch & Judy Festival
Covent Garden Piazza, Covent Garden, WC2 (7836 9136/www.coventgardenmarket.co.uk). Covent Garden tube. **Map** p401 L7. **Date** 1st wk Oct 2002 (call for exact date).
Another opportunity to watch Punch and Judy duff each other up (*see also p263*, Covent Garden May Fayre & Puppet Festival).

Pearly Kings & Queens Harvest Festival
St Martin-in-the-Fields, Trafalgar Square, Westminster, WC2 (7766 1100/www.pearlies.co.uk). Charing Cross tube/rail. **Map** p401 L7. **Date** 6 Oct 2002.
Pearly kings and queens have their origins in the 'aristocracy' of London's early Victorian coster-mongers, who elected their own royalty to safeguard their interests. Now charity representatives, today's pearly monarchy gathers for this 3pm thanksgiving service in their traditional 'flash boy' outfits.

Trafalgar Day Parade
Trafalgar Square, Westminster, WC2 (7928 8978/www.sea-cadets.org). Charing Cross tube/rail. **Map** p401 K7. **Date** 20 Oct 2002.
To commemorate Nelson's victory at the Battle of Trafalgar (21 Oct 1805), 500 sea cadets parade with marching bands and musical performances. The culmination is the laying of a wreath at the foot of Nelson's Column.

London Film Festival
National Film Theatre, South Bank, SE1 (7928 3535/box office 7928 3232/www.lff.org.uk). Embankment tube/Waterloo tube/rail. **Map** p401 M8. **Date** early Nov 2002 (call for details).
Attracting big-name actors and directors and offering the public the chance to see new films at decent prices, the LFF centres on the NFT (*see p293*) and

The best Events

For local colour
Chinese New Year Festival (*see p262*); Brick Lane Festival (*see p266*).

For a summer of fun
Coin Street Festival (*see p263*).

For talking with the animals
London Wildlife Week (*see p263*).

For chilling out
London Garden Squares Day (*see p264*).

For surreal goings-on
Soho Festival (*see p265*); Horseman's Sunday (*see left*).

For spectacular fireworks
The Mayor's Thames Festival (*see p266*); Bonfire Night (*see below*).

the Odeon West End (*see p291*), but has screenings across the capital. One of the biggest film festivals in the world, it screens more than 150 British and international features over two weeks. For more on film festivals, *see p294*.

State Opening of Parliament
House of Lords, Palace of Westminster, Westminster, SW1 (7219 4272/www.parliament.uk). Westminster tube. **Map** p401 L9. **Date** early/mid Nov 2002 (call for details).
In a ceremony that has changed little since the 16th century, the Queen officially reopens Parliament after its summer recess. You can only see what goes on inside on telly, but you can watch HRH arrive and depart in her Irish or Australian State Coach, attended by the Household Cavalry.

London to Brighton Veteran Car Run
from Serpentine Road, Hyde Park, W2 (01753 681736/www.msauk.org). Hyde Park Corner tube. **Map** p395 E8. **Date** 3 Nov 2002.
You need to be an early bird to catch the start of this procession of vintage motors (they set off from Hyde Park at 7.30am, aiming to reach Brighton before 4pm); otherwise join the crowds lining the rest of the route (via Westminster Bridge).

Bonfire Night
Date 5 Nov 2002.
This annual pyrotechnic frenzy sees Britons across the country gather to burn a 'guy' (an effigy of Guy Fawkes, who notoriously failed to blow up James I and his Parliament in the Gunpowder Plot of 1605) on a giant bonfire and set off loads of fireworks. Most public displays are held on the weekend

Arts & Entertainment

Grand openings

The annual event known as Open House, which allows architecture lovers free access to more than 500 fascinating buildings all over the capital, from palaces to pumping stations, celebrates its 10th birthday in September 2002, and aims to be bigger and better than ever. Part of the European Heritage Days initiative, a Council of Europe-promoted programme of architectural celebration that in 2001 took place in 46 European countries, the weekend-long event is the highlight of year-round activities organised by the architectural education charity London Open House.

Among new buildings on show for the first time in 2001 was the controversial Portcullis House, the deluxe office block for Members of Parliament built by Michael Hopkins & Partners in 2000 (*see p30* **Love 'em or hate 'em?**). Derided by many as scandalously costly (it is the most expensive office space in the country) and compared, variously, to a crematorium and a Victorian prison, it nonetheless won – together with Westminster tube station, which forms its foundations (and was built in the deepest excavation ever carried out in central London) – a RIBA Award for Architecture last year (for RIBA, *see p300*) and made it to the seven-stong shortlist of the coveted Stirling Prize 2001. A jury of experts decreed that the use of oak and green leather and the provision of generous office space and a sweeping staircase are a 'visual reminder that one is not in a superior office block but in the mother of parliaments'.

For more information on the event and on other London Open House initiatives, including workshops for children, see www.londonopenhouse.org.

nearest 5 Nov; among the best in London are those at Primrose Hill, Alexandra Palace and Crystal Palace. Alternatively, try to book a late ride on the relevant nights on the London Eye (*see p73*).

Lord Mayor's Show
various streets in the City (7606 3030/ www.lordmayorsshow.org). **Date** 9 Nov 2002.
Today's the day when, under the conditions of the Magna Carta of 1215, the newly elected Lord Mayor of London has to be presented to the monarch or to their justices for approval. Amid a procession of about 140 floats, the Mayor leaves Mansion House at 11am and travels through the City to the Royal Courts of Justice on the Strand, where he makes some vows before returning to Mansion House by 2.20pm. The event is rounded off by a firework display from a barge moored between Waterloo and Blackfriars bridges on the Thames.

Remembrance Sunday Ceremony
Cenotaph, Whitehall, Westminster, SW1. Westminster tube/Charing Cross tube/rail. **Map** p401 L8. **Date** 10 Nov 2002.
In honour of those who lost their lives in World Wars I and II, the Queen, the Prime Minister and other dignitaries lay wreaths at the Cenotaph, Britain's memorial to 'the Glorious Dead'. After a minute's silence at 11am, the Bishop of London leads a service of remembrance.

Christmas Lights & Tree
Covent Garden, WC2 (7836 9136/ www.coventgardenmarket.co.uk); Oxford Street, W1 (7629 2738/www.oxfordstreet.co.uk); Regent Street, W1 (7491 4429/www.regent-street.co.uk); Bond Street, W1 (7821 5230/ www.bondstreetassociation.com); Trafalgar Square, SW1 (7983 4234/www.london.gov.uk). **Date** Nov-Dec 2002.
Though the Christmas lights on London's main shopping streets have become increasingly commercialised over recent years (those on Regent Street are switched on by some jobbing celeb in early November), the lights on St Christopher's Place, Marylebone High Street and Bond Street, W1, and Kensington High Street, W8, are usually more charming. The giant fir tree that's put up in Trafalgar Square each year is a gift from the Norwegian people, in thanks for Britain's role in liberating their country from the Nazis.

International Showjumping Championships
Olympia, Hammersmith Road, Kensington, W14 (7370 8202/www.olympiashowjumping.com). Kensington (Olympia) tube/rail. **Date** 18-22 Dec 2002.
This annual jamboree for equestrian enthusiasts has more than 100 trade stands. Events run the gamut from international riders' competitions to the Shetland Pony Grand National.

New Year's Eve Celebrations
Date 31 Dec 2002.
Celebratory events in London tend to be local in nature, though Trafalgar Square (*see p129*) has traditionally been an unofficial gathering point at the turn of the year. Otherwise, many of the city's nightclubs (*see chapter* **Clubs**) hold expensive New Year parties. If you're feeling up to it the next morning, the extremely raucous New Year's Day Parade through central London includes more than 10,000 performers, from marching bands to clowns. The parade starts at Parliament Square, SW1, at noon, and finishes at Berkeley Square, W1, taking in Whitehall, Trafalgar Square, Lower Regent Street and Piccadilly along the way.

Children

A child's-eye view of London.

Indoor and outdoor activities in the capital should keep children entertained whichever part of the city they're in. For fuller details of children's events and activities, see *Time Out London for Children* (£8.99), available from good bookshops and newsagents. If you need specific assistance or advice, **Parentline** (0808 800 2222/www.parentlineplus.org.uk) is a free and confidential parent helpline, and **Simply Childcare The Register** (7701 6111/www.simplychildcare.com) is a fortnightly childcare listings magazine.

Grand days out

For family days out, central London and the surrounding areas are usually the best, but there are also a few quirky places in the city's less densely populated areas.

The South Bank & Bankside p71

The pride of the South Bank is the **British Airways London Eye** (*see p73*); the relentless queuing is worth it for the chance to soar 443 feet (135 metres) above London. You'll need about an hour and a half at the **London Aquarium** (*see p73*) to learn all about the world's oceans, as well as rainforests, tropical freshwater, seashores and beaches, and to spot sharks and other sea-dwelling life. From here, it's a ten-minute walk to the **BFI London IMAX Cinema** (*see p294*), which shows 3D films year-round and also caters for children's parties. The **National Film Theatre** (*see p293*) has Junior NFT film sessions, showing films for kids on weekends and weekday afternoons, while the **Coin Street Festival** (*see p263*) takes place on the South Bank over much of the summer.

A short distance from the South Bank, up-and-coming Bankside has open spaces and riverside access. **Tate Modern** (*see p79*) has free foyer events and activities for families: these include the Start tours (£1), whereby kids are given a map of the galleries and a kitbag with games and puzzles. At **Shakespeare's Globe** (*see p77*), aspiring thespians aged eight to 11 can take part in workshops that serve as an introduction to Shakespeare through drama, storytelling and art. For kids with a yen for the sea, the nearby **Golden Hinde** (*see p77*), a

reconstructed 16th-century flagship, offers Tudor and Elizabethan workshops and the chance to live like a sailor of yesteryear. Similarly, the **HMS Belfast** (*see p77*), Europe's largest surviving World War II warship, can cater for birthday parties (7940 6320). Among Bankside's other options is the creepy **London Dungeon** (*see p80*).

The City p83

Though this is not the most child-oriented area of London, **St Paul's Cathedral** (*see p89*) has breathtaking views from its dome, **Tower Bridge** and the **Tower of London** (for both, *see p94*) are winners with little ones, and **Museum of London** (*see p94*) never fails to impress. Meanwhile, the **Bank of England Museum** (*see p91*) has an excellent exhibition on London's monetary history, featuring moving models, past and present legal tender and a mini-cinema, all for free.

Piccadilly Circus p113

While not top of the list among adults, Piccadilly Circus has more than just bright lights and burger joints. Among the shops and cafés of the **Trocadero** (*see p113*), Funland has a relentless array of slot machines, games and virtual reality rides. Nearby **Chinatown** offers more interesting food options than the overpriced **Planet Hollywood**, while the cinemas of **Leicester Square** (*see p290*) offer all the latest blockbusters.

Covent Garden p123

Though considered by many a bit of a tourist trap, Covent Garden, with its array of street entertainers, is a good place to bring the kids. The magical **Theatre Museum** (*see p125*) has lots of child-oriented, hands-on displays, as well as horror make-up workshops and the like, while **London's Transport Museum** (*see p125*) has themed zones for all ages and some brilliant interactive displays, including a Tube simulator.

Just south of Covent Garden, **Somerset House** (*see p97*) has a gorgeous courtyard in which to sit and have a picnic, as well as a fantastic fountain display through which kids

Arts & Entertainment

Close to the bones at the **Natural History Museum**. *See p271.*

(and adults) love to run. Free family entertainment at weekends ranges from music and workshops to walks and talks.

Trafalgar Square p129

The **National Gallery** (*see p129*) has excellent (and free) paintings trails for kids to follow, while at the neighbouring **National Portrait Gallery** (*see p130*), children love putting names to faces, from Henry VIII to David Beckham. Nearby, **St Martin-in-the-Fields** (*see p130*) has a Brass Rubbing Centre and the excellent Café in the Crypt (*see p216* **Pit stops**).

From Trafalgar Square, the Mall leads to **Buckingham Palace** (*see p131*) and **St James's Park** (*see p130*) with its lake providing sanctuary for interesting waterfowl.

Greenwich p165

This area, especially the gardens at Greenwich, the museums and Blackheath, will keep children happy for an unlimited time. The **Cutty Sark** (*see p167*), the world's only surviving tea and wool clipper, has decks and the crew's quarters to explore, plus costume

storytelling sessions and workshops on summer weekends. The **National Maritime Museum** (*see p167*) incorporates the Old Royal Observatory, where planetarium days mean looking at the moon and the stars, and the Queen's House Museum. It also boasts an interactive bridge, where kids can try 'steering' a range of boats.

Boat trips

Trips run along the **Regent's Canal** in north London between Little Venice and London Zoo (phone the London Waterbus Company on 7482 2550 or Jason's Trip on 7286 3428), as well as along the **Thames** between Hampton Court in the west and the Thames Barrier in the east, calling at all points and piers on the way. For more information on specific trips and operators, *see p359*.

Museums & collections

Often the first choice for a museum visit, the **Science Museum** (*see p140*) has a wealth of attractions, including Launch Pad with its hands-on activities for all ages. There are also Science Nights and sleepovers for eight- to

11-year-olds who want to explore the museum after dark. The Wellcome Wing, which opened in 2000, includes an IMAX cinema (*see p276*).

You'd need more than a month of Sundays to get round the nearby **Natural History Museum** (*see p140*), with its collection of 68 million plants, animals, fossils, rocks and minerals. Highlights for children include the Dinosaurs Gallery, which houses the animatronic *Tyrannosaurus rex*, bloodstained teeth and all; the Predators exhibition (until May 2002), featuring huge moving models of a great white shark, a toxic spider and an interactive chameleon; the Creepy Crawlies gallery with its live ant colony; and the revolving globe in the Earth Galleries.

Meanwhile, the Young Friends of the **British Museum** (YFBM; *see p103*) offers events and activities for kids aged eight to 15. An annual fee (£17.50) allows entry to the Sunday Club, which offers holiday events, behind-the-scenes visits and free entry to all paying exhibitions. Other activities include drama workshops and the chance to chat to curators, conservators, scientists and security guards to find out what it's like to work in a museum. Egyptian sleepovers take place from time to time.

A division of the **V&A** (*see p140*), the **Bethnal Green Museum of Childhood** (*see p157*) contains all manner of child-related paraphernalia, from familiar games and toys to spectacular dolls' houses completely furnished right down to carpets and mousetraps. There are also puppets, peepshows, models, teddies, magic lanterns, dolls and children's fashion.

The **Ragged School Museum** (*see p162*) has a recreated Victorian classroom in which you can experience how children of that period were taught. There are also displays on East End history, temporary exhibitions and activities for all ages, including workshops, history talks, treasure hunts and canal walks.

The multi-million-pound **Croydon Clocktower** offers film, theatre and other live performances for all ages; there's a full programme of regular children's events. Organised workshops such as the free Bookstart Baby Rhyme Time offer babies, parents and carers the chance to share songs and rhymes in the Children's Library, as do other storytime and play sessions.

Parks & green spaces

The most popular of London's green spaces, **Regent's Park** (*see p109*) has two boating lakes (one for children), three playgrounds and an open-air theatre, as well as the fabulous **London Zoo** (*see p110*). Merging with Hyde

Park, **Kensington Gardens** (*see p137*) has the Round Pond for sailing model boats, two playgrounds and puppet shows in the summer, as well as the enchanting Elfin Oak. Further west, **Syon House** (*see p185*) has a Butterfly House and an Aquatic Experience in its riverside gardens.

Hampstead Heath (*see p149*), particularly **Parliament Hill**, is great for views and kite-flying, while at **Richmond Park** (*see p176*) kids can cycle, spot herds of red and fallow deer and visit the Isabella Plantation, a woodland with a stream, ponds and flower displays. Down south, **Battersea Park** (*see p173*) has a good adventure playground and a small children's zoo (*see p275*). In east London, **Victoria Park** (*see p161*) has a central playground, tennis courts, a bowling green and an animal enclosure.

Camley Street Natural Park
12 Camley Street, King's Cross, NW1 (7833 2311/ www.wildlondon.org.uk). King's Cross tube/rail. **Open** *Summer* 9am-5pm Mon-Thur; 11am-5pm Sat, Sun. *Winter* 9am-5pm/dusk Mon-Thur; 10am-4pm Sat, Sun. **Admission** free. **Map** p399 L2.

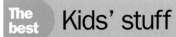

Kids' stuff
The best

For ace animatronics
Natural History Museum (*see p140*).

For animal magic
Camley Street Natural Park (*see above*);
Battersea Park Children's Zoo (*see p275*);
London Zoo (*see p110*).

For Bob the Builder wannabes
Legoland (*see p272*).

For clowning around
Clown Town (*see p272*).

For explosive fun
Royal Gunpowder Mills (*see p276*).

For fab food
Giraffe (*see p274*).

For hair-raising rides
Thorpe Park (*see p272*).

For inner-city adventures
Coram's Fields (*see p272*).

For messing about on the water
Islington Boat Club (*see p276*).

For spellbinding puppetry
Puppet Theatre Barge (*see p276*).

Arts & Entertainment

Internationally acclaimed, Camley Street Natural Park on the banks of the Regent's Canal is great for wildlife spotters. Its pond, meadow and woodland provide a natural environment for birds, bees and amphibians and a lush variety of teeming plantlife.

Coram's Fields
93 Guilford Place, Bloomsbury, WC1 (7837 6138). Russell Square tube. **Open** *Apr-Sept* 9am-7pm daily. *Oct-Mar* 9am-6pm daily. **Admission** free (adults only admitted if accompanied by child under 16). **Map** p399 L4/M4.

This wonderful adventure playground was established by newspaper magnate Lord Rothermere on the site of the 18th-century Foundling Hospital. The grounds are now given over to lawns, huge sandpits, an AstroTurf football pitch, an asphalt basketball court, a toddlers' gym and fenced-off play areas with a three-storey wooden climbing tower, a helterskelter chute, swings and an assault-course pulley (the ground is covered in soft bark to ensure pain-free landings). There's also a café and a petting zoo for sheep, goats, geese and peacocks. Sporting activities, such as informal footie and cricket matches, are organised year round, and for the under-threes there's a drop-in centre with daily painting sessions and occasional clowns' visits in summer.

Theme parks

For a reliable dose of high-energy theme park action, you'll need to make a jaunt outside London.

Chessington World of Adventures
Leatherhead Road, Chessington, Surrey (0870 444 7777/www.chessington.com). By train Chessington South rail. By car M25 or A3 (Junction 9). **Open** *late Mar-end Nov* times vary; phone for details. **Height restrictions** varies, depending on rides. **Admission** *on the day* £19.95, £12 concessions; £16 4-12s; £63 family (2+2 or 1+3); free under-4s. *Online advance bookings (undated)* £18; £14 4-12s; £59 family. *Online advance bookings (dated)* £17; £13 4-12s; £55 family. Allow minimum 2 days to process advance ticket purchases. *Unlimited entry pass* (includes all Tussaud's attractions) £219 family; £70 individual, valid for 1 yr. **Credit** MC, V. **Map** p389.

Is it a zoo or is it a theme park? Well, actually it's a bit of both. The zoo aspect of the park has recently been enhanced by the Trail of the Kings enclosures in Animal Land, where you can be a whisker away from some big cats or whoop it up with the gorillas. Aside from this there are also more traditional rides to experience; the two biggest are Samurai, with its gyrating rotor arms, and Rameses Revenge (which re-opens in revamped form for serious thrill-seekers in 2002). Of the themed restaurants, the best are the Mexican Diner and the Krazy Keg family inn.

Legoland
Winkfield Road, Windsor, Berks (08705 040404/www.legoland.co.uk). By train Windsor & Eton Riverside or Windsor Central rail. By car B3022 Windsor/Ascot Road. **Open** *mid Mar-early Nov* 10am-5pm or 6pm daily (until 7pm during school hols). **Admission** £19; £16 3-15s; £13 concessions. *Two-day peak pass* £26; £23 children. *Two-day off-peak pass* £36; £29 children. *Annual peak pass* £55; £46 children. *Annual off-peak pass* £36; £29. **Credit** AmEx, MC, V. **Map** p389.

Putting the 'theme' back in theme park, Legoland's cute characters hold the fort with their particular brand of construction-brick fun. Catering solely to the younger end of the market, it offers no hair-raising adventures, but kids can pan for gold, float in balloons, drive their own boats, and thrash through the water on jet skis into the bargain. Arrive early to avoid the queues.

Thorpe Park
Staines Road, Chertsey, Surrey (0870 444 4466/www.thorpepark.co.uk). By train Staines rail. By car M25 (Junction 11 or 13). **Open** *late Mar-early Nov* various times depending on season between 10am-5.15pm daily. **Height restrictions** varies, depending on rides. **Admission** *on the day* £19; £12-£14 concessions; £15 4-12s; £59 family (2+2 or 1+3); free under-4s. *Online advance bookings (open)* £17; £13 4-12s; £55 family. *Online advance bookings (dated)* £16; £12 4-12s; £51 family. *Advance phone bookings (open)* £18; £14 concessions, 4-12s; £57 family. *Advance phone bookings (dated)* £17; £14 concessions; £13 4-12s; £55 family. Allow minimum 2 days to process advance ticket purchases. **Credit** AmEx, MC, V. **Map** p389.

A visit to Thorpe Park is bound to include at least one close encounter with a large body of water, especially in Neptune's Kingdom, where chutes, flumes and slides abound. And if that doesn't satisfy your thirst for thrills, how does a backwards rollercoaster ride in the pitch dark grab you? But big spills aside, you can take a waterbus or train to an enchanting turn-of-this-century working farm complete with duck pond, rare breeds and petting area. Newer attractions include Detonator, with its 100ft (30m) vertical drop, and Vortex, a kind of sideways-on Ferris wheel.

Playgrounds

Supervised play areas

Kids Active
Info 7731 1435/www.kidsactive.org.uk.
Kids Active has a total of six playgrounds across London where both disabled and able-bodied children aged from five to 15 can play safely, supervised by fully trained staff.

Indoor adventure playgrounds

Clown Town
222 Green Lanes, Palmers Green, N13 (8886 7520). Palmers Green rail. **Open** 10am-7pm Mon-Tue, Thur-Sun. **Height restrictions** children must be over 4' 9". **Admission** £2.75 per child (adults free). **No credit cards.**

Formerly called Monkey Business, this indoor adventure playground has had a total refurbishment, and clowns are now the theme, though ball ponds, net climbs, slides and a toddler area still feature. Call for details of special children's parties.

Kimber BMX/Adventure Playground

King George's Park, Kimber Road, Wandsworth, SW18 (8870 2168). Earlsfield rail. **Open** *Termtime* 3.30-7pm Tue-Fri; 11am-6pm Sat. *School holidays* 11am-6pm Mon-Sat. **Admission** free.
One of three Wandsworth-run adventure playgrounds (Battersea Park and York Gardens are the others), Kimber has a BMX track, rope swings, monkey bars, a basketball court and a kitchen where kids can try out their culinary skills, plus indoor activities such as table tennis and arts and crafts.

Spike's Madhouse

Crystal Palace National Sports Centre, Ledrington Road, Crystal Palace, SE19 (8778 9876/www.crystalpalace.co.uk). Crystal Palace rail. **Open** *School hols* noon-4pm Mon-Fri; 10am-5pm Sat, Sun. **Admission** £2 1hr; £1 30min. **Credit** (over £5) MC, V.
An indoor playground specifically designed for children aged two to 13. The four storeys of facilities include ballpools, scramble nets, slides, rope swings and biff 'n' bash bags. Kids' parties can also be arranged (phone for details).

Swimming

Below we've listed some of the best pools for children, plus two venues – the Dolphin and Swimming Nature – that specialise in classes. For more pools, *see p325*.
   By law, a maximum of two children below the age of five per adult are allowed into a public swimming pool.

Dolphin Swimming Club *ULU Pool, Malet Street, Bloomsbury, WC1 (8349 1844). Russell Square tube/Euston tube/rail.* **Open** 9.15am-2.45pm Sat, Sun. **Admission** *swimming course* £209 per person (group rates also available). **No credit cards.** **Map** p399 K4.
Finchley Lido *Great North Leisure Park, High Road, Finchley, N12 (8343 9830). East Finchley or Finchley Central tube.* **Open** 6.45-8.30am, 9am-6.30pm Mon; 6.45-8.30am, 9am-9.30pm Tue, Thur, Fri; 6.45-8.30am, 9-8pm Wed; 9am-4.30pm Sat, Sun. *Last entry* 30min before closing. **Admission** £2.70; £1.50 5-16s, concessions; free under-5s. **Credit** MC, V.
Latchmere Leisure Centre *Burns Road, Battersea, SW11 (7207 8004). Clapham Common tube then 345 bus/Clapham Junction rail then 49, 319, 344 bus.* **Open** 7am-9.30pm Mon-Thur, Sun; 7am-6pm Fri; 7am-7.30pm Sat. **Admission** £2.70; £2.20 parent & baby; £1.90 5-16s; £1 concessions; free under-5s. **Credit** (over £5) MC, V.

The fun of the fair at **Legoland**. See p272.

Swimming Nature *Various venues in London* (0870 900 8002/www.swimmingnature.co.uk). **Open** *Administration* 9.30am-5.30pm Mon-Fri; 9.30am-1pm Sat. **Admission** *Phone for details of classes & prices.*

Waterfront Leisure Centre *High Street Woolwich, Woolwich, SE18 (8317 5000). Woolwich Arsenal rail/177, 180, 472 bus.* **Open** 7am-11pm Mon-Fri; 9am-10pm Sat; 9am-9.30pm Sun. *Wet & Wild Adventure Park* 3-8pm Mon-Fri; 9am-5pm Sat; 9am-5pm, 6-8pm Sun. **Admission** £1.30-£4.25; 80p-£3.10 3-16s; free under-3s (additional charge for activities). **Credit** MC, V.

Aside from **London Zoo**, which offers birthday parties and Rampage sessions of art activities, zoo tours, games, fancy dress and playtimes for kids aged five and over (10am-1pm Mon-Sat; *see also p110*), and aside from the good smattering of animal enclosures in the city's parks, there are assorted city farms in and around the capital. Here, kids can commune with the likes of pigs, geese and cattle, and learn about farming in the process. For a full list, contact the Federation of City Farms &

Top tucker

The following eateries were all finalists in the Best Family Restaurant category in the *Time Out* Eating & Drinking Awards 2001, as voted by readers of *Time Out* magazine. For other child-friendly establishments, see the 'Where to...' section of the *Time Out Eating & Drinking Guide 2002*.

Bread & Roses

68 Clapham Manor Street, Clapham, SW4 (7498 1779). Clapham Common or Clapham North tube. **Open** 11am-11pm Mon-Sat; noon-10.30pm Sun. **Food served** noon-3pm, 7-9.30pm Mon-Fri; noon-4pm (African buffet only), 6-9.30pm Sat, Sun. **Credit** MC, V. This veteran family haunt, which is non-smoking till 6pm, has a small back room with kids' toys and games, an outside space for fine weather and a larger space upstairs for children's activities (films, games and art workshops) on Sundays. The food (meat, fish or vegetable platters with mixed salad and rice buffet-style) is great value at £3.95 for a kid's platter and £5.95-£7.95 for adult portions.

fish!

3B Belvedere Road, Waterloo, SE1 (7234 3333). Waterloo tube/rail. **Meals served** 11.30am-10.30pm Mon-Sat; noon-10pm Sun. **Set meal** £9.95 two courses. **Credit** AmEx, DC, MC, V. **Map** p401 M9. This light and airy branch of the fish! mini-chain has good pushchair-access and kid-friendly staff. The food isn't cheap, but the huge prawn cocktail starters are good value, and the kid's menu offers a choice of main, dessert and drink for £6.95. The paved area outside is a good place for little 'uns to let off steam, and you're within spitting distance of the London Eye and London Aquarium.

Branches: (*all* 7234 333) 296-8 Upper Richmond Road, SW15; 92-4 Waterford Road, SW6; 41A Queenstown Road, SW8; Hanover House, 33 Westferry Circus, E14; Cathedral Street, SE1.

Giraffe

46 Rosslyn Hill, Hampstead, NW3 (7435 0343). Hampstead tube. **Brunch served** 8am-4pm Mon-Fri; 9am-4pm Sat, Sun. **Lunch served** noon-4pm Mon-Fri; noon-5pm Sat, Sun. **Dinner served** 5-11pm Mon-Fri; 6-11pm Sat, Sun. **Credit** AmEx, MC, V. Each of this *Time Out* award-winner's branches has a great family location: Hampstead is good for kite-flying on the heath; Marylebone is handy for Madame Tussaud's and Regent's Park; Islington is good for shopping. Giraffe's flexibility is also a draw: you can pop in for breakfast, brunch, lunch, dinner or just a quick snack from the globally eclectic menu. The children's menu has both meat-based and veggie options. Kids also love the huge shakes and juices with the giraffe-shaped skewers, while adults can relax over a killer Bloody Mary.

Smollenksy's

O2 Centre, 255 Finchley Road, West Hampstead, NW3 (7431 5007/ www.smollenskys.co.uk). Finchley Road tube/rail. **Meals served** noon-11pm Mon-Fri; noon-11.15pm Sat; noon-10.30pm Sun. **Credit** AmEx, DC, MC, V. This new sister restaurant to Smollenky's on the Strand provides the same quality US diner fare, including great steaks, but gives families more space in which to spread out and relax. While the kids are entertained on Sundays from noon to 3pm with computer games, clowns, a raffle and face painting,

Community Gardens (The Green House, Hereford Street, Bedminster, Bristol BS3 4NA, 0117 923 1800/www.farmgarden.org.uk).

Battersea Park Children's Zoo

Battersea Park, SW11 (zoo 7924 5826/Splodge 7350 1477). Sloane Square tube then 19, 137 bus/Battersea Park or Queenstown Road rail. **Admission** £2; £1 2-15s, concessions; free under-2s. **No credit cards.**

This little zoo is home to some of the smallest monkeys in the world (marmosets), loveable pot-bellied pig Tum Tum, and otters, reptiles and meerkats. Parties run by Splodge are held daily from March to October (Saturdays and Sundays only in winter); call for times. There are also art activities, treasure hunts and puppet shows, in tailored packages (from £150).

Freightliner's City Farm

Paradise Park, Sheringham Road, off Liverpool Road, Barnsbury, N7 (7609 0467). Holloway Road tube/Highbury & Islington tube/rail. **Open** *Termtime* 10am-1pm, 2-5pm Wed, Sat, Sun. *Holidays* 10am-1pm, 2-5pm Tue-Thur, Sat, Sun. **Admission** free; donations welcome.

A working farm with livestock such as chickens, ducks, geese, sheep, goats and cows that children can touch, help care for and learn about.

Waiter, there's a hair in my bib – a junior diner at **Giraffe**.

parents can enjoy half-price cocktails. There's a cinema right nearby. **Branches**: 105 Strand, Covent Garden, WC2 (7497 2101); Bradmore House, Queen Caroline Street, W6 (8741 8124).

Strada

11-13 Battersea Rise, SW11 (7801 0794/ www.strada.co.uk). Clapham Junction rail. **Meals served** noon-11pm Mon-Sat; noon-10.30pm Sun. **Credit** AmEx, DC, MC, V.

This expanding pizza chain serves up delectable pizzas from its wood-fired ovens, as well as intriguing handmade pasta dishes. There's no special kids' menu but the hospitality and comfy banquette seats make for an unhurried and family-friendly experience. Added extras include free bottled water, and it's also worth watching out for the lunch and early evening offers. **Branches**: 15-16 New Burlington Street, W1 (7287 5967); 105-6 Upper Street, N1 (7226 9742); 8-10 Exmouth Market, EC1 (7278 0800); 175 New King's Road, SW6 (7731 6404); 6 Great Queen Street, WC2 (7405 6293).

The **Puppet Theatre Barge**.

Entertainment

Islington Boat Club
16-34 Graham Street, N1 (7253 0778). Angel tube.
Open 4.30-7.30pm Tue, Thur; 5-8pm Wed; 11am-4pm Sun. **Admission** £1 per day. **No credit cards.**
This 30-year-old water-based youth club for nine- to 18- year-olds offers canoeing, sailing, rowing and the use of mountain bikes. It also works with school groups and children with special needs.

National Film Theatre
South Bank, SE1 (box office 7928 3232/ www.bfi.org.uk/nft). Waterloo tube/rail.
Admission varies depending on screenings £6.85; £5.25 concessions; £1 discount for members. **Credit** AmEx, MC, V. **Map** p401 M7.
There are kids' matinées every Saturday at 3pm, with workshops to accompany the screenings at 2pm. It gets busy, so it's worth booking ahead.

Puppet Theatre Barge
Blomfield Road, Little Venice, W9 (07836 202745/ www.puppetbarge.com). Warwick Avenue tube. **Open** *Box office* 10am-8pm daily. *Children's shows* times vary, phone to check. **Tickets** £7; £6.50 under-16s, concessions. **Credit** MC, V. **Map** p395 D4.
A visit to the Puppet Theatre Barge is an experience even before the curtain goes up. Moored at Little Venice from October to June, and travelling to different locations in Henley, Marlow and Richmond the rest of the year, this floating marionette theatre stages regular family shows suitable for children aged over two. It's tiny, so book ahead. They also offer a programme of activities and workshops for schoolgroups.

Royal Gunpowder Mills
Beaulieu Drive, Waltham Abbey, Essex (01992 767022/www.royalgunpowdermills.com). Waltham Cross rail then 211, 212, 213, 240, 250, 505 or 517 bus. **Open** *Mar-Oct* 10am-6pm daily (last entry 5pm). *Nov-Feb* pre-booked groups only (10 people minimum). **Admission** £5.90; £3.25 5-16s; £5.25 concessions; family £17 (2+up to 3); free under-5s. **Credit** MC, V.
One of the UK's best-kept secrets, this 300-year-old mill opened to the public in May 2000, and though closed when we went to press (except to booked groups) it will open again on 16 March 2002. A day out here includes exhibitions and a visit to a viewing tower with a panoramic view of the grounds, plus a mural showing the animals that inhabit the site.

Science Museum IMAX Cinema
Wellcome Wing, Science Museum, Exhibition Road, South Kensington, SW7 (7942 4454/4455/ www.sciencemuseum.org.uk). South Kensington tube.
Admission Before 4.30pm daily *museum & film* £12.50; £9.50 students; £5.75 concessions. *After 4.30pm* (admission to museum free) £6.75; £5.75 concessions, students. **Time** *Shows* 10.45am, 11.55am, 1.05pm, 2.15pm, 3.25pm, 4.35pm daily; extra show 5.45pm Sat, Sun during busy periods. **Credit** AmEx, DC, MC, V. **Map** p397 D9.
Housed within the space-age Wellcome Wing of the Science Museum (*see p140*), this cinema has 2- and 3D films for kids of all ages.

Taking a break

Childminders
*6 Nottingham Street, Marylebone, W1 (7935 3000/ 2049/www.babysitters.co.uk). **Open** 8.45am-5.30pm Mon-Thur; 8.45am-5pm Fri; 9am-4.30pm Sat.*
Credit AmEx, MC, V. **Map** p398 G5.
A large agency with more than 1,500 babysitters, mainly nurses, nannies and infant teachers (all with references), who live in London or the suburbs.

Pippa Pop-ins
*430 Fulham Road, Chelsea, SW6 (7385 2458/ www.pippapop-ins.com). **Open** 8.15am-6pm Mon-Fri.*
Fees *sessions* from £35 (2.15-6pm); £45 (8.15am-2.15pm); £65 (8.15am-6pm). **Credit** MC, V.
Map p396 B13.
This nursery school and kindergarten run by NNEB-and Montessori-trained nursery teachers and nannies offers parties, holiday activities and a crèche.
Branch: 165 New King's Road, SW6 (7385 2458).

Universal Aunts
Daytime childminding 7738 8937/evening babysitting 7386 5900. **Open** 9.30am-5pm Mon-Thur; 9.30am-4pm Fri. **Rates** *Childminding* from £6/hr. *Babysitting* from £5/hr. **No credit cards.**
This London agency, founded in 1921, provides reliable people to babysit, meet children from trains, planes or boats, or take them sightseeing.

Clubs

Whether you want sweet '60s soul or a huge banging night of garage or house, you'll find something to suit just about every night of the week.

After a decade in which superclubs rammed in the punters, the prevailing fashion in London is for relatively intimate venues that create a sense of something underground. Londoners have always liked to be one step ahead of the game when it comes to music anyway, so the city has always had vibrant subcultural clubbing scenes that blow up and filter into the mainstream.

The city's nightlife functions largely by area – if you stick to Hoxton, Brixton or Soho, you're bound to fall into a club or one of its numerous satellite bars. Even within each club, the variety can be enormous: at clubs such as **Fabric** (*see p279*) or the **333** (*see p281*) you can have three types of music in three separate rooms. Bar hopping is a popular alternative – if one place doesn't appeal, there are usually numerous club-bars nearby that may be preferable.

And this proliferation shows no sign of abating, as the British have always had a large appetite for a hedonistic night out. Scheduled to open as we went to press is the long-awaited **Pacha London**, an Ibiza superclub that promises to provide big house music on the site of the former SW1 club opposite Victoria

Station. Meanwhile, the Leicester Square site of the shortlived Home has been acquired by a group headed up by the Mean Fiddler, though as yet no plans have been announced regarding its reopening or name change. One definitive loss, however, has been that of the legendary Wag (*see p280* **Whatever happened to?**).

In most places the precise music and style of a club varies from night to night. In the reviews below we've highlighted nights worth looking out for, but for full details see the extensive weekly club listings in *Time Out* magazine. It's also a good idea to keep your eyes open for the many long-running one-off nights, such as Soul Jazz's 100% Dynamite, held in venues that are not normally clubs. You'll also find events promoted on radio, on flyers and in specialist club magazines. The more underground scenes are harder to infiltrate, though hanging around in record shops and tuning in to pirate radio are good places to start. Expect to pay £2-£5 to get into a club between Sunday and Thursday, and £6-£12 on Fridays and Saturdays.

For clubs with mainly gay-oriented nights, *see p301* **Gay & Lesbian**.

Tripping the light fantastic at **Bar Rumba**. *See p278*.

Clubs

Bagley's Studios

King's Cross Freight Depot, off York Way,
King's Cross, N1 (7278 2777/www.bagleys.net).
King's Cross tube/rail. **Open** 10.30pm-6am Fri;
10.30pm-7am Sat. **Admission** £10-£15 (more on
the door). **Map** p399 L2.

This pioneering warehouse party venue has been
renovated into a warren of interconnected rooms
pumping with large-scale house and garage bashes.
The most popular night is Saturday's Freedom,
when suburban kids and glammed-up weekenders
come in droves to get their rocks off. Also of note is
Rollerdisco, an old and nu-disco night where clubbers hire rollerskates and relive their childhoods.

Bar Rumba

36 Shaftesbury Avenue, Soho, W1 (7287 2715/
www.barrumba.co.uk). Piccadilly Circus tube. **Open**
5pm-3.30am Mon, Thur; 5pm-3am Tue, Wed; 5pm-
4am Fri; 9pm-6am Sat; 8pm-1am Sun. **Admission**
£3-£12 (cheaper before 11pm). **Map** p401 K7.

One of the best dance clubs in town, Bar Rumba
hosts a series of excellent one-nighters: there's jazz,
funk and drum 'n' bass on Monday; Latin on
Tuesday; deep house on Wednesday; drum 'n' bass
on Thursday; funky disco-house classics on Friday;
and soulful garage on Saturday. Each night is among
the best of its kind and attracts high-class DJs.

Browns

4 Great Queen Street, Covent Garden, WC2
(7831 0802). Holborn tube. **Open** 11pm-3am daily.
Admission £15. **Map** p399 L6.

If you're looking for a nightclub where you can
dress up and party in style, the West End's Browns
fits the bill. This sleek and chic two-floor club,
which was once the New Romantic hangout Blitz
(*see p126*), has long been known as a haunt of
celebs and as a location for after-show parties.
Members are favoured, so non-members should
inform the club in advance, preferably by fax.

Café de Paris

3 Coventry Street, St James's, W1 (7734 7700/
www.cafedeparis.com). Leicester Square or Piccadilly
Circus tube. **Open** 10pm-3am Wed; 8.30pm-3am
Thur; 7pm-4am Fri, Sat. **Admission** £10 Wed;
£15 Thur-Sat. **Map** p401 K7.

This classic art deco ballroom with its lovely balcony and restaurant has been on the high-flying
bar circuit for decades. Warped cabaret night
'Merkin does Vegas!' features Pam Hogg and Boy
George as DJs, though Saturday nights are more
conventional. Expensive, dressed-up nights for rich
babes and young rakes.

Camden Palace

1A Camden High Street, Camden, NW1 (09062
100 200/www.camdenpalace.com). Camden Town or
Mornington Crescent tube. **Open** 10pm-2.30am Tue;
10pm-6am Fri, Sat. **Admission** £3-£5 Tue; £9, £12
after 11pm Fri; £15-£25 Sat.

Transformed into a multilevel inferno of sound and
light back in the early '80s, this huge old music hall
is showing its age now, but it's still worth visiting,
if only for Tuesday's indie-rock club Feet First, and
for some of the special events on weekends, such as
trancey, tribal house and garage night Peach.

Cargo

83 Rivington Street, Shoreditch, EC2 (7739 3440/
www.cargo-london.com). Old Street tube/rail.
Open noon-1am Mon-Thur; noon-3am Fri;
6pm-3am Sat; noon-midnight Sun. **Admission**
free-£8. **Map** p403 R4.

This club has gone from strength to strength since it
opened in January 2001. The incredibly varied music
includes live bands on stage alongside a plethora of
DJs. If the line-up is good, the queues can spread
round the corner, but even if there are lesser-known
names on the bill, Cargo is still a great choice for good
drink and some fresh music. The bar food and restaurant are also highly recommended.

The Clinic

13 Gerrard Street, Chinatown, W1 (7734 9836).
Leicester Square or Tottenham Court Road tube.
Open 5.30pm-3am Mon-Thur (occasional Sun;
phone for details); 5.30pm-4am Fri, Sat.
Admission £3-£6.

This venue has been popular, under various guises,
since the 1960s. The slightly seedy small bar is great
for an early evening drink, but the upstairs dancefloor
is often empty. Club nights such as funky Hammond,
ska night Tighten Up and midweek chillout
Mellodramatic are relaxed and not too loud. On
Tuesdays there's the Portobello Film Festival night
– bring your own movie to play and you get in free.

Colosseum

1 Nine Elms Lane, Nine Elms, SW8 (7627 1283/
www.clubcolosseum.com/www.ticketweb.co.uk).
Vauxhall tube/rail. **Open** 10pm-5am Fri;
10pm-6am Sat. **Admission** £8-£10 (can vary
depending on promoter).

Club Colosseum is about big nights with a steamy
selection of hard house, drum 'n' bass (Trouble on
Vinyl) and hip hop (Emission). The space-age decor
is a little flat but the punters are friendly and the DJs
(DJ Craze, Grooverider) are top notch. This is also
the current venue for the monthly blowout by drum
'n' bass night Movement. Security is very tight.

The Cross

Goods Way Depot, off York Way, King's Cross,
N1 (7837 0828/www.the-cross.co.uk). King's Cross
tube/rail. **Open** 11pm-5am Fri; 10pm-6am Sat;
11pm-5am every other Sun (phone for details).
Admission £12-£15. **Map** p399 L2.

The Cross has a reputation for great weekend dance
parties, including Renaissance and Serious, when
the brick arches shake to the latest glam house
grooves. It's worth the cab fare, but like so many of
these clubs, it's already a hit with dressed-up (but
not too self-conscious) locals, so arriving early is
always a smart move.

Back to school at the **Hanover Grand**.

Emporium

62 Kingly Street, Soho, W1 (7734 3190/
www.emporiumlondon.com). Oxford Circus or
Piccadilly Circus tube. **Open** 11pm-4am Fri, Sat
(members night). **Admission** £10-£15 girls; £15-£20
guys (admission by guest list only). **Map** p398 J6.
The best way to get into this spacious but choosy
Ibizan-style club just off Regent Street is to phone
in advance to ask about dress requirements and the
best time to arrive, and to be patient, polite and persistent. The daunting entrance with its elaborate
gate is worth braving if you want to spot B-list
celebrities wigging out to funky house and future
disco in their best clothes.

The End

18 West Central Street, St Giles's, WC1 (7419
9199/www.the-end.co.uk). Holborn or Tottenham
Court Road tube. **Open** 10pm-3am Mon; 10pm-4am
Thur; 10pm-5am Fri; 10pm-7am Sat; Sun phone for
details. **Admission** £4 Mon; £5 Thur; £8-£12 Fri;
£15 Sat. **Map** p399 L6.
The most sophisticated dance venue in central
London, the End is a homage to minimal styling and
maximum sound quality. Its monthly funky techno,
drum 'n' bass, garage and deep house parties are the
best in London, while on Mondays there's the indie-
rock-dance session Trash. All this, and smart toilets
and proper air-conditioning too.

Equinox

5-7 Leicester Square, WC2 (7437 1446/
www.nightclub.co.uk/equinox). Leicester Square
tube. **Open** 9pm-3am Mon-Thur; 9pm-4am Fri, Sat;
6pm-1am Sun. **Admission** £5, £7 after 10.30pm
Mon-Thur; £8, £10 after 10pm Fri; £10, £12 after
10pm Sat; £2 Sun. **Map** p401 K7.
Cheesy music for a cheesy clientele who should know
better: this club is only an option if you're too drunk
to see where you're going.

Fabric

77A Charterhouse Street, Farringdon, EC1
(7336 8898/advance tickets for Fri 7344 4444/
www.fabriclondon.com). Farringdon tube/rail.
Open 10pm-5am Fri; 10pm-7am Sat.
Admission £12 Fri; £15 Sat. **Map** p402 O5.
One of the hottest clubs in London, maze-like Fabric
manages to be simultaneously large and intimate.
Apart from the diverse music – breakbeat and drum
'n' bass on Fridays, tech-house and house on
Saturday, tribal house on Sunday's gay night – the
main attraction is the Bodysonic dancefloor, which
pumps the music through your body. Punters are
friendly and unpretentious.

Fridge

1 Town Hall Parade, Brixton Hill, Brixton, SW2
(7326 5100/www.fridge.co.uk). Brixton tube/rail.
Open 10pm-6am Fri, Sat. **Admission** £8-£14.
The largest venue in and around Brixton, this former theatre is hardly glamorous, though it can look
spectacular with the clever use of visuals. Saturday
features monthly parties, while Fridays major on
tough, uplifting trance at Escape from Samsara
– the club of choice for techno dreads and cyber clubbers who like their nights to last.

Glasshouse

The Mermaid Building, Puddle Dock, off
Upper Thames Street, City, EC4 (7680 0415/
www.glasshouse-club.com). Blackfriars tube/rail.
Open 10.30pm-5am Fri, Sat. **Admission** £8
members, £12 non-members Fri; £10 members,
£15 non-members Sat. **Map** p404 O7.
The main attraction for this posh club by the river
in Blackfriars is that it's made of glass. The three
dancefloors play house beats for the rather smart
city boys and girls letting loose for the night. Make
sure you dress to impress.

Hanover Grand

6 Hanover Street, Mayfair, W1 (7499 7977/
www.hanovergrand.com). Oxford Circus tube.
Open 10.30pm-3am Wed; 10.30pm-4am Thur, Sat;
10pm-3am Fri. **Admission** £3-£12.**Map** p398 J6.
With its balconied dancefloor and groovy bar down
a sweeping staircase, the Hanover Grand is home to
the best midweek R&B and hip hop at Fresh 'n'
Funky on Wednesdays. The rest of the week attracts
gorgeous club-people, who are the only ones likely
to get past the style police on the door. This is also
the venue for the unbelievably popular school-
disco.com, a tongue-in-cheek retro night where the
punters come in school uniform on Fridays.

Madame Jo Jos

8 Brewer Street, Soho, W1 (7734 3040). Leicester
Square or Piccadilly Circus tube. **Open** 10.30pm-
3am Wed, Fri; 9.30pm-3am Thur; 10pm-3am Sat.
Admission £5 Wed; £3 before 10.30pm, £5 after,
Thur; £6 before 11pm, £8 after, Fri; Sat.
A great venue that still has a touch of the strip club
or cabaret bar to it – something that only adds to its
atmosphere (it even features in *Eyes Wide Shut*; *see*

p290 **On location: Kubrick's London**). Though it's launched some promising midweek funk and hip hop nights, the big draw is Keb Darge's Deep Funk night – one of London's best-kept secrets for years. Perfect for jazz dancers (and the rest of us) to strut their stuff to brilliant, obscure '60s and '70s funk.

Mass

The Brix, St Matthew's Church, Brixton Hill, Brixton, SW9 (7737 1016/www.ticketweb.co.uk/ www.massclub.com). Brixton tube/rail. **Open** 10pm-6am Fri, Sat. **Admission** £12 members; £15 non members; £20 on the door.

Right opposite the Fridge, this three-room club high up a circular stairwell in a converted church is a great space boasting a series of cutting-edge monthly line-ups at nights such as Movement and Dekefex. The rather undramatic sound and lack of air-con can detract from the atmosphere.

Ministry of Sound

103 Gaunt Street, Walworth, SE1 (7378 6528/ www.ministryofsound.co.uk). Elephant & Castle tube/rail. **Open** 10.30pm-6am Fri; 11pm-8am Sat. **Admission** £12 Fri; £15 Sat. **Map** p404 O10.

The most famous club in the whole of London may resemble a prison yard from the outside, but after celebrating its tenth birthday in 2001 it still manages to draw all-night dancers like moths to a flame. Big-name guest DJs from the United States and the UK spinning house and garage are the Ministry's principal attraction.

93 Feet East

150 Brick Lane, Spitalfields, E2 (7247 3293/ www.93feeteast.co.uk). Aldgate East tube. **Open** 6-11pm Mon-Wed, Sun; 6pm-late Thur-Sat. **Admission** £5-£10. **Map** p403 S5.

This large three-room venue on Brick Lane in east London may not have the greatest sound system in the world but it still knows how to put on a really great night. With everything from label showcases from future-folk label Twisted Nerve to free Wall of Sound night Sizzler, you're assured of varied but consistently cutting-edge music. There's a downstairs bar that's white, stylish and always heaving, while the large upstairs bar and dancefloor are more kitsch. The outdoor tables and terrace are also a real bonus in summer.

Whatever happened to? the Wag

Ask almost any seasoned clubber about the Wag and you'll hear a litany of reminiscences. The Soho institution, which closed down in May 2001 after 20 years in business, was the place where many Londoners first experienced 'proper' clubbing, from 1980s celeb-spotting cool to pill-fuelled acid house.

The venue – on the site of an underground drinking club on Wardour Street – was opened by Chris Sullivan as a reaction against the synthetic cheese of New Romantics.

'At the time, all the West End clubs were playing shit pop music. I wanted to open somewhere for people like me, a cool club with a great mix of music, whether it be jazz or funk or disco or reggae,' he explained.

The result was phenomenally popular, attracting hordes of trendsetters and celebrities (Robert de Niro, Neneh Cherry, John Galliano; the list goes on). Musically, it became the birthplace for rare groove, launching the career of Gilles Peterson, and it was the first venue to play hip hop in London. Grandmaster Flash and Afrika Bambaataa, the Beastie Boys, De La Soul, the JBs, Sade and even Bananarama played there.

As the '80s moved on, the club became increasingly elitist, and the door police were notoriously harsh on non-members, though the snobby reputation belied the

Wag's reality as a sweaty den of indulgence. Towards the end, when rent and rates had risen to such an extent that it had to sell up, it had dwindled away to little more than a venue for cheap '80s retro and student nights, though Camden's Mod night Blow Up settled there for a while, and bands such as Air and Pizzicato Five proved there was life in the old dog.

The venue has become a three-storey Irish theme pub, providing a perfect example of the commercialisation that has changed Soho over the decades, but its influence on modern clubbing is considerable. The varied music policy that Sullivan strove towards can be seen in clubs such as Cargo and Bar Rumba (for both, *see p278*) and in the sets of Justin Robertson and the Chemical Brothers.

Plastic People

147-9 Curtain Road, Shoreditch, EC2 (7739 6471/ www.plasticpeople.co.uk). Old Street tube/rail. **Open** 10pm-2am Mon-Thur; 10pm-3am Fri, Sat; 7pm-midnight Sun. **Admission** £3-£7. **Map** p403 R4.

This tiny club is an easy and cheap place to come to for some post-pub drinking. The monthly house and hip hop nights are good enough, but the venue can be rammed or empty at seemingly random intervals. A nice place to go to if the queues at Cargo (*see p278*) get too big.

Rock

Hungerford House, Victoria Embankment, Westminster, WC2 (7976 2006/www.rockclubs.co.uk). Embankment tube. **Open** 6pm-4am Thur, Fri; 10pm-4am Sat. **Admission** £5 1pm-midnight, £7.50 after, Thur; £10 after 10pm Fri; £12-£15 Sat. **Map** p401 L7.

For those who can get in, Rock offers the chance to party in style (that's slick '70s lounge style) along with a host of celebrities and Euro hedonists.

Roof Gardens

99 Kensington High Street (entrance in Derry Street), Kensington, W8 (7937 7994/www.roofgardens.com). High Street Kensington tube. **Open** 6.30pm-3am Thur, Sat. **Admission** free for diners. **Map** p396 B9.

Probably the most beautiful location in town, the Roof Gardens boasts three stunning garden areas in addition to the restaurant and dancefloor. Punters tend towards the affluent, but though the £40 admission sounds steep it does include a three-course dinner. Members are favoured but non-members are also admitted on Thursdays and Saturdays (call in advance).

Scala

275 Pentonville Road, King's Cross, N1 (7833 2022/ www.scala-london.co.uk). King's Cross tube/rail. **Open** 7.30pm-midnight Mon-Thur; 10pm-5am Fri, Sat. **Admission** £6-£14. **Map** p399 L3.

This venue was once the largest repertory cinema in London, and its main room still has a 'swimming pool' feel that reflects its former use. Always busy, it focuses on body rockin' beats from big names for a relaxed, trainer-friendly clientele. Gay indie night Popstarz is extremely popular (*see p303*), as is the monthly hip hop institution Scratch.

Sound

Swiss Centre, Leicester Square, WC2 (7287 1010/ www.soundlondon.com). Leicester Square or Piccadilly Circus tube. **Open** 5pm-4am Mon-Sat; 6pm-2am Sun. **Admission** £8-£12 (free before 9pm).

Sound is doing its bit for much-maligned Leicester Square; it even provides its punters with a classy blue velvet chill-out room. The Kerrang! Club's weekly goth-metal fest (Wednesday nights) provides an amusing contrast to Trevor Nelson's sexy R&B and phat soul night Rare on Fridays, which is very popular with the ladeeez. Long-running disco night Carwash has now been replaced with '80s retro night Love Shack – perfect fodder for the Leicester Square herd.

Subterania

12 Acklam Road (under the Westway), Ladbroke Grove, W10 (8960 4590/www.meanfiddler.com). Ladbroke Grove tube. **Open** 8pm-2am Mon-Sat. **Admission** £5-£8.

This small, dark club has ska and dub on Wednesdays with Rodigan's Reggae, while DJs spin funky sounds at the weekend to a trendy west London crowd. Both Friday's Rotation and Saturday's Soulsonic are hard to get into unless you arrive early (and be sure to dress up for the latter).

333

333 Old Street, Hoxton, EC1 (7739 5949). Old Street tube/rail. **Open** 10pm-3am 1st Thur of mth; 10pm-5am Fri, Sat; 10pm-4am Sun. **Admission** £8, £5 with flyer Thur; £5 before 11pm, £10 after, Fri, Sat; £5 before midnight, £7 after, Sun. **Map** p403 Q4.

This three-storey club is always a laugh, and queues can be very long. Rotating nights include Revolver and the excellent Off Centre (which has the best club flyers in London). Someone's usually playing hip hop or drum 'n' bass in the basement and funky soul or US garage in the main room. The top-floor bar, Mother, is also a great midweek spot with a number of independent club nights of its own.

Turnmills

63 Clerkenwell Road, Clerkenwell, EC1 (7250 3409/www.turnmills.com). Farringdon tube/rail. **Open** 6.30pm-midnight Tue; 10.30pm-7.30am Fri; 10pm-5am Sat; 4am-1pm Sun. **Admission** £5 Tue. £10 members, £12 non-members Fri, Sat. £10 members, £15 non-members Sun. **Map** p402 N4.

Famous for its 'underground' dance nights, Turnmills has nooks and crannies galore and plenty of space to sit and chill. The Gallery, Friday's full-on housey party with uplifting DJs, is jammed. Gay marathon Trade (*see p303*) takes place here every Sunday. Strictly hardcore.

Velvet Room

143 Charing Cross Road, Soho, WC2 (7734 4687/ www.velvetroom.co.uk). Tottenham Court Road tube. **Open** 10pm-3am Mon-Thur; 10pm-4am Fri, Sat; 7.30pm-midnight Sun. **Admission** £5-£10. **Map** p399 K6.

This luxuriously appointed club bar hosts a top drum 'n' bass Wednesday-nighter (Swerve) and a great techno and deep house night on Thursdays (Ultimate BASE). A good, midweek club in the West End, and a precious find; stylish club clothes should normally guarantee admission.

Club-bars

'Club-bars' – bars that stick on a DJ, clear a small dancefloor space and stay open past 11pm – have grown like germs over London's streets in the past five years. Much more relaxed than 'proper' clubs, they usually offer great value for money and retain the nonchalance of bar culture.

AKA

18 West Central Street, St Giles's, WC2 (7836 0110/www.akalondon.com). Holborn or Tottenham Court Road tube. **Open** 6-11pm Mon; 6pm-3am Wed-Fri; 7pm-7am Sat; varies Sun (phone for details). **Admission** £5 after10pm Fri; £8 after 9pm Sat. **Map** p399 L6.

A companion to the End next door (*see p279*), this highly rated bar and restaurant is incorporated into the latter's club nights on Saturdays. Expect to queue on busy nights, for house (21st Century Soul), electro and tech house (Armadillo).

Bug Bar

The Crypt, St Matthew's Peace Garden, Brixton Hill, Brixton, SW2 (7738 3184/www.bugbar.co.uk). Brixton tube/rail. **Open** 7pm-1am Wed, Thur; 7pm-3am Sat; 7pm-2am Sun. **Admission** £4 9-11pm, £6 after 11pm, Fri, Sat.

Perenially popular, the laid-back but lively Bug Bar has regular entertainment, including bands, stand-ups and DJs. A fixture in the Brixton club-bar scene, it often has free entry. Popular with the south London massive.

Dogstar

389 Coldharbour Lane, Brixton, SW9 (7733 7515/www.dogstarbar.com). Brixton tube/rail. **Open** noon-2.30am Mon-Thur; noon-3am Fri, Sat; noon-2.30pm Sun. **Admission** £2-£7 Thur-Sat (free before 10pm).

Relaxed and friendly with students, proper locals and random old men, this vibey and happening converted pub is home to a lot of fine and occasionally properly havin'-it party nights. Some nights you have to pay to get in.

Dust

27 Clerkenwell Road, Clerkenwell, EC1 (7490 5120). Farringdon tube/rail. **Open** noon-midnight Mon-Wed; noon-2am Thur, Fri; 7pm-2am Sat. **Admission** £3 after 11pm Fri; £4 after 9pm Sat. **Map** p402 N4.

A classy, simple but clever space clad in wood and coppery paintwork, Dust has great drinks. The flow of beautiful people has dried up a bit in recent months, but it's worth popping in if you're nearby.

Form

4-5 Greek Street, Soho, W1 (7434 3323). Tottenham Court Road tube. **Open** 5-11pm Mon; 5pm-1am Tue; 5pm-2am Wed, Thur; 5pm-3am Fri, Sat. **Admission** £3 after 10pm Wed; £5 after 9pm Fri, Sat. **Map** p399 K6.

Form offers some very groovy dance midweekers, including hip hop night on Wednesdays and disco and house (Chill Bitch) on Thursdays.

Fridge Bar

1 Town Hall Parade, Brixton Hill, Brixton, SW2 (7326 5100/www.fridge.co.uk). Brixton tube/rail. **Open** 6pm-2am Mon-Thur; 6pm-4am Fri; 6-11am, 6pm-4am Sat; 6-11am, 6pm-2am Sun. **Admission** £5-£8 Fri-Sun.

Operating as a fairly agreeable chill-down session (6-11am) for the club next door (see the Fridge, *p279*), the Fridge Bar is sometimes laid-back, sometimes packed. It adopts a more global dance perspective than the Fridge itself, with a dark basement dancefloor that generates an old-school funky-sweaty party atmosphere.

Ion

161-5 Ladbroke Grove, W10 (8960 1702/ www.meanfiddler.com). Ladbroke Grove tube. **Open** noon-midnight daily.

Almost underneath Ladbroke Grove station, Ion is a light and airy meeting place with a great terrace and a mezzanine restaurant.

Medicine Bar

181 Upper Street, Islington, N1 (7704 9536/ www.liquid-life.com). Highbury & Islington tube/rail. **Open** 5pm-midnight Mon-Thur; 5pm-2am Fri; noon-2am Sat; noon-10.30pm Sun.

This stylish but comfortable Islington hangout fills with pre-clubbers as the after-work drinkers begin to fade away. With its newly added upper floor, it's a great place to hear classic soul, disco and funk. Membership may be required.

Pop

14 Soho Street, Soho, W1 (7734 4004/ www.thebreakfastgroup.co.uk). Tottenham Court Road tube. **Open** 5pm-3am Mon-Thur; 5pm-4am Fri; 8pm-5am Sat; 6-11pm Sun. **Admission** £5 after 9pm Mon-Thur; £10, £8 guestlist Fri; £12, £10 guestlist Sat; £5 Sun. **Map** p399 K6.

This colourful, pop arty venue hosts a diverse mix of groovy and glamorous parties. Dress to impress.

Redstar

319 Camberwell Road, Camberwell, SE5 (7737 0831/www.redstarbar.co.uk). Oval tube then 36, 185 bus. **Open** 5pm-1am Mon-Thur; noon-4am Sat; noon-midnight Sun. **Admission** £4 after 11pm Fri, Sat.

This wonderful club-bar has massive windows over-looking Camberwell Green and superb DJ line-ups. It's usually free, which means its popular with students from the local art college. Great for lounging.

Salmon & Compasses

58 Penton Street, Islington, N1 (7837 3891). Angel tube. **Open** 5pm-late Mon-Wed; 5pm-2am Thur-Sat; 5pm-midnight Sun. **Admission** £3 after 9.30pm Fri, Sat.

This pub venue moves its pool table aside on the weekends for full-to-capacity nights that are refreshingly unpretentious. The People Show breaks and beats slot (Fridays) is always worth a visit, as are tongue-in-cheek monthlies such as Pigeonhold.

Social Bar

5 Little Portland Street, Marylebone, W1 (7636 4992/www.thesocial.co.uk). Oxford Circus tube. **Open** noon-midnight Mon-Fri; 1pm-midnight Sat. **Map** p398 J5.

This starkly minimalist two-storey bar offers fine music nightly and swarms with music business types. Arrive early if you want a seat on club nights, when it gets tighter than a tin of sardines.

Comedy

How – and where – to have the last laugh.

Summer 2001 saw the first London Comedy Festival, but many questioned the validity of such an event in a town where every night's a comedy night, and where most of the nights that fell under the LCF banner were regular events that were happening in the capital's plethora of purpose-built venues, function rooms and pub basements anyway. Yet although the festival served to make it clear why the world's capital city of comedy has never needed a festival before, it will keep getting one anyway; this year's will be in May (phone 08700 119611 for further details).

The festival was set up by the founder of the **Jongleurs** chain (*see p284*), which, along with the **Comedy Store** (*see p284*), **Bound & Gagged** (*see below*) and **Lee Hurst's Backyard** (*see p284*), attract the lion's share of the circuit's big names. You'll pay hefty prices at such places, of course: for cheaper laughs, or to uncover newish or untried acts, head to the **Bearcat Club** (*see below*), the **Chuckle Club** (*see p284*), the **Comedy Café** (*see p284*), or best of all, **Downstairs at the King's Head** (*see p284*): the latter is famed for its try-out nights on Thursdays.

Comedy

Major venues

Amused Moose Soho
Bar Code basement, 3-4 Archer Street, Soho, W1 (8341 1341/www.amusedmoose.co.uk). Leicester Square or Piccadilly Circus tube. **Shows** 8.30pm Thur, Sun, Mon, occasional Wed; 7.45pm Fri, Sat. **Admission** £5-£7; £1 discount members. **No credit cards.**
It's moved around many-a-time in the past, but this time the Amused Moose seems to have found its happiest spot beneath one of Soho's gay staples. Simple, smart and a must for those hunting for sketch shows and double acts.

Banana Cabaret
The Bedford, 77 Bedford Hill, Balham, SW12 (8673 8904/www.bananacabaret.co.uk). Balham tube/rail. **Shows** 9pm Fri, Sat; 8.30pm 2nd Sun of mth. **Admission** £10-£13; £7-£8 concessions. **No credit cards.**
Heralded by one punter as the 'most unusual venue in London' (it's drum-shaped), the Banana rolls on much as it has done for the last 19 years: with great comics and a friendly atmosphere. Its popularity

means you should arrive early (by 8.30pm on Fridays and 7.30pm on Saturdays). A post-laughter DJ entertains until 2am.

Bearcat Club
Turk's Head, 28 Winchester Road, Twickenham, Middx (8892 1972). St Margaret's rail. **Shows** *weekly* 9.15pm Sat. **Admission** £8; £7 members. **No credit cards.**
'It's a bit like a big scout hut,' reckons promoter James Punnett, but it's no bad thing that he's right: the decor's plain, but the lights, music and hordes of twentysomethings (get there early for a seat) have made one of the circuit's old-timers (it's been around since 1984) one of the liveliest venues on the circuit. As for the humour, you'll find that it's the sophisticated stuff that works best here (slapstick in St Margaret's? – c'mon), but the open slots each week make for some surprises.

Bound & Gagged
Palmers Green *The Fox, 413 Green Lanes, N13 (8450 4100/www.boundandgagged.com). Palmers Green rail.* **Tufnell Park** *Tufnell Park Tavern, 162 Tufnell Park Road, N7 (7272 2078). Tufnell Park tube.* **Shows** *Palmers Green* weekly 9.15pm Fri. *Tufnell Park* (closed mid June-mid Sept) weekly 9.30pm Sat. **Admission** *Palmers Green* £7, £5 concessions. Membership (annual) £2.50. *Tufnell Park* £7, £5 concessions. Membership (annual) £1. **No credit cards.**
Bound & Gagged offers some of the most experienced and talented acts on the circuit. The newly refurbished 200-seater venue in Palmers Green is a lively, classy affair, and has turned the adjoining Fox pub into a local landmark. The smaller Tufnell Park venue – situated above the Tufnell Park Tavern – is a poorer cousin in comparison, but both treat a keen young crowd to some of the biggest and most exciting names on the circuit. There's a bar until 1am at both venues.

Canal Café Theatre
The Bridge House, Delamere Terrace, Little Venice, W2 (7289 6054/www.newsrevue.com). Royal Oak or Warwick Avenue tube. **Shows** 7.30pm, 9.30pm Mon-Sat; 7pm, 9pm Sun. **Admission** £5-£10; £1-£2 reduction concessions; phone for details. *Membership* (annual) £1. **Credit** MC, V. **Map** p394 C4.
The topical sketch show 'Newsrevue' (Thur-Sun) began way back in 1985 and remains the welcoming Canal Café Theatre's greatest asset. A regular rotation of casts still sends up the important issues of the day through a series of (constantly updated) sketches and songs.

For topical satire
Newsrevue at the **Canal Café Theatre** (*see p283*).

For sharp improv
Comedy Store Players (*see below*).

For up close and personal
Hampstead Clinic (*see below*).

For try-out nights
Comedy Café (*see below*); **Downstairs at the King's Head** (*see below*).

Chuckle Club
Three Tuns Bar, London School of Economics, Houghton Street, Holborn, WC2 (7476 1672/ www.chuckleclub.com). Covent Garden or Holborn tube. **Shows** *weekly* 7.45pm Sat. **Admission** £10; £8 concessions. **No credit cards. Map** p399 M6.
Still going strong after 16 years, this comfortable club has a matey atmosphere thanks to its location in LSE, and, in an industry where silly names abound, resident host Eugene Cheese has one of the best.

Comedy Café
66 Rivington Street, Shoreditch, EC2 (7739 5706/ www.comedycafe.co.uk). Old Street tube/rail. **Shows** *weekly* 9pm Wed-Sat. **Admission** Wed free; *Thur* £3; *Fri* £10; *Sat* £12. **Credit** MC, V. **Map** p403 R4.
A favourite with comics and punters, and it's easy to see why: one of only a few purpose-built comedy clubs in the capital, the Café has a friendly buzz and terrific line-ups. Wednesday's try-out nights are a Freudian eye-opener: are humans courageous exhibitionists or merely gluttons for punishment?

Comedy Store
1A Oxendon Street, St James's, SW1 (7344 0234/ www.thecomedystore.co.uk). Leicester Square or Piccadilly Circus tube. **Shows** *weekly* 8pm Tue-Sun; also midnight Fri, Sat. **Admission** £12-£15; £8 concessions. **Credit** MC, V. **Map** p401 K7.
The Comedy Store, which is widely regarded as having kick-started alternative comedy, began life in a Soho strip joint in the late 1970s. Big-name stand-ups are the standard fare: on Wednesdays and Sundays the Comedy Store Players provide improv, while Tuesdays see a twist on stand-up with the highly regarded Cutting Edge.

Downstairs at the King's Head
2 Crouch End Hill, Crouch End, N8 (8340 1028/ office 01920 823265). Finsbury Park tube/rail then W7 bus/Crouch Hill rail. **Shows** *weekly* 8.30pm Thur, Sat, Sun. **Admission** free-£7. **No credit cards.**

A popular haunt for many of today's big names in their early days, this admirable and entertaining long-running club features a try-out night every Thursday and a mixture of bigger names and new acts on Saturday nights.

Hampstead Clinic
Downstairs at the White Horse, 154 Fleet Road, Hampstead, NW3 (7485 2112). Belsize Park tube/Hampstead Heath rail. **Shows** *weekly* 9pm Sat. **Admission** £6.50; £5 concessions. **Credit** *food & drink only* MC, V.
The eight-year-old Clinic will most likely have been refurbished by the time you read this, but rest assured the dimly lit intimacy will remain. That also means that you're unlikely to find double acts or sketch shows; instead there are experienced stand-ups with a couple of years under their belt, plus the odd US comic thrown in for good measure. The notoriously great food is an added draw.

Jongleurs Comedy Club
Battersea *Bar Risa, 49 Lavender Gardens, SW11. Clapham Junction rail.* **Bow** *221 Grove Road, E3. Mile End tube.* **Camden** *Dingwalls, Middle Yard, Camden Lock, Chalk Farm Road, NW1. Camden Town or Chalk Farm tube.* **Watford** *76 The Parade, Watford, Herts. Watford tube/Watford Junction rail.* **All** *(box office 7564 2500/info 0870 787 0707/ www.jongleurs.com)* **Shows** *Battersea* 8.45pm Fri; 7.15pm, 11.15pm Sat. *Bow* 8.15pm Fri, Sat. *Camden* 8.45pm Fri; 7.15pm, 11.15pm Sat. *Watford* 8pm Thur-Sat. **Admission** *Battersea, Camden* £14 Fri; £12 Sat. *Watford* £6 Thur; £12 Fri; £13 Sat. *Bow* £13 Fri; £14 Sat. **Credit** AmEx, MC, V.
Often unfairly called the 'McDonald's of comedy' (the 'Pret-à-Manger' is perhaps a more appropriate name), Jongleur puts on biggish names of a high quality at all four of its London venues: the first-floor hall in Battersea, the purpose-built Bow and Camden clubs and the 400-capacity Watford operation. Food is available, and there's an after-show disco every night at Bow and Watford, and on Fridays at Battersea and Camden. It's always a good idea to book for all the Jongleurs.

Lee Hurst's Backyard Comedy Club
231 Cambridge Heath Road, Bethnal Green, E2 (7739 3122/www.leehurst.com). Bethnal Green tube/rail. **Shows** *weekly* 8.30pm Fri, Sat. **Admission** *Fri* £10; £7 concessions; £5 members. *Sat* £12; £11 advance; £9-£10 members. *Membership* free. **Credit** AmEx, MC, V.
Now in its third year, the Backyard Comedy Club is owned by comic Lee Hurst, who has used his industry clout and desire to treat comics with the respect they don't always command in other clubs to ensure consistently top-notch bills. Food is available, and there are post-show discos.

Meccano Club
The Dove Regent, 65 Graham Street, Islington, N1 (7813 4478/www.themeccanoclub.co.uk). Angel tube. **Shows** *weekly* 9pm Sat. **Admission** £7; £5 concessions. **No credit cards. Map** p402 O2.

If watching as an open-spot candidate crashes and burns is your idea of hell, then come here – the Meccano Club doesn't have them. Instead, they invite more practised up-and-comers to mix with the circuit's older hands.

Red Rose Comedy Club

129 Seven Sisters Road, Finsbury Park, N7 (7281 3051/www.redrosecomedy.co.uk). Finsbury Park tube/rail. **Shows** *weekly* 9pm Sat. **Admission** £7; £5 concessions. *Membership* (annual) £1. **No credit cards.**

The Red Rose's founder, comic Ivor Dembina, is an outspoken critic of bland comedy, new act competitions, dodgy promoters, disco-led comedy nights and timing constraints – none of which you'll find here. 'If you fancy paying up to £15 admission, then go elsewhere,' says Dembina. Terrific stuff.

Up the Creek

302 Creek Road, Greenwich, SE10 (8858 4581/ www.up-the-creek.com). Greenwich DLR/rail. **Shows** *weekly* 8.30pm Sat; 9pm Fri, Sun. **Admission** *Fri* £10; £6 concessions. *Sat* £14; £10 concessions. *Sun* £6; £4 concessions; £2 local students. **Credit** AmEx, MC, V.

A noisy bearpit of a club run by the eccentric London comedy legend Malcolm Hardee. The atmosphere may be unforgiving – especially when it comes to new acts – but some sort of entertainment is guaranteed. There's also food and a disco until 2am on Fridays and Saturdays.

Other venues

You'll discover that, aside from the main clubs, many of London's other comedy nights come, go and shift venues with alarming rapidity, so it's always a good idea to phone in advance prior to your visit.

July is the hottest month for comedy, with many comics trying out new shows in the capital before heading north to Edinburgh for the Fringe Festival the following month. By extension, August is London's quietest month for comedy: call the clubs below to check they're running nights before you turn up with your comedy pound.

Aztec Comedy Club *The Borderland, 47-9 Westow Street, Norwood, SE19 (8771 0885).* **Shows** *weekly* 9pm Fri.
Buccaneers Comedy *The Hope, 15 Tottenham Street, Fitzrovia, W1 (7637 0896/07931 551520).* **Shows** *weekly* 9pm Tue. **Map** p398 J5.
Comedy Brewhouse *Camden Head, 2 Camden Walk, Camden Passage, Islington, N1 (7359 0851).* **Shows** *weekly* 9pm Fri, Sat. **Map** p402 O2.
Comedy Pit *The Alexandra, 14 Clapham Common Southside, Clapham, SW4 (7274 5591).* **Shows** *weekly* 8.30pm Sun.
Ha Bloody Ha *(all venues 8566 4067) Ealing Studios, Ealing Green, St Mary's Road, Ealing, W5.* **Shows** *weekly* 9pm Fri, Sat.

Chiswick Town Hall, Heathfield Terrace, Chiswick, W4. **Shows** *fortnightly* 8.45pm Sat.
King's Head, 214 Acton High Street, Acton, W3. **Shows** *weekly* 9pm Fri.
Princess Royal Hall, Ealing Road, Brentford, Middx. **Shows** *monthly* 9pm Thur.
Hackney Empire Bullion Rooms *117 Wilton Way, Hackney, E8 (8985 2424/ www.hackneyempire.co.uk).* **Shows** days & comedy programmes vary.
Hampstead Comedy Club *The Washington, England's Lane, Hampstead, NW3 (8299 2601/ www.hampsteadcomedy.co.uk).* **Shows** *weekly* 9pm Sat.
Hen & Chickens Theatre *109 St Paul's Road, Highbury Corner, Highbury, N1 (7704 2001/ www.henandchickens.com).* **Shows** days vary.
Laughing Horse *Black Horse, 181 Sheen Road, Richmond, Surrey (8940 0424).* **Shows** *weekly* 8pm Sun.
Laughing Horse Camden *Liberties Bar, 100 Camden High Street, Camden, NW1 (7485 4019).* **Shows** *comedy* 8.30pm Wed. *Cabaret* 8.30pm Thur.
Mirth Control Tottenham *Railway Tavern, 65 White Hart Lane, N17 (8808 2102).* **Shows** *weekly* (phone to check) 9pm Tue.
Mirth Control West Hampstead *Lower Ground Bar, 269 West End Lane, West Hampstead, NW6 (7431 2211).* **Shows** *weekly* 8pm Wed.
Pear Shaped in Fitzrovia *The Fitzroy Tavern, 16 Charlotte Street, Fitzrovia, W1 (7580 3714).* **Shows** *weekly* 7.30pm Wed.
Shake-up Comedy Club *Atlantic Bar & Grill, 20 Glasshouse Street, Soho, W1 (7734 4888).* **Shows** call for details.
Soho Laughter Lounge *The John Snow, 39 Broadwick Street, Soho, W1 (7437 1344).* **Shows** *weekly* 8.30pm Sat.
Well Hard Comedy Club *Distillers Arms, 64 Fulham Palace Road, Hammersmith, W6 (8748 2834).* **Shows** *weekly* 9pm Thur.

The **Comedy Café**. *See p284.*

Dance

Whether you're a ballet buff, a flamenco fan or yearn to learn to salsa, London can provide both the shows and the classes.

The capital's thriving dance scene can be measured by the sheer range of work regularly on view, as well as the plethora of workshops or more intensive study options that are available year-round. Venues such as the **Barbican Centre**, the **Royal Opera House** (for both, *see below*) and **Sadler's Wells** (*see p287*) attract the world's top talent, while the dance schools (*see p288*) that operate out of the city's many studios, halls and arts centres can teach you to swing, strut or spin like the stars.

As well as the performances and venues below, check the dance pages in *Time Out* magazine. For up-to-the-minute dance information, see www.londondance.com.

Major venues

Barbican Centre
Silk Street, The City, EC2 (gallery 7382 7105/box office 7638 8891/www.barbican.org.uk). Barbican tube/Moorgate tube/rail. **Box office** 10am-8pm daily. **Tickets** £6-£30. **Credit** AmEx, MC, V. **Map** p402 P5.
This City arts centre (*see also p310*) has become a major player in terms of hosting dance. The fifth Barbican International Theatre Event (BITE, July-Dec 2002) contains a real coup: a world première (10-14 Sept) by choreographer Merce Cunningham.

ICA
The Mall, Westminster, SW1 (box office 7930 3647/membership 7766 1439/www.ica.org.uk). Piccadilly Circus tube/Charing Cross tube/rail. **Box office** noon-9.30pm daily. **Tickets** prices vary; average £8. **Membership** Daily £1.50, £1 concessions Mon-Fri;

£2.50, £1.50 concessions Sat, Sun; under-14s free. *Annual* £25; £15 concessions. **Credit** AmEx, DC, MC, V. **Map** p401 K8.
This intimate space hosts experimental, movement-based theatre and performance with an avant-garde flavour. The London International Mime Festival is a regular visitor (*see p262*), as is Dance Umbrella (*see p288* **Dance festivals**).

London Coliseum
St Martin's Lane, Covent Garden, WC2 (box office 7632 8300/textphone 7836 7666/www.eno.org). Leicester Square tube/Charing Cross tube/rail. **Box office** 10am-8pm Mon-Sat. **Tickets** £3-£66; day tickets on sale to personal callers after 10am Mon-Sat; by phone from 12.30pm Mon-Sat. **Credit** AmEx, DC, MC, V. **Map** p401 L7.
The beautiful, spacious Coliseum is home to the English National Opera (ENO) for most of the year and is usually visited by major dance companies over summer and at Christmas, but no dance is scheduled between mid January and late 2002 because of restoration work.

The Place
17 Duke's Road, Somers Town, WC1 (7380 1268/www.theplace.org.uk). Euston tube/rail. **Box office** 10.30am-6pm Mon-Fri; noon-6pm Sat. **Tickets** £5-£15. **Credit** MC, V. **Map** p399 K3.
This dance venue has had a £7-million renovation that has made it more accessible to both students and audiences. Top-notch professional training is available, as well as classes in all genres for all levels. The 300-seat theatre programmes high-quality international contemporary dance. The 2002 season kicks off with Resolution!, an annual platform for up-and-coming artists (7 Jan-16 Feb). Other highlights are Canada's striking Compagnie Marie Chouinard (26-27 Mar) and Dance Umbrella (*see p288* **Dance festivals**).

Riverside Studios
Crisp Road, Hammersmith, W6 (8237 1000/box office 8237 1111/www.riversidestudios.co.uk). Hammersmith tube. **Box office** noon-9pm daily. **Tickets** £7-£18. **Credit** MC, V.
This leading arts and media centre occasionally hosts British contemporary dance and physical theatre in three auditoria.

Royal Opera House
Bow Street, Covent Garden, WC2 (box office 7304 4000/enquiries 7240 1200/textphone 7212 9228/www.royaloperahouse.org). Covent Garden tube. **Box office** 10am-8pm Mon-Sat. **Tickets** £3-£155. **Credit** AmEx, DC, MC, V. **Map** p401 L7.

Sadler's Wells
Great performance possibilities in a wonderfully modern theatre. *See p287.*

The Place
This terrific contemporary dance centre has had a facelift. *See above.*

Dance Umbrella
Excitingly eclectic, and one of London's best arts festivals. *See p288.*

Arts & Entertainment

Prima ballerina: Darcey Bussell at the **ROH**.

This magnificent theatre is no longer strictly the preserve of ballet classics and the moneyed elite. In addition to the main stage, home to the Royal Ballet, the building now houses two much more affordable spaces: the Linbury Studio Theatre, a handsome space seating up to 420 people, and the Clore Studio Upstairs, used for rehearsals, workshops, events, and small-scale or experimental performances. Ticket prices were cut following the refurbishment, although the best seats remain horrendously pricey.

The Royal Ballet's standards of performance and programming can be variable, but you still can see stars of the calibre of Tamara Rojo, Darcey Bussell and Johan Kobborg. The coming season includes John Cranko's *Onegin* (Jan-Feb and July-Aug) and guest artist Sylvie Guillem in *Marguerite & Armand* (Jan-Feb). The rest of the season balances traditional fare with more modern work from European hotshots William Forsythe and Nacho Duato (Mar, Apr and July-Aug), plus Mats Ek's vivid take on *Carmen*. Birmingham Royal Ballet returns with two programmes in May.

The Linbury is earning a reputation as a leading mid-scale West End venue for music and dance. Programming responsibility for the Linbury and Clore now lies with ex-Royal dancer Deborah Bull.

Sadler's Wells

Rosebery Avenue, Islington, EC1 (7863 8000/ textphone 7863 7863/www.sadlers-wells.com). Angel tube. **Box office** 10am-8.30pm Mon-Sat. **Tickets** £7-£35. **Credit** AmEx, MC, V. **Map** 402 N3. **Peacock Theatre**, *Portugal Street, off Kingsway, Holborn, WC2 (7863 8222/www.sadlers-wells.com). Holborn*

tube. **Box office** noon-8.30pm performance days, 10am-6pm when no performances Mon-Sat. **Tickets** £8.50-£30. **Credit** AmEx, MC, V. **Map** p399 M6.
Sadler's Wells attracts world-class companies to its ultra-modern theatre. The 2002 season begins with Germany's influential Pina Bausch (31 Jan-3 Feb). Other highlights are Cuadra de Sevilla in a flamenco theatre *Carmen* (18-26 Feb); resident company Random working with Jim Henson's Creature Workshop on *Nemesis* (1, 2 Mar); *Moonwater* from Taiwan's Cloud Gate Dance Theatre (28 May-1 June); and hot young contemporary flamenco dancer Eva La Yerbabuena (9-14 July).

The considerably smaller Lilian Baylis Theatre, also in Islington, showcases younger or smaller-scale companies. The Wells retains a second venue, the Peacock Theatre in Holborn, for longer runs of more populist fare. The legendary Lindsay Kemp kicks off the 2002 season with *Dreamdances* (29 Jan-9 Feb). Later on there's flamenco guitarist Paco Pena's dance company (6 Oct-9 Nov).

South Bank Centre

Belvedere Road, South Bank, SE1 (box office 7960 4242/recorded info 7921 0682/www.sbc.org.uk). Embankment tube/Waterloo tube/rail. **Box office** 10am-9pm daily. **Tickets** £5-£60. **Credit** AmEx, DC, MC, V. **Map** p401 M8.
This huge arts complex hosts regular shows by both British and international dance companies at its three venues: the massive Royal Festival Hall, the medium-sized Queen Elizabeth Hall and the smaller Purcell Room. Highlights for 2002 include the rousing Adzido Pan-African Dance Ensemble (12-16 Feb) and a major new work from resident choreographer Akram Khan (11, 12 May), a collaboration with musician Nitin Sawhney and sculptor Anish Kapoor. In August the SBC hosts Summer on the South Bank. Some higher-profile Dance Umbrella artists appear here as well. For both, *see p288* **Dance festivals**; for more on the South Bank Centre, *see p312*.

Stratford Circus

Theatre Square, E15 (8279 1000/www.stratford-circus.org.uk). Stratford tube/rail/DLR. **Box office** 11am-6pm or 30min after show starts Mon-Sat. **Tickets** £10; £3-£5 concessions. *Go-card* £24 (6 shows). **Credit** MC, V.
Dance is a key part of this new east London arts centre's programme, which has four performance spaces and involved British and international artists. The 2002 schedule includes Shobana Jeyasingh's company (1-2 Feb), and, later in the year, the Cholmondeleys and the Featherstonehaughs.

Other venues

Chisenhale Dance Space

64-84 Chisenhale Road, Bow, E3 (8981 6617/ www.chisenhaledancespace.co.uk). Bethnal Green or Mile End tube. **Open** Box office 10am-6pm Mon-Sat. **Tickets** free-£4. **No credit cards**.

Dance festivals

Held over a five-week stretch from early October and currently in its 24th year, **Dance Umbrella** (8741 5881/ www.danceumbrella.co.uk) is one of the world's top contemporary dance festivals. It features a stimulating mix of proven British and international companies, as well as a number of lesser-known discoveries, at a range of venues.

The fifth **BITE** season, which opens in July 2002, brings a wide-ranging programme of theatre, dance and music to the Barbican Centre (*see p286*). This year's treats include a visit by Deborah Colker, the irrepressible Brazilian.

Each August the South Bank Centre (*see p287*) presents **Summer on the South Bank**, Britain's biggest and most diverse community dance festival, and a cornucopia of free dance performances, lectures and workshops.

The Place (*see p286*) is the place to be in January and February, for **Resolution!**, a six-week showcase of nightly triple-bills. It's a hit-and-miss yet lively affair. The Friday/Saturday (and occasional Sunday) gigs incorporate Aerowaves into the schedule, featuring top European artists and companies.

A seminal research centre for contemporary dance and movement-based disciplines of an experimental nature. It also runs workshops and a summer school.

Jacksons Lane Dancebase
269A Archway Road, Highgate, N6 (8341 4421/ www.jacksonslane.org.uk). Highgate tube. **Open** 10am-10pm daily. **Tickets** varies depending on show; £4-£9. **Credit** MC, V.
This community centre puts on lots of performances and activities, including contemporary dance.

Laban Centre
Laurie Grove, New Cross, SE14 (8692 4070/ www.laban.co.uk). New Cross tube/rail. **Open** 8.30am-5.30pm Mon-Fri; 9am-3.30pm Sat, Sun. **Tickets** £6.50; £5 concessions. **No credit cards**.
This independent conservatory for contemporary dance training and research runs undergraduate and postgrad courses, dance classes, short courses and Easter and summer schools. It regularly presents the work of Transitions, its resident company, and performances by contemporary choreographers. The Laban's new £22-million home beside Deptford Creek in Lewisham is being designed by Herzog & de Meuron, the Swiss firm behind Tate Modern (*see p79*), and is set to open in early autumn 2002.

Dance classes

Cecil Sharp House
English Folk Dance and Song Society, 2 Regent's Park Road, NW1 (7485 2206/www.efdss.org). Camden Town tube. **Open** *Enquiries* 9.30am-5.30pm Mon-Fri. **Classes** £5-£8.50. **No credit cards**.
Social dances, day workshops and classes in Cajun, clog, morris, Scottish ceilidh and more.

Dance Attic
368 North End Road, Fulham, SW6 (7610 2055). Fulham Broadway tube. **Open** 9am-10pm Mon-Fri; 10am-5pm Sat, Sun. **Membership** £1.50/day; £30/6mths; £50/yr. **Classes** £3-£6. **No credit cards**. **Map** p396 A12.
Dance Attic offers a wide range of classes for all levels of ability, including ballet, lambada and hip hop; membership is required.

Danceworks
16 Balderton Street, Mayfair, W1 (7629 6183/ www.danceworks.co.uk). Bond Street tube. **Open** 8am-10.15pm Mon-Fri; 9am-6.15pm Sat, Sun. **Membership** £1-£4/day; £40/mth; £99/yr. **Classes** £4-£7. **Credit** MC, V. **Map** p398 G6.
Danceworks runs a variety of classes including contemporary, salsa, ballet, funky street jazz and fitness. Day or annual membership is required.

Drill Hall
16 Chenies Street, Fitzrovia, WC1 (7307 5060/ www.drillhall.co.uk). Goodge Street tube. **Open** 10am-9.30pm Mon-Sat; 11am-6pm Sun. **Courses** £25-£60. **Credit** AmEx, MC, V. **Map** p399 K5.
This central fringe venue runs classes in Latin American, tango, lindy hop, t'ai chi, yoga and more.

Greenwich Dance Agency
Borough Hall, Royal Hill, Greenwich, SE10 (8293 9741). Greenwich rail/DLR. **Open** *Enquiries* 9.30am-5.30pm Mon-Fri. **Classes** £3.75-£5. **No credit cards**.
Professional-level contemporary classes, workshops and intensives run by established artists.

London School of Capoeira
Units 1 & 2, Leeds Place, Tollington Park, Finsbury Park, N4 (7281 2020). Finsbury Park tube/rail. **Classes** 7-9pm Mon, Wed-Fri. **Fees** *Beginners' course* (4 lessons) £75; £65 concessions; £60 under-18s. **No credit cards**. **Map** p399 K3.
Capoeira is a fusion of dance, gymnastics and martial arts. Free demonstration sessions are held every Friday (7-9pm), and introductory workshops take place every month.

Pineapple Dance Studio
7 Langley Street, Covent Garden, WC2 (7836 4004/www.pineapple.uk.com). Covent Garden tube. **Open** 9am-9.30pm Mon-Fri; 9.30am-6pm Sat. **Membership** £1-£4/day; £50-£100/yr. **Classes** £4-£6. **Credit** AmEx, MC, V. **Map** p399 L6.
Pineapple offers a wide choice of classes, with an emphasis on ballet, jazz and commercial genres.

Film

Keep your eyes peeled for London's vast array of cinematic offerings from around the globe.

Like just about everywhere else in western Europe, London has seen many of its cinemas transformed into US-style multiplexes. Though sometimes, as in the case of the awesome 1,943-seat screen at the **Odeon Leicester Square** (*see p290*), this can enhance the cinematic experience (especially if you're watching a big Hollywood blockbuster), all too often it results in tiny cinemas that owe their awkward shape to the fact that they were carved out from one big auditorium.

Having said all this, London is a great city for catching films in terms of the variety on offer, though prices are high, particularly in the West End, where you'll rarely see change from a tenner (except at the wonderful cheapie **Prince Charles**, which is now also famous for its Sing-along-a-Sound-of-Music evenings; *see p293*). For fans of old classics or new but smaller-scale or foreign productions, the **National Film Theatre** (*see p293*) is one of the best rep cinemas in Europe, while the **Everyman** (*see p291*) and the **Ritzy** (*see p292*) offer a welcome change from the flat-packed norm. Sadly, 2001 saw the sudden demise of the arty Lux Centre in Hoxton due to a massive rent increase, but staff are adamant that it will be revived in a new location before too long.

For cinema news and full details on screenings in London, see *Time Out*'s weekly listings and reviews. Films released in the UK are classified under the following categories: **U** – suitable for all ages; **PG** – open to all, parental guidance is advised; **12** – no one under the age of 12 is admitted; **15** – no one under 15 is admitted; **18** – no one under 18 is admitted.

Cinemas

First-run cinemas

First-runs range from multiplexes such as the **Warner Village West End** and **UCI Whiteleys** to the **Metro** and **Renoir**, which devote themselves to artier new releases, and from big chains such as **UGC** to independents along the lines of the **Ritzy** and the **Tricycle**. Prices vary greatly, but generally, the closer you are to Leicester Square the more you pay (many cinemas charge less if you go on Mondays or before 5pm from Tuesday to Friday; call them

for the times of their 'Early shows' in our listings below). Book ahead if you're planning to see a blockbuster on the weekend of its release (new films emerge in the UK every Friday).

The City

Barbican *Silk Street, EC2 (information 7382 7000/bookings 7638 8891/www.barbican.org.uk). Barbican tube/Moorgate tube/rail.* **Screens** 2. **Tickets** £6.50; £5 concessions. *Monday shows* £4. **Credit** AmEx, MC, V. **Map** p402 P5.

Bloomsbury & Fitzrovia

Odeon Tottenham Court Road *Tottenham Court Road, W1 (0870 505 0007/ www.odeon.co.uk). Tottenham Court Road tube.* **Screens** 3. **Tickets** £8; £5 concessions. *Early shows* £5. **Credit** AmEx, DC, JCB, MC, V. **Map** p399 K5.

Renoir *Brunswick Centre, Brunswick Square, WC1 (7837 8402). Russell Square tube.* **Screens** 2. **Tickets** £6.80. *Early shows* £4.50; £3 concessions. **Credit** MC, V. **Map** p401 L4.

The hills are alive at the **Prince Charles**. *See p293.*

Arts & Entertainment

Marylebone

Odeon Marble Arch *10 Edgware Road, W2 (0870 505 0007/www.odeon.co.uk). Marble Arch tube.* **Screens** 5. **Tickets** £8; £5.50 concessions (select times). *Early shows £5.50.* **Credit** AmEx, MC, V. **Map** p395 F6.

Screen on Baker Street *96 Baker Street, NW1 (info 7486 0036/bookings 7935 2772/ www.screencinemas.co.uk). Baker Street tube/ Marylebone tube/rail.* **Screens** 2. **Tickets** £6.80. *Early shows £4.* **Credit** MC, V. **Map** p398 G5.

Mayfair & St James's

Curzon Mayfair *38 Curzon Street, W1 (7465 8865). Green Park or Hyde Park Corner tube.* **Screens** 1. **Tickets** £7.50; £4-£5 concessions (select times). *Early shows £5.* **Credit** AmEx, MC, V. **Map** p400 H8.

ICA Cinema *Nash House, The Mall, SW1 (info 7930 6393/bookings 7930 3647/www.ica.org.uk). Piccadilly Circus tube/Charing Cross tube/rail.* **Screens** 2. **Tickets** £6.50; £5.50 concessions. *Early shows £4.50. Membership £15-£25/yr, allows £2 off all tickets.* **Credit** AmEx, DC, MC, V. **Map** p401 K8.

Odeon Panton Street (formerly ABC) *Panton Street, SW1 (0870 505 0007/www.odeon.co.uk). Piccadilly Circus tube.* **Screens** 4. **Tickets** £7.50; £4 concessions (select times). *Early shows £4.50.* **Credit** AmEx, MC, V. **Map** p401 K7.

Plaza *17-25 Lower Regent Street, W1 (0870 010 2030/www.uci-cinemas.co.uk). Piccadilly Circus tube.* **Screens** 4. **Tickets** £6; £4 concessions. *Early shows £4.* **Credit** AmEx, MC, V. **Map** p401 K7.

UGC Haymarket *63-5 Haymarket, W1 (0870 907 0712). Piccadilly Circus tube.* **Screens** 3. **Tickets** £8.50; £5-£6 concessions (select times). **Credit** AmEx, MC, V. **Map** p401 K7.

UGC Trocadero *Trocadero, WC2 (0870 907 0716). Leicester Square or Piccadilly Circus tube.* **Screens** 7. **Tickets** £8.50; £5-£6 concessions (select times). **Credit** AmEx, MC, V. **Map** p401 K7.

Soho & Leicester Square

Curzon Soho *93-107 Shaftesbury Avenue, W1 (info 7439 4805/bookings 7734 2255). Leicester Square or Piccadilly Circus tube.* **Screens** 3. **Tickets** £8; £5 concessions (select times). *Early shows £5.* **Credit** AmEx, MC, V. **Map** p401 K6.

Empire *Leicester Square, WC2 (08700 102030/ www.uci-cinemas.co.uk). Leicester Square or Piccadilly Circus tube.* **Screens** 3. **Tickets** £7.50-£8.50; £5-£5.50 concessions (select times). *Early shows £5-£6.* **Credit** AmEx, MC, V. **Map** p401 K7.

Metro *Rupert Street, W1 (info 7437 0757/bookings 7734 1506/www.metrocinema.co.uk). Leicester Square or Piccadilly Circus tube.* **Screens** 2. **Tickets** £6.50; £4 concessions (select times). *Early shows & Mon £4.* **Credit** MC, V. **Map** p401 K7.

Odeon Leicester Square *Leicester Square, WC2 (0870 505 0007/www.odeon.co.uk). Leicester Square tube.* **Screens** 6. **Tickets** £10-£11. *Early shows £6-£6.50.* **Credit** AmEx, MC, V. **Map** p401 K7.

Odeon Mezzanine *next to Odeon Leicester Square, WC2 (0870 505 0007/www.odeon.co.uk). Leicester Square tube.* **Screens** 5. **Tickets** £8. *Early shows £5.* **Credit** AmEx, MC, V. **Map** p401 K7.

On location: Kubrick's London

Stanley Kubrick was the last of the truly great Hollywood film directors, a man you could mention in the same breath as Hitchcock, John Ford, John Huston and Billy Wilder. Uniquely, he was able to command total control over his films, the production companies allowing him carte blanche despite the fact that the films were usually late and seldom brought in the kind of revenue that financial bigwigs want to see in Tinseltown.

Kubrick was a true auteur. He would select his scriptwriter and expect to see pages while the screenplay was being fashioned, more often than not requesting that they be faxed to his Hertfordshire retreat. But being the perfectionist he was, he would badger the writer to hone the script until it fitted his vision. Many a scriptwriter has bemoaned the co-credit Kubrick awarded himself after the completion of the final draft.

Perhaps unusually for a director of international repute, Kubrick – especially in his later films, when his influence was

becoming unquestionable – would stress the need for UK-based locations, regardless of how exotic the sites in the source material might be. This wasn't down to some munificent gesture to save the film companies money; rather, it was due to a chronic fear of flying. Kubrick no longer went to Hollywood; Hollywood came to him. A gadget freak, he must have kitted out his study like the control room at NASA. He didn't see the need for travel when global communication was at one's fingertips.

Kubrick's location managers probably didn't see it in such black and white terms. You can imagine the nervous looks that financiers of Kubrick's epic Vietnam flick *Full Metal Jacket* (1987) cast each other when the great man insisted that the film be shot in England. But he pulled it off. Gallions Reach, the site of the old Beckton Gas Works in east London (*see p163*), was perfect for the desolate, bullet-ridden battlegrounds of the Far East. *A Clockwork Orange* (1971) also benefited

Odeon Swiss Centre *10 Wardour Street, W1 (0870 505 0007/www.odeon.co.uk). Leicester Square or Piccadilly Circus tube.* **Screens** 4. **Tickets** £7.50; £4.50 concessions (select times). *Early shows* £4.50. **Credit** AmEx, MC, V. **Map** p401 K7.

Odeon West End *Leicester Square, WC2 (0870 505 0007/www.odeon.co.uk). Leicester Square tube.* **Screens** 2. **Tickets** £10; £6 concessions (select times). *Early shows* £6. **Credit** AmEx, JCB, MC, V. **Map** p401 K7.

Warner Village West End *Leicester Square, WC2 (08702 406020/www.warnervillage.co.uk). Leicester Square tube.* **Screens** 9. **Tickets** £11; £5-£7 concessions (select times). *Early shows* £7. **Credit** MC, V. **Map** p401 K7.

Covent Garden & St Giles's

Odeon Covent Garden *135 Shaftesbury Avenue, WC2 (0870 505 0007/www.odeon.co.uk). Leicester Square or Tottenham Court Road tube.* **Tickets** £8; £5 concessions (select times). *Early shows* £5. **Screens** 4. **Credit** AmEx, MC, V. **Map** p399 K6.

Chelsea & South Kensington

Chelsea Cinema *206 King's Road, SW3 (7351 3742). Sloane Square tube.* **Screens** 1. **Tickets** £7-£8. *Early shows* £5; £3 concessions. **Credit** AmEx, MC, V. **Map** p397 E12.

UGC Chelsea *279 King's Road, SW3 (0870 907 0710). Sloane Square tube then 11, 19, 22 bus.* **Screens** 4. **Tickets** £8.20; £4.50 concessions. **Credit** AmEx, MC, V. **Map** p397 E12.

North London

Everyman Hampstead *5 Hollybush Vale, Hampstead, NW3 (info 7431 1818/bookings 7431 1777/www.everymancinema.com). Hampstead tube.* **Screens** 1. **Tickets** £7.50 (£12 luxury); £5 concessions (select times). *Early shows & Mon* £5. **Credit** MC, V.

Odeon Camden *14 Parkway, Camden, NW1 (0870 505 0007/www.odeon.co.uk). Camden Town tube.* **Screens** 5. **Tickets** £7; £4-£4.50 concessions (select times). **Credit** AmEx, MC, V.

Odeon Swiss Cottage *96 Finchley Road, Swiss Cottage, NW3 (0870 505 0007/www.odeon.co.uk). Swiss Cottage tube.* **Screens** 6. **Tickets** £7; £4.50-£5 concessions (select times). *Early show* £4.50. **Credit** AmEx, MC, V.

Phoenix *52 High Road, Finchley, N2 (info 8883 2233/bookings 8444 6789). East Finchley tube.* **Screens** 1. **Tickets** £4-£6; £3.50-£4 concessions (select times). *Early shows* £3.50-£4.50. **Credit** MC, V.

Screen on the Green *83 Upper Street, Islington, N1 (7226 3520/www.screencinemas.co.uk). Angel tube.* **Screens** 1. **Tickets** £6.80. *Early shows* £4.50. **Credit** MC, V. **Map** p402 O2.

Screen on the Hill *203 Haverstock Hill, Belsize Park, NW3 (7435 3366/www.screencinemas.co.uk). Belsize Park tube.* **Screens** 1. **Tickets** £6.80. *Early shows* £4.50. **Credit** MC, V.

Tricycle Cinema *269 Kilburn High Road, Kilburn, NW6 (info 7328 1900/bookings 7328 1000/www.tricycle.co.uk). Kilburn tube.* **Screens** 1. **Tickets** £7; £6 concessions (select times). *Early shows* £4.50; £3.50 concessions. **Credit** MC, V.

Kubrick's final film *Eyes Wide Shut* (1999; *pictured*), though set in New York, was filmed in the United Kingdom, with those battered Big Apple streets replicated in a Borehamwood studio. The key interior scenes at the masked ceremony were shot over ten days in the sumptuous Royal Suite at the Lanesborough Hotel, Hyde Park Corner, where a one-night stay will cost you more than £5,000 (*see p62* **Rock hotels**). Soho club Madam JoJo's (*see p279*) became a louche New York jazz club; Greenwich Village was fashioned out of Hatton Garden (*see p100*), London's exclusive diamond quarter (the climax of this part of the film, where Tom Cruise is pursued by a shadowy figure, took place on Worship Street, EC2, not a million miles from Liverpool Street Station, where part of *Mission: Impossible* was filmed – Cruise must be getting to know east London quite well); and the final scene was shot in Hamleys toyshop on Regent Street.

from London's atmospheric locations: the notorious scene in which Alex and his 'Droogs' beat up a tramp was filmed in a shopping centre subway in the Thamesmead housing estate (*see p164*).

East London

Rio Cinema *107 Kingsland High Street, Dalston, E8 (7254 6677/www.riocinema.org.uk). Dalston Kingsland rail/30, 38, 56, 76, 149, 242, 243, 277 bus.* **Screens** 1. **Tickets** £6.50; £5 concessions. *Early shows* £4.50; £3.50 concessions. **Credit** MC, V.

South London

Clapham Picture House *76 Venn Street, Clapham, SW4 (info 7498 2242/bookings 7498 3323/www.picturehouse-cinemas.co.uk). Clapham Common tube.* **Screens** 4. **Tickets** £6.50. *Early shows* £5; concessions £4. **Credit** MC, V.
Greenwich Cinema *180 Greenwich High Road, Greenwich, SE10 (info 01426 919020/bookings 8293 0101/www.networkcinemas.com). Greenwich rail.* **Screens** 3. **Tickets** £5.75; £4 concessions (select times). *Early shows* £4.30. **Credit** MC, V.
Ritzy *Brixton Oval, Coldharbour Lane, Brixton, SW2 (info 7737 2121/bookings 7733 2229). Brixton tube/rail.* **Screens** 5. **Tickets** £6.50; £2.50-£3.50 concessions. *Early shows* £4.50. **Credit** MC, V.
UGC Fulham Road *142 Fulham Road, Chelsea, SW10 (0870 907 0711). South Kensington tube.* **Screens** 6. **Tickets** £8.20; £4.50 concessions (select times). *Early shows* £4.50. **Credit** AmEx, MC, V. **Map** p397 D11.

West London

Gate Cinema *87 Notting Hill Gate, Notting Hill, W11 (7727 4043). Notting Hill Gate tube.* **Screens** 1. **Tickets** £7; £3.50 concessions (select times). *Early shows* £4. **Credit** MC, V. **Map** p394 A7.
Notting Hill Coronet *103-5 Notting Hill Gate, Notting Hill, W11 (7727 6705). Notting Hill Gate tube.* **Screens** 2. **Tickets** £6.50; £4 concessions (select times). *Early shows* £4. **Credit** MC, V. **Map** p394 A7.
Odeon Kensington *263 Kensington High Street, Kensington, W8 (0870 505 0007/ www.odeon.co.uk). High Street Kensington tube.* **Screens** 6. **Tickets** £8.20; children £5.20. *Early shows (before 3pm)* £5.20. **Credit** AmEx, MC, V. **Map** p396 A9.
UCI Whiteleys *2nd floor, Whiteleys Shopping Centre, Queensway, Bayswater, W2 (0870 010 2030/ www.uci-cinemas.co.uk). Bayswater or Queensway tube.* **Screens** 8. **Tickets** £8; £4-£5 concessions (select times). *Early shows* £5.75. **Credit** AmEx, MC, V. **Map** p394 C6.

Repertory & art house cinemas

The old classics never die, and this is where you'll find them, along with new movies that haven't managed to secure a commercial release and all manner of mad underground flicks. In addition to the cinemas listed below, several cinemas listed above in the First-run section offer a more limited selection of rep-style fare, including the **Curzon Soho**, **Phoenix**, **Rio**, **ICA Cinema** and **Ritzy**. Conversely, the **Watermans Arts Centre** (40 High Street,

Brentford, Middx, 8232 1010), scheduled to reopen in spring 2002, shows new releases alongside its repertory selections.

A welcome revitalisation of the scene came about in 2001 with the rebirth of the Electric in Portobello (*see p293* **Electric dreams**). If you're looking for something truly small-scale, call the **Charlotte Street Hotel** (*see p48*) for details of its 'Big Chill' Sunday night film club showing classics ranging from *A Streetcar Named Desire* to *Grease*.
Ciné Lumière *Institut Français, 17 Queensberry Place, South Kensington, SW7 (7838 2144/2146/ www.institut.ambafrance.org.uk). South Kensington tube.* **Screens** 1. **Tickets** £6; £4.50 concessions; £4 members. *Membership* £18/yr. **Credit** MC, V. **Map** p397 D10.
Electric Cinema *191 Portobello Road, Ladbroke Grove, W11 (info 7727 9958/bookings 7229 8688/www.the-electric.co.uk). Ladbroke Grove*

or Notting Hill Gate tube. **Screens** 1. **Tickets**
£6.50-£7.50; £4 concessions. *Early shows* £4.
Credit MC, V.
National Film Theatre (NFT) *South Bank,
SE1 (info 7633 0274/bookings 7928 3232/
www.bfi.org.uk/nft). Embankment tube/
Waterloo tube/rail.* **Screens** 3. **Tickets** £6.85;
£5.25 concessions. *Membership* £11-£15.95/yr,
allows £1 off all tickets. **Credit** AmEx, MC, V.
Map p401 M7.
Prince Charles *7 Leicester Place, Leicester
Square, WC2 (today's films 7734 9127/
week's films 0901 272 7007 premium rate/
www.princecharlescinema.com). Leicester Square
or Piccadilly Circus tube.* **Screens** 1. **Tickets**
£1.75-£3.50 non-members; £1.50-£2.50 members.
Membership £5/yr. **Credit** MC, V. **Map** p401 K7.
Riverside Studios *Crisp Road, Hammersmith,
W6 (8237 1111/www.riversidestudios.co.uk).
Hammersmith tube.* **Screens** 1. **Tickets** £5.50;
£4.50 concessions. **Credit** MC, V.

Bollywood cinemas

Boasting what some contend is the biggest
film industry in the world (in terms of output;
it releases about 900 films a year), Bollywood
is famous for its long, racy potboilers and
all-singing, all-dancing romances. Among the
following cinemas, the Grade II-listed Himalaya
Palace, which has just been restored to its 1920s
glory, is especially noteworthy.
Cineworld Wood Green *Shopping City,
High Street, Wood Green, N22 (8829 1400/
www.cineworld.co.uk). Wood Green tube.* **Tickets**
£5; £3.50 concessions; *Early shows* £3 (before 6pm
& Tue); £1 Kids Club (10am Sat). **Credit** MC, V.
Cineworld Feltham *Leisure West, Air Park Way,
Feltham, Middx (8867 0555/www.cineworld.co.uk).
Feltham rail.* **Tickets** £5.70-£6; £4 concessions.
Early shows £4 (before 5pm); £3.70 Tue; £1 Kids Club
(Sat). **Credit** MC, V.

Electric dreams

The multiplex is swiftly taking over the
planet, and these days a night out at the
cinema offers you more film choices than
you'd find dishes on an à la carte menu.
Once upon a time it was queues around the
block, breathtakingly amateurish local ads,
'Patrons are reminded that the right-hand
side of the auditorium is designated no
smoking', a short film, a woman with a tray
of ice-creams, a feature film and the debate
over whether to plump for the orange or mint
Matchmakers. Some of us preferred it that
way. One huge screen that contained your
idols was somehow better than the shrunken
canvases in claustrophobic rooms that you
find in many cinemas now.

Perhaps it's such waves of nostalgia
that have brought the Electric Cinema on
Portobello Road back to life. Arguably the
oldest surviving purpose-built cinema in
the UK, it was designed by Gerald Seymour
Valentin, whose vision for the building was
based on the popular music halls of the
time, the logical environment in which to
view silent films. Although his plans for the
cinema weren't followed rigidly, perhaps due
to construction costs, it nevertheless boasted
some beautiful features, including a picture
frame around the screen, a vaulted ceiling
and an entrance hall with terrazzo flooring.
Built in one of the most popular west London
shopping zones, it opened to the public on
Christmas Eve 1910. It had a capacity of 600
(including standing room), and sometimes the

images on the screen would be accompanied
by music – a piano was situated at the front
of the auditorium. For a while, the Electric
was very popular.

But times changed. Newer, larger cinemas
such as the Odeons and Ritzes sprang up in
the 1930s, hoovering up the Electric's
clientele (a decade or so later, incidentally, it
had as its reserve projectionist John Christie,
one of Britain's most notorious serial killers).
Portobello Road's exclusive status went
south, and by the 1960s it was a fleapit,
stuck in the middle of a street market in what
had developed into a dodgy area.

The Electric, however, has proved to be
a bit of a stayer. The '70s and '80s saw it
ticking over as a repertory cinema run by
Peter Simon, who, despite a string of
different owners and various failed facelifts,
has remained connected with the Electric
ever since, like a concerned parent nursing
a sick child through to recovery. It is
Simon's finances (he founded his fashion
empire, the Monsoon Group, from a stall
outside the cinema) that meant the Electric
could enjoy a new lease of life, and a Grade
II-listed status. The number of seats has
been reduced to 240, but they are big and
comfortable and there are even some
leather armchairs on the back row for those
with more than just the film on their mind.
Nice to know that in this day and age of
70mm, Dolby surround-sound and CGI,
some things haven't changed at all.

The best Cinemas

For Hollywood blockbusters
Odeon Leicester Square (*see p290*).

For underground weirdness
ICA Cinema (*see p290*).

For classics on a Sunday afternoon
Curzon Soho (*see p290*).

For decor
Curzon Mayfair (*see p290*);
Electric (*see p292*).

For modern architecture buffs
Renoir (*see p289*).

For a big, big screen
BFI London Imax (*see p294*).

For French chic
Ciné Lumière (*see p292*).

For smokers
Notting Hill Coronet (*see p292*).

For great value
Prince Charles (*see p293*).

For free film fun
Rushes Soho Shorts Festival (*see p294*).

Himalaya Palace *14 South Road, Southall, Middx* (*8813 8844*). *Southall rail.* **Tickets** £4 Mon-Thur; £6 Fri-Sun; £3.50 concessions. **Credit** MC, V
Safari Cinema, Harrow *Station Road, Harrow, Middx (8426 0303). Harrow & Wealdstone tube/rail.* **Tickets** £6; £4 concessions. *Early show* £3.50 (before 5pm Tue-Fri). **Credit** AmEx, JCB, MC, V.
Safari Cinema, Croydon *193 London Road, Croydon, Surrey (8688 3422). West Croydon rail.* **Tickets** £5; £4 concessions; £3.50 Tue. **Credit** AmEx, JCB, MC, V.
Boleyn Cinema *11 Barking Road, Newham E10 (8471 4884).* **Tickets** £5; £3.50 Wed. **Credit** MC, V.
Uxbridge Odeon *The Chimes Shopping Centre, Uxbridge, Middx (0870 505 0007/www.odeon.co.uk).* **Tickets** £5.50; £3.50 concessions. *Early show* £4. **Credit** AmEx, MC, V.
Ilford Cinema, *300-310 High Road, Ilford, Essex (8514 4400).* **Tickets** £5. *Early show & Wed* £3.50. **Credit** MC, V.

IMAX

The IMAX cinema in the Wellcome Wing of the **Science Museum** (*see p140*) has a capacity of 450 and is only accessible to museum visitors. The 480-seater **BFI London IMAX Cinema** on the South Bank boasts the biggest film screen in the country.

BFI London IMAX Cinema *1 Charlie Chaplin Walk, South Bank, SE1 (7902 1234/ www.bfi.org.uk/imax). Embankment tube/Waterloo tube/rail.* **Screens** 1. **Tickets** £6.95; £4.95-£5.95 concessions; free under-3s. **Credit** AmEx, MC, V. **Map** p401 M8.
Science Museum IMAX Theatre *Exhibition Road, South Kensington, SW7 (0870 870 4868/ www.sciencemuseum.org.uk). South Kensington tube.* **Screens** 1. **Tickets** *Before 4.30pm museum & film* £12.50; £9 students; £5.75 concessions. *After 4.30pm museum* free. *Film* £6.75; £5.75 concessions. **Credit** AmEx, MC, V. **Map** p397 D9.

Festivals

London Lesbian & Gay Film Festival
National Film Theatre, South Bank, SE1 (7928 3232/www.llgff.org.uk/www.bfi.org.uk). Embankment tube/Waterloo tube/rail. **Dates** 3-17 April 2002. **Map** p401 M7.
More than 186 new and restored films from around the world, plus a range of special events.

Rushes Soho Shorts Festival
venues around Soho, W1 (7851 6207/ www.sohoshorts.com). Leicester Square, Piccadilly Circus or Tottenham Court Road tube. **Dates** 27 July-2 Aug 2002. **Map** p398, p399.
Around 60 short films, music videos and idents by new directors are screened for free at venues across Soho, from cafés to cinemas.

BFM International Film Festival
Various venues in London (8531 9199/ www.bfmfilmfestival.com). **Dates** 6-15 Sept 2002.
The fourth *Black Filmmaker*-programmed festival shows a variety of work both inside and outside the mainstream.

Latin American Film Festival
Metro, Rupert Street, Chinatown, W1 (7434 3357/ www.latinamericanfilmfestival.com/). Leicester Square or Piccadilly Circus tube. **Dates** 6-19 Sept 2002. **Map** p401 K7.
This festival offers a range of new movies from Latin America each autumn.

Raindance
Metro, Rupert Street, Chinatown, W1 (7287 3833/ www.raindance.co.uk). Leicester Square or Piccadilly Circus tube. **Date** Oct 2002 (check website for exact dates). **Map** p401 K7.
Britain's largest indie film festival concentrates on first-time directors.

London Film Festival
venues around London (7928 3232/www.lff.org.uk). **Date** Nov 2002 (check website for exact dates).
The biggest film festival in the UK, now in its 46th year, is a broad church; for further details, *see p267.*

Galleries

It's never say die for London's small-scale art venues.

That two key gallery closures announced within a few weeks of each other in summer/autumn 2001 failed to prick the confidence bubble of the London art scene demonstrates its irrepressible vitality. Shortly after Mayfair's Anthony D'Offay put up the closing-down signs, Hoxton's Lux admitted it had lost the fight to keep up with spiralling rents – cinema, workshop and gallery were felled in a single blow. Victim of its own success, you might say, but the loss of the Lux will be felt long after the ripple effect of D'Offay's retirement has ceased to be felt. Also closed for redevelopment in 2001 was Delfina Project Space on Southwark Street, SE1; the Delfina Studio Café and residency programme remain in action at 50 Bermondsey Street, SE1, but as far as exhibitions and shows are concerned, that's it for Delfina for the foreseeable future.

Still, many of the existing galleries continue to put on interesting shows, and new spaces are opening up like buds in spring. Those listed below are a representative sample, but only a sample. Check these out first, but don't assume

that smaller, more out-of-the-way galleries will show work that's any less rewarding. As for bigger, more celebrated spaces, you'll find them listed in the relevant sighteeing chapters of the guide. These include the **Barbican Art Gallery** (*see p95*), **Camden Arts Centre** (*see p147*), the **Courtauld Gallery** and the **Hermitage Rooms** (*see p97*), the **Dulwich Picture Gallery** (*see p171*), the **Hayward Gallery** (*see p74*), the **ICA** (*see p131*), the **National Gallery** (*see p130*), the **Royal Academy** (*see p114*), the **Saatchi Gallery** (*see p146*), the **Serpentine Gallery** (*see p137*), **Tate Britain** (*see p134*), **Tate Modern** (*see p79*) and the **Whitechapel Art Gallery** (*see p156*).

Be aware that some of the galleries listed below close in August; many also have little to see, if they're open at all, between shows, so do phone ahead or check any websites before setting out. *Time Out* magazine has weekly art listings, as well as reviews of new shows. A free brochure, New Exhibitions of Contemporary Art, can be picked up at most galleries or viewed online at www.newexhibitions.com.

Art space: Jay Jopling's **White Cube²**. *See p299.*

Galleries

For vision and ambition
Matt's Gallery. See p299.

For a reliably interesting programme
Photographers' Gallery. See p300.

For good use of a limited space
Percy Miller Gallery. See p299.

Central

Eagle

159 Farringdon Road, Farringdon, EC1 (7833 2674). Farringdon tube/rail. **Open** 11am-6pm Wed-Fri; 11am-4pm Sat; also by appointment. **Credit** AmEx. **Map** p402 N4.
An excellent space located upstairs from the gastropub of the same name (see p100). A highlight in 2001 was the fine Rock Drawings of Jacqueline Jeffries. Other recent exhibitors have included Tom Hammick and Andrew Bick.

Entwistle

6 Cork Street, Mayfair, W1 (7734 6440/ info@entwistle.net). Green Park or Piccadilly Circus tube. **Open** 10am-5.30pm Tue-Sat. **Credit** MC, V. **Map** p400 J7.
Situated in the heart of Mayfair, Entwistle may have young American and British artists as its speciality, but one of the most interesting exhibitions that it hosted in 2001 was by the Austrian Constanze Ruhm, whose *A Memory of the Players in a Mirror at Midnight* took the interior architecture of Irving Kerschner's 1978 film *The Eyes of Laura Mars* as its starting point.

Frith Street

60 Frith Street, Soho, W1 (7494 1550/ www.frithstreetgallery.co.uk). Tottenham Court Road tube. **Open** 10am-6pm Wed-Fri; 11am-4pm Sat. **No credit cards. Map** p399 K6.
Providing a haven from the hectic pace of Soho, Frith Street's interlinked rooms have hosted some truly excellent shows in recent years. Dayanita Singh's black and white photos of Indian interiors worked well in 2001.

Gagosian

8 Heddon Street, Mayfair, W1 (7292 8222/ www.gagosian.com). Oxford Circus or Piccadilly Circus tube. **Open** 10am-6pm Tue-Sat; by appointment Mon. **No credit cards. Map** p400 J7.
This immaculate space has polished stone floors, plus a basement with some smaller rooms. Pop artist John Wesley's paintings were among the shows put on in 2001.

Lisson

52-4 Bell Street, Marylebone, NW1 (7724 2739/ www.lissongallery.com). Edgware Road tube. **Open** 10am-6pm Mon-Fri; 10am-5pm Sat. **Credit** MC, V. **Map** p395 E5.
Among the top five galleries in the whole of London, Marylebone's Lisson boasts a beautiful space (designed by Tony Fretton) and an impressive list of artists, including Douglas Gordon, Jane and Louise Wilson, and Francis Alys.

Sadie Coles HQ

35 Heddon Street, Mayfair, W1 (7434 2227/ www.sadiecoles.com). Oxford Circus or Piccadilly Circus tube. **Open** 10am-6pm Tue-Sat. **No credit cards. Map** p400 J7.
In 2001 John Bock's incomprehensible sculptures made out of old clothes came with a video of the artist explaining his work. None the wiser, we still enjoyed the light and airy first-floor space with its south-facing windows.

Stephen Friedman

25-8 Old Burlington Street, Mayfair, W1 (7494 1434/www.stephenfriedman.com). Green Park or Piccadilly Circus tube. **Open** 10am-6pm Tue-Fri; 11am-5pm Sat. **No credit cards. Map** p399 K6.
Stephen Friedman represents an interesting variety of international artists, including Yinka Shonibare, Vong Phaophanit, David Shrigley and Nikki S Lee.

Waddington Galleries

11 Cork Street, Mayfair, W1 (7437 8611/ www.waddington-galleries.com). Green Park or Piccadilly Circus tube. **Open** 10am-5.30pm Mon-Fri; 10.30am-1.30pm Sat. **No credit cards. Map** p400 J7.
US artist Peter Halley's colourful abstract paintings brightened up Cork Street here in 2001. Waddington Galleries remains one of the major dealers in town.

White Cube

44 Duke Street, St James's, SW1 (7930 5373/ www.whitecube.com). Green Park or Piccadilly Circus tube. **Open** 10am-6pm Tue-Sat. **Credit** AmEx, MC, V. **Map** p400 J7.
Gavin Turk, Sam Taylor-Wood, Marc Quinn, Jake & Dinos Chapman, Mona Hatoum, Damien Hirst: White Cube trades in household names these days, having been instrumental in helping to make them so. This Duke Street space is smaller than the newer White Cube[2] (see p299).

Zwemmer Gallery

1st floor, 24 Litchfield Street, Covent Garden WC2 (7240 4158/www.zwemmer.com). Leicester Square tube. **Open** 11am-6.30pm Tue-Sat. **Credit** AmEx, MC, V.
Just because this tiny gallery is located directly upstairs from the excellent bookshop of the same name (see p233) should not be taken as an indication that it's immune from art bollocks, as James Hyde's *Aircushion*, a giant, inflated painted canvas completely filling the room, showed in 2001.

East

Anthony Wilkinson Gallery

242 Cambridge Heath Road, Bethnal Green, E2 (8980 2662/www.anthonywilkinsongallery.com). Bethnal Green tube. **Open** 11am-6pm Thur-Sat; noon-6pm Sun; also by appointment. **No credit cards.**

An excellent space that's well worth the trip out of town. George Shaw's superb hyper-realistic paintings of the housing estate where he grew up showed here in 2001; it was his second solo exhibition at the gallery.

The Approach

1st floor, Approach Tavern, 47 Approach Road, Bethnal Green, E2 (8983 3878). Bethnal Green tube. **Open** noon-6pm Thur-Sun; also by appointment. **No credit cards.**

The Approach gallery is an extremely pleasant, airy room located above an equally pleasant Bethnal Green pub. Among the artistic highlights in 2001 was an exhibition of deceptively simple figurative paintings by Finnish artist Mari Sunna, who is currently based in London.

Chisenhale Gallery

64 Chisenhale Road, Bow, E3 (8981 4518/www.chisenhale.org.uk). Bethnal Green or Mile End tube/D6, 8, 277 bus. **Open** 1-6pm Wed-Sun; also by appointment. **No credit cards.**

In 2001 Shen Yuan recreated the entire rooftop of a traditional Chinese house in the Chisenhale Gallery, incorporating typical smells and sounds; it would be hard to create a more lifelike representation without offering gallery-goers air tickets to Beijing. At the other extreme, the gallery has shrewdly co-commissioned an Internet work from London artist Mike Nelson, whose love of labyrinths should make the Net an ideal location for his art (*see below* **A full Nelson**).

Flowers East

199-205 Richmond Road, Hackney, E8 (8985 3333/www.flowerseast.com). Bethnal Green tube or Hackney Central rail then 106, 253 bus. **Open** 10am-6pm Tue-Sat. **Credit** AmEx, MC, V.

Painting dominates at Flowers East – and indeed at its two other spaces: Flowers Central, a recent addition to the Mayfair scene at 21 Cork Street, W1, and Flowers West, which is in Santa Monica, so a little

A full Nelson

If Mike Nelson's installation, *Nothing is true, everything is permitted*, in autumn 2001 was a bit of an anticlimax for Nelson-watchers, that was only because his two previous works were outstanding. His transformation of Matt's Gallery (*see p299*) into *The Coral Reef* in spring 2000 and subsequent appearance at the Venice Biennale with *The Deliverance and the Patience* meant that whatever the London artist did next would have to be truly extraordinary. The fact that his next show happened to be at the ICA (*see p131*) was perhaps unfortunate: it seems to have proved a difficult space to re-imagine, less willing than Matt's Gallery to offer itself up as a blank canvas.

For *The Coral Reef*, a ground-breaking work that nevertheless drew on and appeared to evolve from his earlier installations both in the UK and on the Continent, Nelson built a disorienting warren of passageways and doorways, antechambers and waiting rooms, car workshops, druggie squats, minicab offices and hotel lobbies that stimulated the gallery-goer's imagination almost to excess, so that one stumbled from room to room in a state of growing deliriousness. The fictional possibilities were endless, each space suggesting its own narrative while at the same time encouraging different interpretations. By creating a double room at the end of the labyrinth, Nelson

Truth and illusion: Nelson's **ICA** show.

ensured that your experience would conclude with a shock that was as visceral as it was psychologically profound. It messed with your mind in a similar way to the fiction writers he constantly references in his work – HP Lovecraft, Stanislaw Lem, Jorge Luis Borges.

Shortlisted for the Turner Prize in 2001, Nelson found himself a favourite to win. This guide went to press before the announcement, and while we wish Nelson the very best of luck and believe he's without doubt the most exciting and challenging artist on the list, we somehow can't quite picture this reticent, biker jacket-clad artist popping up on live TV to receive the award from, of all people, Madonna.

Arts & Entertainment

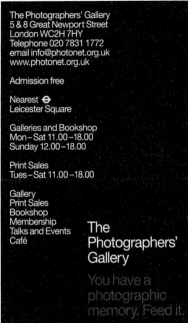
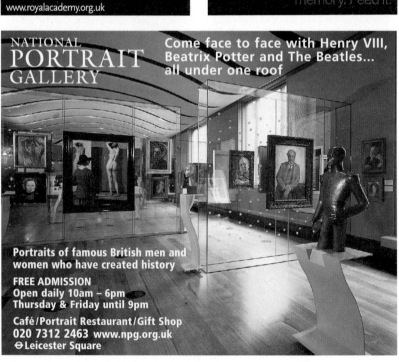

outside of this guide's remit. John McLean, Henry Kondracki, Tai-Shan Schierenberg and Rachel Heller were among those exhibiting in 2001.

Gallery Westland Place
13 Westland Place, Hoxton, N1 (7251 6456/ www.westlandplace.co.uk). Old Street tube/rail. **Open** 8am-6pm Mon-Fri. **Credit** MC, V.
A gorgeous gallery with exposed brick walls that shares ground-floor space with a friendly, relaxed café and extends into the basement. Photographer Rut Blees Luxemburg showed her potent, ominous long exposures of night-time London here.

Interim Art
21 Herald Street, Bethnal Green, E2 (7729 4112). Bethnal Green tube. **Open** 11am-6pm Thur-Sun; also by appointment. **No credit cards**. **Map** p403 R3.
Maureen Paley provides a temporary home for UK and US artists, and for UK artists who have also exhibited widely in the States, such as Paul Noble, whose large-scale pencil drawings of structures located in his fictitious new town, Nobson, make essential viewing.

Matt's Gallery
42-4 Copperfield Road, Mile End, E3 (8983 1771/ www.mattsgallery.org). Mile End tube. **Open** noon-6pm Wed-Sun; also by appointment. **No credit cards**.
One of the most ambitious galleries in the city, Matt's allowed itself to be transformed into a mind-boggling warren of antechambers, truncated corridors and doubled rooms in Mike Nelson's The *Coral Reef* (2000), his strongest work to date (*see p297* **A full Nelson**). It also hosted Daily Hayley, performance art inspired by the news, which just goes to show that no gallery is perfect.

The Millinery Works
85-7 Southgate Road, Islington, N1 (7359 2019/ www.milleryworks.co.uk). Old Street tube/rail then 76, 141 bus. **Open** 11am-6pm Tue-Sat; noon-5pm Sun. **Credit** AmEx, MC, V.
Not strictly east, but just east of north, the Millinery Works puts on an eclectic programme of exhibitions. Painters feature, although not exclusively, including those inclined to both abstract and figurative work: in 2001 Michael Peckham's paintings confused the boundary between the two. Most notable in recent years have been the hallucinatory anatomical paintings of Susan Rosenberg, horrors located somewhere on a scale between Francis Bacon and Barry Burman.

The Showroom
44 Bonner Road, Bethnal Green, E2 (8983 4115/ www.theshowroom.org). Bethnal Green tube. **Open** 1-6pm Wed-Sun. **No credit cards**.
Artists often make work specifically for the unusual triangular space at the Showroom, but Dave Allen, in 2001, was not one of them; instead he created studio 'recordings' and other riffs on the technology of music production.

Victoria Miro
16 Wharf Road, Islington, N1 (7336 8109/ www.victoria-miro.com). Angel tube/Old Street tube/rail. **Open** 10am-6pm Tue-Sat. **Credit** AmEx. **Map** p402 P3.
This huge converted Victorian factory is one of the most fabulous art spaces anywhere. Responsible for launching the careers of Chris Ofili, Jake and Dinos Chapman and Peter Doig, as well as introducing hot overseas talent to a British audience, the Victoria Miro is always worth keeping an eye on.

Wapping Project
Wapping Hydraulic Power Station, Wapping Wall, Wapping, E1 (7680 2080/www.wapping-wpt.com). Wapping tube. **Open** noon-11pm Tue-Sat; noon-6pm Sun. **Credit** AmEx, DC, MC, V.
This magnificent converted hydraulic power station was intended to attract those working with film, video and the digital arts. Finnish artist Elina Brotherus's 2001 show was its first large-scale video and photographic commission.

White Cube²
48 Hoxton Square, Hoxton, N1 (7930 5373/ www.whitecube.com). Old Street tube/rail. **Open** 10am-6pm Tue-Sat. **Credit** AmEx, MC, V. **Map** p403 R3.
Jay Jopling's eastern outpost is a symbol of all that's good and bad about the faux bohemianisation of Hoxton – a moribund district was revitalised, but rents rose and the lovely Lux was forced to close.

South

Hales Gallery
70 Deptford High Street, Deptford, SE8 (8694 1194/ www.halesgallery.com). New Cross tube/Deptford Bridge DLR/Deptford rail. **Open** 9am-5pm Mon-Sat. **Credit** AmEx, DC, MC, V.
Hales represents, among other artists, Spencer Tunick, Judith Dean, Ben Ravenscroft and Danny Rolph, whose vivid abstract paintings were aired in a solo show here in 2001.

Jerwood Space
171 Union Street, Bankside, SE1 (7654 0171/ www.jerwoodspace.co.uk). Borough or Southwark tube. **Open** *during exhibitions* 10am-6pm daily (phone to check). **No credit cards**. **Map** p404 O8.
Still operating the Jerwood Sculpture Prize and associated exhibition, the Jerwood no longer has a programme of curated shows, which is a shame, because it's a fine space.

Percy Miller Gallery
39 Snowsfields, Bankside, SE1 (7207 4578/ www.percymillergallery.com). London Bridge tube/rail. **Open** 11am-6pm Tue-Fri; noon-4pm Sat. **No credit cards**. **Map** p405 Q9.
This likeable little gallery is divided into two distinct spaces: the ground floor is used for exhibitions, such as the joint show in autumn 2001 by Tom Chamberlain (abstract paintings that play optical

tricks) and Tracey Rowledge (found texts reproduced on paper and leather); in the basement you'll find works by other artists, including, if you're lucky, photographs by Philippine Hoegen and David Spero.

South London Gallery

65 Peckham Road, Camberwell, SE5 (7703 9799/ www.southlondongallery.org). Oval tube then 36 bus/Elephant & Castle tube/rail then 12, 171 bus. **Open** 11am-6pm Tue, Wed, Fri; 11am-7pm Thur; 2-6pm Sat, Sun. **No credit cards.**

A fascinating gallery with an ambitious, eclectic programme that's always worth checking out. Among 2001's highlights was the exhibition of film and video by Norwegian artist Anne Katrine Dolven – a trained painter, she makes direct reference to Edvard Munch in her video work.

Other spaces

Further spaces listed in the sightseeing chapters include the **Design Museum** (*see p82*), the **Geffrye Museum** (*see p156*), the **Museum of London** (*see p94*) and the **V&A** (*see p140*).

Architectural Association

36 Bedford Square, Fitzrovia, WC1 (7887 4000/ www.arch-assoc.org.uk). Tottenham Court Road tube. **Open** 10am-7pm Mon-Fri; 10am-3pm Sat. **Credit** *Shop* MC, V. **Map** p399 K5.

Talks, events, discussions and exhibitions: four good reasons for visiting the elegant premises of the Architectural Association.

British Cartoon Centre

7 Brunswick Centre, Bernard Street, Bloomsbury, WC1 (7278 7172/www.cartooncentre.com). Russell Square tube. **Open** 10am-6pm Tue. **Credit** MC, V. **Map** p402 N5.

With two premises in the Brunswick Centre, which is currently being revamped, this is an essential stop for anyone interested in the art form. The excellent Skoob Books (*see p233*) is in nearby Russell Square.

Crafts Council

44A Pentonville Road, Islington, N1 (7278 7700/ www.craftscouncil.org.uk). Angel tube. **Open** 11am-6pm Tue-Sat; 2-6pm Sun. **Credit** AmEx, MC, V. **Map** p402 N2.

The Council showcases the nation's craft output in a range of fields. Shows often take a theme and demonstrate work in that area. The finalists of the Jerwood Applied Art Prize: Jewellery are shown in autumn.

Royal Institute of British Architects

66 Portland Place, Marylebone, W1 (7580 5533/ www.architecture.com). Oxford Circus or Regent's Park tube. **Open** 9am-6.30pm Mon-Fri; 9am-5pm Sat. **Credit** MC, V. **Map** p398 H5.

Based in a monumental edifice built by Grey Wornham in 1934 (*see p32*), RIBA has a gallery that both celebrates the profession's great and good and checks emerging architecture from around the world. RIBA also hosts a programme of discussions.

Photography

Photofusion

17A Electric Lane, Brixton, SW9 (7738 5774/ www.photofusion.org). Brixton tube/rail. **Open** 10am-6pm Tue, Thur, Fri; 10am-8pm Wed; 10am-6pm Sat. **Credit** MC, V.

The gallery at Photofusion, which is London's largest independent photography resource centre, puts on regular shows that are always worth trip down to Brixton. A highlight of the 2001 programme was Eulogy to Beauty, an eclectic catalogue of female representation.

Photographers' Gallery

5 & 8 Great Newport Street, Covent Garden, WC2 (7831 1772/www.photonet.org.uk). Leicester Square tube. **Open** 11am-6pm Mon-Sat; noon-6pm Sun. **Membership** £30/yr; £20/yr concessions. **Credit** AmEx, DC, MC, V. **Map** p401 K6.

A giant among photography galleries, this space hosts 24 shows a year while doing a ton of work to promote photography around the country. With its long opening hours and excellent programme, the Photographers' Gallery is always a good bet for a spontaneous visit.

Shine Gallery

3 Jubilee Place, Chelsea, SW3 (7352 4499/ www.shinegallery.co.uk). Sloane Square or South Kensington tube. **Open** noon-6pm Tue-Sat; by appointment Mon. **Credit** AmEx, MC, V.

This small second-floor white space, located above the Hulton Getty Picture Library (7376 4525) and Michael Hoppen Photography (7352 3649) on the ground and first floors respectively, specialises in cutting-edge, 21st-century photography. A top-drawer exhibition in summer 2001, Light Matters, featured Florencia Durante, Renata Hegyi, Nahako Kudo and Neil Reddy.

Special Photographers Company

21 Kensington Park Road, Notting Hill, W11 (7221 3489/www.specialphotographers.com). Ladbroke Grove or Notting Hill Gate tube. **Open** 10am-6pm Mon-Thur; 10am-5.30pm Fri; 11am-5pm Sat. **Credit** AmEx, MC, V. **Map** p394 A6.

A highlight of the Special Photographers Company 2001 calendar was the exhibition by the American photographer Robert Mann, whose mysterious and sometimes apocalyptic black and white prints seem to bathe the viewer in their own glow.

Zelda Cheatle Gallery

99 Mount Street, Mayfair, W1 (7408 4448/ photo@zcgall.demon.co.uk). Bond Street or Green Park tube. **Open** 10am-6pm Tue-Fri; 11am-4pm Sat. **Credit** AmEx, MC, V. **Map** p400 G7.

The Angus McBean show in 2001 was typical of the high standards set and always met by this specialist in the exhibition and sale of vintage and contemporary photography.

Arts & Entertainment

Gay & Lesbian

Whether you're an all-out scene-queen, a lipstick lesbian or just a queer movie buff, we show you how to navigate London's ever-expanding gay scene.

London's gay scene grows ever larger and more commercial as the queer community squeezes itself more and more obviously into the mainstream. Hardly a month seems to go by without a new venue opening, and Soho in particular – especially around Old Compton Street – is becoming more and more colonised by high-concept, high-energy gay drinking dens.

Similarly, the political climate has changed dramatically. The age of consent for gay men is finally in line with that for straight people (16) and the beginning of a second term of office for Labour has triggered a political explosion of 'sensitive' and 'open' policies from all sides of the political spectrum. Not only is being a gay MP fairly old news, but it's increasingly difficult to find a representative of a mainstream political party who will say anything anti-queer (whatever their private views on the subject).

And still the media's love affair with all things pink continues – over the last year prime-time television series have examined relationships between gay men and straight women, a gay musical, *Closer to Heaven*, has opened (and closed), and the TV phenomenon that is *Big Brother* has trapped two very different queens in a secluded house with no access to hair products or *EastEnders*.

Yet all is not necessarily well in the gay state, – a rush of commercialisation has made central London less of a supportive, community-based place for gay people, and more of an endless party zone. If you're looking for sex, drink and fun around the centre, you're unlikely to be disappointed – there's something for everyone and it's reasonably easy to get your hands on. But if you're looking to meet new people or make new friends, then London's gay village can appear huge, money driven, fashion obsessed and desperately impersonal.

The annual Mardi Gras festival is a good example of this trend – the Gay Pride march increasingly plays second fiddle to gay-friendly bands promoting their Greatest Hits albums at the 'main event'. And inside the festival itself, community stalls and social organisations seem more and more sidelined (*see p306* **Whatever happened to? Gay Pride**).

If you get tired of the spectacle and excitement of the centre and pine for something more convivial, you can still find pockets of friendly folk drinking at their local pubs and bars outside of the centre. There are smaller gay venues all over the city – they can be more sedate, but for many of London's gay citizens they are a home from home. And they can also be a good place to visit when you first arrive in the city – chat to some locals and you may soon find yourself tagging along to some of London's best nights out in the company of your new friends.

If that's not your cup of tea, there are events in the gay calendar that may help you meet people with similar interests. For gay film-goers, the annual **London Lesbian & Gay Film Festival** (*see p294*) at the National Film Theatre is a great opportunity to meet other

The big city lights of **Old Compton Street**.

film-obsessed queers. Another way to meet up with people is through online personal ad websites such as **www.gaydar.co.uk**. Unexpectedly for a site that was designed to help gay men find no-strings sex, gaydar can be quite effective at bringing together people with interests that extend beyond the bedroom. More importantly, if you are travelling from outside the UK, you can talk to people online before you arrive – hopefully helping you find people to spend time with when you're here. Other websites with good community areas include **www.gingerbeer.co.uk** for lesbian visitors and **uk.gay.com**.

For up-to-the-minute information on events in and around London, as well as a comprehensive list of local venues across the city, you can't go far wrong with a copy of *Time Out* tucked under your arm. There are also a number of gay magazines that will help you find what's cool in the capital; some are free (*Boyz*, *QX*) and can be picked up in most gay venues, others (*Attitude*, *Fluid* and *Diva*) are more lifestyle oriented and are available in newsagents.

Clubs

Before you look any further, you should be aware that club nights come and go in London at a tremendous speed. Apart from the staples, such as **G.A.Y.** (*see p303*), **Heaven** (*see p303*) and **Popstarz** (*see p303*), almost any of the events listed below could disappear without warning. Call ahead if you're new in town, or wander around some of the Soho bars, where you'll find the latest happenings advertised and listed in free papers such as *QX* and *Boyz*.

Clubbing in London is never cheap – you can expect to pay in excess of £10 for the most fashionable places, and that's before you factor in the often inflated drinks prices. And when you fall out of the club, you'll probably have to get a taxi (although, if you can stand to wait, London's network of night buses may get you home in one piece; *see p358*).

Atelier
The End, 18 West Central Street, St Giles's, WC1 (7419 9199/www.the-end.co.uk). Holborn or Tottenham Court Road tube. **Open** *Club* 10pm-4am Thur. **Admission** £5; free w/flyer before 11pm. **No credit cards. Map** p399 L6.
From the people who brought you Coco Latte, Atelier is a trendy night with laid-back house for a well-dressed gay crowd.

Beaver
Oak Bar, 79 Green Lanes, Newington Green, N16 (7354 2791). Manor House tube/141, 341 bus. **Open** *Club* 9pm-2am 2nd Sat of mth. **Admission** £5; £4 concessions. **No credit cards.**

Taking the stage at **Heaven**. *See p303*.

Retro-girls love the funk and indie that's played at this monthly lesbian night at the Oak Bar. Men are welcome as guests only.

Crash
Arch 66, Goding Street, Vauxhall, SE11 (7820 1500/www.crashlondon.co.uk). Vauxhall tube/rail. **Open** *Club* 10.30pm-6am Sat. **Admission** £10; £5 w/flyer before midnight. **Credit** AmEx, DC, MC, V.
The south London club of choice for Muscle Marys, Crash is arranged over four bars and has two dance-floors and two chill-out areas. Sexy fun for men.

Dolly Mixtures
Candy Bar, 23-4 Bateman Street, Soho, W1 (7437 1977/www.candybar.easynet.co.uk). Tottenham Court Road tube. **Open** *Club* 9pm-3am Sat. **Admission** £5. **Credit** *Bar only* MC, V.
Girls' party night for the sexy and precocious at London's premier lesbian venue.

DTPM
Fabric, 77A Charterhouse Street, Clerkenwell, EC1 (7439 9009/www.dtpm.net). Barbican tube/ Farringdon tube/rail. **Open** *Club* 10pm-late Sun. **Admission** £12; £8 concessions, members. **Credit** *Bar only* MC, V. **Map** p402 O5.
Soul, jazz, R&B, hip hop and disco arranged over three floors for DTPM's 'polysexual' devotees, most of whom look like firm, bare-chested young men.

Exilio Latino
Houghton Street, Holborn, WC2 (7731 3342/07931 374391 mobile/www.exilio.co.uk). Holborn tube. **Open** *Club* 10pm-3am Sat. **Admission** £6; £5 w/flyer, students. **No credit cards. Map** p399 M6.
A popular, relaxed gay salsa night with a happy mixed crowd of all ages.

Factor 25
Hanover Grand, Hanover Street, W1 (7499 7977/ www.hanovergrand.com). Oxford Circus tube. **Open** 10.30pm-5am Sat. **Admission** £12; £10 members. **Credit** *Bar only* MC, V. **Map** p398 6J.
House and funk over two rooms for muscular men, in a popular venue that encourages stylish dress.

Fiction

The Cross, King's Cross Goods Yard, off York Way, King's Cross, N1 (7439 9009/www.dtpm.net). King's Cross tube/rail. **Open** *Club* 11pm-late Fri. **Admission** £12; £8 before 11.30pm. **Credit** *Bar only* MC, V. **Map** p399 L2.

Another DTPM (*see p302*) mixed 'polysexual' crowd enjoys progressive house and mellow moods.

Fist

Imperial Gardens, 299 Camberwell New Road, SE5 (7252 6000/www.fist.co.uk). Bus 36, 185. **Open** 10pm-6am 2nd Sat of mth. **Admission** £13; £8 members. **No credit cards**.

This monthly fetish club is a well-attended, mixed affair with a darkroom, gallery and fully stocked 'playroom' for people of specific tastes. The dress code is strict, with leather, rubber, skin-gear and uniform the order of the day. Regular erotic performances take place here.

G.A.Y.

Astoria & Mean Fiddler, 157 Charing Cross Road, Soho, WC2 (7734 6963/premium rate 0906 100 0160/www.g-a-y.co.uk). Tottenham Court Road tube. **Open** *Club* 10.30pm-4am Mon, Thur; 11pm-4am Fri; 10.30pm-5am Sat. **Admission** £3-10; reductions w/flyer. **Map** p399 K6.

Probably London's landmark gay night out, G.A.Y. is unpretentious fun for hundreds of mainly young men and their (straight) female friends. Mondays and Thursdays are Pink Pounder nights with cheap drinks and entry, Friday is the larger-scale Camp Attack, and Saturdays feature guest appearances by pop princesses such as Kylie and Atomic Kitten.

Heaven

The Arches, Villiers Street, Charing Cross, WC2 (7930 2020/www.heaven-london.com). Embankment tube/Charing Cross tube/rail. **Open** 10.30pm-3am Mon, Wed; 10.30pm-5am Fri; 10pm-5am Sat. **Admission** £1-£12. **Credit** AmEx, DC, MC, V. **Map** p401 L7.

A London institution with three main rooms, each of which plays variations on the 'theme of the night'. Popcorn (Mondays) and Fruit Machine (Wednesdays) offer upbeat early-week fun, while Fridays are house-focused 'There' nights attracting a mix of straight Antipodeans, Japanese club-kids and gay men. But it's Saturday nights when Heaven lives up to its name, with commercial house and a diverse crowd of gay party boys.

Popstarz

Scala, 275 Pentonville Road, King's Cross, N1 (7833 2022/www.popstarznightclub.com). King's Cross tube/rail. **Open** *Club* 10pm-5am Fri. **Admission** £8; £7 w/flyer after 11pm; £5 members; £4 students before 11pm, £5 after. Free for all before 11pm w/flyer. **Credit** MC, V. **Map** p399 L3.

Popular with students and the indie crowd, Popstarz has maintained its position as the premier club night for less scene-oriented boys and girls. The large main floor plays classic alternative and Britpop tunes to a bouncy, scruffy crowd, while the chill-out bar plays cooler tunes for those who need a break. The most amusing feature is the always crowded Rubbish Room – it's like G.A.Y. but with a healthy dose of irony, so be prepared for Dolly Parton and Bananarama 'classics'.

Substation South

9 Brighton Terrace, Brixton, SW9 (7737 2095). Brixton tube/rail/N2, N3, N37, N109 bus. **Open** 10pm-3am Mon; 10.30pm-2am Tue; 10.30pm-3am Wed; 10.30pm-late Thur; 10.30pm-5am Fri; 10.30pm-6am Sat; 10pm-late Sun. **Admission** £3-£10. **No credit cards**.

Undeniably a club that gets straight to the point, Substation South is about hot and sweaty, down and dirty, sexy ways to spend your evenings. Monday is underwear-only night with Y-front; Tuesday is Sub FC, for those who have a penchant for sportswear; Wednesday is pure uniform, leather, rubber and boots at Boot Camp; Thursday is for hot and hard cruising; Friday is Dirty Dishes, with funky house attitude; and Saturday brings Queer Nation, with New York style house and garage. The grinding only rests on Sunday, when cheap and cheerful indie kids take charge for the night with Marvellous.

Arts & Entertainment

The best Gay nights out

For the gay 'eating experience'
Balans (*see p308*).

For a friendly, fun evening out
Escape Bar (*see p304*).

For camp value
Krystals (*see p306*).

For cabaret
Two Brewers (*see p307*).

For drooling (women)
Candy Bar (*see p304*).

For drooling (men)
Crash (*see p302*).

For dirty, dirty boys
Boot Camp at **Substation South** (*see p303*).

For a conversation
Upstairs at **The Yard** (*see p308*).

Cheap thrills at the **Glass Bar**. See p305.

Trade

*Turnmills, 63B Clerkenwell Road, Clerkenwell,
EC1 (7700 5352/www.tradeuk.net). Farringdon
tube/rail.* **Open** *Club* 4.30am-late Sun. **Admission**
£15; £12 w/flyer; £10 members. **No credit cards.**
Map p402 N4.

Commencing just before sunrise, Trade is for the
toned and tanned, not the faint-hearted. One of
London's clubbing institutions, it's been going for
11 years and shows no sign of flagging. Hard
sounds, harder bodies, cavernous rooms and a
cruisy atmosphere predominate.

Up

*Rhythm Factory, 16-18 Whitechapel Road,
Whitechapel, E1 (7375 3774). Aldgate East or
Whitechapel tube.* **Open** *Club* 10pm-4am every other
Sat. **Admission** £10; £8 members; £7 before 11pm
w/flyer; £5 w/token. **No credit cards. Map** p405 S6.
This fortnightly club offers deep and progressive
house to a good-looking crowd.

Pubs & bars

Most of London's bars are open to gay men and
lesbians. In our reviews below, we've tried to
indicate where a given place has less to offer
either male or female party-goers.

Admiral Duncan

*54 Old Compton Street, Soho, W1 (7437 5300).
Leicester Square tube.* **Open** noon-11pm Mon-Sat;
noon-10.30pm Sun. **Credit** AmEx, MC, V.
Map p399 K6.

This small, traditional gay pub was made notorious
after a homophobic bomb attack in 1999. But it made
a valiant recovery and is once again a popular con-
tributor to the Old Compton Street scene. Expect a
slightly older, down-to-earth, male clientele.

Barcode

*3-4 Archer Street, Soho, W1 (7734 3342/www.bar-
code.co.uk). Piccadilly Circus tube.* **Open** 1pm-1am
Mon-Sat; 1-10.30pm Sun. **Admission** £3 after 11pm.
Credit MC, V. **Map** p401 K7.

Catering for relatively rough-and-ready men,
Barcode is attitude-free, cheaper than most other
Soho haunts and comes complete with a cruisy base-
ment that is open most evenings.

Black Cap

*171 Camden High Street, Camden, NW1 (7428
2721). Camden Town tube.* **Open** noon-2am
Mon-Thur; noon-3am Fri, Sat; noon-12.30am Sun.
Credit AmEx, MC, V.

Camden's gay drinking den with a split personality:
during the day the upstairs bar and beer garden are
as pub-like as they come, but in the evenings the
basement opens up for drag shows and partying.

Brompton's

*294 Old Brompton Road, Earl's Court, SW5 (7370
1344). Earl's Court tube.* **Open** 8pm-2am Mon-Sat;
6pm-midnight Sun. **Admission** £3 after 11pm Mon-
Thur; £3 after 10.30pm Fri, Sat; £2 after 10.30pm
Sun. **Credit** MC, V. **Map** p396 B11.

Two bars and a cabaret stage make Brompton's a
popular destination for men.

Candy Bar

*23-4 Bateman Street, Soho, W1 (7437 1977/
www.candybar.easynet.co.uk). Tottenham Court Road
tube.* **Open** 5pm-1am Mon, Tue; 5pm-3am Thur, Fri,
Sat; 5pm-midnight Sun. **Admission** £5 after 9pm
Fri, Sat; £3 after 10pm Thur. **Credit** *Bar only* MC, V.
Map p399 K6.

London's leading gay women's establishment is
popular with lesbians, bisexual women and their
male guests. Regular DJs and extended opening
hours are part of the appeal.

Compton's of Soho

*53-5 Old Compton Street, Soho, W1 (7479 7961/
www.comptons-of-soho.co.uk). Piccadilly Circus tube.*
Open noon-11pm Mon-Sat; 11am-10.30pm Sun.
Credit MC, V. **Map** p399 K6.

If cruising, shaved heads and bomber jackets are
your cup of tea, you can't go far wrong at Compton's.

The Edge

*11 Soho Square, Soho, W1 (7439 1313). Tottenham
Court Road tube.* **Open** noon-1am Mon-Sat; 1-10.30pm
Sun. **Credit** AmEx, MC, V. **Map** p399 K6.

A multi-floored Soho staple for men and women,
the Edge is the ideal place to meet friends and
colleagues and to hang out – particularly in summer, when it spills out into the street. Fairly non-
cruisy, it still manages to attract some of the
better-looking residents of gay land.

Escape Bar

*10A Brewer Street, Soho, W1 (7734 2626/
www.kudosgroup.com). Leicester Square tube.*
Open 4pm-3am Mon-Sat; 3-10.30pm Sun.
Admission £2 after 11pm Tue-Sat.
Credit AmEx, MC, V. **Map** p401 K7.

Arts & Entertainment

A hidden gem of unpretentious fun in the middle of Soho, Escape attracts young gay men and women more interested in chatting, getting a bit drunk and dancing to music videos than posing, preening and trying to look butch. A refreshing change from many of its more self-conscious W1 neighbours, Escape comes highly recommended.

Freedom Café-Bar

60-66 Wardour Street, Soho, W1 (7734 0071). Leicester Square, Oxford Circus or Tottenham Court Road tube. **Open** 11am-3am Mon-Sat; noon-midnight Sun. **Admission** £3 after 11pm Mon-Thur, Sun; £5 after 10pm, £6 after 10.30pm Fri, Sat. **Credit** MC, V. **Map** p399 K6.

Though it errs more and more on the straight side of 'mixed', Freedom remains a stylish (if expensive) destination for gay men and women. As we went to press, Freedom was closed for a major refurbishment, so expect an even more polished look to be ushered in for 2001.

Friendly Society

Basement, 79 Wardour Street (entrance in Tisbury Court), Soho, W1 (7434 3805). Leicester Square, Oxford Circus or Tottenham Court Road tube. **Open** 4-11pm Mon-Fri; 2-11pm Sat; 2-10.30pm Sun. **Admission** free. **Credit** MC, V.

Early-'80s *Doctor Who* sets have nothing on this entertaining and low-lit underground bar for the 'imaginatively' stylish. The set-up includes a large bed area for lounging on.

Glass Bar

West Lodge, Euston Square Gardens, 190 Euston Road, Bloomsbury, NW1 (7387 6184/ www.glassbar.ndo.co.uk). Euston tube/rail. **Open** 5pm-late Mon-Fri; 6pm-late Sat. **Admission** £1 Mon-Sat. **No credit cards. Map** p398 J4.

Easy on the wallet, this friendly and stylish women-only venue located, atmospherically, in one of the old lodges at Euston Station, has drinks at pub prices. Dress smart-casual.

London: the new San Fran?

In 2001, announcing the introduction of a London Partnerships Register whereby lesbian and gay relationships can now be recorded (it was immediately dubbed the 'gay marriage licence'), mayor Ken Livingstone stated his aim of transforming London into a new San Francisco. But could London ever really rival San Fran's gay-friendly reputation and popularity as a destination for travelling queers, and if so, what needs to be done?

There's certainly no shortage of gay people in London, and there's no shortage of places for them to go. Every taste and style is accommodated, and it shouldn't be difficult to find a bar, club or restaurant that suits your particular attitude. There's no dearth of gay-themed entertainment either, if you're prepared to dig around a bit – London's theatreland carries good-quality drama all year around, and it isn't afraid to explore gay territory, as Mark Ravenhill's *Mother Clap's Molly House* demonstrated at the National Theatre in the second half of 2001. If it's more down-and-dirty action you're looking for, London's sauna scene has exploded to such an extent that it may even put San Francisco's to shame (*see p308* **Saunas**).

Of course, one of the most important things about visiting any city as a gay tourist is how comfortable and welcome you feel. Britain's laws about sexuality still have some slightly draconian aspects, but these are mostly fragments left over from more

reactionary times and are ignored by residents, tourists and the police. In fact, the general climate is very positive towards gay people – the age of consent has been brought in line with that for heterosexuals and the police encourage the reporting of any homophobic violence. You're unlikely to experience any trouble from the locals about being gay, either, although out of the centre it can pay to be more discreet. Within the centre, you can feel completely comfortable – taxi and minicab drivers often queue up outside gay venues to take people home, and Soho continues to be a powerful draw to gay people out looking for a good time.

Yet gay big-city tourists used to round-the-clock fun and an endless choice of places to go may find London a disappointment – like everything else in the city, most of the bars shut at around 11pm, and not many of the clubs stay open all night. Until this changes, London can never be as carefree and relaxed as San Francisco or other world-class gay destinations such as Sydney. If and when our licensing laws get a much-needed overhaul, London will be an infinitely better place to be, and that goes for everyone.

But of course, gay visitors don't only travel to visit gay places, and London has two things that neither of these other cities can offer: a wealth of history going back to the Romans; and the best place to go Queen-spotting on the planet – Buckingham Palace.

The Hoist

Railway Arch, 47B&C South Lambeth Road,
Vauxhall Cross, Vauxhall, SW8 (7735 9972).
Vauxhall tube/rail. **Open** 10pm-3am Fri;
10pm-4am Sat; 9pm-2am Sun. **No credit cards.**
A cruisy bar for men into leather, rubber and uniform
action. Leave your inhibitions at the door.

King William IV

77 Hampstead High Street, Hampstead, NW3
(7435 5747). Hampstead tube. **Open** noon-11pm
Mon-Sat; noon-10.30pm Sun. **Credit** AmEx,
DC, MC, V.
A sedate local pub with a family atmosphere (not only
for those returning from encounters on the heath).

Krystals

97 Stoke Newington Road, Stoke Newington, N16
(7254 1967/www.krystals.org). Dalston Kingsland
rail/149, 156, 243 bus. **Open** 5-11pm Mon-Fri;
1-11pm Sat; 1-10.30pm Sun. **Credit** *Bar only* MC, V.
More or less successful drag-queen action, plus occasional karaoke and quiz nights. The atmosphere and
the clientele are friendly.

Kudos

10 Adelaide Street, Covent Garden, WC2 (7379
4573/www.kudosgroup.com). Charing Cross tube/rail.
Open 11am-11pm Mon-Sat; noon-10.30pm Sun.
Credit AmEx, MC, V. **Map** p401 L7.
Two floors of fun for fashionable scene-queens (a
huge video screen plays fun pop in the evenings).

Manto

30 Old Compton Street, Soho, W1 (7494 2756/
www.mantogroup.com). Leicester Square or Piccadilly
Circus tube. **Open** noon-midnight Mon-Sat; noon-
10.30pm Sun. **Credit** AmEx, MC, V. **Map** p399 K6.
You'll need attitude and money at this popular three-
floored bar. There's a lounge bar and a decent
restaurant, while the main bar attracts a young,
fashionable mixed crowd.

Popstarz Liquid Lounge

257 Pentonville Road, King's Cross, N1
(07956 549246/www.popstarz.org). King's Cross
tube/rail. **Open** 8pm-2am Thur; 5.30pm-1am Fri;
8pm-3am Sat. **Admission** free-£5. **No credit
cards. Map** p399 M3.

Whatever happened to? Gay Pride

There had been a few stirrings and demos
before, but the first event in the UK actually
to be billed as 'Gay Pride' was held on 1
July 1972, when around 2,000 lesbians
and gay men marched down Oxford Street
protesting the unequal gay age of consent
and asking for equal rights for gay people.
In the social climate of the early '70s
this was an astonishing event, since gay
sex had only been decriminalised in the
UK four years previously. Even some gay
people disapproved of it – or at least
decided to avoid it – preferring to keep
a relatively low profile.

Thirty years later, many of the political
battles of the past decades have been
fought and won. Throughout most of its
existence, Gay Pride has been a focus
of many of these battles, becoming a
space where people could safely protest
Section 28 (a law that tried to stop local
authorities 'promoting the acceptability
of homosexuality as a pretend family
relationship') and a place where people
could fight the perception of AIDS as a
'gay disease'. But more importantly, it
existed as a space where individual gay
men and women could discover a sense
of belonging to a larger community, of
feeling 'normal', accepted, proud of
what they were rather than ashamed.

Pride, if it really still exists today at all,
has a very different flavour. Over the years,
the need to cater for ever-larger crowds has
forced the organisers to take a much more
hard-nosed commercial view of the event,
turning it into more of a festival than a
political event. In 1998, when the event
was cancelled because of administrative
problems, it seemed that Pride might
actually have finally died. And in a way it
did, because when Mardi Gras appeared
in 1999, the emphasis had turned very
firmly towards pop acts and money-making.

Today, Mardi Gras is an event comparable
with the Reading Festival or Glastonbury
(for both, *see p318* **The sounds of summer**)
and much of its grassroots enthusiasm
has gone. Instead of being a place where
individual gay people go to feel connected
and accepted, it's become an expensive
if entertaining way to drink, party and watch
gay culture's divas and pop heroes promote
their new albums. There's much to enjoy,
if you can afford the tickets, from club
tents, music stages and bars to fairgrounds
and celebrity appearances, but the true
sense of community can only really be
found in the march that happens each year
before the 'main event'.

For information on Mardi Gras 2002, check
out www.londonmardigras.com.

Boys, boys, boys: the new **Shadow Lounge** is for the starry-eyed.

The refurbishment may have made it feel more student bar than hip, post-Britpop happening, but the Liquid Lounge remains the main pre-Popstarz (*see p303*) bar of choice for indie students and rock fans.

Retro Bar

2 George Court, off Strand, Charing Cross, WC2 (7321 2811). Charing Cross tube/rail. **Open** noon-11pm Mon-Fri; 5-11pm Sat; 5-10.30pm Sun. **Credit** MC, V. **Map** p401 L7.
Unpretentious, relaxed and friendly, the Retro Bar's two floors are a good place for those tired of the style excesses of Soho. Music is '70s, '80s and alternative, and there are regular theme nights and quizzes.

Rupert Street

50 Rupert Street, Soho, W1 (7292 7141). Leicester Square or Piccadilly Circus tube. **Open** noon-11pm Mon-Sat; noon-10.30pm Sun. **Credit** AmEx, MC, V. **Map** p401 K7.
A more expensive bar for the image-conscious and professional sets. While the evenings can be over-crowded with men in suits, the atmosphere during the day is much more relaxed.

The Shadow Lounge

5 Brewer Street, Soho, W1 (7287 7988). Piccadilly Circus tube. **Open** 7pm-3am Mon-Sat. **Admission** £5 before 10.30pm, £10 after 10.30pm Fri, Sat. **Credit** AmEx, MC, V.
Popular with minor celebrities and lounge lovers, this plush new upmarket nightclub offers valet parking and cocktail waiters.

Two Brewers

114 Clapham High Street, Clapham, SW4 (7498 4971). Clapham Common tube. **Open** 4pm-2am Mon-Thur; 4pm-3am Fri, Sat; 2pm-12.30am Sun.

Admission free before 11pm, £2 after 11pm Tue-Thur; free before 9.30pm, £3 9.30-11pm, £4 after 11pm Fri, Sat; free Sun. **Credit** AmEx, MC, V.
There's something for most men – and most tastes – at south London's finest cabaret bar and club.

Vespa Lounge

Upstairs at The Conservatory Bar, 15 St Giles High Street, St Giles's, WC2 (7836 8956). Tottenham Court Road tube. **Open** 6-11pm Mon-Sat; 6-10.30pm last Sun of mth. **No credit cards. Map** p399 K6.
A centrally located, easy-to-find bar for girls and their male guests. The clientele is laid-back and stylish, although the music varies in quality.

Village Soho

81 Wardour Street, Soho, W1 (7434 2124). Piccadilly Circus tube. **Open** 4pm-1am Mon-Sat; 1-10.30pm Sun. **Admission** £2 after 11pm Fri, Sat. **Credit** MC, V. **Map** p398 J6.
Village Soho offers three floors of mostly male bar action for fun-loving, relatively attitude-free lads. The main bar features go-go boys pole-dancing on busy evenings. Upstairs is chilled, and offers a superb view over the gay strip, while the basement has a busy dancefloor.

West Central

29-30 Lisle Street, Soho, WC2 (7479 7981). Leicester Square tube. **Open** 3-11pm Mon-Sat; 3-10.30pm Sun. *Basement bar* 10.30pm-2am Wed, Thur; 10.30pm-3am Fri, Sat. **Admission** £1-£4. **Credit** MC, V. **Map** p401 K7.
This is a fun, camp bar for men, playing show tunes to theatrical types upstairs and pop tunes to a more up-for-it crowd on the ground floor. The small club in the basement is popular with the more undemanding punters.

Arts & Entertainment

The Yard

57 Rupert Street, Soho, W1 (7437 2652/
www.yardbar.co.uk). Piccadilly Circus tube.
Open noon-11pm Mon-Sat; noon-10.30pm Sun.
Credit AmEx, MC, V. **Map** p401 K7.
Summer's choice for relaxed drinking, the Yard has
a courtyard and a comfortable loft in addition to its
small, buzzy main bar. Mainly for men.

Gay cafés & restaurants

In these relatively enlightened times, you're
unlikely to encounter any prejudice in any
London restaurant. Indeed, there are some
restaurants that positively target the gay
community, and with this in mind, we've
chosen a few of what we consider to be the
most queer-friendly eateries in town. For
more on London's restaurants, *see p188*.

Balans

60 Old Compton Street, Soho, W1 (7437 5212/
www.balans.co.uk). Leicester Square or Piccadilly
Circus tube. **Open** 8am-5am Mon-Thur; 8am-6am
Fri, Sat; 8am-2am Sun. **Door charge** £2 midnight-
3am. **Credit** AmEx, MC, V. **Map** p399 6K.
A stylish and affordable brasserie serving trendy
but substantial food to a mainly gay clientele,
Balans remains the premier London restaurant for
queens and company. Its recent refurbishment
means you can no longer use the mirrors to check
out minor queer celebs on other tables, but the
food remains good, there's more space, and the
staff (also mostly gay) will cheerfully give you
relationship advice if you ask nicely.

First Out

52 St Giles High Street, St Giles's, WC2 (7240
8042). Tottenham Court Road tube. **Open**
10am-11pm Mon-Sat; 11am-10.30pm Sun.
No credit cards.
A very friendly and popular café that's more
favoured by London's gay women than men, First
Out is a wonderful day-time destination and a popular pre-club venue on Friday evenings. All the gay
magazines are at hand, the atmosphere is relaxed
and the food is healthy and tasty.

Old Compton Café

34 Old Compton Street, Soho, W1 (7439 3309).
Leicester Square tube. **Open** 24hrs daily.
No credit cards. Map p399 6K.
The Old Compton Café is a much-loved Soho staple for an almost exclusively gay clientele. The food
consists mostly of cheap and tasty sandwiches,
soups and snacks, but the atmosphere is fun and
friendly, you can sit outside in summer, and
many of the regulars are good-looking people-
watchers happy to chat (and chat up) visitors. It's
particularly good for very late-night after-clubbing
meals – expect to see drag queens with big shoes
and attitude queuing for a club sandwich while you
wait for the tube to re-open.

Saunas

London's sauna scene has exploded in the last
few years, giving thousands of gay men each
week yet another opportunity for brief sexual
liaisons. And the growing popularity of this
scene has spawned one hugely successful chain,
Chariots, and a host of smaller independent
venues, all promising an extensive and
semi-naked clientele. Check the gay press
for further listings and offers.

Chariots I

Fairchild Street, EC2 (7247 5333/
www.gaysauna.co.uk). Liverpool Street tube/rail.
Open noon-9am daily. **Admission** £13; £11
concessions. **Credit** AmEx, MC, V. **Map** p403 4R.
The centre of the Chariots empire, this Shoreditch
venue is very well equipped – there are two steam
rooms, two saunas, a Jacuzzi, a Roman-style swimming pool, dozens of private rooms, an extensive
dark area, a bar, a snack bar and a gymnasium. It's
a huge and popular destination; most evenings you'll
find hundreds of men here.

The Sauna Bar

29 Endell Street, Covent Garden, WC2 (7836 2236/
www.thesaunabar.com). Covent Garden tube.
Open noon-midnight daily. **Admission** £12;
£10 concessions. **Credit** MC, V. **Map** p399 L6.
A relatively small men-only sauna for a more discerning clientele, this Covent Garden venue contains
a small bar area, a steam room, a sauna, a splash
pool and showers, plus private rooms for those of a
less public disposition.

Accommodation

For more accommodation, *see p45*.

Accommodation Outlet

32 Old Compton Street, Soho, W1D 4TP (7287
4244/fax 7734 7217/www.outlet.co.uk). Leicester
Square tube. **Open** 10am-7pm Mon-Fri; noon-5pm
Sat. **Map** p399 K6.
This service for lesbian and gay flat-seekers, landlords and people looking for short-term holiday
accommodation can find rooms in the West End
from £45 per night.

Number Seven

7 Josephine Avenue, Brixton, SW2 (8674 1880/
www.no7.com). Brixton tube/rail. **Rooms** 4 (all
en suite). **Rates** £69-£89 single; £99-£149 double.
Credit AmEx, MC, V.
Run by friendly John and Paul (and their dog
Dougal), this small B&B in a Victorian townhouse
is clean, comfortable and quiet, though handy for
Brixton venues such as Substation South (*see p303*)
and the Fridge (*see p279*).
Hotel services *Fax. Garden. Laundry. Parking.*
Safe. **Room services** *Air-conditioning. Hairdryer.*
Radio. Refrigerator. Satellite TV. Tea/coffee.

Music

Listen up: London's music scene is one of the world's best.

Classical & Opera

It's a useful maxim that when you're having no luck, you've got to make your own. Thus, without a truly world-class composer to its name and not a whole lot of promise, a burgeoning aristocracy and a fat pile of cash did just that for London's classical music scene. From Handel to Haydn and from Mendelssohn to Mozart, there's hardly a single musical genius who didn't spend significant time in London under the patronage of the great and good. The legacy remains today in the remarkable array of orchestras, ensembles and eager young students plying their trade in and around town.

The vanguard of London's classical pedigree lies in its orchestras, four of which could easily grace any stage in the world. The London Symphony Orchestra, based at the **Barbican Centre** (*see p310*), is the pick of the bunch, and following the recent renovations to the venue's concert facilities it can look forward to an even brighter future. The LSO is closely backed up by the Philharmonia, which shares its **South Bank Centre** base (*see p312*) with the increasingly impressive London Philharmonic and the itinerant Royal Philharmonic. The **Royal Opera House** (*see p310*) and the English National Opera continue to vie for operatic supremacy, a contest that has been spiced up by the efforts of the ROH to shake off the accursed luck of the past few years, and the promise of a spruced up **London Coliseum** (*see p310*) as the ENO strives to enhance its already impressive reputation for openness and excellence.

On top of these, smaller ensembles such as the Sinfonietta, the Gabrieli Consort and the Nash Ensemble are ever active, while the city's four esteemed music colleges continue to serve up a surfeit of young talent for little or no cost – catch them in residence or in one of the smaller venues or City churches (*see p315*).

As if there wasn't enough home-grown talent, the biggest acts from around the world continue to roll into town to crack the boards of London's numerous concert halls and festival sites, while in the Proms (*see p313*) London has pretty much the best musical festival the world over in terms of both size and quality.

Bush Hall. *See p310.*

Venues

For intimacy
Bush Hall (*see below*); **12 Bar Club** (*see p322*).

For accessible opera
London Coliseum (*see right*).

For impeccable acoustics
Wigmore Hall (*see p312*).

For riverside jazz
Bull's Head (*see p322*).

For utter kookiness
Public Life (*see p321*).

Major venues

Barbican Centre
Silk Street, The City, EC2 (7638 4141/box office 7638 8891/www.barbican.org.uk). Barbican tube/ Moorgate tube/rail. **Box office** 9am-8pm daily. **Tickets** £6.50-£35. **Credit** AmEx, MC, V. **Map** p402 P5.

The Queen remarked at its official opening in 1982 that the Barbican was 'one of the wonders of the modern world'. A more frequent proclamation of first-time visitors is 'what in God's name is that?' Twenty years later and despite the best efforts of the centre's patriarchs, the Barbican remains as notorious for its lack of aesthetic value and its bewildering inaccessibility as it is celebrated for its cultural prowess. And what prowess: the world-class resident London Symphony Orchestra plays more than 80 concerts a year, while the annual Great Performers series boasts an array of internationally acclaimed soloists and orchestras. The City of London Sinfonia, the BBC Symphony Orchestra and the English Chamber Orchestra guest on a regular basis, and the free foyer music is of a fine standard. Throw in a combination of cinemas, galleries and theatres, a blend of contemporary music and a £7-million, four-month refurbishment (although, sadly, only to the inside) and blow me, maybe old Liz wasn't that far off the mark after all.

Bush Hall
310 Uxbridge Road, Shepherd's Bush, W12 (8222 6955/www.bushmusichall.co.uk). Shepherd's Bush tube. **Box office** 9.30am-6pm Mon-Fri. **Tickets** £6-£15; *membership* £95/year (50% off all tickets). **Credit** AmEx, MC, V.

This quirky little Edwardian hall has had something of a varied history– opened in 1904 as the Carlton Ballroom (the plasterwork is dotted with musical motifs) and then for many years a snooker hall, Bush Hall has only recently reverted to a music venue. It

holds a maximum of 150 people, and performances are generally set in the centre of the room, with spectators sitting at tables arranged as if for a cabaret act. You'll typically find decent piano trios and string or even recorder quartets, though performances are currently limited to one or two a week (the hall also hosts jazz evenings) as the fledgling venue finds its feet once more. The omens are good, however, and given time Bush Hall could develop into a smashing place to hear music.

London Coliseum
St Martin's Lane, Covent Garden, WC2 (box office 7632 8300/fax credit card bookings 7379 1264/ minicom 7836 7666/www.eno.org). Leicester Square tube/Charing Cross tube/rail. **Box office** *By phone* 24hrs daily. **Tickets** £3-£61. *Day tickets* to personal callers after 10am Mon-Sat and by phone from 12.30pm Mon-Sat. **Credit** AmEx, DC, MC, V. **Map** p401 L7.

If the Royal Opera House represents the traditional black-tie operatic aristocrat, the English National Opera (which resides at the Coliseum) is in many ways its tousle-haired, jeans and T-shirt wearing cousin. As the ROH fights tooth and nail to shake off its exclusive (and expensive) image, the ENO continues to take considerable pride in making opera available to as wide an audience as possible. Everything is performed in English, and a number of balcony tickets are always available on the day for as little as £3. Yet quality doesn't suffer and the ENO's reputation for ambitious productions of a high standard is as strong as it has ever been. The venue itself has recently undertaken the first serious programme of repair and restoration in its 100-year history, which will be ongoing until 2004, though the programme should proceed unhindered for the next couple of years.

Royal Albert Hall
Kensington Gore, South Kensington, SW7 (info 7589 3203/box office 7589 8212/www.royalalberthall.com). South Kensington tube/9, 10, 52 bus. **Box office** 9am-9pm daily. **Tickets** £3-£50. **Credit** AmEx, MC, V. **Map** p397 D9.

Were the Albert Hall not synonymous with the annual Proms revelry (*see p313*), it would lack much of its international stature, for the simple reason that (whisper it quietly) it's not very good. The Proms aside, the (mostly operatic) programme is extremely conservative and rather stale, the acoustics are underwhelming, and it's not uncommon for the roof to leak on to the balcony during a performance. It's all a bit of a shame, really, because the building itself, if grand old place, is otherwise an incredibly fitting venue for what is arguably the greatest music festival in the world – the Proms wouldn't be the same without it.

Royal Opera House
Covent Garden, WC2 (7304 4000/ www.royaloperahouse.org). Covent Garden tube. **Box office** 10am-8pm Mon-Sat. **Tickets** £3-£175. **Credit** AmEx, DC, MC, V. **Map** p399 L6.

Jingoistic, us? **The Last Night of the Proms** is beamed out to Hyde Park. *See p313.*

Year after year we ask whether the Royal Opera House will emerge in all its glory after years of renovation, arguments over public money and political scrapping – this year is no different. New supremo Tony Hall will hopefully steady the ship following Michael Kaiser's departure from the helm amid mutterings of an intractable board, though the task is not a small one. For years the ROH has been paid for by the public and played with by the elite, and the absorption of countless millions from the public coffers by its (admittedly stunning) renovation has only sharpened calls for a reversal of this trend. Pricing remains restrictive, however, and attempts to stage a more adventurous contemporary programme have failed owing to poor ticket sales. The upshot is a tried and tested formula of classic shows with a star turn guaranteed to sell out and an audience that remains largely unchanged. That said, Icelandic songstress Björk played to a full house in late 2001, and attempts to lure in the broader public are intensifying.

St James's Church Piccadilly

197 Piccadilly, St James's, W1 (7734 4511/ www.st-james-piccadilly.org). Piccadilly Circus tube. **Open** 8am-6.30pm daily. **Admission** free-£17; tickets available at the door 1hr before start of performance. **No credit cards. Map** p400 J7.
A curious little place this. Set amid the bustle of the craft market adjoining Piccadilly, much of the Wren-designed church (*see p114*) was flattened by enemy action during World War II and subsequently rebuilt to its original form. Nowadays it hosts regular free lunchtime recitals (Mon, Wed, Fri) and an excellent range of evening concerts on odd days, following no particular theme. Aside from simply

Christian and musical activities there are frequent exhibitions, lectures, poetry readings, debates and, curiously, Zen meditation sessions.

St John's, Smith Square

Smith Square, Westminster, SW1 (7222 1061/ www.sjss.org.uk). St James's Park or Westminster tube. **Box office** 10am-5pm Mon-Fri, or until start of performance on concert nights; from 1hr before start of performance Sat, Sun. **Tickets** £5-£30 but prices vary so call for details. **Credit** MC, V. **Map** p401 K10.
Just a short walk from the Palace of Westminster and a stone's throw from the political headquarters of the Conservative and Labour parties, St John's is famed for its rich selection of concerts and recitals. The magnificent Sainsbury Organ is recognised as one of Britain's finest, and recitals are enhanced by a projection system affording a view of the organist in action. Conditions are fairly cramped and it gets bloody cold in winter, though the quality is generally good, and the crypt is home to a wonderfully secluded bar and restaurant.

St Martin-in-the-Fields

Trafalgar Square, Westminster, WC2 (concert info 7839 8362/www.stmartin-in-the-fields.org). Charing Cross tube/rail. **Box office** 10am-5pm Mon-Sat, or until start of that evening's performance. **Admission** *Lunchtime concerts* donations requested. *Evening concerts* £6-£16. **Credit** MC, V. **Map** p401 L7.
A church has stood on this spot for the last 700 years. Step inside nowadays and it's almost possible to forget that you're on the edge of Trafalgar Square, arguably the biggest traffic island in Europe. Free lunchtime recitals (Mon, Tue, Fri) are

Who he? George Frideric Handel

Handel's *Messiah*, his most enduring work, was one of those labours of love that seem to come to genius figures in moments of desperation. In 1741, at the age of 56, Handel was struck down by a stroke and partially paralysed. In extremis, he composed his masterwork in just 21 days. Wildly applauded during its première in Dublin, it was received more dubiously by the London audience – indeed, in certain quarters, Handel's work was described as 'profane'.

Born in Halle in 1685, Handel first visited London in 1710, having taken on the role of court composer to the Elector of Hannover (who later became King George I). He moved here permanently two years later, spending most of his time writing Italian operas, though he turned his attention to oratorios after varying degrees of success. A favourite of George II (who was spotted belting out the *Messiah*'s 'Hallelujiah' chorus at one of the early performances), Handel enjoyed the attention of royalty and aristocracy alike.

Ludwig van Beethoven was a big fan of his, going so far as to call him 'the greatest of all of us'. Perhaps, as a deaf composer in his latter years, Beethoven was sensitive to the physical travails that Handel underwent, including blindness in his old age. Rumour has it that Handel's blindness and strokes were the result of lead poisoning due to the cheap port of which he was so fond.

Handel was buried at Westminster Abbey (*see p134*) in the presence of more than 3,000 mourners. His spirit lives on in his music, of course, and also in the brand new **Handel Museum** at 23-5 Brook Street, where the composer lived for more than 35 years until his death in 1759 (*see p113*).

---

generally performed by students, occasionally from the Royal Academy of Music and the Royal College of Music (for both, *see p315*), while evening concerts (Thur, Fri, Sat, occasional Tue) are soaked in candlelit ambience. Music on offer is generally baroque in bent. *See also p131*.

South Bank Centre

Belvedere Road, South Bank, SE1 (7960 4242/ www.sbc.org.uk). Embankment tube/Waterloo tube/rail. **Box office** 9am-9pm Mon-Sat; 9.30am-9pm Sun. **Tickets** £5-£60. **Credit** AmEx, DC, MC, V. **Map** p401 M8.

Whatever you happen to think of its functional concrete exterior, there's no denying that the South Bank Centre offers an incredible musical melting pot. The **Royal Festival Hall** stages mainly symphony concerts and those of a more popular bent; thankfully, the acoustic imperfections that have plagued larger productions should be ironed out by improvements that are currently under way (*see p74*). The **Queen Elizabeth Hall**, roughly a third of the size of the RFH, shares chamber group duties with the even smaller **Purcell Room**. Whereas the former tends to stage theatrical productions as a supplement, the PR otherwise devotes itself to organ recitals. Aside from this illustrious triumvirate, there's free foyer music, a decent bookshop, an overpriced record store, a poetry library and a performance room, and a number of cafés, bars and restaurants, including the classy People's Palace.

Wigmore Hall

36 Wigmore Street, Marylebone, W1 (7935 2141/ www.wigmore-hall.org.uk). Bond Street tube. **Box office** *In person Apr-Oct* 10am-8.30pm Mon-Sat; 10.30am-6.30pm Sun. *Nov-Mar* 10am-5pm Mon-Sat; 10.30am-4pm Sun. *By phone Apr-Oct* 10am-7pm Mon-Sat; 10.30am-6.30pm Sun. *Nov-Mar* 10am-7pm Mon-Sat; 10.30am-4pm Sun. **Tickets** £5-£35. **Credit** AmEx, DC, MC, V. **Map** p398 G6.

Many a superlative has been uttered in praise of this grand old building when just one is needed – perfection. Opened in 1901 as Bechstein Hall, 36 Wigmore Street acquired its present guise following its acquisition by Debenhams at a knock-down price, having previously been closed by the Board of Trade as enemy property in World War I. A century on, there's more to Wigmore Hall than its famously impeccable acoustics and old-fashioned intimacy. The alabaster and marble walls, flooring and stairway act as an enchanting prelude to the performance to follow, and the grand cupola (symbolising humanity's quest after the elusiveness of music in all its abstraction) presides authoritatively over the concerts and recitals unfolding below. The Monday lunchtime concerts, recorded for Radio 3, continue to offer good value for money, though all tickets here are reasonably priced. In short, there's nothing to criticise, so put down this book and go now.

Festivals

With the **Proms** (*see p313*) alone, London is spoiled in terms of music festivals. There's plenty more besides, however, all of it worth investigating. We've stuck to the annual festivals here, though many of the major venues – the Barbican (*see p310*), the Royal Festival Hall (*see p312*) and, occasionally, the Wigmore Hall (*see p312*) present themed events and seasons throughout the year. Also, the Covent Garden festival, a splendid and imaginative little event, is not scheduled for 2002, though it will be relaunched in time for 2003.

BBC Sir Henry Wood Promenade Concerts

Royal Albert Hall, Kensington Gore, South Kensington, SW7 (info 7765 5575/box office 7589 8212/www.bbc.co.uk/proms). South Kensington tube/9, 10, 52 bus. **Date** 19 July-14 Sept 2002. **Tickets** £3-£35. **Credit** AmEx, MC, V. **Map** p397 D9.

If the Proms isn't actually the best classical festival in the world, it's almost certainly the best known, and definitely the best loved. Based solely in the Royal Albert Hall, it mixes old favourites with modern pieces and premières for a series that is nothing if not full of surprises, and that is careful not to attach itself too much to a specific genre. Considering the startling number of performances, the quality is consistently high, though the odd duff one creeps in. Tickets can be purchased in advance, but not joining the 'Prommers' in the seatless arena at the front (tickets for which are only available on the day) would be a missed opportunity indeed, not to mention much more of a strain on the wallet. You can't get a ticket for the Last Night without having been to numerous other performances, though in recent years the spectacle has been beamed on to a big screen in Hyde Park, with additional live performances from the likes of José Carreras. If you're in town, it's a must-see.

City of London Festival

Venues in & around The City (info 7377 0540/ box office 7638 8891/www.colf.org.). Date 24 June-11 July 2002. **Tickets** free-£40. **Credit** AmEx, MC, V.

Now in its 40th year, this festival comprises three weeks of remarkably diverse entertainment amid the magnificent architecture of the square mile, catering for every taste and every wallet. St Paul's and the City's churches and livery halls see most of the action; the Barbican (*see p310*), the Tower of London (*see p94*) and the Spitz (*see p320*) also host events.

Hampton Court Palace Festival

Hampton Court, East Molesey, Surrey (Ticketmaster 7344 4444/www.hamptoncourtfestival.com). Hampton Court rail/riverboat from Westminster or Richmond to Hampton Court Pier (Apr-Oct). **Date** 13-22 June 2002 (tbc). **Tickets** £15-£85 (approx). **Credit** AmEx, MC, V.

More perhaps a celebration of the venue than the music on offer, the Hampton Court Palace Festival represents a pleasant evening out with a few classical big guns thrown in for good measure, and maybe a few fireworks if you're lucky.

Holland Park Theatre

Holland Park, Kensington High Street, Kensington, W8 (7602 7856). High Street Kensington or Holland Park tube. **Date** 11 June-early Aug 2002. **Tickets** £26-£29. **Credit** AmEx, MC, V. **Map** p394 A8.

Set in the delicious surroundings of Holland House, this open-air theatre hosts mainly opera throughout the summer. If the weather holds, it's wonderful, though a canopy covering the stage and the audience ensures against a complete washout. *See also p338.*

Kenwood Lakeside Concerts

Kenwood House, Hampstead Lane, Highgate, NW3 (info 8233 7435/box office 7413 1443/ ww.picnicconcerts.com). Golders Green or East Finchley tube then courtesy bus on concert nights. **Date** July, Aug 2002. **Tickets** £12.50-£30 (approx). **Credit** AmEx, MC, V.

A pleasant if uninspiring programme of tried and tested acts in the expansive grounds of Kenwood House – a charming place to enjoy a picnic at dusk. It's best enjoyed on a fireworks night.

London Bach Festival

Venues around central London (info 01883 717372/www.bachlive.co.uk). Date 27 Oct-9 Nov 2002. **Tickets** free-£20. **Credit** MC, V (phone bookings only).

This short series of concerts and recitals in celebration of one man's genius takes place largely around Marylebone Road (Royal Academy of Music and St Marylebone Parish Church), though there are odd events in the City and at St John's Smith Square.

Marble Hill Concerts

Marble Hill Park, Richmond Road, Twickenham, Middx (info 8233 7435/box office 7413 1443/ www.picnicconcerts.com). St Margaret's rail or Richmond tube/rail then 33, 90, 290, H22, R70 bus. **Date** July, Aug 2002. **Tickets** £10-£20. **Credit** AmEx, MC, V.

Held at a leafy west London venue, this event is pretty similar in feel to the Hampton Court and Kenwood concerts (for both, *see above*). Marble Hill

Arts & Entertainment

provides a fine setting in which to enjoy the standard classical repertoire, which is performed on Saturdays in summer.

Spitalfields Festival

Christ Church, Commercial Street, Spitalfields, E1 (7377 1362/www.spitalfieldsfestival.org.uk). Aldgate East tube/Liverpool Street tube/rail. **Date** 10-28 June 2002, 11-20 Dec 2002. **Tickets** free-£27. **Credit** MC, V. **Map** p403 S5.

A twice-yearly musical dose that reflects the cultural diversity of the Spitalfields area. Most of the concerts take place in Nicholas Hawksmoor's truly splendid Christ Church.

City lunchtime concerts

Of the plethora of old churches that are scattered amid the high-rise blocks and hordes of wheeler-dealers in the City, many capitalise on their historic musical associations by putting on regular lunchtime concerts by local musicians, many of whom are students. The acoustics are naturally impressive, the settings intimate and the quality excellent. Concerts are either free or with an 'admission by donation' policy. Pick up a copy of City Events from the City Information Centre across the road from St Paul's Cathedral for more information.

In addition to venues that we have listed below, regular lunchtime organ concerts are held at several churches outside the City, including **Temple Church** (off Fleet Street, EC4, 7353 8559), **Grosvenor Chapel** (South Audley Street, W1, 7499 1684) and **St James's** (Clerkenwell Close, EC1, 7251 1190); call for details.

St Anne & St Agnes *Gresham Street, EC2 (7606 4986). St Paul's tube.* **Performances** 1.10pm Mon, Fri. **Map** p404 P6.

St Bride's *Fleet Street, EC4 (7427 0133). Blackfriars tube/rail.* **Performances** 1.15pm Tue, Fri (except Aug, Advent, Lent). **Map** p404 N6.

St Lawrence Jewry *Guildhall, EC2 (7600 9478). Mansion House, Bank or St Paul's tube.* **Performances** 1pm Mon, Tue. **Map** p404 P6.

St Magnus the Martyr *Lower Thames Street, EC3 (7626 4481). Monument tube.* **Performances** 1.05pm Tue.

St Margaret Lothbury *Lothbury, EC2 (7606 8330). Bank tube.* **Performances** 1.10pm Thur (except Aug & between Christmas & New Year). **Map** p405 Q6.

St Martin within Ludgate *Ludgate Hill, EC4 (7248 6054). St Paul's tube/Blackfriars tube/rail/ City Thameslink rail.* **Performances** 1.15pm Wed. **Map** p404 O6.

St Mary-le-Bow *Cheapside, EC2 (7248 5139). Bank, Mansion House or St Paul's tube.* **Performances** 1.05pm Thur. **Map** p404 P6.

St Michael Cornhill *Cornhill, EC3 (7626 8841). Bank or Monument tube.* **Performances** 1pm Mon. **Map** p405 Q6.

Other venues

With four top-class music colleges, London enjoys an embarrassment of riches in terms of talented young hopefuls. The best thing is that most of the frequent lunchtime recitals are free and open to all. The **Royal Academy of Music** (Marylebone Road, NW1, 7873 7373/ www.ram.ac.uk) has benefited in recent times from a fruitful collaboration with the London Sinfonietta, and the 'Free on Friday' series of lunchtime concerts (1.05pm) often act as a prelude to a repeat performance in the evening at a larger venue with a paying audience. The recent completion of its imaginatively titled New Recital Hall (*see also p108*) is a worthy addition to the fine recital facilities on offer, while the new specialist postgraduate Opera course offered by the Academy will add another fine string to the bow of very fine chamber and orchestra music already available at a reasonable price in the evenings.

The **Royal College of Music** (Prince Consort Road, Knightsbridge, SW7, 7589 3643/www.rcm.ac.uk) stages chamber concerts on most weekdays during termtime (1.05pm) as well as occasional larger events in the evenings, while **Trinity College of Music** (King Charles Court, Old Royal Naval College, Greenwich, SE10) has recently started a free series of lunchtime concerts in the magnificent setting of the chapel of the Old Royal Naval College in Greenwich (1pm Tue; *see p168*), as well as in its elegant Peacock Room (1pm Wed). As if that wasn't enough, the **Guildhall School of Music & Drama** (Silk Street, the City, EC2, 7628 2571) also operates a regular series of lunchtime recitals and evening events featuring soloists and ensembles from the college.

Blackheath Halls

23 Lee Road, Blackheath, SE3 (8463 0100/ www.blackheathhalls.com). Blackheath rail/54, 89, 108, 202, N53 bus. **Box office** 10am-7pm Mon-Sat; 11am-5pm Sun. **Tickets** £2.50-£25. **Credit** AmEx, MC, V.

South-east London's premier music venue is well located a short walk from leafy Blackheath and presents a variety of different styles and genres. Though not as easily accessible as other major venues, it still attracts a number of top performers, and it's worth the trek for the right occasion.

Resources

British Music Information Centre

10 Stratford Place, Marylebone, W1 (7499 8567/ www.bmic.co.uk). Bond Street tube. **Open** noon-5pm Mon-Fri. **Concerts** 7.30pm Tue, Thur (except Aug). **Tickets** £3-£7. **No credit cards. Map** p398 H6.

Arts & Entertainment

Riding the tide: the all-new **Ocean**. *See p317.*

A mine of information on any aspect of musical repertoire. As well as an astonishing collection of books, scores and recordings (audio and video), there are occasional lectures and weekly recitals of modern British music, many of which are premières.

National Sound Archive

British Library, 96 Euston Road, Somers Town, NW1 (7412 7440/www.bl.uk/collections/ sound-archive). Euston or King's Cross tube/rail. **Open** 10am-8pm Mon; 9.30am-8pm Tue-Thur; 9.30am-5pm Fri, Sat. **Map** p399 K3.
From music to drama and from vox pops to wildlife sounds, it's here. The NSA also offers public access to a wide range of specialist publications, books, magazines and journals covering every aspect of recorded sound. Listening is free, though membership of the British Library is required and it is advisable to call ahead with your request.

Rock, Roots & Jazz

There's something of a rock 'n' roll renaissance going on at the moment.
For a start, various cool venues (such as **Public Life**, *see p321,* and the **Arts Café at Toynbee Hall**, *see p320*) are opening or reopening and fast making a name for themselves. Then there's the fact that some of the best gigs in town can be free (for instance, at **Borders**, *see p232*; outside the **Royal Festival Hall**, *see p312*; and at the **Betsey Trotwood**, *see p320*). Lastly, there are a bunch of cool places in which to hang out now on Sundays, including Twisted

Arm Lounge at the **Windmill** (*see p321)*, which means that you can round off the weekend in style. Out in clubland things are getting more eclectic too; venues such as **Cargo** (*see p278*), **Fabric** (*see p279*), **333** (*see p281*) and **93 Feet East** (*see p280*) regularly put on some refreshing bills that include bands/dance acts among the usual rash of superstar DJs.

Tickets

Prices for gigs can go as high as £80 for the stellar names, though average ticket prices for a well-known band at most of the biggish venues are £10-£25, and you can check out lesser-known indie, jazz and folk groups for around a fiver at the pubs and bars detailed below (*see p320*). While tickets for the latter are usually available only on the door, you should try to buy tickets in advance (and direct from the venue, if possible, if you want to avoid paying a booking fee) for most big gigs: anything halfway decent will sell out astonishingly quickly. If the venue has sold out, or you can't make it there, try one of the agencies: **Ticketmaster** (7344 4444/ www.ticketmaster.co.uk), **Stargreen** (7734 8932/www.stargreen.co.uk) and **Ticketweb** (7771 2000/www.ticketweb.co.uk). Avoid at all costs buying from the scamming chancers with violent tendencies – otherwise known as touts – who hang around outside bigger venues: you'll pay a fortune for what may be a forged ticket.

Rock venues

If you want to be the first on the block to catch the well-regarded, hotly tipped and buzzing new acts as they break, see what's on at **Notting Hill Arts Café** (*see p321*) or the **Arts Café at Toynbee Hall** (*see p320*). Remember – there's also a whole bunch of new talents just gagging to be discovered/supported, so if you want to catch the next would-be indie superstar on the way up, check what's on at places such as the **Hope & Anchor** (*see p321*), though don't imagine that every band on this 'circuit' will be the next effortlessly cool Mercury Prize winner. If you still feel compelled to buy into the latest over-hyped charade by some enormo-celebrity, then start the long and tedious journey towards one of the three arena venues and marvel at just how user-unfriendly an experience it is.

Major venues

In addition to the venues listed below, the **South Bank Centre** (*see p312*), the **Royal Albert Hall** (*see p310*) and the **Barbican**

Centre (*see p310*) attract all kinds of big-name acts, from Nina Simone to Extreme Noise Terror, and programme variously themed mini-festivals (*see p318* **The sounds of summer**), which are well worth a visit.

Astoria

157 Charing Cross Road, Soho, WC2 (box office 7344 0044/ info 8963 0940/www.meanfiddler.com). Tottenham Court Road tube. **Box office** *In person* 11am-7pm Mon-Sat. *By phone* 24hrs daily. **Tickets** £8-£15. **Credit** AmEx, MC, V. **Map** p399 K6.

This large-ish rock venue is unusually central, and reasonably user-friendly. What's more, it boasts decent sightlines and seems to attract some reasonably big names, playing host to everything from populist indie rock to chart pop (both Kylie and Marc Almond have trodden the boards at its popular G.A.Y. night; *see p303*).

Brixton Academy

211 Stockwell Road, Brixton, SW9 (info 7771 3000/box office 0870 771 2000/www.brixton-academy.co.uk). Brixton tube/rail. **Box office** *By phone* 24hrs daily. **Tickets** £10-£20. **Credit** MC, V.

The Brixton Academy is one of the better places in which to see the bigger acts passing through town, a fact that's due largely to the fact that the venue's sloping floor actually allows you to see the stage. It thus seems relatively intimate for a venue its size (it holds more than 4,000 people), but be warned – toilet queues (especially for the Ladies) can be bladder-bustingly huge.

Earl's Court Exhibition Centre

Warwick Road, Earl's Court, SW5 (7385 1200/ www.eco.co.uk). Earl's Court tube. **Box office** 9am-6pm daily; 9am-2pm Sat. **Tickets** £17-£50. **Credit** AmEx, MC, V. **Map** p396 A11.

As the name tells you, this place was never designed to host live music. The acoustics are dreadful, the concessions a rip-off, and the atmosphere deadly – our advice is to stay well away.

Forum

9-17 Highgate Road, Kentish Town, NW5 (info 7284 1001/box office 7344 0044/www.meanfiddler.com). Kentish Town tube/rail/N2 bus. **Box office** *In person* from the Astoria or the Jazz Café (no credit cards). *By phone* 24hrs daily. **Tickets** £5-£15. **Credit** AmEx, MC, V (phone bookings only).

The Forum is the capital's leading mid-sized venue, closely followed by the Brixton Academy (*see p317*). Decent sound and views are part of the appeal, of course, but the atmosphere's the thing. It's worth coming along to catch your fave stars performing in this beautiful old theatre before they hit the stadium circuit.

Hammersmith Apollo

Queen Caroline Street, Hammersmith, W6 (0870 4000 700). Hammersmith tube. **Box office** *In person* 10am-6pm Mon-Sat. *By phone* 24hrs daily. **Admission** £10-£40. **Credit** AmEx, MC, V.

After being dominated by lame *Riverdance*-type snooze-athons for quite a while, this huge all-seater theatre has started hosting more gigs. The acoustics and sightlines are generally excellent.

London Arena

Limeharbour, Isle of Dogs, E14 (7538 1212/ www.londonarena.co.uk). Crossharbour & London Arena DLR. **Box office** *In person* 9am-7pm Mon-Fri; 10am-3pm Sat. *By phone* 9am-8pm Mon-Fri; 10am-3pm Sat. **Tickets** £5-£50. **Credit** MC, V.

A mammoth aircraft hangar better suited to ice hockey games than rock concerts: its acoustics are terrible, its concessions are shockingly priced, and it's got all the ambience of a school gymnasium (except there's no cloakroom).

Ocean

270 Mare Street, Hackney, E8 (switchboard 8986 5336/box office 8533 0111/24hr bookings 7314 2800/www.ocean.org.uk). Hackney Central or Hackney Downs rail. **Box office** *In person* 10am-6pm daily; later on performance nights. *By phone* 24hrs daily. **Tickets** £1-£30. **Credit** MC, V.

London's newest mid-size venue/entertainment complex in the heart of Hackney was opened by Chris Smith and Soft Cell. The music programming veers from world music to the Wonderstuff via Lee Perry and Howard Marks. The main space is a great place to see and hear bands, possessing superb sightlines, state-of-the-art PA (and lights) and funky toilets, but it can sometimes feel a little like you're watching a band perform in a leisure centre. There's also a bar/café (open all day), club nights at weekends, and two smaller spaces (holding up to 300 and 100) to check out.

Shepherd's Bush Empire

Shepherd's Bush Green, Shepherd's Bush, W12 (7771 2000/www.shepherds-bush-empire.co.uk). Shepherd's Bush tube. **Box office** *In person* noon-5pm Mon-Fri. *By phone* 24hrs daily. **Tickets** £5-£25. **Credit** MC, V.

This former television theatre (Terry Wogan used to host his chat shows here) is now a delightful venue with wonderful acoustics, though its sightlines are below average (it can be quite difficult to see from the stalls), and fire regulations mean that the two balconies are both no-smoking (this is a rock venue, for chrissakes…).

Wembley Arena

Empire Way, Wembley, Middx (8902 0902/ www.wembleyticket.com). Wembley Park tube/ Wembley Central tube/rail. **Box office** *By phone* 24hrs daily. **Tickets** £5-£100. **Credit** AmEx, MC, V.

The closure of Wembley Stadium has left the 12,500-capacity Wembley Arena and, though a lot less frequently, the 7,500-capacity Conference Centre as Wembley's music venues. The Arena is draughty and tacky, and it takes an age to get there; when you do, you'll find it has all the rock 'n' roll fun of a dentists' convention.

Arts & Entertainment

Club venues

100 Club
100 Oxford Street, W1 (7636 0933/
www.the100club.co.uk). Oxford Circus or Tottenham
Court Road tube. **Open** *Gigs* 7.30pm-midnight
Mon-Thur; noon-3pm, 8.30pm-2am Fri; 7.30pm-1am
Sat; 7.30-11.30pm Sun. **Admission** £6-£12.
No credit cards. Map p399 K6.
Now dividing its time between trad jazz, swing and
indie of a cool and cultish variety, this central club
is notorious for having hosted what many believe
was the first ever punk festival, back in 1976. The
Rolling Stones and the Kinks both appeared here
in the swinging '60s.

Borderline
Orange Yard, Manette Street, Soho, W1 (7734
2095/www.borderline.co.uk). Tottenham Court Road
tube. **Box office** 10am-6pm Mon-Fri. **Open** *Gigs*

8-11pm Mon-Fri, some Sats. *Clubs* 11.30pm-3am
Mon-Thur; 11.30pm-4am Fri, Sat. **Admission** *Gigs*
£6-£16. *Clubs* £3-£8. **Credit** MC, V. **Map** p399 K6.
Don't be put off by the ersatz Mexican cantina decor
– this subterranean venue programmes a vibrant
mixture of Americana, roots rock and indie. On a
busy night there's an exciting vibe about the place,
as you can get up close and personal with your
favourite combos. Expect to-die-for shows by alt-
rock heavyweights such as Sparklehorse, the Dirty
Three and Johnny Dowd. Check out the list of everyone who has played there on your way in.

Dingwalls
Middle Yard, Camden Lock, Chalk Farm Road,
Camden, NW1 (info 7267 1577/box office 7428
5929/www.dingwalls.com). Camden Town or Chalk
Farm tube. **Box office** tickets available from
Rhythm Records, 281 Camden High Street (7267
0123). **Open** *Gigs* 7.30pm-midnight, nights vary.
Admission £5-£15. **Credit** AmEx, MC, V.

The sounds of summer

Britain's summer music festival season is
dominated by large-scale, big-name events
such as **Glastonbury**, the **Reading Festival**
(for both, *see below*) and the **Notting Hill
Carnival** (*see p266*), with **All Tomorrow's
Parties** (*see below*) giving them a run for
their money for coolness, if not numbers.
Yet there are still lots of smaller events going
on, with most of the capital's fields and open
spaces staging some sort of bash (usually
free) during the year: keep an eye on *Time
Out* magazine for breaking news of festival
line-ups. For confirmation of dates or prices,
phone or check the websites nearer the time.
  If Britain has an equivalent to Woodstock,
Glastonbury is it. Founded by farmer Michael
Eavis in the 1960s, it's since snowballed
into a gigantic stoner-fest that generations
of weekend-wasters have grown to love. The
atmosphere draws as many people as the
music (which covers everything from rock
to jug band music), though whether acres
of muddy fields, appalling toilet facilities
and every juggler in the western world are
really all they're cracked up to be is a
moot point. Find out for yourself between
28 and 30 June 2002. Details will be
available on www.glastonburyfestivals.co.uk
or www.glastonbury.co.uk (01458 834596),
or in *Time Out* from around March.
  If roughing it in a muddy field doesn't grab
you, how about three days of indie music and
post-rock noise in a holiday camp in Camber
Sands on the south coast? – that's what

you'll get if you attend **All Tomorrow's Parties**
in April. Previous events were hosted by Sonic
Youth and Mogwai and featured the likes of
Television and Belle & Sebastian; the 2002
shindig on the sea is curated by Steve Albini
(call 0871 220 0260 for details, or see
www.alltomorrowsparties.co.uk).
  Meltdown, which takes over the Royal
Festival Hall for two weeks in June and July,
is a brilliant idea that doesn't always live up
to its full potential. The point here is that the
choices of performers reflect the personal
taste of the curator, who changes each year:
previous incumbents have been Nick Cave,
John Peel, and, in 2001, Robert Wyatt, whose
programming ranged from Baaba Maal to
Tricky (*pictured*). Call 7960 4242 or see
either www.sbc.org.uk or www.rfh.org.uk for
the latest news on this year's curator and
the acts he or she is lining up.
  The traditionally Brighton-based **Essential**
is a funky but chilled-out affair featuring
some great names (along the lines of Gil
Scott Heron, George Clinton and Ice T). On
the Saturday (dance day) it attracts a young
and clubby crowd, while roots-reggae Sunday
draws a more laid-back mob. In 2002 it
will take place in Bristol in May, and later
in the year, in Hackney in east London – on
2 August (indie/rock £35); 3 August (dance
£37.50); and 4 August (roots £37.50).There
may also be some events in Brighton. Call
the information line (09068 230 190) for
details nearer the time.

Though Fridays and Saturdays are block-booked by Jongleurs comedy club (*see p284*), there are often great gigs here during the week (and Saturday does have a rockabilly record hop too). Due to the multiple levels, this is a bit of a sit-down venue.

Garage

20-22 Highbury Corner, Highbury, N5 (info 8963 0940/box office 7344 0044/www.meanfiddler.com). Highbury & Islington tube/rail. **Box office** *In person* 7pm on show nights. *By phone* 24hrs daily. **Open** *Gigs* 8pm-midnight Mon-Thur, some Suns; 8pm-3am Fri, Sat. **Admission** £4-£10. **Credit** MC, V.

This is just about the right size if you want to check out hotly tipped US and UK indie acts on their way up, but though the line-ups are usually strong and the decor is suitably grungey, the sound can be poor, and the place is a sweatbox in summer. More obscure/cultish acts play Upstairs At The Garage, which is much smaller; on a good night it's pleasantly rammed and full of atmosphere.

Mean Fiddler

165 Charing Cross Road, Soho, WC2 (info 7434 9592/ box office 7344 0044/www.meanfiddler.com). Tottenham Court Road tube. **Box office** *In person* 10am-6pm Mon-Sat. *By phone* 24hrs daily. **Tickets** £8-£18.50. **Credit** AmEx, MC, V. **Map** p399 K6.

Though the views are not uniformly great for gigs here (if you want to watch from upstairs, you have to do so through a glass window), the sound usually is, and it does have some fantastic names (Big Star, Jon Spencer Blues Explosion and the like).

Rock Garden

6-7 The Piazza, Covent Garden, WC2 (7240 3961/ www.rockgarden.co.uk). Covent Garden tube. **Open** 5pm-3am Mon-Thur; 5pm-4am Fri, Sat; 7pm-2am Sun. *Gigs* noon & 7pm Sun. **Admission** free-£12. **Credit** AmEx, DC, MC, V. **Map** p401 L6.

This Covent Garden venue features mainly clueless pop-rocker wannabes playing to those who don't know any better.

The **Reading Festival**, held over the August Bank Holiday weekend, ostensibly marks the end of the English summer. The three-day, big-budget Mean Fiddler-organised fandango takes place a short train ride from London, so you can just go for the day. It usually provides an excellent line-up spread over several stages, with big names matching decibels with up-and-comers and flavours of the month. Reading is an exhausting experience, and so it should be – it's a rock festival, after all. Expect lots of bad boy rawk acts on Sunday. For information, call 8963 0940.

For something entirely different, the **Charles Wells Cambridge Folk Festival** at the tail end of July offers folk, cajun, blues and gospel. Even if they're not your bag, if you're even slightly open to hearing things outside your normal sphere of listening and you like the idea of hanging out in the grounds of a lovely country house with a bunch of like-minded individuals, book quickly; details can be had on 01223 357851 (Cambridge Corn Exchange box office) or on 01223 457245, or see www.camfolkfest.co.uk).

Fleadh (pronounced 'flar' – it's Gaelic for party), is now about as Irish as Jack Charlton, though if a line-up of vaguely Celtic acts in Finsbury Park in June or July appeals, call 8961 5490 or see www.fleadhfestival.com.

Jazz enthusiasts will be heading for the year's two big productions: the autumn **Soho Jazz & Heritage Festival** (*see p267*) and the **London Jazz Festival** (call 08700 100300 or check out www.serious.org.uk for details). In addition, the **Coin Street Festival** (*see p263*) offers a wide array of performances.

The year should also see the second coming of the anti-racist **Respect!** festival, held in north London in 2001; *see p266* for further information and contact details.

Ronnie Scott's. *See p322.*

Spitz

Old Spitalfields Market, 109 Commercial Street, Spitalfields, E1 (7392 9032/www.spitz.co.uk). Aldgate East tube/Liverpool Street tube/rail. **Open** 11am-11pm Mon-Sat; 11am-10.30pm Sun. *Gigs* 8-11pm Mon-Sat. **Admission** £4-£10. **Credit** MC, V. **Map** p403 R5.

The Spitz – practically part of Spitalfields Market – is a bar, a café/restaurant, an art gallery, a club and a music venue. Expect a gleefully eclectic mixture of acts (from Klezmer to anti-folk), though the trendy location may attract the more fashionable outfits on the scene.

Underworld

174 Camden High Street, Camden, NW1 (7482 1932). Camden Town tube. **Open** *Gigs* 7pm-3am, nights vary. **Admission** £3-£12. **No credit cards.**

Though it's bigger than the other Camden indie venues, Underworld's weirdly shaped basement room has awful sightlines and too many pillars. Worse still, staff throw everyone out at 10.30pm on a Saturday night (they have a club on afterwards). Indie stuff is the main bill of fare.

University of London Union (ULU)

Manning Hall, Malet Street, Bloomsbury, WC1 (7664 2030/www.ulu.lon.ac.uk). Goodge Street tube. **Open** *Gigs* 8-11pm, nights vary. **Admission** £5-£10. **Credit** MC, V. **Map** p399 K4.

Given that this is a uni venue, you won't be surprised to hear that the acts who play here are invariably *NME*-endorsed indie guitar types currently riding high on the student circuit. The hall itself is large and characterless, though the ludicrously cheap beer means you probably won't care too much.

Pubs & bars

The Arts Café at Toynbee Hall

28 Commercial Street, Spitalfields, E1 (7247 5681). Aldgate East tube. **Open** 10am-9pm Mon-Wed; 10am-11pm Thur; 10am-midnight Fri, Sat. *Gigs* 8.30pm Fri, Sat. **Admission** £3-£5. **Credit** MC, V.

It's a café and restaurant, it's a bar, it's an art gallery, and it's also one of the very few rock venues in London where you can munch on a pizza while you're listening to a hardcore band. There are different nights organised by a variety of clubs here, so the programme is varied, though it's generally of a lo-fi/alt rock bent.

Barfly

The Monarch, 49 Chalk Farm Road, Camden, NW1 (7691 4244/ticketline 0870 907 0999/ www.barflyclub.com). Chalk Farm tube. **Open** 7.30-11pm Mon-Thur; 7.30pm-2am Fri, Sat; 7.30-10.30pm Sun. *Gigs* 8.15pm daily. **Admission** £4-£6. **Credit** *ticketline only* AmEx, MC, V.

The Barfly club, formerly at the Falcon, is now firmly settled in at the recently renovated Monarch, which is one of the nicer Camden boozers. Expect an array of up-and-coming indie bands.

Betsey Trotwood

56 Farringdon Road, Clerkenwell, EC1 (7253 4285). Farringdon tube. **Open** noon-11pm Mon-Sat; noon-10.30pm Sun. **No credit cards.**

Various independently promoted nights of indie-kid bliss take place in the upstairs room at this groovy little pub. Pleasantly tiny, it's an ideal place for checking out your local lo-fi underground celeb. The occasional club nights (call for details) are also well worth a butcher's.

Boston Arms

178 Junction Road, Tufnell Park, N19 (7272 8153/ www.dirtywaterclub.com). Tufnell Park tube. **Open** 11am-midnight Mon-Wed, Sun; 11am-1am Thur-Sat. *Gigs* 10pm, day varies. *Club* 9pm every other Fri. **Admission** £4-£6. **No credit cards.**

This briefly became the trendiest venue in Britain when the White Stripes rolled into town last summer. On alternate Fridays the Dirty Water club turns it into a swinging '60s-style retro-bash – expect DJs playing R&B, classic beats and mod grooves, plus bands of the trashy garage punk variety.

Bull & Gate

389 Kentish Town Road, Kentish Town, NW5 (7485 5358). Kentish Town tube/rail. **Open** 11am-11pm Mon-Sat; noon-10.30pm Sun. *Gigs* 8.30pm daily. **Admission** £3-£5. **No credit cards.**

It would be all too easy to write off this Kentish Town venue as the stamping ground of indie chancers and no-hopers, but fair's fair – it has been renovated of late, and it does manage to pull the occasional good bill out of the bag (this is where *NME*-friendly big-hitters such as Suede learnt their trade, so you may be surprised).

Dublin Castle

94 Parkway, Camden, NW1 (7485 1773/ www.dublincastle.co.uk). Camden Town tube. **Open** noon-1am Mon-Sat; noon-midnight Sun. *Gigs* 9pm Mon-Sat; 8.30pm Sun. **Admission** £3.50-£5. **No credit cards.**

This is everything an indie venue should be: a big pub with a small, hot and sweaty backroom, open relatively late, with all sorts of up-and-coming talent to be discovered/ignored. At weekends the bar heaves with indie kids.

Hope & Anchor

207 Upper Street, Islington, N1 (7354 1312).
Highbury & Islington tube/rail. **Open** noon-1am
daily. *Gigs* 8.45pm daily. **Admission** £3.50-£5.
Credit MC, V. **Map** p402 O1.
One of the smaller venues, the Hope & Anchor
started holding gigs again a few years back, hav-
ing made its name in the 1970s with pub rock (Ian
Dury, Dr Feelgood and their ilk) and punk (the Sex
Pistols and the Stranglers). Expect lots of off-kilter
indie and alt-rock hopefuls.

Notting Hill Arts Club

21 Notting Hill Gate, W11 (7460 4459). Notting Hill
Gate tube. **Open** 6pm-1am Mon-Wed; 6pm-2am
Thur, Fri; 4pm-2am Sat; 4-11pm Sun. *Gigs* times
vary. **Admission** £3-£6. **No credit cards.**
There are various different club nights and afternoons, many of them free, to be sampled in this
swanky little basement, including Radio4 and Lazy
Dog. Saturdays play host to Rough Trade's Rota
sessions – this is possibly your best chance to see
various indie scene big names strut their impecca-
bly cool stuff (and it's free too).

Public Life

82A Commercial Street, Spitalfields, E1 (7375
2425/www.publiclife.org). Liverpool Street tube/rail.
Open 6.30pm-midnight Tue-Sun. *Gigs* 8pm daily.
Admission free-£2 (voluntary donation).
Credit MC, V.
This swish basement (it's actually a converted public toilet) is probably both the smallest and kookiest
venue in town. Doubling as a bar/café/exhibition
space, it offers various nights of off-kilter acts (lo-fi
indie, electronica and dance).

The Verge

147 Kentish Town Road, Camden, NW1 (7284
1178/www.theverge.co.uk). Camden Town or
Kentish Town tube. **Open** 8pm-midnight Mon-Wed,
Sun; 8pm-2am Thur-Sat. **Admission** £3-£10.
Credit AmEx, V.
This Camden/Kentish Town boozer stays open
until late at weekends, and boasts a well-stocked
bar and a much better sound system than many of
its competitors. There are usually mixed bills of
indie guitar types, plus occasional big names from
the roots rock circuit at weekends (Hank Wangford,
John Otway and co.).

Water Rats

328 Gray's Inn Road, Bloomsbury, WC1 (7837 7269/
www.plumpromotions.co.uk). King's Cross tube/rail.
Open *Gigs* 7.30pm-midnight Mon-Sat. **Admission**
£4-£6. **No credit cards. Map** p399 M3.
This is where Oasis were discovered after playing
their first headline gig here, and where, 30 years earlier, Bob Dylan made his UK debut, though there
isn't so much of a buzz about it these days. Which
is a shame, as it's a beautiful pub with a great PA
and a little back room with a plush red curtain. Still,
you may find the occasional indie-flavoured gem
here in among the usual slew of pop/rock hopefuls.

Windmill

22 Blenheim Gardens, Brixton, SW2 (8671 0700).
Brixton tube. **Open** *Gigs* 7-11pm Mon-Sat; 7-10.30pm
Sun. **Admission** free-£3. **No credit cards.**
This groovy little place located just off Brixton Hill
has free barbecues on Sunday afternoons in summer, regular Twisted nights of country and hip
hop, and an usually relaxed and friendly atmosphere. Punters should prepare themselves for
anything from ska and punk to poetry.

Roots venues

Africa Centre

38 King Street, Covent Garden, WC2 (7836 1973/
www.africacentre.org.uk). Covent Garden tube.
Open *Gigs* 11.30pm Fri. *Clubs* 9.30pm-3am Fri, Sat.
Admission £6-£8. **Credit** MC, V. **Map** p401 L7.
Situated in the heart of Covent Garden, the Africa
Centre offers top African bands most Friday nights,
plus occasional gigs on other nights.

Bread & Roses

68 Clapham Manor Street, Clapham, SW4 (7498
1779). Clapham Common or Clapham North tube/
37, 88, 133, 137, 345 bus. **Open** 11am-11pm
Mon-Sat; noon-10.30pm Sun. *Gigs* 1-5pm Sun.
Admission free. **Credit** MC, V.
The Mwalimu Express, one of the best world music
events in London, is held here every Sunday, focusing on the music and food of a different city each
week. *See also p228.*

Cecil Sharp House

2 Regent's Park Road, Camden, NW1 (7485
2206/www.efdss.org). Camden Town tube.
Open *Gigs* 7pm, nights vary. **Admission** £3-£7.
No credit cards.
This is the centre of the English Folk Dance and
Song Society. The club on Tuesdays is fun in a hey-
nonny-nonny kind of way, while there are regular
cajun nights, and all sorts of classes (from flamenco
to clog-dancing) to be sampled.

Hammersmith & Fulham Irish Centre

Blacks Road, Hammersmith, W6 (8563 8232/
www.lbhf.gov.uk/irishcentre). Hammersmith tube.
Open *Gigs* nights vary. **Admission** £4-£10.
No credit cards.
You'll find all kinds of Irish music events, from free
ceilidhs to biggish-name Irish acts such as the
Popes, on offer at this small, friendly craic dealer.

Swan

215 Clapham Road, Stockwell, SW9 (7978 9778/
www.theswanstockwell.com). Stockwell tube. **Open**
5pm-midnight Wed; 5pm-2am Thur; 5pm-3am Fri;
7pm-3am Sat; 7pm-2am Sun. *Gigs* 9.30pm Wed; 10pm
Thur, Sat; 10pm & midnight Fri. **Admission** £2-£6
(normally free Wed & before 11pm Thur, 10pm Sun).
Credit MC, V.
This usually raucous Irish pub specialises in semi-
trad music most evenings, though there are tribute
bands in the upstairs dancehall at weekends.

Arts & Entertainment

12 Bar Club

22-3 Denmark Place, off Denmark Street, St Giles's,
WC2 (info 7916 6989/box office 7209 2248/
www.12barclub.com). Tottenham Court Road tube.
Open 8pm-1am daily. *Gigs* 8.30pm daily.
Admission £5-£10. **Credit** MC, V. **Map** p399 K6.
This Tin Pan Alley venue has had everyone from
Mark Eitzel to Kristin Hersh treading its boards.
Though it's split over two levels, the 12 Bar Club
is tiny and intimate, and has a sawdusty vibe that
is truly welcoming. Hang out at the bar while
you're waiting for the coolest acts in town, or from
out of town, to nip in and do a sneaky secret show
in the early hours of the morning.

Union Chapel

Compton Terrace, Islington, N1 (7226 1686/
box office 0870 120 1349/www.unionchapel.org.uk).
Highbury & Islington tube/rail/N19, N65, N92 bus.
Open *Gigs* 7.30pm, nights vary. **Tickets** £3-£13
(subject to booking fee from the booking line).
No credit cards.
A former church (it still has the pews to prove it),
the atmospheric Union Chapel stages semi-regular
gigs of various kinds, from folk to electronica. This
is a great place in which to take in brooding
Radiohead-style acts that demand a kind of religious silence or ethereal acts such as Goldfrapp,
though the sound can be a tad echoey.

Jazz venues

606 Club

90 Lots Road, Chelsea, SW10 (7352 5953/
www.606club.co.uk). Earl's Court or Fulham
Broadway tube/11, 22 bus. **Open** 7.30pm-1.30am
Mon-Wed; 8pm-2am Thur-Sat; 8pm-midnight Sun.
Gigs 8pm-1am Mon-Wed; 9.30pm-1.30am Thur;
10pm-2am Fri, Sat; 9.30-midnight Sun.
Admission *Music charge* £5 Mon-Thur, Sun;
£6 Fri, Sat. **Credit** MC, V. **Map** p396 C13.
A restaurant, late-night club and popular hangout
for musicians, this venue has the laudable policy of
booking British-based jazz musicians. There's no
entry fee – the musicians are funded from a music
charge that is added to your bill at the end of the
night. Alcohol is only served with meals.

Bull's Head

373 Lonsdale Road, Barnes, SW13 (8876 5241/
www.thebullshead.com). Barnes Bridge rail.
Open 11am-11pm Mon-Sat; noon-10.30pm Sun.
Gigs 8.30pm Mon-Sat; 2-4.30pm, 8-10.30pm Sun.
Admission £3-£10. **Credit** AmEx, DC, MC, V.
This delightful riverside pub (and Thai bistro),
which is something of a jazz landmark, still offers
gigs by musicians both from here and the States. It
has a particularly well-stocked bar (check out the
selection of malt whiskies).

Jazz Café

5 Parkway, Camden, NW1 (info 7916 6060/
box office 7344 0044/www.jazzcafe.co.uk).
Camden Town tube. **Open** 7pm-1am Mon-Thur;

7pm-2am Fri, Sat; 7pm-midnight Sun. *Gigs*
9pm daily. **Admission** £8-£20. **Credit** AmEx,
MC, V.
The ambience at the Jazz Café is good, but that's in
spite of the '80s decor and incessant nattering of
industry types on the balcony. The jazz tag is something of a misnomer, however: though music here is
usually jazzy-ish, you can expect anything from
funk and soul to singer-songwriters.

Pizza Express Jazz Club

10 Dean Street, Soho, W1 (restaurant 7437 9595/
Jazz Club 7439 8722/www.pizzaexpress.co.uk).
Tottenham Court Road tube. **Open** *Restaurant*
11.30am-midnight daily. *Jazz Club* 7.45pm-midnight
daily. *Gigs* 9pm daily. **Admission** £10-£20.
Credit AmEx, DC, MC, V. **Map** p399 K6.
There's all sorts of contemporary jazz to be sampled in the basement of this Soho eatery, with
everyone from Mose Allison to Annie Whitehead
playing here (most other Pizza Express branches
offer some form of live music; call or see the website for further details).

Pizza on the Park

11 Knightsbridge, Knightsbridge, SW1 (7235 5273).
Hyde Park Corner tube. **Open** 8.30am-midnight
Mon-Fri; 9.30am-midnight Sat, Sun. *Gigs* 9.15pm
daily. **Admission** £10-£20. **Credit** AmEx, DC,
MC, V. **Map** p400 G8.
A former branch of Pizza Express, this restaurant
just across the road from Hyde Park hosts decent
mainstream jazz artists.

Ronnie Scott's

47 Frith Street, Soho, W1 (7439 0747/
www.ronniescotts.co.uk). Leicester Square or
Tottenham Court Road tube. **Open** 8.30pm-3am
Mon-Sat; 7.30-11pm Sun. *Gigs* 9.30pm Mon-Sat;
8.30pm Sun. **Admission** £4-£20. **Credit** AmEx,
DC, MC, V. **Map** p399 K6.
One of the most famous jazz clubs in the world,
Ronnie Scott's venue in the heart of Soho continues
to dominate the scene in spite of the death of its
founder a few years back. It's certainly not cheap,
either to get into or to drink (or eat) in, but the atmosphere really is spot on, and the quality of the acts
(who play two sets a night here for a week at a time,
sometimes longer) rarely falters.

Vortex

139-41 Stoke Newington Church Street, Stoke
Newington, N16 (7254 6516/www.palay.ndirect.co.uk/
vortex.jazz). Stoke Newington rail/67, 73, 76,
106, 243 bus. **Open** 10am-11.30pm Mon-Thur;
10am-midnight Fri, Sat; 11am-11pm Sun. *Gigs* 9pm
daily. **Admission** free-£10. **Credit** MC, V.
This relaxed and very cosy café/restaurant/venue
situated in the heart of Stoke Newington is a firm
favourite among London's jazz buffs. Music ranges
from modern jazz and standards to free jazz and
karaoke. It's a great place for a coffee and for
watching the world go by from the window, or to
have some excellent (mainly veggie) food.

Sport & Fitness

Whether you're looking for a climbing wall, a yoga class or the best in spectator sports, London won't disappoint.

The weekly Sport section of *Time Out* magazine gives a rundown of the main action in everything from basketball to rugby union, while fitness, complementary therapy and alternative living are covered in the Body & Mind section. Alternatively, contact **Sportsline** (7222 8000) or your nearest leisure centre.

Participation sports

Athletics

The following are open to casual users, but are also home to athletics clubs, which can offer a more structured and competitive approach.

Barnet Copthall Stadium *Great North Way, Hendon, NW4 (8457 9915). Mill Hill East tube.* **Cost** £2/day; £53 (6mths); £73 (1yr) season ticket.
Crystal Palace National Sports Centre *Ledrington Road, Crystal Palace, SE19 (8778 0131/ www.crystalpalace.co.uk). Crystal Palace rail.* **Cost** £1.60-£2.30/day.
Millennium Arena *Battersea Park, East Carriage Drive, Battersea, SW11 (8871 7537). Battersea Park rail.* **Cost** £1.80/day.
Parliament Hill Track *Highgate Road, Hampstead Heath, NW5 (7435 8998). Gospel Oak rail.* **Cost** £2/day; £28 (1yr) season ticket.

Baseball & softball

For details of playing opportunities and to find your nearest team, contact BaseballSoftball UK.

BaseballSoftball UK *Ariel House, 74A Charlotte Street, Fitzrovia, London W1T 4QJ (7453 7055/ www.baseballsoftballuk.com).*

Cycling

Herne Hill is the oldest cycle stadium in the UK and London's only velodrome, while Lee Valley caters for BMX, road racing, time-trialling, cyclo-cross and mountain biking on various purpose-built tracks. For bike hire, *see p361*.

Herne Hill Velodrome *Burbage Road, Herne Hill, SE24 (7737 4647). Herne Hill or North Dulwich rail.* **Open** *Summer* 10am-12pm, 6-8.30pm Tue, Thur; 6-8.30pm Fri; 9am-1.30pm Sat. *Winter* noon-3.30pm Sat. **Cost** £5.30; £1.90 under-16s.
Lee Valley Cycle Circuit *Quartermile Lane, Stratford, E15 (8534 6085/www.leevalleypark.com).*

Leyton tube. **Open** *Summer* 8am-8pm daily, but check availability. *Winter* 8am-4pm daily. **Cost** *With bike hire* £4.50; £3.50 under-16s. *With own bike* £2.30; £1.20 under-16s.

Golf

Membership is not essential at the 18-hole public courses listed below. There's no course at Regent's Park, but there is a driving range and lessons can be booked. For more on courses in the capital, contact the English Golf Union (01526 354500/www.englishgolfunion.org).

Airlinks Golf Course *Southall Lane, Hounslow, Middx (8561 1418). Hounslow West tube/Hayes & Harlington rail then 195 bus.* **Fees per round** £12 Mon-Fri; £18 Sat, Sun.
Brent Valley Golf Course *Church Road, Hanwell, W7 (8567 1287). Ealing Broadway tube/rail.* **Fees per round** £7.70 Mon; £10 Tue-Fri; £14.85 before noon Sat, Sun; £12.30 after noon Sat, Sun.
Chingford Golf Course *Bury Road, Chingford, E4 (8529 5708). Chingford rail.* **Fees per round** £11 Mon-Fri; £15.25 Sat, Sun; £6.20 under-18s, OAPs after 10am Mon-Fri. (Note: golfers must wear a red shirt as the course is on a public thoroughfare.)
Lee Valley Golf Course *Picketts Lock Lane, Edmonton, N9 (8803 3611/ www.leevalleypark.org. uk). Ponders End rail.* **Fees per round** *Members* £10 Mon-Fri; £12.50 Sat, Sun. *Non-members* £12 Mon-Fri; £15 Sat, Sun.
Regent's Park Golf & Tennis School *Outer Circle, Regent's Park, NW1 (7724 0643/ www.rpgts.co.uk). Baker Street tube.* **Open** 8am-9pm daily. **Map** p398 G2.
Richmond Park Golf Course *Roehampton Gate, Priory Lane, Richmond, SW15 (8876 3205). Richmond rail/tube.* **Fees per round** £15 Mon-Fri; £18 Sat, Sun (cost drops the later in the day you play).
Stockley Park Golf Course *off Stockley Road (A408), Uxbridge, Middx (8813 5700). Heathrow Terminals 1, 2 & 3 tube then U5 bus.* **Fees per round** *Hillingdon residents* £22 Mon-Fri; £32 Sat, Sun. *Non-residents* £24 Mon-Fri; £34 Sat, Sun.

Horse riding

For a pleasant ride through Hyde Park, you need to book ahead. Wimbledon Village Stables offers classes and horses to suit riders of all ages (from three up) and abilities, with rides on the common, Putney Heath and Richmond Park.

Hyde Park Stables *63 Bathurst Mews, Paddington, W2 (7723 2813/www.hydeparkstables.com). Lancaster*

In the swim

Some of the most congenial places for swimming in the capital are afforded by its lidos, which were once a major part of London life, echoing the days when Romans introduced bathing for pleasure (though the word 'lido' itself is derived from a 17th-century beach resort near Venice).

Among the best, and without doubt the hippest of London's lidos, is **Brockwell Evian Lido** (Dulwich Road, Herne Hill, SE24, 7274 3088), renamed in 2001 after the French water bottler stepped in to save it. Built in the 1930s in the middle of a national craze for 'healthy public resorts', it also provided relief for those who couldn't get to the seaside on hot days. Along with nine other lidos, it closed and fell into disrepair during the dark days of Thatcherism, when the screws were tightened on council coffers, and from 1993, when squatters moved in, it was given a new lease of life as a venue for alternative parties, film screenings and the like. It was rescued from this ignoble fate a year later by two former council employees.

Other surviving lidos include **Parliament Hill Lido** (Gordon House Road, NW3; 7485 3873) and **Tooting Bec Lido** (Tooting Bec Road,

SW17; 8871 7198). The **Serpentine Lido** in Hyde Park, W2 (7298 2100), is most famous for the Christmas morning dips undertaken by some of London's hardier types, though it's usually only open for two months during the summer.

Other outdoor swimming venues include **Richmond Pools on the Park** (Old Deer Park, Twickenham Road, Richmond, Surrey; 8940 0561); the very central and gay-friendly **Oasis Sports Centre** (*pictured* – 32 Endell Street, Covent Garden, WC2; 7831 1804), which also has an indoor pool; and, for real back-to-nature types, the free **Hampstead Heath Ponds** (NW3; 7485 4491), which were originally brick pits. There's one pond each for single-sex bathing and one mixed pond for both sexes.

In terms of indoor facilities, we recommend **Highbury Pool** (Highbury Crescent, N5; 7704 2312), which has a women-only session from 7.30pm to 9.30pm on Tuesdays, and **Ironmonger Row Baths** (Finsbury, EC1; 7253 4011). To find your nearest swimming pool, try the *Yellow Pages* or Sportsline (7222 8000). *See also p325* **Sport & leisure centres**, and, for pools particularly suited to children, *see p273.*

Gate tube. **Open** *Summer* 10am-5pm Tue-Fri; 8.30am-5pm Sat, Sun. *Winter* 10am-sunset Tue-Fri; 8.30am-sunset Sat, Sun. **Fees** *Group lessons* £32/hr; £30/hr children. *Individual lessons* £55/hr. *Ride around Hyde Park* £30. **Map** p395 D6.
Branch: *Kensington Stables* 11 Elvaston Mews, South Kensington, SW7 (7589 2299).
Wimbledon Village Stables *24 High Street, Wimbledon, SW19 (8946 8579/www.wvstables.com). Wimbledon tube/rail.* **Open** 8am-5pm Tue-Sun. **Fees** £25-£35/hr.

Ice skating

Aside from the rinks listed below (of which only Broadgate is outdoors), the courtyard of **Somerset House** (*see p97*) has an outside rink for a few weeks over Christmas (5 Dec-20 Jan, dedicated info/ticket line 7845 4670, tickets £8 adults, £6 under-12s).

Broadgate Ice Arena *Broadgate Circus, Eldon Street, the City, EC2 (7505 4068). Liverpool Street tube/rail.* **Open** *Late Oct-Apr* noon-2.30pm, 3.30-6pm Mon-Thur; noon-2.30pm, 3.30-6pm, 7-10pm Fri; 11am-1pm, 2-4pm, 5-8.30pm Sat; 11am-1pm, 2-4pm, 5-7pm Sun. **Admission** (incl skate hire) £7; £4 children. **Map** p403 Q5.
Lee Valley Ice Centre *Lea Bridge Road, Lea Bridge, E10 (8533 3154/www.leevalleypark.org.uk). Blackhorse Road or Walthamstow Central tube/rail then 158 bus.* **Open** noon-4pm, 8.30-11pm daily. **Admission** £5.90; £4.90 children.
Leisurebox *First Bowl, 17 Queensway, Bayswater, W2 (7229 0172). Bayswater or Queensway tube.* **Open** 10am-1.45pm, 2-4.45pm, 5-6.45pm, 8-10pm Mon-Thur; 10am-1.45pm, 2-4.45pm, 5-6.45pm, 7.30-10.45pm Fri, Sat; 10am-1.45pm, 2-4.45pm, 5-6.45pm, 8-10pm Sun. **Admission** £6; £6.50 from 7.30pm Fri, Sat. **Map** p394 C6.
Streatham Ice Arena *386 Streatham High Road, Streatham, SW16 (8769 7771/www.streatham*

icearena.co.uk). Streatham rail. **Open** 10am-4pm,
4.15-7pm, 7.30-10pm Mon-Fri; 10.30am-5pm,
5.30-7.30pm, 8-11pm Sat; 10.30am-5pm Sun.
Admission £6; £5.50 under-12s; £2.50 under-4s.
Alexandra Palace Ice Rink *Alexandra Palace
Way, N22 (8365 4386). Wood Green tube/W3 bus.*
Open 11am-1.30pm, 2-5pm Mon-Thur; 11am-1.30pm,
2-5pm, 8.30-11pm Fri; 10.30am-12.30pm, 2-4.30pm,
8.30-11pm Sat, Sun. **Admission** *Mon-Fri* £3.90;
£3.30 children. *Sat, Sun* £5.20; £4.20 children.
Fri, Sat evening £5.50 per person.

Karting

All these tracks have bookable day and evening
sessions; phone for availability and prices.
Daytona Raceway *Atlas Road, Acton, NW10
(8961 3616/www.daytona.co.uk). North Acton tube.*
Playscape Pro Racing *Streatham Kart Raceway,
390 Streatham High Road, Streatham, SW16 (8677
8677/www.playscape.co.uk/karting). Streatham rail.*
Raceway *Central Warehouse, North London
Freight Terminal, York Way, King's Cross, N1
(7833 1000/www.theraceway.net). King's Cross
tube/rail.*
Teamworks Karting *Upper Level, Bishopsgate
Goods Yard, 33 Shoreditch High Street, Shoreditch,
E1 (0870 900 3020/www.teamworkskarting.com).
Liverpool Street tube/rail.*

Rollerblading

Skate Night takes place every Thursday in
Hyde Park (*see p136*); participants meet by the
the hot dog stand on the north side of the
Serpentine at 7pm. Nearby kit shops/rental

outlets include Queen's Skate Shop at 52
Queensway (7727 4669) and Slick Willies
(41 Kensington High Street; 7937 3824).

Sport & leisure centres

London's public sports centres offer various
indoor sports, plus swimming, gyms and
exercise classes. Courts or halls get booked up
well in advance. The following centres are open
to anyone, but ask about membership rates if
you're planning to use the facilities over a long
period of time. For further centres, look in the
Yellow Pages under 'Leisure Centres', or call
Sportsline (7222 8000).

Chelsea Sports Centre
*Chelsea Manor Street, Chelsea, SW3 (7352 6985).
Sloane Square tube.* **Open** 7am-10pm Mon-Fri;
8am-6.30pm Sat; 8am-10pm Sun. **Map** p397 E12.
The Chelsea Sports Centre has a 25m swimming pool
plus a teaching pool, weights, badminton, yoga and
exercise classes.

Jubilee Hall Leisure Centre
*30 The Piazza, Covent Garden, WC2 (7836 4835/
www.jubileehallclubs.co.uk). Covent Garden tube.*
Open 7am-10pm Mon-Fri; 10am-5pm Sat, Sun.
Last entry 45min before closing time. **Map** p401 L7.
A well-equipped but busy gym with plenty of free
weights. Martial arts, exercise classes and complementary therapies are also on offer.

Michael Sobell Leisure Centre
*Hornsey Road, Holloway, N7 (7609 2166/
www.aquaterra.org). Holloway Road tube/Finsbury*

Cruisin': **Skate Night** in Hyde Park.

Park tube/rail. **Open** 7am-10pm Mon-Fri; 9am-6pm Sat; 9am-9.30pm Sun.

Activities at this north London centre include squash, trampolining, exercise classes, skating and a wide range of sports in the massive main arena.

Mornington Sports & Leisure Centre

142-50 Arlington Road, Camden, NW1 (7267 3600/ www.hp-mornington.freeservers.com). Camden Town tube. **Open** 7am-9pm Mon-Fri; 10am-5pm Sat, Sun. **Map** p398 J2.

A small centre with the usual range of team sports – volleyball, basketball and football – plus a gym and plenty of exercise classes.

Queen Mother Sports Centre

223 Vauxhall Bridge Road, Victoria, SW1 (7630 5522). Victoria tube/rail. **Open** 6.30am-8pm Mon; 9.30am-8pm Tue; 7.30am-8pm Wed, Fri; 8am-5.30pm Sat, Sun. **Map** p400 J10.

This centre is Victoria has a well-equipped gym, with two exercise studios, and facilities for badminton, swimming and diving, and martial arts. Beauty treatments are also available.

Seymour Leisure Centre

Seymour Place, Marylebone, W1 (7723 8019). Edgware Road or Marble Arch tube. **Open** 7am-10pm Mon-Fri; 7am-8pm Sat; 8am-8pm Sun. **Map** p395 F5.

A '30s-style centre with a swimming pool, sports hall, fitness room, steam and sauna suite, plus a Courtney's gym with separate tariffs. The 'Move It' programme of exercise classes is justly renowned.

Westway Sports Centre

1 Crowthorne Road, Ladbroke Grove, W10 (8969 0992). Latimer Road tube. **Open** 9am-10pm Mon, Wed, Fri; 7am-10pm Tue, Thur, Sat; 10am-10pm Sun.

After a recent £10-million overhaul, this is one of London's most advanced sports centres. It now boasts the UK's biggest climbing facility, a floodlit riding arena, indoor tennis courts, all-weather football pitches and even four courts for the obscure game of Eton Fives.

Tennis

Private facilities and coaching – available at, among other places, the Islington Tennis Centre with its two outdoor courts and six indoor courts – can be pricey, but many of London's public parks have tennis courts that cost little or nothing to use; ring your nearest park for details. **Sportsline** (7222 8000) may also be able to help you find venues.

If you want to test your shots on grass, phone or write (with a stamped SAE) to the Information Department at the **Lawn Tennis Association**, Queen's Club, Palliser Road, West Kensington, London W14 9EG (7381 7000/www.lta.org.uk) for a leaflet on venues (the Middlesex one includes central London).

Islington Tennis Centre *Market Road, Barnsbury, N7 (7700 1370/www.aquaterra.org). Caledonian Road tube.* **Open** 7am-11pm Mon-Thur; 7am-10pm Fri; 8am-10pm Sat, Sun. **Fees** *Outdoor* £6-£7/hr. *Indoor* £14-£15.50/hr.

Tenpin bowling

Listed here are a few of London's best bowling centres; for other choices call the **British Tenpin Bowling Association** (8478 1745/ www.btba.org.uk). The average price is around £5 per game, including the hire of shoes. *See also p324 Leisurebox.*

Rowans Bowl *10 Stroud Green Road, Finsbury Park, N4 (8800 1950/www.rowans.co.uk). Finsbury Park tube/rail.* **Open** 10.30am-1am Mon-Thur; 10.30am-3.30am Fri, Sat; 10.30am-1.30am Sun. **Lanes** 24.

Streatham Mega Bowl *142 Streatham Hill, Streatham, SW2 (8671 5021/www.megabowl.co.uk). Streatham Hill rail.* **Open** 10am-midnight Mon, Sun; 10am-1am Tue-Sat. **Lanes** 36.

XS Superbowl *15-17 Alpine Way, Beckton, E6 (7511 4440). East Ham tube then 101 bus/Beckton DLR.* **Open** noon-midnight Mon-Thur, Sun; noon-2am Fri, Sat. **Lanes** 22.

Watersports

Of the companies listed, Capital specialises in rowing; DS&WC offers dragonboat racing, sailing, rowing and canoeing; the DWC has jet-skiing; and Lee Valley has windsurfing, sailing, water-skiing and canoeing.

Capital Rowing Centre *Kingston Rowing Club, Lower Ham Road, off Richmond Road, Kingston-upon-Thames, Surrey (07973 314199). Kingston rail.* **Open** daily, times vary.

Docklands Sailing & Watersports Centre *Millwall Dock, Westferry Road, Docklands, E14 (7537 2626/www.dswc.org). Crossharbour DLR.* **Open** *Summer* 9.30am-11pm Mon-Fri; 9.30am-5pm Sat, Sun. *Winter* times vary; phone for details.

Docklands Watersports Club *Tereza Joanne, Gate 14, King George V Dock, Woolwich Manor Way, Woolwich, E16 (7511 7000/www.tereza-joanne.com). Gallions Reach DLR/North Woolwich rail.* **Open** *Summer* 10am-dusk Wed-Sun. *Winter* 10am-dusk Thur-Sun.

Lee Valley Watersports Centre *Banbury Reservoir, Harbet Road, Chingford, E4 (8531 1129/ www.leevalleypark.org.uk). Angel Road rail.* **Open** *Apr-Oct* times vary Mon-Fri; 10am-dusk Sat, Sun.

Spectator sports

Basketball

This increasingly popular sport has a number of teams in the capital. The London Towers play in the elite Dairylea Dunkers Championship and two European competitions. For more details,

contact the **English Basketball Association** (0113 236 1166/www.basketballengland.org.uk).
London Towers *Crystal Palace National Sports Centre, Ledrington Road, Crystal Palace, SE19 (8776 7755/www.london-towers.co.uk). Crystal Palace rail.* **Admission** £8; £6 concessions.

Boxing

Though its dissenters have recently been more vocal, there are still legions of fans paying good money to see major fights around London. Seats can cost from £20 to £200; more for a big world-title bout. Most promotions take place at York Hall Leisure Centre on Old Ford Road, Bethnal Green, E2 (8980 2243), though major championship fights are staged at bigger venues such as Earl's Court, Wembley Arena or the London Arena (*see p330*). For info, contact the **BBBC** (7403 5879/www.bbbofc.com).

Cricket

If time is of the essence, catch a one-day match in the NatWest Trophy or Norwich Union National League rather than a County Championship match staged over four days. For regular games (everything except the semi-finals and finals of knockout competitions), tickets cost £10 or less; tickets for internationals are far harder to come by.

Lord's and the Oval host internationals, one-day games and cup finals and semi-finals, and are home to Middlesex and Surrey cricket clubs respectively. The season is April to September.

Foster's Oval *Kennington Oval, Kennington, SE11 (7582 7764/www.surreyccc.co.uk). Oval tube.*
Lord's *St John's Wood Road, St John's Wood, NW8 (MCC info 7289 1611/tickets 7432 1066/ www.lords.org.uk). St John's Wood tube.*

Football

Tickets for FA Barclaycard Premiership matches are now virtually impossible to come by for casual spectators, and each of London's Premier League clubs attracts sell-out crowds most weeks. Yet London clubs also feature in all three divisions of the Nationwide League, and at this level tickets are cheaper and easier to get. The prices quoted are for adult non-members buying on a match-by-match basis.

Clubs

Arsenal *Arsenal Stadium, Avenell Road, Highbury, N5 (7704 4000/www.arsenal.com). Arsenal tube.* **Tickets** £21-£39. FA Barclaycard Premiership.
Brentford *Griffin Park, Braemar Road, Brentford, Middx (8847 2511/www.brentfordfc.com). South Ealing tube/Brentford rail.* **Tickets** £10 standing; £10-£15 seated. Nationwide League Division 2.

Charlton Athletic *The Valley, Floyd Road, Charlton, SE7 (8333 4010/www.cafc.co.uk). Charlton rail.* **Tickets** £20-£25. FA Barclaycard Premiership.
Chelsea *Stamford Bridge, Fulham Road, Chelsea, SW6 (7386 7799/www.chelseafc.co.uk). Fulham Broadway tube.* **Tickets** £27-£40. FA Barclaycard Premiership. **Map** p396 B13.
Crystal Palace *Selhurst Park, Whitehorse Lane, Selhurst, SE25 (8771 8841/www.cpfc.co.uk). Selhurst rail.* **Tickets** £18-£25. Nationwide League Division 1.
Fulham *Craven Cottage, Stevenage Road, Fulham, SW6 (7893 8383/www.fulhamfc.co.uk). Putney Bridge tube.* **Tickets** £16 standing; £22-£26 seated. FA Barclaycard Premiership.
Leyton Orient *Matchroom Stadium, Brisbane Road, Leyton, E10 (8926 1111/www.leytonorient.com). Leyton tube.* **Tickets** £12-£16. Nationwide League Division 3.
Millwall *The Den, Zampa Road, Bermondsey, SE16 (7231 9999/www.millwallfc.co.uk). South Bermondsey rail.* **Tickets** £15-£20. Nationwide League Division 1.
Queens Park Rangers *Loftus Road Stadium, South Africa Road, Shepherd's Bush, W12 (8740 2575/www.qpr.co.uk). White City tube.* **Tickets** £15-£18. Nationwide League Division 2.
Tottenham Hotspur *White Hart Lane, Bill Nicholson Way, High Road, Tottenham, N17 (08700 112222/www.spurs.co.uk). White Hart Lane rail.* **Tickets** £27-£55. FA Barclaycard Premiership.
Watford *Vicarage Road, Watford, Hertfordshire (01923 496010/www.watfordfc.com). Watford High Street rail.* **Tickets** £16-£25. Nationwide League Division 1.
West Ham United *Boleyn Ground, Green Street, West Ham, E13 (8548 2700/www.whufc.com). Upton Park tube.* **Tickets** £26-£46. FA Barclaycard Premiership.
Wimbledon *Selhurst Park, Whitehorse Lane, Selhurst, SE25 (8771 8841/www.wimbledon-fc.co.uk). Selhurst rail.* **Tickets** £16-£25. Nationwide League Division 1.

Golf

Two of the UK's most famous courses lie within easy reach of London. Wentworth hosts the World Matchplay tournament every October.

Sunningdale *Ridgemount Road, Sunningdale, near Ascot, Berkshire (01344 621681/ www.sunningdale-golfclub.co.uk). Sunningdale rail.*
Wentworth *Wentworth Drive, Virginia Water, Surrey (01344 842201/www.wentworthclub.com). Virginia Water rail.*

Greyhound racing

One of Britain's most popular spectator sports is great fun for an evening out, and very user-friendly for the uninitiated. All tracks have bars and restaurants. For more general information and venue details, see www.thedogs.co.uk.

Catford Stadium *Adenmore Road, Catford, SE6 (8690 8000). Catford or Catford Bridge rail.* **Races** 7.30pm Mon; 7.20pm Thur, Sat. **Admission** £4.50.

Arts & Entertainment

Relax!

However much you love London, the noise, the pollution, the crowds, the pace of life and the sheer cost of living are sometimes going to get you down. For times when you can't escape with the help of our Trips Out of Town chapter (*see p339*), or, better still, the latest edition of the popular *Time Out Book of Weekend Breaks*, we asked Barefoot Doctor (healer, *Observer* 'Wellbeing' columnist and author of *Return of the Urban Warrior*; £12.99) for his tips on how to stay sane in the city.

'No matter what you're doing,' he told us, 'always remember to keep your breath flowing. Stop holding your breath, in other words. As tensions accumulate, imagine yourself to be releasing them on the exhalation. Breathing is the greatest key to staying sane (and alive).

'At all times, keep checking your body for muscular tension and whenever you find some, release it with an outbreath and the internal command, "relax!". Relaxing your muscles is the key to relaxing your mind. Do this through the day and night no matter what else you're engaged in.

'Lastly, no matter how tough things get, keep reminding yourself to be grateful for the privilege of being alive to witness the extraordinary theatre of human life on the planet at this time, however insane it appears to be. Just keep muttering under your breath, "thank you!", but don't move your lips too much or they may come and take you away.'

For those who need help in getting into a meditative frame of mind, yoga has really taken off again over the past few years, largely thanks to glamorous converts such as Sting, Madonna and Gwyneth Paltrow. Whether you're a beginner or an advanced student, London is now full of places where you can stretch your aching muscles and ease your tired mind.

The **Iyengar Institute** (223A Randolph Avenue, Maida Vale, W9; 7624 3080/ www.iyi.org.uk) specialises, as the name suggests, in Iyengar, a focused and precise style of yoga, while relative newcomer **Triyoga** (*pictured* – 6 Erskine Road, Primrose Hill, NW3;, 7586 5939) is a bright, funky centre offering classes, therapies and Pilates. Unsurprisingly, new agey Stoke Newington has its own dedicated centre in the form of **Yogahome** (11 Allen Road, N16; 7249 2425/ www.yogahome.com), which offers classes in almost every style, from £6 for a drop-in class to £36 for six-week course.

Romford Stadium *London Road, Romford, Essex (01708 762345). Romford rail.* **Races** 7.35pm Mon, Wed, Fri; 7.30pm Sat. **Admission** £1.50-£5.50.
Walthamstow Stadium *Chingford Road, Chingford, E4 (8531 4255/www.wsgreyhound.co.uk). Walthamstow Central tube/rail then 97, 215 bus.* **Races** 7.30pm Tue, Thur, Sat. **Admission** free-£6.
Wimbledon Stadium *Plough Lane, Wimbledon, SW17 (8946 8000/www.wimbledondogs.co.uk). Tooting Broadway tube/Wimbledon tube/rail/ Haydons Road rail.* **Races** 7.30pm Tue, Fri, Sat. **Admission** £3-£5.50.

Horse racing

The horse racing year is roughly divided into the flat racing season (Apr-Sept) and the National Hunt season (ie jumps racing; Oct-Apr). Evening meetings are held in summer. Courses have plenty of places to eat and drink.

Ascot

High Street, Ascot, Berkshire (01344 622211/ www.ascot.co.uk). Ascot rail. **Admission** £6-£50. Britain's premier flat racing course is best known for the Royal Meeting in June, when the Queen – and countless other toffs in hats – drop in for a flutter and admission prices rocket. In 2002, the Royal Meeting will be held from 18-22 June (Ladies' Day is on 20 June); booking is essential. *See also p264.*

Epsom

Epsom Downs, Epsom, Surrey (01372 726311/ www.epsomderby.co.uk). Epsom, Epsom Downs or Tattenham Corner rail. **Admission** *(for ordinary meetings)* £5-£18.
The Oaks and the Derby are both run at Epsom (7 June 2002 is the Vodafone Oaks & Vodafone Coronation Cup, tickets £5-£60; 8 June 2002 is the Vodafone Derby, tickets £5-£95). In contrast to the exclusive Royal Meeting at Ascot, 'Derby Day' is a traditional Londoners' day out; *see p263.*

Those with ailments such as asthma, ME, hypertension, arthritis, diabetes, menstrual problems and stress-related illness can find helpful courses at the **Yoga Therapy Centre** (Homeopathic Hospital, 60 Great Ormond Street, Bloomsbury, WC1; 7419 7195), as well as general drop-in classes (£6 to £8.50). A charitable institution, it boasts large, airy premises and excellent teachers.

For those who want to just lie back and let it all wash over them, London's spa scene has also improved of late. For a dose of true luxury, head to one of the posh hotels. The **Dorchester Spa** (Dorchester Hotel, Park Lane, W1; 7495 7335) offers art deco splendour for a £35 day membership charge (treatments are extra, but day membership then drops to just £15); the **Spa at the Mandarin Oriental** (66 Knightsbridge, SW1; 7838 9888) pampers you with outrageously good treatments (a customised personal treatment starts at £140, including the use

of spa facilities); and **Agua at the Sanderson** (50 Berners Street, W1; 7300 1414) is an all-white, Philippe Starck-designed nirvana with heavenly treatments costing from £44 for a 30-minute massage to £226 for a package of four chosen treatments.

Those whose flesh is willing but whose finances are weak could check out the **Porchester Spa** (*pictured* – Queensway, Bayswater, W2; 7792 3980), with its bargain admission fee of £18.95, which includes use of the swimming pool in the adjoining leisure centre. The spa itself boasts art deco-style relaxation areas, Turkish hot rooms, Russian steam rooms, a sauna, a plunge pool and a range of complementary therapies that come in at around the £30 mark.

If you can't really spare the time for a full-on relaxation session, try a reviving 20-minute massage (£16.95) at the **Walk-in Backrub** (14 Neal's Yard, Covent Garden, WC2; 7836 9111; 11 Charlotte Place, Fitzrovia, W1; 7436 9876; and Selfridges – *see p236*) or a fabulous shiatsu head and shoulders massage at one of London's skilled Japanese hairdressers: we particularly recommend **J Moriyama** (58 Upper Montagu Street, W1; 7724 8860; £15 for a massage, or free with a haircut).

For more spas, beauty salons, herbalists and complementary clinics, see the annual *Time Out Shopping Guide* for detailed listings. For more urban wisdom from Barefoot Doctor, visit www.barefootdoctorglobal.com.

Kempton Park

Staines Road East, Sunbury-on-Thames, Middx (01932 782292/www.kempton.co.uk). Kempton Park rail. **Admission** £6-£17.
The King George VI Stakes, run on Boxing Day (26 Dec), is an annual highlight at this popular course.

Sandown Park

Portsmouth Road, Esher, Surrey (01372 463072/ www.sandown.co.uk). Esher rail. **Admission** £5-£17.
Sandown is generally considered the best equipped of the South-east tracks. Its major occasions include the Whitbread Gold Cup (27 Apr 2002) and the Coral Eclipse Stakes (6 July 2002).

Windsor

Maidenhead Road, Windsor, Berkshire (01753 865234/www.windsorracing.co.uk). Windsor & Eton Riverside rail. **Admission** £5-£18.
Though Windsor hosts meetings year round, it's better known as a flat racing course and its summer evening meetings are particularly popular.

Ice hockey

Created in 1998 to spearhead British ice hockey's expansion, the London Knights play (with some success) in the Sekonda Superleague. Slough play in the lower-grade British National League. The season is from September to March.

London Knights *London Arena, Limeharbour, Docklands, E14 (7538 1212/www.knightice.co.uk). Crossharbour & London Arena DLR.* **Admission** £12-£18; £7 concessions.
Slough Jets *Ice Arena, Montem Lane, Slough, Berkshire (01753 822658/www.sloughjets.co.uk). Slough rail.* **Admission** £8; £4.50 children.

Motor sport

Every Sunday evening a range of bangers, hot rods and stock cars provide a bout of family-oriented mayhem at this stadium in Wimbledon.

Wimbledon Stadium *Plough Lane, Wimbledon, SW17 (8946 8000/www.wimbledonstadium.co.uk). Tooting Broadway tube/Wimbledon tube/rail/ Earlsfield or Haydons Road rail.* **Admission** £10; £5 concessions.

Rugby league

The Broncos are the only professional rugby league team outside the game's traditional northern heartland; they work hard to overcome local indifference to the 13-a-side code. The Super League season runs March to September.

London Broncos *The Valley, Floyd Road, Charlton, SE7 (8853 8800/www.londonbroncos.co.uk). Charlton rail.* **Admission** £10-£15; £3-£5 children. As we go to press, the Broncos have announced that they will not be playing at the Valley in 2002, due to relaying of the pitch. For further information, consult the team's website.

Rugby union

With a capacity of more than 60,000, Twickenham is the home of English rugby union, playing host to most internationals and major domestic cup finals. Tickets for matches in the Six Nations Championship (January to March) are almost impossible for casual spectators to obtain, but those for cup finals and other matches are easier to come by; call for details.

Many leading internationals play their club rugby in London, notably with Harlequins, London Wasps and Saracens. The Zurich Premiership and lower-grade National League seasons run from August to May; most games are played on Saturday and Sunday afternoons.

Twickenham *Whitton Road, Twickenham, Middx (info 8892 2000/tickets 8831 6666/www.rfu.com). Twickenham rail.*

Clubs

Esher *369 Molesey Road, Hersham, Surrey (01932 220295/www.esherrfc.org). Hersham rail.* **Admission** £5; free under-16s. National League Division 2.

London Wasps *Loftus Road Stadium, South Africa Road, Shepherd's Bush, W12 (8740 2545/ www.wasps.co.uk). White City tube.* **Admission** £10-£15. Zurich Premiership.

London Welsh *Old Deer Park, Kew Road, Richmond, Surrey (8940 2368/www.london-welsh. co.uk). Richmond tube/rail.* **Admission** £10 standing; £13 seated. National League Division 1.

NEC Harlequins *Stoop Memorial Ground, Langhorn Drive, Twickenham, Middx (8410 6000/ www.quins.co.uk). Twickenham rail.* **Admission** £10-£25. Zurich Premiership.

Rosslyn Park *Priory Lane, Upper Richmond Road, Roehampton, SW15 (8876 6044/ www.rosslynpark.co.uk). Barnes rail.* **Admission** £8; £4 concessions. National League Division 2.

Saracens *Vicarage Road Stadium, Watford, Hertfordshire (01923 496200/www.saracens.com). Watford High Street rail.* **Admission** £10-£35. Zurich Premiership.

Tennis

Britain's most famous tournament runs from 24 June to 7 July 2002. Seats on Centre and Number One courts are allocated by ballot and must be applied for the previous year. However, if you're prepared to spend a few hours queuing, you can get into the outer courts, where the freedom to wander from match to match means you're never far from the action. Later in the day, you can buy returned show-court tickets for a fraction of their face value.

Wimbledon is preceded by the Stella Artois tournament, where stars from the men's circuit warm up for the main event. The 2002 event will be held from 10 to 16 June at Queen's Club.

All England Lawn Tennis Club (Wimbledon) *PO Box 98, Church Road, Wimbledon, SW19 (8944 1066/info 8946 2244/www.wimbledon.org). Southfields tube.*

Queen's Club *Palliser Road, Hammersmith, W14 (7385 3421/www.queensclub.co.uk). Barons Court tube.*

Major venues

Crystal Palace National Sports Centre

Ledrington Road, Crystal Palace, SE19 (8778 0131/ www.crystalpalace.co.uk). Crystal Palace rail. London's only major athletics stadium is in dire need of some refurbishment, but it still stages a Grand Prix athletics meeting every summer. The sports centre hosts a huge variety of activities and competitions, including basketball, netball, martial arts, hockey and weightlifting.

London Arena

Limeharbour, Docklands, E14 (7538 1212/ www.londonarena.co.uk). Crossharbour & London Arena DLR/D8, D9 bus. Though it looks like a warehouse from outside, the London Arena provides an impressively modern and comfortable setting for major indoor sports. As well as being home to ice hockey's London Knights team (*see p329*), it plays host to big boxing promotions (*see p327*).

Wembley Arena/Conference Centre

Empire Way, Wembley, Middx (8902 0902/ www.wembley.co.uk). Wembley Park tube/Wembley Stadium rail. Since the closure of Wembley stadium in 2000, sporting activity here has diminished significantly, though you can still see the likes of showjumping and basketball at the Arena, while the nearby Conference Centre hosts boxing and snooker.

Theatre

London's theatre scene has taken some knocks but remains vibrant.

London's West End theatres aren't packing in the punters like they used to. The dire events of 2001 – from the countryside-closing foot-and-mouth epidemic to the tragedy of 11 September – have meant a general reduction in tourist numbers, and London's theatres were among the first to feel the pinch: in autumn 2001 a number of long-running big productions, including *The Witches of Eastwick* and *Peggy Sue Got Married*, were forced to close early, while *Starlight Express* is grinding to a halt in January 2002. But there are other problems: iniquitous booking fees, which can add £1.50 to the price of an already expensive ticket, pricey programmes and interval drinks, and, in some of the older theatres, uncomfy seats and poor sightlines, can all too often make an evening at the theatre feel like an assault course.

But it's not all bad news. The resilient West End continues to roll out big new productions – Andrew Lloyd Webber's *Bombay Dreams*, stage versions of *The Full Monty* and *Chitty Chitty Bang Bang* and a new Queen musical scripted by Ben Elton are all scheduled to open in 2002. At the other end of the scale, there's the unmissable world of fringe performances, often in intimate, low-key venues.

The West End is a cultural, rather than a geographic, term. Some of its leading theatres lie well outside the traditional boundaries of London's theatreland. The most reliable of West End venues, with an exciting repertory of new plays and classics rather than fixed, long-running programmes, are the building-based companies such as the South Bank's **Royal National Theatre** (*see p333*), the **Royal Shakespeare Company** (*see p333*; two theatres in the Barbican during the winter season) and **Shakespeare's Globe** (*see p77 and p334*).

Off-West End refers to the next rung down in terms of financial means, and generally offers the best mix of quality and originality. These theatres are usually heavily subsidised, paying minimum wages or, in some cases, no wages at all. Top writers, directors and actors are lured, instead, by the prospect of artistic liberty. But even these places have their own pecking order: wealthier theatres such as the **Young Vic** (*see p338*) and the **Almeida** (*see p337*) lead the pack, with the likes of the **Gate** and the **King's Head** (for both, *see p338*) often dependent on fresh-out-of-drama-college hopefuls prepared to work for nothing to make their names.

The Fringe, meanwhile, is scattered all over London. It's the theatrical underclass where standards are much more variable. There is, of course, a lot of good work to be found, and many of the biggest names in British theatre

The best Theatres

For young writers
Royal Court (*see p333*); The Bush (*see p337*).

For alfresco productions
Shakespeare's Globe (*see p334*); Holland Park Theatre (*see p338*); Open Air Theatre (*see p338*).

For glimpses of flesh
The Graduate (*see p335*).

For classic Cole Porter
Kiss Me Kate (*see p335*).

For breathtaking costumes
The Lion King (*see p335*).

Engage with the elements at the **Open Air Theatre** in Regent's Park. See p338.

GREAT NIGHTS OUT

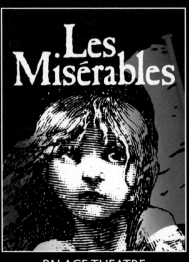

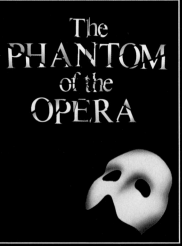

started their careers in these more humble venues, but finding such shows is, in practice, like winning the lottery. Among the most reliable venues are the Finborough Theatre (118 Finborough Road, SW10, 7373 3842), the New End Theatre (27 New End, NW3, 7794 0022) and the Grace Theatre (503 Battersea Park Road, SW11, 7794 0022), all three struggling in adverse financial circumstances to develop bold artistic policies.

For the latest fringe productions, see *Time Out* magazine's comprehensive weekly theatre listings, which also take in the West End and Off-West End.

Tickets & information

Tickets for big musicals are pricey and can be hard to obtain. **Ticketmaster** (7344 4444, www.ticketmaster.co.uk) and **First Call** (7420 0000, www.firstcalltickets.com) offer advance tickets, but watch out for those big bad booking fees, which can bump up the price by at least ten per cent. The cheapest option is to buy your tickets in person with cash direct from the theatre. Bear in mind that many theatres offer 24-hour phone sales by rolling over to a big ticket merchant – such as the two mentioned above – when the box office closes, which means that tickets are subject to booking fees; to avoid extra fees, call during office hours.

Many West End theatres also offer reduced-price tickets for performances that have not sold out. These seats, available only on the night, are known as 'standby' tickets, and sell for about half what a top-priced ticket would cost. We've listed standby prices in this section, but be sure to call to check both availability and conditions (some standby tickets are limited to students, and it varies from theatre to theatre as to when standbys are put on sale).

Alternatively, try **tkts**, a non-profit-making organisation run by the Society of London Theatres that sells tickets for West End shows on a first-come, first-served basis on the day of the performance only. Though each ticket is subject to a service charge of £2.50, and a maximum of four are allowed per customer, the discounts available are often spectacular: tickets for almost every West End show can often be snapped up with as much as 50 per cent off face value. You should be aware that most of the gaudy booths advertising cheap theatre seats around the rest of Leicester Square are unofficial and, often, more than a little dodgy. Avoid them at all costs.

tkts

Leicester Square, WC2 (www.officiallondontheatre.co.uk). Leicester Square tube. **Open** 10am-7pm Mon-Sat; noon-3pm Sun. **Credit** AmEx, DC, MC, V. **Map** p401 K7.

The Lion King. *See p335.*

West End

Repertory companies

Royal Court

Sloane Square, Chelsea, SW1 (7565 5000/ www.royalcourttheatre.com). Sloane Square tube. **Box office** 10am-6pm Mon-Sat. **Tickets** 10p-£26; all tickets £5 Mon. **Credit** AmEx, MC, V. **Map** p400 G11. The Royal Court is the undisputed epicentre of new writing in Britain. Now firmly re-established in its long-time Sloane Square home after a £25 million refurbishment, it boasts two performing spaces – the imaginatively titled 'Upstairs' (a small studio theatre) and 'Downstairs' (a proscenium arch main stage) – plus a snazzy restaurant and bar.

Royal National Theatre

South Bank, SE1 (info 7452 3400/box office 7452 3000/www.nationaltheatre.org.uk). Embankment tube/Charing Cross or Waterloo tube/rail. **Box office** 10am-8pm Mon-Sat. **Tickets** *Olivier & Lyttelton* £10-£32. *Cottesloe* £13-£24. *Standby* £8, £15. **Credit** AmEx, DC, MC, V. **Map** p401 M7. It's all change at the National, which has announced the appointment of Nicholas Hytner as director, succeeding Trevor Nunn in April 2003. In addition, Trevor Nunn has announced proposals for the transformation of the unlovely proscenium-arched Lyttleton Theatre, one of the National's three performance spaces, into two new spaces: a 650-seat 'arena' and a 100-seat loft (a new, flexible performance space dedicated to presenting the work of young writers, directors and artists). Meanwhile, Nunn's impressive development of the work of the core repertory company looks set to continue. Productions planned for 2002 include Molière's *Tartuffe*, the *Bacchae* by Euripides, a new trilogy by Tom Stoppard and, to celebrate the centenary of Richard Rodgers' birth, a new production of *South Pacific*, not seen in London for 13 years.

Royal Shakespeare Company

Barbican Centre, Silk Street, The City, EC2 (7638 8891/www.rsc.org.uk). Barbican tube/Moorgate tube/rail. **Box office** 9am-8pm daily. **Tickets** £5-£35. *Standby* £12, £7. **Credit** AmEx, MC, V. **Map** p402 P5.

The principal custodian of Shakespeare's legacy in Britain, the RSC also stages works by new and classical writers of relevance to the Bard, as well as doing a sideline in money-spinning musicals such as *Les Misérables*. Aside from national tours, it divides its time between its main home in Stratford-upon-Avon (*see p350*) at the Royal Shakespeare Theatre, the Swan and the Other Place in Stratford, and, between October and May, the Barbican Centre (the huge Barbican Theatre and the more intimate space of the Pit); *see also p95*. In 2002 the RSC plans to renew its award-winning collaboration with the Lyric Hammersmith (*see p338*), co-producing Henrich von Kleist's *The Prince of Homburg*. Other productions planned for 2002 include *Hamlet*, *Twelfth Night*, *King John* and a new play entitled *The Prisoner's Dilemma*. As we go to press, plans are afoot for the RSC to move location in April 2002 – where it will end up is, as yet, undecided.

Shakespeare's Globe

21 New Globe Walk, Bankside, SE1 (7401 9919/ www.shakespeares-globe.org). Blackfriars or Mansion House tube. **Box office** *Off season* 10am-5pm Mon-Fri. *Theatre season* 10am-8pm daily. **Tickets** £5-£27. **Credit** AmEx, MC, V. **Map** p404 O7.

More than a heritage gimmick, the Globe has established itself as a serious theatre under Mark Rylance, staging plays in the open-air theatre that replicates the original Globe from October to April. With the background noise of modern life and the transient interest of coach parties, the theatre is no friend of artistic nuance, but it does offer interesting insights into how Will dealt with mob dynamics, and the productions are rarely less than fun. *See also p77.*

Long-runners & musicals

Most theatres have evening shows Monday to Saturday (starting 7.30-8pm) and matinées on one weekday (usually Wednesday) and Saturday. Check *Time Out* magazine for details.

An Inspector Calls

Playhouse Theatre, Northumberland Avenue, WC2 (7494 5372). Embankment tube. **Box office** 10am-7.45pm Tue-Fri; 10am-8.15pm Sat. **Tickets** £14-£35. *Standby* £15. **Credit** AmEx, MC, V.

After a change in venue, Stephen Daldry's production of JB Priestley's repertory warhorse continues to run. An expressionist psychological and social parable, it's set in a sort of giant dolls' house on stilts in the middle of an Edwardian slum. No performances on Saturdays and Sundays.

Art

Whitehall Theatre, Whitehall (south of Trafalgar Square), SW1 (7321 5405). Embankment tube/ Charing Cross tube/rail. **Box office** *In person* 10am-8.15pm Mon-Sat. *By phone* 9am-9pm Mon-Sat; 10am-6pm Sun. *Ticketmaster* 24hrs daily. **Tickets** £18-£35. *Day seats* £1. **Credit** AmEx, MC, V. **Map** p401 L8.

Yasmina Reza's lightweight satire involves three men whose friendship is blown apart when one buys an overpriced painting. The perennially popular show is subject to frequent cast changes but usually features at least one big name.

Blood Brothers

Phoenix Theatre, Charing Cross Road, St Giles's, WC2 (7369 1733/www.theambassadors.com). Tottenham Court Road tube. **Box office** *In person* 10am-7.45pm

Who they? the Generating Company

Though cirque nouveau, with its dazzling brand of modern, animal-free circus focusing on physical skills and bravura, took the world by storm in the '90s, Britain had to content itself with occasional shows by visiting overseas companies such as Cirque du Soleil and Cirque Eloize from Canada, De La Guarda from Argentina and Circus Oz from, you've guessed it, Australia. But the closing of the ill-fated Millennium Dome Experience put paid to this lack: when the Central Arena show that was the Dome's high point packed up its harnesses and bungee stilts, the Generating Company (or Genco for short) was born, giving Britain a young, sexy and vibrant circus company all of its own.

Resident at the Circus Space in Hoxton, Genco made its debut with *Storm*, a big, flashy show about 24 hours in the life of a city as an all-engulfing storm approaches.

Performed by 25 of the world's most innovative aerial performers and musicians, *Storm* played to packed houses in London for four weeks before touring Britain and Ireland to acclaim. In 2002 the troupe will take the show to six European cities, but British fans will be able to catch it again in London in August. In summer, meanwhile, party-goers in Ibiza will be able to see Genco in action in its second season at raunchy club Manumission.

Those who can't wait that long will be pleased to hear that there are plans to open a new circus/theatre performance in London in April prior to a 14-week UK tour; for details of this and for further information on the Circus Space, including its summer school for would-be jugglers or tightwire artists, call 7613 4141 or check out the website www.thecircusspace.co.uk.

Mon-Sat. *By phone* 9am-9pm Mon-Sat; 10am-6pm Sun. *Ticketmaster* 24hrs daily. **Tickets** £14.50-£37.50. *Standby* £15. **Credit** AmEx, MC, V. **Map** p399 K6. Scouse sentiment and toe-tapping songs in Willy Russell's likeable, long-running melodrama about two brothers separated at birth and exiled to opposite ends of the social ladder.

Buddy

Strand Theatre, Aldwych, Holborn, WC2 (7930 8800/ www.trh.co.uk). Covent Garden tube. **Box office** *In person* 10am-6pm Mon; 10am-8pm Tue-Sat; 12.30-4pm Sun. *By phone* 10am-8pm Mon-Sat; 12.30-4pm Sun. **Tickets** £14.50-£35. **Credit** AmEx, MC, V. **Map** p399 M6. A singalong, dance-in-the-aisles review of the rise and nose-dive of Buddy Holly.

Cats

New London Theatre, Drury Lane, Covent Garden, WC2 (7405 0072/www.catsthemusical.com). Covent Garden or Holborn tube. **Box office** *In person* 10am-7.45pm Mon-Sat. *By phone* 10am-8pm Mon-Sat. *Ticketmaster* 24hrs daily. **Tickets** £10.50-£37.50. *Standby* £15. **Credit** AmEx, DC, MC, V. **Map** p399 L6. London's longest-running musical, a Lloyd Webber offering based on TS Eliot's *Old Possum's Book of Practical Cats*, refuses to die. Won't somebody please put it out of its misery?

Chicago

Adelphi Theatre, Strand, Covent Garden, WC2 (Ticketmaster 7344 0055). Charing Cross tube/rail. **Box office** *In person* 10am-8pm Mon-Sat. *By phone* 24hrs daily. **Tickets** £16-£38.50. **Credit** AmEx, MC, V. **Map** p401 L7. Kander and Ebb's Easy Street has established itself as a West End staple.

Fame

Cambridge Theatre, Earlham Street, Covent Garden WC2 (7494 5080). Covent Garden tube. **Box office** *In person* 10am-7.30pm Mon-Thur, Sat; 10am-8.30pm Fri. *By phone* 24hrs daily. **Tickets** £12.50-£35. *Fri mat (5.30pm)* all tickets half price. **Credit** AmEx, MC, V. Based on the 1980s film and television series and set in the New York High School for Performing Arts, this relentlessly upbeat show is strong on high-octane dancing.

The Graduate

Gielgud Theatre, 33 Shaftesbury Avenue, Soho, W1 (7494 5065). Piccadilly Circus tube. **Box office** *In person* 10am-6pm Mon-Sat. *By phone* 24hrs daily. **Tickets** £15-£35. **Credit** AmEx, JCB, MC, V. A Terry Johnson adapted and directed version of the quintessential '60s classic. If the verbal gags fail to amuse, the bewildering array of leading ladies (from Jerry Hall to Linda Gray), each appearing for a limited season, is always intriguing.

Kiss Me Kate

Victoria Palace Theatre, Victoria Street, SW1 (7834 1317/www.kissmekate.co.uk). Victoria tube/rail. **Box office** *In person* 10am-8.30pm Mon-Sat. *Ticketmaster* 24 hrs daily. **Tickets** £7.50-£37.50. *Standby* £15. **Credit** AmEx, MC, V. This ever-enduring Cole Porter classic, with Shakespeare's *Taming of the Shrew* as the play within the play, has arrived in London fresh from Broadway, with some of the award-winning cast members still in place.

Les Misérables

Palace Theatre, Shaftesbury Avenue, Soho, W1 (7434 0909/www.lesmis.com). Leicester Square tube. **Box office** 10am-8pm Mon-Sat. *Ticketmaster* 24hrs daily. **Tickets** £7-£37.50. *Standby* £17.50. **Credit** AmEx, DC, MC, V. **Map** p399 K6. Boubil and Schonberg's 15-year-old money-spinner idealises the struggle between paupers and villains in Victor Hugo's revolutionary Paris.

The Lion King

Lyceum Theatre, Wellington Street, WC2 (0870 243 9000). Covent Garden tube/Charing Cross tube/rail. **Box office** *In person* 10am-6pm Tue-Sat. *Ticketmaster* 24hrs daily. **Tickets** £15-£40. **Credit** AmEx, MC, V. **Map** p401 L7. This Disney extravaganza about a lion cub struggling to grow up has been wildly acclaimed for its breathtaking choreography and costumes.

Mamma Mia!

Prince Edward Theatre, 30 Old Compton Street, Soho, W1 (7447 5400/www.mamma-mia.com). Leicester Square or Tottenham Court Road tube. **Box office** *In person* 10am-7pm Mon-Sat. *By phone* 24hrs daily. **Tickets** £18.50-£40. **Credit** AmEx, MC, V. **Map** p399 K6. Perpetually sold out, this 1970s musical links Swedish supergroup Abba's greatest hits into a continuous but entirely spurious story.

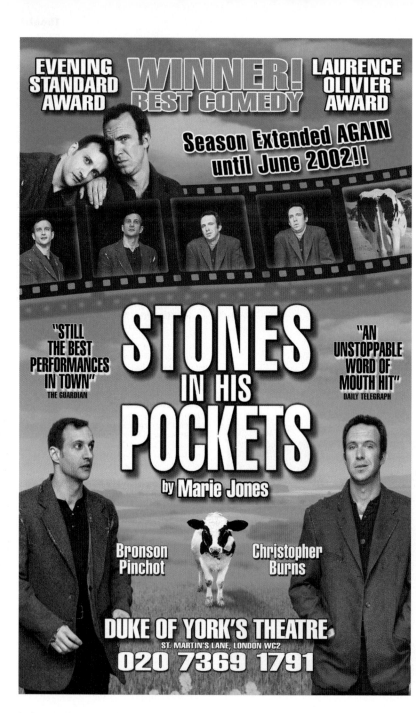

The Mousetrap

St Martin's Theatre, West Street, Covent Garden, WC2 (7836 1443). Leicester Square or Tottenham Court Road tube. **Box office** 10am-8pm Mon-Sat. **Tickets** £11.50-£29. **Credit** AmEx, MC, V. **Map** p399 K6.

An absurdly long-running mystery (it's been going now for a full half-century) from the mistress of suspense, Agatha Christie.

My Fair Lady

Theatre Royal Drury Lane, Catherine Street, WC2 (7494 5000/www.ruttheatres.com). Covent Garden tube. **Box office** 10am-8pm Mon-Sat. **Tickets** £7.50-£40. **Credit** AmEx, MC, V.

A strong cast succeeds in extracting the comedy and pathos from Lerner and Loewe's famous musical version of George Bernard Shaw's class-conscious romance, *Pygmalion*.

Phantom of the Opera

Her Majesty's Theatre, Haymarket, St James's, SW1 (7494 5400/www.thephantomoftheopera.com). Piccadilly Circus tube. **Box office** *In person* 10am-6pm Mon-Sat. *By phone* 24hrs daily. **Tickets** £15-£40. **Credit** AmEx, MC, V. **Map** p401 K7.

Lloyd Webber's best musical to date, this long-runner concerns a deformed theatre-goer who becomes obsessed with a beautiful opera singer.

Stones in His Pockets

Duke of York's, St Martin's Lane, WC2 (7369 1791). Charing Cross tube/rail. **Box office** *In person* 10am-7.30pm Mon-Sat. *By phone* 9am-9pm Mon-Sat; 10am-6pm Sun. **Tickets** £8.50-£29.50. **Credit** AmEx, MC, V.

The impact of a Hollywood film crew on a small, rural Irish community is the subject of this delightful comedy. With a virtuoso cast of two playing a total of 15 characters, this award-winning show is fast becoming a West End favourite.

The Woman in Black

Fortune Theatre, Russell Street, WC2 (7836 2238/www.thewomaninblack.com). Covent Garden tube. **Box office** 10am-8pm Mon-Sat. **Tickets** £10-£29.50. *Standby* £10. **Credit** AmEx, MC, V. **Map** p399 L6.

A persistently popular West End spine-chiller written by Susan Hill.

Off-West End

Almeida

Omega Place, off Caledonian Road, King's Cross, N1 (7359 4404/www.almeida.co.uk). King's Cross tube/rail. **Box office** *In person* 5-7pm Mon-Fri; 10am-7pm Sat. *By phone* 24hrs daily. **Tickets** £5-£27.50. **Credit** AmEx, MC, V. **Map** p399 L2.

Jonathan Kent and Ian McDiarmid, the co-directors of the Almeida Theatre Company for the past ten years, have announced their retirement in summer 2002. They will bequeath an outstanding legacy: a bold choice of lively, highbrow drama, substantial injections of sponsorship, and a list of London's

The **Almeida** in exile.

finest directors and actors queuing up to work at the Almeida. While the Islington theatre is being refurbished, the Almeida is located at a converted coach station in King's Cross, which houses two auditoria. The company is planning to return to Islington during the winter of 2002/3.

BAC (Battersea Arts Centre)

Lavender Hill, Battersea, SW11 (7223 2223/www.bac.org.uk). Clapham Common tube/Clapham Junction rail/77, 77A, 345 bus. **Box office** *In person* 10.30am-6pm Mon; 10.30am-9pm Tue-Sun. *By phone* 10.30am-6pm Mon-Sat; 3.30-6pm Sun. **Tickets** £3.50-£12.75; 'pay what you can' Tue. **Credit** MC, V.

The self-appointed 'National Theatre of the Fringe', the BAC has three theatres (a main house and two studios) that together carry much of the capital's very best fringe work.

The Bush

Shepherd's Bush Green, Shepherd's Bush, W12 (7610 4224/www.bushtheatre.co.uk). Goldhawk Road or Shepherd's Bush tube. **Box office** *In person* 5-8pm Mon-Sat. *By phone* 10am-7pm Mon-Sat. **Tickets** £8-£13. **Credit** AmEx, JCB, MC, V.

One of the most important venues for new writing in London, the refurbished Bush is a springboard for young writers into the bigger theatres (such as Conor McPherson, author of *The Weir*).

Donmar Warehouse

41 Earlham Street, Covent Garden, WC2 (7369 1732/www.donmar-warehouse.com). Covent Garden tube. **Box office** *In person* 10am-7.30pm Mon-Sat. *By phone* 9am-9pm Mon-Sat; 10am-6pm Sun. *Ticketmaster* 24hrs daily. **Tickets** £14-£25. *Standby* £12. **Credit** AmEx, MC, V. **Map** p399 L6.

Under the direction of Sam Mendes (who, at the end of 2001, announced that he's to step down), the Donmar continued to produce a variety of old and new plays, visiting and in-house shows to a very high standard with casts often peppered with big names. In 2002 it launches its tenth anniversary season with a production of *Privates on Parade* by Peter Nichols.

Drill Hall

16 Chenies Street, Fitzrovia, WC1 (7637 8270/ www.drillhall.co.uk). Goodge Street tube. **Box office** *In person* 10am-7.30pm Mon-Fri; 11am-7.30pm Sat. *By phone* 10am-9pm Mon-Sat; 10am-7pm Sun. **Tickets** £5-£15. **Credit** AmEx, MC, V. **Map** p399 K5.

Staging its own work and shows from all over the world, London's biggest gay and lesbian theatre is not generally a separatist venue, though Mondays are women-only from 6pm and Thursdays are non-smoking days.

The Gate

The Prince Albert, 11 Pembridge Road, Notting Hill, W11 (7229 0706). Notting Hill Gate tube. **Box office** 10am-6pm Mon-Fri. **Tickets** £6-£12; 'pay what you can' Mon. **Credit** MC, V. **Map** p394 A7.

Located above a pub in the heart of Notting Hill, the Gate is renowned for its high-quality, low-budget drama and radical set design.

Hampstead Theatre

98 Avenue Road, Swiss Cottage, NW3 (7722 9301/ www.hampstead-theatre.co.uk). Swiss Cottage tube. **Box office** 10am-7.30pm Mon-Sat. **Tickets** £7-£17. **Credit** MC, V.

Under the direction of Jenny Topper, the Hampstead is widely respected for its contemporary drama. In autumn 2002 it will move from the dilapidated prefab that has been its home for 40 years into a new building, complete with a 350-seat auditorium, landscaped gardens, educational facilities and a café-bar.

Holland Park Theatre

Holland Park, off Kensington High Street, Kensington, W8 (7602 7856/ www.operahollandpark.com). High Street Kensington tube. **Box office** *11 Jun-Aug* 10am-6pm, 10am-8pm (performance nights) Mon-Sat. **Tickets** £26; £20.50 concessions. **Credit** AmEx, MC, V. **Map** p394 A8.

This 720-seater outdoor theatre against the backdrop of Holland House also runs a ten-week summer season of opera and ballet. *See also p313.*

King's Head

115 Upper Street, Islington, N1 (7226 1916). Angel tube/Highbury & Islington tube/rail. **Box office** 10am-8pm Mon-Sat; 10am-4pm Sun. **Tickets** £4-£14. **Credit** MC, V. **Map** p402 O1.

The oldest pub theatre in the city stages a variable diet of small-scale musicals, plays and revues. The bar's late licence and the musical evenings held here make it a very busy all-round winner, and the good news is that it's still operating despite having lost its local council funding.

Lyric Hammersmith

King Street, Hammersmith, W6 (8741 2311/ www.lyric.co.uk). Hammersmith tube. **Box office** *In person* 10am-8pm Mon-Sat. *By phone* 10am-7pm Mon-Sat. **Tickets** £5-£20. **Credit** AmEx, DC, MC, V.

The Lyric has great facilities and a reputation for alternative mainstream work. There are two theatres here: a proscenium main stage and a smaller-scale studio space.

Open Air Theatre

Regent's Park, NW1 (7486 2431/www.open-air-theatre.org.uk). Baker Street tube. **Repertory season** May-Sept, phone for details. **Tickets** £9-£23. *Standby* £9 (approx). **Credit** AmEx, DC, MC, V. **Map** p398 G3.

Set in the midst of Regent's Park, this is a beautiful summer venue. Count on a couple of alfresco Shakespeares, a musical and a family show.

Orange Tree

1 Clarence Street, Richmond, Surrey (8940 3633/ www.orangetreetheatre.co.uk). Richmond tube/rail. **Box office** 10am-7pm Mon-Sat. **Tickets** £5-£15.50. **Credit** MC, V.

A small, smart bearpit of a venue that's been quietly flourishing under the directorship of Sam Walters and his prescribed diet of wholesome, closely directed (often) costume drama in the round, with little or no set.

Theatre Royal Stratford East

Gerry Raffles Square, Stratford, E15 (8534 0310/ www.stratfordeast.com). Stratford DLR/tube/rail. **Box office** 10am-7pm Mon-Sat. **Tickets** £3-£16. **Credit** MC, V.

This powerhouse of popular community-oriented drama, musicals and revue has launched West End hits such as *East is East*. Having reopened in December 2001 after a three-year refurbishment programme, the Theatre Royal still boasts the same well-loved Victorian auditorium, but the front-of-house facilities, rehearsal rooms, offices and bars have all been revamped.

Tricycle

269 Kilburn High Road, Kilburn, NW6 (7328 1000/ www.tricycle.co.uk). Kilburn tube. **Box office** 10am-9pm Mon-Sat; 2-9pm Sun. **Tickets** £9-£20.50. **Credit** MC, V.

The Tricycle specialises in high-quality black and Irish shows aimed at its local population. The centre also incorporates its own art gallery and super-comfortable cinema, plus one of Kilburn's more agreeable bars.

Young Vic

66 The Cut, Waterloo, SE1 (7928 6363/ www.youngvic.org). Southwark tube/Waterloo tube/ rail. **Box office** 10am-7pm Mon-Sat. **Tickets** £9-£18. **Credit** MC, V. **Map** p404 N8.

The Young Vic has a well-proportioned studio space and large main house that regularly plays host to touring companies and big-name thesps.

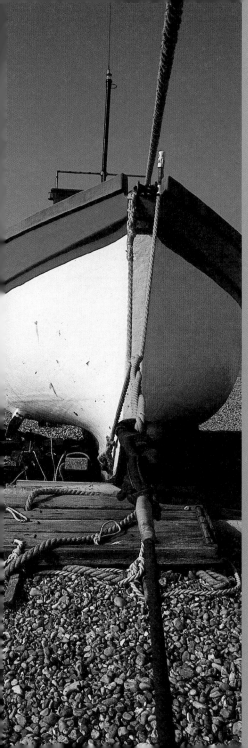

Trips Out of Town

Trips Out of Town

Highlights of the great beyond.

Map p389

When the big city becomes all too much, escape to one of the often little-known but easily accessible attractions that lie beyond the M25. Most of the places we've listed are within an hour and a half's train journey from London (though some require a further bus or taxi ride).

For a more in-depth look at getaways within easy reach of London, pick up a copy of *Time Out Weekend Breaks from London*, £12.99. Many of the destinations in this chapter are great for families, particularly the castles and seaside towns. For details of theme parks within easy reach of London, *see p272*.

PLANNING A TRIP

The **Britain Visitor Centre** (*see below*) stocks guidebooks and free leaflets and offers advice on any destination in the UK and Ireland; you can also book rail, bus, air or car travel, reserve tours, theatre tickets and accommodation, and there's even a bureau de change, a branch of Thomas Cook, a ticket agency and a bookshop. The **British Tourist Authority** website, www.visitbritain.com, contains masses of useful information and advice on destinations across the country.

Travellers should also visit the tourist information centre as soon as they arrive in a town; these can provide leaflets, further information about accommodation and where to eat, and details of local attractions.

Britain Visitor Centre

1 Regent Street (south of Piccadilly Circus), SW1 (no phone/www.visitbritain.com). Piccadilly Circus tube (3rd exit). **Open** *Oct-May* 9.30am-6.30pm Mon; 9am-6.30pm Tue-Fri; 10am-4pm Sat, Sun. *June-Sept* 9.30am-6.30pm Mon; 9am-6.30pm Tue-Fri; 9am-5pm Sat; 10am-4pm Sun. **Credit** AmEx, MC, V. **Map** p401 K7.
This centre is open to personal callers only, but the website has lots of useful information.

OPENING TIMES & PRICES

For the main entries below, we've included full details of opening times, admission and transport details, but be aware that these can change without notice so **always phone to check that a particular sight is open** if you're planning a visit around it. Major sights are open throughout the year, but many more minor attractions close in winter (Nov-Mar).

In the 'Where to stay' sections, the accommodation prices listed are the range for a double room.

Getting there

By train

For information on train times and ticket prices, call **08457 484950**. (To reserve tickets in advance by credit card, ask for the appropriate number.) Make sure you ask about the cheapest ticket for the journey you are planning, and be aware that for longer journeys, the earlier you book, the cheaper the ticket. The **rail travel centres** in all London's mainline stations, as well as in Heathrow and Gatwick airports and the British Visitor Centre (*see above*), will also be able to help with timetable information and ticket booking. The train journey times we give are the fastest available.

For online timetable info on any British train company, see www.virgintrains.co.uk. Tickets for any train operator in the UK can be bought on the Net at www.thetrainline.com.

London mainline rail stations

Charing Cross *Strand, WC2.* **Map** p401 L7.
For trains to and from south-east England (including Dover, Folkestone and Ramsgate).

Euston *Euston Road, Euston, NW1.* **Map** p399 K3.
For trains to and from north and north-west England and Scotland, and a suburban line north to Watford.

King's Cross *Euston Road, King's Cross, N1.* **Map** p399 L2.
For trains to and from north and north-east England and Scotland, and suburban lines to north London and Hertfordshire.

Liverpool Street *Liverpool Street, The City, EC2.* **Map** p403 R5.
For trains to and from the east coast (including Harwich) and Stansted Airport; also for trains to East Anglia and suburban services to east and north-east London.

Paddington *Praed Street, Paddington, W2.* **Map** p395 D5.
For trains to and from south-west and west England, south Wales and the Midlands.

Victoria *Terminus Place, Victoria, SW1.* **Map** p400 H10.
For fast trains to and from the Channel ports (Folkestone, Dover, Newhaven); also trains to and from Gatwick Airport, plus suburban services to south and south-east London.

Waterloo *York Road, Waterloo, SE1.*
Map p401 M8.
For fast trains to and from the south and
south-west of England (Portsmouth, Southampton,
Dorset, Devon), plus suburban services to
south-west London.

By coach

Coach and bus travel is almost always cheaper
than rail travel, but more often than not it's
also slower. **National Express** (08705
808080) runs routes to most parts of the
country; its coaches depart from Victoria Coach
Station on Buckingham Palace Road, five
minutes' walk from Victoria rail and tube
stations. **Green Line** (0870 608 7261) operates
within an approximate 40-mile (64-kilometre)
radius of London. Most buses depart from
Eccleston Bridge, SW1 (Colonnades Coach
Station, behind Victoria Station).

Victoria Coach Station

*164 Buckingham Palace Road, Victoria, SW1
(7730 3466). Victoria tube/rail.* **Map** p400 H11.
Britain's most comprehensive coach company
National Express (*see p356*) and **Eurolines**
(01582 404511), which travels to the Continent,
are based at Victoria Coach Station. There are many
other companies operating to and from London
(some departing from Marble Arch).

By car

If you're in a group of three or four, it may
be cheaper to hire a car (*see p361*), especially
if you plan to take in several sights within an
area. The road directions given in the listings
below should be used in conjunction with a
map. (Note that, for example, 'J13 off M11'
means 'exit the M11 motorway at junction 13'.)

Town & city breaks

Bath

London resident Daniel Defoe once said of
this city: 'Bath is a spot of ground which our
countrymen ought to esteem as a particular
favour of heaven.' The city's most famous
literary resident, however, was Jane Austen.
'Oh, who can ever be tired of Bath?' sighed the
heroine of *Northanger Abbey*, echoing the
sentiment of many a social butterfly who flitted
from the Pump Room to the new Theatre Royal,
between the promenades, balls and assemblies
that confirmed the city as high society's
favourite watering hole in the 1800s.

It wasn't until the 1880s that the cellars of
the Pump Room finally gave up their secret of
the Great Roman Bath and temple to Minerva,
providing yet more ungodliness for good old

Spa quality: **Bath**'s famed waters.

Brighton's **Royal Pavilion**. *See p344.*

Queen Victoria to contend with: she is said to have snapped shut the curtains of her carriage when she was being driven through the city, for fear of clapping eyes on half-naked bathers. Today the **Roman Baths Museum** (01225 477785) is the city's most famous attraction and the most impressive non-military Roman remains in Britain. Plans are afoot to restore the baths as a spa (the current timetable for the opening of five listed buildings and a new four-storey complex is October 2002; further details are available on 01225 477710). In the meantime, you can taste the waters, which still bubble up from the earth here at a rate of 250,000 gallons a day, in the adjoining **Pump Room**, though a pot of Earl Grey might go down better.

Overlooking the baths is **Bath Abbey** (01225 422462), a 15th-century reworking of an earlier Norman structure, itself built on the site of the Saxon church where Edgar, the first king of a united England, was crowned back in 973. It's a beautifully light, harmonious building, boasting some fine fan vaulting and stained glass.

Bath has close on 20 museums, most of them excellent. These include the **Building of Bath Museum** on Lansdown Road (01225 333895), the highlight of which is a spectacular model of the city, and, in Bennett Street, the **Museum of East Asian Art** (01225 464640), which contains a fine collection of Chinese jade carvings. Opposite, in the grand Assembly Rooms (once the social focus of Georgian high society in Bath), there's the renowned **Museum**

of Costume (01225 477789), with posh togs dating back to the late 16th century. The **Victoria Art Gallery** on Bridge Street (01225 477233) houses the region's permanent collection of British and European art from the 15th century to the present day, and at Claverton Manor the **American Museum & Gardens** (01225 460503) offers a fascinating series of reconstructed 17th- to 19th-century US domestic interiors.

But Bath's greatest attraction is simply its streets, the grandest of which is the much-photographed **Royal Crescent**, a breathtaking sweep of 30 houses designed by John Wood the Younger (1767-75). **No.1 Royal Crescent** (01225 428126), designated a World Heritage building, is furnished in authentic period style with a fully restored Georgian garden and is open to the public from mid February to the end of November. Nearby is the magnificent **Circus**, designed by the elder John Wood and completed by his son in 1767, composed of three crescents forming a circle. With its three tiers of columns, it's been described as 'the Colosseum turned outside in', and is in many ways an even finer creation than Royal Crescent.

The **River Avon**, which adds greatly to the appeal of the city, is spanned by the shop-lined **Pulteney Bridge**, an Italianate masterpiece by Robert Adam. There are walks beside the river and the adjacent Kennet and Avon Canal, and in summer boats can be hired from the Victorian **Bath Boating Station** (Forester Road, 01225 466407).

Trips Out of Town

Cambridge's **Kettle's Yard**. *See p347.*

Further information

Where to eat & drink: Sally Lunn's
Refreshment House & Museum (01225 461634)
in North Parade Passage is the oldest house in
Bath; here you can sample the famous buns made
fashionable by Sally Lunn in the 1680s. The best of
Bath's many restaurants are top-rank curry house
Jamuna at 9-10 High Street (01225 464631), Michelin
two-star **Restaurant Lettonie** at 35 Kelston Road
(01225 446676), the classy, cosy **Moody Goose**
(01225 466688) with its Modern British cuisine on
Kingsmead Square, and the excellent low-priced
Hullaballoos at 36 Broad Street (01225 443323).
Popular pubs include the **Bell** in Walcot Street, the
Old Green Tree on Green Street, and the **Cross
Keys** on the corner of Midgord Road and Southstoke
Road – its garden and aviary make it great for kids.
Where to stay: **Harington's Hotel** (8-10 Queen
Street, 01225 461728; £88-£108) is the best-value
central hotel. **Holly Lodge** (8 Upper Oldfield Park,
01225 424042; £79-£97) is a classy B&B perched
high above the city. The **Queensberry Hotel**
(Russell Street, 01225 447928; £120-£210) provides
Regency elegance in the centre of town. **Royal
Crescent** (16 Royal Crescent, 01225 823333;
£220-£320) has possibly the best address of any
hotel in Britain and is the place to come for a splurge.
Getting there: *By train* from Paddington (1hr
25min). *By coach* National Express (3hrs 20min).
By car J18 off M4 then A46, use park 'n' rides to
get into the centre.
Tourist information centre: *Abbey Chambers,
Abbey Churchyard (01225 477101/www.visitbath.
co.uk)*. **Open** *May-Sept* 9.30am-6pm Mon-Sat;
10am-4pm Sun. *Oct-Apr* 9.30am-5pm Mon-Sat;
10am-4pm Sun.

Brighton

From political party conference delegates to
dirty weekenders (they often overlap), Brighton
looks after its visitors: it has endless hotels,
guesthouses and restaurants, lots of intriguing
shops, and a vibrant and sophisticated cultural
scene and nightlife that all thrive on close
connections to the capital. And with all the
gaudy fun of a relatively sunny British beach
town (even if the shoreline is full of pebbles
rather than sand, and even if, since 2001, it's
technically been a city), there's a constant influx
of coach parties and day-trippers to soak up
some beer, buy a stick of rock and play on the
dodgems on the pier.

In addition, a lot of people come down for
the weekend, get bitten by the Brighton bug,
and never manage to leave again. The city
is of famously liberal persuasion and greets
outsiders, new agers, artists, freaks and
eccentrics with open arms and a warm heart.
These persecuted hipsters, along with an array
of rat-race absconders, relocate to Brighton's
pebbly shore to tune in, turn on and drop out.
A thriving gay and lesbian scene has also done
a lot to put Brighton on the map, and even
the local authorities have had to acknowledge
the power of the pink pound.

Nowhere in Brighton better reflects this
diversity, extravagance and exuberance than its
best-known landmark, the outrageous **Royal
Pavilion** (01273 290900). Built by John Nash
in 1823 for the Prince Regent (later George IV),
it none too subtly blends elements of Indian,
Chinese and Islamic architecture. Next door,
the freshly revamped **Brighton Museum &
Art Gallery** (01273 290900) has a good crop
of 20th-century and ethnic art and artefacts.

Down at the waterfront, the gaudy **Palace
Pier** is packed with archetypal seaside
attractions – slot machines, funfair and fish
and chips stalls. On a clear day you can gaze
west from the top of the helter-skelter to
the Isle of Wight, or along the shore to the
derelict, skeletal but Grade I-listed West Pier
(restoration is finally getting underway in

2002) and genteel Hove. Ocean lovers should also visit the **Brighton Fishing Museum** (01273 723064) on the lower prom between the piers and the **Sea-Life Centre** (01273 604234), housed in a beautiful 19th-century aquarium on Marine Parade.

When the sea loses its fascination, duck into the **Lanes**, a warren of old fishermen's cottages that now house a variety of antiques and specialist shops punctuated by pubs and cafés, between West Street and the Old Steine. If these prove too expensive, cross North Street and explore the vibrant **North Laine** area for vintage clothing, street fashion, records, kitsch and cafés of every kind, or visit the **Duke of York's** (01273 626261) at Preston Circus, quite possibly the cosiest indie cinema in the UK.

On a less sedate note, Brighton is also a mecca for clubbers; located on the seafront, the **Zap** (01273 202407) is the grandaddy of the city's clubs. Also in King's Road Arches are the **Honey Club** (01273 202807), **Beach** (01273 722272) and the **Funky Buddha Lounge** (01273 725541).

Further information

Where to eat & drink: For food, try the enticing Anglo-Asian dishes at the unpromisingly sited **Black Chapati** (12 Circus Parade, New England Road, 01273 699011), the famous vegetarian fare at **Terre à Terre** (71 East Street; 01273 729051), the magnificent French food at **La Fourchette** at 101 Western Road (01273 722556), or the Modern European dishes at the ultra-cool **C Restaurant** (01273 645755) at Blanch House, 17 Atlingworth Street (*see above*). The most charming trad boozers are the **Cricketers** in Black Lion Street, the **Eastern** in Trafalgar Street and the **Battle of Trafalgar** in Guildford Road. For soemthing trendier, try the **St James** in Madeira Place, the **Sidewinder** in Upper St James Street, or, for camping it up large style, the **Regency Tavern** in Russell Square.

Where to stay: **Blanch House** (17 Atlingworth Street, 01273 603504; £90-£110) is petite but seriously funky. **Hotel Pelirocco** (10 Regency Square, 01273 733845; £85-£115) offers kitschy decor to a party-hard crowd; **Hotel Twenty One** (21 Charlotte Street, 01273 686450; £60-£95) is a well-run B&B with Victorian furniture; **Nineteen** (19 Broad Street, 01273 675529; £95-£150) is chic, stylish and intimate; the **Oriental** (9 Oriental Place, 01273 205050; £55-£70) is a bohemian budget option near the sea.

Events: The **Brighton Festival** (01273 700747) fills the first three weeks of May with theatre, comedy, art, music and literature. On Sundays throughout the year Madeira Drive on the seafront hosts a range of diverse events – notably the **London to Brighton Bike Ride** in June and the **London to Brighton Veteran Car Run** in November. Monthly listings guides *Impact* and *The List* are available from newsagents, or find out what's going down by tuning in to the what's-on run-down on Surf 107FM (6.30-7pm Mon-Fri). For gay listings, see the monthly *G Scene* or visit www.scene22.com.

Getting there: *By train* from Victoria (from 50min), or from King's Cross (1hr 10min). *By coach* National Express (1hr 50min). *By car* M23 then A23.

Tourist information centres: *10 Bartholomew Square (0906 711 2255/www.visitbrighton.com).* **Open** *Jan-June, Sept-Dec* 9am-5pm Mon-Fri; 10am-5pm Sat; 10am-4pm Sun. *July, Aug* 9am-5.30pm Mon-Fri; 10am-6pm Sat; 10am-4pm Sun. *Hove Town Hall, Church Road, Hove (0906 711 2255).* **Open** *Jan-June, Sept-Dec* 9am-5pm Mon-Fri. *July, Aug* 11am-5pm Mon-Fri.

The best Trips

For getting lost
The maze at **Leeds Castle** (*see p351*); Marlborough Maze at **Blenheim Palace** (*see p352*).

For Britain's only World Heritage city
Bath (*see p341*).

For hedonism by the sea
Brighton's beachfront clubs (*see p344*).

For messing about on the water
Oxford (*see p348*) and **Cambridge** (*see p345*).

For gardens to inspire
Groombridge Place Gardens (*see p352*).

Cambridge

Cambridge stretches out across its commons and pastures, but its historic centre (where most of the sights are situated) can easily be covered on foot. Indeed, much of the central area is semi-pedestrianised, the red-brick roads encouraging the unwary to wander with carefree abandon. This, however, is just what the cyclists are waiting for, and with a stealthy silence they will mow you down with an equally free abandon, chiming their little bells in celebration.

Most of these bell-ringing free-wheelers are students of the **university**, which has dominated Cambridge life since the 14th century. The oldest college is **Peterhouse** on Trumpington Street, endowed in 1284. The original hall survives, though most of the present buildings are 19th century. Just up the road is **Corpus Christi**, founded in 1352. Its Old Court dates from that time and is linked by a gallery to the 11th-century **St Bene't's Church**, the oldest building in town. Just across the road is 15th-century **Queens'**; most of its original buildings, including the beautiful timbered president's lodge, remain. The inner courts are wonderfully picturesque.

Next to Queens', **King's** was founded by Henry VI in 1441 and is renowned for its **chapel** (01223 331155), built between 1446 and 1515. Considered one of the greatest Gothic buildings in Europe, it has a breathtaking interior with its original stained glass intact.

If you visit in termtime, be sure to attend a service, when the choirboys' otherworldly voices provide a sublime counterpoint to the beauty of the building.

To the north is **Trinity**, founded in 1336 by Edward III and refounded by Henry VIII in 1546. A fine collection of Tudor buildings surrounds the Great Court where, legend has it, Lord Byron used to bathe naked in the fountain with his pet bear. Wittgenstein studied and taught here; the library where he occasionally worked, designed by Wren, is open to visitors

A sea change

Cool, liberal and vibrant, and a mere hour's jaunt from the capital, Brighton will never shake off its reputation as London-on-sea; more city-dwellers than ever now either use the city as a regular weekend base or have upped sticks entirely to take up permanent residence there, and in fine weather you'll find yourself sharing the pebbly expanse of its shore with hundreds of other locals and daytrippers who've had the same idea. Venture further afield, however, to wilder, remoter beaches in Kent, and you'll find that the British seaside has far more to offer than games arcades, sticks of rock and kiss-me-quick hats.

Clinging to Kent's North Sea coastline, **Whitstable** has a superb, ramshackle seafront cluttered with toy-like cottages, fishermen's huts and sailmakers – horror-meister Peter Cushing was a great fan and lived here for many years, as a viewpoint plaque attests. But whatever other fame this gently bohemian town has garnered is purely down to its succulent, uniquely flavoured native oysters, which thrive in Whitstable's warm, silty waters. Though the number of oystermen has inevitably dwindled over the last century, you can still walk along the seafront, treading on the millions of oyster shells shucked up and spat out by the harbour businesses, and nosing in the fishermen's boats and cages.

To get the full flavour of Whitstable, time your visit to coincide with the annual week-long Oyster Festival at the end of July; some of the old working yawls are raced in a regatta, and a pre-season catch of oysters is paraded round town by locals doing the Fish Slapping Dance, a king of maritime morris dance with seaweed and shell costumes – expect traditional songs and,

of course, much fish slapping. As for eating the critters, it's best to come in season, which runs from September through to the end of March.The **Whitstable Oyster Fishery Company** (Horsebridge, 01227 276856) is an upmarket choice offering simple, unfussy dishes, while the more basic **Wheeler's** (8 High Street, 01227 273311) was founded in the mid 19th century and is the town's oldest oyster bar.

You can learn more about the oysters at the **Whitstable Museum** (5A Oxford Street, 01227 276998), which also has a Peter Cushing display. Those wishing to spend a night or two here can even bed down in one of the old **Fishermen's Huts** (01227 280280; £75-£115), which were rescued from dilapidation a few years ago and provide minimalist but comfortable accommodation right on the seafront. For more information on Whitstable, contact the **tourist office** (34 St Margaret's Street, 01227 766567).

South of Whitstable, on Kent's Channel coast, **Dungeness** is a remote and gloriously desolate little world apart that just 1,000 years ago didn't even exist – the promontory on which it sits (actually, the world's biggest accumulation of shingle) has been built up by longshore drift over the last millennium. The light here, reflected from the sea on both sides, adds to the peculiar, almost eerie atmosphere of the place.

One of the town's most extraordinary sights is the garden created by filmmaker Derek Jarman around the little cottage he inhabited here in the latter stages of his life, when he was gradually succumbing to AIDS. The choice of Dungeness, the site of a massive nuclear power station with a hum that's famously audible for miles, was a gesture

at certain times (1-2pm Mon-Fri, 10.30am-12.30pm Sat termtime only, 01223 338400). Further on, at the corner of Bridge and St John's Streets, is the **Round Church**, the oldest of the four remaining round churches in England. Behind the main group of colleges is the **Backs**, a series of beautiful meadows, some still grazed by cows, bordering the willow-shaded **River Cam**, which is spanned by several fine footbridges. It's a perfect spot for summer strolling, or you can hire a punt and drift lazily along the river.

Among Cambridge's non-collegiate attractions are the **Fitzwilliam Museum** on Trumpington Street (01223 332900), which has outstanding collections of antiquities and Old Masters; **Kettle's Yard** (Castle Street, 01223 352124), which has fine displays of 20th-century art; and the quite formal **Botanic Gardens** (01223 336265) in Bateman Street, which belong to the university.

Unsurprisingly, Cambridge is an excellent place to buy books – new, second-hand and antiquarian – and the daily market in **Market**

On the waterfront: **Whitstable**.

Derek Jarman's garden at **Dungeness**.

of defiance: he was determined to create beauty in the face of such ugliness. You can see the results today in the surreal but intoxicatingly beautiful garden he made from stones, objects found while beachcombing, and unusual plantlife. Visitors are free to wander around the garden but don't be too intrusive – this is still a private residence.

There's little else to do here but watch the minature railway that puffs its way across the bleak landscape (it was built by millionaire racing driver Captain Howey in 1927), walk on the flinty beach with its row of fishing boats, flags flapping in the wind, and its discarded fish heads, investigate the area's fragile ecology at the **Dungeness RSPB Nature Reserve** (01797 320588, or enjoy the views over the power station and

the Ness from the **Old Lighthouse** (01797 321300). For sustenance and shelter from the biting winds, treat yourself to a pint and a plate of fish and chips in the **Britannia** (Dungeness Road, 01797 321959).

Heading back towards to the M20 to London, stop off at the more hospitable stretch of Camber Sands just east of Rye along the coastal road; in summer it hosts an indie music festival (*see p318* **The sounds of summer**). Fans of Derek Jarman should also make the minor detour to St Clement church at Old Romney, which has pink pews inside and a yew tree in the churchyard, beneath which Jarman is buried.

For more information on the Dungeness area, contact the **Tourist Information Centre** at Rye (01797 226696).

Square is always a pleasure to browse, whether for books, clothes, antique, flowers or something good to eat.

Further information
Where to eat & drink: For posh nosh, the inventive French cooking at **Midsummer House** (01223 369299) on Midsummer Common, the global cuisine at the tiny, candlelit **22 Chesterton Road** (01223 351880) or the bargain goodies at **Dojo Noodle Bar** in Miller's Yard, Mill Lane (01223 363471). Pub-wise, though the **Eagle** on St Bene't Street receives all the plaudits, there are many of equal merit, including the **Pickerel Inn** on Magdalene Street, **Fort St George** by the river on Midsummer Common, the **Mill** and the **Anchor**, practically next door to each other between Granta Place and Silver Street.

Where to stay: Cambridge is notoriously short on characterful accommodation; the newish **Meadowcroft Hotel** (16 Trumpington Road, 01223 346120; £130-£150) is head and shoulders above the competition. For something different and more youthful, **Sleeperz Hotel** (Station Road, 01223 304050; £55), another recent addition, has simple modern cells betraying both Scandinavian and Japanese influences.

Events: The **Cambridge Shakespeare Festival** is held once a year in July and August. Performances mainly take place outside, and remain as true to the text as possible.

Getting there: *By train* from King's Cross (50min). *By coach* National Express (1hr 50min). *By car* J11 or J12 off M11.

Tourist information centre: *The Old Library, Wheeler Street (01223 322640/ www.tourismcambridge.com)*. **Open** *Apr-Oct* 10am-6.30pm Mon, Wed-Fri; 10am-6.30pm Tue; 10am-5pm Sat; 11am-4pm Sun. *Nov-Mar* 10am-5.30pm Mon-Fri; 10am-5pm Sat.

Canterbury

England has many medieval cathedral cities, some better preserved and others more idyllically situated than Canterbury. But it is not fanciful to say that so significant were the events of its early history – the coming of Christianity with St Augustine in the sixth century, and the murder of the Archbishop of Canterbury in 1170 – that they continue to reverberate in its narrow streets and landmark **cathedral** (01227 762862).

The latter, with its superb stained glass, stone vaulting and vast Norman crypt, is now the mother church of Anglicans worldwide. A plaque near the altar marks the spot where Archbishop Thomas à Becket was murdered in 1170 by four overzealous knights who had overheard King Henry II moaning, 'Will no one rid me of this turbulent priest?' and decided to do the troubled king a favour. Becket's tomb has been a site of pilgrimage

ever since. **Trinity Chapel** contains the site of the original shrine plus the tombs of Henry IV and the Black Prince.

Though it gets overcrowded in summer, the small city centre is charming. **Eastbridge Hospital** (01227 471688) on the High Street was founded to meet the growing kipping needs of pilgrims in the wake of Becket's murder and retains the smell and damp of ages past; there are the remains of a Roman townhouse and mosaic floor at the **Roman Museum** on Butchery Lane (01227 785575); and the **Heritage Museum** (01227 452747) on Stour Street is the best museum on the history of the city. Meanwhile, **Canterbury Tales** (01227 479227) clunkily but endearingly recreates the experience of Chaucer's 14th-century pilgrims.

Further information
Where to eat & drink: **Tue e Mio** at 16 The Borough (01227 761471) is a stylish Italian with matching food; **Café des Amis du Mexique** at 95 St Dunstan's Street (01227 464390) is upbeat and deservedly popular; and newcomer **Lloyds** (89-90 St Dunstan's Street, 01227 768222) has ambitious international cuisine. Drink in the ancient and sedate **Thomas Becket** in Best Lane or, further afield on St Dunstan's Street, the pretty and peaceful **Unicorn** with its charmingly kitsch garden.

Where to stay: **Acacia Lodge & Tanglewood** (39-40 London Road, 01227 769955; £40-£48) is a well-priced B&B formed from 1880s farm cottages and run by a former town guide. The **Coach House** (34 Watling Street, 01227 784324; £40-£48) is a fresh, new B&B with fleamarket decor; the **Falstaff** (8-10 St Dunstan's Street, 01227 462138; double £100) is Canterbury's loveliest historic hotel.

Getting there: *By train* from Victoria to Canterbury East (1hr 20min), or from Charing Cross to Canterbury West (1hr 30min). *By coach* National Express (1hr 50min). *By car* A2 then M2 then A2 again.

Tourist information centre: *34 St Margaret's Street (01227 766567/www.canterbury.co.uk)*. **Open** *Jan-Mar* 9.30am-5pm Mon-Sat. *Apr-Oct* 9.30am-5.30pm Mon-Sat; 10-4pm Sun. *Nov, Dec* 9.30am-5pm Mon-Sat; 10-4pm Sun.

Oxford

Of the 118,000 inhabitants that live in this city, approximately 15 per cent are reckoned to be the transient university population, and in addition to that the streets throb all year round with tourists and rucksacked European school parties. The city centre is dominated by the university and its colleges, although there are other parts of town – notably Jericho and Summertown to the north, and Headington and Cowley to the east – that have their own distinct identities and considerably fewer sightseers and students. There is also

Norman conquest: **Leeds Castle**. See p351.

a wealth of museums, from the quirky **Pitt Rivers** (01865 270927) on Parks Road, with its voodoo dolls, shrunken heads and other ethnological delights, to the all-embracing **Ashmolean** (Beaumont Street, 01865 278000), which is the country's oldest museum and houses the university's collection of art and antiquities.

Founded by the Saxons, Oxford began its development in the early eighth century around a priory established on the site where Christ Church now stands. Its steady growth in importance and influence received the royal seal of approval when Henry I built his Palace of Beaumont here in the early 12th century, at much the same time as the first students were beginning to gather. By the end of the century Oxford was firmly established as England's first university town.

Most of the university's architecturally spectacular buildings are usually open to the public. Among the finest are **Christ Church**, with its famous Tom Tower and chapel that serves as Oxford's cathedral. Nearby **Merton**, founded in 1264, boasts a marvellous medieval library and garden. **Magdalen** (pronounced 'mord-lin'), often said to be the loveliest college, has a deer park and a meadow where the rare snakeshead fritillary still blooms every April. Other centres of academia include the **Bodleian Library** (01865 277000), begun in 1598, and the dinky, elegant **Radcliffe Camera**, England's earliest example of a round reading room (1737).

But Oxford's attractions do not begin and end with the colleges. **Carfax Tower** (01865 792653), the only surviving part of the 14th-century church of St Martin, is notable for its two 'quarter-boy' clocks that chime every quarter-hour; it also provides great views of the town if you climb the 99 steps to the top. The **Museum of Modern Art** (01865 722733) in Pembroke Street has established an international reputation for its pioneering exhibitions of contemporary and 20th-century work.

A browse around the town's boutiques is a gentler pastime. Little Clarendon Street and Gloucester Green offer some interesting specialist shops, while the classy **Covered Market**, linking High Street and Market Street, opened in 1774, is a foodie's delight.

The countryside pushes green fingers into the heart of the town, with the **Oxford Canal**, the **River Thames** (sometimes called the Isis, from the Latin 'Tamesis'), and the **Cherwell** (pronounced 'Char-well') providing fine strolling and punting opportunities. For the classic view of Matthew Arnold's 'dreaming spires', climb Boar's Hill three miles (two kilometres) to the south-west.

Further information

Where to eat & drink: Cherwell Boathouse (01865 552746) off Bardwell Road offers upmarket fare, while at 71-2 Walton Street, Raymond Blanc's swish, metropolitan brasserie **Le Petit Blanc** (01865 510999) is outstanding value. **Branca Bar Italian Brasserie** (111 Walton Street, 01865

Trips Out of Town

Earthly delights at **Sissinghurst**. *See p353.*

556111) is a funky newcomer. Oxford has loads
of pubs, but few are cheap or quiet – the busy
16th-century **King's Arms** in Holywell Street is
a studenty choice with good beer and decent pub
grub; the **White House** behind the station is
a gastropub offering live trad jazz at Sunday
lunchtime; and the part-thatched **Perch** on Binsey
Lane has a big garden and a children's play area.

Where to stay: Burlington House (374 Banbury
Road, 01865 513513; £70-£75) is an outstanding
small hotel with B&B prices. The 17th-century **Old
Parsonage** (01865 310210; £165-£200) at 1 Banbury
Road, one-time home to the undergraduate Oscar
Wilde, is classy. The **Old Bank Hotel** (01865
799599; £155-£300) at 92-4 High Street is sleek,
modernist and arty.

Getting there: *By train* from Paddington (1hr),
then use your rail ticket for a free ride into the
centre on one of Oxford's pioneering electric
buses (every 10min). *By coach* frequent, cheap,
fast services from several London departure
points; details from National Express (1hr 40min),
Stagecoach (01865 727000) and Oxford Bus
Company (01865 785410). *By car* J8 off M40
then A40; use the park 'n' rides.

Tourist information centre: *The Old School,
Gloucester Green (01865 726871/www.visitoxford.org).*
Open *Easter-Oct* 9.30am-5pm Mon-Sat; 10am-3.30pm
Sun. *Nov-Easter* 9.30am-5pm Mon-Sat.

Stratford-upon-Avon

Stratford's cutesy half-timbered architecture,
cobbled mews and teashop culture aren't
everyone's cup of char. Local proprietors aren't
shy when it comes to milking Shakespeare's
connection with the town – Sheep Street, in
particular, has fallen prey to pricey boutiques
and restaurants, and ghastly souvenir shops.

Yet it's all worth braving if you're a
genuine Shakespeare junkie. In the town
centre are **Shakespeare's Birthplace**
(01789 204016) on Henley Street, which
underwent major restoration in 2000,
adding period room-settings to the hall,
parlour, kitchen and bedchambers; **Hall's
Croft** (01789 292107) on Old Town, named
after Dr John Hall, who married the Bard's
daughter Susanna; and **Nash's House**
(01789 292325) on Chapel Street, which
belonged to the first husband of his
granddaughter, Elizabeth. In the garden of
the latter are the foundations of **New Place**,
his last home, which was demolished in 1759.

A mile and a half (2.5 kilometres) away at
Shottery, and accessible from Stratford by
public path, is **Anne Hathaway's
Cottage** (01789 292100), where Shakespeare's
wife lived before she married. The girlhood
home of his mother, **Mary Arden's House**
(01789 293455), at Wilmcote, a pleasant
four-mile (6.5-kilometre) stroll along the
Stratford Canal. Both may also be reached
by bus; there are trains to Wilmcote.

Shakespeare was educated at **Stratford
Grammar School**, which you can see on
Church Street, and buried in **Holy Trinity
Church**, which has a fine riverside setting
and supposedly the playwright's tomb
(although the location of his body is disputed).
But of course, his most meaningful memorials
are his plays, and the **Royal Shakespeare
Company** (01789 403403) is the place to see
them. If you can't get a ticket (they sell out
fast), do a backstage tour and visit the **RSC
Collection** museum of props and costumes
(for tours call 01789 403405).

Stratford has been a market town since
1169 and, in a way, that's still what it does best.
See it on a Friday, when the awnings go up over
the stalls at the top of Wood Street and locals
flock in from outlying villages. In the town
centre, which still maintains its medieval grid
pattern, many fine old buildings survive,
among them **Harvard House** (open around
June-Oct; 01789 204016) on the High Street,
dating from 1596. The home of Katharine
Rogers, mother of John Harvard, founder of
Harvard University, it now houses a nationally
important collection of pewter.

The town's charms are enhanced by the presence of the **River Avon** and the **Stratford Canal**. The canal basin is usually crammed with narrowboats and there are walks alongside both waterways. **Avon Boating** (01789 267073) can provide punts, rowing boats, Canadian canoes and more.

Further information

Where to eat & drink: The **Opposition** (01789 269980) on Sheep Street is a great bistro, **Russon's** (01789 268822) at 8 Church Street specialises in imaginative fish dishes, and **Desport's** (01789 269304) at 13-14 Meer Street offers eclectic modern cooking. Drink with the thesps at the **Dirty Duck** (aka the **Black Swan**) on Stratford Way.

Where to stay: Caterham House Hotel (01789 267309; £80-£85) at 58 Rother Street is close to the Royal Shakespeare Theatre and popular with both audience and actors. Another good choice, **Victoria Spa Lodge** (01789 267985; £65) on Bishopton Lane has the feel of a grand country house; Queen Victoria stayed here before ascending to the throne in 1837.

Tourist information centre: *Bridgefoot (01789 293127)*. **Open** *Easter-Oct* 9am-6pm Mon-Sat; 11am-5pm Sun. *Nov-Easter* 9am-5pm Mon-Sat.

Getting there: *By train* from Paddington (2hrs 10min). *By coach* National Express (2hrs 45min) or Guide Friday (01789 294466) from Euston. *By car* J15 off M40 then A46.

Castles

Arundel

Arundel, West Sussex (01903 882173/www. arundelcastle.org). **Getting there** *By train* from Victoria (1hr 30min). *By car* A24 then A280 and A27. **Open** *Apr-Oct* noon-5pm Mon-Fri, Sun (last entry 4pm). **Admission** £7.50; £5-£6.50 concessions; £21 family (2+2). **Credit** MC, V.

This wonderful, imposing pile has its origins in the 11th century, although the original castle was heavily damaged during the Civil War, then extensively remodelled in the 18th and 19th centuries. Inside is a fine collection of 16th-century furniture and paintings by Van Dyck, Gainsborough and Reynolds, among others. Don't miss the 14th-century Fitzalan Chapel, a Roman Catholic chapel tucked inside an Anglican church so that the dukes and their families could worship according to Catholic rites. Home to a clutch of tombs of Dukes of Norfolk past, it mercifully shows no signs of the time when Oliver Cromwell used it as a stable.

Arundel also has its own neo-Gothic 19th-century **cathedral**, which is actually more impressive outside than inside, plus a number of agreeable shops and some decent alehouses.

Hever

Hever, near Edenbridge, Kent (01732 865224/ www.hevercastle.co.uk). **Getting there** *By train* Victoria to Edenbridge (1hr), then 5-min taxi journey, or Victoria to Hever (1hr), then 1-mile walk. *By car* J5 off M25 then B2042 and B269, or J6 off M25 then A22, A25 and B269. **Open** House & Gardens *Mar-Nov* 11am-6pm daily. **Admission** *Castle & Gardens* £8; £4.40-£6.80 concessions; £20.40 family (2+2). *Garden only* £6.30; £4.20-£5.40 concessions; £16.80 family (2+2). **Credit** MC, V.

The childhood home of Henry VIII's ill-fated second wife Anne Boleyn, this 13th-century castle is surrounded by a double moat and has a splashing water maze with water jets for visitors to negotiate. Hever was bought and restored by William Waldorf Astor in 1903 and it was he who built the 'Tudor' village that lies behind it and created the magnificent gardens and lake. Other attractions inside the house include a miniature model houses exhibition and a fairly gruesome display of instruments of execution and torture that date back over the past few hundred years. Special events include Easter egg trails, jousting demonstrations and music festivals.

Leeds Castle

Broomfield, near Maidstone, Kent (01622 765400/www.leeds-castle.co.uk). **Getting there** *By train* Victoria to Bearsted (1hr), then 10-min bus transfer. *By car* J8 off M20. **Open** *Mar-Oct* 10am-7pm daily (last entry 6pm). *Nov-Feb* 10am-5pm daily (last entry 4pm). **Admission** *Castle & park* £10; £6.50-£8.50 concessions; £29 family (2+ up to 3). *Park only* £8.50; £5.20-£7 concessions; £24 family (2+ up to 3). **Credit** MC, V.

Stunningly sited on two small islands in the middle of a lake, Leeds was built by the Normans shortly after 1066 on the site of a Saxon manor house, converted into a royal palace by Henry VIII and now contains a mishmash of medieval furnishings, paintings, tapestries and, bizarrely, the world's finest collection of antique dog collars. The castle's greatest attractions are external; apart from the flower-filled gardens, there's the Culpeper Garden (an outsize cottage garden), a duckery and an aviary containing more than 100 rare bird species. Best of all is the maze, which centres on a spectacular underground grotto adorned with stone mythical beasts and shell mosaics. Facilities for disabled visitors are good. Special events are held year round, including a grand firework spectacular for Guy Fawkes' night.

Windsor

High Street, Windsor (01753 831118/24hr recorded info 01753 831118/www.royalresidences.com). **Getting there** *By train* Paddington to Slough, then change for Windsor Central (45min); Waterloo to Eton & Windsor Riverside (1hr). *By car* J6 off M4. **Open** *Mar-Oct* 9.45am-4pm (last entry) daily. *Nov-Feb* 9.45am-3pm (last entry) daily. *Changing of the Guard* (weather permitting) Apr-June 11am daily. July-Mar check info line. **Admission** £11; £5.50-£9 concessions; £27.50 family (2+2). **Credit** AmEx, MC, V.

Admission to Windsor Castle normally includes entry to the state apartments, St George's Chapel, Queen Mary's Dolls' House, the Albert Memorial

Chapel, the castle precincts and the gallery. The state rooms, destroyed by the 1992 fire, have now been fully restored and are open to the public: they include the opulent Waterloo Chamber, which was built to celebrate the famous victory over the French in 1815. The gorgeous 15th-century St George's Chapel is the burial place of ten monarchs, including Henry VIII (note that it's closed to visitors on Sunday, although worshippers are welcome). Edward Lutyens' amazing dolls' house (complete with flushing loos and electricity) involved the work of about 1,500 men and took three years to complete.

Country houses & gardens

Althorp, the burial place of Diana, Princess of Wales, is a 90-minute drive from London in Northamptonshire. For more information phone 0870 167 9000 or see www.althorp.com. Note that the house is open only during the months of July and August.

Audley End

Saffron Walden, Essex (01799 522399). **Getting there** *By train* Liverpool Street to Audley End (1hr) then 1-mile (1.5km) walk or 2-min taxi ride. *By car* J8 off M11 then B1383. **Open** *Apr-Sept* 11am-5pm Wed-Sun. *Oct guided tours only* 10am-3pm Wed-Sun. **Admission** £6; £3 5-16s; £4.50 OAPs, students; £15 family. **Credit** MC, V.

The magnificent Jacobean mansion of **Audley End** was the largest house in the entire country when it was built for Thomas Howard, 1st Earl of Suffolk, way back in 1614. It was later owned by Charles II, but was given back to the Howards in the 18th century. The latter demolished two-thirds of it in order to make the place more manageable. More than 30 rooms are open to the public today, many of them restored to Robert Adam's 1760s designs. 'Capability' Brown landscaped the gardens. Call ahead to book a tour.

Saffron Walden (1 mile/1.5km from Audley End) is an appealing market town containing many timber-framed houses with decorative plastering ('pargeting'). Eight miles (13km) south-west of here is the village of Thaxted, where Gustav Holst wrote much of *The Planets*; it's also the site of a superb three-tiered, half-timbered Guildhall dating from the 15th century (01371 831339). There are many other fine villages and much great walking in the area.

Blenheim Palace

Woodstock, Oxfordshire (24hr recorded info 01993 811325/www.blenheimpalace.com). **Getting there** *By train* Paddington to Oxford (1hr) then 30-40-min bus ride. *By car* J9 off M40 then A34 and A44. **Open** Palace, park & gardens *mid Mar-Oct* 10.30am-4.45pm (last entry) daily. *Park* 9am-4.45pm daily. **Admission** *Palace, park & gardens* £10; £5-£7.50 concessions. *Park only* £5-£6 per car (incl occupants), £1-£2 per person; 50p-£1 per person concessions. **Credit** AmEx, DC, MC, V.

After defeating the French at the Battle of Blenheim in 1704, John Churchill, first Duke of Marlborough, was so handsomely rewarded that he could afford to build this fabulous palace. Designed by Sir John Vanbrugh and set in huge grounds landscaped by 'Capability' Brown, it's the only non-royal residence in the country grand enough to be given the title 'palace'. Even if you decided not to tour the palace itself – with its remarkable long library, gilded state rooms, and Churchill exhibition (Sir Winston was born here, and is buried at nearby Bladon) – there's plenty to keep you occupied in the grounds, including a butterfly house, miniature railway, lake for boating and fishing, and the Marlborough Maze, the world's biggest symbolic hedge maze.

The handsome, well-scrubbed Oxfordshire town of **Woodstock** has a long history of royal connections but now chiefly services visitors to Blenheim and the Cotswolds (*see p354*).

Groombridge Place Gardens

Groombridge, near Tunbridge Wells, Kent (01892 863999/www.groombridge.co.uk). **Getting there** *By rail* Charing Cross to Tunbridge Wells (53min) then 10-min taxi ride. *By car* J5 off M25 then A21, A26 and B2176. **Open** *Easter-Oct* 9am-6pm/dusk daily. **Admission** £7.50; £6.50 concessions. **Credit** AmEx, MC, V.

The Manor of Groombridge has passed through many hands since its early life as a medieval pig pasture, flourishing and wilting as its owners' fortunes fluctuated. Much of what we can see today is down to Philip Packer, a barrister and academic who in the mid 17th century demolished the old manor house, constructed Groombridge Place and enlisted the help of the diarist John Evelyn to design brand new gardens.

In 1994, having inspired artists and writers for several centuries (Sir Arthur Conan Doyle modelled Birlstone Manor in *The Valley of Fear* on the house and Peter Greenaway filmed most of *The Draughtsman's Contract* here in the 1980s), they were finally opened to the public. Come to see peacocks strut around spring-fed pools and waterfalls, the strangely cut topiary and the giant chess set. Visitors can also take a canal boat to the award-winning 'Enchanting Forest', or stroll through the vineyard. A magical day out.

Hatfield House

Hatfield, Hertfordshire (01707 262823/www.hatfield-house.co.uk). **Getting there** *By train* from King's Cross to Hatfield (25min). *By car* J4 off A1(M). **Open** House *Easter-Sept* noon-4pm daily. Guided tours noon-4pm Mon-Fri. *West Gardens* Easter-Sept 11am-5.30pm daily. *East Gardens* Easter-Sept 11am-5.30pm Fri. **Admission** *House, park & gardens* £7; £3.50 concessions. *Park & gardens* £4.50; £3.50 concessions. *Park only* £2; £1 concessions. **Credit** MC, V.

Built by Robert Cecil, Earl of Salisbury, in 1611, this superb Jacobean mansion oozes history. In the grounds stands the remaining wing of the Royal Palace of Hatfield, the childhood home of Queen

If you go down to the woods today, make **Epping Forest** your first choice. *See p354.*

Elizabeth I, where in 1558 she held her first Council of State. The gardens include herb terraces, orchards and fountains restored to their former glory by the present-day marchioness.

Sissinghurst Castle Garden

Sissinghurst, Cranbrook, Kent (01580 712850/ www.nationaltrust.org.uk). **Getting there** *By train* Charing Cross to Staplehurst (53min) then 10-min taxi ride. *By car* J5 off M25 then A21 and A262. **Open** *Apr-mid Oct* 1-6pm (last entry) Tue-Fri; 10am-5.30pm (last entry) Sat, Sun. **Admission** £6.50; £3 concessions. **Credit** AmEx, MC, V.
Sissinghurst is famous not only for its wonderful inspirational garden but also for its celebrity creators, poet and novelist Vita Sackville-West and her husband Harold Nicolson, an historian and diplomat. There's tremendous individuality evident in the varied gardens, which have something to offer whatever the season. Visitors can also see the 15th-century long library and tower.

Stowe

Buckinghamshire (gardens 01280 822850/house 01280 818282/www.nationaltrust.org.uk). **Getting there** *By train* Euston to Milton Keynes (40min) then bus to Buckingham (30min) then 5-min taxi ride. *By car* J10 off M40 then A43 and A422, or J14 off M1 then A5 and A422. **Open** seasonal hours; phone for details. **Admission** *Gardens* £4.60; £2.30 concessions; £11.50 family (2+3). *House* £3; £1.50 concessions. **No credit cards.**
Three miles (5km) north-west of Buckingham, Stowe is quite possibly the most important and spectacular 18th-century landscaped garden in the country. Its 325 acres (132 hectares) were first laid out in 1680 but were transformed over the following century by the addition of trees, six lakes and

32 temples. To 'Capability' Brown's naturalistic landscape-shaping were added monuments by almost every big-name architect of the time, including James Gibbs and John Vanbrugh. The overall effect is beautiful, idyllic and, above all, quintessentially English. Little of the house can be seen because it's occupied by Stowe School.

Waddesdon Manor

Waddesdon, near Aylesbury, Buckinghamshire (01296 653226/www.waddesdon.org.uk). **Getting there** *By train* Marylebone to Aylesbury (53min) then bus. *By car* J9 off M40 then A41. **Open** *House end Mar-3 Nov* 11am-4pm Wed-Sun, bank hol Mon. *Grounds 27 Feb-22 Dec* 10am-5pm Wed-Sun, bank hol Mon. **Admission** £10; £7.50 5-16s; free under-5s. *Grounds only* £3; £1.50 5-16s; free under-5s. **Credit** MC, V.
Baron Ferdinand de Rothschild's truly magnificent French Renaissance-style château was constructed in the 1870s and houses some of the world's foremost collections of 18th-century French decorative art, together with some important English paintings. The garden is famous for its specimen trees, seasonal bedding displays and rococo-style aviary of exotic birds. Check the website for the seasonal events held here, including wine tastings, and talks on paintings and textiles.

Out in the country

There's wonderful walking country within easy reach of the city, particularly in the North Downs, which lie south of London; the Chilterns to the north-west; and the Cotswolds to the west. You could also walk a stretch of the **Thames Path**, which follows a 180-mile (288-kilometre) stretch of river from its source near Kemble in Gloucestershire via the Cotswolds, Oxford, the Chilterns, Windsor and through London to the Thames Barrier at Woolwich. Leaflets are available from tourist information centres.
Country Lanes *9 Shaftesbury Street, Fordingbridge, Hampshire SP6 1JF (01425 655022/ www.countrylanes.co.uk).*
Representatives from Country Lanes will meet you off your train from London and lead you on cycling or walking tours of the New Forest and the Cotswolds. There are day trips, short breaks and six-day tours. Visit the website or phone for a brochure.

The Chilterns

Getting there: *By train* from Paddington to Henley (55min); Paddington to Bourne End then change for Marlow (1hr 5min). *By car Henley/Marlow* J8 off M4 then A404(M) and A4130, or J4 off M40 then A404 and A4155. *Wendover* J20 off M25 then A41 and A4011, or A40 and A413.
Stretching in a broad arc around the north-west of London, the Chilterns rarely receive more than a cursory glance out of the window from the coachloads of tourists powering through to Oxford

and Stratford. Yet this gently hilly region has some great walking and excellent pubs (if also some charmless towns) and is easily and quickly accessible from the capital.

At the place where Oxfordshire, Berkshire and Buckinghamshire meet sits cocky little **Henley** (tourist office: 01491 578034). This wealthy commuter burgh becomes the epicentre of braying-toff life for five loud days at the tail-end of June, when the Henley **Royal Regatta** is in full swing (*see p265*), but it's otherwise most useful as a base from which to explore the wonderful villages and countryside that lie to the north of it. Some of the best walking in the Chilterns can be found around **Frieth** and **Nettlebed**, as well as further north around **Wendover**.

Another good (if very popular) place from which to explore the southern Chilterns and the Thames Valley, **Marlow** is a relaxed little town with some good Georgian architecture and a fine pub – the Two Brewers on St Peter's Street – where the author Jerome K Jerome is said to have penned much of *Three Men in a Boat*. Other notable literary residents of Marlow have included Percy and Mary Shelley and TS Eliot.

The cutesy village of **Cookham**, four miles (7 km) east of Marlow, is famed as the home of one of Britain's greatest and most idiosyncratic 20th-century painters, **Stanley Spencer**. Several of his deceptively naïve, sex-and-God-obsessed works are displayed in the **Stanley Spencer Gallery** (01628 471885) on the High Street.

The Cotswolds

Getting there *By train* Paddington to Moreton-in-Marsh (1hr 20min). *By car* M40 then A40 and A44.

Nowhere in England is there such a harmonious relationship between buildings and landscape as there is in the Cotswolds. The enchanting stone villages and incomparable 'wool churches' that characterise the area were built by the medieval merchants who grew rich from the profits of the local wool trade. Routinely described as 'honey-coloured', the stone here is actually very variable, yet its ubiquitous use helps to unify a region that sprawls over six counties.

Certain parts of the Cotswolds suffer horrible congestion during summer weekends, but this problem is always localised. While crowds tend to buzz around **Bourton** and **Bibury**, equally charming villages such as **Stanton** and **Stanway** slumber gently on, remaining almost undisturbed. The small Cotswold towns are often even more memorable than the villages themselves: places such as **Stow-on-the-Wold**, with its elegant 17th-century houses that look down on the square (the area's tourist information centre can found here; 01451 831082); **Winchcombe**, with its church encrusted with gargoyles and its great setting; **Broadway**, where cottage gardens full of wisteria, clematis and old roses spill out on to the High Street; and, best of all, **Chipping Campden**, with its 600-year-old houses and its glorious wool church.

Chipping Campden is also the starting point of the **Cotswold Way** long-distance path. Fortunately, Cotswold footpaths are as suitable for Sunday strollers as they are for hardened hikers. Well-maintained and waymarked, they converge on every town and village. The ancient **Eight Bells Inn** (01386 840371) and the **Cotswold House Hotel** (01386 840330) in Chipping Campden, as well as the **Malt House Hotel** (01386 840295) in Broad Campden, are highly recommended as bases. For **Stratford-upon-Avon**, *see p350*.

Epping Forest

Information Centre, High Beech, Loughton, Essex (020 8508 0028/www.eppingforest.org.uk). **Getting there** *By train* Loughton tube then 2-mile walk or 5-min taxi ride. *By car* J26 off M25. **Open** *Apr-Oct* 10am-5pm Mon-Sat; 11am-5pm Sun. *Nov-Mar* 11am-3pm Mon-Fri; 10am-dusk Sat; 11am-dusk Sun.

The 6,000 acres (2,430 hectares) left of this once massive ancient forest are still mightily impressive, and perfect for walking, cycling, horse riding, picnicking, blackberrying and mushrooming. Wander down wheelchair- (and pushchair-) friendly paths, among ancient oaks adjacent to the visitors' centre and around Connaught Water. The friendly staff can offer suggestions for walks or supply leaflets and a detailed map to help with explorations. Be warned that the visitors' centre is a two-mile (3km) uphill walk from Loughton tube station. You're best off buying a map of the forest beforehand (try Edward Stanford; *see p232*), having a coffee in Loughton town when you get off the tube and then walking to the information centre through the forest rather than along the main roads. Alternatively, continue on the tube for a couple of stops to Theydon Bois, a pretty, largely unspoiled village with a green and duck pond, and wander into the forest from there.

The North Downs

Getting there *By train* Waterloo to Boxhill & Westhumble or Dorking (40-50min) then 10-min taxi ride. *By car* A3 then A243 and A24.

The bones of the landscape of England south of London are the Downs – North and South – long chalk ridges facing each other across the Weald. The South Downs are the more spectacular of the two, but the North Downs are far closer to the capital; so close, in fact, that you can enjoy some of the South-east's best views little more than 20 miles (32km) from the heart of London.

A long-distance footpath, the **North Downs Way** runs for 140 miles (224km) from Farnham in Surrey to the White Cliffs of Dover. Opportunities for shorter walks are plentiful, and the ancient market town of **Dorking** is a good centre. There's easy access from here to **Box Hill**, which has been a popular picnic spot since the days of Charles II – avoid weekends if you can. Not far away is **Ranmore Common**, which offers good walks on the south slopes of the Downs. Another good spot for walking, six miles (9km) south-west of Dorking, is **Leith Hill**, the highest point in south-east England.

Directory

Directory

Getting Around

For London's domestic rail and coach stations, *see p340*.

By air

Gatwick Airport

01293 535353/www.baa.co.uk/ gatwick. About 30 miles (50km) south of central London, off the M23.
Of the three rail services that link Gatwick to London, the quickest is the **Gatwick Express** (08705 301530, www.gatwickexpress.co.uk) to Victoria Station, which takes about 30 minutes and runs 24 hours daily: every 15 minutes between 5.50am and 12.50am, then hourly between 1.35am and 4.35am, with an additional service at 5.20am. Tickets cost £10.50 for a single, £11.70 for a day return (after 9.30am) and £20 for a period return (valid for 30 days). Under-15s get half-price tickets; under-5s travel for free. British Airways and American Airlines offer check-in services at Victoria.

Connex South Central (08457 484950, www.connex.co.uk) also runs a rail service between Gatwick and Victoria, with trains running approximately every 15 minutes during the day and every hour from 1am to 4am. It takes between three and eight minutes longer than the Gatwick Express but tickets are cheaper – £8.20 for a single, £8.30 for a day return (after 9.30am) and £16.40 for a period return (valid for one month). Under-15s get half-price tickets, and under-5s go for free.

For those who are staying in the Bloomsbury area or connecting with trains at King's Cross or Euston, the **Thameslink** (08457 484950, www.thameslink.co.uk) service might prove more convenient. It runs through Blackfriars, City Thameslink, London Bridge Farringdon and King's Cross; frequency and journey times vary with the time of day. Tickets (to King's Cross) cost £9.80 (single) and £19.60 (return).

Forget travelling to London from Gatwick by coach: your only option is an arduous trip to Brighton to get a connecting service to Victoria.

If you want your hand held from airport to hotel and don't mind paying £20 per person each way, try Hotelink (01293 532244, fax 01293 531131, www.hotelink.co.uk). You can book in advance by fax or online with a credit card, giving them your flight details, and someone will meet your plane and shuttle you in to your hotel in central London.

Unless you have more money than sense and/or an expense account to die for, forget **taxis**. You'll end up paying £90 for the torporific, hour-plus journey into central London.

Heathrow Airport

0870 000 0123/www.baa.co.uk/ heathrow. About 15 miles (24km) west of central London, off the M4.
The **Heathrow Express** (0845 600 1515, www.heathrowexpress.co.uk), which runs from the airport to Paddington Station every 15 minutes between 5am and midnight daily, takes 15-20 minutes and is the quickest and most efficient way of travelling between Heathrow and central London. The train can be boarded at one of the airport's two underground stations (Terminals 1, 2 and 3, or Terminal 4). Tickets cost £12 each way or £23 return (£11 or £20 return if booked over the Internet); under-16s travel free (up to four children per paying adult). Many airlines, including British Airways, American Airlines and United Airlines, now have check-in desks at Paddington for both hand and hold luggage.

A longer but far cheaper journey is by tube on the **Piccadilly line**. Tickets for the 50- to 60-minute ride into central London cost £3.60 one way (£1.50 under-16s). Trains run every few minutes from about 5am-11.45pm every day except Sunday, when they run 6am to 11pm. There are tube stations at Terminal 4 and Terminals 1, 2 and 3.

National Express (08705 808080) runs daily services to London Victoria between 5.30am and 9.30pm daily, leaving Heathrow Central bus terminal roughly every 30 minutes at peak times. For a 40-minute journey to London, you'll pay £7 for a single (£3.50 under-15s) or £10 return (£5 under-15s).

As at Gatwick, **Hotelink** (*see above*) offers a hand-holding service for £14 per person each way.

Taxi fares to central London are high (around £45) and the journey time is about 45-60 minutes, often far longer during the rush hour.

London City Airport

7646 0000/ www.londoncityairport.com. About 9 miles (14km) east of central London, Docklands.
Silvertown & City Airport rail station, on the Silverlink Line (*see p359*), is a couple of minutes' walk from the London City Airport terminal, and offers a service that runs approximately every 20 minutes via Stratford, where you can pick up a Central line tube.

Most people, though, head into London on the blue **Shuttlebus** (7646 0088), whose 25-minute ride to Liverpool Street Station goes via Canary Wharf. The shuttle bus leaves every ten minutes (6.50am-10pm during the week; 6.50am-1.15pm on Saturdays; and 11am-10pm on Sundays). Tickets to Liverpool Street Station cost £6 one-way, and just £3 to Canary Wharf.

The journey by **taxi** to the City takes about 30-40 minutes and will cost around £20.

Luton Airport

01582 405100/www.london-luton.co.uk. About 30 miles (50km) north of central London, J10 off the M1.
Luton Airport Parkway Station is close to the airport, but not in it: there's still a short shuttle-bus ride. The **Thameslink** service (*see above*) calls at a number of central London stations including King's Cross and has a journey time of 30-40 minutes. Trains leave roughly every 15 minutes and cost £9.50 single and £18 return, or £9.60 for a cheap day return (available only after 9.30am Monday to Friday).

It takes between an hour and an hour and 30 minutes to get to Victoria by coach. **National Express** (*see above*) runs a 24-hour service with a frequency of around 30 minutes at peak times. An adult single costs £7 (under-15s travel for £3.30), while returns cost £10 and £5 respectively.

A **taxi** from the airport into central London will take an hour at the very least, and will set you back a not inconsiderable £65 or so.

Stansted Airport

0870 000 0303/www.baa.co.uk/ stansted. About 35 miles (60km) north-east of central London, J8 off the M11.
The quickest way to get to London from Stansted is on the **Stansted Express** train (08457 484950) to Liverpool Street Station; the journey time is 40-45 minutes. Trains leave every 15-30 minutes depending on the time of day, and tickets cost £13 for a single and £21 for a return; under-15s get all tickets at half-price.

The **Airbus A6** (08705 808080) coach service from Stansted to Victoria takes at least an hour and 40 minutes and runs from 12.20am to 11.20pm. Coaches run roughly every 30 minutes, more frequently during peak times. An adult single costs £8 (£4 for under-15s), a return is £12 (£5.50 for under-15s).

The hour-plus **taxi** ride to central London will cost around £80.

By rail

Eurostar

Waterloo International Terminal, SE1 (08705 186186/ www.eurostar.co/ Waterloo tube/rail. **Map** p401 M8.
Eurostar now operates five routes from London: Paris, Disneyland Paris, Brussels, Lille, and the ski train, which goes to Bourg St Maurice and Moutiers during the season (Saturdays only).

Standard-class fares to Brussels and Paris range from £70 for a weekend day return (£110 for first class) to £500. If you book at least 14 days in advance and stay two nights or over a Saturday, the Leisure Apex 14 return fare is a bargain at £79. Look out for other special offers nearer the time.

The journey time to Paris is three hours, while it takes just two hours 40 minutes to get to Brussels (the tunnel section takes a measly 22 minutes). Services are frequent: there are currently 16-20 trains a day to Paris from Monday to Saturday, and either ten or 11 to Brussels. On Sundays, ten to 12 trains run to Paris, with seven or eight heading to Brussels.

Public transport

Information

All the information below can be accessed online at www.londontransport.co.uk and www.thetube.com, or by phoning 7222 1234. Transport for London (TfL; formerly London Transport) also runs Travel Information Centres that provide maps and info about the tube, buses and Docklands Light Railway (DLR; *see below*). You can find them in the stations listed below. For lost property, s*ee p369.*

Travel Information Centres

Euston 7.15am-6pm Mon-Sat; 8.30am-5pm Sun.
Heathrow Airport *Terminals 1, 2 & 3 underground station* 6.30am-7pm Mon-Sat; 7.15am-7pm Sun. *Terminal 4 Arrivals Hall* 6am-3pm Mon-Sat; 7.15am-3pm Sun.
King's Cross *Underground station* 8am-6pm Mon-Sat; 8.30am-5pm Sun.
Liverpool Street 8am-6pm Mon-Fri 8.45am-5.30pm Sat, Sun.
Victoria 7.45am-7pm Mon-Sat; 8.45am-7pm Sun.
Waterloo *Eurostar Arrival Hall* 8am-11pm daily.

Fares & tickets

Bus and tube fares are based on a zone system. There are six zones stretching 12 miles (20 kilometres) out from the centre of London. For most visitors to London, the Travelcard (*see below*) is by far the cheapest way of getting around. Beware of on-the-spot £10 penalty fares – fines by any other name – for anyone caught travelling without a valid ticket. Staff aren't known for accepting excuses, so buy your ticket before you travel.

Adult fares

The single underground fare for adults within Zone 1 is £1.50; for zones 1 and 2 it's £1.90, while an all-zones single fare is £3.60. Single bus fares are 70p for a journey outside Zone 1 and £1 for a trip within Zone 1 or crossing the Zone 1 boundary.

Buying individual tickets is the most expensive way to travel. If you're likely to make three or more journeys in one day, or if you're staying in London for more than a day, it's always better value to buy a Travelcard (*see below*).

Child fares

On all buses, tubes and local trains, under-16s are classified as children; under-5s travel free. Under-16s pay a child's fare until 10pm; after 10pm (buses only) they pay an adult fare.

Fourteen- and 15-year-olds must carry Child Rate Photocards, available from any post office: take a passport-size photo and proof of age (passport or birth certificate) with you. The single underground fare for children in Zone 1 is 60p, or 80p for zones 1 and 2, rising to £1.50 for an all-zone ticket. Single child bus fares cost 40p to go anywhere in London.

One-Day LT Cards

One-Day LT Cards will only be of interest if you intend to travel during peak times (ie before 9.30am on weekdays) and make several journeys during the day. They are valid on buses (including night buses), underground services (except those running to and from Bakerloo line stations north of Queen's Park; this section of track is not run by Transport for London), and Docklands Light Railway (DLR) services, but not on overland rail services or airbuses. The cards cost £5.10 for zones 1 and 2; £6.20 for zones 1-4 and £7.70 for zones 1-6 (child £2.50 zones 1 and 2; £3 zones 1-4; £3.30 zones 1-6).

Travelcards

The most economical way to get around London is with a Travelcard, which can be used on the tube system, buses, rail services, Docklands Light Railway and some Green Line buses, and can be bought at all tube and rail stations as well as at appointed newsagents. The most convenient cards for short-term visitors are the One-Day or One-Week Travelcards, though monthly and yearly tickets are also available.

One-Day Travelcards can be used after 9.30am on weekdays and all day at weekends. You can make unlimited journeys within the zones you select. A One-Day Travelcard costs £4 for zones 1 and 2, £4.30 for zones 1-4 or £4.90 for zones 1-6 (£2 for a child all-zone ticket). They're now valid until 4.30am and can be used on N-prefixed night buses.

Family Travelcards are available for families and groups of one or two adults travelling with between one and four children. Like regular One-Day Travelcards, they're valid after 9.30am from Monday to Friday and all day on weekends and public holidays, and can be used until 4.30am; they cost £2.60 for zones 1 and 2, £2.80 for zones 1-4 or £3.20 for zones 1-6 (child 80p zones 1-6).

If you think you'll be travelling on consecutive weekend days, it's probably worth getting a Weekend Travelcard, which allows travel on consecutive weekend days or public holidays, though not on N-prefixed night buses. It costs £6 for zones 1 and 2, £6.40 for zones 1-4 or £7.30 for zones 1-6 (child £3 zones 1-6).

One-Week Travelcards offer unlimited journeys throughout the selected zones for seven days, including use of N-prefixed night buses, and are valid around the clock. Weekly Travelcards cost £15.90 for Zone 1; £18.90 for zones 1 and 2; £22.40 for zones 1-3; £27.60 for zones 1-4; £33.30 for zones 1-5; £36.40 for all zones (child £6.60 Zone 1; £7.70 zones 1 and 2; £10.30 zones 1-3; £12.80 zones 1-4; £14.10 zones 1-5; £15.40 zones 1-6).

Carnet

If you're planning on making a lot of short-hop journeys within Zone 1 over a period of several days, it makes sense to buy a carnet of ten tickets for £11.50 (£5 for children). This brings down the cost of each journey to £1.15 rather than the standard £1.50. Note that if you exit a station outside of Zone 1 and are caught with only a carnet ticket, you'll be liable to a £10 penalty fare.

Photocards

Photocards are required for all bus passes and Travelcards except the One-Day and Weekend versions. Child-rate photocards are required for five- to 15-year-olds using child-rate Travelcards and bus passes. Fourteen- and 15-year-olds need a child-rate photocard in order to buy any ticket at the discounted rate.

London Underground

Though short distances are best covered on foot, travelling on the capital's underground rail system – known as the tube – is the quickest way to get around London (*see p70* **Rumblings**). That said, there are frequent delays, escalators are sometimes out of action and, occasionally, there are station and line closures (typically at weekends due to engineering work).

Crime is not a major problem on the tube, though you'd be wise to avoid getting into an empty carriage on your own, and beware of pickpockets. Smoking is illegal anywhere on the underground system.

Using the system

Tickets can be purchased from a station ticket office or from self-service machines. Unfortunately, staff in ticket offices rarely speak foreign languages and can be remarkably gruff and unhelpful.

You can buy most tickets, including carnets and One-Day LT Cards (*see p357*), from self-service machines, but for anything covering a longer period you'll need to show a valid photocard to a ticket officer. Note that, because of staff shortages, ticket offices in some of the less busy stations often close early (around 7.30pm). In any case, try and keep a little change with you at all times: the queues at ticket offices can be time-consuming, and using a ticket machine is usually far quicker. Ticket machines are supposed to give change, but often run out – and they don't accept cards.

To enter the tube, insert your ticket in the automatic checking gates with the black magnetic strip facing down, and pull it out of the top to open the gates. Exiting the system at your destination is done in much the same way, though if you have a single journey ticket, it will be retained by the gate as you leave.

There are 12 underground lines, colour-coded on the tube map, of which the newest is the much-delayed Jubilee line extension, which opened in late 1999 and links Green Park in the West End to Stratford in east London via Waterloo, Bermondsey, Canary Wharf and North Greenwich.

Underground timetable

Tube trains run daily, starting at around 5.30am every day except Sunday, when they start an hour to two hours later, depending on the line. The only exception is Christmas Day, when there is no service. Generally, you won't have to wait more than ten minutes for a train, and during peak times the service should run every two or three minutes. Times of last trains vary, though they're usually around 11.30pm-1am every day except Sunday, when they finish 30 minutes to an hour earlier. The only all-night public transport is by night bus (*see below*). Try to avoid the rush-hour crush between about 8am and 9.30am, and 4.30pm and 6.30pm.

Docklands Light Railway (DLR)

7363 9700/www.dlr.co.uk.
The DLR is administered as part of the tube system. Its driverless trains run on a raised track from Bank (Central or Waterloo & City lines) or Tower Gateway, close to Tower Hill tube (Circle and District lines), to Stratford, Beckton and down the Isle of Dogs to Island Gardens, Greenwich and Lewisham. Trains run from 5.30am to around 12.30am Monday to Friday, 6am-12.30am Saturday and 7.30am-11.30pm Sunday.

Docklands Shuttle South (Lewisham to Canary Wharf) adult tickets cost £1.50; Docklands Shuttle East (valid between Beckton/Stratford and Island Gardens via Westferry) tickets are £2.10; City Flyer South (valid between Bank and Lewisham) tickets are £2.90; and City Flyer East (valid between Beckton/Stratford and Bank) tickets are £3.30. Expect to pay around half price for child tickets (under-18s; no photocard required).

The DLR is keen to promote itself as much as a tourist attraction as a transport system. To this end it offers 'Sail and Rail' tickets that combine unlimited travel on the DLR with a riverboat trip between Greenwich and Westminster Piers (boats depart from 10.30am to 6.30pm; *see p359*) plus discounts on selected museums and sights. Starting at Tower Gateway, special trains leave on the hour (from 10am), with a DLR guide giving passengers the low-down on the area as the train glides along. Tickets are about £8.50 for adults, £4.50 for kids.

Buses

Travelling on London's extensive bus network has to be one of the most pleasurable and enlightening ways of discovering the city, but be warned: progress through the invariably dreadful traffic can be very slow in the morning and evening rush hours, and even outside these times, the buses are hardly about to break any land speed records.

Certain routes still use the venerable red Routemaster buses – the ones you can hop on and off at the back – but modern buses are taking over.

Night buses

Night buses are the only form of public transport that runs through the night, operating from around 11pm to 6am at a frequency of about once an hour on most routes (more often on Fridays and Saturdays). All pass through central London and the majority stop at Trafalgar Square, so head there if you're unsure which bus to get. Night buses have the letter 'N' before their number, and are now free to holders of One-Day Travelcards, Weekend Travelcards, Family Travelcards and One-Day LT cards. You'll find free maps and timetables at the LT Travel Information Centres (*see p357*).

Directory

Fares for night buses are now the same as for day buses: £1 for any journey that includes travelling into or through central London (Zone 1), 70p for the rest of London.

Green Line buses

Green Line buses (0870 608 7261, www.greenline.co.uk) serve the suburbs and towns within a 40-mile (64km) radius of London. Their main departure point is Eccleston Bridge, SW1 (Colonnades Coach Station, behind Victoria).

Stationlink buses

The red and yellow Stationlink buses (7222 1234) are convenient for the disabled, the elderly, people laden with luggage or those with small children. The service connects all the main London rail termini (with the exception of Charing Cross) on a circular trip. Buses run every hour from about 9am to 7pm (phone for details). The fare is £1 for adults, 40p for five- to 15-year-olds.

Rail services

Independently owned commuter services run out of all the city's main line rail stations (*see p340*). Travelcards are valid on these services within the relevant zones. **Silverlink** (01923 207258, www.silverlinktrains.com; or National Rail Enquiries on 08457 484950) is a useful and underused overground service that carves a huge arc through the north of the city, running from Richmond (in the south-west) to North Woolwich (in the east) via London City Airport. The line connects with the tube network at several stations. Trains run about every 20 minutes every day except Sunday, when they run every half-hour, and offer a refreshing alternative to the tube, with great views of London's back gardens.

For more information about train travel, *see p340*. To retrieve property that has been left on trains, *see p369*.

Water transport

Often overlooked, the river makes for a speedy way of getting about, and is less congested than other modes of transport. The times of services vary, but most operate every 20 minutes to one hour between about 10.30am and 5pm. Services may be more frequent and run later in summer. Call the individual operators below for details of schedules and fares, or see TfL's website, www.tfl.gov.uk. The names in bold below are the names of piers: the central ones are on the maps at the back of this guide.
Westminster–Greenwich (1hr) Westminster Passenger Services 7930 4097.
Westminster–Tower (25-30min) City Cruises 7930 9033.
Westminster–Festival (5min)–**London Bridge City** (20min)–**St Katharine's** (5min) Crown River Cruises 7936 2033.
Westminster–(Thames) Barrier Gardens (1hr 30min) Thames Cruises 7930 3373.
Westminster–Kew (1hr 30min)–**Richmond** (30min)–**Hampton Court** (1hr 30min) Westminster Passenger Service Association 7930 2062.
Embankment–Tower (30min)–**Greenwich** (30min) Catamaran Cruises 7987 1185.
Greenland Dock–Canary Wharf (8mins)–**St Katherine's** (7min)–**London Bridge City** (4min)–**Bankside** (3min)–**Blackfriars** (3mins)–**Savoy** (3min) Collins River Enterprises 7977 6892.
Savoy–Cadogan (15-20min)–**Chelsea** (2min) Riverside Launches 07831 574774.
Greenwich–(Thames) Barrier Gardens (25min) Campion Launches 8305 0300.
Lunch & dinner cruises Lunch cruises daily from Embankment (1hr-1hr 30min): Woods River Cruises 7480 7770/ Bateaux London 7925 2215. Dinner cruises (2 days a week to daily) from Westminster, Embankment and Savoy (2hrs 45min-3hrs 30min): City Cruises 7237 5134/Bateaux London 7925 2215.

Taxis

Black cabs

Licensed London taxis are commonly known as black cabs (even though they now come in a wide variety of colours thanks to the advent of on-cab advertising) and are a quintessential feature of London life. They all have a yellow 'For Hire' sign and a white licence plate on the back of the vehicle. Drivers of black cabs must pass a test called 'The Knowledge' to prove they know the name of every street in central London, where it is and the shortest route to it.

When a taxi's 'For Hire' sign is switched on, it can be hailed in the street (though, annoyingly, some cabbies switch off the sign even if they're free, picking up fares as and when they please). If a taxi stops, it's the cabbie's responsibility to take you to your destination, provided it's within seven miles. In reality, some – albeit a minority – turn their noses up at south London, or, indeed, anywhere that they don't fancy going. Also, thanks to a hike in prices during autumn 2001, you can expect to pay a higher fare after 8pm and during the day at weekends.

Radio Taxis (7272 0272; credit cards only) and **Dial-a-Cab** (7253 5000) both run 24-hour services for black cabs (with a pick-up charge).

Any enquiries or, indeed, complaints about black cabs should be made to the Public Carriage Office (*see below*). Remember to note the badge number of the offending cab, which should be clearly displayed in the rear of the cab as well as on its back bumper. For lost property, *see p369*.
Public Carriage Office *200 Baker Street, Marylebone, NW1 5RZ (7918 2000). Baker Street tube.* **Open** *By phone* 9am-4pm Mon-Fri. *In person* 9pm-2am Mon-Fri.

Minicabs

Minicabs (saloon cars) are generally cheaper than black cabs, especially at night and weekends, but the drivers are usually unlicensed, often untrained, sometimes uninsured, frequently unreliable and, occasionally, dangerous. In some places – Victoria Station, or in and around Soho late at night, to name but two – drivers tout for business on the street. Avoid them at all costs: aside from the fact that minicabs can't legally be hailed in the street, the drivers are often imbecilic ruffians who barely know their own way home, let alone to your front door, and will charge you the earth in order to get you there.

This dire situation is supposed to be improving with the introduction of licences for all minicabs, but with just 20 inspectors and around 20,000 unlicensed cars at present, real change looks like it'll be a long time coming.

In the meantime, there are plenty of trustworthy and licensed minicab firms; ask for a recommendation. **Addison Lee** (7387 8888) is one of the bigger companies, and claims to do pick-ups from all areas. Women travelling alone may prefer to use **Lady Cabs** (7254 3501), which employs only women drivers. Whoever you use, ask the price when you book and confirm it with the driver when the car arrives.

Driving

If you've heard that driving in central London is tough, just wait until you try to find somewhere to park. If you park illegally, you'll probably get a £60-£80 parking ticket (which will be reduced by 50 per cent if you pay within 14 days). Worse still, you may find your car has been immobilised by a yellow triangular wheel clamp, or even towed away and impounded. And the retrieval procedure, to put it mildly, is no easy ride (*see below*). So, if you can avoid driving in central London, for God's sake do so, especially since there are so many public transport options to choose from.

Breakdown services

If you're a member of a motoring organisation in another country, check to see if it has a reciprocal agreement with a British organisation.

AA (Automobile Association)
Info 08705 500600/ breakdown 0800 887766/ new members 0800 444999/ www.theaa.co.uk. **Open** 24hrs daily. **Credit** V.
You can call the AA if your car breaks down. Membership prices start at £44 a year for standard roadside assistance, going up to £164 a year. It only offers annual membership for the UK, but you can get temporary breakdown cover from the AA for Europe (or free European cover for 72 hours).

ETA (Environmental Transport Association)
10 Church Street, Weybridge, Surrey KT13 8RS (01932 828882/ www.eta.co.uk). **Open** *Office* 8am-6pm Mon-Fri; 9am-4pm Sat. *Breakdown service* 24hrs daily. **Credit** MC, V.
The green alternative, if you don't want part of your membership fees used for lobbying the government into building more roads, as happens with the AA and RAC. Basic membership is £25 a year for individuals, and there's also a one-off joining fee of £10, but this is waived if you pay by direct debit or credit card.

RAC (Royal Automobile Club)
RAC House, 1 Forest Road, Feltham, Middx TW13 7RR (emergency breakdown 0800 828282/office & membership 08705 722722/ www.rac.co.uk). **Open** *Office* 8am-9pm Mon-Fri; 8.30am-4pm Sat; 10am-4pm Sun. *Breakdown service* 24hrs daily. **Credit** AmEx, DC, MC, V.
Ring the enquiries number and ask for the Rescue Service. Membership costs from £39 for basic cover to £198 for the most comprehensive. European cover starts at £90.

Parking

Central London is scattered with parking meters, but finding a free one could take several hours, and when you do it'll cost you up to £1 for every 15 minutes to park there, and you'll be limited to two

hours on the meter. Parking on a single yellow line, a double yellow line or a red line at any time during the day is illegal, and you're likely to end up being fined, clamped or towed.

However, in the evening (from 6pm or 7pm in much of central London) and at various times at weekends, parking on single yellow lines is legal and free. If you find a clear spot on a single yellow line during the evening, check a nearby sign before you leave your car: this sign should tell you at which times parking is legal on this particular yellow line, as times vary from council to council and even from street to street.

It's a similar story with meters, which become free after a certain time in the evening and at various times on weekends: check before paying, as it could save you several quid. Parking on double yellow lines and red routes is, by and large, illegal at all times.

NCP 24-hour car parks (7499 7050/www.ncp.co.uk) in and around central London are numerous but phenomenally expensive. Prices vary with location, but expect to pay £6-£10 for two hours and £30-£50 for 24 hours. Among its central car parks are those at Arlington House, Arlington Street, St James's, W1; Upper Ground, Southwark, SE1; and 2 Lexington Street, Soho, W1.

A word of warning: almost all NCPs in central London are underground, and a select few – such as the car park on Adeline Place behind Tottenham Court Road – are frequented by drug users looking for a quiet place in which to smoke, snort or inject. In other words, take care if you're using them.

Clamping
The immobilising of illegally parked vehicles by attaching a clamp to one wheel is commonplace in London. There will be a label attached to the car telling you which payment centre

to phone or visit. Some boroughs let you pay over the phone with a credit card, others insist you go in person. Either way, you'll have to stump up an £80 clamp release fee and show a valid licence (there's a 50% discount on the fine if you pay within two weeks). If you can't show a valid licence, you'll have to pay a release fee of £120 for motorcycles and cars, £600 for any other vehicle.

Staff at the payment centre will promise to de-clamp your car some time within the next four hours, but they won't tell you exactly when. You are also warned that if you don't remove your car immediately, they might clamp it again. This Kafkaesque system means you may have to spend quite some time waiting by your car.

If you feel you've been clamped unfairly, look for the appeals procedure and contact number printed on the back of your ticket. If your appeal is turned down and you still wish to take things further, call the Clamping and Vehicle Section (7747 4700), an independent governing body.

Vehicle removal

If your car has mysteriously disappeared, chances are that, if it was legally parked, it's been nicked; if not, it's probably been hoisted on to the back of a truck and taken to a car pound, and you're facing a stiff penalty: a fee of £160 is levied for removal, plus £15 per day from the first midnight after removal. To add insult to injury, you'll probably get a parking ticket of £40-£80 when you collect the car (there's a 50% discount if you pay within 14 days). To find out where your car has been taken and how to retrieve it, call the Trace service hotline (7747 4747).

Vehicle hire

To hire a car, you must have at least one year's driving experience with a full current driving licence; in addition, many car hire firms refuse to hire vehicles out to people under the age of 23. If you're an overseas visitor, your current driving licence is valid in Britain for a year.

Prices for car hire vary considerably; always ring several competitors for a quote (see the *Yellow Pages* or www.yell.com). As well as the companies listed below – call or check the web to find out the location of your nearest

office – Easycar's online-only service, at www.easycar.co.uk, offers extremely competitive rates, so long as you don't mind driving a heavily branded car around town.
Avis *08705 900500/www.avis.co.uk.* **Open** 24hrs daily. **Credit** AmEx, DC, MC, V.
Budget *0800 181181/ www.gobudget.com).* **Open** 8am-10pm daily. **Credit** AmEx, DC, MC, V.
Europcar *0870 607 5000/ www.europcar.com.* **Open** 24hrs daily. **Credit** AmEx, DC, MC, V.
Hertz *0870 599 6699/ www.hertz.com.* **Open** 24hrs daily. **Credit** AmEx, MC, V.

Motorbike hire

Scootabout *1-3 Leeke Street, King's Cross, WC1 (7833 4607/ www.hgbmotorcycles.co.uk).* King's Cross tube/rail. **Open** 9am-6pm Mon-Fri. **Credit** MC, V. **Map** p399 M3.
It costs £73.50 a day or £385 a week to hire an ST1100 Pan European. All rental prices include 250 miles (402km) a day, with excess mileage at 10p a mile, AA cover, insurance and VAT. Bikes can only be hired with a credit card and after a £350 deposit has been made. No crash helmet hire.

Cycling

Central London is, on the whole, an unfriendly place for cyclists. The traffic is overwhelming, fumes can be appalling in summer, and potholes proliferate. A safety helmet, a filter-mask and a determined attitude are advisable.

London Cycling Campaign

30 Great Guildford Street, SE1 0HS (7928 7220/www.lcc.org.uk). **Open** Phone enquiries 2-5pm Mon-Fri. Individual membership (which costs £23.50 a year) allows discounts at LCC-member bike shops, advice and information on bike maintenance, insurance deals, cycle route maps and subscription to *London Cyclist* magazine.

Cycle hire & storage

Bikepark

11-13 Macklin Street, Covent Garden, WC2 (7430 0083/ www.bikepark.co.uk). Covent Garden or Holborn tube. **Open** 8.30am-7pm Mon-Fri; 10am-6pm Sat. **Credit** MC, V. **Map** p399 L6.

This Bikepark branch allows you to leave your bike in secure parking (at a charge of £2 for 24 hours, £7.50 for a week, and £20 for a month); it also has changing facilities that you can make use of. In addition, there's a repair service and the possibility of hiring a hybrid or mountain bike and accessories for commuting or touring. For bike hire services, head to the SW3 branch.
Branch: 67 New King's Road, SW3 (7731 7012). **Hire** £12 first day; £6 second day; £4 per day thereafter. **Deposit** £200.

London Bicycle Tour Company

1A Gabriel's Wharf, 56 Upper Ground, South Bank, SE1 (7928 6838/www.londonbicycle.com). Southwark tube/Blackfriars or Waterloo tube/rail. **Open** Easter-Oct 10am-6pm daily. Nov-Easter by appointment. **Hire** £2.50 per hr; £12 first day; £6 per day thereafter. **Deposit** £100 (unless paying by credit card). **Credit** AmEx, DC, MC, V. **Map** p404 N7.
In addition to bike hire and the increasingly popular rickshaw hire (which costs £20 per hour with driver), this company, as its name implies, conducts daily bicycle tours covering either west London, east London or the centre of town. All tours cost £11.95 and last approximately three hours. The firm also offers weekend breaks in the countryside around London.

Walking

As is the case with any city, the best way to see London is on foot. However, unlike many other great cities, London is extremely complicated in terms of its street layout – so much so, in fact, that even locals carry maps around with them most, if not all, of the time. This means that you should be prepared to get lost on at least a semi-regular basis.

We've included a selection of street maps covering central London in the back of this book (starting on page 394), but we recommend that you also buy a separate map of the city: both the standard Geographers' *A–Z* and Collins' *London Street Atlas* versions come in a variety of sizes and are very easy to use.

Directory

Resources A-Z

Addresses

London addresses invariably come with a postcode attached. This helps determine where the street is found, but also helps differentiate between streets with the same name in different parts of London (there are 20 Park Roads in the city, for example).

A London postcode written in its most basic form takes a point of the compass – N, E, SE, SW, W and NW, plus EC (East Central) and WC (West Central) – and then a number; for example, N1, WC2, SE24, etc. With the exception of those numbered 1, which denote the area nearest the centre of London, the numbers are ordered alphabetically by area. For example, in east London, Whitechapel takes E1 as it's closest to central London, but then E2 is Bethnal Green, E3 is Bow and so on.

Age restrictions

You must be 17 or older to drive in the United Kingdom, and 18 to buy cigarettes or be served alcohol (to be safe, carry photo ID if you're under 22 years of age, or look as if you might be).

The age of consent in Britain is 16 for both heterosexuals and homosexuals.

Business

The proudly pink *Financial Times* (daily) is the most recognisable (due to its distinctive colour) and authoritative newspaper for facts and figures in the City and all over the world. But if you're more in the market for in-depth analysis, as well as some considered domestic and international news, then you should try *The Economist* magazine (weekly).

Conventions & conferences

London Tourist Board & Convention Bureaux

7932 2020/www.londontown.com. The LTB runs a venue enquiry service for conventions and exhibitions. You can call or email for an information pack, which lists hotels and centres that host events, together with their facilities.

Queen Elizabeth II Conference Centre

Broad Sanctuary, Westminster, SW1 (7222 5000/www.qeiicc.co.uk). St James's Park tube. **Open** 8am-6pm Mon-Fri. *Conference facilities* 24hrs daily. **Map** p401 K9.
This unattractive, purpose-built centre has some of the best conference facilities in the capital. There are rooms with capacities ranging from 40 to 1,100, and communications equipment is available (including wireless LAN technology installed throughout).

Couriers & shippers

DHL and FedEx offer local and international courier services; Excess Baggage is the UK's largest shipper of baggage.

DHL *181 Strand, Covent Garden, WC2 (08701 100 300/ www.dhl.co.uk). Charing Cross tube/rail.* **Open** 8am-8pm Mon-Fri. **Credit** AmEx, DC, MC, V. **Map** p401 L7.
Excess Baggage Company *168 Earl's Court Road, Earl's Court, SW5 (020 7373 1977/www.excess-baggage.com). Earl's Court tube.* **Open** 8am-6pm Mon-Fri; 9am-1pm Sat. **Credit** AmEx, MC, V. **Map** p396 B10.
Federal Express *0800 123800/ www.fedex.com/gb.* **Open** 7.30am-7.30pm Mon-Fri. **Credit** AmEx, DC, MC, V.

Office hire & business centres

ABC Business Machines

59 Chiltern Street, Marylebone, W1 (7486 5634/www.abcbusiness.co.uk). Baker Street tube. **Open** 9am-5.30pm Mon-Fri; 9.30am-12.30pm Sat. **Credit** MC, V. **Map** p398 G5.

Faxes, answerphones, computers, photocopiers and audio equipment are among the items on hire at ABC.

British Monomarks

Monomarks House, 27 Old Gloucester Street, Bloomsbury, WC1 (7419 5000/7404 5011/ www.britishmonomarks.co.uk). Holborn tube. **Open** 9am-6pm Mon-Fri. **Credit** AmEx, MC, V. **Map** p399 L5.
Services available here include mail forwarding, email, fax and 24-hour telephone answering.

Secretarial services

Reed Employment, Staff Agency

143 Victoria Street, Westminster, SW1 (7834 1801/www.reed.co.uk). Victoria tube/rail. **Open** 8am-6pm Mon-Fri. **Map** p400 J10.
Reed supplies secretarial, computing, accountancy and technical services to registered companies. This branch specialises in secretarial and admin.

Typing Overload

67 Chancery Lane, Holborn, WC1 (7404 5464/ www.typingoverload.com). Chancery Lane tube. **Open** 9.30am-5.30pm Mon-Fri. **Credit** AmEx, MC, V. **Map** p399 M5.
A speedy and professional typing service is offered.
Branch: 35 Brompton Road, Knightsbridge, SW3 (7823 9955).

Translators & interpreters

Central Translations

21 Woodstock Street, Mayfair, W1 (7493 5511/ www.centraltranslations.co.uk). Bond Street tube. **Open** 9am-5pm Mon-Fri. **Map** p398 H6.
Be it typesetting, proofreading, translation or the use of an interpreter, Central can work with almost every language under the sun.

1st Translation Company

24 Holborn Viaduct, The City, EC1 (7329 0032). Chancery Lane or Holborn tube. **Open** 9am-8pm Mon-Fri. **Map** p404 N5.
More than 50 languages can be translated by this firm. Interpreters are available from £220.

Consumer

Most shops will happily offer a full refund for faulty or defective goods. However, should you experience any difficulty in obtaining a refund, contact the Trading Standards department of your local council, which can provide help and legal advice.

Customs

When entering the UK, non-European Union citizens and anyone buying duty-free goods should be aware of the following import limits:

● 200 cigarettes or 100 cigarillos or 50 cigars or 250 grams (8.82 ounces) of tobacco;
● wine plus either 1 litre of spirits or strong liqueurs (more than 22% alcohol by volume) or 2 litres of fortified wine (under 22% abv), sparkling wine or other liqueurs;
● 60cc/ml of perfume;
● 250cc/ml of toilet water;
● other goods to the value of £145 for non-commercial use;
● the import of meat, meat products, fruit, plants, flowers and protected animals is restricted or forbidden.

Since the Single European Market agreement came into force at the beginning of 1993, people over the age of 17 arriving from an EU country have been able to import large quantities of goods for their own personal use, but Customs officials may need convincing that you do not intend to sell any of the goods.

Disabled

Compared to some European cities, London is relatively friendly to the mobility-impaired. But it's only relative. While many of the capital's sights make provision for wheelchair users, the great headache for those who have problems getting around is transport. For information on provisions for the disabled on the tube, check out the *Access to the Underground* booklet, available free from ticket offices, TfL's Access to Mobility (42-50 Victoria Street, SW1H 0TL, 7918 3312) and Travel Information Centres (*see p357*). Access to Mobility also has details on buses and Braille maps. All DLR stations have wheelchair access.

We recommend *Access in London* by Gordon Couch, William Forrester and Justin Irwin (Quiller Press, 1997), which has detailed maps of step-free routes and accessible tube stations alongside a guide to adapted toilets, and sections on shopping, accommodation and entertainment. The guide is available at some bookshops for £7.95, or from Access Project, 39 Bradley Gardens, W13 8HE (7250 3222).

The organisations below offer help to disabled visitors to London. For the National Bureau for Students with Disabilities, *see p374*.

Artsline

54 Chalton Street, Somers Town, NW1 (tel/minicom 7388 2227/ www.artsline.org.uk). Euston tube/rail. **Open** 9.30am-5.30pm Mon-Fri. **Map** p399 K3.
Information on disabled access to arts and entertainment events in London and on adapted facilities in cinemas, art galleries, theatres and the like.

Can Be Done

7-11 Kensington High Street, Kensington, W8 5NP (8907 2400/ www.canbedone.co.uk). High Street Kensington tube. **Open** Phone enquiries 9am-5.30pm Mon-Fri. **Map** p396 A9.
Holidays and tours in London that are tailored to the needs of disabled people.

DAIL (Disability Arts in London)

Diorama Arts Centre, 34 Osnaburgh Street, Fitzrovia, NW1 (7916 6351/ minicom 7691 4201/www.dail.dircon. co.uk). Great Portland Street tube. **Open** 11am-4pm Mon-Fri. **Map** p398 H4.
DAIL produces a 32-page monthly magazine with listings, reviews and articles on the arts and the disabled (it costs £10 per year, or £30 for overseas subscribers). DAIL is part of LDAF (London Disability Arts Forum; 7916 5484), which organises events for disabled people in London.

DIAL (National Association of Disablement Information & Advice Lines)

01302 310123. **Open** 9am-5pm Mon-Fri.
DIAL holds details of local groups in the United Kingdom that can offer free information and advice on all aspects of disability.

William Forrester

1 Belvedere Close, Guildford, Surrey, GU2 6NP (01483 575401).
William Forrester is a London Registered Guide and, since he's a wheelchair user himself, has extensive experience in leading tours in the capital for disabled individuals and groups. Very popular, so make sure you book early.

Greater London Action on Disability (GLAD)

336 Brixton Road, Brixton, SW9 (7346 5800/info line 7346 5808/ minicom 7346 5811). Brixton tube/rail. **Open** Phone enquiries 9am-5pm Mon-Fri. *Info line* 1.30-4.30pm Mon, Wed, Fri.
GLAD is a voluntary organisation that provides valuable information for disabled visitors and residents. Among its publications are the fortnightly *Update*, containing relevant extracts from national newspapers, and magazines relating to the disabled, the monthly *London Disability News*, and the bi-monthly *Boadicea*, for disabled women.

Holiday Care Service

Open Helpline 9am-5pm Mon, Tue; 9am-1pm Wed-Fri.
An advisory service specialising in disabled holiday accommodation.

Royal Association for Disability & Rehabilitation (RADAR)

12 City Forum, 250 City Road, Islington, EC1 (7250 3222/ www.radar.org.uk). Old Street tube/rail. **Open** 9am-4pm Mon-Fri. **Map** p402 P3.
This central organisation for disabled voluntary groups gives advice on almost any aspect of life. Every month the Association publishes *Bulletin*, a newsletter containing articles on issues such as housing and education.

Tripscope

Vassall Centre, Guill Avenue, Fishpond, Bristol BS16 2QQ (tel/minicom 08457 585641/ www.justmobility.co.uk). **Open** *Phone* enquiries 9am-5pm Mon-Thur; 9am-4.30pm Fri.

Directory

Jim Bennett and Adrian Drew's advice and information service for the elderly and disabled can help with all aspects of getting around London, the UK and overseas. It's chiefly an enquiry line, but you can write in or email them via the website if you have difficulty with the telephone.

Wheelchair Travel & Access Mini Buses

1 Johnston Green, Guildford, Surrey GU2 9XS (01483 233640/ www.wheelchair-travel.co.uk). **Open** 9am-5pm Mon-Fri. An excellent source of converted vehicles for hire, including adapted minibuses (with or without driver), plus cars with hand controls and 'Chairman' cars.

Electricity

As in the rest of Europe, the United Kingdom uses a standard 220-240V, 50-cycle AC voltage. British plugs use three cumbersome pins rather than the standard two-pin variety, so travellers with appliances from mainland Europe will need to bring an adaptor, as will travellers planning on using US appliances, which run off 110-120V, 60-cycle.

Embassies & consulates

Check the telephone directory and *Yellow Pages* under 'Embassies' for embassies, consulates and high commissions. For individual departmental opening times for the places listed below, check their websites.

American Embassy *24 Grosvenor Square, Mayfair, W1 (7499 9000/ www.usembassy.org.uk). Bond Street or Marble Arch tube.* **Open** 9am-5.20pm Mon-Fri. **Map** p400 G7.
Australian High Commission *Australia House, Strand, Holborn, WC2 (7379 4334/ www.australia.org.uk). Holborn or Temple tube.* **Open** 9.30am-3.30pm Mon-Fri. **Map** p401 M6.
Canadian High Commission *38 Grosvenor Street, Mayfair, W1 (7258 6600/www.canada.org.uk). Bond Street or Oxford Circus tube.* **Open** 8-11am Mon-Fri. **Map** p400 H7.

Irish Embassy *17 Grosvenor Place, Belgravia, SW1 (7235 2171). Hyde Park Corner tube.* **Open** 9.30am-1pm, 2.30-5pm Mon-Fri. **Map** p400 G9.
New Zealand High Commission *New Zealand House, 80 Haymarket, St James's, SW1 (7930 8422/ www.nzembassy.com). Piccadilly Circus tube.* **Open** 9am-5pm Mon-Fri. **Map** p401 K7.
South African High Commission *South Africa House, Trafalgar Square, St James's, WC2 (7451 7299/ www.southafricahouse.com). Charing Cross tube/rail.* **Open** 8.30am-1pm, 2-5pm Mon-Fri. **Map** p401 K7.

Emergencies

In the event of a serious accident, fire or incident, call **999** – free from any phone, including payphones – and specify whether you require ambulance, fire service or police. For addresses of London hospitals, *see p366*; for helplines, *see p367*; and for city police stations, *see p372*.

Gay & lesbian

Help & information

Jewish AIDS Trust
Walsingham House, 1331 High Road, Whetstone, N20 9HR (8446 8228/www.jat-uk.org). **Open** 9.30am-5pm Mon-Thur; 9.30am-1pm Fri. Info, counselling, financial, practical and social support and education.

London Friend
7837 3337. **Open** 7.30-10pm daily. A lesbian and gay helpline offering confidential information and support.

London Lesbian & Gay Switchboard
7837 7324. **Open** 24hrs daily. Everything you want to know about queer life in the capital, but prepare for a long wait to get through.

Naz Project
Palingswick House, 241 King Street, Hammersmith, W6 (8741 1879). **Open** 9.30am-5.30pm Mon-Fri. The Naz Project serves the (gay and straight) Asian community with counselling and information on HIV, AIDS and sexual health in South Asian, Middle Eastern, South American, Horn of African and North African languages.

Health

Free emergency medical treatment under the National Health Service (NHS) is available to:

● European Union nationals, plus those of Iceland, Norway and Liechtenstein. People from these countries are also entitled to specific treatment for a non-emergency condition on production of form E112 or E128.
● Nationals (on production of a passport) of Bulgaria, the Czech and Slovak Republics, Gibraltar, Hungary, Malta, New Zealand, Russia, former Soviet Union states (not Latvia, Lithuania and Estonia) and the former Yugoslavia.
● Residents, irrespective of nationality, of Anguilla, Australia, Barbados, British Virgin Islands, Channel Islands, Falkland Islands, Iceland, Isle of Man, Montserrat, Poland, Romania, St Helena, Sweden, Turks & Caicos Islands.
● Anyone who has been in the UK for the previous 12 months.
● Anyone who has come to the UK to take up permanent residence.
● Students and trainees who are on a course that requires them to spend more than 12 weeks in employment during their first year. Students and others living in the UK for a settled purpose for more than six months may be accepted as ordinarily resident and not liable to charges.
● Refugees and others who have sought refuge in the UK.
● Anyone formally detained by the immigration authorities.
● People with HIV/AIDS at a special clinic for the treatment of sexually transmitted diseases. The treatment covered is limited to a diagnostic test and counselling associated with that test.

There are no NHS charges for the following:

● Treatment in Accident & Emergency departments.
● Certain district nursing, midwifery or health visiting.
● Emergency ambulance transport.
● Diagnosis and treatment of certain communicable diseases, including STDs.
● Family planning services.
● Compulsory psychiatric treatment.

Any further advice should be obtained from the Patient Services Manager at the hospital where treatment is to be sought.

Directory

Accident & emergency

Below are listed most of the London hospitals that have 24-hour accident and emergency departments.

Charing Cross Hospital
Fulham Palace Road, Hammersmith, W6 (8846 1234). Barons Court or Hammersmith tube.

Chelsea & Westminster Hospital *369 Fulham Road, Chelsea, SW10 (8746 8000). South Kensington tube.* **Map** p396 C12.

Guy's Hospital *St Thomas Street (entrance Snowsfields, off Weston Street), Bankside, SE1 (7955 5000). London Bridge tube/rail.* **Map** p404 P8.

Homerton Hospital *Homerton Row, Homerton, E9 (8510 5555). Homerton rail.*

Royal Free Hospital *Pond Street, Hampstead, NW3 (7794 0500). Belsize Park tube/Hampstead Heath rail.*

Royal London Hospital *Whitechapel Road, Whitechapel, E1 (7377 7000). Whitechapel tube.*

St George's Hospital *Blackshaw Road, Tooting, SW17 (8672 1255). Tooting Broadway tube.*

St Mary's Hospital *Praed Street, Paddington, W2 (7886 6666). Paddington tube/rail.* **Map** p395 D5.

St Thomas's Hospital *Lambeth Palace Road, Lambeth, SE1 (7928 9292). Westminster tube/Waterloo tube/rail.* **Map** p401 M9.

University College Hospital *Grafton Way, Fitzrovia, WC1 (7387 9300). Euston Square or Warren Street tube.* **Map** p398 J4.

Whittington Hospital *St Mary's Wing, Highgate Hill, Archway, N19 (7272 3070). Archway tube.*

Complementary medicine

British Homeopathic Association

15 Clerkenwell Close, Clerkenwell, EC1R OAA (7566 7800/ www.trusthomeopathy.org). **Open** *Phone enquiries 9am-5pm Mon-Fri.*
You can call the BHA for the address of your nearest homeopathic chemist and/or doctor.

Institute for Complementary Medicine

PO Box 194, SE16 7QZ (7237 5165/www.icmedicine.co.uk).
Send the Institute an SAE and two loose stamps for a list of registered practitioners or training advice.

Contraception & abortion

Family planning advice, contraceptive supplies and abortions are free to British citizens on the National Health Service. This also applies to EU residents and foreign nationals living, working and studying in Britain. If you decide to go private, contact one of the organisations listed below. You can also phone 7837 4044 for your nearest branch of the **Family Planning Association**.

The 'morning after' pill, effective up to 72 hours after intercourse, is now available over the counter, though the convenience comes with a hefty £20 price tag.

British Pregnancy Advisory Service

0845 304030/ www.bpas.demon.co.uk. **Map** p400 H10.
Callers are referred to their nearest clinic. Contraception advice and contraceptives are available, as is pregnancy testing.

Brook Advisory Centre

92-4 Chalton Street, Euston, NW1 (7387 8700/www.brook.org.uk). **Open** *noon-7pm Mon-Thur; noon-3pm Fri; noon-2pm Sat.* **Map** p399 K2.
Advice and referrals are given on sexual health, contraception and abortion, plus there are free pregnancy tests for the under-25s. Call for your nearest clinic.

Marie Stopes House

Family Planning Clinic/Well Woman Centre *108 Whitfield Street, Fitzrovia, W1 (family planning 7388 0662/termination 0845 300 8090/www.mariestopes.org.uk). Warren Street tube.* **Open** *7am-10pm Mon-Fri.* **Map** p398 J5.
For contraceptive advice, emergency contraception, pregnancy testing, unplanned pregnancy counselling, an abortion service, cervical and health screening and gynaecological services; fees vary.

Dentists

Dental care is free under the National Health Service to the British residents included in the list below:

- Under-18s.
- Under-19s in full-time education.
- Pregnant women and those with a baby under the age of one when treatment begins.
- People receiving Income Support, Jobseeker's Allowance, Family Credit or Disability Working Allowance.

All other patients, NHS or private, must pay. NHS charges start from around £4 for a check-up or a filling. To find an NHS dentist, get in touch with the local Health Authority or a Citizens' Advice Bureau *(see p367)*, or visit one of the following.

Dental Emergency Care Service

7955 2186. **Open** *9am-3pm Mon-Fri.*
The DECS refers callers to a surgery open for treatment (private or NHS). Arrive before 1.30pm if possible.

Guy's Hospital Dental School

Guy's Tower, St Thomas Street, Bankside, SE1 (7955 4317). London Bridge tube/rail. **Open** *9am-noon, 1.30-3pm Mon-Fri.* **Map** p405 Q8.
The Dental School provides a free walk-in dental emergency service for all-comers.

Doctors

If you're a British citizen or if you are working in the United Kingdom, you can go to any general practitioner (GP). If you're not visiting your usual GP, you'll be asked for details of the doctor with whom you are registered, in order that your records can be updated. People who are ordinarily resident in the UK, including overseas students, are also permitted to register with an NHS doctor.

Great Chapel Street Medical Centre

13 Great Chapel Street, Soho, W1 (7437 9360). Leicester Square, Oxford Circus or Tottenham Court Road tube. **Open** *11.30am-12.30pm, 2-4pm Mon, Tue; 2-4pm Wed-Fri.* **Map** p399 K6.
A walk-in NHS surgery for anyone without a doctor. Phone first, as they operate different clinics each day.

Hospitals

For a list of hospitals with A&E departments, *see p366*; for other hospitals, see the

Yellow Pages; and for details on what to do in an emergency, *see p365*.

Opticians

For details of opticians in London, *see p254*.

Pharmacies

Most pharmacies keep regular shop hours – usually around 9am to 6pm every day except Sunday, when most are closed. However, there are a handful of late-opening pharmacies in London, for which *see p260*.

Prescriptions

Though some drugs can be bought over the counter in the UK, many more are only available on prescription. A pharmacist will dispense medicines on receipt of a prescription from a GP. An NHS prescription costs £6.10 at present (some people, including children under the age of 16 and people over 60, are exempt, and contraception is free for all). If you're not eligible to see an NHS doctor, you'll be charged cost price for medicines prescribed by a private doctor.

Pharmacists, who must be qualified, can advise on the appropriate treatments for minor ailments from behind the counter.

STDs, HIV & AIDS

NHS Genito-Urinary Clinics (such as the Centre for Sexual Health; *see below*) are affiliated to major hospitals. They provide free, confidential treatment of sexually transmitted diseases (STDs) and other problems, such as thrush and cystitis, offer info and counselling about HIV and other STDs, and can conduct a confidential blood test to determine HIV status.

For other helplines, *see below*, and for details on abortion and contraception services, *see p367*.

National AIDS Helpline

0800 567123/minicom 0800 521361. **Open** 24hrs daily.
A free and confidential information service. Another helpline (0800 917227) caters for various languages from 6-10pm on specific days: Bengali (Mon), Urdu (Tue), Arabic (Wed), Gujerati (Thur), Hindi (Fri), Punjabi (Sat) and Cantonese (Sun).

Ambrose King Centre

Royal London Hospital, Turner Street, Whitechapel, E1 (7377 7312). Whitechapel tube. **Open** 9.30am-5pm Fri (appointments only).
A weekly lesbian health clinic offering smears, HIV testing, information and counselling.

Centre for Sexual Health

Genito-Urinary Clinic, Jefferiss Wing, St Mary's Hospital, Praed Street, Paddington, W2 (7886 1697). Paddington tube/rail. **Open** *Walk-in clinic* 8.45am-5pm Mon; 8.45am-6pm Tue, Fri; 11.45am-6pm Wed; 8am-1pm Thur. *Appointments* 5-7pm Mon; 10am-noon Sat. **Map** p395 D5.
A free and confidential walk-in clinic. New patients must arrive at least 30 minutes before closing.

Mortimer Market Centre for Sexual Health

Mortimer Market Centre, Mortimer Market, off Capper Street, Bloomsbury, W1 (appointments 7530 5050). Warren Street tube. **Open** 9am-6pm Mon, Tue, Thur; 1-7pm Wed; 9am-2.45pm Fri. **Map** p398 J4.
A sexual health clinic for gay and bisexual men and women under 26. An appointment is recommended but not essential. The centre also offers drugs information for gay men.

Terrence Higgins Trust Lighthouse

52-4 Gray's Inn Road, Bloomsbury, WC1 (office 7831 0330/helpline 7242 1010/www.tht.org.uk). Chancery Lane tube. **Open** *Office* 9.30am-6pm Mon-Fri; *helpline* noon-10pm daily.
This charity, formed from a merger of the UK's two largest HIV charities in October 2000, advises and counsels those with HIV/AIDS, their relatives, lovers and friends. Free leaflets about AIDS are available. The Trust also provides advice about safer sex.

See also above **STDs, HIV & AIDS**. For gay and lesbian helplines, *see p365*.

Alcoholics Anonymous

7833 0022/www.alcoholics-anonymous.org.uk. **Open** *Helpline* 10am-10pm daily.
Operators put you in touch with a member in your area who can act as an escort to your first meeting.

Childline

Freepost 1111, London N1 0BR (0800 1111/7239 1000/www.childline.org.uk). **Open** *Phone lines* 24hrs daily.
Free helpline for children and young people in trouble or danger.

Citizens' Advice Bureaux

CABs are run by local councils and offer free advice on legal, financial and personal matters. Check the phone book for your nearest branch.

Just Ask

Daniel Gilbert House, 1 Coate Street, Bethnal Green, E2 (7247 0180). Bethnal Green rail. **Open** 10am-6pm Mon-Thur; 10am-5pm Fri. **Map** p403 R6.
Counselling is targeted at people aged 35 and under who are homeless, unemployed or on a low income, but advice will be given to anyone with a personal problem.

NHS Direct

0845 4647/www.nhsdirect.nhs.uk. **Open** 24hrs daily.
NHS Direct is a first-stop service for medical advice on all subjects from trained health professionals.

MIND

Granta House, 15-19 Broadway, Stratford, E15 4BQ (info line 8522 1728/0845 766 0163/www.mind.org.uk). **Open** *Info line* 9.15am-5.15pm Mon-Fri.
MIND has more than 60 factsheets on all facets of mental health. Its staff can also tell you where to get help for mental distress.

Narcotics Anonymous

7730 0009/www.ukna.org. **Open** 10am-10pm daily.
NA offers advice and informs callers of their nearest meeting. Opening times may vary.

National Missing Persons Helpline

0500 700700/www.missingpersons.org. **Open** 24hrs daily.

Directory

The volunteer-run NMPH publicises information on anyone reported missing. They can artificially age photographs, and will help find missing persons through a network of contacts. A 'Message Home' freephone service (0800 700 740) allows runaways to reassure friends or family of their wellbeing without revealing their whereabouts.

Rape & Sexual Abuse Support Centre
8683 3300/www.rasasc.org.uk. **Open** noon-2.30pm, 7-9.30pm Mon-Fri; 2.30-5pm Sat, Sun.
Provides support and information for those who have experienced rape or sexual abuse.

Refuge Helpline
08705 995443. **Open** 24hrs daily.
Refuge referral for women suffering domestic violence. When phones are not manned, an answerphone will give alternative numbers where you can get immediate help.

Rights of Women
7251 6577. **Open** *Helpline* 2-4pm, 7-9pm Tue-Thur; noon-2pm Fri.
Legal advice for women.

Samaritans
08457 909090/ www.samaritans.org.uk. **Open** 24hrs daily.
The Samaritans listen to anyone with emotional problems. It's a popular service, so persevere when phoning.

Victim Support
PO Box 11431, SW9 6ZH (0845 303 0900/www.victimsupport.com). **Open** *Support line* 9am-9pm Mon-Fri; 9am-7pm Sat, Sun.
Victims of crime are put in touch with a volunteer who provides emotional and practical support, including information on legal procedures and advice on compensation. Interpreters can be arranged where necessary.

Insurance

Insuring personal belongings is highly advisable, and difficult to arrange once you've arrived in London, so organise it before you travel.

Medical insurance is often included in travel insurance packages, and it's important to have it unless your country has a reciprocal medical treatment arrangement with Britain (*see p365*). EU citizens (and those from Iceland,

Norway and Liechtenstein) are entitled to free emergency healthcare in hospitals under the NHS. Those wanting specific treatment under the NHS will need form E112, while citizens of these countries studying in the UK for less than six months are entitled to full NHS treatment if they have form E128.

Internet

A great many hotel rooms have modem points, and some of those that don't offer surfing facilities in a bar or café. There are also a huge number of cybercafés around town (*see below*), of which the biggest are those in the **easyEverything** chain.

If you want to get set up online over here, you're also in luck. Massive competition in the ISP sector has meant that prices have plummeted, and there are now a great many ISPs that do not charge a subscription fee, only billing for calls. We suggest that you check one of the UK's many Internet publications for details on current deals at the time you arrive; the best is *Internet* magazine.

For the best London websites, *see p379*.

Internet access

Café Internet *22-24 Buckingham Palace Road, Belgravia, SW1 (7233 5786). Victoria tube/rail.* **Open** 9am-9pm Mon-Fri; 10am-8pm Sat, Sun. **Net access** £2/hr. **Terminals** 20. **Map** p400 H10.
Cybergate *3 Leigh Street, Bloomsbury, WC1 (7387 6560/www.c-gate.com).* **Open** 9am-11pm daily. **Net access** £1/20min. **Terminals** 25.
Cyberia Cyber Café *39 Whitfield Street, Fitzrovia, W1 (7681 4200/ www.cyberiacafe.net). Goodge Street tube.* **Open** 9am-8pm Mon-Fri; 11am-7pm Sat. **Net access** 50p/15min. **Credit** MC, V. **Map** p399 K5.
easyEverything *160-166 Kensington High Street (7938 1841/ www.easyeverything.com). High Street Kensington tube.* **Open** 24hrs daily.

Net access £1/30min-2hrs (varies depending on number of other users). **Terminals** 550+. **Map** p396 B9. **Branches** are numerous; check the phone book.
Global Café *15 Golden Square, Soho, W1 (7287 2242/ www.globalcafe.net). Oxford Circus or Piccadilly Circus tube.* **Open** 9am-11pm Mon-Fri; 10am-11pm Sat; noon-10.30pm Sun. **Net access** £5/hr. **Terminals** 15. **Map** p400 J7.
Webshack *15 Dean Street, Soho, W1 (7439 8000/www.webshack-cafe.com). Tottenham Court Road tube.* **Open** 10am-11pm Mon-Sat; 1-11pm Sun. **Net access** 50p/10min; £1/40min; £2/80min. **Terminals** 32. **Map** p399 K6.

Left luggage

Airports

Call the following numbers for details on left luggage.

Gatwick Airport *South Terminal 01293 502014/North Terminal 01293 502013.*
Heathrow Airport *Terminal 1 8745 5301/Terminals 2 & 3 8759 3344/Terminal 4 8745 7460.*
London City Airport *7646 0162.*
Luton Airport *01582 394063.*
Stansted Airport *01279 663213.*

Rail & bus stations

With terrorism a very real issue to be considered, London stations tend to have left-luggage desks rather than lockers. To find out if a train station offers this facility, call 08457 484950.

Legal help

If you get into legal difficulties, visit a Citizens' Advice Bureau (*see p367*) or contact one of the groups that are listed below. Otherwise, if you require an explanation of the legal aid system, you can contact the Legal Aid Board (7759 0000).

Community Legal Services Directory
0845 608 1122/www.justask.org.uk. **Open** 9am-10pm daily.
This free telephone service guides those with legal problems to government agencies and law firms that may be able to help.

Joint Council for the Welfare of Immigrants (JCWI)
115 Old Street, Hoxton, EC1 (7251 8706). Old Street tube/rail. **Open** *Phone enquiries* 2-5pm Tue-Thur.
This telephone-only advice line for immigrants with legal troubles offers guidance and referrals.

Law Centres Federation
Duchess House, 18-19 Warren Street, Fitzrovia, W1 (7387 8570). Warren Street tube/rail. **Open** *Phone enquiries* 10am-6pm Mon-Fri.
Free legal help to people who can't afford a lawyer. This central office will connect you with your nearest centre, though bear in mind that the centres only offer advice to those who live or work in the immediate area.

Release
388 Old Street, Hoxton, EC1 (7729 9904/after-hours 7603 8654). Old Street tube/rail. **Open** 10am-5pm Mon-Fri.
This group offers free addiction counselling and legal advice to those with drug problems, or whose drug dependency has left them in legal trouble. It also provides referrals to addiction counsellors, law firms and governmental organisations.

Libraries

Unless you're a London resident, you won't be able to join a lending library. Access to the British Library is limited to the exhibition centre for non-members: the others listed below are open for reference, copying and browsing.

British Library
96 Euston Road, Somers Town, NW1 (7412 7000). King's Cross tube/rail. **Open** 9.30am-6pm Mon, Wed-Fri; 9.30am-8pm Tue; 9.30am-5pm Sat; 11am-5pm Sun. **Map** p399 K3.

Holborn Library
32-8 Theobald's Road, Bloomsbury, WC1 (7974 6345). Chancery Lane tube. **Open** 10am-7pm Mon, Thur; 10am-6pm Tue, Fri; 10am-5pm Sat. **Map** p399 M5.

Kensington & Chelsea Central Library
Philimore Walk, Kensington, W8 (7937 2542). High Street Kensington tube. **Open** 9.30am-8pm Mon, Tue, Thur; 9.30am-5pm Wed, Fri, Sat. **Map** p396 A9.

Victoria Library
160 Buckingham Palace Road, Belgravia, SW1 (7641 4287). Victoria tube/rail. **Open** 9.30am-7pm Mon, Tue, Thur, Fri; 10am-7pm Wed; 9.30am-5pm Sat. *Music library* 11am-7pm Mon-Fri; 10am-5pm Sat. **Map** p400 H10.

Westminster Reference Library
35 St Martin's Street, Westminster, WC2 (7641 4636). Leicester Square tube. **Open** 10am-8pm Mon-Fri; 10am-5pm Sat. **Map** p401 K7.

Lost property

Always inform the police if you lose anything, if only to validate insurance claims. *See p372* or the *Yellow Pages* for your nearest police station. Only dial the emergency number (999) if violence has occurred. Lost passports should be reported both to the police and to your embassy (*see p365*).

Airports

The following lost property offices deal only with items lost in the airports concerned. For property lost on the plane, contact the airline or handling agents dealing with the flight.

Gatwick Airport *01293 503162.*
Heathrow Airport *8745 7727.*
London City Airport *7646 0000.*
Luton Airport *01582 395 219.*
Stansted Airport *01279 663293.*

Public transport

If you've lost property in an overground station or on a train, call 08700 005151; an operator will connect you to the appropriate station. For property lost on a tube or bus, *see below*.

Transport For London
Lost Property Office, 200 Baker Street, Marylebone, NW1 5RZ (recorded info 7486 2496). Baker Street tube. **Open** 9.30am-2pm Mon-Fri. **Map** p398 G4.
Allow three full working days from the time of loss. If you lose something on a bus, call 7222 1234 and ask for the phone numbers of the depots at either end of the route.
If you lose something on a tube, pick up a lost property form from any station.

Taxis

Taxi Lost Property
200 Baker Street, Marylebone, NW1 (07918 2000). Baker Street tube. **Open** *phone enquiries* 9am-4pm Mon-Fri. **Map** p398 N2.
This office deals only with property that has been found in registered black cabs. For items lost in a minicab, contact the office from which you hired the cab.

Media

Magazines

After years of boom in the magazine industry, 2001 saw a heavy downturn, with several titles falling by the wayside. The market for women's magazines had actually been declining since 1996, but this slowdown had been hidden by a number of high-profile launches, the most recent of which, *Glamour* and *In Style* in 2001, are UK versions of existing US titles. For its part, the men's market has proven unable to sustain its growth of 283 per cent between 1995 and 1999, though *Loaded*, *FHM* and *Maxim* seem invincible. In the women's sector, *Cosmopolitan*, *Vogue*, *Marie Claire* and *Elle* continue to rule the roost.

Otherwise, celebrity magazines have had a boost after difficult times, with the glossy *Heat* doing particularly well, while at the opposite end of the spectrum style mags such as *i-D* and *Dazed and Confused* have found a profitable little niche.

Those looking for something more serious and hard-hitting aren't spoilt for choice; *The Spectator*, *New Statesman* and *Prospect* are about as good as it gets. *Private Eye* offers a fortnightly satirical look at politics and news. *The Big Issue*, sold on the street by homeless people, is also worth a look. *The Economist* covers political and business issues, while you'll find international editions of *Time* and *Newsweek* at most newsagents.

Newspapers

National newspapers fall broadly into three categories. At the lofty, serious end of the scale are the broadsheets: the right-wing *Daily Telegraph* and *The Times* (which is best for sport) are balanced by the *Independent* and the *Guardian* (best for arts coverage). All have bulging Sunday equivalents bar the *Guardian*, which has a sister Sunday paper, the *Observer*).

The right-wing middle-market leader has long been the truly odious *Daily Mail* (and *Mail on Sunday*). Its rival, the *Daily Express* (and *Sunday Express*), has struggled for some time, and in 2000 was bought out by a man behind an array of top-shelf publications.

At the bottom of the pile are the most popular papers of them all: the tabloids. Still the undisputed leader of the rat pack is the *Sun* (and the Sunday *News of the World*), which sells around 3.5 million copies daily – more than half the daily total of all newspapers sold. The *Daily Star* and the *Mirror* are the other main lowbrow contenders, with the *People* and the *Sunday Mirror* providing sleaze on Sunday.

London's main daily paper, which comes out in several editions through the day (Monday to Friday only), is the right-wing *Evening Standard*, a sort of *Mail* for London. *Metro*, London's free morning paper, is distributed at tube stations and contains just enough news and features to sustain you through the average journey (and the discarded copies clog the tube by mid morning).

Radio

BBC Radio 1 *98.8 FM*. Youth-oriented music station dealing mostly in pop, rock and dance.
BBC Radio 2 *89.1 FM*. Bland and middle-of-the-road during the day, but adventurous (if still retro) at night.
BBC Radio 3 *91.3 FM*. The Beeb's classical music station.
BBC Radio 4 *93.5 FM, 720 MW, 198 LW*. Speech-only station, loved for its *Today* morning news show and for its soap, *The Archers*.
BBC Radio 5 Live *693, 909 MW*. News and sport 24 hours a day. Live coverage of major sporting events.
BBC London 94.9 *94.9 FM*. Not a patch on GLR, the station it replaced, but Robert Elms (9am-noon Mon-Fri) is still a must-listen.
BBC World Service *648 MW*. Transmitted worldwide but available in the UK for a distillation of the best of all the other BBC stations.
Capital FM *95.8 FM*. Popular commercial station with irritating DJs and repetitive playlist.
Capital Gold *1548 MW*. Retro 'classics' from the '60s to the '80s.
Choice FM *96.9, 107.1 FM*. Pioneering black-music channel.
Classic FM *100.9 FM*. Lowbrow classical station.
Heart *106.2 FM*. MOR.
Jazz FM *102.2 FM*. Smooth jazz.
Kiss *100.0 FM*. London's dance station. Not for the faint-hearted.
Liberty *963, 972 MW*. Faux kitschy, largely retro music station.
LBC *1152 MW*. Non-stop phone-ins and chat. The cabbies' favourite.
News Direct *97.3 FM*. News, weather, travel and business.
Ritz *1035 MW*. Country music.
Spectrum *558 MW*. Researched, produced and presented by various ethnic communities.
TalkSport *1053, 1089 MW*. One for sports buffs.
Virgin *105.8 FM*. MOR and chat.

Television

The next generation of television in the UK is now here: Sky Digital, ONdigital and various digital cable TV companies offer services that reproduce and expand on the established analogue offerings listed here.

Network channels

BBC1 The Corporation's mass-market station. There's a smattering of soaps and game shows, and the odd quality programme. Daytime programming, however, stinks. As

with all BBC radio and TV stations, there are no commercials.
BBC2 In general, BBC2 is also free of crass programmes. That doesn't mean the output is riveting, just that it's not insulting. It offers a cultural cross-section and plenty of documentaries.
ITV1 Carlton, which provides the weekday programming for ITV, crams its schedules with mass-appeal shows and frequent ad breaks. Any successful formula is repeated ad infinitum, with little of merit to break up the monotony. LWT (London Weekend Television) takes over from Carlton at the weekend to offer more of the same. ITV2 is on digital.
Channel 4 C4's output includes some pretty mainstream fare, especially its extremely successful US imports (*Friends*, *ER*, *The Sopranos* and so on), but it still comes up with some gems, particularly films (often shown first on its film channel, Film Four; *see below*).
Channel 5 Britain's newest terrestrial channel offers a mix of sex, US TV movies, sex, rubbish comedy, sex, more sex and US sport.

Satellite, digital & cable channels

The non-network sector is crammed to bursting with stations on a variety of formats (satellite, cable and fast-expanding digital). Most are not worth bothering with; listed below are the pick of the pack.

BBC News 24 The Beeb's rolling news network.
Bravo B-movies and cult TV.
CNN News and current affairs.
Discovery Channel Science and nature documentaries.
FilmFour Channel 4's movie outlet, with 12 hours of programming daily.
History Channel Self-explanatory.
MTV Rock/pop channel that borrows from its US counterpart.
Paramount US and Brit sitcoms.
Performance Dance, theatre and opera, plus interviews with the stars.
Sky Moviemax Blockbusters.
Sky News Rolling news.
Sky One Sky's version of ITV.
Sky Sports Sports. There are also Sky Sports 2 and Sky Sports 3.
UK Gold Reruns of yesteryear's BBC and ITV successes.
UK Horizon Science documentaries.
VH-1 MTV for grown-ups.

Money

As much of Europe switches over to the euro (€), Britain's currency remains the pound sterling (£); you'll probably find an increasing number of places pre-empting the government and accepting euros, but don't rely on it. One pound equals 100 pence (p). One pence and 2 pence coins are copper; 5p, 10p, 20p and the seven-sided 50p coins are silver; the £1 coin is yellowy-gold; the £2 coin is silver in the centre with a circle of yellowy-gold around the edge. Paper notes are as follows: blue £5, orange £10, purple £20 and red £50.

You can exchange foreign currency at banks and bureaux de change (*see below*). If you're here for a long stay, you may need to open a bank or building society account. To do this, you'll probably need to present a reference from your bank at home, and certainly a passport as identification.

Western Union
0800 833833.
The old standby for bailing cash-challenged travellers out of trouble, but it's pricey.

ATMs

Aside from inside and outside banks themselves, cash machines can also be found in some supermarkets, selected other shops (such as the Virgin Megastore; *see p257*), and in tube and rail stations. The vast majority accept withdrawals on major credit cards, and most also allow withdrawals using the Maestro/Cirrus debit system.

Banks

Minimum banking hours are 9.30am to 3.30pm Monday to Friday, but most branches close at 4.30pm and a few even stay open until 5pm.

Exchange and commission rates on currency vary hugely, and it pays to shop around. Commission is sometimes charged for cashing travellers' cheques in foreign currencies, but not for sterling travellers'

cheques, provided you cash the cheques at a bank affiliated to the issuing bank (get a list when you buy your cheques); it's also charged if you change cash into another currency. You always need ID, such as a passport, when exchanging travellers' cheques.

Bureaux de change

You'll be charged for cashing travellers' cheques or buying and selling foreign currency at a bureau de change. Commission rates, which should be clearly displayed, vary. **Chequepoint**, **Lenlyn** and **Thomas Cook** are reputable bureaux with branches all over town. Major rail and tube stations in central London have bureaux de change, and there are many in tourist areas. Most are open 8am-10pm, but those listed below are open 24 hours daily.

Chequepoint
548 Oxford Street, Marylebone, W1 (7723 1005). Marble Arch tube. **Map** p398 G6.
2 Queensway, Bayswater, W2 (7229 0093). Queensway tube. **Map** p394 C6.
71 Gloucester Road, South Kensington, SW7 (7473 9682). Gloucester Road tube.

Credit cards

Most shops, restaurants, ticket agents, garages, box offices and the like, as well as selected bars and museums, accept credit cards. Visa and Mastercard are the most widely accepted, while American Express and Diners Club tend to be accepted in fewer establishments.

Lost/stolen credit cards

Report lost or stolen credit cards immediately to both the police and the 24-hour services listed below. Inform your bank by phone and in writing.

American Express
01273 696933.
Diners Club *01252 513500.*
JCB *7499 3000.*
MasterCard/Eurocard
0800 964767.
Switch *08706 000459.*
Visa/Connect *0800 895082.*

Tax

With the exception of a few choice items (food, books, newspapers, children's clothing, etc), purchases in the UK are subject to VAT – value-added tax, AKA sales tax – of 17.5 per cent. However, unlike in the US, this tax is always included in prices quoted in shops, so a price tag of £10 means you pay £10 rather than £11.75.

Beware, though, hotels, which often naughtily quote room rates exclusive of VAT: always be sure to ask whether or not the rate you have been quoted includes tax.

Opening hours

Listed below are some general guidelines on opening hours in London. However, hours can vary in all cases. If you're after the opening hours of a specific establishment, see the listing in the chapter in question.

Banks 9am-4.30pm (some close at 3.30pm) Mon-Fri.
Bars 11am-11pm Mon-Sat; noon-10.30pm Sun.
Businesses 9am-5pm Mon-Fri (except media/Internet, which generally operate later hours).
Post offices 9am-5.30pm Mon-Fri; 9am-noon Sat.
Shops 10am-6pm Mon-Sat.

Police stations

The police are a good source of information about the locality and are used to helping visitors find their way. We have listed a handful of central London police stations in this section (*see p372*). If you've been robbed, assaulted or involved in an infringement of the law, go to your nearest police station (if it's not listed here, either look under 'Police' in the phone book or call Directory Enquiries on 192).

If you have a complaint to make about the police, there are several things you can do. Ensure that you take the offending police officer's identifying number, which should be displayed on his or her epaulette. You can then register a complaint with the **Police Complaints Authority**, 10 Great George Street, SW1P 3AE (7273 6450). Alternatively, contact any police station or visit a solicitor or a Law Centre.

Police stations

Belgravia Police Station
202-6 Buckingham Palace Road, Pimlico, SW1 (7730 1212). Victoria tube/rail. Map p400 H10.

Charing Cross Police Station
Agar Street, Covent Garden, WC2 (7240 1212). Charing Cross tube/rail. Map p401 L7.

Chelsea Police Station
2 Lucan Place, Chelsea, SW3 (7589 1212). Sloane Square tube. Map p397 E10.

Euston Road Police Station
Euston Station, Euston Road, NW1 (7704 1212). Euston tube/rail. Map p401 K3.

Islington Police Station
2 Tolpuddle Street, Islington, N1 (7704 1212). Angel tube. Map p402 N2.

Kensington Police Station
72-4 Earl's Court Road, Kensington, W8 (7376 1212). High Street Kensington tube. Map p396 B11.

King's Cross Police Station
76 King's Cross Road, King's Cross, WC1 (7704 1212). King's Cross tube/rail. Map p399 M3.

Marylebone Police Station
1-9 Seymour Street, Marylebone, W1 (7486 1212). Baker Street tube/Marylebone tube/rail. Map p395 F6.

Paddington Green Police Station *2-4 Harrow Road, Paddington, W2 (7402 1212). Edgware Road tube.* Map p396 E5.

West End Central Police Station *27 Savile Row, Mayfair, W1 (7437 1212). Piccadilly Circus tube.* Map p400 J7.

Postal services

You can buy stamps at all post offices and many newsagents. Current prices are 19p for second-class, 27p for first-class

letters and 37p for letters to EU countries. Postcards cost 37p to send within Europe and 40p to countries outside Europe. Rates for other letters and parcels vary according to weight and destination.

Post offices

Post offices are usually open 9am-5.30pm Monday to Friday and 9am-noon Saturday, with the exception of **Trafalgar Square Post Office** (24-8 William IV Street, WC2, 7484 9307; Charing Cross tube/rail), which is open 8am-8pm Monday to Friday and 9am-8pm Saturday. The busiest time of day is usually 1-2pm.

Listed below are the other main central London offices. For general post office enquiries, call the central information line on 08457 223344 or consult www.postoffice.co.uk.

43-4 Albemarle Street *Mayfair, W1 (7493 5620). Green Park tube.* Map p400 J7.

111 Baker Street *Marylebone, W1 (7935 3701). Baker Street tube.* Map p398 G5.

202 Great Portland Street *Marylebone, W1 (7636 9935). Great Portland Street tube.* Map p398 H4.

32A Grosvenor Street *Mayfair, W1 (7629 2480). Bond Street tube.* Map p400 H7.

19 Newman Street *Fitzrovia, W1 (7636 9995). Tottenham Court Road tube.* Map p398 J5.

43 Seymour Street *Marylebone, W1 (7723 0867). Marble Arch tube.* Map p395 F6.

Poste restante

If you need to receive mail while you are away, you can (as is the case in most countries around the world) have it sent to a post office, where it will be kept at the enquiry desk for up to one month. Your name and 'Poste Restante' must be clearly marked on the letter above the following address: Post Office, 24-8 William IV Street, London WC2N 4DL. Bring ID when you come to collect it.

Religion

Anglican

St Paul's Cathedral *For listings details, see p89.* **Services** 7.30am, 8am, 12.30pm, 5pm Mon-Fri; 8am, 8.30am, 12.30pm, 5pm Sat; 8am, 10.15am, 11.30am, 3.15pm, 6pm Sun. Map p404 O6.
Times vary due to special events; phone to check.
Westminster Abbey *For listings details, see p134.* **Services** 7.30am, 8am, 12.30pm, 5pm Mon-Fri; 8am, 9am, 12.30pm, 3pm Sat; 8am, 10am, 11.15am, 3pm, 5.45pm Sun.
Map p401 K9.

Baptist

Bloomsbury Central Baptist Church *235 Shaftesbury Avenue, Covent Garden, WC2 (7240 0544/ www.bloomsbury.org.uk).* Tottenham Court Road tube. **Open** 10am-4pm Mon-Fri; 10am-8.30pm Sun. Friendship Centre noon-2.30pm Tue; 10.30am-8.30pm Sun; closed during services, Aug. **Services** 5.30pm Tue; 11am, 6.30pm Sun. Map p399 L6.

Buddhist

Buddhapadipa Temple
14 Calonne Road, Wimbledon, SW19 (8946 1357/www.buddhapadipa.org). Wimbledon tube then 93 bus. **Open** *Temple* 1-6pm Sat, Sun. *Meditation retreat* 7-9pm Tue, Thur; 4-6pm Sat, Sun.

Catholic

London Oratory *For listings details, see p138.* **Services** 7am, 8am (Latin mass), 10am, 12.30am, 6pm Mon-Fri; 7am, 8.30am, 10am, 6pm Sat; 7am, 8.30am, 10am (tridentine), 11am (sung Latin), 12.30pm, 3.30pm, 4.30pm, 7pm Sun. Map p397 E10.
Westminster Cathedral
For listings details, see p135. **Services** 7am, 8am, 9am, 10.30am, 12.30pm, 5pm Mon-Fri; 8am, 9am, 12.30pm, 6pm Sat; 7am, 8am, 9am, 10.30am, noon, 5.30pm, 7pm Sun. Map p400 J10.

Hindu

Swaminarayan Hindu Mission
105-19 Brentfield Road, Church End, NW10 (enquiries Amrish Patel 8961 5031). Neasden tube/Harlesden tube/rail. **Services** 11.45am, 7pm daily. In addition to a large prayer hall, this huge complex contains a conference hall, a marriage suite, sports facilities, a library and a health clinic.

Islamic

London Central Mosque
146 Park Road, St John's Wood, NW8 (7724 3363). Baker Street

tube/bus 74. **Open** dawn-dusk daily.
Services 5.30am, 1pm, 4pm, 7pm,
8.30pm daily.
East London Mosque *82-92*
Whitechapel Road, E1 (7247 1357/
www.eastlondon-mosque.org.uk).
Aldgate East or Whitechapel tube.
Open 10am-8.30pm daily. **Services**
Friday prayer 1.30pm (1pm in
winter). **Map** p405 S6.

Jewish
Liberal Jewish Synagogue
28 St John's Wood Road, St John's
Wood, NW8 (7286 5181/
www.ljs.org). St John's Wood tube.
Open *Enquiries* 9am-5pm Mon-Thur;
9am-1pm Fri. **Services** 6.45pm Fri;
11am Sat.
West Central Liberal
Synagogue *109 Whitfield Street,*
Fitzrovia, W1 (7636 7627). Warren
Street tube. **Services** 3pm Sat.
Map p398 J4.

Methodist
Methodist Central Hall
Westminster Central Hall, Storey's
Gate, Westminster, SW1 (7222
8010/www.wch.co.uk). St James's
Park tube. **Open** *Chapel* 9am-6pm
Mon-Fri. **Services** 12.45pm Wed;
11am, 6.30pm Sun. **Map** p401 K9.

Quaker
Religious Society of Friends
(Quakers) *Friends House, 173-7*
Euston Road, Bloomsbury, NW1
(7387 3601/www.quaker.org.uk).
Euston tube/rail. **Open** 8.30am-
9.30pm Mon-Fri. **Meetings** 11am
Sun. **Map** p399 K3.

Safety & security

Violent crime is a relatively
rare occurrence in London, but,
just as in any major city, you
would be unwise to take any
risks. Pickpockets and thieves
target unwary tourists. Use
common sense and follow
these basic rules:

● Keep your wallet and purse out
of sight. Don't wear a wrist watch
(they're easily snatched). Keep
your handbag securely closed.
● Don't leave a handbag, briefcase,
bag or coat unattended, especially
in pubs, cinemas or fast-food
restaurants, on public transport,
or in crowds.
● Don't leave your bag or coat
beside, under or on the back of
your chair.
● Don't put your bag on the floor
near the door of a public toilet.
● Don't wear expensive jewellery
or wrist watches that can be
easily snatched.

● Don't keep your passport, money,
credit cards, etc, together. If you
lose one, you'll lose all.
● Don't put your purse down on the
table in a restaurant or on a shop
counter while you check the bill.
● Don't carry a wallet in your back
pocket, and don't flash your
money or credit cards around.

Smoking

Smoking is permitted in almost
all pubs and bars – though an
increasing number have non-
smoking areas – and in most
restaurants, though specify
when you book that you'd like
a table in the smoking section.
Smoking is forbidden in shops
and on public transport.

Study

Being a student in London
will be an exciting if expensive
affair. Whether you're here to
study or just visiting, *Time
Out*'s *Student Guide*, available
from many bookshops and
newsagents from October
each year, provides the
lowdown on what London
has to offer students and
how to survive in the big city.

Throughout this guide,
entry prices for students
at museums, art galleries,
sights, sports venues and
other places are usually
designated ('concessions').
You'll have to show ID (an
NUS or ISIC card) to get these
rates. Students, whether EU
citizens or not, wanting or
needing to find work in the
UK as a way of boosting their
funds should turn to *p377*.

Language classes

All the places listed below
offer a variety of language
courses; call for full details.

Aspect Covent Garden
Language Centre
3-4 Southampton Place, WC1
(7404 3080/www.aspectworld.com).
Holborn tube. **Map** p399 L5.
Central School of English
1 Tottenham Court Road, W1
(7580 2863/www.centralschool.co.uk).

Tottenham Court Road tube.
Map p397 K5.
Frances King School of English
77 Gloucester Road, SW7 (070
0011 2233/www.francesking.co.uk).
Gloucester Road tube. **Map** p395 F9.
London Study Centre
Munster House, 676 Fulham Road,
SW6 (7731 3549/www.londonstudy
centre.com). Parsons Green tube.
Sels College *64-5 Long Acre,*
WC2 (7240 2581/www.sels.co.uk).
Covent Garden tube. **Map** p399 L6.
Shane English School
59 South Molton Street, W1
(7499 8533/www.saxoncourt.com).
Bond Street tube. **Map** p398 H6.

Students' unions

Many unions only let students
with the relevant ID in, so
always carry your NUS or ISIC
card. Below, taken from the
Time Out Student Guide, are
those with the five best student
bars, which offer a good night
out at student-friendly prices.
Imperial College *Beit Quad,*
Prince Consort Road, SW7 (7589
5111). South Kensington tube. **Open**
noon-2pm, 5-11pm Mon, Tue, Thur;
noon-2pm, 5pm-midnight Wed; noon-
2pm, 5pm-1am Fri; noon-11pm Sat;
noon-10.30pm Sun (times vary out of
termtime). **Map** p397 D9.
International Students House
229 Great Portland Street, W1
(7631 8300). Great Portland Street
tube. **Open** noon-2pm, 5-11pm Mon,
Tue; noon-2pm, 5pm-midnight Wed;
noon-2pm; 5pm-1am Thur; noon-
2pm, 5pm-3am Fri; noon-3am Sat;
noon-10.30pm Sun. **Map** p398 H4.
King's College *Macadam Building,*
Surrey Street, WC2 (7836 7132).
Temple tube. **Open** *Waterfront*
noon-11pm Mon-Fri; 7-11pm Sat.
Tutu's 9pm-3am Fri; 10.30pm-3am
Sat. **Map** p401 M7.
University of London Union
(ULU) *Malet Street, WC1 (7664*
2000). Goodge Street or Russell
Square tube. **Open** 11am-11pm
Mon-Fri; 11am-2am Sat; noon-
10.30pm Sun. **Map** p399 K4.
University of North London *166-*
220 Holloway Road, N7 (7607 2789).
Holloway Road tube. **Open** 11am-
11pm Mon, Tue, Thur; 11am-2am
Wed; 11am-late Fri; 11am-6am Sat.

Universities

Brunel University *Cleveland*
Road, Uxbridge, Middlesex (01895
274000/students' union 01895
462200). Uxbridge tube.
City University *Northampton*
Square, EC1 (7477 8000/students'

Directory

union 7505 5600). *Angel tube.*
Map p402 O3.
Guildhall University *Calcutta House, Old Castle Street, E1 (7320 1000/students' union 7320 2233). Aldgate East tube.* Map p405 S6.
South Bank University *Borough Road, SE1 (7928 8989/students' union 7815 7815). Elephant & Castle tube/rail.* Map p404 O9.
University of East London (Stratford Campus) *Romford Road, E15 (8223 3000/students' union ext 4210). Stratford tube/rail.*
University of Greenwich *Wellington Street, SE18 (8331 8000/students' union 8331 8268). Woolwich Arsenal rail.*
University of London *see below.*
University of Middlesex *Trent Park, Bramley Road, N14 (8362 5000/students' union 8362 6450). Cockfosters or Oakwood tube.*
University of North London *166-220 Holloway Road, N7 (7607 2789/students' union 7753 3367). Holloway Road tube.*
University of Westminster *309 Regent Street, W1 (7911 5000/students' union 7915 5454). Oxford Circus tube.* Map p398 H4.

University of London

Many students in London attend one of the 34 colleges, spread across the city, that make up the huge University of London; only the six largest are listed below. All London universities (with the exception of Imperial College) are affiliated to the National Union of Students (NUS).

NUS London Regional Office *7272 8900/www.nus.org.uk.*
Goldsmiths' College *Lewisham Way, SE14 (7919 7171/students' union 8692 1406). New Cross/New Cross Gate tube/rail.*
Imperial College *Exhibition Road, SW7 (7589 5111/students' union 7594 8060). South Kensington tube.* Map p397 D9.
King's College *Strand, WC2 (7836 5454/students' union 7836 7132). Temple tube.* Map p401 M7.
Kingston University *Penrhyn Road, Kingston, Surrey (8547 2000/students' union 8547 8868). Kingston rail.*
London School of Economics (LSE) *Houghton Street, WC2 (7405 7686/students' union 7955 7158). Holborn tube.* Map p399 M6.
Queen Mary & Westfield College (QMW) *327 Mile End Road, E1 (7882 5555/students' union 7975 5390). Mile End or Stepney Green tube.*
University College London (UCL) *Gower Street, WC1 (7679 2000/students' union 7387 3611). Goodge Street or Warren Street tube/Euston tube/rail.* Map p399 K4.

Useful organisations

For BUNAC and the Council on International Educational Exchange, *see p377.*

National Bureau for Students with Disabilities *Chapter House, 18-20 Crucifix Lane, SE1 (0800 328 5050/www.skill.org.uk/minicom 0800 068 2422).* **Open** *Phone enquiries 1.30-4.30pm Mon-Thur.* Information and advice.

Telephones

Dialling & codes

The codes for London changed in 2000. The old 0171 and 0181 codes – not long in operation themselves – were replaced by a single new code, 020, with a **7** or **8** added to the original seven-digit number to create a new 11-digit number. For example, 0171 813 3000 became 020 7813 3000. Throughout this book, London numbers have been listed without their code.

Making a call

If you want to call a London number from within London, you omit the code (020) and dial the last eight digits. If you are calling from outside the UK, dial the international access code from the country from which you're calling, then the UK code 44, then the full London number, omitting the first 0 from the code. For example, to make a call to 020 7813 3000 from the US, dial 011 44 20 7813 3000.

To dial abroad from the UK, first dial 00, then the country code (see below for a list).

International codes

Australia 61; Austria 43; Belgium 32; Brazil 55; Canada 1; Czech Republic 420; Denmark 45; France 33; Germany 49; Greece 30; Hong Kong 852; Iceland 354; India 91; Ireland 353; Israel 972; Italy 39; Japan 81; Netherlands 31; New Zealand 64; Norway 47; Portugal 351; South Africa 27; Spain 34; Sweden 46; Switzerland 41; USA 1.

Public phones

Public payphones take coins, credit cards or prepaid phonecards (sometimes all three). The minimum cost is 20p: this buys you a 110-second local phone call, which works out at 11p per minute. But be careful: some payphones, such as the counter-top ones found in many pubs, require more.

British Telecom Phonecard Plus

Available from post offices & many newsagents. **Cost** *20p per unit; cards in denominations of £3, £5, £10 and £20.*
The traditional Phonecard has been replaced with BT's Phonecard Plus: call boxes with the green Phonecard symbol take the prepaid cards, which can be charged using a credit or debit card too. A digital display shows the units remaining on your card.

Operator services

Operator

Call **100** for the operator if you have difficulty in dialling; for an early-morning alarm call; to make a credit card call; for information about the cost of a call; and for help with international person-to-person calls.

Dial **155** if you need to reverse the charges (call collect) or if you can't dial direct, but be warned that this service is very expensive.

Directory enquiries

Dial **192** for any number in Britain, or **153** for international numbers. Phoning directory enquiries from a private phone is expensive, and only two enquiries are allowed per call. If you phone from a public call box, calls are free.

Talking Pages

This 24-hour free service lists the numbers of thousands of businesses in the UK. Dial **0800 600900** and say what type of business you require, and in what area of London.

Telephone directories

There are three phone directories for London: two for private numbers and one for companies. These are available at post offices and libraries. Hotels have them too and they are issued free to all residents, as is the *Yellow Pages* directory, which lists businesses and services. A searchable *Yellow Pages* is available at www.yell.com.

Mobile phones

Mobile phones in the UK work on either the 900 or 1800 GSM system used throughout much of Europe. If you're travelling to the UK from Europe, check whether your service provider has a reciprocal arrangement with a UK-based service provider before setting out.

The situation is more complex for US travellers. If your service provider in the US uses the GSM system, it will probably run on the 1900 band; this being the case, you will need a tri-band phone, and your provider needs to have a reciprocal arrangement with a UK provider.

The simplest option, though, may be to buy a 'pay as you go' phone (about £40-£200). There's no monthly fee and calls are charged not by billing but by buying (widely available) cards that slot into your phone in denominations of £10 and up. Check before you buy whether the phone is capable of making and receiving international calls.

Telegrams

There is no longer a domestic telegram service, but you can still send telegrams abroad: call 0800 190190. This is also the number to call to send an international telemessage: phone in your message and it will be delivered by post the next day (at a cost of 92p a word, including the recipient's name and address).

Time

London operates on Greenwich Mean Time, which is five hours ahead of the US's Eastern Standard time. In spring (31

Mar 2002) the UK puts its clocks forward by one hour to British Summer Time (BST). In autumn (27 Oct 2002) the clocks go back to GMT again.

Tipping

In Britain it's accepted that you tip in taxis, minicabs, restaurants (some waiting staff rely heavily on tips), hairdressers, hotels and some bars (not pubs). Ten per cent is normal, with some restaurants adding as much as 15 per cent. Always check if service has been included in your bill: some restaurants include service and then leave the space for a gratuity on your credit card slip blank.

Toilets

Public toilets are few and far between in London, a situation exacerbated by the fact that pubs and restaurants reserve their toilets for customers only. However, all main-line rail stations and a very few tube stations – Piccadilly Circus, for one – have public toilets (you may be charged a small fee), while it's usually possible to sneak into a large department store such as John Lewis.

Tourist information

The **London Tourist Board** (LTB; 7932 2000) runs the information centres listed below, all of which can supply a free map of central London. For more details, check online at www.londontown.com.

The opening times given are for winter; hours are usually longer for the rest of the year.

Britain Visitor Centre
1 Regent Street, Piccadilly Circus, W1 (no phone/www.visitbritain.com). Piccadilly Circus tube. **Open** *Oct-May* 9.30am-6.30pm Mon; 9am-6.30pm Tue-Fri; 10am-4pm Sat, Sun. *June-Sept* 9.30am-6.30pm Mon; 9am-6.30pm Tue-Fri; 9am-5pm Sat; 10am-4pm Sun. **Map** p401 K7.

Heathrow Airport *Terminals 1, 2 & 3 tube station, Heathrow Airport, TW6.* **Open** 8am-6pm daily.
Liverpool Street *Liverpool Street, The City, EC2.* **Open** 8am-6pm Mon-Fri; 8am-5.30pm Sat; 9am-5.30pm Sun. **Map** p401 R5.
London Visitor Centre *Arrivals Hall, Waterloo International Terminal, SE1.* **Open** 8.30am-10.30pm daily. **Map** p405 M9.
Southwark Information Centre *London Bridge, 6 Tooley Street, SE1.* **Open** *Easter-Oct* 10am-6pm Mon-Sat; 10.30am-5.30pm Sun. *Nov-Easter* 10am-6pm Mon-Sat; 11am-4pm Sun. **Map** p407 Q8.
Victoria *Station Forecourt, Pimlico, SW1.* **Open** 7.45am-7pm Mon-Sat; 8.45am-7pm Sun. **Map** p400 H10.
There are also tourist information offices in Greenwich and next to St Paul's (**Map** p404 O6). However, if you require information on travel throughout the rest of Britain, *see p340*.

Visas & immigration

Citizens of EU countries don't require a visa to visit the United Kingdom; citizens of other countries, including the USA, Canada and New Zealand, require a valid passport for a visit of up to six months in duration.

To apply for a visa to the United Kingdom, and to check your visa status **before you travel**, you should contact the British embassy, high commission or consulate in your own country. The visa allows you entry for a maximum of six months. For information about work permits, *see p377*.

The immigration department of the Home Office deals with queries about immigration, visas and work permits from Commonwealth countries.

Home Office *Immigration & Nationality Bureau, Lunar House, 40 Wellesley Road, Croydon CR9 1AT (0870 606 7766/application forms 0870 241 0645/ www.homeoffice.gov.uk).* **Open** *Phone* enquiries 9am-4.45pm Mon-Thur; 9am-4.30pm Fri.

Weights & measures

The United Kingdom is gradually moving towards full metrication. Distances continue to be measured in miles but recent legislation means that all goods are now officially sold in metric quantities, with no legal requirement for the imperial equivalent to be given.

Conversions

1 centimetre (cm) = 0.39 inches (in)
1 inch (in) = 2.54 centimetres (cm)
1 yard (yd) = 0.91 metres (m)
1 metre (m) = 1.094 yards (yd)
1 mile = 1.6 kilometres (km)
1 kilometre (km) = 0.62 miles
1 ounce (oz) = 28.35 grammes (g)
1 gramme (g) = 0.035 ounces (oz)
1 pound (lb) = 0.45 kilogrammes (kg)
1 kilogramme = 2.2 pounds (lb)
1 pint (US) = 0.8 pints (UK)
1 pint (UK) = 0.55 litres (l)
1 litre (l) = 1.75 pints (UK).

When to go

Climate

Prepare yourself for the unpredictability of the British climate. For some guidance try **Weathercall** on 0870 600 4242 (60p per minute). See *also p377* **Weather report** and www.met-office.gov.uk.

Spring extends approximately from March to May, though winter often seems to stretch well beyond February. March winds and April showers may turn up either a month early or a month late. May is generally very pleasant.
Summer (June, July and August) can be unpredictable, with searing heat one day followed by sultry greyness and thunderstorms the next. The combination of high temperatures, humidity and pollution can create problems for anyone with hayfever or breathing difficulties. Temperatures down in the tube can reach sweltering levels, with many commuters arriving to work soaked through after enduring the rush-hour crowds.
Autumn starts in September, although the weather can still have a mild, summery feel. Real autumn comes with October, when the leaves start to fall. Then the cold sets in and November hits with a reminder that London is situated on a fairly northerly latitude.

Winter may contain the odd mild day, but don't bank on it. As a general rule, December, January and February are pretty chilly in London, although snow is rare. But that said, a crisp, sunny winter's day in the capital is hard to beat.

Public holidays

On public holidays (known as bank holidays), many shops remain open, but public transport services are less frequent, generally running to a Sunday timetable. The exception is Christmas Day, when almost everything shuts.
New Year's Day Tue 1 Jan 2002; Wed 1 Jan 2003.
Good Friday Fri 29 Mar 2002; Fri 18 Apr 2003.
Easter Monday Mon 1 Apr 2002; Mon 21 Apr 2003.
May Day Holiday Mon 6 May 2002; Mon 5 May 2003.
Spring Bank Holiday Mon 3 June 2002; Mon 26 May 2003.
Golden Jubilee Bank Holiday Tue 4 June 2002.
Summer Bank Holiday Mon 26 Aug 2002; Mon 25 Aug 2003.
Christmas Day Wed 25 Dec 2002; Thur 25 Dec 2003.
Boxing Day Thur 26 Dec 2002; Fri 26 Dec 2003.

Women

The women's movement may now keep a low profile, but London is home to dozens of women's groups and networks, from day centres to rights campaigners, as a browse through websites such as www.gn.apc.org/womeninlond on or www.wrc.uninet.co.uk will reveal.

SAFETY/HARASSMENT

Visiting women are unlikely to be harassed. Bar the very occasional sexually motivated attack, the streets of London are no more dangerous to women than they are to men, if you follow the usual precautions (*see p373*).

National Library of Women

Old Castle Street, Whitechapel, E1 (7320 1189/www.lgu.ac.uk/fawcett). *Aldgate or Aldgate East tube.* **Open** call for details.

Europe's largest women's studies archive has made a £4-million move to larger premises (on the same road). Exhibitions include such subjects as the suffragette movement. Staff are usually happy to help with general women-related queries.

Working in London

Finding temporary work in London can be a full-time job in itself. But providing you can speak a reasonable level of English, are an EU citizen or have a work permit, you should be able to find something in catering, labouring, bar/pub or shop work. Graduates with an English or foreign-language degree could try teaching.

If your English isn't that great, there's always the mind-numbing task of distributing free magazines. You can also try for seasonal work in tourist spots. Ideas can be found in *Summer Jobs in Britain*, published by Vacation Work, 9 Park End Street, Oxford OX1 1HJ (£9.99 plus £1.50 p&p). The **Central Bureau for Educational Visits & Exchanges** (*see below*) has other useful publications.

Other ways of finding work are to look in the *Evening Standard*, in the local and national papers and in newsagents' windows. Employers advertise vacancies on Jobcentre noticeboards; there is often temporary and unskilled work available. Most districts of London have a Jobcentre; look in the *Yellow Pages* under 'Employment Agencies'.

If you're interested in relatively lucrative office work and you have good typing (40 words per minute upwards) or word processing skills and know how to dress the part, you could sign on with some of the temp agencies, many of which have specialisms beyond the obvious admin/secretarial roles, such as translation.

Weather report

Average daytime temperatures, rainfall and hours of sunshine in London

	Temp (°C/°F)	Rainfall (mm/in)	Sunshine (hrs/dy)
Jan	6/43	54/2.1	1.5
Feb	7/44	40/1.6	2.3
Mar	10/50	37/1.5	3.6
Apr	13/55	37/1.5	5.3
May	17/63	46/1.8	6.4
June	20/68	45/1.8	7.1
July	22/72	57/2.2	6.4
Aug	21/70	59/2.3	6.1
Sept	19/66	49/1.9	4.7
Oct	14/57	57/2.2	3.2
Nov	10/50	64/2.5	1.8
Dec	7/44	48/1.9	1.3

Work permits

With few exceptions, citizens of non-European Economic Area (EEA) countries have to have a work permit before they are legally able to work in the United Kingdom, which they must obtain before making the journey over here.

Employers who have vacancies that they are unable to fill with a resident or EEA national must apply for a permit to the Department for Education and Employment (*see below*). Permits are issued only for jobs that carry a high level of skill and experience.

Au pairs

The option of au pairing is only open to citizens of the countries listed below aged between 17 and 27. Try contacting an agency in your own country or look in the *Yellow Pages* under 'Employment Agencies'. The positive aspect to work of this kind is that it usually includes free accommodation, but on the down side, wages do tend to be on the low side.

The following countries are all in the **Au Pair Scheme**: Andorra, Bosnia-Herzegovina, Croatia, Cyprus, Czech Republic, Faroe Islands, Greenland, Hungary, Macedonia, Malta, Monaco, San Marino, Slovak Republic, Slovenia, Switzerland and Turkey.

Sandwich students

Students should note that approval for course-compulsory sandwich placements at recognised UK colleges must be obtained by the college from the DfEE's **Overseas Labour Service** (*see below* **Dept for Education & Employment**).

Students

Visiting students from the US, Canada, Australia or Jamaica can get a blue BUNAC card enabling them to work in the UK for up to six months. BUNAC cards are not difficult to obtain, but they must be acquired in advance. Either contact the Work in Britain Department of the **Council on International Educational Exchange** or call **BUNAC** (*see below*). BUNAC students should obtain an application form OSS1 (BUNAC) from BUNAC. This should be submitted to the nearest Jobcentre to obtain permission to work.

Working holidaymakers

Citizens of Commonwealth countries aged 17-27 may apply to come to the UK as a working holidaymaker. This allows them to take part-time work without a DfEE permit. In order to do this, they must contact their nearest British Diplomatic Post in advance.

Useful addresses

BUNAC

16 Bowling Green Lane, Clerkenwell, EC1 (7251 3472/www.bunac.org.uk). Farringdon tube/rail. **Open** 9.30am-5.30pm Mon-Thur; 9.30am-5pm Fri. **Map** p402 N4.

Central Bureau for Educational Visits & Exchanges

British Council, 10 Spring Gardens, St James's, SW1 (7930 8466/ www.britishcouncil.org). Charing Cross tube/rail. **Open** 9am-5pm Mon-Fri. **Map** p401 K8.

While the Central Bureau for Educational Visits & Exchanges only deals with the organisation of visits outside the United Kingdom, you can obtain copies of its very useful publications here.

Council on International Educational Exchange

Work in Britain Department, 633 3rd Avenue, New York, NY 10017, USA (00 1 212 822 7244/ www.ciee.org). **Open** 9.30am-5.30pm Mon-Fri.

Set up more than half a century ago, the Council on International Educational Exchange aids young people to study, work and travel abroad. It's divided into two interrelated but independent operations: international study programmes, and exchanges.

Department for Education & Employment

Work Permits UK helpline (0114 259 4074/www.workpermits.gov.uk). **Open** *Phone enquiries* 9am-5pm Mon-Fri.

Employers who are seeking work permit application forms should phone the enquiry line on 08705 210224 or visit the website.

Home Office

Immigration & Nationality Directorate, Lunar House, 40 Wellesley Road, Croydon CR9 2BY (0870 606 7766/ www.ind.homeoffice. gov.uk). **Open** *Phone enquiries* 9am-4.45pm Mon-Thur; 9am-4.30pm Fri.

The Home Office is able to provide advice on whether or not a work permit is required.

Overseas Visitors Records Office

180 Borough High Street, Borough, SE1 (7230 1208). Borough tube/Elephant & Castle or London Bridge tube/rail. **Open** 9am-4.30pm Mon-Fri. **Map** p404 P9.

In a former incarnation this was the Aliens Registration Office run by the Metropolitan Police. These days, though, it's known as the vastly less scary Overseas Visitors Records Office, and it charges £34 to register a person if they have a work permit.

Directory

Further Reference

Books

Fiction

Peter Ackroyd
Hawksmoor; The House of Doctor Dee; Great Fire of London
Intricate studies of arcane London.
Martin Amis *London Fields*
Darts and drinking way out east.
Jonathan Coe
The Dwarves of Death
Mystery, music, mirth, malevolence.
Norman Collins
London Belongs to Me
A witty saga of '30s Kennington.
Wilkie Collins
The Woman in White
Spooky goings-on.
Joseph Conrad *The Secret Agent*
Anarchism in seedy Soho.
Charles Dickens
Oliver Twist; David Copperfield; Bleak House; Our Mutual Friend
Four of the master's most London-centric novels.
Sir Arthur Conan Doyle
The Complete Sherlock Holmes
Reassuring sleuthing shenanigans.
Maureen Duffy *Capital*
The bones beneath our feet and the stories they tell.
Bernadine Evaristo
The Emperor's Babe
Verse-novel romp through Londinium AD 211.
Christopher Fowler *Soho Black*
Walking dead in Soho.
Anthony Frewin *London Blues*
One-time Kubrick assistant explores '60s porn movie industry.
Neil Gaiman *Neverwhere*
A new world above and below the streets by *Sandman* creator.
Graham Greene
The End of the Affair
Adultery and catholicism.
Patrick Hamilton *20,000 Streets Under the Sky; Hangover Square*
A romantic trilogy among Soho sleaze; love and death in Earl's Court.
Tobias Hill *Underground*
Women are being pushed under tube trains, and secret tunnels abound.
Alan Hollinghurst
The Swimming Pool Library
Gay life around Russell Square.
**Maria Lexton (vol 1)/
Nicholas Royle (vol 2) (eds)**
Time Out Book of London Short Stories Volumes 1 & 2
Writers pay homage to their city.
Colin MacInnes
City of Spades; Absolute Beginners
Coffee 'n' jazz, Soho 'n' Notting Hill.
Derek Marlowe *A Dandy in Aspic*
A capital-set Cold War classic.
China Miéville *King Rat*
Myth, murder and drum 'n' bass.

Michael Moorcock *Mother London*
A love-letter to London.
Iris Murdoch *Under the Net*
The adventures of a talented but wastrel writer.
Courttia Newland *The Scholar*
Life is full of choices for a kid on a west London estate.
Kim Newman *The Quorum*
Docklands-based media intrigue.
Geoff Nicholson *Bleeding London*
London as it is and as we think it is.
George Orwell
Keep the Aspidistra Flying
Saga of a struggling writer.
Derek Raymond
I Was Dora Suarez
The blackest London noir.
Jean Rhys *After Leaving Mr Mackenzie; Good Morning, Midnight*
Sad, lost women haunt the streets and squares of Bloomsbury.
Nicholas Royle *The Matter of the Heart; The Director's Cut*
Abandoned buildings and secrets from the past.
Geoff Ryman *253*
The lives of tube travellers.
William Sansom
Selected Short Stories
Lyrical tales of Londoners at large.
Will Self *Grey Area*
Short stories.
Iain Sinclair
Downriver; Radon Daughters; White Chappell, Scarlet Tracings
The Thames' own *Heart of Darkness* by London's laureate; William Hope Hodgson via the London Hospital; Ripper murders and book dealers.
Muriel Spark
The Ballad of Peckham Rye
Mayhem in Peckham.
Jane Stevenson *London Bridges*
Greek monks and murder.
Barbara Vine *King Solomon's Carpet; Grasshopper*
From the underground to a rooftop love story.
Evelyn Waugh *Vile Bodies*
Shameful antics in 1920s Mayfair.
Angus Wilson
The Old Men at the Zoo
London faces down oblivion.
Virginia Woolf *Mrs Dalloway*
A kind of London *Ulysses*.

Non-fiction

Peter Ackroyd
London: The Biography
Wilfully obscurantist city history.
Marc Atkins & Iain Sinclair
Liquid City
Sinclair haunts photographed.
Felix Barker & Ralph Hyde
London as it Might Have Been
Schemes that never made it past the drawing board.

Anthony Burgess
A Dead Man in Deptford
The life and murder of Elizabethan playwright Christopher Marlowe.
Margaret Cox *Life and Death in Spitalfields 1700-1850*
The removal and analysis of bodies from Christ Church Spitalfields.
Daniel Farson *Soho in the Fifties*
An affectionate portrait.
Stephen Halliday
The Great Stink of London
The sewage crisis in London in 1858.
Derek Hammond *London, England*
A witty celebration of the capital.
Derek Hanson
The Dreadful Judgement
The embers of the Great Fire re-raked.
Stephen Inwood
A History of London
A recent, readable history.
Ian Jack (ed)
Granta, London: the Lives of the City
Fiction, reportage and travel writing.
**Rachel Lichtenstein
& Iain Sinclair**
Rodinsky's Room
The mysterious disappearance of an East End Jew.
Jack London
The People of the Abyss
Extreme poverty in the East End.
Nick Merriman (ed)
The Peopling of London
A fascinating account of 2,000 years of settlement.
George Orwell
Down and Out in Paris and London
Waitering and starving.
Samuel Pepys *Diaries*
Fires, plagues, bordellos and more.
Patricia Pierce *Old London Bridge*
The story of the world's longest inhabited bridge.
Roy Porter *London: A Social History*
An all-encompassing history.
Jonathan Raban *Soft City*
The city as state of mind; a classic.
Denis Severs *18 Folgate Street*
The late eccentric on his museum-cum-piece of performance art.
Iain Sinclair
Lights Out for the Territory
Time-warp visionary crosses London.
Richard Trench
London Under London
Investigation of the subterranean city.
Ben Weinreb & Christopher Hibbert (eds)
The London Encyclopaedia
Fascinating, thorough, indispensable.
Andrew White (ed)
Time Out Book of London Walks Volumes 1 & 2.
Writers, cartoonists, comedians and historians take a walk through town.
Jerry White *London in the 20th Century: A City and Its People.*
The radical transformation of the city.

Films

Alfie *dir. Lewis Gilbert* (1966)
What's it all about, Michael?
Beautiful Thing
dir. Hettie MacDonald (1996)
A tender, amusing coming-of-age
flick set in south-east London.
A Clockwork Orange
dir. Stanley Kubrick (1971)
Kubrick's vision still shocks.
Blow-Up
dir. Michelangelo Antonioni (1966)
Swingin' London captured in
unintentionally hysterical fashion.
Croupier *dir. Mike Hodges* (1997)
Gambling and drinking dominate
Hodges' terrific flick.
Death Line *dir. Gary Sherman* (1972)
Cannibalism on the tube. Yikes.
Jubilee *dir. Derek Jarman* (1978)
A horribly dated but still interesting
romp through the punk era.
The Krays *dir. Peter Medak* (1990)
The Kemp brothers excel as the
notorious East End gangsters.
**Life is Sweet; Naked;
Secrets & Lies; Career Girls**
dir. Mike Leigh (1990; 1993; 1996; 1997)
A mocking but affectionate look at
Metroland; a bleak but compelling
character study; familial tensions in
1990s Britain; the past and present
lives of old friends.
**Lock, Stock & Two
Smoking Barrels; Snatch**
dir. Guy Ritchie (1998; 2000)
Mr Madonna's pair of East End faux-
gangster flicks.
London; Robinson in Space
dir. Patrick Keiller (1994; 1997)
Fiction meets documentary.
The Long Good Friday
dir. John MacKenzie (1989)
Bob Hoskins stars in the classic
London gangster flick.
Mona Lisa; The Crying Game
dir. Neil Jordan (1986; 1992)
Prostitution, terrorism, transvestism.
Mrs Dalloway
dir. Marleen Goris (1997)
Vanessa Redgrave stars in this
adaptation of the Woolf novel.
Nil by Mouth
dir. Gary Oldman (1997)
A violent, uncompromising but truly
compelling tale of working-class life.
Notting Hill
dir. Roger Michell (1999)
Hugh Grant and Julia Roberts get it
on in west London.
Peeping Tom
dir. Michael Powell (1960)
Powell's creepy murder flick still
shocks 40 years after release.
Performance *dir. Nicolas
Roeg, Donald Cammell* (1970)
The cult movie to end all cult movies
made west London cool for life.
Wonderland
dir. Michael Winterbottom (1999)
A gritty, verité London classic of love,
loss and deprivation.

Music

Albums

Alabama 3
Exile on Coldharbour Lane (1997)
Brixtonian gospel/rap fusion.
Blur *Modern Life is Rubbish*
(1993); *Park Life* (1994)
Modern classics by the Essex exiles.
The Clash *London Calling* (1979)
Epoch-making punk classic.
MJ Cole *Sincere* (2000)
The best UK garage long-player yet.
Ian Dury & The Blockheads
New Boots & Panties (1977)
The late Dury's seminal work.
Handel *Water Music; Music For
the Royal Fireworks* (1717; 1749)
The glory days of the 18th century.
The Jam
This is the Modern World (1977)
Paul Weller at his splenetic finest.
Madness *Rise & Fall* (1982)
The nutty boys wax lyrical about
their beloved home.
Morrissey *Vauxhall & I* (1994)
The former Smiths frontman's finest
solo album.
Anthony Newley
The Very Best of… (1997)
Swingin' retrospective of everyone's
favourite Cockney scallywag.
The Rolling Stones *December's
Children (and Everybody's)* (1965)
Moodily cool evocation of the city.
The Sex Pistols
Never Mind the Bollocks (1977)
The best ever punk album.

Songs

assorted *A Foggy Day (in London
Town); A Nightingale Sang in Berkeley
Square; Let's All Go Down the Strand;
London Bridge is Falling Down; Maybe
It's Because I'm a Londoner*
David Bowie *London Boys*
Lloyd Cole *Charlotte Street*
Elvis Costello & The Attractions
(I Don't Want to Go to) Chelsea
Ray Davies *London Song*
Donovan *Sunny Goodge Street*
Nick Drake *Mayfair*
Eddy Grant *Electric Avenue*
The Kinks *Denmark Street; Muswell
Hillbillies; Waterloo Sunset*
Phil Lynott *Solo in Soho*
Pet Shop Boys
King's Cross; West End Girls
The Pogues *A Rainy Night in Soho;
Misty Morning, Albert Bridge*
Gerry Rafferty *Baker Street*
Diana Ross *Big Ben*
Roxy Music *Do the Strand*
St Etienne *London Belongs to Me*
Sham 69 *Hersham Boys*
Simple Minds *Chelsea Girl*
Frank Sinatra *London by Night*
Squeeze *Up the Junction*
Sugar Minott *Riot Inna Brixton*
XTC *Towers of London*

Websites

BBC London 94.9
www.bbc.co.uk/london
The successor to the much-loved
GLR, BBC London 94.9 offers
online news, travel, weather,
entertainment and sport, as well
as providing details of London's
radio and television schedules.
Book2Eat *www.book2eat.com*
You can make your reservations
for London's restaurants through
this website.
Classic Cafés
www.classiccafes.co.uk
Resources on London's surviving
'50s and '60s caffs.
Greater London Authority
www.london.gov.uk
See what Ken and co are up to at
the London Assembly.
London Active Map
*www.uktravel.com/london/
londonmap.asp*
Click on a tube station and find
out which attractions are nearby.
LondonTown *www.londontown.com*
The official tourist board website is
stuffed full of information and offers.
London Underground Online
www.thetube.com
A website devoted to the capital's
beleaguered Underground network.
Meteorological Office
www.met-office.gov.uk
Find out what the Met Office says
before you head out. Not always
accurate, but the best you'll get.
Pubs.com *www.pubs.com*
London's traditional boozers.
The River Thames Guide
www.riverthames.co.uk
Useful info on places and events
along the banks of the Thames.
Street Map
www.streetmap.co.uk
Search for a road name or area,
then zoom in, zoom out and find
grid references and postcodes.
This is London
www.thisislondon.co.uk
The online version of the London
Evening Standard.
Time Out *www.timeout.com*
An essential source of info, with
an online guide and a wealth
of recommendations from *Time
Out*'s sharpest critics.
Transport for London
www.londontransport.co.uk
The official website for buses,
DLR, river services and other forms
of transport in the capital, with real-
time travel information and journey
planning resources. See **London
Underground Online**, *above*, for
information on the Underground.
Yellow Pages Online
www.yell.com
This business directory can help you
find a specific company or service in
your area.

Directory

Advertisers' Index

Please refer to relevant sections for addresses and telephone numbers

Section sponsored by

Teamsys.
A WORLD OF SERVICES

Places of interest or entertainment	▬
Railway stations	▬
Underground stations	⊖
Parks	▬
Hospitals	▬
Casualty units	✚
Churches	✚
Synagogues	✡
Districts	**MAYFAIR**

Maps

Teamsys.

A WORLD OF SERVICES

Teamsys is always with you, ready to assure you all the tranquillity and serenity that you desire for your journeys, 365 days a year.

Roadside assistance always and everywhere, infomobility so not to have surprises, insurance... and lots more.

To get to know us better contact us at the toll-free number **00-800-55555555**.

...and to discover Connect's exclusive and innovative integrated infotelematic services onboard system visit us at:

www.targaconnect.com

Trips Out of Town

© Copyright Time Out Group 2002

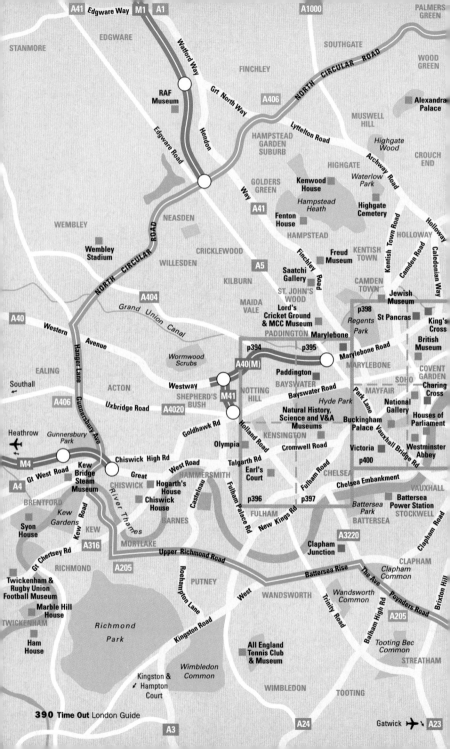

London Overview

© Copyright Time Out Group 2002

Central London
by Area

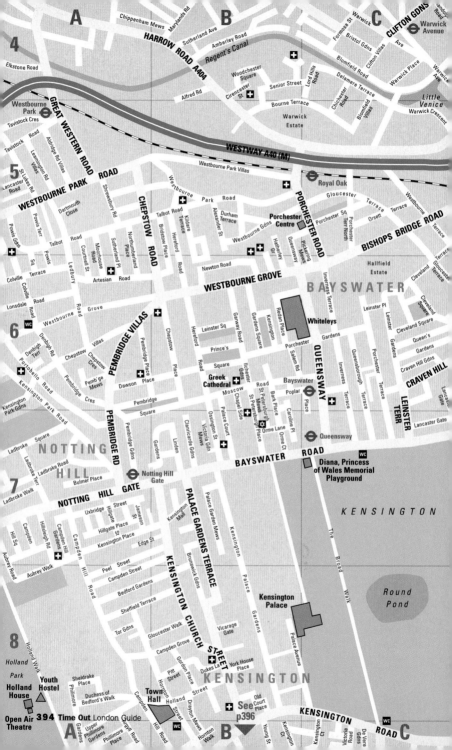

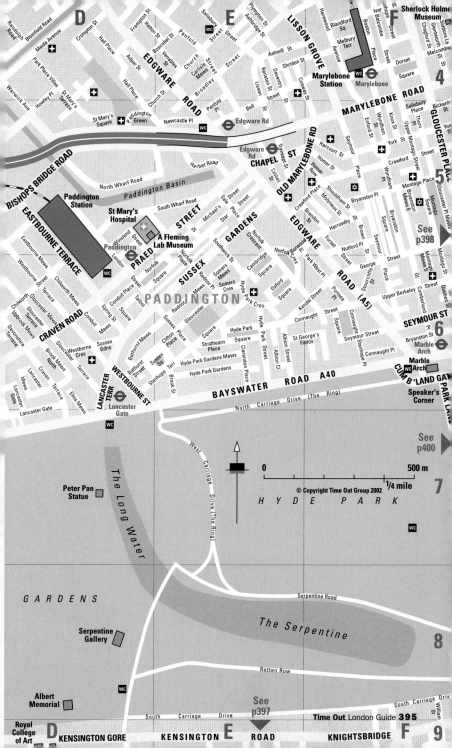

See p398

See p400

See p397

© Copyright Time Out Group 2002

0   500 m

1/4 mile

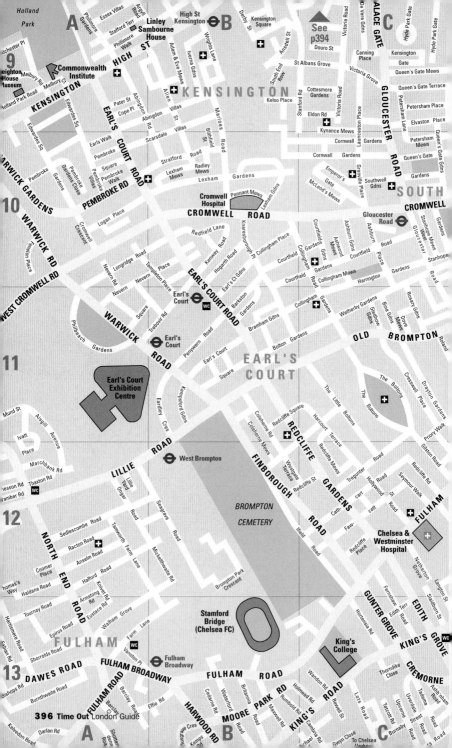

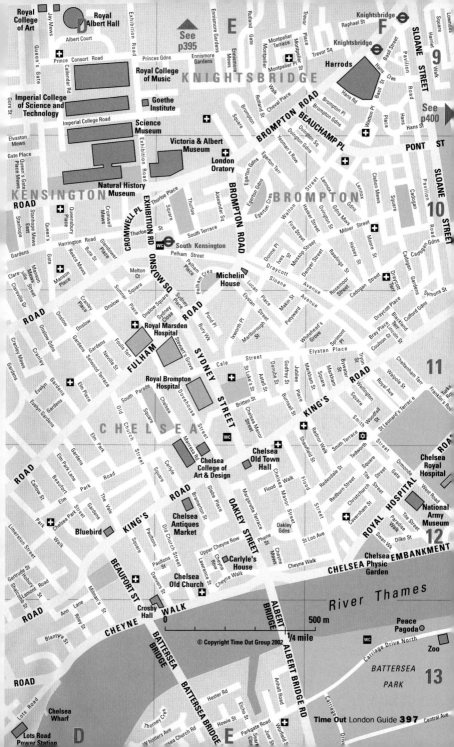

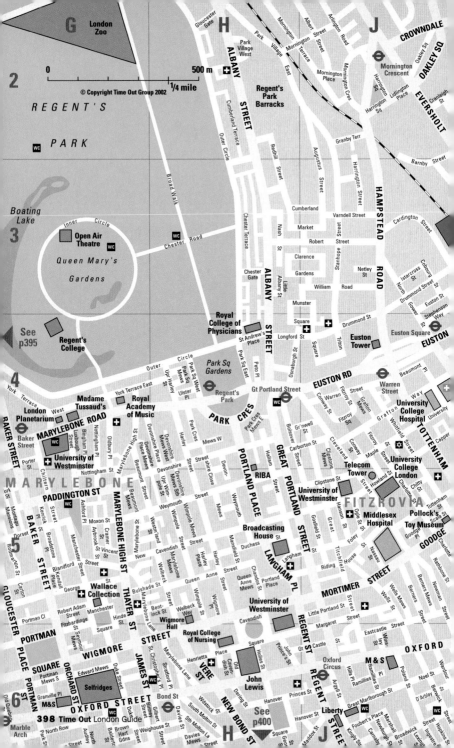

G London Zoo

H **J** CROWNDALE

REGENT'S

PARK [wc]

Boating Lake

Queen Mary's Gardens

Open Air Theatre [wc]

See p395

Regent's College

Royal College of Physicians

Madame Tussaud's

London Planetarium

Royal Academy of Music

University of Westminster

University College Hospital

University College London

Telecom Tower

FITZROVIA

RIBA

University of Westminster

Broadcasting House

Middlesex Hospital

Pollock's Toy Museum

GOODGE

Wallace Collection

University of Westminster

Wigmore Hall

Royal College of Nursing

MORTIMER STREET

Oxford Circus

M&S

OXFORD

Selfridges

John Lewis

Liberty [wc]

Marble Arch

398 Time Out London Guide

H **J**

ALBANY STREET

Regent's Park Barracks

HAMPSTEAD ROAD

Mornington Crescent

EVERSHOLT

EUSTON

Euston Tower

Euston Square

EUSTON RD

Warren Street

TOTTENHAM

PORTLAND PLACE

GREAT PORTLAND STREET

LANGHAM PL

REGENT ST

VERE ST

NEW BOND ST

See p400

© Copyright Time Out Group 2002

0   500 m
       ¼ mile

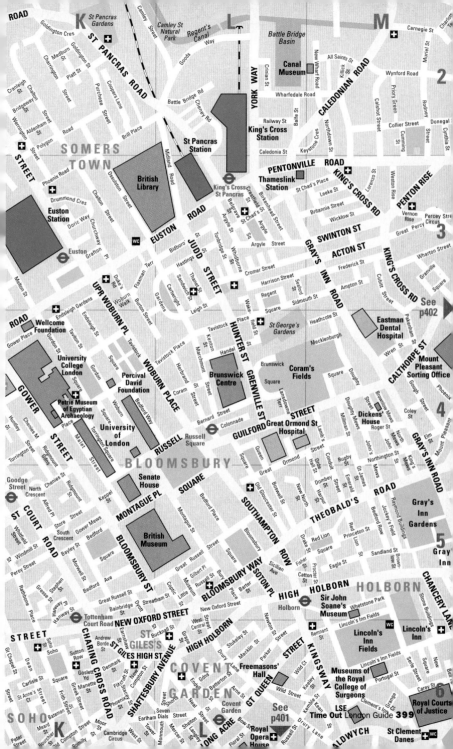

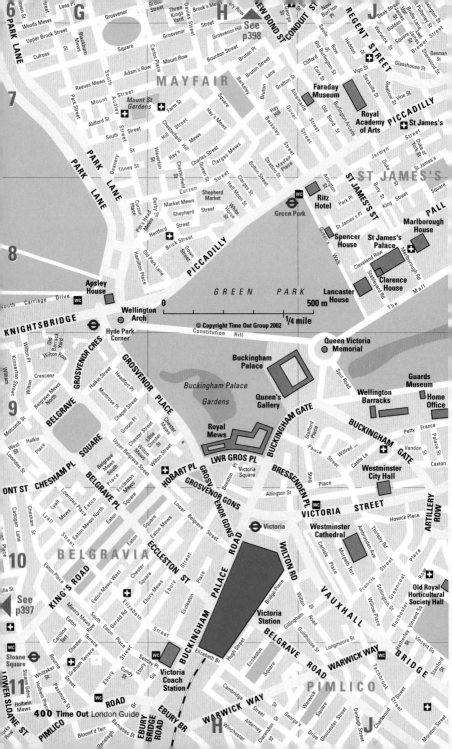

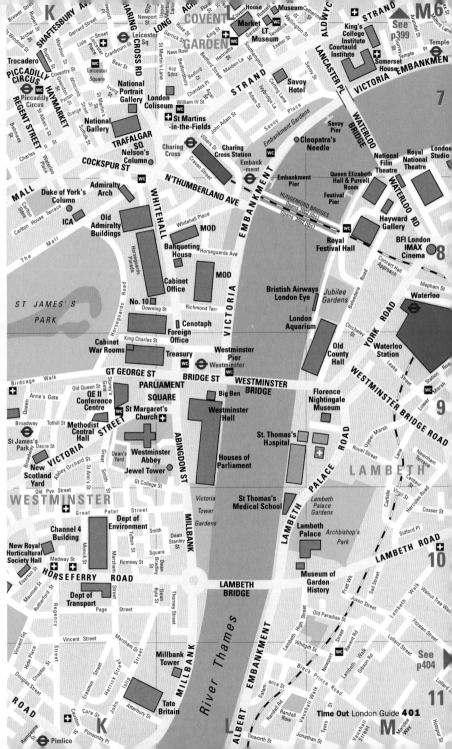

N O P

Lofting Road
Barnsbury Street

1
Ripplevale Grove
Richmond
Barnard Park

Lonsdale
Square
Waterloo Terr
Florence St
Sebbon St
Hawes St

Essex Road
rail station

Braes St
anonbury Villas

Eccleshbourne Rd
Rotherfield Rd
Moreton Rd
St

NEW NORTH ROAD

Cross Street
Dagmar Terr
Dibden St

ESSEX ROAD
Britannia Row

Greenman St
Popham Road

Popham St
Popham Rd

Basire Street

St Paul
Linton Street

Arlington Avenue

ISLINGTON

Business
Design Centre

Barford St

ISLINGTON GREEN

Camden Passage
Charlton Place

Gaskin St

St Peters Street

Cruden St

Raleigh Rd
Chantry St

Rheidol Terrace

Packington Square

Regent's Canal

Eagle Wharf Road

Napier Grove

2
Dewey Rd
Ritchie St
Tolpuddle Street

WC

Chapel Market

White Lion Street

Angel

UPPER STREET

Islington High St
Duncan Street

Devonia Road
Grantbridge St

Gerrard Road

Danbury St
Burgh St

Frome St

Baldwin Terr

0   500 m

© Copyright Time Out Group 2002   ¼ mile

Shaftesbury St

PENTONVILLE ROAD

Claremont
Square

See
p399

Claremont Cl
Myddelton
Square
Chadwell
Street

GOSWELL STREET

Wakley St

Nelson Terr

CITY ROAD

City Garden Row
Coombs St

City Road Basin

Wharf Road

Wenlock Rd

Sturt St

Wenlock St
Bletchley St

Wenlock
Terr

Micawber St

Windsor
Terr

Under-
wood St

Taplow Street

Shepherdess Walk

3
Lloyd
Sq

Margery Street
Merlin
Hardwick St

ROSEBERY AVENUE

ST JOHN STREET

Friend St

Rawstone Street

Spencer Street

Moreland Street

Central Street

Macclesfield Rd

Dingley Road

Mora St

Galway St

Bath St

LEVER STREET

Ironmonger
Row

Radnor Street

SKINNER ST

WC

PERCIVAL ST

Cyrus St

Seward Street

BUNHILL

Bartholomew
Sq

4
Mount
Pleasant
Sorting
Office

ROSEBERY AVENUE

House of
Detention

FARRINGDON ROAD

Corporation
Row

Woodbridge St

Compton Street

Dallington St
Northburgh Street

Bastwick St
Gee Street

GOSWELL ROAD

Pear Tree St

Mitchell St

Helmet
Row

Garrett St

Banner Street
Street

OLD   STREET

Whitecross

Chequer St

Dufferin St

Errol Street

5
CLERKENWELL RD

CLERKENWELL

FARRINGDON ROAD

Clerkenwell Grn

Museum of
the Order
of St John

Charterhouse

St Barts
Medical
College

ST JOHN   ROAD

Charterhouse
Square

Barbican

GOSWELL ROAD

Fann St

Golden Lane

Fortune St

WC

CHISWELL

402 Time Out London Guide

HOLBORN   N

Farringdon

Cowcross Street

CHARTERHOUSE STREET

LONG LANE

Cloth
Fair
Little Britain

WEST SMITHFIELD   O

Hosier Lane

Smithfield
Market

St Bartholomew
the Great

See
p404

BEECH   STREET

Arts
Centre

Barbican
Centre

St Giles

Museum of
London

Silk Street

Fore Street

Moor

**Guildhall School
of Music & Drama**

St Alphage
Garden   P

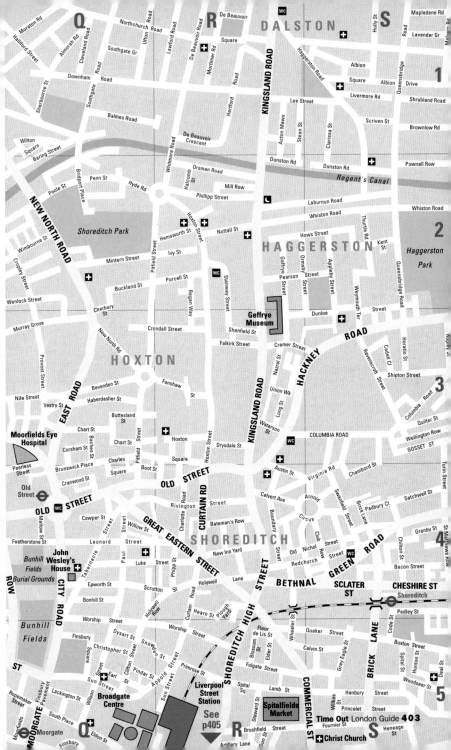

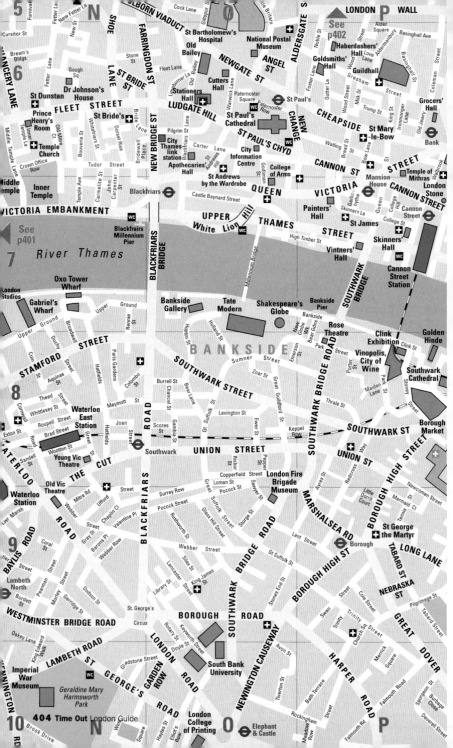

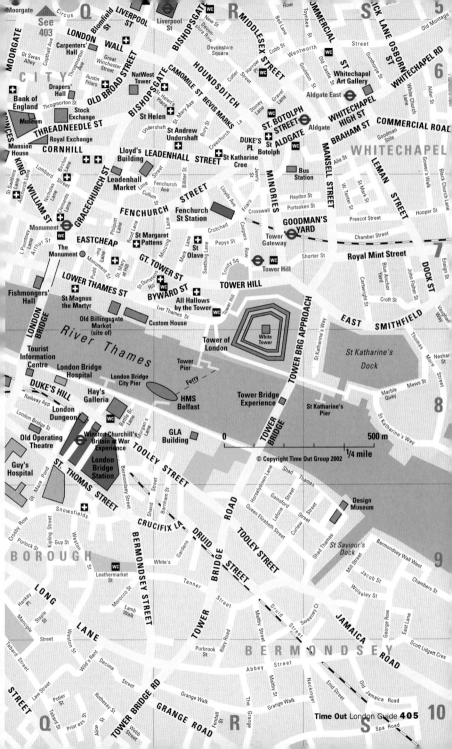

Street Index

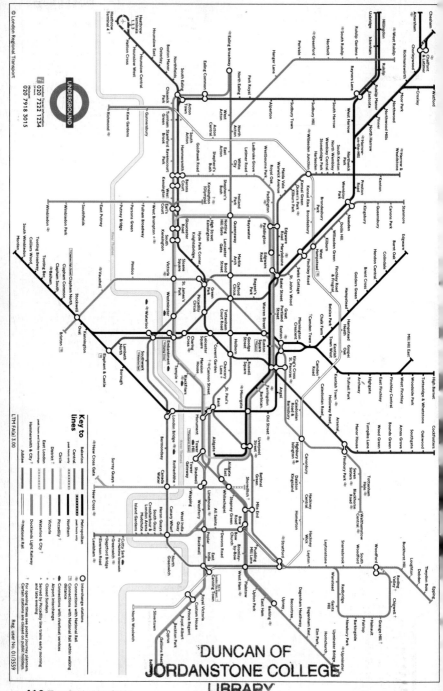